OCCUPATIONAL INJURIES AND ILLNESSES

DANIEL J. STONE, M.D.

Editor–In–Chief

Mosby

MATTHEW◆BENDER

QUESTIONS ABOUT THIS PUBLICATION?

For questions about **Editorial Content** in this volume or reprint permission, please call:

Beverly Lieberman . . . . .1-800-252-9257 (ext. 8629)
Rina Cascone. 1-800-252-9257 (ext.8858)
Outside the United States and Canada please call. . . . .(212) 967-7707

For assistance with shipments, billing or other customer service matters,
refer to book code 30875. Please call:

Customer Services Department at . . . .(800) 426-4545
Outside the United States and Canada, please call. . .(314) 872-8370
Fax Number. . . . .(800) 535-9935
Outside the United States and Canada, please fax. . .(314) 453-4379

LIBRARY OF CONGRESS CATALOGING IN PUBLICATION DATA
Library of Congress Cataloging Publication Data

Stone, Daniel
    Occupational Injuries and Illnesses / Daniel J. Stone, editor-in-chief
      p. cm.
    "Times Mirror books."
    Includes index.
    ISBN 0-8205-1884-0
    1. Occupational diseases. 2. Industrial accidents. I. Stone, Daniel J.
RC964.0258 1992
616.9803--dc20
92-25361

This publication is designed to provide accurate and authoritative information in regard to
the subject matter covered. It is sold with the understanding that the publisher is not engaged in
rendering professional services. If expert assistance is required, the services of a competent
professional should be sought.

MATTHEW BENDER & Co., INC.
Editorial Offices
11 Penn Plaza, New York, NY 10001-2006 (212) 967-7707
2101 Webster St., Oakland, CA 94612-3027 (510)-446-7100

MOSBY-YEAR BOOK, INC.
11830 Westline Industrial Drive
St. Louis, MO 63146
(800) 325-4177; (314) 872-8370

Table of Contents

A COMPLETE SYNOPSIS FOR EACH CHAPTER APPEARS
AT THE BEGINNING OF THE CHAPTER

Table of Contents

Table of Contents

Table of Contents

Table of Contents

Table of Contents

Table of Contents

Table of Contents

Table of Contents

Preface

Occupational health has become in very recent years one of the most rapidly evolving health disciplines. No longer an area neglected by physicians, nurses, health care workers, economists, industry and government, it has developed nationally and internationally into a major area of health concern.

Indeed, in the past several years, the United Nations, through its International Labor Organization, has published numerous compendia relating to occupational health. In the United States, the legislation that created OSHA (Occupational Safety and Health Act) and NIOSH (National Institute for Occupational Safety and Health) has led to the development of standards to regulate and educate concerned parties as to the health concerns associated with various occupations.

Industrial health organizations have developed a parallel approach to occupational health care, not only emphasizing treatment of work–related illnesses and injuries but initiating carefully evaluated programs to prevent occupationally related illness and injury.

The result of this multiphase approach to occupational health has been a widespread, well–organized effort to perform basic and clinical scientific research in order to determine the effects of toxic substances and specific occupations on the health of American workers. The medical profession has also become more aware of the relationships among work hazards, occupational exposure and health consequences.

The net result has been a growing volume of literature dealing with many occupationally related illnesses and injuries. It has, therefore, become a Herculean task for anyone interested in occupational health issues to keep abreast of the literature.

For these reasons, there is an obvious need for a thorough analysis of the current state of the art that will be of value to all concerned with occupational health. Thus, the aim of this volume is to provide background information and critical appraisal of work–related illnesses and injuries.

The staff engaged in the writing of this volume are experienced medical writers with complete access to bibliographic sources. The chapters have been carefully reviewed in several stages for both content, style and accuracy. The subjects covered include injuries to multiple body areas and the effects of hazardous occurrences such as exposure to noise and to known toxic substances such as asbestos. A chapter on reproductive disorders is designed to accommodate a growing concern with this area. Occupationally related cancer also receives a carefully documented analysis. The bibliographies at the end of each chapter have been selected to provide ready reference to articles reflecting the current state of the art.

Preface

The chapter design, bibliographies and technical information clearly will serve as an important resource for professionals in any field dealing with health care matters. The technical information and bibliographies, however, are complete enough so that health professionals, including physicians, nurses, industrial hygienists and others, will find this volume a valuable resource for clinical, educational and preventive medicine uses.

Daniel J. Stone, M.D.

Publisher's Editorial Staff

Beverly R. Lieberman
Managing Editor

Rina Cascone
Project Editor

Editor - In - Chief

DANIEL J. STONE, M.D.

Daniel J. Stone, M.D., is a Professor of Medicine and faculty member of the New York Medical College at Valhalla. A pulmonary specialist for 40 years, Dr. Stone is the author of several textbooks on pulmonary physiology and disease and has written numerous articles in the field of pulmonary medicine. He has served as a member of the Board of Directors of the New York Lung Association, and was vice president of the association as well as chairman of several committees. He is a fellow of the American College of Occupational Medicine, the American College of Physicians and the American College of Chest Physicians, and a Senior Member of the American Thoracic Society. In addition to being Medical Director Emeritus of the University Sleep Center and Director Emeritus of the Pulmonary Division of New York Medical College, he currently serves as a consultant on academic affairs for the American Lung Association of Southeast Florida.

CHAPTER 1

Hand Injuries

SCOPE

Acute hand injuries are common occupational mishaps. The most frequent types of hand injuries include lacerations, avulsions (tearing away or forcible separation), puncture wounds, burns, bites, fractures, vascular injuries, crush injuries and amputations. The full extent of a hand injury may not be obvious from an examination of the wound itself; rather, complete diagnosis is best made by evaluating the motor and sensory function of the whole hand. The therapy of any serious hand injury usually requires both surgery and extensive rehabilitation. The outcome is often less than perfect, in that function does not return to the level it was before the injury. Any injury may result in some deficit in motor and/or sensory function, which, even if it is small, may disable a worker who depends on a high degree of precision in hand function.

SYNOPSIS

1.01 INTRODUCTION

The hand is a vital piece of human anatomy. It is a finely tuned instrument that performs with a high degree of precision, strength and agility. A wide variety of occupations place heavy demands on hand function, requiring exquisite sensory activity and precise fine motor control. It is not unusual for a small loss in either of these abilities to result in a major loss for the affected individual in terms of occupation and livelihood. Hands also have cosmetic and social importance; hand injury can therefore have far-reaching consequences for many individuals, and these factors may complicate rehabilitation.

Occupational hand injuries may be classified into two categories: acute and chronic. The most common form of chronic injury is overuse, also known as repetitive motion disorder. These injuries, which can be disabling, include carpal tunnel syndrome *(see Figure 1–1), tenosynovitis and other syndromes.* [1]

Acute hand injuries include lacerations to skin, nerves and tendons; puncture wounds; thermal, chemical and electrical injuries; fractures; vascular injuries; and complex injuries, including avulsion (tearing away), amputation and crush injuries.

1.02   ANATOMY AND TERMINOLOGY

The hand is anatomically thought of as having two surfaces: these are referred to as the dorsum (the dorsal surface or back) and the palm (the palmar surface, also called the volar surface). In addition, there are two sides: the thumb is located on the radial side, and the little finger on the ulnar side. These terms are derived from the bones of the forearm, the radius and the ulna, which articulate (connect together loosely) at the wrist. (*See Figure 1–2.*)

[1]   Bone Structure

There are 27 bones in the hand. The wrist is made up of 8 bones— the carpal bones. These articulate with the radius and the ulna of the forearm proximally, and with the metacarpals distally. The metacarpals can be felt beneath the palm; they extend to the base of the fingers and thumb. (*See Figure 1–3.*) There are 5 of them and they are usually referred to by number, with the thumb extending from the first metacarpal, the index finger from the second, and so forth.

The bones of the fingers and thumb are referred to as phalanges; the fingers have three phalanges, the thumb has two. These are proximal, middle and distal in the case of the fingers; proximal and distal in the case of the thumb.

In the fingers, the joints are the metacarpophalangeal (MCP), proximal interphalangeal (PIP) and distal interphalangeal (DIP). (*See Figure 1–4.*) The wrist joint contains many articulations between the various bones.

---

[1] *See also* ch. 8.

DORSUM

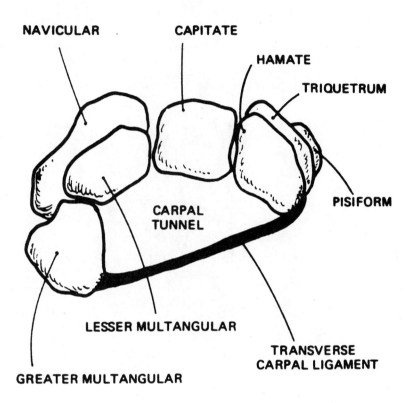

Fig. 1-1. A transverse section of the wrist joint (from the hand side) shows the capitate as the "keystone" of the arch of the wrist joint. The concave contour of the wrist bones on the volar (palm) surface of the wrist forms the carpal tunnel, with the transverse carpal ligament closing in on the volar (palm) side.

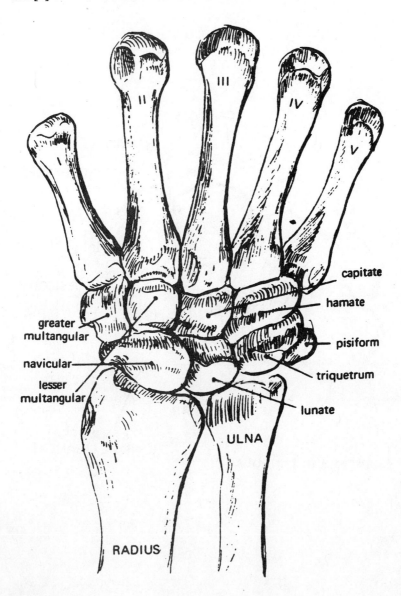

Fig. 1-2. The wrist is composed of the distal 2 inches of the radius and the carpal bones. The radius forms a joint with the carpal bones nearest the forearm. The carpal bones are arranged in a proximal row and distal row of four bones each.

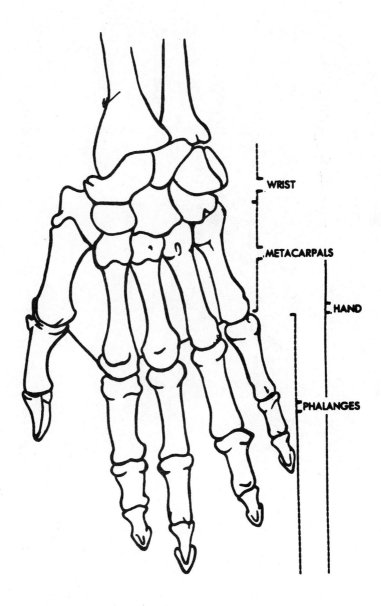

Fig. 1-3. Bone structure of the hand and wrist.

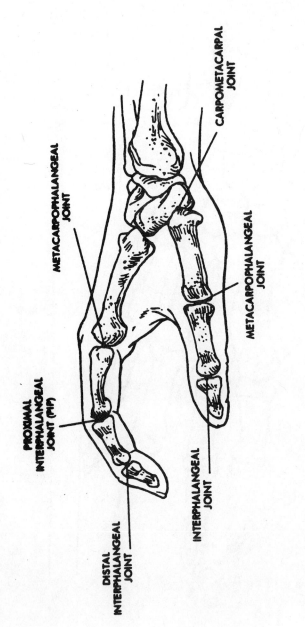

Fig. 1-4.   The joints of the hand.

[2] Muscles and Tendons

The hand is capable of a wide variety of motions. Closing the hand to make a fist is referred to as *flexion*. *Extension* is the opposite motion, straightening the fingers. Many of the muscles that produce these motions are located in the forearm as well as the hand. Thus, a forearm injury can produce a deficit in the hand. The muscles are attached to their respective bones by tendons. Ligaments, in contrast, attach bones to bones. The tendons of the hand must frequently glide over very mobile joints and are aided in this by synovial sheaths, which encase them. (The term *tendinitis* refers to an inflamed tendon; whereas the term *tenosynovitis* refers to inflammation of both the tendon and its protective sheath.) The extensor tendons are easily felt on the dorsal aspect of the hand; extending the fingers causes them to stand out so they are visible. The flexor tendons are less easily palpable in the hand, though they may be felt at the wrist.

[3] Nerves and Blood Vessels

The major nerves of the hand are the radial, median and ulnar. Each has multiple branches, serving motor and sensory functions. The three nerves that supply the hand exit the spinal cord through a total of four cervical and one thoracic nerve roots. Injuries at many different points may produce deficits in the hand.

There are two major arteries of the hand: the radial and the ulnar. (*See Figure 1–5.*) The branches of these arteries join in the hand to form arterial arches.

1.03 MECHANISMS OF INJURY

The hand is more frequently injured than any other part of the body. Hand and finger injuries constitute approximately a third of all occupational injuries requiring emergency room treatment. The most common injuries are lacerations produced by knives, followed by hypodermic needle punctures and, finally, accidents involving industrial equipment, which may result in lacerations, abrasions, fractures and more complex injuries.

Hand injuries are common in a wide variety of agricultural and industrial occupations. Laborers, clerks and food service workers are frequently affected. In one study, it was machine operators and

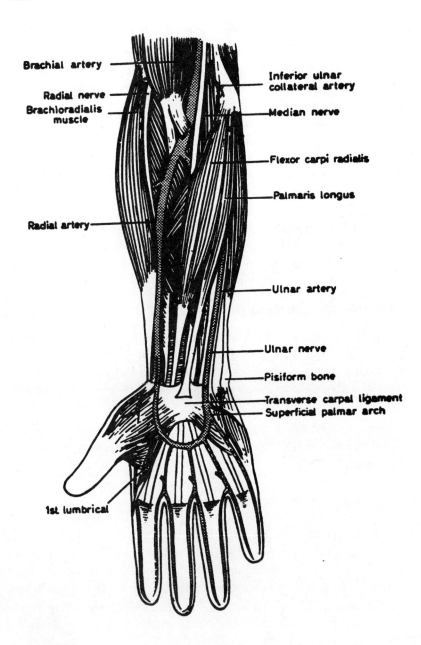

Fig. 1-5. Front of the right arm, showing the arteries and the superficial palmar arch.

assemblers who were most frequently injured (Centers for Disease Control, 1989).

[1] Agricultural Machinery

Injuries associated with machinery are relatively infrequent but may be much more serious than those that do not involve machines. Agricultural machinery, particularly grain augers and corn huskers, has been associated with severe and complex injuries, including amputations.

[2] Industrial Machinery

Industrial machinery is also associated with the risk of serious injury. A common mechanism of injury is entrapment of the hand in gears, rollers, mixers and other machine parts. The mechanical power press is frequently implicated in severe hand injuries. What is worse, approximately 49 percent of power press injuries result in amputations (Centers for Disease Control, 1988). Drill presses, milling machines and cut-off saws are also important sources of hand injury.

In addition to specific occupation, several other factors have been identified as risks for work-related hand injuries. Youth has consistently been identified as a statistic risk factor: individuals under the age of 25 run the highest chance of injury. The use of defective equipment and lack of familiarity with the task also place the operator at risk.

1.04 CLINICAL APPROACH TO THE INJURED HAND

Diagnosing the true extent of a hand injury is often the critical factor in designing the appropriate therapy. In general, the examination should take place as soon as possible after the injury. The clinical approach involves four components: history taking, physical examination, x-rays and examination under anesthesia.

[1] History

The critical components of the patient history are the timing and mechanism of the injury. The length of time that passes before the injury is evaluated by a physician has important implications for its prognosis. If many days or weeks have passed, a tendon injury may have already scarred. If an open wound is more than eight hours old, it is considered to be contaminated and should be left open, at least initially, to allow the infection to drain.

The position of the hand at the time of injury is also important, particularly with regard to tendon lacerations in the fingers. The hand is always examined in the extended position (with fingers straight). If the fingers were extended at the time of injury, the tendons were generally cut at the same level as the skin. But if the injury occurred during flexion, the cut skin will not be in the same place as the tendon laceration when the hand is extended for examination.

It is also important to document any previous injury to the hand, as well as any underlying disease, such as arthritis, that may compound the injury or mimic another. Diabetes, too, can mimic injury, either through diabetic neuropathy injuries (more frequent in the lower extremities) or through aseptic necrosis or skin infections secondary to the diabetic state.

[2] Physical Examination

The examination of the injured hand generally involves a close look at the entire affected extremity, with constant comparison to the uninjured limb. In the case of an acute open injury limited to the hand, such as a laceration, it may not be necessary to examine the rest of the body. However, in some cases, symptoms the patient experiences in the hand may actually be referred from elsewhere, necessitating a more complete examination, especially of the arm, neck and spine. This is particularly true of disorders involving nerves. Weakness and sensory disturbances in the distribution of the median nerve (the thumb, index, middle and part of the fourth fingers) may be due to nerve injury anywhere from the hand to the spine. (*See Figure 1–6.*) Only careful attention to the wrist, elbow, shoulder and neck will determine the site(s) of the injury.

The key to diagnosing a hand injury lies not in the examination of the wound itself but in examining the rest of the hand. The site of the injury is important, of course, but only a systematic evaluation of total hand function will reveal the full extent of the damage.

The appearance of the skin in the area of a wound is important. Abnormalities of color, swelling and temperature may indicate infection, compromise of the blood supply or other disease processes. In an open wound and particularly in burns, the viability of the skin must

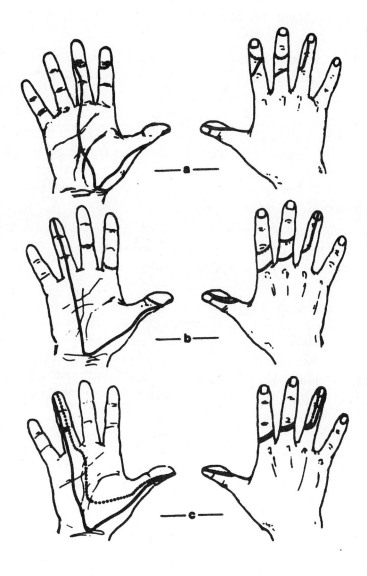

Fig. 1-6. Sensory changes after median nerve injury. The approximate areas within which sensory changes may be found in lesions of the median nerve: (a) small area, (b) average area and (c) large area.

be assessed; nonviable tissue will require excision at some point (referred to as debridement).

Tendon and muscle functions are evaluated by examining active and passive movement of the hand and digits, as well as strength and range of motion.

Tendon injuries are often apparent from the position of the fingers. For example, in the case of a lacerated flexor tendon, all the fingers will be flexed when they are relaxed except the one with the lacerated tendon. If the tendon is partially torn, the patient may experience pain when asked to flex the affected finger; there may be weakness even though there is full range of motion.

Bones and joints are evaluated by palpation (manual examination) for tenderness and deformity, active and passive movement and range of motion. However, the definitive examination of bony structures is the x-ray.[2]

Nerves are assessed by motor and sensory functions, particularly pinprick sensation and the discrimination of two points. In this procedure, an opened paper clip is usually used, starting with the ends widely separated. The examiner touches the skin with both ends of the clip simultaneously. This is repeated with the ends gradually brought closer together, to locate the distance at which the patient feels the two points as a single stimulus.

[3]   X-rays

An adequate radiologic examination is critical to the diagnosis of bone and joint injuries as well as to the detection of some foreign bodies. X-rays must be taken from at least two views, usually the anterior-posterior (front view) and the lateral (side view). Other views from a variety of angles are frequently important—these are referred to as oblique views.

[4]   Examination Under Anesthesia

In isolated instances, a complete diagnostic examination requires the use of local, regional or even general anesthesia. A hand wound is usually not probed, for example, until it is anesthetized. This permits a more extensive and careful examination with the right instruments.

---

2 *See* 1.04[3] *infra.*

General anesthesia is required for cases in which there are multiple operative sites, for example, when tissue must be taken from elsewhere in the body to use as a graft to repair the hand injury. *Local anesthesia* refers to injection of anesthetics into the area immediately surrounding the wound. *Regional anesthesia* involves nerve blocks and may be applied to any nerve in the arm or hand.

Hand surgery is usually performed with a tourniquet wrapped around the upper arm to stop the blood supply to the area. This allows the surgeon to operate in a bloodless field, which greatly improves visibility and shortens operating time. It is safe in most cases, provided the pressure applied and the duration of its use are carefully monitored. Tourniquets have been associated with some complications, however, the most serious of which are nerve palsies (McGraw and McEwen, 1987).

1.05 TYPES OF INJURIES

The major types of occupational injuries include lacerations, punctures, burns, crush injuries, avulsion (tearing) injuries and amputations. Abrasions, fractures and animal bites may also occur.

[1] Abrasions and Avulsion Injuries

An *abrasion* is an injury in which there is partial skin loss. Although the outermost layers of skin are lost, the layers responsible for regeneration remain intact, and the skin will heal spontaneously. This is in contrast to *avulsion* injuries, in which all skin layers are lost. Such injuries usually require skin grafting or tissue flaps to cover the underlying structures.

Abrasions may be associated with damage to the underlying structures caused at the time of injury. Abrasions may also be complicated by infection, and "tattoos" may occur when foreign material (usually dirt) is not removed and the skin heals over it.

An avulsion injury occurs when tissue is torn from its attachment site. Skin and nerves may be avulsed, and ligaments and tendons may also be avulsed from their attachments to bone. A severe avulsion injury involving many tissues may in fact amount to an amputation.

Skin avulsions may be complete or incomplete. An incomplete avulsion creates a flap of skin that may or may not be viable. It may take several days of observation to determine whether such a flap will survive; in the meantime, the skin flap can be taped or loosely sutured. Any nonviable tissue is removed surgically, and coverage of the defect will require a skin graft or composite tissue flap, depending on the defect.

Avulsed tendons may sometimes be repaired using tendon grafts or transfers. Since skin grafting and other operative procedures are usually necessary to treat the same wound, reconstruction may involve multiple stages over several months.

[2]   Degloving Injuries

A degloving injury is one in which the skin and possibly some soft tissue has been stripped off. In treatment, nonviable tissue must be excised to prevent infection. Skin grafting, tendon grafting and microsurgical reattachment of blood vessels may also be required. Although this may produce an acceptable cosmetic result, the functional outcome is variable. Amputation may occasionally be preferable to salvage, depending on the injury and the wishes and needs of the patient (Brown, 1988).

[3]   Ring Avulsion Injuries

A ring avulsion is essentially a degloving injury to the ring finger. When a ring is caught on a stationary object, it may strip tissues off the finger. Classically, the individual is jumping down, falling or running, and catches the ring on a fixed object; the force of the movement jerks the ring off, taking the skin, and possibly nerves and tendons, with it. The bones may fracture as well. Falling this way from a height of five feet or more can avulse all the soft tissues of the ring finger, leaving only denuded bone. This injury generally requires surgical amputation, while lesser degrees of injury may be reconstructed or skin grafted, depending on the extent and type of tissue loss.

Ring avulsion injuries are not uncommon in industry. They may be avoided by not wearing rings.

1.06   LACERATIONS

Lacerations or cuts of the fingers and hand are very common occupational injuries. In a majority of cases, the injury results from either being struck by an object or striking against a stationary object.

Knives and other sharp metal items, saws, glass, nails and machines are most frequently implicated. Those who work in food service, construction and meat packing are at great risk.

Lacerations are medically important for two reasons. First, skin injury exists that must be repaired in such a manner as to maximize function. Second, and frequently more important, there may be a deeper injury that is not apparent without a detailed physical examination.

[1] Simple Lacerations

Skin lacerations may be associated with lacerations of the nerves and tendons immediately underlying the skin. These structures are frequently not visible in the wound (cut tendons may retract a considerable distance), and their status must be assessed by a functional examination. A careful examination of range of motion and sensation will pick up subtle indications of nerve and tendon damage.

A common error occurs with small lacerations along the creases of the palmar surface of the fingers (the flexion creases). The flexor tendons and digital nerves are very close to the skin at these points and may easily be severed with a skin laceration (Brown, 1988). If the examination reveals loss of full flexion or sensory loss, then the injured tendons and nerves must be located and repaired. This often means extending the original laceration surgically for adequate visualization.

Simple lacerations of the skin and soft tissues can usually be repaired easily. When the wound is contaminated, it is preferable to allow the wound to stay open as it heals, which permits infected material to drain; this is referred to as secondary closure. If an infected wound is sutured closed, an abscess is likely to result, with further tissue damage.

Wounds that go without treatment for over seven to eight hours are presumed to be contaminated and are treated the same way. Wounds created by objects that are highly likely to be contaminated (such as broken glass in a garbage can, or a meat knife) may also be left open.

[2] Tendon Lacerations

Tendons attach muscles to bone. When the muscle contracts, it shortens, pulling on the tendon, which moves the bone in the direction of the muscle. Tendons in the hand must travel considerable distances.

Many of the muscles that operate the fingers are located in the forearm; the tendons must cross the wrist, traverse the palm and then travel up the finger to their insertion sites. When muscles contract, the attached tendons must be able to glide smoothly through all the surrounding structures for full range of motion to occur. This gliding motion is facilitated in the hand by sheaths that encase the tendons.

The severed hand tendon is one of the most challenging injuries to repair and rehabilitate, even for an experienced hand surgeon. That is because the scars formed after any tendon injury or surgical repair tend to glue together all the surrounding tissues and can prevent smooth motion of the tendon; the tendon may even be glued into a fixed position.

One of the most important factors favoring a good prognosis is the site of injury. The relationships of the structures surrounding the tendon vary from site to site. When the lacerated tendon is in a tight space, the resulting scar invariably hampers the motion of the tendon.

[3]   Flexor Tendon Lacerations

Lacerations of the flexor tendon are very common because of their location just under the skin in the palm and the palmar aspect of the fingers: this is the gripping surface of the hand. Severed flexor tendons present major problems for both patient and surgeon. Surgical repair is often difficult even for experienced hand surgeons, and rehabilitation is long and arduous, demanding considerable motivation on the part of the patient. For these reasons, the outcome of a flexor tendon repair is frequently suboptimal and leaves the patient with some degree of impairment. Unfortunately, because of the function of flexor tendons, this impairment will be in gripping, the most important function of the hand.

[a]   Classification

Flexor tendon injuries are usually classified by location, or zone. The hand is divided into five zones. Zone 1 extends from the fingertip to the middle of the finger; zone 2, from the mid-finger to the first (distal) palmar crease. The mid-palm contains zone 3. Zone 4 is the most proximal (closer to the point of origin) third of the palm and contains the carpal tunnel, and zone 5 is in the forearm. The thumb is subdivided into its own two zones, zone 1 and zone 2.

This classification scheme is useful for prognosis. Lacerations in zones 3 (mid-palm) and 5 (forearm) are more likely to have satisfactory results than lacerations in other zones. Severed tendons in zone 4 are compounded by the tight fit through the carpal tunnel. Zone 2 lacerations have the worst prognosis, and the prognosis for zone 1 injuries is only slightly more favorable than for those in zone 2 (Burke and Pulvertaft, 1987).

In zone 2, there are eight flexor tendons, two for each finger. Each pair of tendons runs together in a single, tightly fitting sheath that passes through a tight fibro-osseous tunnel. Lacerations of the tendons invariably also cut through the sheath, and the inevitable scar will restrict motion of the tendons to some degree, even with the best repair.

[b]   Diagnosis

The diagnosis of flexor tendon injuries is made by physical examination and requires a detailed knowledge of the functional anatomy of the hand. The diagnosis is not made by the site of the skin wound, which can easily lead the examiner astray. The relationships of tendon relative to skin change, depending on whether the hand is flexed or extended. A laceration may occur with the hand flexed, but any palmar surface wound is examined with the hand extended. Tendon injuries are not diagnosed by examining the wound; many tendons retract when they are cut, so the ends may not be visible in the wound.

There are two flexor tendons for each finger, the superficialis and the profundus, both of which originate in the forearm. The superficialis inserts at the middle phalanx of the finger and bends the finger at the proximal interphalangeal joint PIP). The profundus inserts at the base of the distal phalanx and flexes the fingertip.

Flexor tendons are examined by observing active movements of the hand and digits. The hand is laid on a flat surface while the examiner presses on the fingers. The profundus tendon is tested by seeing if the patient can raise the tip of the finger while the examiner holds the middle portion down. The examiner may push gently against the tip, to see if it raises against resistance. The superficialis tendon is tested similarly, with the examiner holding down the other fingers.

The diagnosis of injury to these tendons is sometimes straightforward, as when the patient closes the hand to make a fist and one finger remains straight. Frequently it is not this easy, particularly if the tendon is only partially severed. In this case, there may well be full range of motion of the finger, but there is weakness and pain.

Weakness and pain due to tendon injury may be compounded by weakness and pain due to associated nerve, muscle or skin injury, which complicates the diagnosis. The motor and sensory functions of the rest of the hand must also be evaluated.

[c]   Treatment

There have been several longstanding controversies in tendon repair. First, the timing of repair has been disputed, particularly for zone 2 injuries. Repair may be performed early (referred to as primary or delayed primary repair) or late (secondary repair), in which case the wound is closed and the tendon repaired by graft later. The graft is a tendon harvested from elsewhere in the body. Currently the consensus favors a primary or delayed primary repair. Secondary repair by grafting may be required when considerable time has passed since the injury or when other conditions or injuries render early repair impossible.

Other controversies concern the tendons themselves: when both tendons to a finger are cut, there has been disagreement over whether both or only one should be repaired. It is the general concensus that whenever possible, both should be repaired. There is also some disagreement over sheath repairs (Leddy, 1988).

Tendon repair surgery is an extensive and involved subject that cannot be covered here in detail. The reader is referred to the Bibliography for further information.

[d]   Complications

Great care must be exercised by the surgeon to avoid further trauma to the tendons and their sheaths; the greater the trauma, the larger the resulting scar, and the worse the functional outcome. This is not a simple procedure. Sutures must be strong enough and numerous enough to hold together a structure that routinely undergoes significant tension, but the more extensive the suturing, the more the tendon is traumatized.

Repaired tendons may rupture. This may be precipitated by a number of factors during the rehabilitation phase of treatment.

1. Poor cooperation, inappropriate splinting or activity may occur.

2. Postoperative infection may occur with or without a hematoma and can greatly increase the local trauma and scarring, resulting in a much worse outcome.

3. Joint contractures often occur following tendon repair. These require careful rehabilitation if they are to be avoided (Burke and Pulvertaft, 1987).

4. Adhesions or scars may complicate recovery. In certain cases, these may be surgically treated using a procedure called tenolysis, which releases the tendon from its scar.

[e] Rehabilitation and Prognosis

Rehabilitation is as critical to the outcome as the surgical repair. It is lengthy and detailed. The best outcome requires considerable motivation on the part of the patient.

Rehabilitation can begin on the first postoperative day and continues for at least three months in most cases. It involves splinting and a graduated program of exercise, progressing from passive to active motion, then to motion against resistance and finally to work-related activities. For optimal results, the patient must be closely supervised by an experienced hand therapist.

The prognosis is determined by a number of factors. The site of a laceration is very important. Additional injuries, particularly crush injuries and fractures, can seriously interfere with repair and rehabilitation, resulting in a poor outcome. However, tendon healing is slow and scarring inevitable; thus even the simplest tendon laceration has a guarded prognosis for good functional outcome.

[4] Extensor Tendon Lacerations

Extensor tendon laceration repair is complicated by the fact that these tendons are thinner and less able to hold sutures well. In addition, most extensor tendon injuries occur at a joint. When the hand makes a fist, the flexor tendons are on the inside, whereas the extensors are on the outside and hence more vulnerable to injury from objects striking the hand.

Also, any tendon laceration at a joint is quite likely to penetrate the joint, which greatly complicates the injury and the treatment (Doyle, 1988). In addition to the severed tendon, there may be extensive soft tissue loss and bone injury, as is seen in injuries with planers, sanders, circular and other types of saws. In addition, crush injuries to the hand are likely to involve the extensor tendons.

Six extrinsic extensor tendons originate in the forearm, one for each finger and two for the thumb. When the fingers are stretched out, the extensor tendons can be felt easily, especially where they cross the joints. All these originate on muscles in the forearm and enter the hand by passing under a fibrous band, the extensor retinaculum, at the wrist (this band holds the tendons in place at the wrist).

The extensor mechanism for the fingers is complicated and involves both the long extensor tendons (the extrinsic muscles) and the short intrinsic muscles that originate in the hand itself. In the finger, each long extensor tendon divides into three: the central band (called the central slip) attaches to the middle phalanx, and the other two (the lateral bands) travel up the sides of the finger to insert on the distal phalanx.

[a] Diagnosis

The diagnosis of extensor tendon laceration is made by physical examination of tendon function; the tendons do not retract and are easily visible in the wound. The full extensor mechanism of the finger is complex, and extensor tendon lacerations may easily be missed. A high index of suspicion and diligent search for subtle findings are required.

The examiner may palpate for tenderness, and then the extension of each phalanx is tested. Sensation and motor function of the rest of the hand are also assessed, since abnormalities in movement can result from nerve damage.

[b] Treatment

The surgical treatment of extensor tendon lacerations is complex. The exact procedure is determined by the level at which lacerations occur, from the forearm to the fingertip. In some cases, no surgery is necessary, because the ends of the tendon are in close proximity and will unite in healing if held in place by a splint. This is true of extensor tendon injuries in the finger. Splinting and prolonged immobilization are all that is necessary. Other cases will need tendon repair, grafting or tendon transfer, depending on the nature of the injury.

[c] Complications

When the injury involves the joint and other structures as well as the tendon, adhesions formed during the healing process can cement the structures together.

A common problem with extensor tendon injuries is delay in treatment, either because the diagnosis was missed by the clinician or because the patient misjudged the seriousness of the injury and failed to seek early treatment. If the delay is sufficiently long, a contracture will develop, and the treatment will be more complicated.

Problems with splints are another common source of complications, particularly removal of the splint before the tendon has healed. Tendons may take as long as 12 weeks to heal.

Rupture, infection and contracture are likely to complicate extensor tendon repair.

[d] Rehabilitation and Prognosis

Extensor tendon injuries in the finger are the exception to the rule of early mobilization. Fingers are immobilized for prolonged periods. Elsewhere in the hand and in the forearm, extensor tendon injuries are rehabilitated using the same principles as those of flexor tendons.[3] The healing process is just as slow, and the prognosis for a good outcome equally guarded.

[e] Secretan's Disease

Secretan's disease, also called peritendinous fibrosis, is a condition of uncertain etiology that has been seen in workers who report a blow to the back of the hand. There are no accompanying lacerations or fractures, and there may be psychologic abnormalities. It is characterized by a firm swelling over the dorsum (back) of the hand, which progresses until the patient is unable to flex the fingers; prolonged disability is the usual result (Doyle, 1988).

Surgical treatment of Secretan's disease has met with poor results. Problems have included failure to improve, faulty healing, prolonged recovery and high recurrence rate. Conservative management is not very successful either in terms of cure, but most authors prefer not to operate (Doyle, 1988).

[f] Boutonnière Deformity

When that portion of the extensor tendon to the middle phalanx is disrupted, the proximal interphalangeal joint becomes fixed in the flexed position (the proximal joint of the finger is bent). This is usually associated with hyperextension at the distal finger joint. The resulting deformity is called a Boutonnière deformity.

---

[3] *See* 1.06[3] [e] *supra.*

Classically, the patient sustains a closed injury to the proximal interphalangeal joint, frequently a jam or a sprain. The joint is swollen and painful but otherwise not deformed. On examination, there is some loss of extension, but it may not be more than 15 or 20 degrees and so may easily be missed by an inexperienced observer (Doyle, 1988).

In spite of tendon disruption, the joint can still be extended, because other small muscles participate in extension at this point. However, without the long extensor tendon present, the extensor mechanism is unbalanced, and repeated use of the finger will lead to the boutonnière deformity over time.

The usual treatment consists of splinting the joint in the extended position. Surgery may be required in some cases.

[g]   Mallet Finger

When the lateral bands (the distalmost portion of the extensor tendon) are disrupted, the patient is unable to straighten the distal phalanx, and the distalmost part of the finger is permanently bent. This condition is referred to as a mallet finger. The injury may be penetrating, as in a laceration or crush injury. More frequently, the tip of the finger is suddenly flexed with enough force that the tendon is avulsed (torn) from the bone. In many cases, the tendon itself is intact but its bony attachment site is avulsed from the rest of the bone.

Mallet finger resulting from closed injury usually heals with splinting alone. Surgery may be necessary in some cases.

[5]   Nerve Lacerations

Intact nerves are vital to the function of the hand. A severed peripheral nerve renders an area of hand insensate, with potentially disastrous effects on function.

Nerve repair is greatly complicated by the internal anatomy of the nerve. Each nerve contains thousands of individual nerve cell fibers (called axons), each originating from and terminating at specific locations, and it is impossible to reconnect them precisely with current techniques. Axons are organized into bundles, or fascicles, and these may be reapproximated using microsurgical instruments, but even this is suboptimal.

A severed axon undergoes a degeneration process that takes about three weeks. The nerve cell body will regenerate a new axon, which will grow along the path of the old neural tube, but this does not necessarily grow to terminate at and stimulate the same structure as the original axon. Regenerating a connection to the correct structure obviously depends on several factors: the availability of the right path, reapproximation of all the individual severed axons and minimal scarring.

In some injuries, the nerve is damaged but not actually cut; this is referred to as neurapraxia. Greater damage may produce an axonotmesis: some of the axons in the nerve are torn, but the tubes that encase them are not. Recovery from either of these injuries will occur spontaneously, although the recovery time in axonotmesis is much longer. Neurotmesis is the most severe injury: in this case, all the components of the nerve have been cut. The nerve ends must be reapproximated surgically if there is to be any recovery at all.

[a] Diagnosis

The diagnosis of nerve injuries is made by physical examination and a knowledge of the anatomy of nerve distributions. Sensory and motor functions are tested.

[b] Treatment

If the two ends of the nerve can be brought together without tension, then the nerve can be repaired by suturing the severed ends. If there is a gap, then a nerve graft is necessary. The suturing is usually done under a microscope, which greatly improves the ability of the surgeon to see and appropriately align the fascicles. Surgery may involve suturing the epineurium (tissue that encases the nerve) or suturing the groups of fascicles.

[c] Complications and Prognosis

There are two major complications of nerve injuries: suboptimal nerve function and pain. Pain may result from reflex sympathetic dystrophy[4] or from neuromas—small but extremely painful masses of nerve fibers that form during healing.

Neuropraxias heal spontaneously, and usually completely. The prognosis for axonotmesis is fair, although the recovery time is longer.

When the nerve is completely severed and repaired, there will be some recovery of function, but it will never return to preinjury levels.

---

[4] *See* 1.14[2] *infra.*

Complete surgical realignment is impossible, and there will be some scar, all of which will interfere with nerve function. Generally the prognosis is good if recovery is clearly progressing within the first few months after repair, and poor if it is not. Nerve recovery continues for years, so the full extent of recovery does not become apparent for some time.

The ultimate outcome also depends on features of the initial injury: the smaller the nerve, the smaller the affected territory, and the less the effect on overall function of the hand. Similarly, the more distal the injury, the better the prognosis. Nonetheless, for certain individuals, such as musicians, even a small loss of nerve function can be devastating to a career.

Age also affects prognosis: generally the younger the patient, the better the nerve will regenerate.

1.07   PUNCTURE AND INJECTION INJURIES

Two types of puncture wounds will be considered here: needle-stick injuries, which are very common among health care workers, and high-pressure injection injuries, which are industrial accidents.

[1]   Needle-Stick Injuries

Needle-stick injuries are usually accidental skin punctures with a hypodermic or surgical needle. The wound, most frequently located on a finger, is almost always trivial. However, the injury may be associated with transmission of one or more infectious diseases, most notably hepatitis or acquired immunodeficiency syndrome (AIDS), which may result in serious disability or loss of life.

[2]   High-Pressure Injection Injuries

The other type of puncture injury that deserves mention is more accurately called an injection injury and is caused by an industrial high pressure device. Grease guns, spray guns and diesel fuel injectors are the most common instruments involved. Such guns generate a pressure in excess of 5000 pounds per square inch, which propels material through a nozzle that may be less than 1 mm in size. Injuries often occur when the operator attempts to wipe the nozzle with his free hand.

The entry wound is frequently pinpoint in size, but the injected substance causes severe irritation and may destroy substantial amounts of tissue. Certain substances, such as paints and paint solvents, are capable of entering the lymphatics, which transports them proximally, causing such extensive tissue destruction that amputation may be required.

[a] Symptoms

The initial penetration is usually almost painless and may be dismissed by anyone not acquainted with these types of injuries. Subsequently pain and swelling develop, and within hours, there may be fever and an elevation of the white blood cell count (those cells that respond to inflammation). The outcome depends largely on the type of material that was injected. Grease and oil create a more localized response, with formation of an oleoma (collection of oil and the tissue response to it) and ulceration. Paints and paint solvents spread rapidly and create intense tissue reaction over a much larger area.

[b] Treatment

These injuries are treated by decompression and debridement (removal of all devitalized tissue) as soon as possible. Time is particularly critical in the case of solvents. Surgery must be performed under specific conditions that avoid increasing the pressure in the tissues (local injections of anesthetics are contraindicated, as well as pressure bandages). As much of the material as possible must be removed through as large an incision as is necessary.

1.08 BURNS

Many different types of burn injuries may occur in the workplace. The mechanisms of injury include chemical and electrical burns, scalds, flash burns and contact burns.

Electrical burns often involve the hand as the point of entry. Extensive damage usually occurs elsewhere in the body, along the path of the electric current and at the exit site, which is often on the leg.

[1] Classification of Burns

Burns are classified according to their depth. In the past, it was common to refer to first-, second-, third-and fourth-degree burns. The first-degree burn is characterized by erythema (redness, as in a sunburn). Blisters are the main feature of second-degree burns. In a third-degree burn, the epidermis and the dermis are destroyed (all layers of skin, including those responsible for regeneration). A third-degree burn lacks the capacity to re-epithelialize, or to cover itself with skin in the process of healing, because the layers of skin responsible for re-epithelialization have been destroyed. A fourth-degree burn involves tissues beneath the skin, including fat, muscles, tendons and even bone, in severe cases.

It has now become more common to classify burns in two categories rather than four degrees: These are the partial-thickness or superficial, and full-thickness or deep burns. Partial thickness refers to first- and second-degree burns, where enough skin remains for re-epithelialization; deeper burns (third or fourth degree), in which the regenerative layer of skin is absent, are full thickness.

This latter classification system is more useful clinically. In partial-thickness burns, healing is usually satisfactory without skin grafting, whereas the full-thickness burn requires tissue replacement. However, in the hand, "satisfactory" healing usually means with minimal scarring, since scars lead to contractures and loss of function. Thus a partial-thickness burn elsewhere on the body may be managed medically with satisfactory results, but the same degree of injury on the hand requires a skin graft to maintain maximal mobility of the tissues.

[2]   Evaluation and Treatment

The depth of a burn is not always immediately clear and may not become evident for a few days. Partial-thickness burns are tender and pink or red in color; blisters may be present. In full-thickness burns, the skin itself does not suffer pain (is anesthetic), because the nerve endings in the skin have been destroyed. A full-thickness burn may be white or charred.

[a]   Superficial Burns

The management of a superficial burn is largely symptomatic; the wound should be cleaned and dressed, and the patient is encouraged to exercise the hand. Blisters are left intact in most cases: the blister itself is an effective dressing, and opening it introduces bacteria into the wound (Salisbury and Dingeldein, 1988). Tetanus prophylaxis is routine for all burns as well as for penetrating wounds.

[b] Deep Burns

A deep burn requires a much more aggressive approach. Initially the blood supply to the injured area must be evaluated, especially if the burn is circumferential (encircles the arm, hand or fingers). Severe swelling may develop in the hours following a burn, and when this is circumferential, the swollen tissue acts like a tourniquet, cutting off the blood supply to the distal tissue.

The two methods of evaluating perfusion are first to palpate the pulses at the wrist (in the case of an arm burn) and, second, ultrasound detection of pulses in the hand. If the pulse is no longer detectable, the swollen area must be surgically decompressed immediately, a procedure referred to as *escharotomy*. Incisions are made through the skin in the swollen tissue, which relieves the tension, reduces the pressure and permits blood flow to continue. In addition, it dramatically increases the early mobility of the injured hand, which is vital to preserving function.

The management of deep burns also includes elevation of the arm and hand, to encourage blood flow back to the body and reduce swelling; application of topical antibiotics; and splinting, to maintain the hand in the best position for minimizing a deforming scar. Splinting is particularly important, since the position that is most comfortable is not at all optimal for preserving function. Early physical therapy is also vital to maximizing long-term function (Salisbury and Dingeldein, 1988).

A deep burn creates a wound that generally requires a skin graft for coverage, but the timing of this procedure is a matter of controversy. There are two approaches. In the first, surgery is performed early; the wound is excised (nonviable tissue is removed); and the area is skin grafted immediately. The second approach is more conservative initially: surgery is delayed for up to two weeks. This allows more exact delineation of true full thickness burns, since many areas that initially appear to be full thickness are in fact deep partial thickness and may be capable of spontaneous healing. Data from recent studies tends to favor the delayed approach, except in cases in which the wound is compounded by an underlying bone fracture (Salisbury and Dingeldein, 1988).

[3] Types of Burns

Different types of burns create diverse types of wounds and frequently demand different approaches to management. The most common types of burn are scalds, flash burns, contact burns, chemical burns and electrical burns.

[a] Scalds

Scalds may result from accidents involving hot liquids, steam or molten material such as tar, bitumen, molten metals and molten plastic. In the immediate treatment of a scald with molten material, water should not be used to cool the wound until all the material has been wiped away. Water causes explosive spattering when it comes into contact with the molten material, which will extend the injury. Tar and bitumen, which are used by roofers and road crews, are removed with paraffin oil. Molten plastic can only be removed surgically (Gurdak, 1990).

[b] Contact Burns

Contact burns commonly occur with hot metal materials, rivets and presses (Gurdak, 1990). The burn is usually deep but well localized. In burns associated with presses, there may be associated crush injury and fractures, which complicate the management. High-speed conveyor belts may also produce crush injury compounded by a deep contact burn (due to the heat generated by friction). A fracture under a burn wound requires early surgical treatment. Nonviable tissue is removed (debrided), the fracture is repaired and skin is grafted to the wound for coverage (Salisbury and Dingeldein, 1988).

[c] Chemical Burns

Chemical burns may be caused by acids, alkaline materials, organic chemicals or phosphorus. The degree of injury depends on the type of chemical, its concentration and the duration of exposure. Although some chemical injuries may theoretically be treated with specific neutralizing agents, these are rarely immediately available, and the neutralizing process produces heat that may deepen the burn. Therefore, most experts recommend copious irrigation with water, which both removes and dilutes the offending chemical (Gurdak, 1990). Exceptions to this rule include burns caused by lime (the major component of cement), in which case the dust should be wiped off before irrigation; phenol, which is not soluble in water and requires glycerol or other solvents; and hydrofluoric acid (Salisbury and Dingeldein, 1988).

Sulfuric acid is the most common chemical agent involved in occupational burns. Hydrofluoric acid burns are less common but more severe; this material is absorbed into the tissues, producing a deep burn. Absorbed acid cannot be irrigated but may be treated with calcium gluconate injections or excision (Salisbury and Dingeldein, 1988). The most common alkali burns occur with sodium hydroxide, potassium hydroxide and lime (Gurdak, 1990).

[d] Electrical Burns

The hand is frequently involved in electrical injuries, although damage elsewhere in the body may be more extensive and life threatening. Cardiopulmonary arrest (from cardiac dysrhythmias) and renal failure may occur.

The essential principle of electrical injuries is that they are more severe than they appear on external examination. Injury occurs at the entry site, along the path that the electricity takes, and at the exit site. Extensive muscle damage that is not evident from examination of the skin is common.

The initial management is similar to that for deep circumferential burns: The arm should be elevated and splinted, and the pulses should be carefully monitored. Because injury to deep tissues occurs, severe swelling (edema) may occcur in those tissues, requiring not only immediate escharotomy (surgical decompression of the swollen area) but also fasciotomy (a much deeper incision) to relieve the pressure caused by edema. Extensive surgical debridement, followed by covering the wound with a skin graft or flap (skin and muscle grafting), is often necessary (Salisbury and Dingeldein, 1988).

[4] Rehabilitation and Prognosis

Deep burns can create unsightly scars, which can continue to enlarge for 12 to 18 months after the burn. Such scars are not only a cosmetic problem, but they may seriously interfere with function. Joints may be more severely affected, because motion increases the tension across the wound, which tends to produce yet more scar tissue. Although scarring cannot be prevented, it may be minimized by proper skin care, splinting, positioning and exercise. Antiscar pressure garments are also available.

1.09   ANIMAL BITES

Animal bites are a common occupational hazard for veterinarians, farm workers, laboratory workers and others. The major problems of bite wounds are local tissue damage from the bite itself and infection, which commonly and rapidly spreads up the arm in the form of lymphangitis (inflammation of the lymphatic vessels). Local tissue damage may be extensive, involving both crush and laceration. Bloodstream infections that have spread to other organs may complicate the localized infection.

Most animal bites are not sutured but are left to heal spontaneously, as they are considered to be contaminated. Thorough irrigation is important. Larger wounds require surgical debridement to remove nonviable tissue. If necessary, they can be sutured closed some days later, when infection has been treated (Neviaser, 1988). Physicians and nurses should be aware of specific bacterial infections that are typically associated with particular types of animal bites.

1.10   VASCULAR INJURIES

The two major types of vascular injury are hemorrhage and occlusion. In occupational injuries, hemorrhage generally occurs due to another injury and will not be discussed here.

Occlusions may be primary injuries to the vessels themselves that cause them to spasm or clot, or they may result from external pressure, as in the severe swelling that occurs in compartment syndrome. Occlusions may be arterial or venous, but most such lesions in the hand are arterial.

[1]   Compartment Syndrome

The tissues of an extremity may be subdivided into different compartments that are bordered by bone, fascia (membranes) and skin. The compartments are long, running the full length of the forearm, upper arm, etc., and enclose the muscles (which make up the bulk of the compartment), nerves and blood vessels. Most compartments are a closed space; their boundaries are fixed and cannot expand much to accommodate an increase in pressure or contents.

Several disease processes can increase the pressure in a compartment. When this occurs unchecked, the pressure will eventually reach a degree that prohibits blood flow into the tissues of the compartment. The result is ischemic necrosis (cell death due to inadequate blood supply), which affects the muscles and nerves in that compartment.

In cases in which a single compartment is involved, the muscle dies and is replaced by a fibrous scar that is considerably shorter than the original muscle, thereby considerably deforming the affected limb. The nerves die also, leading to loss of sensation as well as movement. When such arterial compromise is severe enough and affects large areas, gangrene may result.

Compartment syndrome was originally described in 1881 by Volkmann in a patient with fracture of the humerus (the bone in the upper arm). In such an injury, the fracture can elicit spasm of the brachial artery, which cuts off the blood supply to the forearm muscles. Subsequently the muscles die and are replaced by scar tissue, which progressively shortens and produces a permanent contracture, referred to as a Volkmann's ischemic contracture.

Compartment syndrome is not a common consequence of injury, but if it is detected early, it is easy to prevent its further development. Basically the treatment is to surgically open the compartment (fasciotomy).[5]

[a] Causes

Compartment syndrome may occur in the arm and in the hand. It may be produced by a wide variety of injuries, including burns (in which case the syndrome is caused by local tissue swelling), bleeding into the compartment from arterial injury, fractures with associated arterial spasm, high-pressure injection injuries and snakebites. It can also be caused by tight casts or dressings that apply excessive external pressure. Roller crush injuries, such as those associated with printing presses, may also produce this syndrome, even though the skin may be intact.

[b] Diagnosis

The diagnosis of the compartment syndrome depends heavily on the clinical picture. This is characterized by pain, especially with stretching of the affected muscles, and diminished sensation, due to nerve ischemia. In addition, the area is tight and swollen, and the

---

[5] *See* 1.10[1][c] *infra.*

affected muscles are tender to the touch. The pulses may or may not be affected by injury to a single compartment and so are not reliable guides to the detection of inadequate blood supply. The same is true of skin color and temperature.

The integrity of the blood supply may require specialized monitoring techniques, using the Doppler principle, plethysmography (measurement of changes in the volume of an organ or structure resulting from an increase or decrease in the amount of blood circulating through the part) or the use of arterial contrast injections to delineate by x-ray the actual blood supply.

A variety of devices are available for monitoring intracompartmental pressures, and these may be helpful in distinguishing the compartment syndrome from other conditions, such as nerve and arterial injuries (Rowland, 1988). Such injuries may also produce pain and sensory deficits, leading to confusion. In addition, the three conditions—nerve injury, arterial injury and compartment syndrome—may coexist.

[c]   Treatment

Compartment syndrome constitutes an emergency and requires an immediate fasciotomy: an incision through the skin and into each compartment. The incision must be long enough to decompress the entire compartment, which, in the case of the forearm, means from the elbow to the hand. When the individual muscles are directly examined, they may also require an epimysiotomy (incisions through the membranes that envelop them).

The forearm is usually decompressed by a single, long incision. Decompression of the hand usually requires two or more incisions, depending on the number of compartments involved. Fingers may be individually decompressed if necessary.

The wound is left open for several days while the swelling subsides. It may be partially closed on the fifth day but should not be completely closed until the tenth day. This may require skin grafting in some cases. Even when skin grafting is not necessary, the healed decompression wound leaves a long and wide scar.

[d]   Prognosis

Early fasciotomy (surgical opening of the compartment) maximizes the potential for a good outcome. However, fasciotomy may still be helpful if it is done days after injury. If fasciotomy is not performed to treat the compartment syndrome, the muscles will degenerate and fibrose. The resulting scar contracts as part of the normal healing process and produces a contracture that pulls the affected parts into a permanent deformity. The deformity can be minimized by splinting and may be modified later by corrective surgery.

The nerves in the compartment are also involved; if the condition remains untreated, these usually die, resulting in sensory as well as motor impairment.

[2] Thrombosis

Arterial thrombosis occurs when a blood clot obstructs an artery and occludes flow. The tissue normally fed by this artery becomes ischemic (the condition of inadequate blood supply); it is painful, cold, numb and pale. The most common thrombosis in the hand is ulnar artery thrombosis. It is associated primarily with the symptoms of Raynaud's phenomenon,[6] although the typical ischemic symptoms, particularly numbness and coolness, may be present. In some instances, especially if underlying arteriosclerosis is present, gangrene of the fingertips may develop.

[a] Causes

Arterial thrombosis can occur as an occupational injury and usually results from single or recurrent episodes of blunt trauma. The ulnar artery is most frequently involved, with a blow to the side of the hand the usual cause. The best known disorder of this type is the "hammer hand syndrome," in which the hand is repeatedly used as a hammer.[7] A careful occupational history is important to determine the cause of the thrombosis.

Arterial thrombosis has other causes, including embolism (blood clots or other material that circulate in the blood) from elsewhere in the body. In the case of blood clots (thromboembolism), a common source is a thrombosed aneurysm (ballooning out of an artery) in the arm, from which pieces of clot break off and travel downstream.

A rare cause of arterial thrombosis in the hand is an inflammatory disease known as giant cell arteritis. Here the occlusion is due to a

---

[6] *See* 1.10[4] *infra.*

[7] *See* 1.10[2][b] *infra.*

local intra-arterial inflammatory reaction. It most commonly affects the temporal arteries in the head but has been reported to occur in the hand (Newmeyer, 1988).

A number of other ischemic diseases may affect the upper extremity, but most affect the arteries in the arm or more proximal locations.

[b]   Hammer Hand Syndrome

Hammer hand syndrome is the major occupational form of ulnar artery thrombosis and is also associated with ulnar artery aneurysms, which are much less common.[8] The trauma that produces the thrombosis comes from repeated use of the hand as a hammer. Typically the ulnar edge of the hand (the side of the hand, below the little finger) is used to strike an object. The muscular mass on this aspect of the hand is the hypothenar eminence, and the syndrome is also referred to as the hypothenar hammer syndrome.

It is thought that repeated trauma damages the inner lining of the artery, which stimulates clot formation; damage to blood vessel linings is an important stimulus for clotting under normal circumstances. Alternatively, the trauma may induce the formation of an aneurysm, which stimulates clot formation (Aucilino, 1990). The end point either way is occlusion of the lumen (hollow interior of the artery) by a clot.

[c]   Diagnosis

Physical examination usually reveals cool fourth and fifth fingers. There may be sensory loss in this region. Palpation of the hand along the course of the ulnar artery is usually painful.

Blood flow to the hand enters the hand via two arteries, the radial and the ulnar, which are located one on each side of the hand. In 80 percent of normal individuals, these two arteries interconnect in the hand through the palmar arches. Patency of the artery may be examined using the Allen test. (*See Figure 1–7.*) In this test, the examiner occludes both arteries by pressure and then releases them in sequence to see if the hand fills (turns pink). Normally the hand should fill fully when either side is occluded, because blood from one artery passes to the other side through the palmar arches.

If the ulnar artery is occluded, the hand will fill when only the radial side is released. It will remain white when the radial side is pressed

---

[8] *See* 1.10 [3] *infra.*

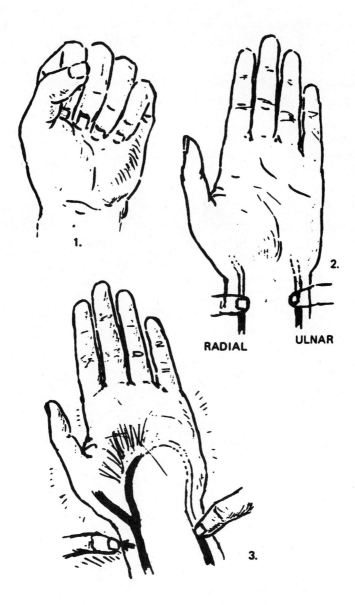

RADIAL   ULNAR

Fig. 1-7. The Allen test is performed by having the patient make a fist several times (1). The physician presses on the radial and ulnar arteries, occluding the pulse prior to having the patient open the hand (2). Either the radial or ulnar artery is released, and the hand is observed to see if the pallor decreases as the blood rushes into the hand to return it to its normal pink color.

and the ulnar side is released. However, many normal individuals do not have complete palmar arches and will therefore have "false-positive" results on the Allen test.

The diagnosis may be confirmed by a variety of laboratory tests, including digital plethysmography, which examines changes in skin impedance that occur when blood flow is obstructed. Doppler flow studies and radionuclide flow studies are also employed (Aucilino, 1990). Some physicians recommend arteriogram of the hand, but this is controversial (Aucilino, 1990).

[d] Treatment

The surgical treatment of thrombosis is also a matter of controversy. Thrombectomy (removal of the clot) is recommended by some, as is resection and reconstruction of the involved segment of artery. The major complications are infection and, if the artery is repaired, recurrent thrombosis. When thrombosis occurs, further repair is not recommended unless digital ischemia develops. In many cases, relief of symptoms persists despite thrombosis of the repair (Newmeyer, 1988).

Physicians who favor a nonsurgical approach to the problem view the pathology of the syndrome differently. Their theory is that ulnar artery disease is primarily a problem of the sympathetic nerves, which induce vasospasm, rather than simple thrombosis. This would explain why the predominant symptoms are typically of the vasospastic or Raynaud's type. Drugs (vasodilators) and surgical approaches (sympathectomy) have also been used to treat this problem (Newmeyer, 1988).

[3] Ulnar Artery Aneurysms

An aneurysm is the dilation of an artery; the wall becomes damaged, weakened and balloons out. The most common cause of ulnar artery aneurysm is repeated blunt trauma due to the hammer hand syndrome. It can also occur in individuals who do sculpture (Rothkopf, et al., 1990). Aneurysms may also develop after a single blow (Aucilino, 1990).

The symptoms include pain and numbness in the fourth and fifth fingers, which develop when a clot forms in the aneurysm and pieces of it break off and travel into the fingers. Physical examination may reveal a pulsatile mass at the wrist. The Allen test is usually normal.[9] Angiography confirms the diagnosis but is not usually necessary.

The treatment is surgical resection. If blood flow to the hand is adequate without the ulnar artery, resection and tying off the two ends may be all that is necessary. In other cases, reconstruction using a vein graft may be necessary.

[4] Raynaud's Phenomenon

Raynaud's phenomenon is caused by a spasm of the small blood vessels in the hands and fingers. This reduces the blood supply and produces pain, numbness and pallor. The stimulus for the spasm is cold; classically the affected digits become painful and turn white on exposure to cold.

Occupationally induced Raynaud's phenomenon is associated with the use of vibrating hand tools. The first symptoms are usually not of the Raynaud's type: sensory abnormalities such as numbness and tingling, but without recognizable vasospasm. Symptoms often begin at the fingertip and, as the disease progresses, affect more of the finger, and then more fingers. With time, the symptoms of Raynaud's phenomenon develop on top of the sensory complaints.

[a] Causes

The Raynaud syndrome has been associated with prolonged exposure to vibration, and because of this, it is often referred to as vibration white finger. It has been reported with long-term use of pneumatic hammers, grinding tools, rock drills, riveters, jackhammers, chain saws and other vibrating hand tools. The prevalence of Raynaud's phenomenon in workers with this history varies greatly.

Smaller tools such as metal burring wheels have also been associated with this syndrome. Such tools are used in welding, painting and sheet metal work. Smaller tools may be more damaging than larger tools, and they may require less exposure to produce the symptoms (Cherniak, 1990).

Raynaud's phenomenon has a wide variety of causes. It occurs in 8 to 10 percent of normal young women and also occurs in certain immunologic diseases, such as scleroderma and rheumatoid arthritis. It may occur as a late sequela of frostbite or crush injuries (Cherniak,

---

9 *See* 1.10[2][c] *supra.*

1990) and can be caused by ulnar artery thrombosis.[10] In addition, it must be distinguished from other causes of arterial occlusion and sensory impairment, such as carpal tunnel syndrome and other compression neuropathies.[11] It also occurs in the peripheral nerve diseases, or polyneuropathies, which may accompany diabetes, thyroid disease and many other disorders.

[b]   Diagnosis

A number of blood tests will help screen out diabetes, thyroid disease and other medical causes of neuropathy. Once the signs and symptoms of Raynaud's phenomenon become evident (and can be duplicated by the clinician), immunologic disorders can be ruled out to some extent by other laboratory tests, such as erythrocyte sedimentation rate and rheumatoid factor.

The major diagnostic problems of the vibration-induced syndrome arise before the symptoms of Raynaud's phenomenon become prominent, when neurologic complaints and sensory deficits are the major findings. It may be difficult to distinguish the vibration-induced syndrome from carpal tunnel syndrome. Nerve conduction studies may be abnormal in both. Recently developed tests such as cold challenge plethysmography and segmental nerve conduction studies may help distinguish between these two diseases (Cherniak, 1990).

[c]   Treatment

There is no surgical treatment for vibration-induced disorders. Vasospastic symptoms may respond to vasodilators and calcium channel blockers, which are reputed to have an antispasmodic effect, although the response to such drugs is usually suboptimal. Symptoms are likely to improve if the use of vibratory tools can be avoided, although in advanced cases, symptoms usually persist after exposure ceases (Cherniak, 1990).

The course of occupational Raynaud's phenomenon may be modified but not prevented by certain protective measures, including using coated tool handles and antivibration gloves (Cherniak, 1990).

---

[10] *See* 1.10[2] *supra.*

[11] *See also* ch. 8.

1.11 CRUSH INJURIES AND MACHINE MANGLING

Conveyor belts, industrial presses, gears and pistons are common sources of crush injuries. Machinery with rotating blades, grinders, shredders, corn pickers, harvesters and other power machinery are all capable of mangling or crushing any body part inserted into them. There is usually extensive skin and soft tissue damage, often with disruption of vessels, tendons and nerves, and bone fractures, and—particularly in the case of farm machinery—risk of heavy bacterial contamination.

[1] Arterial Injuries

The most urgent problem with a crush or mangling injury is the state of the blood vessels. Arterial injuries must be repaired immediately if the hand is to be salvaged. Attention is then directed to debridement of all nonsalvageable tissue, cleaning the wound and decompression (if the swelling is sufficient to cause a compartment syndrome).[12] When the damage is extensive, the best therapeutic option may be amputation.

[2] Bone Fractures

Bone fractures are usually repaired within the first 48 hours, but reconstruction of other tissues is delayed. Successive debridements are often necessary as the condition of the tissues evolves (Brown, 1988). Reconstruction is usually done in several stages over time.

1.12 AMPUTATIONS

The most severe form of injury involves loss of fingers, thumb or larger fragments of hand. The usual mechanism of injury involves crush and tearing, which devitalizes a substantial amount of tissue. The usual industrial and agricultural causes are similar to those listed for crush and mangling injuries.[13] Single finger amputations are the most common.

The simplest treatment is to discard the amputated part, clean up the amputation site and cover it with skin graft, if necessary. Replantation is an option for some amputation wounds. This is a lengthy

---

[12] *See* 1.10[1] *supra.*

[13] *See* 1.11 *supra.*

procedure with prolonged rehabilitation and variable functional results. Its feasability depends on the viability of the amputated part, the mechanism of injury, the time that passes between injury and treatment, and the proximity to an institution where such procedures are performed. Its desirability depends on the particular amputated part (the thumb is considered more critical than the other fingers) and the cosmetic importance to the patient.

If feasible, the amputated member should be put in a plastic bag, surrounded by cooled sterile saline and brought to the hospital with the injured worker. The finger or thumb should not be frozen.

1.13 FRACTURES AND DISLOCATIONS

Fractures and dislocations are very common occupational injuries. They may occur alone or as a component of a more complex injury, such as a crush or an avulsion.

Hand fractures in the workplace may be associated with blunt trauma from objects striking the hand, or the hand striking a stationary object or getting caught in a door. Falls on slippery floors or over obstacles as well as other mechanisms can also cause fractures.

Wrist fractures and dislocations are most commonly due to a fall on the outstretched hand. The most common bone fractured is the navicular, also called the scaphoid. (*See Figure 1–1.*) However, a fall on the outstretched hand is much more likely to fracture the distal radius rather than one of the wrist bones. The best known is a Colles' fracture, in which the radius is fractured just proximal to its articulation with the wrist. This produces a characteristic "dinner fork" deformity.

[1] Diagnosis

A fracture may be clinically obvious on physical examination, due to swelling and deformity. X-rays are essential in all cases, and these confirm the diagnosis. Any fracture should be viewed from at least two angles—anteroposterior and lateral. In many cases, particularly when a joint is involved, an oblique view is also necessary. With finger fractures, it is essential to have a lateral view of the injured finger alone, with the uninjured fingers out of the way so that they do not obscure the pathology.

The major pitfall of fracture diagnosis is missing associated injury: vascular, nerve or tendon injury, or additional bony injury such as dislocation.

[2] Treatment

The treatment of fractures varies from case to case, depending on the precise injury. In general, the bone fragments are realigned and then maintained in place by a splint or cast, or by internal hardware (wires, screws and plates).

[3] Complications

Malunion, or healing in an unsatisfactory position, is the most common complication of finger and hand fractures. Frequently the problem is one of malrotation. If the fragments are not properly aligned and one is slightly rotated on the other, after healing, the finger may appear to be straight when it is fully extended, but when flexed, it veers off to one side. Malrotation of metacarpals may lead to gaps between the fingers and may obstruct flexion of adjacent fingers. Treatment requires an osteotomy (resection of bone).

Fracture fragments may also deviate in one direction or another. In addition, fragments may be malaligned in such a way as to shorten the healed bone.

Weakness is a common problem in fracture rehabilitation, due to the prolonged periods of immobilization required to heal the fracture.

Navicular (scaphoid) fractures are plagued by one particular complication: nonunion. This is diagnosed when x-rays of the navicular fail to show healing three months after the injury. Nonunion can produce significant pain and disability in some patients.

Complications of Colles' fractures are common. They include tendon damage, median or ulnar nerve damage, carpal tunnel syndrome, stiffness, reduction in grip strength and arthritis.

1.14 INJURY COMPLICATIONS

Common complications of any open injury include infection and bleeding. In a closed space, particularly postoperatively, a hematoma may develop, which then forms a focus for infection. Many individual hand injuries have their own unique complications.

[1] Foreign Bodies

When the hand is lacerated by an object that breaks, pieces of the object may remain in the hand tissue. These may not be clinically obvious, but they are important to detect and remove, because they introduce infection and interfere with healing. Routine x-rays will detect any metallic object, and although it is popularly thought that only leaded glass shows up on plain x-ray film, in fact, all glass objects will (Russell, et al., 1991).

The visibility of gravel on plain x-ray film is variable, depending on its precise composition. Wood fragments are difficult to visualize using this technique; computed tomography (CT) scanning is preferred. Plastic fragments are difficult to see on CT scanning but can be seen on magnetic resonance imaging (MRI) (Russell, et al., 1991).

[2]   Reflex Sympathetic Dystrophy

Reflex sympathetic dystrophy (RSD) is a local disease of the sympathetic nervous system that may follow trauma or surgery. When it occurs in the hand, the stimulus may have been in the arm or the hand, and on occasion, the initiating event was a more distant injury, such as disease in the neck or chest (this form involves the whole upper extremity and is referred to as the shoulder-hand syndrome).

The symptoms are pain, swelling, discoloration (usually redness) and stiffness. The pain may be severe and disabling; it is often aggravated by movement and may be accompanied by hypersensitivity to touch. The stiffness is also disabling; it eventually involves the whole hand, even if the original injury was minor or involved only a single finger. Other findings include sweating abnormalities, osteoporosis and changes in the skin that make it shiny.

Several other conditions may resemble reflex sympathetic dystrophy (RSD). A "flare" reaction, in which the hand is transiently red, can occur after surgery for carpal tunnel syndrome and other conditions. Symptoms mimicking RSD may be seen postoperatively in patients with underlying vascular disease, such as diabetes or atherosclerosis.

The etiology of RSD is not clear, but it is thought to be in part an exaggeration and a prolongation of the normal sympathetic nervous system response to injury in which vasoconstriction (to prevent blood loss) predominates. The symptoms respond to a sympathetic block, which involves injecting anesthetic agents into the sympathetic centers in the neck. In longstanding severe cases, a sympathectomy may be indicated (this involves removal of portions of the sympathetic chain in the chest).

[3] The Stiff Hand

Stiffness of the joints in the hand follows immobilization. Swelling, fibrosis and ligament shortening all contribute to stiffness. The edema (swelling) that accompanies most injuries represents a particular problem. Hand function depends on very precise small movements between accurately fitted anatomic parts, and it takes very little edema fluid to interfere with these movements. If edema and immobility persist, fibrin from the edema fluid invades the ligaments, tendons and joints and cements the tissues in place.

Stiffness may be minimized by appropriate physiotherapy and rehabilitation methods, particularly such measures as dynamic splinting (splints that move).

1.15 PSYCHOLOGICAL ASPECTS OF REHABILITATION

Rehabilitation is critical in hand surgery, because a high level of function, strength and precision are vital. The best surgical repair is futile if not followed by appropriate rehabilitative efforts; inadequate exercise in the postoperative period can yield a contracted, stiff and useless hand. However, for many hand injuries, rehabilitation is a lengthy and demanding process. A good outcome therefore usually requires a highly motivated patient.

[1] Motivation

The factors that influence motivation are many and varied, and all these factors come into play in an occupational injury. Financial compensation for injury, the adversarial nature of compensation claims, the degree to which the patient desires to work and his or her psychological background all influence the course of rehabilitation (Louis, 1990). A thorough psychological assessment at the outset may help to uncover all the variables that might interfere with successful rehabilitation.

[2] "Clenched Fist" Syndrome

The previously mentioned factors may complicate rehabilitation from all types of injury. Hand injury may also be complicated by a particular set of symptoms, known as the clenched-fist syndrome. These symptoms include pain, swelling and tight clenching of the hand. The patient is apparently unable to extend the fingers, although this may be easily accomplished under anesthesia. Psychological evaluation of such patients reveals a great deal of anger and poor defense mechanisms. The prognosis is poor.

1.16 EVALUATION OF IMPAIRMENT

Residual impairment is not uncommon following repair of a hand injury. The evaluation of such impairment begins with a full review of the medical records since the onset of the injury. Then the patient is examined, and a physical evaluation of the injured hand is made, using standards such as the *Guides to the Evaluation of Permanent Impairment,* published by the American Medical Association (1993). This text outlines in detail a system for assessing and quantifying impairment based on specific measurements and specific parameters: amputation, sensory loss, abnormal motion and ankylosis (fixed joint deformities). Each measurement is converted to a percentage impairment, based on the principle that amputation represents 100 percent impairment of that part of the body.

In addition, each part of the body is assigned a value, so that impairment of one body part can be expressed as a fraction of the total individual. For example, a 50 percent thumb impairment (which might result from amputation at the interphalangeal joint, or total sensory loss, or a specific amount of motion restriction and joint stiffness) is equivalent to a 20 percent hand impairment, which is considered to represent an 18 percent upper extremity impairment or 11 percent impairment of the whole person.

[1] Sensation

Sensory impairment is determined largely by measuring two-point discrimination. The impairment is rated by its location (sensory loss is more critical at some sites than others) and extent (the distance between the two points at which the patient feels two discrete stimuli). Total sensory loss is considered to be equivalent to 50 percent of the impairment that results from amputation; lesser degrees of sensory impairment can be rated by referring to tables in the *Guides*.

[2] Motion

Motion abnormalities are evaluated by measuring the extent of movement possible in all directions at each joint. Each motion is assigned a relative value that allows a motor loss to be quantified according to both the extent of loss and the relative importance of that particular motion. For example, in the thumb, the motion with the greatest value is opposition (the movement of the thumb toward the fingers that permits the hand to grasp). Thus, a 25 percent loss of opposition will represent a greater impairment in hand function than a 25 percent loss of extension (American Medical Association, 1993).

1.17 PREVENTION

Prevention of occupational hand injuries involves education, use of safety equipment, ergonomics (that branch of engineering that aims to fit the job to the worker) and tool design (Centers for Disease Control, 1989). Also important is a monitoring system to ensure that safety procedures are in use. For example, many injured workers admit to removing or altering safety devices in order to improve the efficiency of the machines with which they work.

1.100   BIBLIOGRAPHY

Reference Bibliography

American Medical Association: Guides to the Evaluation of Permanent Impairment, 4th ed. Chicago: American Medical Association, 1993.

Aucilino, P. L.: Neurovascular Injuries in the Hands of Athletes. Hand Clin. 6(3):455–466, August 1990.

Brown, P. W.: Open Injuries of the Hand. In: Green, D. P. (Ed.): Operative Hand Surgery, 2nd ed. New York: Churchill Livingstone, 1988.

Burke, F. D. and Pulvertaft, R. G.: Flexor Tendons. In: McFarlane, R. M. (Ed.): Unsatisfactory Results in Hand Surgery. New York: Churchill Livingstone, 1987.

Centers for Disease Control: Work-related Injuries and Illnesses in an Automotive Parts Manufacturing Company-Chicago. Morb. Mort. Wkly. Rep. 38(23):413–416, June 1989.

Centers for Disease Control: Injuries and Amputations Resulting from Work with Mechanical Power Presses. Morb. Mort. Wkly. Rep. 37(6):96, Feb. 1988.

Cherniak, M. G.: Raynaud's Phenomenon of Occupational Origin. Arch. Int. Med. 150(3):519–522, Mar. 1990.

Doyle, J. R.: Extensor Tendons-Acute Injuries. In: Green, D. P. (Ed.): Operative Hand Surgery, 2nd ed. New York: Churchill Livingstone, 1988.

Gurdak, C.: Thermal Injuries in the Workplace. A.A.O.H.N. J. 38(10):492–496, Oct. 1990.

Leddy, J. P.: Flexor Tendons-Acute Injury. In: Green, D. P. (Ed.): Operative Hand Surgery, 2nd ed. New York: Churchill Livingstone, 1988.

Louis, D. S.: Evolving Concerns Relating to Occupational Disorders of the Upper Extremity. Clin. Orthop. Rel. Res. (254):140–143, May, 1990.

McGraw, R. W. and McEwen, J. A.: The Tourniquet. In: McFarlane, R. M. (Ed.): Unsatisfactory Results in Hand Surgery. New York: Churchill Livingstone, 1987.

Neviaser, R. J.: Infections. In: Green, D. P. (Ed.): Operative Hand Surgery, 2nd ed. New York: Churchill Livingstone, 1988.

Newmeyer, W. L.: Vascular Disorders. In: Green, D. P. (Ed.): Operative Hand Surgery, 2nd ed. New York: Churchill Livingstone, 1988.

Rothkopf, D. M., et al.: Surgical Management of Ulnar Artery Thrombosis. J. Hand Surg. 15A(6):891–897, Nov. 1990.

Rowland, S. A.: Fasciotomy: The Treatment of Compartment Syndrome. In: Green, D. P. (Ed.): Operative Hand Surgery, 2nd ed. New York: Churchill Livingstone, 1988.

Russell, R. C., et al.: Detection of Foreign Bodies in the Hand. J. Hand. Surg. 16A(1):2–11, Jan. 1991.

Salisbury, R. E. and Dingeldein, G. P.: The Burned Hand and Upper Extremity. In: Green, D. P. (Ed.): Operative Hand Surgery, 2nd ed. New York: Churchill Livingstone, 1988.

CHAPTER 2

Shoulder and Upper Extremity Injuries

SCOPE
Occupational injuries to the upper extremity may be caused by acute trauma or chronic overuse. The major causes of acute upper extremity injury are falls and blows. Fractures are the most common acute injuries with potential for long-term disability. Moreover, fractures are often complicated by neurovascular problems that result from damage to the surrounding tissues by fracture fragments. Burns of the upper extremity may cause scarring that results in disability. Vascular and crush injuries can predispose to secondary complications that cause permanent disabling muscle contractures. Chronic problems from overuse of the upper extremity include bursitis, tendinitis, adhesive capsulitis and microtrauma to the rotator cuff. Proper diagnosis of soft tissue derangement and reduction of fractures and dislocations of the bones of the upper extremity are critical to prevent impairment not only of the shoulder and elbow but also the hand and fingers.

2.01   INTRODUCTION

Injuries to the shoulder and upper extremity fall into two broad categories: acute and chronic. The acute injuries include accidents, such as a fall on the outstretched arm or an electric burn. The chronic injuries are largely those associated with overuse or repetitive motion.[1]

The acute and chronic categories of injury are not mutually exclusive, and they frequently overlap. An acute event may reveal an underlying chronic condition or be superimposed on a chronic process. This is seen, for example, in rotator cuff tears, when a fall or an acute injury produces a tear in an already degenerated tendinous cuff.[2]

In addition to occupational overuse, degeneration associated with aging also plays an important role in some chronic injuries.

2.02 ANATOMY

For the purposes of this chapter, the upper extremity is defined as the shoulder, upper arm, elbow and forearm.[3]

[1] The Shoulder

The bony architecture of the shoulder consists of three bones: the scapula (shoulder blade), the humerus (bone of the upper arm) and the clavicle (collarbone). These bones form three joints: the glenohumeral joint (the ball-and-socket joint of the shoulder), the acromioclavicular joint (formed by the articulation of the clavicle and the acromion process of the scapula) and the sternoclavicular joint (which joins the clavicle and the sternum at the base of the neck). The sternoclavicular joint is the only point at which the bony structure of the upper limb connects directly with the axial (central) skeleton. (*See Figure 2–1.*)

The shoulder is designed more for mobility than stability. Its mobility derives from its ball-and-socket joint, in which the socket is shaped much more like a saucer than a cup and barely encloses the head of the humerus (the ball). Much of the shoulder's stability derives from flexible ligaments, tendons and muscles rather than from bone.

The rotator cuff, an important stabilizer, is formed from four short muscles whose tendons blend to form a continuous cuff that surrounds the anterior, superior and posterior aspects of the humeral head. Other

---

[1] *See also* ch. 8 for additional information on repetitive motion disorders.

[2] *See* 2.17 [1] *infra.*

[3] *See also* ch. 1 for information on hand injuries.

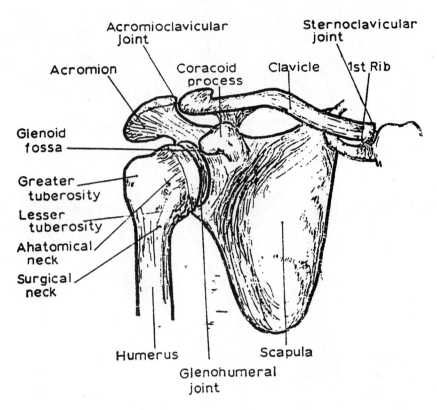

Fig. 2-1. Anterior view of the shoulder bones and joints.

stabilizers include the joint capsule and the labrum (a fibrocartilaginous lip that lines the perimeter of the socket and reinforces the joint capsule).

The musculature of the shoulder is complex; it includes muscles attached to the chest wall (front and back), clavicle, scapula and humerus.

The nerves that supply the upper limb originate in the cervical spinal cord. Regions of the spinal cord involved with the upper limb extend from the fifth cervical vertebra (C5) down to the first thoracic vertebra (T1). Nerve roots exit at C5, C6, C7, C8 and T1 levels and interconnect at the brachial plexus (the nerve bundle that innervates the upper extremity). Emerging from the brachial plexus are the radial, median and ulnar nerves, the major nerves to the forearm and hand, as well as several smaller nerves that innervate the structures of the shoulder and upper arm. (*See Figure 2–2.*)

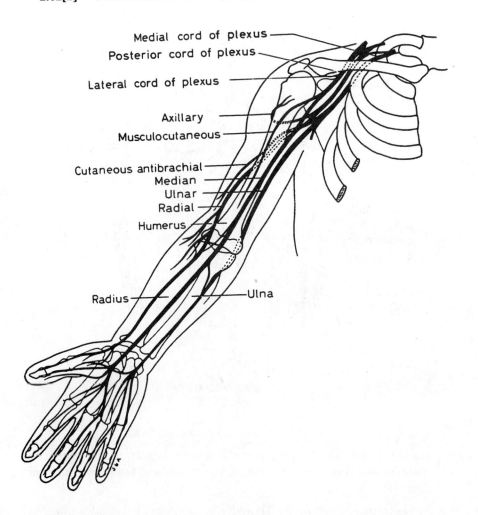

Medial cord of plexus
Posterior cord of plexus
Lateral cord of plexus
Axillary
Musculocutaneous
Cutaneous antibrachial
Median
Ulnar
Radial
Humerus
Radius
Ulna

Fig. 2-2. The brachial plexus and its divisions into the median, radial and ulnar nerves.

The major artery to the upper extremity leaves the aorta as the subclavian artery. Upon crossing the axilla (armpit), it becomes the axillary artery. In its course down the upper arm, it is called the brachial artery. (*See Figure 2–3.*)

[2] The Upper Arm

The humerus extends from the shoulder to the elbow. The upper end of the humerus, called the humeral head, forms the ball of the

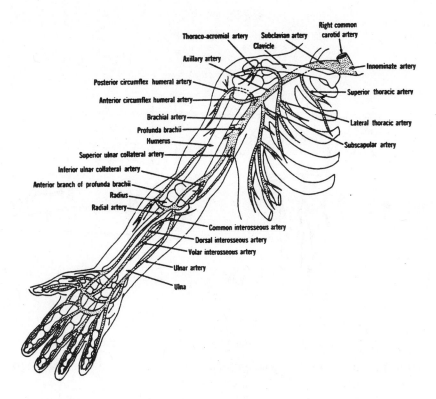

Fig. 2-3. The blood supply of the upper extremity. The subclavian artery emerges from the aorta and becomes the axillary artery at the armpit and the brachial artery at the elbow.

shoulder joint. At its distal (lower) end, the humerus has articular surfaces for the elbow joint and two bony projections, which can be felt as bony bumps, one on each side of the elbow. These are the epicondyles, which provide attachment sites for the long tendons that flex and extend the wrist, thumb and fingers. (*See Figure 2–4.*)

The major muscles of the upper arm are the biceps, which bends (flexes) the elbow, and the triceps, which straightens (extends) the elbow. Numerous other muscles involved in shoulder, forearm and hand function also have attachments on the humerus.

[3]　The Elbow

The humerus articulates with the two bones of the forearm—the radius and ulna—at the elbow. Several muscles that operate the elbow,

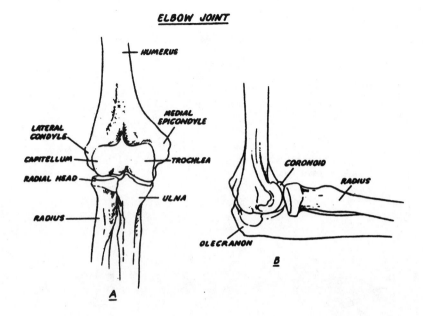

Fig. 2-4. The bones of the elbow joint in extension (A) and flexion (B).

forearm and hand, the brachial artery and the three major nerves to the forearm and hand all cross the elbow.

[4] The Forearm

The radius and the ulna are constructed in such a way that one can rotate around the other. This allows the hand to rotate approximately 180 degrees. The three major nerves of the upper arm and their branches course down the forearm to the hand. The brachial artery divides just below the elbow into the radial and ulnar arteries.

2.03 MECHANISMS OF INJURY

The major mechanisms of injury to the upper extremity are falls, blows and exertion, such as lifting, working with the arm continuously abducted and extended (out and up) and repetitive motions.

Falls are a hazard in many occupations and particularly affect construction workers, miners and machine operators. A fall on the outstretched hand may produce any of several skeletal injuries, including fractures of the wrist, radius, ulna or humerus, as well as ligamentous and muscle injuries. Falls directly on the shoulder or elbow may produce serious fractures or dislocations.

Blows to the shoulder, elbow or arm are a common mechanism of injury. Being struck by a moving object, such as something that falls on the shoulder, is a common problem that can result in fracture, contusion, laceration or other injury. Being caught between or within pieces of equipment is another source of injury.

Acute trauma is only one component of the total picture of occupational injuries to the upper limb. The worker who spends all day repeatedly rotating the forearm and hand, as in turning a screwdriver, subjects his or her wrist extensor tendon to chronic stress, which may result in what is commonly known as tennis elbow.[4] Repetitive motion injury (also called overuse syndrome), repetitive stress injury and cumulative trauma disorder are increasingly identified as sources of occupational injury.

Some injuries are combinations of acute and chronic trauma, as, for example, a tendon that degenerates and then ruptures acutely when subjected to a relatively minor degree of stress. In such instances, it may be difficult to determine the extent to which the cause is acute or chronic, and the extent to which the chronic problem is due to work, recreation, previous injury or normal aging.

2.04 CLINICAL APPROACH TO INJURIES OF THE UPPER EXTREMITY

Examination of any injury to the upper extremity should begin with the patient history and physical examination. In cases in which there are no obvious signs of injury, the history may help elucidate the source of the patient's complaints. Physical examination can help determine the extent of injury. Both the history and physical examination are important for determining whether more extensive diagnostic procedures, such as x-ray or arthrography (x-ray study using injection of radiopaque dye to outline pathologic changes in the soft tissue), are necessary.

[1] History

The importance of the injury history varies with the type of injury. In acute trauma such as a fall, particularly when fractures are involved,

---

[4] See 2.17 [2] infra.

the diagnosis is made by x-ray, and the injury history is essentially limited to the details of the fall. In other cases, an extensive history of all previous occupational and recreational activity is vital to the diagnosis of a seemingly acute injury.

Any history of upper extremity injury should include important details such as age, dominant hand and general state of health. The features of the major symptom must be extensively documented: its onset, duration and severity; motions that produce it; and actions that alleviate it. Additional symptoms must also be considered. Questions should be asked about the entire upper extremity, including the neck, since a variety of neck problems may produce shoulder and arm symptoms.

The history also entails evaluation of present and past use of the upper limb. This should include details on current occupation, including the position and motions of the arm at work, weight of tools and use of equipment. It may be important to obtain the same information regarding past occupations or employers.

Finally, a full history of previous injuries since childhood is vital. Any previous damage may set the stage for the current injury. For example, an old neck injury may be the cause of symptoms in the shoulder; shoulder pain referred from the neck may be so severe as to limit shoulder motion and produce a frozen shoulder in some cases.

[2] Physical Examination

Physical examination includes the neck as well as both upper extremities, with the uninjured limb serving as a comparison. Skin color, swelling, deformity and any palpable abnormalities are inspected. Vascularity is assessed by palpating the pulses, with the arm in various positions. Strength and the range of motion of each joint, including the neck, is thoroughly tested to the fullest extent possible. Finally, reflexes and sensation are evaluated.

[3] Radiologic Techniques

X-rays are vital to the diagnosis of skeletal injuries such as fracture and dislocation. Joint injuries may require arthrography (x-ray study using injection of radiopaque dye to outline pathologic changes in the soft tissue). Ultrasonography has been used in the evaluation of rotator cuff tears and other soft tissue injuries.

[4] Procedures

Arthroscopy has become an important diagnostic aid in the evaluation of some shoulder injuries. It is performed under anesthesia in the operating room by inserting a small fiberoptic tube (arthroscope) into the shoulder joint. Although the field of vision through the tube is somewhat limited, by manipulating the arthroscope, the examiner can adequately assess many structures much better than through conventional techniques. In selected cases, the injury diagnosed by arthroscopy may be treated during the same procedure.

2.05 CONTUSIONS AND LACERATIONS

Contusions (bruises) and lacerations are often only skin injuries. Their significance lies in their association with deeper injury, such as a fracture or damage to a nerve, muscle or tendon. With knowledge of the site of the injury and the anatomy of the underlying structures, the clinician can look for deeper injury by testing the motor and sensory function of the injured limb.

2.06 BURNS

Occupational burns to the upper extremity are common and include thermal (including scalds, flash and contact burns), chemical, microwave and electrical burns. Thermal and chemical burns are more common on the hand. Electrical burns usually involve the hand as the point of entry, but a great deal of additional tissue may be destroyed as the current passes through the upper extremity.[5]

[1] Classification of Burns

The most important feature of a burn is its depth, more specifically, whether the burn extends to the deep layer of skin responsible for regeneration. The traditional degree classifications (first through fourth degree) have gradually been replaced by thickness descriptions (epidermal; superficial, partial thickness; deep, partial thickness; full thickness). Epidermal burns, formerly called first-degree burns, are the least severe type of burn. They involve only the superficial layers of the skin. These burns are painful for only a couple of days, causing little or no anatomic disturbance and healing within three to five days.

---

[5] *See also* ch. 1.

The burned area is reddened immediately after injury, but the redness will disappear without any scarring.

The distinguishing characteristic of superficial burns is that they heal spontaneously. This is in contrast to full-thickness or deep (third- and fourth-degree) burns, in which the regenerative layers of skin are damaged. A third-degree burn includes all layers of skin, and a fourth-degree burn extends into the subcutaneous tissue or deeper. These wounds destroy the skin's ability to re-epithelialize (generate new skin).

Currently, burns are classified as partial-thickness or full-thickness. A partial-thickness burn usually heals satisfactorily without a skin graft; a full-thickness burn requires coverage with skin transplanted from elsewhere, usually a skin graft or a flap (consisting of skin, subcutaneous tissue and possibly muscle).

[2]   Evaluation and Treatment

The depth of a burn is not always evident initially and may take several days of observation to ascertain. Some areas that appear to be full-thickness injuries at the outset later reveal themselves to be deep partial-thickness burns.

Superficial burns are managed symptomatically, with good hygiene and exercise. Blisters are left intact to prevent bacterial contamination. A deep burn requires a more aggressive approach. In the upper extremity, swelling can become a major problem. A circumferential burn (one that encircles the arm) creates circumferential swelling that may be sufficient to cut off the circulation. If this becomes imminent, incisions are made in the skin (escharotomy) to relieve the pressure.

Burn healing may be complicated by severe scarring or contractures. In the upper extremity, contractures (scars that progressively shorten, pulling anatomic parts together and dramatically reducing mobility) are a major problem, since they can effectively disable an arm. The hand, elbow and axilla (armpit) are the most vulnerable sites in the upper extremity for contractures.

A contracture at the elbow can immobilize it in the flexed position, resulting in ankylosis (a stiff, fixed joint). Similarly, in the axilla, a contracture can tether the arm to the chest. In both sites, skin, tendons and other tissues frequently become involved in the scarring process. Repairing such contractures is often a multistage operation involving numerous skin surgical procedures.

Contractures can be minimized by early splinting techniques. The elbow may be splinted in extension (straight), and the shoulder in the abducted and extended position (with the arm held up in the air). Dynamic splinting (the use of moving splints) is also used as early in the treatment program as possible. Pressure garments are used to minimize scar production.

[3] Thermal Burns

Different burning agents create different types of wounds. Thermal burns include scalds, contact burns and flash burns. Laundry workers are at risk for scalds and contact burns from hot presses; food service and restaurant workers suffer similar injuries. Foundry workers and forge shop workers can experience severe contact burns from hot equipment and scalds from molten metals. Workers in the chemical industry are at risk for several different types of burns, since inadvertent explosions may produce blast, flame and chemical injuries.

[4] Chemical Burns

Chemical burns may be caused by organic and inorganic acids, alkaline substances and phosphorus. Workers at risk and the chemicals commonly involved include (Vannier and Rose, 1991):

- health care workers and plastics manufacturers (phenol);
- steel production workers and other manufacturers (sulfuric and nitric acid);
- chemical and refinery workers (hydrochloric acid);
- tannery workers and dye makers (picric acid) and;
- silicon chip manufacturers, glass makers and workers in the petroleum, drug manufacturing, photography, masonry, ceramics and plastics industries (hydrofluoric acid).

Sulfuric acid is the most common chemical agent involved in occupational burns. Burns from hydrofluoric acid are less common but much more severe, since the agent is rapidly absorbed into the tissues. Once in the tissues, hydrofluoric acid tends to trap the body's supply of free calcium, which can create a serious hypocalcemia (low blood levels of calcium).

Workers at risk for alkali burns and the agents involved include (Vannier, 1991):

- tannery, soap and dye manufacture and petroleum industry workers (sodium hydroxide);

- electroplating, paper and soap production workers (potassium hydroxide); and

- fertilizer manufacture, refrigeration, textile and paper industry workers (ammonium hydroxide).

Chemical burns are treated immediately by copious irrigation with water, which both removes and dilutes the chemical. (Specific neutralizing agents are used in some circumstances but are not always practical.) Burns made by certain chemicals, such as lime dust, phenol and hydrofluoric acid, should not be irrigated immediately, as this may actually aggravate the burn.

[5] Electrical Burns

The upper extremity is frequently involved in electrical injury, since the hand is the most common site of entry or contact with the electric current. Significant injury may be clearly visible at the site of entry and at the site of exit. The major problem with electrical injuries, however, is the extensive internal damage that usually occurs along the path of the current and is not initially visible.

The vast majority of severe electrical injuries occur at work. The most common types of accidents involve direct contact with "live" power lines; energized equipment (particularly metal ladders) and cranes or "cherry pickers" in contact with live lines; and use of improperly installed or broken equipment (Perotta, et al., 1987). Workers at highest risk for electrical injuries include line workers, electricians and construction workers, who frequently use electrical equipment and may work in close proximity to live wires, power supplies and other electrical equipment.

[a] Classification

Electrical injuries are often classified as high-voltage (greater than 1000 volts) or low-voltage injuries (less than 1000 volts). Low-voltage injuries are generally less severe and often produce a local thermal-type burn.

In high-voltage injuries, damage occurs along the path the electricity takes through the body. In the upper extremity, this often produces extensive muscle necrosis (cell death) and nerve injury. In some cases, the injury is focused at certain sites, which appear to be damaged by current traveling outside the body rather than through it. These injuries are referred to as arc injuries (not to be confused with the painful arc syndromes, types of shoulder lesions caused by degenerative disease), because the current is thought to jump, or arc, from site to site. The palm, flexor forearm surface and axilla (underarm) may be involved in this type of injury. Arc injuries are very severe due to extremely high temperatures generated at the site of injury. The energy appears to concentrate at these sites.

[b] Treatment

Treatment of an electrical burn in the upper extremity usually requires a fasciotomy (incision deep into the tissue) to relieve the pressure created by tissue swelling. If this is not done, or if it is inadequate in length, the mounting pressure can occlude the arteries and shut off the blood supply to the extremity, which rapidly destroys any remaining healthy tissue. An adequate fasciotomy incision will often extend from the hand all the way to the shoulder. Later, all devitalized (dead) tissue must be removed to prevent massive infection. In severe cases, amputation is required.

Electrical injuries to the upper extremity are often associated with injuries to other organs and potentially life-threatening complications such as massive fluid loss (into the swollen tissues) and renal failure due to overloading of the kidneys with muscle protein released from damaged muscle and infection.

2.07 VASCULAR INJURIES

Major vascular injuries to the upper extremity include vessel lacerations, which may accompany any severe open injury, fracture or laceration, and the compartment syndrome, in which pressure builds up in the tissue, compressing the arteries and occluding the blood supply to the muscles and nerves of one of the compartments of the upper limb.

The compartment syndrome is a complication seen after a variety of upper extremity injuries, particularly burns, electrical and crush injuries (due to local tissue swelling) and fractures (due to arterial spasm). Injuries that cause bleeding into a compartment (as in arterial laceration) can cause the compartment syndrome, as can tight casts or dressings applied for nonvascular injuries.

When compartment syndrome is left untreated, the tissues in the affected compartment die. This may lead to severe infection in the short term and replacement of the dead muscles and nerves by scar in the long term. When the scar tissue contracts as part of the normal healing process, it can produce a contracture known as Volkmann's ischemic contracture, which is characterized by an insensate, paralyzed and contracted limb.

Treatment of a compartment syndrome involves opening the compartment to relieve the pressure (fasciotomy).

2.08   CRUSH INJURIES

Crush injuries are associated with several types of machinery, such as conveyor belts, industrial presses, gears and pistons. Injuries tend to occur when the machine is inadvertently turned on while the operator's arm is in the press. Cleaning and repairing the machine increase the risk, since guards and other protective devices are usually removed at these times.

Most crush injuries are closed (the skin remains intact). The internal damage may be extreme, however, and this may not be recognized at the outset. Crush injuries may produce severe arterial damage through rupture, spasm or thrombosis (clotting). In addition, there is frequently severe muscle injury, which is often sufficient to produce a compartment syndrome from swelling alone.

Nerves are also susceptible to injury by crushing, particularly from a roller press, which tends to cause laceration. Nerve injury may also result from an inadequately treated compartment syndrome.[6]

The bone fractures that occur in crush injuries are usually comminuted (in multiple fragments). Fractures of this type are at high risk for malunion, nonunion and infection (osteomyelitis). Osteomyelitis may go undetected for 10 years or more (Beatty and Belsole, 1991).

2.09   FRACTURES

Fractures of the upper limb are relatively common and frequently result from falls, particularly on the outstretched arm. Falls may fracture any of the bones in the upper extremity, depending on the

---

[6] *See* 2.19 *infra.*

type of fall and the age of the person. Shoulder fractures may also be caused by falling objects.

A variety of injuries may occur when an object dropped from above falls on the shoulder. Construction workers are particularly susceptible to these injuries; typically a hand tool or other piece of equipment is accidentally dropped or kicked off a scaffold above. Alternatively, materials being hoisted may fall while in transit. Some of these injuries may be prevented by the installation of toeboards on all overhead work platforms, the use of side rails and nets, and enclosing hoisted materials.

Falls that result in injuries to the upper extremity are divided into falls from an elevation and falls on the same level. Approximately half of all falls on the same level are caused by slips, most of which occur when the floor surface changes unexpectedly and becomes wet, oily or highly polished. Slaughterhouses and food processing plants are common sites for slips. Another common mechanism of a fall is tripping over an unexpected object or step. Such falls can be minimized by good housekeeping, good lighting and caution signs.

2.10   FRACTURES OF THE CLAVICLE

Fractures of the clavicle (collarbone) usually result from a blow to the shoulder rather than a direct blow to the clavicle itself. The most common fracture of the clavicle occurs in the middle third of the bone, generally as a result of a blow to the shoulder or a fall on the outstretched hand. In the latter case, either the forces are transmitted through the arm to the shoulder, or the arm does not break the fall and the shoulder strikes the ground.

A clavicle fracture may also result from a blow to the top of the shoulder, such as an object falling on the shoulder, or a fall directly on the shoulder. In this case, the fracture may occur more distally (closer to the shoulder). Fractures of the proximal end of the clavicle (close to the sternum, or breastbone) occur when the shoulder is struck forcefully from the side. This is the least common type of clavicle fracture (Craig, 1990).

The clavicle is located in close proximity to several important structures that may be torn by the sharp ends of the fracture fragments. These include the subclavian blood vessels, the lung and the brachial plexus. Injury to these structures is rare but very serious.

[1]   Diagnosis and Treatment

Clavicular fractures are diagnosed by x-ray. In most instances, two views (anteroposterior or front-to-back, and a 45–degree view from below) are sufficient. Fractures of the distal third of the clavicle require additional investigations both for assessment of the fracture and evaluation of the integrity of the ligaments in the area.

Uncomplicated fractures of the clavicle are usually reduced (set) by a manipulation of the shoulders and then held in place by a cast or sling. Unstable fractures (which occur when ligaments rupture), fractures with displaced fragments (fragments that are out of alignment) or otherwise complicated cases may require internal fixation (the fragments are wired or plated together surgically). Distal fractures are more likely to be treated surgically because of difficulties in immobilization and resulting nonunion.

[2]   Complications

Potential complications of a fractured clavicle and its healing process include associated soft tissue injury, problems with bone union and post-traumatic arthritis.

[a]   Associated Tissue Injury

Fracture fragments may puncture the pleura (membrane surrounding the lung) or the lung itself, resulting in a pneumothorax (air in the pleural cavity around the lung) that may compress or even collapse the lung.

In severe injuries, there may be associated lacerations to the subclavian artery and vein, subclavian aneurysm (a flaw in the wall of the subclavian artery that causes it to dilate and potentiates rupture) or injury to the brachial plexus. Alternatively, neurovascular involvement may occur as healing progresses, when scarring or deformity of the clavicle compresses the vessels and nerves; this may be associated with development of the thoracic outlet syndrome.

Although such complications have been reported, the vast majority of clavicular fractures occur without any associated injury.

[b]   Malunion and Nonunion

Malunion occurs when a fracture does not heal in the correct anatomic position and a bony deformity results. It may involve shortening of the bone or deformity, and may present a functional problem or be purely a cosmetic disturbance.

Nonunion refers to a situation in which fracture fragments fail to heal; they become connected by fibrous tissue instead of bone.

Nonunion of the clavicle is rare. It may occur when the bone is inadequately immobilized or, in cases of severe trauma, when the fragments are severely displaced or otherwise complicated. Nonunion usually, but not always, causes significant pain. Approximately 75 percent of patients with nonunion have pain, and at least 25 percent of patients have neurologic symptoms (Craig, 1990). It is possible, however, for nonunion to be incidental to the sensation of pain, rather than its cause, in a patient whose primary complaint is pain and whose nonunion is only detected upon x-ray.

Nonunion is diagnosed by observing motion at the fracture site and confirmed by x-ray. If it is asymptomatic, nonunion does not require treatment. Symptomatic presentations generally call for surgery.

[c] Post-traumatic Arthritis

Arthritis at the acromioclavicular joint may occur following a fracture of the distal end of the clavicle, usually as a result of an intra-articular fracture that was not recognized as such at the time of injury. Symptoms may include pain at the joint or impingement due to bony intrusion on the rotator cuff.[7] The diagnosis is made by x-rays. Treatment may involve injections into the joint or surgery.

2.11 FRACTURES OF THE PROXIMAL HUMERUS

Fractures of the humerus at the shoulder occur in several situations. A common scenario involves an elderly patient with osteoporosis or other pre-existing disease of the humeral bone, and a relatively trivial episode of trauma, such as a fall on the outstretched hand. Such cases are often referred to as pathologic fractures, since bone pathology (osteoporosis, metabolic bone disease, metastatic cancer, etc.) is a precondition for fracture.

Fractures to the humerus may also occur in younger individuals, but it requires greater force than just described. Severe or multiple trauma, a direct blow to the upper arm, a fall while carrying an object, electric shock injuries and seizures all can fracture the upper humerus.

---

[7] *See* 2.17 *infra.*

[1]   Diagnosis and Treatment

Fractures of the proximal humerus are diagnosed by x-ray. Diagnostic errors usually involve failure to diagnose the full extent of the injury, such as an accompanying dislocation. It has been estimated that 50 percent of posterior fracture dislocations are missed initially, in part because routine x-ray views are inadequate for the diagnosis (Craig, 1990).

Treatment depends on the degree of displacement. Minimally displaced fractures that are stable may require only a sling and range of motion exercises, which start within 7 to 10 days. More severely displaced or complicated fractures may require open reduction (surgical realignment), casts, pins and other aids.

[2]   Complications

Several possible complications of proximal humeral fractures may occur at the time of the initial injury or later, as healing progresses. Acutely, there may be injury to the ribs or lung if the force of injury drives the humeral head into the chest wall. Injury to the brachial plexus or the axillary nerve also may occur acutely. Injury to the axillary artery is uncommon but serious when it does occur, as it can compromise the blood supply to the entire upper extremity.

In chronic conditions, recovery may be complicated by abnormalities of union, frozen shoulder, adhesions that limit motion, avascular necrosis (bone death caused by compromise of blood supply) and myositis ossificans (bone formation in torn muscle fibers).

[a]   Avascular Necrosis

Avascular necrosis is a condition in which bone cells die due to lack of blood supply. Post-traumatic avascular necrosis in the shoulder is not unusual, as the blood supply to the humeral head is precarious. It can occur as a result of trauma or when treatment of other shoulder injuries results in the severance of the small blood vessels.

Avascular necrosis is more common when there has been a comminuted fracture (one with multiple fragments). Once the blood supply is compromised, the bone cells die, and the end result is resorption. When this occurs on the humeral head, its surface becomes irregular and no longer rolls smoothly in the socket. A painful arthritis then develops over the months following injury. Malunion and nonunion may accompany the problem.

[b]   Malunion and Nonunion

Malunion usually results from inadequate treatment at the time of injury. The symptoms may involve significant reduction in range of motion, impingement syndrome and nerve deficits.

Nonunion of a fracture may be attributed to inappropriate mobilization, interposition of soft tissue between the bone fragments, excessive traction and other factors, including osteoporosis. It is usually painful and limits shoulder motion significantly.

[c]   Adhesive Capsulitis

Adhesive capsulitis is one cause of the frozen shoulder syndrome. In post-traumatic cases, the shoulder is rendered stiff by scar tissue in and around the joint. This condition is largely preventable with proper mobilization during rehabilitation.

[3]   Prognosis

Uncomplicated fractures may require six months or longer for recovery of strength and full, pain-free range of motion. More extensive lesions require even longer periods.

2.12   FRACTURES OF THE HUMERAL SHAFT

The shaft of the humerus may be fractured in a fall, a direct blow to the arm, a motor vehicle accident or a crushing injury. Pathologic fractures also occur in the humeral shaft, usually due to metastatic malignancy. The diagnosis is made by x-ray.

[1]   Complications

The most common complication of humeral shaft fractures is injury to the radial nerve. As it courses down the upper arm, the radial nerve lies right next to the humerus, a location that renders it susceptible to injury during fracture. In most cases, the nerve is only contused or stretched rather than severed, and function will return.

Vascular injuries include arterial lacerations and spasm. Lacerations require prompt attention, as they can threaten the viability of the limb and even the life of the patient. Spasm of the brachial artery has been associated with development of the compartment syndrome, with resulting hand and arm deformity if left untreated.[8]

---

[8] *See also* ch. 1.

[2] Prognosis

The prognosis of humeral shaft fractures depends on a number of factors. The greater the degree of injury, the worse the prognosis. Injuries that are close to the elbow or shoulder may affect joint function. The type of immobilization used is also a factor. Some casts permit greater mobility than others, reducing the risk of late joint stiffness.

2.13 FRACTURES OF THE DISTAL HUMERUS

The distal end of the humerus has a complex configuration designed for elbow and hand function. Fractures may occur in any of several planes about this configuration and are generally classified into two groups: intra-articular (within the joint) and extra-articular (outside the joint).

Extra-articular fractures include supracondylar and transcondylar fractures (both of which occur in the humeral shaft just above the elbow) and epicondylar fractures. (Epicondyles are the bony processes that can be easily felt on either side of the humerus at the elbow.) Epicondylar fractures are very rare in adults.

The supracondylar fracture commonly results from a fall on the outstretched hand. Displacement of fracture fragments, with injury to local blood vessels and nerves, is not uncommon. It is usually diagnosed on x-ray and treated by closed reduction (external manipulation under anesthesia). (*See Figure 2–5.*)

There are several different types of intra-articular fracture. The mechanisms of injury include a fall on the flexed elbow, which drives the ulna into the distal humerus; a direct blow to the elbow; and a fall on the outstretched arm with the arm slightly flexed in such a fashion that the radial head is driven into its articulation surface on the humerus (the capitellum).

[1] Diagnosis and Treatment

The diagnosis is made by clinical examination and confirmed by x-ray. Some fractures about the elbow are difficult to see on plain films, which makes the clinical examination critical in diagnosis.

Treatment may be operative or nonoperative, depending on the nature and extent of the lesion.

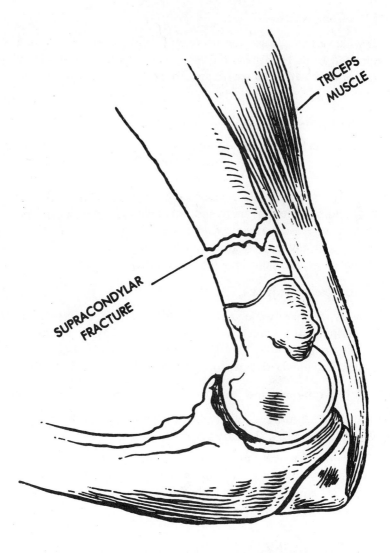

Fig. 2-5. Postreduction of a supracondylar fracture, showing the manner in which the triceps muscle and tendon maintain reduction when the elbow is flexed.

[2]   Complications

A wide variety of vascular, nerve and bony complications have been associated with fractures of the distal humerus, including elbow stiffness and myositis ossificans (bone formation in torn muscle fibers).

[a]   Vascular Complications

Several mechanisms of vascular compromise are possible in fractures about the elbow. The brachial artery may be lacerated or go into spasm. Arterial spasm associated with a supracondylar fracture is classically associated with development of the compartment syndrome. If the condition remains untreated, this results in muscle necrosis and replacement by scar tissue, with eventual contracture (Volkmann's ischemic contracture).[9] This syndrome may also result from severe swelling or hemorrhage into the tissue after injury.

[b]   Nerve Injury

Any of the three major nerves of the arm may be injured acutely in distal humeral fractures. Ulnar nerve injury may occur chronically; ulnar nerve entrapment at the elbow has been associated with a previous fracture in that region (Bryan and Morrey, 1985).[10]

[c]   Malunion and Nonunion

Malunion is more common than nonunion; malunion does not always require surgical treatment.

Nonunion is uncommon in distal humeral fractures, but when it occurs, the symptoms are disabling. Predisposing factors include the severity of injury, infection and the appropriateness of the initial treatment.

2.14   RADIAL FRACTURES

Fractures of the radius (the longer of the two bones of the forearm) are divided into fractures of the radial head, fractures of the radial shaft and fractures of the distal radius that occur just proximal to the wrist.[11]

---

[9] *See* 2.07 *supra.*

[10] *See* 2.19 *infra.*

[11] *See also* ch. 1.

[1] Fractures of the Radial Head

A fracture of the radial head usually occurs through a fall on the outstretched hand with the arm slightly bent at the elbow, as in a fall to the side or backward, rather than forward. Associated injuries are common and include other fractures, injury to the ulnar collateral ligament (a major stabilizer of the elbow) and muscular injury.

[a] Diagnosis and Treatment

The diagnosis is made with x-ray. Treatment depends on the degree of displacement and comminution (multiple fragments). Simple undisplaced fractures are generally treated without surgery. More severe injuries require operative intervention and, often, resection of the radial head.

[b] Complications

Fractures of the radial head are generally considered serious. Suboptimal outcomes are not uncommon, even with minimal radial head injury. Small degrees of extension loss (inability to straighten the arm at the elbow) have been reported in up to a third of patients, depending on the series (Morrey, 1985). Other complications include variable degrees of rotation loss (difficulty rotating the forearm), elbow pain, loss of strength, post-traumatic arthritis and myositis ossificans (bone deposition in the muscle, which may follow compound fracture-dislocation injuries).

Wrist pain may follow radial head fracture, as a result of either concomitant wrist injury or treatment.[12] After radial head excision, the radius migrates proximally in some patients. This occurs slowly over the first few years following excision in a significant number of patients.

[2] Fractures of the Radial Shaft

Fractures of the radial shaft may occur alone or in combination with an ulnar fracture. The most common mechanism of injury is a motor vehicle accident, usually one that involves a direct blow to the forearm. A fall on the outstretched arm with the arm rotated may fracture the radius alone.

---

[12] *See also* ch. 1.

These fractures are usually displaced, and some degree of deformity is clinically apparent. (*See Figure 2–6.*) The diagnosis is confirmed on x-ray. Treatment frequently requires surgery.

Complications include malunion, nonunion, infection and compartment syndrome.[13] In fractures treated surgically, the prognosis is generally good, although it varies with the severity of the injury and the type of surgical fixation used.

[3]   Fractures of the Distal Radius

The most common fracture of the upper extremity is a fracture of the distal radius. There are several variations of distal radius fractures, but they all involve a transverse fracture through the radius about $1\frac{1}{2}$ inches from the wrist. The most common type is the Colles' fracture.[14]

[a]   Diagnosis and Treatment

Distal radial fractures are diagnosed by x-ray. Associated injuries are not infrequent, and these must be included in the diagnostic process. The possibilities of shoulder and elbow dislocations and fractures, wrist fractures, median nerve and vascular injuries should be investigated.

Nondisplaced distal radial fractures are treated with immobilization, usually a splint or cast that immobilizes the wrist without immobilizing the fingers. Displaced fractures may be realigned by traction and manipulation of the anesthetized arm, or by a surgical procedure using pins, plates or other hardware to stabilize the fracture.

[b]   Complications

Fractures of the distal radius in general have a high complication rate, and for intra-articular fractures (fractures within the joint, in this case, where the radius meets the wrist), the rate is even higher. Unsatisfactory results are estimated to occur in at least 30 percent of such fractures (Palmer, 1988). Complications include chronic nerve injury (median nerve compression), arthritis, nonunion, malunion (which frequently causes pain and limited wrist motion), stiffness, Volkmann's ischemic contracture, reflex sympathetic dystrophy and tendon disruption.

---

[13] *See* 2.07 *supra.*

[14] *See also* ch. 1.

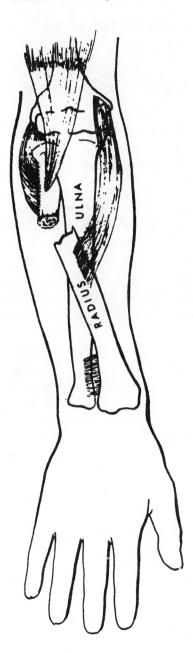

Fig. 2-6. Fracture of the proximal radius. The pull of the supinator muscle tends to rotate the muscle into supination (toward the midline of the body).

2.15   FRACTURES OF THE ULNA

Fractures of the ulna may result from falls on the outstretched arm with the elbow slightly flexed, a direct blow to the tip of the bent elbow or a direct blow to the ulnar side of the arm. Fracture from a direct blow occurs most often when the forearm is poised to protect the head and breaks a blow intended for the head (called a nightstick fracture).

[1]   Diagnosis and Treatment

A direct blow to the elbow may fracture the most proximal portion of the ulna, the olecranon (the bony projection that forms the point of the elbow). The diagnosis is made on x-ray and requires two views for full evaluation. These fractures involve the joint and usually require surgical treatment to ensure precise alignment of the fragments.

Fractures of the ulna below the olecranon include the so-called nightstick fracture and the Monteggia fracture, in which the ulna fracture is accompanied by dislocation of the radial head. (*See Figure 2–7.*)

The diagnosis is made on x-ray evaluation. In the case of the Monteggia fracture, special care must be taken to search for radial head dislocation, as it is easy to miss. Delayed diagnosis of radial head dislocation occurs in about a third of cases. The Monteggia fracture is usually treated with surgery in adults.

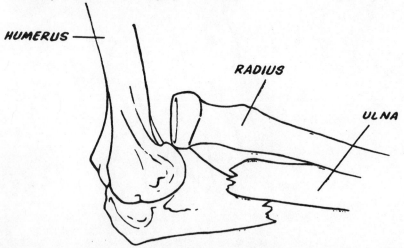

Fig. 2-7. A Monteggia fracture of the ulna, with displacement of the radial head.

[2] Complications

Common complications of olecranon fractures include diminished range of elbow motion and post-traumatic arthritis, both of which can affect a considerable number of patients. Stiffness, ulnar nerve injury, elbow instability and nonunion may also occur.

The most common complication of the Monteggia fracture is acute injury to branches of the radial nerve. Although this is not an uncommon development, it tends to resolve completely. Radial nerve palsy may develop late in recovery, due to missed diagnosis of radial head dislocation, but it is rare.

2.16 JOINT SPRAINS, INSTABILITY AND DISLOCATIONS

The joints of the upper limb are not designed for strength and stability, as are those of the lower extremity, which must bear weight and absorb shock. Thus, joint injuries in the upper extremity are common.

The shoulder is particularly susceptible to instability and is the most frequently dislocated joint in the body (Matsen and Zuckerman, 1990). Of the three joints in the shoulder, dislocation of the glenohumeral joint (the ball and socket) is the most common; acromioclavicular joint dislocations are uncommon, and sternoclavicular joint dislocations are extremely rare.

Joint injuries vary in severity. Primarily they affect the ligaments and other soft tissue structures that stabilize the joint. Ligament stress or tear is referred to as a sprain, which does not alter the bony anatomy of the joint but may render the joint susceptible to instability. Joint instability is defined as increased excursion of the bones of the joint and is not necessarily pathologic. Further injury or stress may produce a subluxation, in which the bones of the joint are transiently displaced during motion but immediately slip back into place. Finally, in dislocation, the joint surfaces are no longer in congruity (the ball is out of the socket).

[1] Glenohumeral Joint

Glenohumeral instability may occur in three ways. One of these involves conditions of ligamentous laxity, in which a person has many naturally "loose" joints. In such persons, it takes little or no injury to sublux the glenohumeral joint; in some cases, the person may even be able to voluntarily sublux one or both shoulders. More commonly, the person has a history of recurrent instability that begins with a minor incident on or off the job.

Another way in which glenohumeral instability occurs is through repetitive motion that renders the shoulder unstable. Finally, glenohumeral instability is seen when the shoulder is subluxed or dislocated by a blow to the proximal humerus or, more frequently, by a force that pulls the arm back over the head (for an anterior dislocation). Shoulder dislocation and subluxation most often occur anteriorly (toward the front). Posterior and inferior dislocations also occur, and instability may also be multidirectional.

[a] Diagnosis and Treatment

The physical signs of instability may be very subtle and hard to elicit in an apprehensive patient. Physical examination under anesthesia is an important mode of diagnosis. X-rays and CT scans may be helpful in revealing a variety of bony defects associated with instability. Arthroscopy (direct visualization of the joint with an arthroscope, a tubelike device) may be required, especially when instability coexists with the impingement syndrome. Dislocation is more obvious clinically, and the details can be confirmed on x-ray.

Conservative treatment of instability focuses on strengthening the muscles that stabilize the shoulder. If this fails, surgery may be necessary.

[b] Complications

Complications of dislocations include fractures, neurologic and vascular compromise and recurrent dislocation owing to extensive ligamentous damage or rotator cuff tears caused by the initial injury. Arthritis has also been reported after dislocation.

Axillary nerve injury during dislocation is particularly common. It is usually caused by traction (stretching) of the nerve, which recovers spontaneously (Matsen, et al., 1990). Injury to the brachial plexus can also occur.[15]

Recurrent dislocation is the most common complication of an acute traumatic dislocation. Most recurrences occur in the first two years

---

[15] See 2.19 infra.

after injury. The incidence of recurrence varies depending on the age of the patient (younger patients are more likely to experience recurrence), use and the severity of the initial trauma (if the initial trauma was minor, the bones were not hard to dislocate and recurrence is more likely) (Matsen, et al., 1990).

Complications of surgery for instability include infection, an excessively tight shoulder and recurrent instability.

[2]   Acromioclavicular Joint

The acromioclavicular joint is the articulation between the lateral end of the clavicle (the end of the collarbone at the shoulder) and the acromion process of the scapula (shoulder blade). The most common mechanism of sprain or dislocation of this joint is a fall on the point of the shoulder. This type of fall will either break the clavicle or rupture the ligaments attaching the clavicle to the scapula.

Other mechanisms of injury include carrying a heavy load that suddenly shifts in position, but this is rare (Rockwood and Young, 1990).

[a]   Diagnosis and Treatment

The diagnosis is made clinically and confirmed on x-ray. When the injury is mild, joint abnormalities may only be revealed on stress x-rays, which are taken while the patient holds a weight in the hand of the affected limb.

Mild sprains are treated conservatively, and surgery is generally used for dislocations. The details of both conservative and surgical management are matters of controversy (Rockwood and Young, 1990).

[b]   Complications

Occasionally patients with acromioclavicular injuries may report symptoms that persist for up to five years after injury. Such symptoms are described as significant in 8 to 40 percent of patients, depending on the severity of the initial injury (Rockwood and Young, 1990).

Associated injuries may include clavicular or scapular fractures. Calcification (hardening or stiffening through deposition of calcium) of the surrounding ligaments may occur following even a mild sprain of the acromioclavicular joint, although this does not appear to have adverse effects.

Osteolysis of the distal clavicle may follow an acute acromio-clavicular joint injury. In this condition, the end of the clavicle at the shoulder undergoes degenerative destruction. The symptoms include weakness and pain that limit flexion and abduction (raising the arm forward and out). X-rays of the distal clavicle show a variety of abnormalities, including osteoporosis (demineralization of bone). Bone scans may be helpful in the diagnosis.

Destructive bony abnormalities of the distal clavicle, such as osteolysis, are associated with a wide range of activities and diseases. Lifting weights and occupational chronic stresses on the shoulder were among the first causes identified. Rheumatoid arthritis, hyper-parathyroidism (overactivity of the parathyroid glands), scleroderma (connective tissue disease that manifests as thickening of the skin), gout (deposition of uric acid crystals in the joints) and multiple myeloma (malignant neoplasm that originates in bone marrow) are some of the medical conditions that may produce a similar picture.

The treatment is initially conservative, with patients avoiding shoulder-straining activities. Most patients experience relief with rest alone, but this may take up to a year. Surgery may be required if rest is ineffective.

Surgical repair of acromioclavicular joint injuries may be complicated by infection, arthritis, migration or erosion of pins and other fixation devices, fractures through drill holes and other unfortunate events. The nonoperative approach to treatment is not without problems, which are chiefly related to immobilization. These include stiffness, skin breakdown due to pressure from the immobilization device and arthritis.

[3]   Elbow

Dislocations of the elbow are usually a result of a fall on the outstretched arm. Other mechanisms include motor vehicle accidents and direct trauma. The dislocation is commonly not the only injury sustained during the accident. Additional elbow injuries may include radial head[16] and epicondylar[17] fractures. Shoulder and wrist injuries, damage to nerves and blood vessels, and the compartment syndrome[18] may also complicate the picture.

---

16 *See* 2.14[1] *supra.*

17 *See* 2.13 *supra.*

18 *See* 2.07 *supra.*

Although recurrent dislocation of the elbow is uncommon, previous injury to the major elbow stabilizer, the medial collateral ligament, may render the elbow more susceptible to dislocation.

[a] Diagnosis and Treatment

Elbow dislocation is diagnosed by clinical examination and x-ray. Assessment for associated neurovascular injury must be undertaken before treatment. The dislocation is usually reduced by manual manipulation or traction followed by splinting. Surgery may be required when there are concomitant fractures.

[b] Complications

The most common complication is a limitation of extension (inability to fully straighten the arm), which results from scarring in the soft tissues injured by the dislocation. Physiotherapy may be helpful, but if the limitation persists longer than 6 to 12 months, surgery may be required to release the scar.

Nerve damage is a common component of an elbow dislocation. The ulnar nerve is most susceptible, and traction or stretch is the most common injury. The impairment may be transient or permanent. The median nerve may also be involved.

Dislocation may be complicated by the formation of new bone (ossification) in abnormal locations, such as the joint capsule, and in the ligaments and muscles around the joint. This is a problem if it involves the muscle, since this can severely limit elbow motion. Treatment requires surgical removal, but only after the new bone has matured—a process that takes about a year.

2.17 TENDON INJURIES

The majority of tendon injuries not involving those of the hand are chronic, resulting from a combination of factors including overuse and degeneration due to aging. Tendon injuries may also occur acutely, as in a laceration, or may present as an acute event superimposed on chronic wear and tear, as in the case of a worn-out tendon that suddenly ruptures under minor stress.

The two major sites for tendon injury in the upper extremity, excluding the hand, are the rotator cuff of the shoulder and the epicondyles at the elbow, which serve as insertion sites for the common extensor and flexor tendons of the forearm. The two most common pathologic entities involving tendons are the impingement syndrome (in which the acromion impinges on the rotator cuff) and tennis elbow (usually tendinitis of the common extensor tendon at the elbow). Tendinitis of individual tendons also occurs.

[1]   Rotator Cuff Injuries

The rotator cuff is comprised of four short muscles and their tendons, which fuse to form a cuff that wraps around the humeral head and encases its anterior, posterior and superior aspects. The muscles are the supraspinatus, infraspinatus, teres minor and subscapularis. (*See Figure 2–8.*) Once the arm is raised, these muscles contract to hold the humeral head in the glenoid fossa (when the shoulder is in motion, the cuff keeps the ball in the socket).

There are two theories of the pathogenesis of rotator cuff tears—the degenerative theory and the traumatic theory. The degenerative theory holds that degeneration due to age and routine shoulder use is a prerequisite for rotator cuff tears. Evidence supporting this theory includes the fact that tears generally do not occur in individuals under the age of 40, regardless of the degree of trauma. In addition, there is frequently no history of trauma, repetitive or otherwise. Some patients sustain a rotator cuff tear with a fall or other trauma, but many do not recall an acute traumatic episode. Accordingly, "tendinitis" of cuff tendons may not be inflammatory, as the name suggests, but caused by degenerative cuff failure at the microscopic level. When sufficient fibers have failed, an acute traumatic episode—even a minor fall—may produce a cuff tear.

According to the traumatic theory of rotator cuff tears, microtrauma (i.e., overuse) or repetitive motion is a critical factor. Anatomy plays an important role here. On the top of the shoulder, the rotator cuff is sandwiched between two bony structures—the humeral head and the acromion. It is here that much of the damage occurs, and it is thought to result from impingement of the acromion on the rotator cuff. As the cuff weakens, it is less able to hold down the humeral head, leading to more impingement, which leads in turn to more damage.

Motions associated with this pathology are those that occur with the arm held up and forward. Painting, carpentry, tree pruning, fruit picking, welding and assembly line work are all associated with an increased risk of rotator cuff pathology.

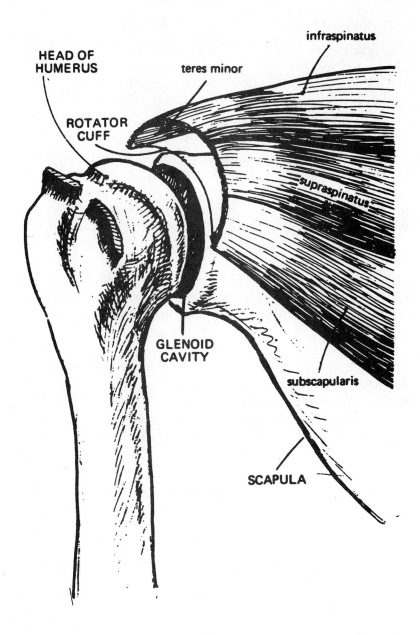

Fig. 2-8. The rotator cuff is composed of the tendons of the subscapularis, supraspinatus, infraspinatus and teres minor muscles. The rotator cuff stabilizes the head of the humerus against the glenoid cavity of the scapula.

[2]   Tendinitis

Tendinitis at the shoulder may involve the supraspinatus, biceps or infraspinatus tendon. The supraspinatus and infraspinatus form part of the rotator cuff. Biceps tendinitis is usually thought of as a component of the impingement syndrome, since the biceps tendon is also sandwiched between the acromion and the humeral head. Primary bicipital tendinitis is thought to be unusual.

At the elbow, the most common form of tendinitis is tennis elbow. This occurs at the insertion site of the common tendons on the epicondyles of the humerus (the two bony processes at the sides of the elbow). It may be referred to as epicondylitis and may be lateral (lateral tennis elbow), involving the common extensor tendon; or medial (medial tennis elbow), involving the common flexor tendon. The tendons are attached to muscles that operate the fingers and wrist. Tennis elbow is seen in occupations that require repetitive twisting motions of the forearm, such as carpentry (due to use of screwdrivers and wrenches), plumbing, some assembly line work and meat cutting.

[3]   Tendon Ruptures

Tendon ruptures are uncommon but do occur during acute episodes of trauma. Several underlying medical conditions predispose to tendon rupture. These include renal osteodystrophy (a bone disorder that accompanies kidney disease), hyperparathyroidism, Marfan's syndrome (an inherited disease of connective tissue) and chronic corticosteroid use.

The biceps tendon can rupture at the shoulder and, very rarely, at the elbow. At the shoulder, the biceps tendon rides in a groove of the humerus. It may slip out of its groove (subluxation) or abnormalities of the groove may promote wear and tear, predisposing to rupture. Repeated overhead lifting is thought to be an important factor in rupture as well as tendinitis and subluxation of the biceps tendon. The biceps tendon may rupture in lifting a heavy load, but some degree of underlying degeneration is usually present in such cases.

Triceps tendon rupture is very rare and is generally caused by a fall or a blow.

[4]   Tendon Lacerations

Tendon lacerations are common in the hand, where the tendons are abundant and superficially located.[19] In the arm, a deep laceration may cut a tendon but is more likely to involve muscle and other structures.

2.18   MUSCLE INJURIES

Muscle ailments are frequent occupational health problems. In the arm and shoulder, the most common syndrome is the occupational cervicobrachial disorder, a painful condition of the neck, shoulder and arm that is of muscular origin. It is commonly seen in sedentary workers whose shoulders remain stationary but whose arms are involved in frequent fine-motor activity.

2.19   NERVE INJURIES

Nerve injuries in the upper extremity can occur primarily through direct injury or secondarily through compression by other tissues.

[1]   Traumatic Nerve Palsies

Injuries to the nerves that operate the shoulder are uncommon but may occur in blunt trauma, lacerations, motorcycle accidents and during surgical procedures. Fractures and dislocations are another cause of nerve trauma, particularly humeral fractures, which may injure the radial nerve. Clavicular fractures may occasionally injure the subscapular nerve. Dislocations of the shoulder may injure the axillary nerve, and injuries to the elbow may damage the ulnar nerve.

Generally nerve damage that results from closed injuries, such as a closed fracture or dislocation, have a good prognosis for recovery (Leffert, 1990).

[2]   Thoracic Outlet Syndrome

The thoracic outlet syndrome is a condition in which the major artery, vein and nerves to the upper extremity are compressed at the base of the neck. These structures may be compressed either between the first rib and the neck muscles or between the first rib and the clavicle.

---

[19] *See also* ch. 1.

The symptoms of thoracic outlet syndrome may be vascular, neurologic or both. They are usually brought on or exacerbated by deformity due to old trauma, postural changes or motion of the arm. The wide variety of symptoms that has been attributed to this syndrome has created considerable controversy in the literature about what the precise diagnostic criteria should be. There is also disagreement over treatment.

[3]   Nerve Entrapment Syndromes

Several nerve entrapment syndromes can affect the upper limb. The most common is carpal tunnel syndrome, in which the median nerve is compressed in the carpal tunnel at the wrist. The ulnar nerve may be compressed at the elbow or at the wrist. The thoracic outlet syndrome is an entrapment syndrome and may coexist with other forms of compression, such as carpal tunnel syndrome. When both are active in the same patient (the so-called double crush syndrome), it is important to delineate as fully as possible the extent to which each contributes to the symptoms. Since the symptoms of thoracic outlet syndrome and those of carpal tunnel syndrome sometimes appear similar, it may be difficult to arrive at the correct diagnosis.[20]

2.20   BURSITIS

Bursae are closed sacs filled with fluid that function as lubricating mechanisms. They are located in places where structures must glide over one another, particularly tendons and bones. Bursitis is an inflammation of a bursa. It is a relatively common problem but also a misunderstood phenomenon, particularly in the shoulder. Shoulder pain is frequently attributed to bursitis in cases in which the primary problem is something else. (*See Figure 2–9.*)

[1]   Bursitis at the Shoulder

There are several bursae around the shoulder which can become inflamed, but this usually occurs secondary to the impingement syndrome (impingement of the acromion upon the rotator cuff). Subacromial bursitis and subdeltoid bursitis are commonly used terms but are misleading. Both diagnosis and treatment should be directed at the pathology of the impingement syndrome rather than at the bursa.

---

20 *See also* ch. 8.

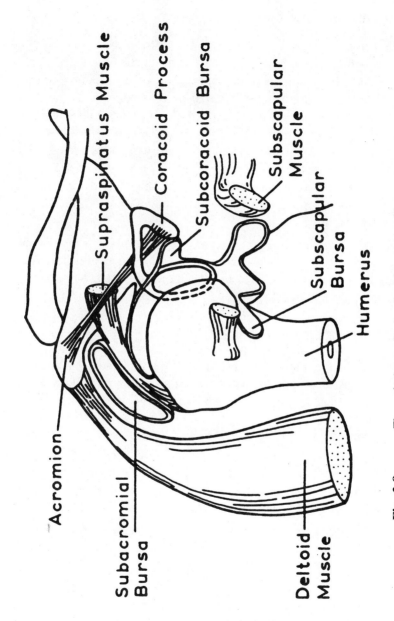

Fig. 2-9.   The main bursae in the shoulder area.

[2]   Bursitis at the Elbow

The most common type of bursitis at the elbow involves the olecranon bursa, which is located at the tip of the elbow and is very superficial. The olecranon bursa may become inflamed through repetitive trauma, a condition referred to as miner's elbow owing to the amount of repetitive leaning on the elbows associated with the occupation. Other workers who frequently lean on their elbows and are at risk of olecranon bursitis are plumbers, carpenters and construction workers. Direct trauma, such as a fall on the tip of the elbow, and systemic inflammatory diseases, such as rheumatoid arthritis, gout or chondrocalcinosis (calcification of cartilage), are other causes of olecranon bursitis.

Olecranon bursitis may produce pain when the elbow is bent or only a swelling at the tip of the elbow. Diagnosis and treatment involve aspirating fluid from the bursa to evaluate it for evidence of infection and to reduce the swelling.

2.21   INJURY COMPLICATIONS

Injuries to the upper extremity may be complicated by a variety of conditions specific to the particular injury. Other complications are less specific and may follow a wide variety of upper limb injuries.

[1]   Reflex Sympathetic Dystrophy

Reflex sympathetic dystrophy is a pathologic condition of the local sympathetic nervous system that may involve the hand alone or extend from the hand to the shoulder. In the latter case, it is often referred to as shoulder-hand syndrome.

This condition may follow an episode of trauma or illness; it has been associated with myocardial infarction (heart attack), cervical disc disease and trauma to the neck, shoulder, arm or hand. However, in many cases, no antecedent event can be identified.

The symptoms include pain and limited motion in the shoulder, accompanied by severe pain and swelling of the hand and arm on the same side. There are changes in the skin of the hand, and there may be personality abnormalities as a result of the pain and the inability to identify a definitive pathology. Bone scans and routine x-rays usually show abnormalities. Most patients respond to corticosteroid therapy and exercise, but some will require surgery on the sympathetic nervous system (sympathectomy).

[2] Frozen Shoulder

Injuries to the shoulder may be followed by the development of stiffness, also called the frozen shoulder. This term has been used confusingly to refer to two different entities. The first is adhesive capsulitis, marked by inflammation and scarring of the joint capsule. The exact cause of this condition is unknown, but any prolonged form of immobilization with the arm hanging dependent may produce it. Persons with this condition may have no history of trauma.

The term frozen shoulder is also used to refer to the clinical appearance of the stiff shoulder under any number of different pathologic conditions: tendinitis, arthritis, sprains, rotator cuff tears and other abnormalities, all of which can produce a painful, stiff shoulder.

[3] Elbow Contractures

Stiffening or fixation of a joint, referred to as ankylosis, is a relatively common complication of elbow trauma. The risk and extent of ankylosis depends on the severity of the initial injury and the extent to which the joint surfaces are involved. Fractures about the elbow, especially supracondylar and transcondylar fractures of the humerus, are associated with a particularly high risk of subsequent ankylosis. Burns about the elbow are also likely to produce a flexion contracture.

[4] Post-traumatic Arthritis

Arthritis is a relatively common sequel of joint injury in the upper extremity, particularly when the injury produces damage to the articulating surfaces (the cartilaginous surfaces that must glide across one another during joint motion). Injuries that are strongly associated with the development of arthritis include subluxations and dislocations, fractures involving the joint surfaces and fractures complicated by malunion, nonunion or avascular necrosis.

Arthritis has a number of different etiologies. These include osteoarthritis (or degenerative arthritis), rheumatoid arthritis and osteonecrosis. Less common causes of arthritis include gout, hemochromatosis (disorder of iron metabolism), endocrinologic disorders (acromegaly, hyperparathyroidism), amyloidosis (a disorder characterized by extracellular accumulation of the protein amyloid), psoriasis (inflammatory condition of the connective tissues) and Lyme disease.

The diagnosis of post-traumatic arthritis is made on the basis of history: Trauma significant enough to predispose to arthritis is usually remembered in detail. X-rays often reveal evidence of old injury.

[a]   Glenohumeral Arthritis

Recurrent dislocation is associated with sufficient wear and tear on the joint surfaces to produce arthritis. Factors that add to the risk include posterior instability and previous surgery for dislocation, particularly procedures that involved the use of hardware such as screws or pins that intrude on the joint. The interval between the original injury and the diagnosis of arthritis varies.

Rotator cuff tears have been associated with the development of shoulder arthritis in some patients, a syndrome referred to as Milwaukee shoulder or cuff tear arthropathy. The pathogenesis is not clear, but it usually involves an older patient with a large rotator cuff tear.

Osteoarthritis (without a history of trauma) is common in the shoulder after the age of 60, although it is more common in other joints. There is little evidence that occupation influences the development of this degenerative condition (Luck and Andersson, 1990).

[b]   Acromioclavicular Arthritis

Injury to the acromioclavicular joint may be followed by arthritis of that joint, even when the initial injury is mild. Minor injury to the ligaments may be sufficient to allow abnormal excursions of the joint components that lead to the development of arthritis.

The major symptom is pain, which is aggravated by holding the arm straight up. The diagnosis is made on the basis of history, physical examination and x-rays of the acromioclavicular joint.

The acromioclavicular joint is located very superficially. Diseases involving multiple joints (e.g., rheumatoid arthritis) may have acromioclavicular arthritis as a first manifestation.

Osteoarthritis of the acromioclavicular joint is uncommon and tends to affect younger individuals. It has been associated with occupational stress in the form of repetitive motion.

2.22 EVALUATION OF IMPAIRMENT

The evaluation of upper extremity impairment depends significantly on measurements of the extent of joint motion and sensation. Motor strength, pain and joint deformities as well as swelling and instability are rated. All measurements are converted to ratings according to tables in the *Guides to the Evaluation of Permanent Impairment,* 4th edition (American Medical Association, 1993) or another comparable source. The final rating is a percentage impairment of the upper limb, on a scale in which 0 reflects full function and 100 percent impairment is equivalent to amputation of that limb.

Most of the functional value to the upper limb is assigned to the fingers. Hence amputation of (or equivalent injury to) all four fingers and thumb is estimated to be a 90 percent impairment in the upper extremity as a whole. An immobile shoulder is rated as a much lesser impairment, although the actual rating depends on the position in which the shoulder is fixed; some positions are much more functional than others.

Impairment ratings can be calculated for a single impaired part of the upper extremity, such as a frozen shoulder or elbow, or for a combination of problems, such as an impairment of both elbow and shoulder function. Once the impairment to an upper extremity function has been calculated, it can be evaluated against standardized tables in the *Guides to the Evaluation of Permanent Impairment* to determine a percentage of impairment to the whole person.

[1] The Elbow

The elbow supplies 70 percent of upper extremity function: 42 percent (60 percent of elbow function) from the ability to flex and extend the elbow (through a range of 0 degrees extension to 140 degrees flexion) and 28 percent (40 percent of elbow function) from the ability to pronate (to 80 degrees) and supinate (to 80 degrees) at the elbow joint.

An elbow ankylosed in full extension (0 degrees) or full flexion (140 degrees) would constitute a 42 percent impairment of upper extremity function. Impairment of extension and flexion between these extremes can be calculated with the help of standard tables in the *Guides to the Evaluation of Permanent Impairment*. For example, an injury that prevents the arm from flexing beyond 60 degrees (19 percent impairment of upper extremity function) and causes a lag in extension of 40 degrees (4 percent impairment of upper extremity function) results in a combined 23 percent impairment of upper extremity function.

Similarly, an elbow ankylosed in full supination or pronation (80 degrees) would constitute a 28 percent impairment of upper extremity function. An impairment that permits supination of only 30 degrees (2 percent functional impairment) and pronation of only 20 degrees (4 percent functional impairment) would combine for an upper extremity impairment of 6 percent.

If a patient sustained an injury that caused 23 percent impairment of function to the upper extremity due to loss of extension and flexion, and 6 percent impairment of upper extremity function due to loss of supination and pronation, the combined 29 percent impairment of upper extremity function would represent a 17 percent impairment of the whole person.

[2]   The Shoulder

The shoulder supplies 60 percent of upper extremity function contributed by three functional units of motion: flexion and extension; abduction and adduction; and internal and external rotation. Flexion represents 40 percent of shoulder function and extension represents 10 percent, for a combined total of 50 percent of shoulder function (30 percent upper extremity function). Abduction accounts for 20 percent of shoulder function and adduction for 10 percent, for a combined total of 30 percent of shoulder function (18 percent upper extremity function). Internal rotation is responsible for 10 percent of shoulder function and external rotation for 10 percent, for a combined total of 20 percent shoulder function (12 percent upper extremity function).

The shoulder can flex to 180 degrees and extend to 50 degrees. Thus an injury that immobilizes the shoulder at either of these two extremes represents a 50 percent loss of shoulder function (or 30 percent loss of upper extremity function). Similarly, injury that immobilizes the arm in 180 degrees of abduction or 50 degrees adduction would represent a 20 percent loss of shoulder function (or 18 percent loss of upper extremity function), and an injury that immobilizes the arm in 90 degrees of internal or external rotation would represent a loss of 20 percent of shoulder function (or 12 percent of upper extremity function).

[3] Miscellaneous and Combined Disabilities

Upper extremity function can be impaired by disorders of the peripheral nervous system. Each of the nerve roots that innervates the upper extremity is assigned maximum percentages for impairment of upper extremity function due to sensory deficit (or pain) and motor deficit (or loss of power). For example, the C8 nerve root is estimated to cause a maximum of 5 percent impairment of upper extremity function due to sensory deficit and a maximum of 45 percent impairment of upper extremity function due to motor deficit. An injury that causes 20 percent sensory loss and 50 percent motor loss in the area of the upper extremity innervated by C8 would equal a total loss of upper extremity function of 23 percent $(.20 \times .05 + .50 \times .45)$. This 23 percent loss of upper extremity function translates to 14 percent impairment of the whole person.

2.100 BIBLIOGRAPHY

Reference Bibliography

American Medical Association: Guides to the Evaluation of Permanent Impairment, 4th edition. Chicago: American Medical Association, 1993.

Beatty, E. and Belsole, R. J.: Early Repair and Late Reconstruction of Crush Injuries. In: Kasdan, M. L. (Ed.): Occupational Hand and Upper Extremity Injuries and Diseases. Philadelphia: Hanley & Belfus, 1991.

Bryan, R. S. and Morrey, B. F.: Fractures of the Distal Humerus. In: Morrey, B. F. (Ed.): The Elbow and Its Disorders. Philadelphia: Saunders, 1985.

Craig, E. V.: Fractures of the Clavicle. In: Rockwood, C. A. and Matsen, F. A. (Eds.): The Shoulder. Philadelphia: Saunders, 1990.

Leffert, R. D.: Neurological Problems. In: Rockwood, C. A., and Matsen, F. A.: The Shoulder. Philadelphia: Saunders, 1990.

Luck, J. V. and Andersson, G. B.: Occupational Shoulder Disorders. In: Rockwood, C. A. and Matsen, F. A. (Eds.): The Shoulder. Philadelphia: Saunders, 1990.

Matsen, F. A. and Zuckerman, J. D.: Anterior Glenohumeral Instability. Clin. Sports Med. 2(2):319–337, July 1983.

Matsen, F. A., et al.: Anterior Glenohumeral Instability. In: Rockwood, C. A. and Matsen, F. A. (Eds.): The Shoulder. Philadelphia: Saunders, 1990.

Morrey, B. F.: Radial Head Fracture. In: Morrey, B. F. (Ed.): The Elbow and Its Disorders. Philadelphia: Saunders, 1985.

Palmer, A. K.: Fractures of the Distal Radius. In: Green, D. P. (Ed.): Operative Hand Surgery, 2nd ed. New York: Churchill Livingstone, 1988.

Perotta, D. M., et al.: Occupational Electrocution in Texas, 1981–1985. Morb. Mort. Wkly. Rep. 36(44):725, Nov. 1987.

Rockwood, C. A. and Young, D. C.: Disorders of the Acromioclavicular Joint. In: Rockwood, C. A. and Matysen, F. A. (Eds.): The Shoulder. Philadelphia: Saunders, 1990.

Vannier, F. P. and Rose, J. F.: Etiologies and Prevalence of Occupational Injuries to the Upper Extremity. In: Kasdan, M. L. (Ed.):

Occupational Hand and Upper Extremity Injuries and Diseases. Philadelphia: Hanley & Belfus, 1991.

Additional Bibliography

Bigliani, L. U.: Fractures of the Proximal Humerus. In: Rockwood, C. A. and Matsen, F. A. (Eds.): The Shoulder. Philadelphia: Saunders, 1990.

Hachinski, V.: The Thoracic Outlet Syndrome. Arch. Neurol. 47(3):330, Mar. 1990.

Karas, S. E.: Thoracic Outlet Syndrome. Clin. Sports Med. 9(2):297–310, Apr. 1990.

Roos, D. B.: The Thoracic Outlet Syndrome is Underrated. Arch. Neurol. 47(3):327–328, Mar. 1990.

Wilbourn, A. J.: The Thoracic Outlet Syndrome is Overdiagnosed. Arch. Neurol. 47(3):328–330, Mar. 1990.

Yakuboff, K. P. and Kleinert, H. E.: Electrical Injuries. In: Kasdan, M. L. (Ed.): Occupational Hand and Upper Extremity Injuries and Diseases. Philadelphia: Hanley & Belfus, 1991.

CHAPTER 3

Ankle and Foot Injuries

SCOPE

Injuries to the ankle and foot are common in several industries. The most frequent industrial ankle injuries are due to slipping and result in sprains. Foot injuries are usually caused by blunt trauma, specifically an object falling on the foot. Most injuries are acute and relatively minor; only the most severe injuries lead to significant disability. Chronic injuries, such as those attributed to repetitive impact on a hard floor, are very common in dance and are also becoming increasingly recognized in industries requiring prolonged standing or walking. The focus of injury prevention is on floor surface and on footwear, which may be designed to protect the foot against a variety of occupational hazards.

SYNOPSIS

3.01 INTRODUCTION

Injuries to the foot and ankle account for many occupational injuries. Approximately half of the injured workers are involved in heavy manual labor, usually construction. Other high risk occupations include mining, heavy industry, metal manufacturing, some types of engineering and professional dance.

The most common mechanism of foot injury is an object falling on or rolling over the foot, which may produce a contusion (bruise), crush injury, fracture or, very rarely, amputation. The most common ankle injury is a sprain, usually resulting from twisting the ankle during a slip or a fall. Blunt trauma to the ankle also occurs, typically when the ankle is struck by a moving object.

There are several ways to protect against foot and ankle injuries. Foremost is the safety boot, which varies in design depending on the types of injuries that occur in different industries. Attention to floor surface is also important in avoiding trips and slips that result in injury.

3.02 ANATOMY AND TERMINOLOGY

The ankle and foot are designed for two functions: to bear the weight of the body efficiently and to assist in walking by serving as a lever. The bones of the foot are arranged in such a way as to distribute the body weight across the heel, side and ball of the foot. The joints of the foot allow it to turn inward and outward slightly to adapt to uneven terrain, but most foot motion occurs at the ankle joint, which acts as a hinge.

[1] Ankle

The ankle is formed by the two bones of the lower leg—the tibia, which is the larger, weight-bearing bone, and the fibula—and the talus of the foot. The joint formed by these bones is a hinge joint.

The tibia sits directly on the talus and has a projection that hangs over the medial (inner) side. This projection forms the bony bump that is easily felt on the inside of the ankle, called the medial malleolus. The main purpose of the medial malleolus is to stabilize the ankle.

On the lateral (outer) side, the fibula runs alongside the tibia and then down the side of the talus. At the lower end of the fibula is the lateral malleolus, the bump on the outer side of the ankle. (*See Figure 3–1.*)

The bones of the ankle are connected and held in position by strong ligaments. When the ankle is twisted, the ligaments may stretch or tear, resulting in a sprain.[1]

---

[1] *See* 3.06 [2] *infra.*

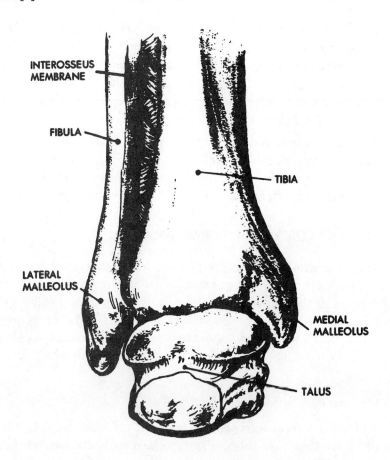

Fig. 3-1. Anterior view of the ankle joint.

Many tendons, nerves and blood vessels cross the ankle. Occupational injury to these structures is unusual.

The ankle joint is a hinge joint and movement occurs in a single plane. Other movements of the foot, such as turning the foot out or in, occur at joints in the foot itself, rather than at the ankle.

The motions of the ankle are referred to as dorsiflexion and plantar flexion. In *dorsiflexion* the toes point up, as in walking on one's heels. *Plantar flexion* describes the ankle motion in walking on the toes; extremes of plantar flexion are seen in classical ballet, in which the dancers frequently stand "en pointe" (on the point of their toes).

[2] Foot

The surfaces of the foot are referred to as "plantar" (sole) and "dorsal" (top). The sides are "lateral" (outside) and "medial" (inside, or on the side of the big toe).

The foot is frequently discussed in terms of three anatomic sections: hindfoot, midfoot and forefoot. The hindfoot is composed of the talus (part of the ankle joint) and the calcaneus (heel bone). The midfoot contains five small bones: the navicular; the medial, middle and lateral cuneiforms; and the cuboid. The forefoot contains the phalanges (toe bones) and the metatarsals (long bones extending from the middle of the foot to the base of each toe). Two sesamoids (small bones buried in tendons that move over bony surfaces, such as joints) sit beneath the head of the first metatarsal (long bone extending to the big toe).

There are five metatarsals, one extending to each toe. The distal end (farther from the limb's attachment to the trunk) of the metatarsal is called the head. Together, all five metatarsal heads form the ball of the foot. The first metatarsal (extending to the big toe) and the fifth metatarsal (extending to the pinkie or little toe) bear most of the weight.

Each digit has three phalangeal bones, except the big toe, which has two. The big toe is often referred to as the hallux. (*See Figure 3–2.*)

The calcaneus sits directly under the talus. The joint between the talus and the calcaneus is frequently referred to as the subtalar joint. This joint enables the foot to tilt inward and outward. When the foot is twisted in either direction beyond the capacity of the subtalar joint, the forces are transmitted to the ankle, producing injury at that level (the twisted ankle).[2]

The foot bones are arranged in the formation of arches. There are three arches: two along the length of the foot and one running across from one side to the other. The arches are supported by ligaments and to some extent by tendons.

The movements of the toes are referred to as flexion (curling under or bending) and extension (straightening). The motion of tilting the foot inward or outward, which occurs at the subtalar joint, may be described by several different terms. Turning the foot inward toward

---

[2] *See* 3.06[2] *infra.*

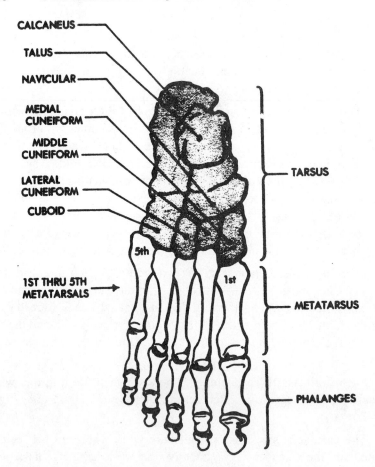

Fig. 3-2. Dorsal view of the bones of the foot.

the midline of the body may be called inversion, adduction or supination. The reverse motion, turning the foot outward, may be called eversion, abduction or pronation. (*See Figure 3–3.*) Inversion and eversion will be used here.

3.03   MECHANISMS OF INJURY

Acute injuries to the foot and ankle usually result from obvious trauma. An object may fall on or roll over the foot, or strike the ankle. Additionally, the ankle may be twisted after a slip or a fall.

Chronic foot pain has been associated with a variety of factors, some of which may be occupational. These factors may involve footwear,

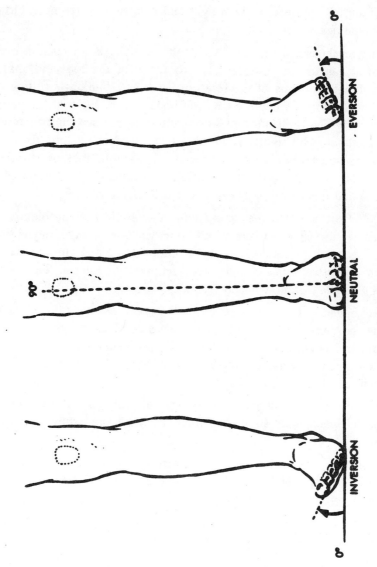

Fig. 3-3. Inversion and eversion of the ankle and foot.

floor surface, posture, body weight and congenital (present at birth) abnormalities.

Proper shoes are vital to foot health. Emphasis on fashion over comfort can create considerable problems for the foot and ankle. Superficial problems of the forefoot, such as a bunion (swelling of the bursa, or fluid-filled sac between bones, of the big toe) and corns (hardening and thickening of skin, caused by pressure and friction), are common with tightly fitted shoes. A high-heeled shoe forces a greater percentage of one's body weight onto the forefoot, overloading the metatarsals and possibly resulting in bursitis (inflammation of a bursa) and metatarsalgia (pain in the ball of the foot).[3]

Floor surface also may contribute to chronic foot problems. In industries in which workers spend hours walking on hard, unyielding surfaces, such as concrete or metal, foot fatigue and chronic injury from repetitive impact[4] may become major problems. The same problems may occur with hot surfaces.

Prolonged standing fatigues the feet as well as the legs and back. Other postures, such as curling the feet around the rungs of a chair while seated, may create more specific problems. Extensive use of a foot pedal in some occupations may lead to fatigue and overuse syndromes.

Obesity contributes to a variety of foot problems. These include chronic ligamentous sprain,[5] plantar fasciitis[6] and generalized foot fatigue.

Congenital abnormalities in foot structure and shape, such as a high arch or flatfoot (lack of an arch), may predispose an individual to painful chronic foot problems.

3.04 CLINICAL APPROACH TO INJURIES

Acute and chronic foot syndromes require slightly different clinical approaches. Acute injuries, such as the most common type in which an object is dropped on the foot, can usually be evaluated fairly

---

[3] See 3.05[6][b] infra.

[4] See 3.05[6] infra.

[5] See 3.06 [2] infra.

[6] See 3.05[6] [c] infra.

rapidly. In chronic or subacute conditions, a more thorough investigation is required.

[1] History

The history of any acute injury involves an account of the accident. This may include the mechanism of a fall or the nature of objects that have penetrated or otherwise injured the tissue.

The evaluation of a chronic problem requires information about the medical history and habits of the patient. This begins with an account of the occupational and recreational stresses on the feet, with attention to shoes and surfaces as well as activity. The physician also should ascertain whether the patient smokes or drinks excessively. Smoking has important effects on the circulation to the lower extremities. Alcoholism may be associated with a neuropathy (nerve disease), which can produce symptoms in the feet.

Diabetes mellitus (a disease in which the metabolism of sugars is impaired due to the faulty secretion of insulin by the pancreas) wreaks havoc on the feet. Symptoms may be directly related to neuropathy or result from the infection and ulceration that frequently occur when sensory loss due to neuropathy prevents the patient from attending to small sores or blisters. Diabetes mellitus is also associated with arteriosclerosis (hardening and thickening of blood vessel walls) of the vessels supplying the foot and leg. Infection, ulceration and even gangrene (death of tissue or a part of the body) of the toes and foot may complicate this disease.

Many common arthritic diseases involve the feet; some even have their first presentation in this region. Gout (a metabolic condition resulting in excessive amounts of uric acid in the blood) and gonococcal arthritis (a manifestation of gonorrhea) may first become manifest in the foot and ankle; other arthritic and systemic disorders may involve the feet, but these usually produce evidence of disease elsewhere. These include rheumatoid arthritis (a form of chronic arthritis usually affecting several joints), osteoarthritis (degenerative arthritis) and pyogenic (pus-producing) osteomyelitis.

[2] Physical Examination

The lower extremity is evaluated for deformity, skin discoloration, laceration, swelling, areas of tenderness and joint stability. Observations of gait (the manner in which a person walks) and footwear may provide clues as to patterns of overuse. In many types of injury, the state of the nerves and blood vessels must also be assessed.

[3] Tests

Standard x-rays of the foot and ankle are invaluable in the diagnosis of bony injuries. X-rays may be taken from a variety of different angles, depending on the suspected injury.

Bone scans are useful in the evaluation of stress fractures (bony injuries consisting of numerous tiny cracks, a result of excessive compression) and bone infections, since it may take several weeks for such abnormalities to show up on x-rays. Computed tomography (CT; cross-sectional x-rays) and magnetic resonance imaging (MRI; diagnostic procedure based on the assessment of the density of hydrogen protons in the cell nuclei of the body) are important in the diagnosis of tumors and other diseases but play a relatively small role in the evaluation of foot and ankle injury.

Blood tests are pertinent when disease such as arthritis, gout or diabetes mellitus is suspected.

[4] Evaluation of Impairment

Foot and ankle impairment are assessed using a rating system that assigns values to different degrees of loss of function. The motion in each joint is measured and compared to the normal function. The extent of fixed deformity (ankylosis) is also measured.

The extent of flexion (bending) or extension (straightening) is calculated and converted to a percent disability, using tables designed for this purpose (American Medical Association, 1993). Sensation is assessed for each peripheral nerve that is affected by the injury. The relative values of the nerves have been assigned, and each loss is assigned a relative value.

To evaluate flexion and extension of the interphalangeal joint of the big toe, for example, the patient's foot is set in a neutral position (with the knee at a 45-degree angle and the ankle at a 90-degree angle). A goniometer (calibrated instrument for measuring range of motion) is centered next to the joint, and the patient is asked to plantar flex the toe (bend it toward the sole) as far as possible. The angle that stretches beneath the arc of motion is recorded and converted to a disability rating, using the AMA tables. The average range of flexion-extension is 30 percent; if the patient can achieve 30 percent active (without assistance) flexion from the neutral position or from maximum extension, he or she has a 0 percent impairment of the toe. However, if the patient can only achieve a 10 or 20 percent range of motion, the disability rating is 30 or 15 percent, respectively.

3.05 FOOT INJURIES

The vast majority of acute industrial foot injuries result from objects being dropped on the toes or the midfoot. In mild cases, there is only contusion. In more severe cases, there may be skin laceration or fracture. Fractures are frequently multiple, due to the close relationship of the bones of the foot.

[1] Contusions

Contusions (bruises) are common injuries. A contusion is an injury to the soft tissues that does not break the skin. Swelling and bleeding under the skin are common and give a bruise its characteristic color.

Contusions usually occur on the dorsal (top) surface of the foot. In most cases, they are mild and of little consequence. However, if an object that falls on the foot is sufficiently heavy, bruising of the soft tissues may be severe. An automobile tire rolling over the foot may produce significant internal hemorrhage (bleeding) without breaking any bones, for example. This is a crush injury and may be complicated by development of the compartment syndrome.[7]

Contusions of the plantar (sole) surface can be more problematic, because they interfere with weight-bearing. Bruises on the heel or the ball of the foot render walking and standing quite painful and can be slow to heal. Padding the shoe with foam rubber helps but may not reduce the pain sufficiently to permit weight-bearing for long periods. Work done while standing may have to be restricted for some time.

[2] Lacerations and Other Skin Wounds

A variety of lacerations and other skin wounds may occur in the occupational setting. They include puncture wounds, high-pressure injection wounds and degloving injuries.

---

[7] *See* 3.05[3] *infra.*

[a]   Puncture Wounds

Puncture wounds result when a worker steps on a sharp object, for example, an upturned nail sticking out of lumber lying on the floor, that pierces the shoe. This was the most common type of industrial foot injury until safety shoes incorporated steel insoles (Hall, 1982).

Puncture wounds are usually more serious than they appear, since the pain is minimal and the visible part of the wound is relatively small. Such wounds may require surgical exploration to assess the extent of injury, remove any devitalized tissue and provide adequate drainage for infection. Tetanus prophylaxis therapy is indicated when such wounds occur.

[b]   High-Pressure Injection Injuries

High-pressure injection injuries are associated with the use of tools such as paint and grease guns. In this type of injury, a chemical substance is inadvertently injected through the skin with a tool designed to generate pressure in the range of 5,000 pounds per square inch. The degree of injury depends on the tool as well as the nature of the chemical; most chemicals are capable of causing severe irritation, and some, particularly organic solvents and paints, spread rapidly and can destroy much tissue. One reported high-pressure injection injury in the foot resulted from a water blaster used to remove paint from pavement, which was inadvertently directed at the foot (Dietz, et al., 1988).

[c]   Degloving Injuries

Degloving injuries, which occasionally affect the foot, occur when a body part is trapped and subjected to forces that shear off the skin and other tissues. This type of injury may occur when a heavy object rolls over the foot, causing an open wound with or without a flap of skin that is usually devitalized (irreparably damaged). A skin graft or myocutaneous flap (muscle, skin and subcutaneous tissue taken from elsewhere in the body) is required to cover such a wound.

[3]   Crush Injuries

Crush injuries are most frequently caused by blunt trauma. The foot may be run over by an automobile or other heavy equipment, stepped on by a horse or struck by a falling object. Although bruising and swelling are evident, the skin is often intact; this conceals the full extent of the injury.

Injury to the soft tissues, particularly the muscles, can create a condition known as the compartment syndrome. The muscles are contained in rigid compartments formed by bones and fascia (membranes). Bleeding or swelling of tissues can raise the intracompartmental pressure to the extent that it cuts off the blood supply. At this point, the muscles and nerves in the compartment start to die.

The compartment syndrome constitutes an emergency. Treatment is by fasciotomy: an incision along the length of the compartment that is left open. This relieves the pressure, thereby restoring circulation. When the swelling subsides, the wound may be closed or grafted.

Fractures are common in crush injuries. Because of the proximity of the bones in the foot, such fractures are usually multiple. Comminution (multiple fragmentation of one fractured bone) is common, as are healing complications such as malunion (nonaligned bone healing).

[4] Burns

Burns are classified according to their depth. In the past, it was common to refer to first-, second-, third- and fourth-degree burns. The first-degree burn is characterized by erythema (redness, as in a sunburn). Blisters are the main feature of second-degree burns. In a third-degree burn, the epidermis and the dermis are destroyed (all layers of skin, including those responsible for regeneration). A third-degree burn lacks the capacity to re-epithelialize, or to cover itself with skin in the process of healing, because the layers of skin responsible for re-epithelialization have been destroyed. A fourth-degree burn involves tissues beneath the skin, including fat, muscles, tendons and even bone, in severe cases.

It has now become more common to classify burns in two categories rather than four degrees: These are the partial-thickness or superficial, and full-thickness or deep burns. Partial thickness refers to first- and second-degree burns, in which enough skin remains for re-epithelialization; deeper burns (third or fourth degree), in which the regenerative layer of skin is absent, are full thickness.

This latter classification system is more useful clinically. In partial-thickness burns, healing is usually satisfactory without skin grafting, whereas the full-thickness burn requires tissue replacement.

[a] Thermal Burns

Scalds, from hot liquids or molten material, commonly involve the foot. The material can spill, leak though a worker's trousers and travel down into the worker's boot. Severe burns may result, in part because the time required to remove the boot prolongs contact with the hot object and deepens the injury. Immediate treatment consists of removing the boot and wiping away the material. In the case of molten material, pouring water into the boot causes explosive spattering and creates further damage (Gurdak, 1990).

Scalds can occur with molten metals, bitumen and molten plastic. Roofers, road crews and felters are some of the workers likely to be affected. Workers in foundries, iron and steelworks are also at risk. Cleaners using hot water may be scalded by inadvertently hosing the water inside their boots. The risk of these injuries is increased by the use of high-top boots worn open at the top, which provides easy access to the foot for any spilled material.

Hot liquid scalds are common among food service and restaurant workers. Although the upper extremity is most frequently involved, burns to the foot may occur.

Flame burns and contact burns, usually associated with hot metal objects, rarely affect the foot. Contact burns have been reported in welders, caused by hot metal fragments falling inside their boots.

Several devices are available for protection against thermal burns. They include foot and leg coverings made of rubber or metal. Shoes that are worn without tongues and are easy to unfasten may also prevent further damage.

[b]   Chemical Burns

Chemical burns to the foot are not common but do occur. Usually acidic or alkaline material spills onto clothing or falls into a boot and is absorbed by the sock. The burn then occurs gradually, with the worker unaware of the problem for some time.

Workers at risk for chemical burns can be protected by the use of synthetic rubber boots. Such boots are tested by exposure to hydrochloric acid.

[c]   Electrical Burns

The feet are almost always involved in any high-voltage electrical injury, since they conduct the current to the ground. In these cases, there is extensive injury elsewhere in the body, usually the upper extremity and the trunk.[8]

---

[8] *See also* ch. 2.

In high-voltage electrical injuries, the hand is the usual site of entry and the foot is the exit site. Wounds created by current entry and exit are different: The entry wound resembles a burn, whereas the tissue at the exit site looks as if it has exploded.

Workers at risk for high-voltage electrical injury are usually required to wear shoes with nonconductive soles. Such footwear protects the entire body from electrical injury and may save the worker's life.

[5] Fractures

Fractures are common foot injuries, usually caused by objects falling on the foot. Forced inversion injuries, such as those that occur when the worker falls on the inturned foot, may produce fractures of the midfoot as well as ankle sprain[9] or fracture.[10] Chronic repetitive impact of the foot on a hard surface may produce stress fractures (bony injuries consisting of numerous tiny cracks, a result of excessive compression) in one of several bones. Stress fractures are most common in professional dancers.

[a] Toe Fractures

Approximately 80 percent of foot fractures involve the toes, most commonly the distal phalanx (toe bone farther from the rest of the foot) of the big toe. Most of these injuries could be prevented by wearing safety shoes with a metal toe cap. The fractures are usually simple and require only protective splinting.

[b] Metatarsal Fractures

The metatarsals are the long bones extending from the middle of the foot to each toe. Direct blows, as in a crush injury,[11] account for the majority of metatarsal fractures. In some cases, the fifth metatarsal (corresponding to the fifth, or pinkie, toe) may fracture in an inversion injury, in which the patient falls on the foot with the foot twisted toward the midline of the body (inverted).

Metatarsal injuries tend to be more serious than toe fractures. Associated injuries are not uncommon, and hemorrhage from these fractures may create a compartment syndrome.[12]

---

[9] *See* 3.06[2] *infra.*

[10] *See* 3.06 [3] *infra.*

[11] *See* 3.05[3] *supra.*

[12] *See* 3.05[3] *supra.*

Single fractures of the second, third or fourth metatarsal (corresponding to the second, third or fourth toe, respectively) are usually quite stable and are splinted by their intact neighbors. Casting is not usually required, and patients can walk on the foot once swelling subsides. A similar approach is taken to inversion injury fracture of the fifth metatarsal, which usually requires only bandage support.

Many industrial crush injuries involve fractures of more than one metatarsal. Surgical treatment is usually required to adequately splint the injured bones in place.

First (big toe) metatarsal fractures may require more aggressive treatment. The first metatarsal is an important weight-bearing structure and is vital to normal locomotion. The fragments must be immobilized for healing; this requires a non-weight-bearing cast for four to six weeks, followed by a protective shoe or walking cast. Displaced or angulated fracture fragments, or involvement of the joints usually requires surgical treatment.

A march fracture is a fracture of a metatarsal, usually the second or third, caused by repeated microtrauma that renders the bone unable to heal itself. It is occasionally encountered in the occupational setting. The patient with such a fracture does not report an accident but rather a history of recent excessive walking or running activity (or marching). The risk of injury is increased when the second metatarsal is longer than the first.

The symptoms of a march fracture consist of pain at the fracture site, which accompanies any form of weight-bearing activity. The patient may become progressively disabled during subsequent weeks if the fracture is not allowed to heal.

The diagnosis of a march fracture may take some time if it is unsuspected, since the fracture does not show up on x-ray for up to six weeks. Bone scans will reveal the defect much earlier.[13] Symptoms may persist for months.

The differential diagnosis of the march fracture includes all other causes of metatarsalgia (pain in the midfoot).[14] Freiberg's disease— avascular necrosis (spontaneous destruction of the bone) of the metatarsal head—may present with similar features. This condition

---

[13] See 3.04 [3] supra.

[14] See 3.05[6][b] supra.

has a characteristic appearance on x-ray that helps distinguish it from other entities.

[c] Calcaneal Fractures

Fractures of the calcaneus (heel bone) are rare but frequently devastating. The usual mechanism is a fall from a height onto one or both feet, producing a crush injury to the bone. Most commonly, the worker falls off scaffolding or a ladder. Falls severe enough to fracture the calcaneus are often associated with other injuries, particularly a vertebral compression fracture (fracture caused by compression of two vertebrae).

The pain from a calcaneal fracture is severe. Diagnosis is confirmed by x-ray, and treatment varies with the type and extent of the fracture. (*See Figure 3–4.*)

The prognosis for calcaneal fractures is not good. The subtalar joint (joint between the talus, or ankle bone, and the calcaneus) is often damaged, with resultant loss of foot motion, difficulty with weight-bearing and chronic pain. No treatment method yields predictably good results, and these injuries are notorious for their poor outcome.

[6] Subacute and Chronic Foot Pain

Some painful conditions of the feet may be at least partially related to occupation. They result from biomechanical stresses on the foot and are created by a combination of factors, including deformity, either congenital or acquired; fatigue from standing and other postures; and suboptimal floor surface and footwear. Included in this group are several common foot ailments: heel pain, metatarsalgia, plantar fasciitis and sesamoiditis.

[a] Heel Pain

Heel pain has many causes. Jumping from a height or working with the feet on a hard surface may cause a forceful pull on the ligaments, followed by inflammation. The symptoms are characteristically worse on first arising in the morning, improving with some activity, but worsening with prolonged standing or walking. Heel pain of this type tends to be chronic but is not usually disabling.

X-rays may show a bony spur on the calcaneus at the point of tenderness. Whether or not this spur is the cause of the pain has been the matter of some debate. Spurs are common in asymptomatic heels,

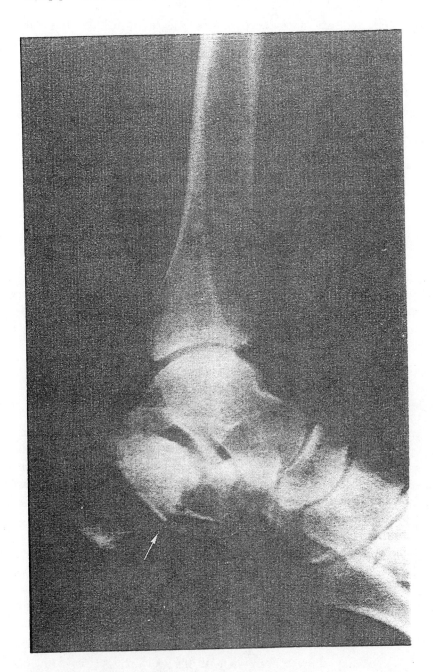

Fig. 3-4. Lateral x-ray of the foot, revealing a fracture of the calcaneus (at arrow). The prognosis for such a fracture is poor.

and frequently an individual will have spurs on both heels but pain in only one. However, occupational factors may help precipitate symptoms in a previously asymptomatic heel spur. Certain workers, such as janitors, have been reported to be more at risk than others for developing symptomatic heel spurs (Gorecki, 1987).

The tarsal tunnel syndrome is another cause of heel pain. This is a nerve compression syndrome involving the posterior tibial nerve (a branch of the sciatic nerve supplying sensory and motor innervation to the foot). It may occur as a complication of ankle trauma. Plantar fasciitis and various forms of arthritis also may cause heel pain.

[b] Metatarsalgia

Metatarsalgia is a nonspecific term referring to pain in the region of the metatarsophalangeal joints (between the metatarsals, or the long bones extending from midfoot to the toes, and the phalanges, or toe bones). One common cause is overload on the forefoot. This may be related to a high arch or another foot deformity, or wearing high-heeled shoes, which force the body weight onto the forefoot. Other possible causes include rheumatoid arthritis (a form of chronic arthritis usually affecting several joints), gout (a metabolic condition resulting in excessive amounts of uric acid in the blood), contusions (bruises), stress fractures (bony injuries consisting of numerous tiny cracks, a result of excessive compression) and bursitis (inflammation of a bursa, one of the fluid-filled sacs interposed between moving body parts). Laxity of the transverse metatarsal ligament—which may be congenital or acquired from prolonged standing or walking, age-related degeneration or obesity—alters foot biomechanics and can produce metatarsalgia.

[c] Plantar Fasciitis

Plantar fasciitis is a common repetitive motion disorder of the foot in which the plantar fascia becomes inflamed. The plantar fascia, or aponeurosis, is a layer of tough connective tissue that extends from the calcaneus and fans out over the sole to the metatarsal heads. (*See Figure 3–5.*) Inflammation can result from repetitive stress on the foot that overloads the bones and ligaments, and shifts some of the load to the plantar fascia. The plantar fascia is then called on to support more load than it can physiologically accommodate.

The most common cause of plantar fasciitis is overuse. Excessive walking on hard, unyielding floor surfaces such as cement is thought

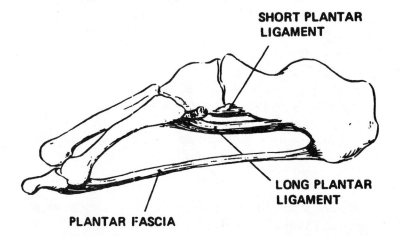

SHORT PLANTAR
LIGAMENT

LONG PLANTAR
LIGAMENT

PLANTAR FASCIA

Fig. 3-5. The plantar fascia and other ligaments of the foot. Plantar fasciitis is caused most often by overuse.

to be a factor in some cases. Steel toe and steel sole shoes frequently worn by workers contribute to the problem; they provide little cushion to assist in absorbing the shock of repetitive impact.

Other factors that increase the risk of plantar fasciitis include a high arch, an externally rotated leg (one that is turned away from the midline of the body) and obesity. The disorder also may be caused by a variety of rheumatic conditions.

The major symptom is pain, usually in the midfoot or heel, which increases on rising and improves with activity. There are no x-ray abnormalities, and the diagnosis is based on the clinical picture. Conservative (nonsurgical) treatment may involve rest, padding, crutches and anti-inflammatory agents. Symptoms may subside within two or three weeks, but improvement may be very slow in some cases, occasionally taking as long as a year (Schepsis, et al., 1991). Surgery is a last resort in chronic cases.

[d]   Sesamoiditis

The sesamoids are two small, pebble-shaped bones under the head of the first metatarsal (long bone extending from midfoot to the base of the big toe). They are located in a region that plays a major role in weight-bearing and is susceptible to injury from chronic repetitive impact. (*See Figure 3–6.*)

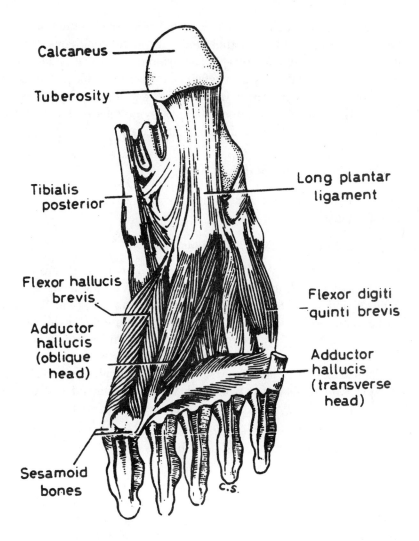

Fig. 3-6. Plantar view of the foot, showing the sesamoids in relation to other structures. The sesamoid bones are enclosed in the tendon of the flexor hallucis brevis.

Dancers are at high risk for sesamoid injuries. Sesamoiditis may occur in the occupational setting under the same conditions as those described for plantar fasciitis.[15] The symptoms are pain and tenderness. The diagnosis rests on excluding a fracture, which requires an x-ray or a bone scan. (Stress fractures will not appear on plain x-rays until several weeks after the onset of symptoms.) The treatment consists of rest, padding and anti-inflammatory agents.

3.06   ANKLE INJURIES

Common ankle injuries include contusions and lacerations, sprains and fractures.

[1]   Contusions and Lacerations

Contusions (bruises) and lacerations (cuts) of the ankle are caused by blunt trauma. Although shoes protect the feet, the ankle is often exposed and vulnerable to injury; objects rolling along the floor that strike the lower extremity are more likely to injure the ankle than the foot. Skin wounds over the malleoli (bony protrusions on either side of the ankle) are at risk for complications. The tissue overlying the malleoli is very thin and has a relatively slow circulation, particularly in older individuals and persons with varicose (enlarged and twisted) veins. Infection and delayed healing are not uncommon.

Protective boots are available for workers at risk for blunt trauma to the ankle, such as those who push carts.

[2]   Sprains

The most common ankle injury is a sprain, which usually results from a fall onto the twisted foot. A sprain is the twisting or straining of a joint so that some of the ligaments and other structures are torn or distorted but the bones remain in place. The ligaments that stabilize the ankle are susceptible to such an injury. The medial (inner) side of the ankle is supported by a thick, wide ligament (medial collateral ligament), which is strong and not easily injured. On the lateral side, three ligaments—the talofibular, calcaneofibular and talocalcaneal—run between the fibula (outer leg bone), the talus (ankle bone) and the calcaneus (heel bone). All three are relatively thin and weak, and it is here that most problems arise.

---

[15] See 3.05[6] [c] supra.

[a] Mechanisms of Injury

The ankle joint is a hinge; it is designed to move in a single plane, not to tilt. Inward and outward tilting of the foot (inversion and eversion) occur at the talar joints. When the foot is forcibly tilted beyond the capacity of the talar joints, the force is transmitted to the ankle, and a sprain is likely. In the most common injuries, the foot is forcibly tilted inward, resulting in damage to the lateral ligaments. (*See Figure 3–7.*)

The majority of ankle sprains result from trips and slips. Slips tend to occur when the floor surface changes unexpectedly and becomes wet, oily or highly polished. Slaughterhouses and food processing plants are common sites for slips. Trips occur when there is an unexpected object or step in the worker's path. These can be minimized by good housekeeping, proper lighting and caution signs.

[b] Diagnosis

Mild sprains, usually involving partial tears of one or two of the three lateral ligaments, are most common. The diagnosis is made based on the clinical picture after concluding that x-rays for fracture are negative.

More severe sprains occur through the same mechanism and involve complete tears of a ligament. A complete tear creates instability in the ankle joint. When a severe sprain is suspected, instability may be evaluated radiologically by stress x-ray views of the ankle. This involves an x-ray of the anesthetized ankle under an inversion stress. If the ligaments are intact, the inversion stress will not be able to invert the talus, and the x-ray will show that the bones remain aligned. If a lateral ligament is torn and the ankle is unstable, an inversion force will invert the talus relative to the tibia (inner leg bone), and x-rays will show a wedge-shaped gap in the joint.

[c] Treatment

Mild sprains are treated initially with elevation of the foot to reduce swelling, then with the use of a cane or a crutch for walking. Healing occurs within three weeks.

Severe sprains may be treated with surgery followed by immobilization or conservatively with immobilization alone. The advantage of surgery is that it may return the ligament to its original length. A ligament left to heal on its own will be longer and looser after healing,

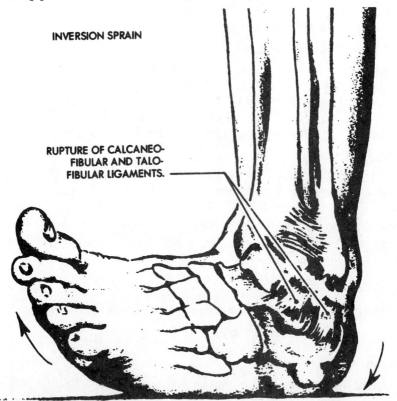

INVERSION SPRAIN

RUPTURE OF CALCANEO-
FIBULAR AND TALO-
FIBULAR LIGAMENTS.

Fig. 3-7. An inversion sprain of the foot usually disrupts the lateral ligaments of the ankle.

which provides less support and predisposes the ankle to recurrent inversion injury and instability.

Surgical success rates range from 80 to 90 percent; the success of conservative treatment is slightly lower (60 to 90 percent, depending on the series). Surgical complications include infection, loss of motion, delayed healing, arthritis and prolonged rehabilitation (Yale, 1987).

Because of the risks of surgery, and because it is generally felt that only very athletic individuals require complete ankle stability, most cases are treated conservatively, with three to six weeks of immobilization in a walking cast, followed by rehabilitation.

[d]   Complications

The most common and troublesome complication of an ankle sprain is recurrent sprain. One inversion injury tends to lengthen and weaken the ligaments, predisposing the ankle to future sprains. In addition, severe sprains may be followed by frequent episodes of pain and swelling after exertion, and patients may also develop a fear of the ankle giving way that interferes with their daily activities. Such symptoms of persistent instability are seen in as many as 40 percent of patients with lateral ligament injuries (Lassiter, et al., 1989). Degenerative arthritis is another possible late complication.

[3] Fractures

The most common type of ankle fracture usually results from an inversion injury, in which the foot is forcibly tilted inward, causing damage to the lateral ligaments. The mechanism is the same as that of the most common type of sprain, but the forces involved are greater. In the fracture, the bony insertion site of one of the lateral ligaments is torn off (an avulsion fracture). This type of fracture is diagnosed by x-ray, evaluated for instability and treated like a sprain,[16] although the period of immobilization (in a walking cast) may be as long as six to nine weeks.

The same mechanism of injury but with still greater force may fracture the tibia (thicker bone of the lower leg). (*See Figure 3–8.*) Such an injury might occur when a worker jumps or falls, landing on the foot on an incline.

Eversion injuries (which occur when the foot is turned out) and other types of more serious ankle fractures may occur in the occupational setting but are uncommon.

[a] Diagnosis and Treatment

The diagnosis of an ankle fracture is based on radiologic findings. Special x-ray views are required in some circumstances for full evaluation of the injury.

Ankle fractures can be treated conservatively or surgically. Conservative therapy, with closed reduction (nonsurgical realignment) of displaced fracture fragments, avoids opening the skin but is plagued by problems in maintaining the fragments in place. Furthermore, a cast is required for as long as 16 weeks after conservative therapy; after surgical reduction, it may be required for only 4 to 6 weeks.

---

[16] *See* 3.06 [2][a] *supra.*

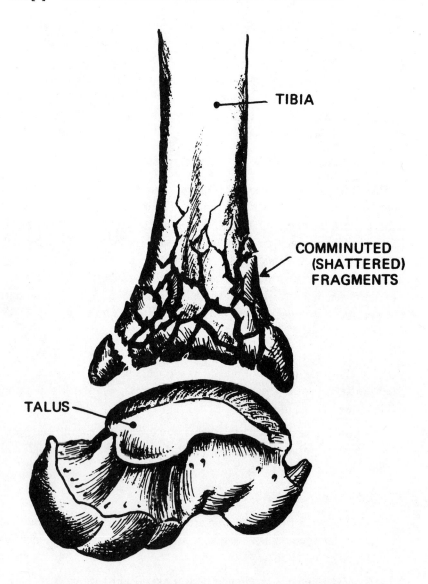

Fig. 3-8. Comminuted fracture of the tibia involving the ankle joint. This fracture usually results from an inversion injury, in which the foot is forcibly tilted inward.

[b] Complications

The major long-term complication of ankle fractures is osteoarthritis (a form of arthritis in which the structures degenerate). The risk of chronic pain and arthritis depends on the severity and type of fracture, and possibly on the method of treatment. For some fractures, operative treatment may carry a lower risk, but for others, the development of chronic symptoms occurs equally in surgically and nonsurgically treated groups (Gumann, 1989).

3.07 PREVENTION OF FOOT AND ANKLE INJURIES

The thrust of injury prevention in the foot is on footwear, which may be designed to protect the foot against a variety of occupational hazards. No less important is attention to floor surface, both in design and maintenance (keeping it dry, well lit and uncluttered).

In 1962, the National Safety Council established the Z–41 Committee, which set standards for protective footwear. There are several classes of shoes, which are designed to withstand different types of hazards and varying degrees of impact. Shoes have been designed to protect against impact, compression, heat, static electricity, high voltage and slippery surfaces.

To be effective, safety shoes must be worn and they must be appropriate for the job. This means that their use must be required and that workers must be educated in their use and upkeep. Early research showed that when they are not required, less than 10 percent of workers will use such footwear. When used, injuries still occur, but 85 percent of these involve an unprotected part of the foot (U.S. Department of Labor, 1981). Safety shoes have been found to be very effective in preventing many types of injuries.

[1] Toe Caps

The steel toe cap is a critical protective device for workers at risk for injury due to objects being dropped on the foot. Toe caps are tested for impact according to the specifications of the Z–41 Committee. The cap must be able to withstand specified amounts of impact and compression, which vary with the forces likely to be found in particular work environments.

[2] Sole Protection

The sole can be designed to prevent slips, puncture wounds and conduction of electric current.

[a] Slip-resistant Soles

The design of a slip-resistant sole depends on the floor surface on which it is to be used. Many different soles with varying tread designs and abrasive components are available. Some are well researched and tested, others are not.

[b] Puncture Protection

The steel insole is the major protective device in use for guarding against puncture wounds. Its use has dramatically reduced the incidence of penetrating wounds in the sole. However, it may increase the risk of certain repetitive impact disorders, such as plantar fasciitis[17] and sesamoiditis,[18] since it reduces the cushioning effect of the shoe.

[c] Protection Against Electricity

Nonconductive soles are used in occupations in which there is potential exposure to high-voltage electricity. To be effective, the sole must be composed of special materials and be of a certain thickness. The sole and heel must be free of metal parts (e.g., nails) and must be either stitched or cemented.

Exposure to static electricity requires a conductive sole. Workers who are exposed may accumulate static electricity on the body and require clothing that will conduct it to the ground. Otherwise, enough charge may build up around the body to create electric shocks or send off sparks that can burn or ignite flammable material in the environment.

Safety shoes for static electricity exposure must be carefully maintained or they will not function correctly. Grit, oils and other types of dirt interfere with the effectiveness of the shoe. Oils, oily cleaning compounds and waxes cannot be used on floors where conductive shoes are in use.

---

[17] See 3.05[6][c] supra.

[18] See 3.05[6][d] supra.

[3] Metatarsal Shields

The most effective form of metatarsal protection is the metatarsal shield. This covers the dorsum (top surface) of the foot. The metatarsal shield is used most widely in steel and foundry work, logging, and the pulp and paper industry.

[4] Ankle Protection

The ankle may be protected against blunt trauma through the use of specially designed gaiters (foot and/or leg coverings) and high-top boots. However, these devices do not protect against sprain.

[5] Floor Surface

In some cases, floor surfaces may be modified to minimize the risk of disorders related to chronic repetitive impact. The harder a floor surface is, the more the foot is required to absorb the shock of impact. The floor may be modified to absorb more of the shock, in effect, to yield slightly on impact. This has been done on some dancing surfaces, where a wood floor may be supported by springs or rafters.

Another modification to the floor surface is the varied terrain floor surface. The human foot was not designed for consistently flat terrain. On the varied terrain surface, the foot assumes a slight tilt, and each time the foot is repositioned, the angle of tilt changes. This type of floor has been reported to reduce the rate of injuries to the foot (Gorecki, 1987).

3.100   BIBLIOGRAPHY

Reference Bibliography

American Medical Association: Guides to the Evaluation of Permanent Impairment, 4th ed. Chicago: American Medical Association, 1993.

Dietz, J. W., et al.: Acinetobacter Calcoaceticus Foot Infection Secondary to High-Pressure Injection Injury: A Case Report. Foot Ankle 8(4):216–222, Feb. 1988.

Gorecki, G. A.: Occupational Foot Health. In: Helfand, A. E. (Ed.): Public Health and Podiatric Medicine. Baltimore: Williams and Wilkins, 1987.

Gumann, G.: Ankle Fractures. In: Scurran, B. L. (Ed.): Foot and Ankle Trauma. New York: Churchill Livingstone, 1989.

Gurdak, C.: Thermal Injuries in the Workplace. A.A.O.H.N. J. 38(10):492–496, Oct. 1990.

Hall, H.: Industrial Injuries to the Foot and Ankle and Their Prevention. In: Jahss, M. H. (Ed.): Disorders of the Foot. Philadelphia: Saunders, 1982.

Lassiter, T. E., et al.: Injury to the Lateral Ligaments of the Ankle. Orthop. Clin. North Am. 20(4):629–640, Oct. 1989.

Schepsis, A. A., et al.: Plantar Fasciitis. Clin. Orthop. 266:185–196, May 1991.

U.S. Department of Labor, Bureau of Labor Statistics: Accidents Involving Foot Injuries, Report No. 626. Washington, D.C.: Government Printing Office, Jan. 1981.

Yale, J. F.: Yale's Podiatric Medicine. Baltimore: Williams and Wilkins, 1987.

CHAPTER 4

Hip, Knee and Leg Injuries

> **SCOPE**
> Hip, knee and leg injuries involve the soft tissues such as the bursae and ligaments as well as the menisci of the knee. Fractures occur, but these are uncommon and usually result from motor vehicle accidents and falls. Workers in certain occupations have a high incidence of chronic injuries involving the hip and knee. These include bus drivers, who tend to get bursitis of the hip, and occupations in which workers kneel frequently, which increases the risk of a variety of chronic knee problems.

SYNOPSIS

4.01   INTRODUCTION

The vast majority of acute occupational injuries to the hip and knee are soft tissue injuries involving ligaments, bursae (closed sacs over exposed or prominent parts of the body) and the menisci (crescent-shaped structures of cartilage or fiber).[1] Outside the joints, leg injuries are uncommon; fractures may occur, but these are usually a result of a traumatic event, such as a motor vehicle accident or a fall.

Chronic occupational problems affect workers who spend long periods kneeling or sitting. These are well-known entities in some

---

[1] *See* 4.02[2] [b] *infra.*

occupations and have common names that link the syndrome with its cause, such as "housemaid's knee"[2] or "weaver's bottom."[3]

4.02 ANATOMY AND TERMINOLOGY

In occupational injuries, the hip and knee joints are much more likely to be involved than the thigh or leg.

[1] Hip and Thigh

The hip is a true ball-and-socket joint and is designed for stability. The socket is a deep cup in the pelvic bones called the acetabulum, and the ball is the head of the femur (the thigh bone). (*See Figure 4–1.*) The position of the femoral head is maintained in part by the bony architecture and in part through strong ligaments that encase the joint and are attached to the pelvis and the femur.

Numerous bursae are located in the region. Bursae are fluid-filled sacs between gliding structures that minimize friction and promote a smooth, gliding motion between moving parts.

The femur is a long, thick bone. At the upper end is the ball-shaped head. This is attached to a short segment of bone called the neck, which connects the head to the shaft, the long segment that extends to the knee. The femoral neck is not vertically oriented; rather, it extends out from the hip joint more or less laterally (the angle between the neck and the shaft is about 125 degrees).

At the junction of the neck and the shaft, the shaft is enlarged and has several large prominences that serve as insertion sites for the muscles that operate the hip joint. The topmost prominence is called the greater trochanter.(*See Figure 4–2.*) This bony projection can be easily felt in the standing position on the side of the hip. It is covered by bursae, which may be a source of occupational problems.

The lower end of the femur is enlarged into two large, rounded condyles (knucklelike prominences) that form the upper part of the knee joint. The hip has a wide range of motion. Flexion is the motion of bringing the knee up to the abdominal wall. Extension is the reverse. Abduction refers to movement of the leg out to the side, and adduction brings the legs back together. The hip may also be rotated out laterally,

---

[2] *See* 4.03[3] *infra.*

[3] *See* 4.05[1][a] *infra.*

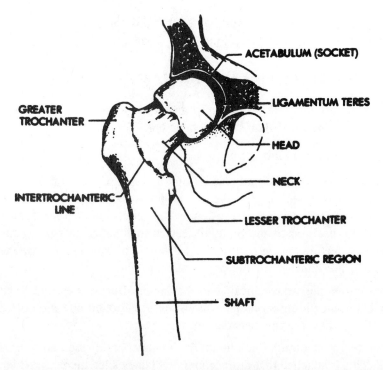

Fig. 4–1. Anatomy of the hip joint. The femoral head inserts into the acetabulum. The joint is buttressed by the lesser and greater trochanters, which serve as muscle attachments. Blood vessels that supply the intracapsular components pass through the ligamentum teres.

which points the knee and foot out to the side. Medial rotation points the knee inward toward the opposite knee.

[2]   Knee and Leg

The knee and leg contain bones that are particularly susceptible to occupational injuries. These include the tibia (shinbone) and fibula (smaller of the two bones of the lower leg).

[a]   Bony Anatomy

The fibula is a thin shaft of bone that runs alongside the larger tibia. It plays an important role in ankle stability, but ends just below the knee and therefore has nothing to do with this joint or with weight-bearing.

The bones that make up the knee joint are the femur, the tibia (the weight-bearing bone of the lower leg) and the patella, or kneecap. The

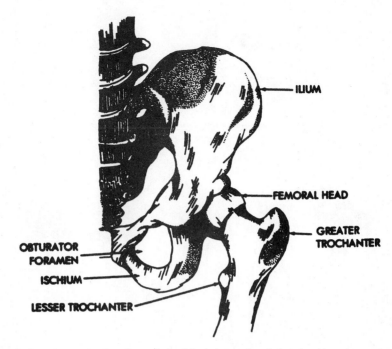

Fig. 4–2. Schematic drawing of the hip joint and pelvis, showing the major features, such as the ilium, the femoral head, the greater and lesser trochanter, the obturator foramen and the ischium.

patella is not part of the true knee joint, but it does form a joint with the anterior (front) surface of the femur. The patella is functionally part of the tendon of the quadriceps muscle, the powerful muscle of the anterior thigh, and it glides up and down with quadriceps motion.

The knee is essentially a hinge joint. (*See Figure 4–3.*) Unlike the hip, stability is not a major feature of its bony architecture. The condyles (knucklelike prominences) of the femur rest on the top of the tibia. The tibial plateau, as the top is called, is more or less flat and contains no bony structures that might prevent the femoral condyles from rolling or sliding off the tibia.

[b] Soft Tissues

The stability of the knee is a function of the thigh muscles, the ligaments and the menisci (crescent-shaped structures). A meniscus is a fibrocartilaginous rim of tissue that converts the flat tibial surface into a saucer for the condyle. There are two in each knee: medial and lateral, one for each condyle.

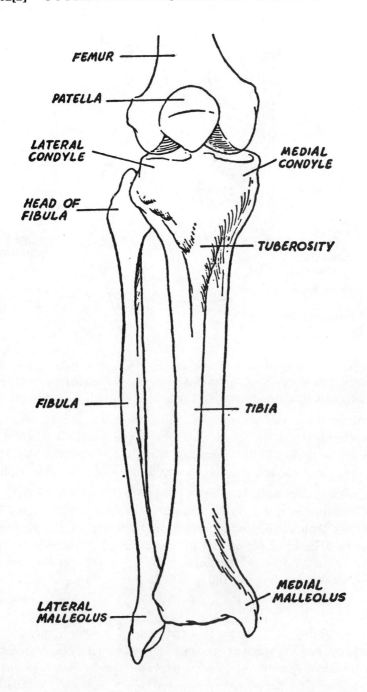

Fig. 4–3. Anterior view of the bones of the right leg articulating at the knee.

The menisci serve several purposes. They provide some stability, and they act as shock absorbers. In addition, they contribute to the lubrication of the joint.

The menisci have no blood supply and are incapable of healing if they are torn. Tearing occurs when the knee is forcibly rotated, which causes the condyles to grind across the menisci, for example, when the hip turns but the foot is anchored in place.

Several ligaments maintain the femoral condyles in position. On the sides, the medial (also called medial collateral) and lateral ligaments keep the femur from sliding sideways off the tibia. The short cruciate ligaments are located in the center of the joint, between the condyles. These prevent forward and backward sliding.

There are several bursae about the knee, and these may become inflamed in occupational activities. One bursa on the posterior side of the knee may become distended and bulge out. In this situation, it may be referred to as a Baker's cyst (or popliteal cyst).

4.03 MECHANISMS OF INJURY

Acute injuries to the hip, knee and leg may be caused by direct trauma, such as a blow or a motor vehicle accident. Falls from a height severe enough to fracture the long bones do occur, but these are uncommon. (*See Figure 4-4.*) Twisting is a common mechanism of acute injury and is associated with meniscal, ligamentous and bony injuries.

Chronic occupational leg injuries are related to the postural demands of specific jobs. A variety of knee problems have been associated with prolonged kneeling,[4] and bursitis around the hip may develop in some cases as a result of prolonged sitting.[5]

[1] Blunt Trauma

A common knee injury results from a blow to the knee. Typically a worker uses a heavy hammer to strike objects in front of him or her and misses, striking the knee. Motor vehicle accidents account for much of the direct trauma to the lower extremity.

---

[4] *See* 4.03 [3] *infra.*

[5] *See* 4.05 *infra.*

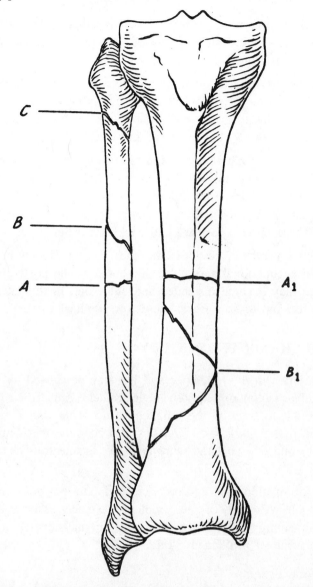

Fig. 4–4. Transverse, spiral and oblique fractures of tibia and fibula.

A) Transverse fracture of fibula.

B) Transverse fracture of tibia.

C) Spiral fracture of fibula.

D) Spiral fracture of tibia.

E) Oblique fracture of fibular neck.

Falls may produce fractures of any of the long bones in the leg. These bones are among the largest of the body, and major forces are required to break them, with one exception. If a patient has osteoporosis, the neck of the femur becomes fragile and susceptible to fracture at the slightest degree of trauma, usually a slip and fall. In some cases, the trauma is so minimal that the fracture occurs first, then the fall. Osteoporosis is most common in elderly women but occurs in individuals with a variety of medical conditions and in individuals on chronic corticosteroid medication.

[2] Twisting

A common mechanism of knee injury involves a twisting motion. Damage to the ligaments and menisci frequently results from twisting.[6] Injury occurs when the foot is fixed and the thigh turns. Twisting of the knee also occurs in situations in which the individual is attempting to escape an external force or object about to roll into the body. This is a common mechanism of acute knee injury in industry.

A twisting injury to the ankle, such as a sprain, is often associated with a fracture of the fibula just below the knee.[7] This fracture may be missed if the examiner focuses only on the ankle.

Meniscal tears may occur in many other situations. In some cases, a healthy meniscus can be torn through apparently minimal trauma, such as a minor fall, stumble or trip. This is particularly likely if the ligaments have been damaged in a previous twisting incident, rendering the knee slightly unstable.

[3] Kneeling

Chronic injury to the knee is a feature of occupations in which workers kneel or squat frequently. One of the first recognized occupational knee problems, called housemaid's knee, occurred in housemaids who spent time kneeling to wash floors.

Currently workers at risk for knee problems include miners who work in cramped spaces, floor layers, carpet layers, stone cutters, gardeners, tile setters, cement and concrete finishers, dry-wall installers and lathers, and carpenters (Thun, et al., 1987). These workers may experience knee joint infections, fluid in the knee (effusion), bursitis

----

[6] *See* 4.02 *supra.*

[7] *See also* ch. 3.

and arthritis. Meniscal tears also occur; over prolonged periods, kneeling and squatting place the menisci under chronic continuous pressure and can cause them to degenerate.

Carpet and floor layers may use a "knee kicker," a tool used to stretch carpet when installing it wall to wall. This device is operated by hitting it with the knee. The use of a knee kicker appears to increase the risk of knee injury (Thun, et al., 1987).

[4]   Sitting

Bursitis about the hip is associated with prolonged sitting. Chronic irritation and pressure on the bursae around the buttock and hip may produce painful symptoms, most commonly ischiogluteal bursitis ("weaver's bottom")[8] and trochanteric bursitis, which is seen in bus drivers.[9]

4.04   CLINICAL APPROACH TO LOWER EXTREMITY INJURIES

The diagnosis of most lower extremity injuries depends largely on the history and physical examination. X-rays and other procedures confirm the diagnosis and help reveal the full extent of the injury.

[1]   History

The history of an acute injury involves principally the actions and objects involved in the accident. In many cases, a history of previous injury to the same region is critical. Past and present recreation and sports activities may set the stage for an acute injury. In the case of chronic symptoms, work posture and activity are important, in addition.

Knee pain is a symptom of a wide variety of disorders. The daily pattern of pain and the precise movements that precipitate symptoms often point to specific diagnoses. Other symptoms are also helpful; "locking" and "giving way" are characteristic of meniscal and ligamentous injuries. Knee pain may also represent referred pain from the hip.

Many medical illnesses can involve the knee. These are usually detected by taking a thorough patient history. Fever, pain in other

---

8 *See* 4.05[1][a] *infra.*

9 *See* 4.05[1][b] *infra.*

joints or symptoms that also involve other systems, such as the skin or gastrointestinal tract, can all indicate an underlying medical condition.

Chronic arthritis involving one knee may result from osteoarthritis, meniscal and ligamentous damage, gout and other diseases involving deposition of crystals in the joint (pseudogout), and infections (tuberculosis, Lyme disease and fungal infections). Gonorrhea, septic arthritis, rheumatoid arthritis and a wide variety of other inflammatory diseases can produce knee symptoms.

Meniscal and ligamentous damage commonly results from trauma, but it may be seen in some forms of arthritis (McCune, et al., 1988).

Hip pain is usually classified by location: anterior, lateral and posterior. Hip joint disease may produce anterior or lateral hip pain. Posterior or buttock pain may result from hip disease but is frequently referred from the low back and may be due to any of the causes of low back pain (muscle strain, intervertebral disc disease, sacroiliitis, etc.).[10] Hip pain rarely results from vascular insufficiency. Internal disorders such as kidney stones may produce anterior pain, but these conditions usually have distinguishing features that become apparent with the history and physical examination.

[2] Physical Examination

The appearance of the joint is an important diagnostic clue. Redness and swelling indicate an acute inflammatory or infectious process. Tenderness is a feature of some disorders, particularly bursitis (inflammation of the bursa, a sac filled with fluid located between moving surfaces). Motion is examined actively and passively; pain on both passive and active motion usually indicates involvement of the joint surfaces themselves. Pain on active motion but not with passive movement of the joint by the examiner points to bursitis and extra-articular disease (occurring outside the joint).

In addition, a number of specific maneuvers are designed to stress the ligaments and test the stability of the knee.

[3] Tests

A wide variety of diagnostic tests are available for the evaluation of hip, knee and leg injuries. The test sequence depends on the differential diagnosis in each case.

---

[10] *See also* ch. 6.

X-rays are useful in the diagnosis of fractures or bone diseases such as tumors, infections, Paget's disease (a disease marked by both loss and overgrowth of bone tissue, resulting in deformities), osteoarthritis and avascular necrosis (death of tissue due to an insufficient blood supply). Bone scans are most useful in the early detection of bone infections and tumors. Magnetic resonance imaging (MRI) is the most sensitive test for the detection of early avascular necrosis and is also useful in the evaluation of the menisci and ligaments.

If fluid is present in the joint, a specimen may be aspirated (removed through a hollow needle) for culture and analyzed. This is particularly easy in the knee and is a common procedure.

Arthroscopy has become a very important diagnostic and therapeutic tool in the evaluation of knee injuries. A thin fiberoptic tube is inserted into the joint, allowing the examiner to see the internal structures. In some cases, the procedure is also therapeutic, since some types of repair may be performed through arthroscopy.

[4]   Evaluation of Impairment

The assessment of impairment is based primarily on the motion of the joints. The hip and knee are put through all ranges of motion, and the extent of the range is measured in degrees (degrees of flexion, extension, etc.). Fixed deformities (ankylosis) are measured. Sensation is also assessed.

Each incremental loss in degrees of motion is converted to a percentage impairment of that limb by the use of tables designed for this purpose by the American Medical Association in its *Guides to the Evaluation of Permanent Impairment* (1993). In the case of the knee, the AMA *Guides* also ranks individual injuries (e.g., meniscal tears, sprains) and some surgical procedures (arthroplasty). Each entity on the list is given a percentage impairment rating.

4.05   HIP INJURIES

Hip fractures in the working population are distinctly unusual and result from major trauma, except in the case of an individual with underlying osteoporosis.[11]

---

[11] *See* 4.03[1] *supra.*

Chronic hip problems may occur in sedentary individuals. One study of bus drivers reported that 15 percent of drivers suffered from hip problems (Kompier, et al., 1987).

[1] Bursitis of the Hip

Ischiogluteal and trochanteric bursitis have been reported as occupational problems. There are several bursae in the region of the hip. These may become irritated and inflamed when they are under constant pressure or friction (bursitis, inflamed bursa).

[a] Ischiogluteal Bursitis

Ischiogluteal bursitis (also called ischial bursitis or "weaver's bottom") has been associated with prolonged sitting. This bursa lies between the lowest point of the ischium (part of the pelvic bone) and the gluteus maximus muscle (the major muscle of the buttock). This bursa lies directly over the sciatic nerve.

The major symptom is pain in the buttock that increases with sitting and may be severe. The pain may radiate down the back of the leg, mimicking sciatica and low back disorders, including herniated disc disease. The straight leg raising test, in which pain is produced upon maneuvers that stretch the sciatic nerve, is positive in both lumbar disc herniation and ischiogluteal bursitis, which may complicate the diagnosis.

The inflamed bursa will be acutely tender, which distinguishes this syndrome from back problems. Steroid injections into the bursa usually provide relief of symptoms, and are therefore both diagnostic and therapeutic.

[b] Chronic Trochanteric Bursitis

Chronic trochanteric bursitis (pain or tenderness on the side of the hip) is a frequent occupational complaint of bus drivers, particularly when the driver's seat is not level but rides up slightly on the sides, to mold to the driver's body. The trochanteric bursa may then be compressed between the greater trochanter and the seat. Movements of the hip, such as those required to operate the foot pedals, may increase the irritation.

The symptoms are pain and tenderness over the greater trochanter, on the lateral aspect (side of the hip). Hip joint disease may elicit lateral hip pain but may be distinguished from bursitis (inflammation of a bursa) in that bursitis produces local tenderness and passive motion of the hip is painless.

Acute trochanteric bursitis is an uncommon disorder that follows local contusion with secondary bleeding into the bursa. It responds to aspiration and/or local steroid injection.

Several factors may contribute to the development of chronic trochanteric bursitis. Anything that causes the driver to lean slightly (even if imperceptibly) to one side increases the pressure on that side and may precipitate bursitis. Painful disorders of the knee, foot and back may produce such a postural change, particularly pain on one side of the back. This may be due to any number of different disorders.[12] Leg length discrepancy may also predispose the individual to trochanteric bursitis (the bursitis occurs on the side of the longer leg) (Roberts and Williams, 1988).

The diagnosis of chronic trochanteric bursitis is based on the clinical examination. Injection of corticosteroids into the affected bursa produces relief of symptoms and also serves as a diagnostic test.

[2]   Arthritis of the Hip

The major form of arthritis involving the hip is osteoarthritis. This is most common in elderly individuals and results from age-related changes in the cartilage of the hip joint. Arthritis may also follow trauma to the hip joint.

4.06   KNEE INJURIES

The most common knee injuries are sprains and meniscal tears (tears in the crescent-shaped fibrocartilaginous pads of the knee). Contusions (bruises), bursitis (inflammation of a bursa, or sac) and chondromalacia patellae (softening of the cartilage in the kneecap) account for the majority of the remainder. Fractures occur but are unusual. Patellar fractures may result from blunt trauma, as in a direct blow to the front of the knee. A fracture of the tibia at the knee (tibial plateau fracture) may occur in a fall from a height.

[1]   Contusions

A contusion (bruise) is an injury to the soft tissues (everything excluding the bone) that does not break the skin. It is usually

---

[12] See also ch. 6.

accompanied by bleeding into the tissues including the skin, which gives the bruise its characteristic black-and-blue color.

A direct blow to the knee may produce a contusion. The most common mechanism is a fall forward onto the hands and knees. This often precipitates bleeding into the joint itself (an effusion). The blood may be confined by the joint capsule that encases the joint, producing severe pain as the capsule is stretched. This is usually treated with ice packs and range of motion exercises once the effusion has resolved.

[2] Bursitis of the Knee

There are several bursae about the knee, any of which may become inflamed (bursitis). The bursa most frequently affected is the prepatellar bursa, located between the patella (kneecap) and the skin. This is the classic "housemaid's knee."[13] The bursa of the medial collateral ligament may become inflamed, usually after repeated squatting and standing activity. Involvement of the bursa at the back of the knee may produce a popliteal cyst.

[a] Prepatellar Bursitis

Prepatellar bursitis, also called housemaid's knee, results from prolonged kneeling and was originally described in women who scrubbed floors on their hands and knees. Coal miners, who work in tunnels with low ceilings and frequently kneel, are also susceptible to the development of prepatellar bursitis; in this case, it is typically combined with a disfiguring cellulitis (inflammation of the connective tissue) of the tissue overlying the patella and has been referred to as *beat knee.*

Today prepatellar bursitis is more common in other workers, but the mechanism of injury—kneeling—is the same. Workers who kneel frequently include carpet and floor layers, miners, tile setters, dry wall installers and lathers, and cement and concrete finishers.[14]

The symptoms usually include pain, tenderness and swelling on top of the kneecap (the bursa becomes filled with fluid). Occasionally the condition becomes chronic, and in rare cases, it may be complicated by infection.

Treatment involves aspirating the fluid from the bursa, with or without a local injection of corticosteroids (a steroid hormone

---

[13] *See* 4.06[2] [a] *infra.*

[14] *See* 4.03[3] *supra.*

produced by the cortex of the adrenal gland). Kneeling must be avoided while the inflammation subsides. In chronic cases, it may be necessary to remove the bursa surgically.

[b] Popliteal Cysts

A popliteal cyst, also called a Baker's cyst, is a painful swelling at the back of the knee. The posterior bursa is involved. It may develop after an activity that hyperextends the knee, such as working on a ladder. In many cases, the posterior bursa communicates with the joint space; in such cases, swelling of the bursa is an indication of pathology in the joint space itself.

The diagnosis of a popliteal cyst is made by transilluminating the cyst (shining a light through it; light passes easily through the cyst fluid). Ultrasound may also be used to confirm the diagnosis. The differential diagnosis includes tumors (lipoma, vascular tumors and fibrosarcoma). In cases in which the cyst or cyst fluid dissects down the calf, it may be difficult to distinguish a popliteal cyst from a deep venous thrombosis (blood clot in the veins of the calf) on physical examination alone.

Treatment consists of aspiration, steroid injection and modification of activities. If treatment fails, a more detailed examination of the knee joint is warranted to make an evaluation of joint pathology.

[3] Sprains

Ligamentous injuries (sprains) are usually a result of some overt traumatic event. The most common injury is a sprain of the medial ligament (on the inner aspect of the knee), which may be caused by a twisting injury or a blow to the lateral side of the knee. Such injuries are often associated with meniscal tears and may be combined with damage to the cruciate ligaments.

Lateral ligament injuries are less common and less disabling. The cruciate ligaments, located inside the joint, may also be sprained by a blow to the front or the back of the knee, but this is rare.

Sprains are graded according to the degree of instability that they create. Grade I sprains are mild and result in minimal instability; the ligaments are stretched but intact. A partial tear is thought to be the cause of a grade II sprain, and complete disruption of the ligament represents a grade III sprain that is associated with marked instability.[15]

[a] Diagnosis and Treatment

The patient with a mild sprain of the medial ligament has pain and tenderness over the medial aspect of the knee. On physical examination, the examiner cannot displace the bony structures of the knee; it is stable. In grade II (moderate) sprains, the tenderness is more widespread. The examiner puts the knee through several maneuvers that stress the joint, and clinical instability is present. In some cases, x-rays of the knee under stress (forces attempting to displace the bones) are used to quantitate instability.

Mild sprains are treated with elastic bandage support and exercise. Healing occurs in about three weeks. Moderate sprains may also be treated conservatively, but a splint or walking cast is required for immobilization, and the healing time is longer. Grade III sprains are usually treated with immobilization and/or surgery.

[b] Complications

Ligaments will heal even when they are completely torn. However, even a stretched or partially torn ligament will be longer after healing than before injury. Joint stability depends on tight ligaments of exactly the right length, and the healed but lax ligament may set the stage for instability and future symptoms.

This is particularly true of cruciate ligament tears, in which the laxity tends to progress and creates stresses that damage the menisci and other structures. Patients complain that the knee gives way, or buckles, at the slightest provocation, including walking on uneven terrain. Surgery appears to improve the outcome for most patients.

[4] Meniscal Tears

An acute meniscal tear frequently occurs in a twisting injury; the foot is fixed to the ground (by an object, or is caught in a hole), and the hip turns, forcing the femur to rotate on the tibia. The femur then grinds over the menisci, tearing them. Because they lack a blood supply, the menisci cannot repair themselves, and loose fragments of meniscus will interfere with knee function until they are removed.

---

[15] *See also* ch. 7.

Forces sufficient to acutely tear the menisci usually disrupt the ligaments also. For this reason, acute tears of the menisci are usually associated with a sprain.

An acute meniscal tear may occur through a slightly different mechanism in the occupational setting. Kneeling with the knee in maximum flexion requires a small amount of rotation of the femoral condyles (prominences) on the tibia. If a worker who has been kneeling for some time suddenly stands up, the force of rapid extension and untwisting of the knee is occasionally sufficient to tear the meniscus. This mechanism of injury has been seen in roofers, carpet and floor layers as well as individuals working on machinery close to the floor.[16]

Chronic meniscal injury may be of occupational origin. Repeated kneeling and squatting have been associated with meniscal tears. This posture creates continuous pressure on the menisci, leading to degeneration. Coal miners have an increased incidence of meniscal lesions, as do other kneeling workers.[17]

[a]   Diagnosis and Treatment

A torn meniscus may present in different ways. In the case of a sudden twisting injury producing a major tear, there is swelling due to effusion (fluid in the joint), "locked knee" (a meniscal fragment preventing hinge motion), pain and tenderness. Small tears are not necessarily disabling and may only produce noticeable symptoms when the individual attempts to pivot. This is popularly described as a "trick knee."

Some patients report symptoms of pain and locking that occur suddenly with squatting or climbing stairs. Others note an insidious onset of knee pain that is usually aggravated by activity but may persist at rest.

The diagnosis of a torn meniscus is best made by arthroscopy (examination of the interior of a joint), and the treatment is surgical removal of the meniscus (meniscectomy), either arthroscopically (using this diagnostic instrument in a therapeutic way) or through an open incision. Recovery following treatment is usually complete, and most individuals return to normal functioning.

---

[16] See 4.03 [3] supra.

[17] See 4.03 [3] supra.

[b] Complications

Meniscectomy is associated with an increased risk of developing degenerative arthritis of the knee in the years following surgery. This has been explained in terms of knee biomechanics: removal of the menisci permanently alters the biomechanical relations of the structures of the knee and increases the friction between them.

It is possible, however, that the same factors that led to the torn meniscus in the first place are responsible for the development of the arthritis. These underlying factors may be unaffected by meniscectomy and may continue to exist in the post-treatment years. This particularly applies in the occupational setting, where the worker returns to the kneeling job after treatment. For this reason, some authors prefer conservative treatment of meniscal tears.

[5] Chondromalacia Patellae

Chondromalacia patellae (softening of the patellar cartilage) is a common degenerative condition of the patella in which cartilage covering the posterior or inside surface of the patella becomes eroded. The posterior surface of the patella articulates with the anterior surface of the femur (the patellofemoral joint). The patellofemoral pain syndrome is the name given to the symptoms that result from this condition.

There are several causes of chondromalacia. The most common is thought to be malalignment, so that the pull exerted by the quadriceps muscle does not draw the patella straight through its groove between the femoral condyles. The posterior contour of the patella is designed to fit the contour of the femoral groove. In individuals with knock-knees, bow-legs or wide hips, the quadriceps may pull at an angle that causes the patella to ride up against one side of the groove. This constant irritation leads to degeneration of the cartilage and chondromalacia.

Injury to the patella may lead to chondromalacia patellae. A blow to the front of the knee that does not fracture the patella may bruise the posterior side and initiate degeneration. Irritation of the cartilage may also result from forceful extension of the knee, as in climbing and standing on a ladder.

The patellofemoral syndrome consists of pain in the knee that is aggravated by climbing stairs and prolonged sitting (activities that require flexion of the knees). In some cases, patients complain of grinding in the knees; in others, the knees "lock." On examination, pressure on the patella produces pain.

The treatment is conservative and consists primarily of keeping the knee straight until the symptoms resolve.

[6]   Fractures about the Knee

Fractures about the knee may involve the patella, the femur or the tibia. These fractures do occur in occupational settings but are not common. As with other fractures, the diagnosis is made by x-ray.

[a]   Patellar Fractures

Patellar fractures may occur through direct trauma, classically, in a motor vehicle accident when the knee strikes the dashboard. The fracture is usually comminuted (in multiple pieces) and requires surgical treatment (the patella may have to be removed). The long-term prognosis for knee function is good, although 6 to 12 months are required to regain full knee function after surgery. However, the majority of patients report problems climbing stairs, walking downhill and kneeling after this injury.

[b]   Tibial Fractures

Tibial fractures may occur in a fall from a height. There are several different types, and they may be associated with ligamentous and meniscal injuries. The treatment may be open (surgical) or closed, depending on the injury. When the fracture involves the joint surface, post-traumatic arthritis is likely to occur as a late complication. The prognosis for most tibial fractures is good, but it depends heavily on the ability to achieve and maintain proper alignment of the fracture fragments.

In fractures in which all or part of the tibial plateau is depressed (dented) or compressed, the prognosis for pain-free motion of the knee is guarded. In some of these cases, the plateau may be replaced by a prosthesis.

[c]   Femoral Fractures

Fractures of the distal femur are classified by their location relative to the femoral condyles: They may be condylar (involving the condyles) or supracondylar (above the condyles).

Extreme force is generally required to fracture a healthy femur. Motor vehicle accidents and falls from a height account for the majority of these injuries. Complications related to the injury include nerve and blood vessel injuries, and damage to the surrounding muscles.

Supracondylar fractures generally take three to four months to heal, although longer healing periods are not uncommon. In most cases, this injury is followed by permanent restriction in knee flexion, due to muscle and tendon injuries, and local scarring.

When the condyles are involved, the prognosis is not so good. Involvement of the joint surface demands precise surgical realignment of the fracture fragments. Long-term mobility depends heavily on early motion to prevent the development of scarring within the joint.

[7]   Arthritis of the Knee

Arthritis of the knee is a common problem. Many different types of arthritis may involve the knee; the most common type is degenerative arthritis, also called osteoarthritis. It is primarily a problem of people over the age of 50.

[a]   Causes

Several factors contribute to the development of osteoarthritis of the knees. Age, obesity and prior knee trauma are known risk factors. The category of prior knee trauma includes all injuries affecting the biomechanics of the joint and includes bony, tendinous, ligamentous and meniscal injuries.

Sports and occupation may also play a role in the origin of osteoarthritis. Coal miners and carpet layers have been reported to have an increased risk of knee arthritis. Occupations requiring repeated bending of the knee have been associated with an increased risk (Anderson and Felson, 1988).

Chronic arthritis of the knee may be caused by several inflammatory diseases. Gout (a disease characterized by excessive amounts of uric acid in the blood, with pain in the joints), pseudogout (hereditary condition in which calcium, not uric acid, is deposited in joints), rheumatoid arthritis, psoriatic arthritis (concurrence of arthritis and the skin disease psoriasis), Reiter's syndrome (association of arthritis with conjunctivitis and urethritis) and Lyme disease may all affect the knee, but the patient history in these cases usually reveals symptoms in other joints. Many of these diagnoses may be supported by blood tests showing anemia and an elevated sedimentation rate (both of which accompany active inflammation) or positive Lyme antibody tests (in the case of Lyme disease). When there are doubts as to the diagnosis, aspiration and examination of the joint fluid may be decisive. In osteoarthritis, the joint fluid is free of crystals and inflammatory elements (high numbers of white blood cells).

Chronic arthritis limited to the knee may, rarely, be caused by tuberculosis. A positive tuberculin skin test (the PPD, or purified protein derivative) and an abnormal chest x-ray may suggest that a workup for tuberculosis be done. A biopsy of the synovium (joint lining) may also be useful. The fluid should be aspirated and carefully cultured for tuberculosis and other bacteria.

A rare condition that mimics arthritis of the knee is a tumor of the synovium called pigmented villonodular synovitis. This disease has a characteristic radiologic appearance and can be diagnosed on synovial biopsy.

[b]   Diagnosis and Treatment

The clinical picture of arthritis in the knee is dominated by knee pain that is initially brought on by weight-bearing and later may persist following activity. Stiffness on first rising, which rapidly improves with activity, is another common symptom. A cold and damp climate characteristically aggravates the symptoms.

On physical examination, the bones of the knee may be enlarged due to thickening of the joint capsule and osteophytes (bony projections associated with chronic irritation). There may be effusion (fluid in the joint) and crepitus (crackling and creaking sounds) on movement.

There are a variety of radiologic features, such as bony deformities, osteophytes, joint space narrowing and cartilage loss. However, the correlation between the clinical picture and the x-ray appearance is notoriously poor.

The diagnosis of osteoarthritis of the knee is based on the clinical picture, supported by x-rays, and the exclusion of other diseases. The treatment consists of anti-inflammatory drugs or analgesic medication. The use of intra-articular injections of corticosteroids (hormones derived from the cortex of the adrenal gland) is controversial. Weight loss reduces the load on the knee and is useful for obese patients. In severe cases, surgical reconstruction of the knee is considered.

4.07 LEG AND THIGH INJURIES

Lower extremity injuries in the workplace (other than those to the foot, ankle and knee) are uncommon. Leg and thigh injuries do occur; in addition to mild contusions (bruising), such injuries range from burns to severe, open fractures.[18]

[1] Burns

Burns are classified according to depth. In the past, it has been common to describe burns as first, second, third or fourth degree. First- and second-degree burns are characterized by partial skin loss; the burn does not extend down to the deepest layer of skin responsible for regeneration. The newer classification approach refers to first- and second-degree burns as partial-thickness, or superficial burns. Third- and fourth-degree injuries are now commonly called full-thickness, or deep, burns.

A partial-thickness or first-degree burn resembles a sunburn; a second-degree burn tends to blister. Full-thickness (third-degree and deeper) burns involve all layers of the skin (and the underlying tissues as well, in fourth-degree burns). These wounds will not heal spontaneously, because the skin cannot replace itself. Skin grafting is required.

There are three types of burns: thermal, chemical and electrical. There are several different mechanisms of thermal burns, including scalds, contact and flash burns. In the leg, the usual type of burn results from a spill of a hot liquid (a scald) or chemical. Electrical injuries involving the leg usually also affect the upper extremity and the rest of the body.

Scalds may be due to hot liquids. Cleaners using hot water, and food service and restaurant workers may be subject to these injuries. Scalds may also occur with spills and spattering of molten metals, bitumen and molten plastic. Roofers, road crews, felters, foundry workers as well as iron and steel workers are at risk.

Although clothing may protect the skin from such injuries to some extent, the use of high-top boots can increase the risk if they are worn

---

[18] *See also* ch. 3.

open at the top: Material may spill into the boot, and contact time is prolonged by the time required to remove the boot. Leg gaiters are used in some occupations to protect the legs.

[2]   Muscle Injuries

Muscle injuries to the leg include contusions, crush injuries and ruptures. Contusions or bruises are generally caused by blunt trauma. When these injuries are severe, there may be significant hemorrhage into the muscle. In some cases, such a hemorrhage may be complicated by the late development of myositis ossificans, a condition in which bone forms in the hematoma or blood clot. This complication aside, contusions may be disabling for several days but then resolve.

Crush injuries may involve the leg, as when a piece of heavy equipment falls on the leg or rolls over it. Crush injuries can be severe, indeed, life threatening if they affect a sufficiently large portion of the body. Damaged muscle swells, and the combination of bleeding and swelling in the muscle may produce a compartment syndrome, in which the pressure in the muscle compartment builds to such a degree that it cuts off the blood supply. The muscles and nerves in the compartment will die if the situation is not rapidly corrected by fasciotomy (an incision along the length of the compartment). If they are severe enough, crush injuries may release myoglobin (a protein) into the bloodstream and result in kidney failure.

Muscle ruptures in the workplace usually involve the gastrocnemius muscle, the major muscle of the calf. The mechanism involves sudden exertion, as in suddenly pushing off from the foot. There is usually considerable pain and hemorrhage, and symptoms may take six to eight weeks to resolve, but permanent disability is rare.

[3]   Fractures

Fractures of the tibia and femur require considerable force and result from major trauma such as a motor vehicle accident, a gunshot wound or a fall from a height. There are several different types of fracture, all of which are diagnosed by x-ray, and many different methods of treatment. (*See Figure 4–4.*)

[a]   Specific Fractures

Femoral fractures are often life threatening. Complications include massive hemorrhage and fat embolism. (The latter is fat from the bone marrow that enters the bloodstream and interferes with circulation in the lung and brain. If such interference is severe, it can lead to acute respiratory failure and death.) The treatment of a femoral fracture may require an extended hospital stay (one to two months), and return to work may be delayed for a considerable time.

Tibial fractures also require much force and result from similar mechanisms. In many cases, the fibula is fractured as well. The healing time for tibial fractures varies from 10 to 26 weeks, depending on the severity of the fracture.

Fractures of the fibula are relatively unimportant, since the fibula is not a weight-bearing bone. These fractures may occur through trauma to the leg or knee, or a twisting injury to either the knee or the ankle (typically, an ankle sprain).

Fibular fractures may be associated with damage to other important structures, such as the lateral capsule and ligaments of the knee (in a twisting knee injury), and the peroneal (relating to the fibula) nerve. Peroneal nerve damage may result from the fibular fracture or from traction or casting (pressure) for a tibial fracture. Damage to the peroneal nerve may result in foot drop (a condition in which the patient is not able to bend the foot upward, usually because of muscular paralysis).

[b] Prognosis

The prognosis for a leg fracture depends largely on the fracture itself: the bones involved, the degree to which the fragments are displaced or comminuted (multiply fragmented), the extent of soft tissue damage and whether the fracture was open (communicating with the skin, with fragments exposed). The force involved in producing the injury also plays a role in prognosis; high-energy wounds (motor vehicle accidents and gunshot wounds) tend to be worse than low-energy insults (falls).

[c] Stress Fractures

One last type of fracture that may occur in the occupational setting but is not as common is the stress fracture. Typical sites for stress fractures in the lower extremity are the lower end of the fibula and the shaft of the tibia. (A fracture of the neck of the femur as typically occurs in the elderly is considered by some to be a stress fracture.)

Stress fractures are associated with considerable activity or movement. The diagnosis may be complicated by the fact that the x-rays are usually negative for the first few weeks. A bone scan confirms the diagnosis.

4.100 BIBLIOGRAPHY

Reference Bibliography

American Medical Association: Guides to the Evaluation of Permanent Impairment, 4th ed. Chicago: American Medical Association, 1993.

Anderson, J. J. and Felson, D. T.: Factors Associated with Osteoarthritis of the Knee in the First National Health and Nutrition Examination Survey (Hanes I). Am. J. Epidem. 128:179–189, July 1988.

Kompier, M., et al.: Physical Work Environment and Musculoskeletal Disorders in the Bus Driver's Profession. In: Buckle, P. (Ed.): Musculoskeletal Disorders at Work. Philadelphia: Taylor and Francis, 1987.

McCune, W. J., et al.: Evaluation of Knee Pain. Primary Care 15(4):795–808, Dec. 1988.

Roberts, W. N. and Williams, R. B.: Hip Pain. Primary Care 15:783–793, Dec. 1988.

Thun, M., et al.: Morbidity from Repetitive Knee Trauma in Carpet and Floor Layers. Brit. J. Indus. Med. 44:611–620, Sept. 1987.

CHAPTER 5

Spinal Cord and Nerve Root Injuries

SCOPE

Spinal cord injury can be caused by both blunt and penetrating trauma. Closed injuries due to blunt trauma are the most common type of occupational spinal cord injury. Major causes are falls, motor vehicle accidents, being hit by falling objects, explosions and crush injuries. These injuries may also compress or damage the spinal nerve roots. Most cases involve the cervical spine, which is more flexible and thus more vulnerable to injury than the thoracic and lumbar spine areas. The severity of injury and consequent disability depend on the level of the spine that is affected and whether the injury is complete or incomplete. Specialized emergency management may prevent further loss of function, and new pharmacologic treatments may preserve function by interrupting secondary neural damage. Spinal cord injury is associated with many complications, including partial or complete paralysis; cardiorespiratory and gastrointestinal problems; skin breakdown; impairment of urinary, rectal and sexual function; pain; spasticity; and psychosocial difficulties. Prognosis depends largely on the level of the lesion and the patient's motivation to engage in comprehensive rehabilitation.

5.01   INTRODUCTION

Throughout history, spinal cord trauma has been a devastating injury resulting in high mortality and severe disability for those few victims who lived (Gutierrez, et al., 1993). As recently as the 1960s, 30 percent of spinal-cord-injured patients died. By the 1980s, however, mortality had been reduced to 6 percent (Ducker, 1990). This means that large numbers of patients are now surviving with disabilities.

The development of well-organized, comprehensive management plans, including early diagnosis of the extent of neurologic damage, prevention of additional primary or secondary damage to the spinal cord, and rehabilitation, has made it possible to restore enough function to most patients to make them productive members of society

(Gutierrez, et al., 1993). Nevertheless, the best form of treatment remains prevention.

[1]   Epidemiology

Since not all states require reporting of spinal cord injury, accurate data on incidence nationally do not exist. It has been estimated that between 8,000 and 10,000 cases occur annually. Of this total, complete and incomplete quadriplegics (individuals with paralysis of all four limbs) and complete and incomplete paraplegics (paralysis of both lower limbs and, generally, the lower trunk) each comprise about 25 percent (Gutierrez, et al., 1993). In Colorado, which has a reporting system, 566 cases of spinal cord injury occurred between January 1986 and June 1991, of which 74, or 13.1 percent, occurred at a workplace (Rosenberg, et al., 1993).

Up to 85 percent of individuals with spinal cord injury are male, mostly single and between the ages of 16 and 30. Half these cases are caused by motor vehicle accidents that involve mostly young people. Falls, mostly sustained by the elderly, account for 20 percent. Sports, especially diving, and violence each account for 15 percent of the total (Gutierrez, et al., 1993).

[2]   Structure of Spinal Column, Spinal Cord and Nerve Roots

The spinal cord, nerve roots and cauda equina ("horse's tail"; tail-like structure at the bottom of the spinal cord) are encased and protected by the bony spinal column and the supporting ligaments that run along its length. *(See Figure 5-1.)* At each segmental level, two spinal nerve roots emerge from the spinal cord and pass through openings between the vertebrae that are known as intervertebral foramina. *(See Figure 5-2.)*

Compression of the nerve roots at any level as a result of narrowing of the foramina increases the impairment (Becker, 1988). The dorsal (posterior) roots transmit sensory impulses coming into the cord, and the ventral (anterior) roots transmit motor impulses coming from it. At each level, the two roots combine to form a spinal nerve.

The spinal cord ends at the top of the L2 (second lumbar) vertebra. Below this level lies the cauda equina, which consists of nerve roots that descend farther through the vertebral canal.

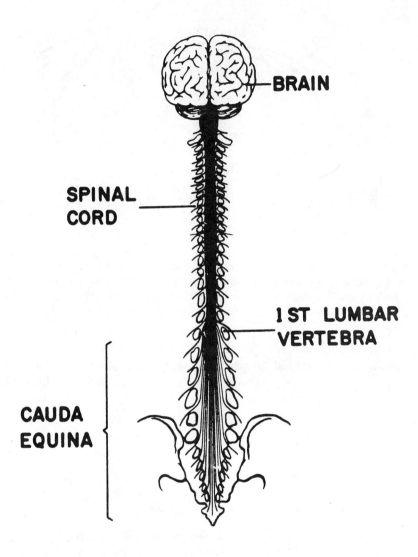

Fig. 5-1. Posterior view of the brain, spinal cord and cauda equina.

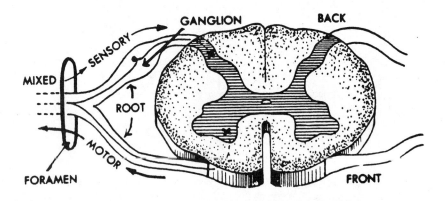

Fig. 5-2. Cross section of the spinal cord, showing how each nerve is formed by the union of a sensory and a motor nerve root. After passing through the foramen (opening) between adjacent vertebrae, the two roots merge to form a spinal nerve. The ganglion is a collection of nerve cells.

The cervical (neck) spine is the most flexible part of the vertebral column and has the least protection. Generally, however, the cervical spinal canal is at least 30 percent larger in diameter than the cord within it, allowing most patients to sustain a fair amount of dislocation without damage to the cord.

By contrast, the thoracic (in the chest area) spine is strongly fixed to the ribs and much less flexible, requiring a great deal of force to dislocate it, and the thoracic canal is not much larger in diameter than the cord.

5.02 GENERAL CAUSES OF INJURY

Spinal cord injuries may be caused by blunt or penetrating trauma. Blunt trauma causing closed injuries is the most common type in civilian life (Jellinger, 1991). Spinal cord injury is frequently associated with head trauma, fractures of the trunk or limbs, and serious chest and thoracic injuries (Gutierrez, et al., 1993).

[1] Closed Injuries

Closed injuries of the spinal cord are those that produce no external wounds. They are caused by a blunt force transmitted to the spine.

Neural (nerve) tissue may be injured even though there is no damage to bony or soft tissue in the spine. In such a case, the lesion may extend to many cord segments above or below the point of impact (Jellinger, 1991).

Motor vehicle accidents—the most important cause of injury—may involve automobiles, motorcycles, snowmobiles and collisions between automobiles and bicycles or pedestrians. *(See Figure 5-3.)* Sports, particularly diving but also cycling, field sports, gymnastics, water-skiing and winter sports, constitute the second most important cause of spinal cord injury. Falls, being hit by a falling object and the blast effect from explosions are other causes (Rosenberg, et al., 1993; Jellinger, 1991).

[2] Penetrating Trauma

Between 5 and 10 percent of civilian spinal cord injuries are due to penetrating trauma, such as from gunshots, knives, high- or low-velocity missiles, or fragments of bone produced by blunt trauma, such as in the blast effects of an explosion. Often the spinal cord itself can sustain a severe direct penetrating injury, such as from a stab wound, without the spine being damaged (Jellinger, 1991).

5.03 MECHANISMS OF INJURY

Spinal cord injury occurs when the spinal column, muscles and ligaments protecting the spine are unable to dispel the energy of a physical force that impacts the spine. Flexion, extension, compression, rotation, distraction and shearing are forces that cause direct injury

Fig. 5-3. Mechanism of injury in a rear-end collision. Severe extension-flexion motion of the cervical spine can damage the spinal cord.

to the cord. Indirect injury results from trauma to the vertebral column, such as fracture-dislocation, which may lead to compression of the cord by fragments of a burst disc or vertebral body. *(See Figure 5-4.)* Most spinal cord injury is in fact a result of a fracture-dislocation (Sonntag and Douglas, 1992).

[1]   Closed Injury

Injuries caused by extension of the cervical spine (in which the neck is stretched up and backward) lead to fracture of the posterior parts of the vertebrae and disruption of the longitudinal ligaments. Flexion

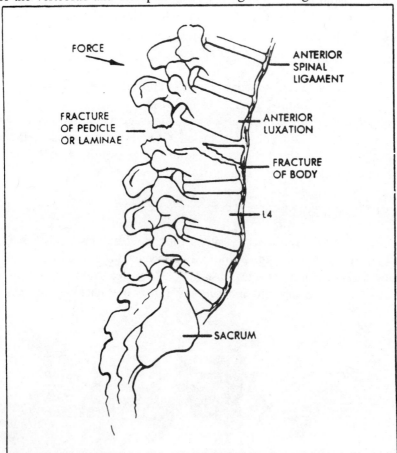

Fig. 5-4. Indirect injury may result in fracture-dislocation of a vertebra. Here the third lumbar vertebra (L3) has suffered a horizontal fracture of the vertebral body, fracture of the articular (joint) processes and disruption of all major ligaments in the area.

injuries (in which the neck is bent forward) may result in rupture of the intervertebral discs and fracture of the vertebral bodies. *(See Figure 5-5.)* In both these cases, rotation may cause additional disruption. Vertebral body fracture and tearing of ligaments may result from compression injuries (Becker, 1988). *(See Figure 5-6.)*

The effect of a disruption of spinal alignment or of a fracture-dislocation is to compress or otherwise distort the tissue of the cord or nerve roots by diminishing the diameter of the spinal canal or of the foramina. Frequently the anterior and posterior spinal arteries, which supply the spinal cord, are compromised as well (Spencer, et al., 1989). Compression may also result from bleeding or swelling in surrounding soft tissues. Protrusion of an intervertebral disc is another cause of cord compression (Briggs, 1994).

Compression begins a progression of pathologic changes in the cord tissue that, over a period of hours to days, can lead to loss of neural function (Spencer, et al., 1989). Recent developments in treatment

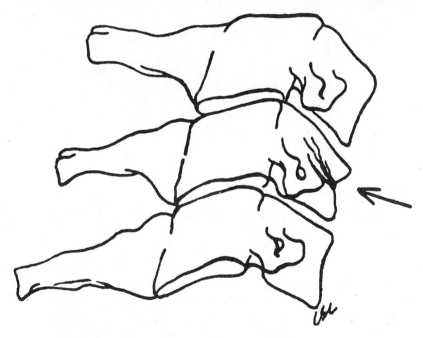

Fig. 5-5. Forced flexion of the cervical spine often results in a compression fracture of a vertebral body (arrow).

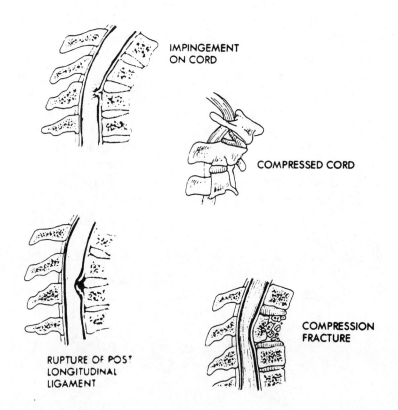

Fig. 5-6. Outward flexion of the cervical spine can cause cord impingement and compression, and rupture of ligaments.

focus on minimizing these changes in order to preserve neural function.

[a]   Cervical Cord Injuries

Between 50 and 60 percent of all cases of spinal cord injury affect the cervical spine, which is the most vulnerable part (Spencer, et al., 1989). Since the cervical spine is the most flexible part of the vertebral column, a relatively modest degree of trauma can fracture or dislocate it.

Individuals who are most vulnerable are those with a spinal canal narrower than normal and older persons whose spinal canal has been diminished by osteoarthritis (degenerative joint disease). In such persons, hyperextension or hyperflexion can result in severe injury even when there is no dislocation of the spinal column. At the same time, cervical injuries are more frequently incomplete (some sensation or voluntary motor function remains below the level of the injury) and reversible than thoracic injuries (Becker, 1988).

[b] Thoracic Cord Injuries

The powerful force required to dislocate the thoracic spine means that thoracic injuries, when they occur, are usually complete and irreversible. Because of the smallness of the thoracic spinal canal, compression is more likely (Becker, 1988). Most thoracic spine injuries are fractures caused by flexion injuries resulting from falls or vehicle accidents (Meyer, 1992).

[c] Lumbar Cord Injuries

The lumbar spinal column is also powerfully constructed and supported by the massive paraspinal muscles, with a wider canal in relation to the diameter of the neural structures inside it. Consequently very strong forces are required to disrupt it. What is more, the cauda equina at its base can tolerate greater levels of compression and other trauma than can the spinal cord. Here, again, injuries are more likely to be incomplete (Becker, 1988).

[d] Spinal Nerve Root Injuries

Injuries that compress the spinal cord can also cause compression or irritation of the spinal nerve roots through a decrease in the size of the intervertebral foramina. Vertebral body bursting fractures, dislocations or fracture-dislocations, and herniating discs that protrude laterally are some causes of compression. Others include soft-tissue injuries that lead to bleeding or swelling in the tissues surrounding the vertebrae. An abnormal motion such as whiplash may cause stretching of the nerve roots (Briggs, 1994). In severe injuries, one or more nerve roots may be completely avulsed (torn) from the spinal cord (Volle, et al., 1992).

[2] Penetrating Injuries

Penetrating injuries of the spinal cord range from superficial lesions to small, localized stab or puncture wounds to total disruption of the cord involving tears in the dura mater (outermost of the membranes that cover the cord), complete transection or hemisection (in which only one side of the cord is cut, resulting in Brown-Séquard syndrome.[1]

Stab wounds tend to produce well-defined, localized lesions that involve only one level of the cord. A missile that traverses the spinal canal or cord and leaves through an exit wound causes a perforating injury with little bleeding or bruising. However, penetrating injuries caused by the effects of high-velocity missiles passing through the spine may result in considerable damage to the cord through contusion (bruising) and other mechanical effects, even without touching the dura mater (Jellinger, 1991).

[3] Pathologic Changes

Most spinal cord injury does not involve complete transection of the cord but, rather, damage affecting only part of it, leaving some viable nerve tissue, which presumably makes some degree of neurologic recovery possible. Unfortunately, however, the response of the spinal cord to injury involves rapid damage to these remaining neurons.

Experts currently believe that spinal cord injury is followed within minutes by a sequence of pathologic events that lead to massive metabolic abnormalities, involving secondary damage to adjacent neurons that results in permanent loss of neural function. There are two theories about how these lesions progress.

The first theory involves mechanical distortion of the neurons of the cord; it suggests that the pathologic changes are initiated by distortion of the neuronal membrane by the trauma. The second theory is vascular. It suggests that decrease or interruption of blood flow to the cord is responsible for the changes.

Inflammatory changes begin two hours after injury. Within six hours, edema (swelling due to abnormal accumulation of fluid) due to vascular occlusion begins to appear, further reducing blood flow through the cord. Complete necrosis (tissue death) may occur within 24 to 48 hours after the injury. Within weeks, contracted scar tissue forms.

Newly developed pharmacologic and surgical treatments for spinal cord injury are based on the assumption that if this progression of

---

[1] *See also* 5.04[7][c] *infra.*

pathologic changes can be stopped, neural function below the level of the injury can be preserved or even regained. It has been found, for example, that injured cats require only 10 percent of the appropriate white-matter nerve tracts to regain the ability to stand and walk (Wilberger, 1993; Sonntag and Douglas, 1992).

5.04 TYPES OF LESIONS

Spinal cord injuries are classified according to the level of the lesion in the cord and whether the injury is complete or incomplete. The newest system of classification is that of the American Spinal Cord Injury Association (ASIA), published in 1992, which has been accepted both in North America and internationally (Pasarin and Green, 1993).

[1] Level of Injury

The segmental level at which a spinal cord injury occurs determines which parts of the body will lose nerve function and which medical complications the patient will probably experience. *(See Figure 5-7.)* The ASIA classification uses x-rays to determine the skeletal level of injury (SkLI). This term refers to the vertebra or two adjacent vertebrae that have sustained the most damage.

The neurologic level of injury (NLI) is determined by the neurologic examination. *(See Figure 5-8.)* ASIA specifies the key muscles and points on the body to be used to test the motor level of injury (MLI) and sensory level of injury (SLI). The NLI is defined as the lowest segment that has good motor and sensory function (Gutierrez, et al., 1993).

[2] Complete and Incomplete Injuries

The completeness of an injury depends on how much neural function remains, not on whether the cord was completely transected. An incomplete injury is one in which there is any nonreflex neurologic function below what is known as the zone of partial preservation or zone of injury. Most patients have such an area, just below the NLI, where some sensory or motor function remains. It may include as many as three adjacent segments, and the injury would still be considered complete if no function remained below these segments.

The definition of complete versus incomplete injury is somewhat controversial. However, the most important prognostic indication is

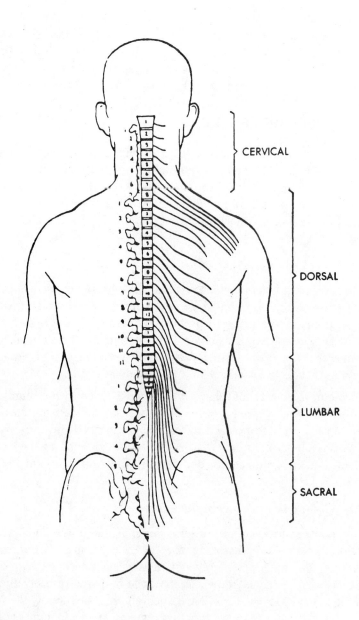

Fig. 5-7. Posterior view of the spinal cord and spinal nerves, illustrating segmentation. The spinal cord extends from the base of the brain to the posterior aspect of the disc between L1 and L2.

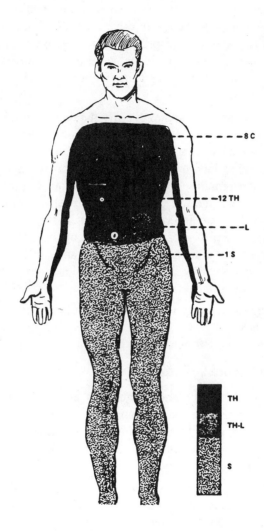

Fig. 5-8. Transection of the spinal cord produces anesthesia or loss of sensation as mapped in this drawing. Injury to the cervical region (C8 and above) involves anesthesia of the upper extremities and trunk muscles, and weakness of the lower extremities; 12 TH refers to the thoracic region; L to the lumbar area and S to the sacral plexus.

whether the patient has any function remaining distally (farther from the point of origin or trunk of the body). For example, a patient with a cervical injury at C5-C6 who has normal motor function in the biceps and weak function in the triceps or other more distal arm muscles does not necessarily have a good prognosis for recovery of foot or leg function; whereas a patient with the same injury who has some foot or leg function has a better prognosis (Gutierrez, et al., 1993; Pasarin and Green, 1993).

The Frankel system is used to classify the degree to which function is preserved below the NLI, on a scale from *A* to *E*. *A* designates a complete injury according to the definition just given. The other categories describe incomplete injuries. In Frankel B injuries, only sensory function remains below the zone of partial preservation. In Frankel C injuries, there is preserved but useless voluntary motor function below the zone. In Frankel D lesions, there is useful voluntary motor function, "useful" meaning that most of the important muscles are able to move the joint against gravity. Frankel E lesions are those in which normal sensory and motor function is regained, though possibly with abnormal reflexes.

Half of patients with spinal cord fractures resulting in neural damage arrive at the hospital in Frankel class A. Ten percent are in class B, 10 percent in C and 30 percent in D (Gutierrez, et al., 1993).

[3] Spinal Shock

After complete injury and sometimes after incomplete injury, patients experience a period of spinal shock, during which there is no function at all in any part of the spinal cord below the level of the injury. After a few weeks, function begins to return in the parts of the cord that were not directly injured (Gutierrez, et al., 1993).

The signs of spinal shock are bradycardia (slowed heartbeat), hypotension (low blood pressure), flaccid paralysis (in which muscles lose their tone and tendon reflexes are decreased or absent), areflexia (absence of reflexes), retention of urine and feces, and poikilothermy (lack of thermoregulation, so that body temperature varies with the environment) (Sommer, et al., 1991).

The first function to return in men is usually the bulbocavernosus reflex (in muscles at the base of the penis), followed by deep tendon reflexes, other involuntary reflexes and autonomic nervous system activity (Gutierrez, et al., 1993).

[4] Concussion

Shock waves resulting from jarring of the spine due to a fall or blast injury can cause concussion—a fairly mild, reversible injury. The patient loses all function immediately after the trauma, but function returns within minutes. The pathogenesis of concussive injury is not understood (Jellinger, 1991; Becker, 1988).

[5] Contusion

Contusion, or bruising, includes all spinal cord injury caused by blunt trauma, such as crush injuries. Contusion disrupts small blood vessels, which bleed into the cord tissue. The extent of injury ranges from small areas of hemorrhage to extensive necrosis involving almost the entire cord. The acute stage of hemorrhage and necrosis leads to a second stage of resorption and organization of the tissue and then, after five years or longer, to formation of scar tissue. The goal of pharmacologic treatment is to inhibit this progression[2] (Jellinger, 1991).

[6] Compression

Compression injury can result from dislocation or fracture-dislocation, the presence of dislocated bone fragments, disc herniation, pressure from distorted ligaments and formation of a hematoma (localized mass of blood). However, most people can tolerate a decrease of 30 to nearly 50 percent in the front-to-back diameter of the spinal canal before the cord suffers damage.

Sudden pinching or squeezing during a flexion-extension injury such as whiplash often causes cervical cord injury. By contrast, injury in the thoracic or lumbar spine is more often caused by permanent compression.

Compression of the cord leads to necrosis, hemorrhage and edema. In unstable fractures, the injured vertebrae can inflict continuing damage on the cord as they continue to move. Even when the vertebral column has been realigned, needlelike bone fragments may continue to compress the cord (Jellinger, 1991).

[7] Syndromes of Spinal Cord Injury

Depending on the specific nature of the injury, patients manifest a variety of typical patterns of functional deficit.

---

[2] *See also* 5.07[5] *infra.*

[a]   Central Cord Syndrome

Central cord syndrome most often occurs after hyperextension injuries of the cervical spine. It is caused by necrosis due to hemorrhage in the central gray matter of the spinal cord, which progresses outward toward the peripheral white matter. The neural tracts of the white matter are organized in such a way that the sensory fibers serving the sacral area are located in the most lateral part of the cord, while the cervical fibers are more medial (closer to the center). Consequently the sacral fibers are more protected from damage in this type of injury (Gutierrez, et al., 1993).

As a result, patients with an incomplete injury may experience what is known as sacral sparing—the ability to feel a touch or pinprick in the area around the anus (Becker, 1988). The physical findings in central cord syndrome have been called *upside down quadriplegia,* since patients have less weakness in the legs than in the arms. Some of these patients are eventually able to walk, although they still experience considerable arm weakness (Gutierrez, et al., 1993).

[b]   Anterior and Posterior Cord Syndromes

In anterior cord syndrome, the front part of the cord is damaged, either by compromise of the anterior spinal artery or anterior cord compression, while the posterior tracts are spared. Anterior cord syndrome may follow flexion injuries and central disc herniations (abnormal protrusions). The patient typically experiences weakness due to loss of voluntary motor function, and loss of temperature and pain sensation below the level of the injury, while retaining sensations of light touch and vibration and a distal position sense.

Posterior cord syndrome involves damage to the posterior part of the cord and has the opposite clinical picture. However, the prognosis is better than in anterior cord syndrome (Gutierrez, et al., 1993; Becker, 1988).

[c]   Brown-Séquard Syndrome

This syndrome is caused by an injury that affects one side of the cord, such as a penetrating wound or lateral compression. It can also be caused by protrusion of an intervertebral disc to one side. The result is motor weakness and loss of fine touch and position sense on the same side of the body as the lesion, and deficits in pain and temperature sensation on the opposite side. In addition, the patient may experience flaccid weakness and anesthesia (lack of sensation) at the NLI, caused by damage to the nerve roots there (Gutierrez, et al., 1993).

[8]   Cauda Equina–Conus Medullaris Syndrome

This syndrome involves damage to spinal nerve roots and sometimes the conus medullaris (the cone-shaped lower end of the spinal cord), resulting from injuries to the lower spine at or below the thoracolumbar junction. Damage to lower motor neurons causes flaccid paralysis, loss of all sensory function and partial or total loss of sacral reflexes, resulting in bladder and bowel dysfunction (Gutierrez, et al., 1993).

[9]   Traumatic Lesions of the Spinal Nerve Roots

Because of the functional separation between dorsal (sensory) and ventral (motor) nerve roots, damage to a dorsal nerve root will cause pain followed by anesthesia, while injury of a ventral root leads to weakness followed by paralysis and loss of reflexes. These changes affect the specific dermatome (skin area innervated by a given nerve) corresponding to the injured nerve root. *(See Figure 5-9.)* Nerve root pain is typically sharp, as opposed to the more diffuse pain resulting from spinal cord injury.

Nerve roots may also be avulsed (torn from the spinal cord). Rupture of posterior nerve roots, which occurs often in acute injury to the cervical cord, occurs primarily adjacent to or at the point where the root enters the cord. Damage to the cord itself or subarachnoid bleeding (occurring between the arachnoid and the pia mater, the two innermost membranes covering the cord), may also be present (Jellinger, 1991).

5.05   SPINAL CORD AND NERVE ROOT INJURIES IN THE WORKPLACE

The trunk and spine are more often injured in work accidents than any other part of the body. They are involved in 29 percent of all cases, and 38 percent of all compensation is paid for such injuries (Briggs, 1994).

[1]   Causes of Injury

Important causes of spinal cord injury in the workplace are falls, motor vehicle accidents, being hit by falling objects, explosions and

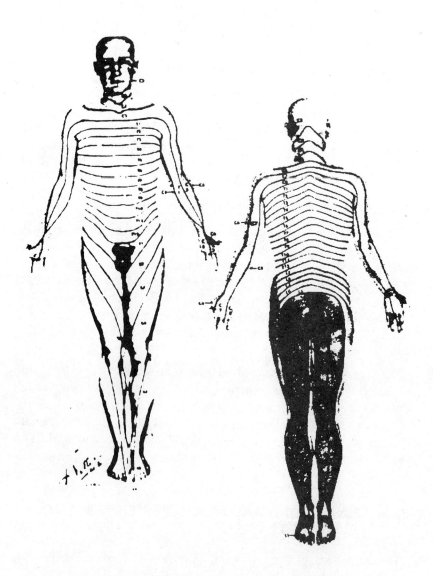

Fig. 5-9. Map of the dermatomes (regions of the surface of the body supplied by nerves passing through a single root). If only one root is severed, some sensation remains in the region, because there is some overlapping of adjacent nerve roots. Knowledge of the region of sensory disturbance often permits precise specification of the site of disturbance in the nervous system.

crush injuries. The most frequent cause of occupational spinal cord injury is falls, which, in a Colorado study, were found to cause 50 percent of all occupational spinal cord injuries. In a Texas study, falls comprised 44 percent of all such injuries. Being hit by a falling object caused 18.9 percent of injuries (Rosenberg, et al., 1993).

[a]   Construction Industry

Falls were particularly common in the construction industry, with its signature risk of falling from one level to a lower one. In fact, 41.9 percent of occupational spinal cord injuries happened to workers in this industry. This is consistent with the fact that the construction industry has the highest overall injury rate of all sectors (Rosenberg, et al., 1993). Other than falls, hazards in this industry include collapse of structures and trenches, and proximity to large machines, such as earth movers, that can back up and hit workers on the ground or tip over and crush the driver.

[b]   Motor Vehicle Accidents

By contrast with the 50 percent figure for nonoccupational spinal cord injury, motor vehicle accidents comprised only 18.9 percent of occupational cases in Colorado. These accidents occurred when the victims were delivering products or services or driving between work sites (Rosenberg, et al., 1993). Occupational motor vehicle accidents also occur at shipping and receiving departments, in parking lots, on roadways around factories and railroad sidings, and in the operation of trucks, tractor-trailers and earth-moving equipment.

[c]   Other Causes

Other causes of occupational spinal cord injury in Colorado were skiing, gunshot wounds and stabbing. The occupations of the victims included professional/managerial, clerical/sales, service, farming, fishing, forestry, processing and bench work, in addition to construction (Rosenberg, et al., 1993).

Injury rates in the manufacturing sector are high (though not as high as in construction), due to risks such as contact with moving machinery, crane loads striking workers, falls from trestles or ladders, explosions of gases, vapors or other inflammable substances, and falling objects (Preventing Illness, 1985).

[2] Prevention of Injury

Prevention of spinal cord injury in the workplace requires incorporation of injury controls into the design of plants and equipment. Industrial hygiene involves recognition of occupational hazards, then taking measures to control them. This is often achieved through a formal occupational safety program concerned with preventing accidents.

Important components of such a program include the following (Prieskop, 1990; Fowler, 1990):

- a safety committee whose members come from the entire work force;

- the presence of emergency medical facilities on site;

- an inspection program designed to recognize hazards in the worksite (frequently this is made a responsibility of the safety committee); and

- investigations carried out following accidents for the purpose of developing measures to prevent recurrence, observing patterns of work flow, environmental conditions and levels of stress to which workers are subject.[3]

[a] Recognition of Hazards

The best method for recognizing materials and processes that may result in harm to workers is to carry out inspections of the workplace. Safety engineers have developed models of "good practice" to prevent injury. Examples would be proper construction of scaffolding and use of ladders that conform to codes on construction sites. During a "walk-through survey," therefore, safety committee members would observe whether actual work practices conform to the model, as well as the effectiveness of control measures. They would also inspect equipment (Fowler, 1990; Preventing Illness, 1985).

[b] Control of Hazards

Control of workplace hazards includes controls on human behavior as well as preventive maintenance of equipment such as motor vehicles. One type of control on behavior is administrative control, such as creating safe pathways through the workplace, scheduling

---

[3] See also 5.08[6] infra.

dangerous operations at times when the fewest number of workers are present and forbidding individuals without proper training to enter such a worksite (Fowler, 1990).

Another important element of hazard control is educating workers to understand hazards and training them in safe operating practices. Occupational Health and Safety Administration standards mandate specialized training programs for workers who operate particular types of equipment, such as forklifts, cranes and powered punch presses.

Control of work practices may require continuous supervision. In the case of workers who will operate vehicles, the safety program may include screening of workers or job applicants and ongoing medical surveillance (Prieskop, 1990; Fowler, 1990).

5.06 DIAGNOSTIC PROCEDURES

Once an injured patient has been medically stabilized, a variety of diagnostic procedures may be used to identify and define the extent of spinal cord injury.

[1] X-rays

Lateral and anteroposterior (front-to-back) x-rays are taken to identify fractures and the extent of dislocation. An open-mouth view and sometimes a view through the armpit are needed to completely visualize the cervical spine. Plain x-rays are also used to monitor attempts at reduction (restoring the spine to its normal alignment) (Sonntag and Douglas, 1992; Spencer, 1989).

[2] Computed Tomography (CT)

Computed tomography (CT) is used to further define areas of suspected injury. Software is available that enables CT to be used to create three-dimensional images that may reveal fractures that are not visible on conventional CT images (Sonntag and Douglas, 1992). CT shows bone pathology well. Modern equipment can also reveal significant soft-tissue pathology in the spinal canal (Greenberg, 1993).

[3] Myelography

Myelography involves removal of cerebrospinal fluid and injection of contrast medium into the subarachnoid space (the area between the inner and middle layers of membrane covering the spinal cord; the subarachnoid space contains cerebrospinal fluid). When the patient is x-rayed, the contrast medium shows the outline of the spinal canal and nerve roots.

CT myelography is CT used with a contrast medium. These modalities may be used to reveal fractured or dislocated fragments of bone that may be impinging on the spinal cord and to detect nerve root avulsion, traumatic meningoceles (protrusion of the meninges, or membranes covering the spinal cord, through a defect in the vertebral column) and masses compressing the cord (Volle, et al., 1992; Sonntag and Douglas, 1992).

[4]   Magnetic Resonance Imaging (MRI)

Magnetic resonance imaging (MRI) uses magnetic fields, radio waves and atomic nuclei to produce detailed cross-sectional images. MRI provides excellent resolution of structures in the spinal canal, and the method is now the procedure of choice for diagnosing acute soft tissue injuries. Relatively fast and noninvasive, it uses differences in proton density between the cerebrospinal fluid, spinal cord, vertebral body marrow and discs to image these structures without the need for injection of contrast medium.

However, MRI cannot image the entire length of the spine, as can contrast myelography. Two or three images may be needed to do this, and the time required may be excessive for a severely injured patient (Greenberg, 1993).

[5]   Electromyography

Electromyography (EMG) tests motor nerve function by inserting needle electrodes into skeletal muscles to detect the electrical potentials generated by muscle fiber contraction. These potentials are then transmitted to an oscilloscope. EMG can confirm motor function loss and radiographic findings of lesions in spinal nerve roots (Trojaborg, 1994).

[6]   Somatosensory Evoked Potentials

This technique evaluates sensory function. Sensory nerves in the legs are stimulated, and the central nervous system response is recorded by means of surface electrodes placed over the cauda equina. A delay in the time required for response indicates nerve damage. Somatosensory evoked potentials (SEPs) are used to detect spared cord function and lesions in the spinal nerve roots, and this method has been reported to be useful, together with clinical indicators such as pinprick tests, for predicting outcome (Trojaborg, 1994; Li, et al., 1990).

[7] Ultrasonography

Ultrasonography (the use of high-frequency sound waves to construct images corresponding to body tissues) is useful for real-time evaluation of intradural (between the membranes covering the spinal cord) and spinal canal structures during surgery. Ultrasonography can detect lesions within the spinal cord or beneath the dura and reveal the degree of decompression achieved within the epidural space (outside the dura mater). However, it can image these structures only when overlying bone is being removed (Greenberg, 1993).

5.07 PATIENT MANAGEMENT

Spinal cord injury requires specialized management, starting at the scene of the accident, since preventing any additional loss of function is critical (Sonntag and Douglas, 1992).

[1] Emergency Care

At the scene of the injury, an adequate airway is first obtained, and shock and hemorrhage are controlled with as little movement of the spine as possible if spinal injury is suspected. Proper handling of the patient is essential to prevent further injury to the cord. The entire spine should remain immobilized until x-rays rule out thoracic or lumbar injury.

When the patient must be extricated from a motor vehicle, log-rolling techniques, scoop stretchers or long spine boards are used to immobilize the entire spine. The patient is then placed on a board, lying on his or her back, with the neck in a neutral position. Towels or sandbags are placed on either side of the head, and the head is taped to the board to immobilize it. This procedure is safer than using a cervical collar.

Between 50 and 60 percent of patients have associated injuries, so a multidisciplinary team should evaluate the patient in the emergency room and provide cardiorespiratory resuscitation if it is needed. Patients with high to midcervical injuries may have impaired diaphragmatic function, and those with low cervical injuries may have impaired intercostal muscle function. Since both types of injuries can create breathing difficulties, these patients may need nasotracheal intubation and/or ventilation with a respirator.

The patient's cardiopulmonary function may be impaired due to associated injuries, creating a need for fluid administration. Maintaining blood pressure is particularly critical, since it is known that perfusion of the spinal cord drops rapidly after injury (Wilberger, 1993). Insertion of a nasogastric tube for suctioning prevents abdominal distension caused by paralytic ileus (intestinal obstruction caused by loss of motility in the intestine). A catheter should be inserted into the bladder to prevent overdistension due to paralysis. Prophylactic antibiotics and tetanus prophylaxis are used for open wounds (Sonntag and Douglas, 1992).

[2]   Early Diagnosis

Once the patient has been stabilized, a history is obtained from the patient or, if necessary, from a relative or a witness to the injury. It is important to discover any pre-existing spinal problems, which may significantly change the way the injury is managed. A physical examination should also be performed, including palpation (manual examination) of the entire length of the spinal column while moving the patient as little as possible. Putting the patient on a rotating treatment table makes unnecessary the excessive use of log-rolling techniques, which have been associated with further disruption of the spinal column (Pasarin and Green, 1993).

A complete neurologic examination is performed to determine the level of the injury and whether it is complete or incomplete. The neurologic examination covers motor and sensory functions. It tests the ability to flex and extend joints, and to perceive position, vibration, touch, pain and temperature. The presence of various reflexes is also tested (Pasarin and Green, 1993; Sonntag and Douglas, 1992).

[a]   Radiographic Evaluation

Since 10 to 15 percent of spinal injuries occur at separate levels of the spinal column (Pasarin and Green, 1993), the entire spine must be imaged radiographically to detect all such fractures. Angiography (x-raying of blood vessels using contrast medium) of the carotid and vertebral arteries may be used when signs indicate that these vessels have been injured (Sonntag and Douglas, 1993). *(See Figure 5-10.)*

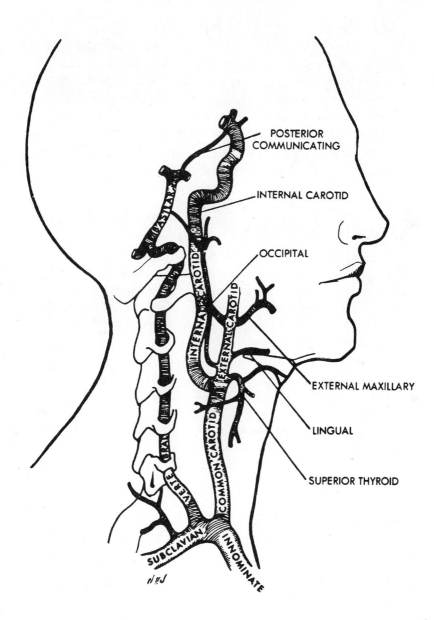

Fig. 5-10. The carotid and vertebral arteries of the neck, leading to the brain.

[b] Signs of Spinal Cord Injury

Weakness, inability to move the extremities, absence of sensation, lacerations or abrasions on the head and neck, and tenderness when the spine is palpated indicate spinal cord injury. Patients with these signs should be treated as though they had such an injury until it is ruled out. The same is true for injured patients who are unconscious (Sonntag and Douglas, 1993).

The ability to move the toes and legs indicates that there is no major cord damage. If the patient cannot move the legs but can move the arms, the lesion is below the cervical area. If the arms are paralyzed, the lesion is at C6 (the sixth cervical vertebra) or above (Briggs, 1994).

[3] Cervical Injuries

If radiography reveals a cervical fracture-dislocation with bone intruding into the spinal canal, immediate reduction (restoration of normal alignment) using traction with tongs or a halo ring is required. The progress of reduction is monitored using x-rays. If reduction is not successful, CT myelography is used to visualize the relation of bone fragments to the spinal cord.

Two different treatment strategies exist for spinal cord injuries. The conservative approach leaves patients in traction for long periods, in the hope of achieving spontaneous fusion. The more aggressive approach advocates early surgery in order to mobilize the patient as soon as possible and thereby avoid the medical complications of prolonged stays in bed. The question of which approach is preferable has not been resolved, because no multicenter prospective randomized trial, which could provide appropriate data, has been done.

In cases in which compression of the spinal cord persists after reduction, the timing of surgery is controversial. If the patient's neurologic status is deteriorating, early surgical decompression may be preferred—even though no statistically significant evidence demonstrates that early decompression is preferable to late decompression—because of the possibility that continued compression may increase the neurologic deficit.

Decompression within 24 hours of injury may improve the functional outcome for patients with complete injuries, but these patients will derive no benefit from surgical decompression performed after the first 24 hours of injury. In quadriplegics, however, decompression may improve nerve root function.

The timing of surgical decompression for patients with incomplete injuries is also controversial, except when bone, disc, blood or subluxation (displacement of vertebrae) is still exerting pressure on the cord and the patient does not improve with traction or begins to deteriorate. In such cases, surgical decompression should be performed.

During the operation, the vertebrae are stabilized using metal plates, bone grafting or wiring (Sonntag and Douglas, 1992). *(See Figure 5-11.)*

[4] Thoracic and Lumbar Injuries

Fracture-dislocations of the thoracic and lumbar spine usually require surgical reduction. After decompression, the spinal column is stabilized using metal rods that exert traction on the laminae (flat plates that extend posteriorly from the vertebrae, forming part of the bony arch through which the spinal cord passes) or bone grafts (Spencer, et al., 1989; Becker, 1988).

[5] Pharmacologic Treatment

The goal of pharmacotherapy is to interrupt the cascade of deleterious physiologic events that cause secondary neural damage after spinal cord injury. A number of drugs affecting various aspects of these biochemical reactions have been studied experimentally, but the complexity of the injury makes it difficult to translate promising laboratory results into the clinical setting (Wilberger, 1993).

[a] Opiate Receptor Antagonists

Spinal cord injury causes a release of endogenous (produced by the body) opioids (endorphins; compounds that have opiatelike effects by interacting with opiate receptors) into the blood, which results in a decrease in spinal cord blood flow. Opiate antagonist drugs, which block opiate receptors, ought therefore to prevent this reduction of blood supply to the cord. Naloxone and thyrotropin-releasing hormone (TRH), both of which are potent antiopiates, have been found effective in preventing this drop in spinal cord blood flow in animal experiments.

In a small clinical trial of TRH, patients with incomplete injuries showed a trend toward improved outcome, but the difference between them and placebo-treated patients was not significant. Naloxone has

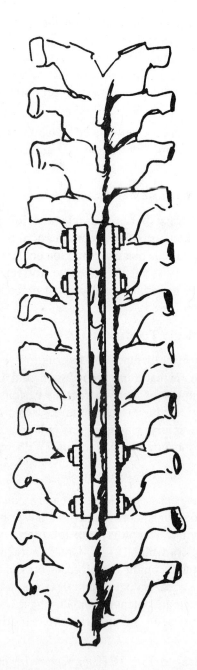

Fig. 5-11. In spinal cord injury, the vertebrae may be stabilized internally with metal plates and screws.

also been studied in clinical trials (Wilberger, 1993; Sonntag and Douglas, 1992).

[b] Steroids

Steroids inhibit lipid peroxidation, a cellular reaction resulting from the activity of free radicals (highly reactive molecules), which destroy the integrity of cell membranes after trauma. Steroids also function as free-radical scavengers and possibly as antioxidants.

After studies reported enhanced motor recovery in animals with its use, the steroid methylprednisolone was widely used clinically. However, there was no evidence that patients derived significant benefit from it. Then it was demonstrated that dose and timing were important for achieving good results. In the second of two clinical trials—the National Acute Spinal Cord Injury Studies (NASCIS) I and II—patients with both complete and incomplete injuries who were given a high dosage of methylprednisolone within eight hours of injury had statistically significant improvement in both motor and sensory function, while patients treated with this drug after eight hours did not show improvement.

The effects of naloxone were also studied in NASCIS II. Patients receiving this drug did not have a neurologic outcome different from those who received a placebo.

The neurologic improvements shown in NASCIS II were small, and their functional significance was questioned. A third NASCIS study was initiated in 1991, in order to study whether administering steroids immediately to four hours after injury is more beneficial than later treatment (four to eight hours).

This third study will also evaluate the effectiveness of Tirilizad®, one of a newly developed group of drugs called 21-aminosteroids. Tirilizad® seems more effective than methylprednisolone in inhibiting lipid peroxidation and does not produce any of the side effects of steroids, such as hyperglycemia (excess level of blood sugar) and immunosuppression (Wilberger, 1993; Sonntag and Douglas, 1992).

[c] DMSO

Another drug that has been studied is dimethyl sulfoxide (DMSO), a vasodilator, free-radical scavenger and anti-inflammatory agent. It may also function as a diuretic to reduce edema (swelling due to accumulation of fluid). However, it has shown only limited effectiveness in animal experiments (Sonntag and Douglas, 1992; Wilberger, 1993).

[d] Hypothermia

Lowering the temperature of injured neural tissue decreases its demand for oxygen and metabolic activity. Hypothermia (low body temperature) has been found to protect the spinal cord against the damaging effects of hypoxia (deficient oxygenation of the blood) and ischemia (lack of oxygen supply to tissues resulting from inadequate blood supply) in experimental animals. In a few cases, it was used to treat human spinal cord injury, but local spinal cord cooling to decrease the temperature by 10 degrees required a difficult surgical procedure. Recent studies, however, suggest that a smaller degree of cooling is adequate to decrease tissue damage (Martinez-Arizala and Green, 1992).

5.08 MEDICAL COMPLICATIONS

Patients with spinal cord injury are subject to a wide variety of complications resulting from surgery, paralysis, long periods of immobilization, tracheal intubation and traction.

[1] Paralysis

The pattern of motor function loss after spinal cord injury depends on the level of the lesion and whether it is complete or incomplete. Cervical cord injury results in quadriplegia (paralysis of most of the body below the upper shoulder and all four limbs). Thoracic cord lesions cause paraplegia (paralysis of the lower body and legs). Injury affecting one side of the cord leads to hemiplegia (paralysis of the arm and leg on one side of the body). Localized lesions of the motor pathways of the cord or of the cauda equina usually result in monoplegia (paralysis of a single limb, usually a leg).

[2] Loss of Sensation

Patterns of sensory loss vary. Loss of pain perception creates a risk of injury because of inability to sense when the body is in a stressful position. Inability to perceive pain sensations from internal organs leads to a risk from conditions such as urinary blockage, ulcers and kidney stones. Lack of pain sensation may also cause pressure necrosis of skin.

[3] Syringomyelia

Syringomyelia is a late complication of spinal cord injury in which cystic cavities filled with fluid develop in the central part of the cord. The fluid acts as a mass that compresses the cord. Patients experience loss of pain and temperature sensations, typically over the shoulders and neck; loss of motor function, with muscle atrophy; pain; respiratory insufficiency and changes in the level of spasticity.

This complication is particularly serious when functional loss occurs above the original level of injury. Diagnosis is by MRI or CT myelography. Treatment involves stabilizing the spine, release of adhesions (scar tissue) that may be tethering the cord and opening the cavity so the fluid can drain. The goal is to preserve function (Gutierrez, et al., 1993).

[4] Cardiorespiratory Complications

Loss of sympathetic nervous system function impairs the regulation of blood pressure, so that patients are subject to sudden hypotension (low blood pressure), usually related to postural changes. Patients should not sit up abruptly and may require the adrenergic drug dobutamine to maintain blood pressure. The efficacy of adrenergic drugs in stabilizing blood pressure is, however, uncertain and should not be the primary therapy in treating any form of shock.

Except for those with low level injury, spinal cord injury patients experience respiratory compromise due to paralysis of the diaphragm and the intercostal (rib cage) or abdominal muscles. Since these muscles are also needed to cough effectively, these patients are at risk for pneumonia. Those with injuries at C4 or above may be unable to maintain adequate ventilation and pulmonary gas exchange, resulting in significant hypoxemia (low blood level of oxygen) and occasionally carbon dioxide retention. Such patients require artificial ventilation.

Another potentially life threatening complication is deep venous thrombosis (inflammation of a vein with formation of thrombi, or clots), due to decreased blood flow resulting from immobilization. Deep venous thrombosis can lead to pulmonary embolism (life-threatening obstruction of an artery in the lung by a blood clot traveling in the bloodstream). Preventive treatments include subcutaneous administration of heparin to prevent clot formation, pneumatic stockings and constant electrical stimulation of the legs (Gutierrez, et al., 1993; Sommer, et al., 1991).

[5]   Gastrointestinal Complications

Gastrointestinal problems are caused mostly by lack of stomach motility. Patients experience nausea and dyspepsia and develop chronic peptic ulcers, sometimes with bleeding. Reflux of acid and pepsin from the stomach can lead to esophagitis (inflammation of the esophagus) and aspiration pneumonitis.

Hypomotility of the gallbladder may lead to gallstones. Hypomotility of the colon and spasticity of the anal sphincter may result in chronic constipation. However, this can be avoided by a bowel training program in which patients perform digital rectal stimulation to promote evacuation. Stool softeners and dietary fiber supplements help avoid fecal impaction (Gutierrez, et al., 1993; Sommer, et al., 1991).

[6]   Dermatologic Complications

Loss of the ability to detect prolonged pressure on the skin and to shift position to relieve it means that patients must move consciously or depend on someone else to move them to relieve this pressure. Pressure that is not relieved causes ischemia and necrosis, leading to development of a pressure sore (decubitus ulcer). Skin covering a bony prominence, such as the sacrum or ischium (part of the pelvis), is especially vulnerable.

Pressure sores may also develop due to fecal or urinary incontinence, friction resulting from muscle spasms, accumulation of metabolic waste products and other factors. A variety of beds have been developed that spread pressure over a wide area, such as air or water flotation beds. Most important is turning the patient every two hours, by hand or using a rotating bed frame (Gutierrez, et al., 1993; Becker, 1988).

[7]   Genitourinary Difficulties

Urinary and sexual functions are often both impaired after spinal cord injury, since the nerves supplying the bladder and sexual organs lie near one another.

[a] Urologic Complications

Renal failure is a life-threatening complication of spinal cord injury. Between 3 and 15 percent of paraplegics die of uremia (toxic condition resulting from excess by-products of protein metabolism in the blood) (Sommer, et al., 1991).

As long as intravenous fluids are being administered, continuous drainage of the bladder via an indwelling catheter is necessary. Once intravenous infusion has been discontinued and the urine is sterile, catheterization can be intermittent. Bacteriostatic (inhibiting the growth of bacteria) drugs such as Bactrim® are given to prevent infection (Chan, 1993).

For some patients, a bladder retraining program may be appropriate. Its goal is to empty the bladder regularly and adequately, thus preventing pyelonephritis (kidney inflammation) and other conditions that lead to renal failure, and to re-establish urinary continence. The program involves adhering to a drinking, voiding and catheterization schedule, as well as learning one or more specific techniques for voiding, depending on the nature of the deficit (Andrews and Opitz, 1993).

[b] Sexual Complications

Disturbance of autonomic nervous system function in the reproductive and genital organs causes sexual dysfunction after spinal cord injury. Sexual behaviors of men and women are often considerably changed by their disability, although they are affected differently. However, both lose the experience of orgasm.

[i] Males

Two types of erections are possible for men with spinal cord injury. The first, psychogenic erections, result from mental stimulation and occur in about 30 percent of males with lower-level injuries (those with complete upper-level injuries do not have them). The second type, reflexogenic erections, are triggered by an external stimulus applied to the genitals or pelvic region. About 90 percent of males with upper-level injuries can have these.

Recent advances in treatment have increased the rates of ejaculation. The two most common techniques for producing ejaculation are vibratory stimulation, which can be done at home, and electroejaculation, which is an office procedure. Both these techniques have resulted in successful pregnancies.

For men who are unable to achieve an erection, penile prostheses are available, although they involve a risk of infection or erosion. Newer techniques developed to treat erectile dysfunction include intracavernous injections of vasoactive substances.

Men with complete spinal cord injury are often infertile because of poor semen quality due to reduced sperm motility and testicular hyperthermia, among other causes (Kirschner, et al., 1993; Rohe, 1993).

[ii]   Females

Women usually remain fertile after spinal cord injury, with menstruation resuming two to three months after the injury (Rohe, 1993). All premenopausal women with spinal cord injuries can have successful pregnancies with vaginal delivery; paraplegia is not necessarily an indication for cesarean section (Ahn, 1991). The major consideration with these patients is preventing complications.

In particular, paraplegic and quadriplegic women are at risk for autonomic hyperreflexia[4] during labor and delivery. Autonomic hyperreflexia has been successfully managed with epidural anesthesia (Kirschner, et al., 1993).

[8]   Pain and Spasticity

Up to 7 percent of patients with spinal cord injury experience painful dysesthesias (unpleasant abnormal sensations produced by normal stimuli), the onset of which may be months or years after the injury. A frequent cause is delayed development of a spinal cyst; in such a case, pain can be relieved by drainage of the cyst. Severe, intractable nerve root pain may be treated by a surgical procedure that involves cutting dorsal nerve roots at the point where they enter the dorsal horn of the spinal cord (Marion and Clifton, 1991).

Once the period of spinal shock is over,[5] reflexes reappear in the areas of the cord below the level of injury that were not directly damaged. Tactile stimuli often cause exaggerated responses, resulting in spasms of extensor and flexor muscles or abdominal contractions.

---

[4] *See also* 5.08[9] *infra.*

[5] *See also* 5.04[3] *supra.*

Spasticity can be exacerbated by noxious stimuli, such as a urinary tract infection or pressure sore. Spasticity causes discomfort and can interfere with rehabilitation and other activities.

Treatment is accomplished with drugs, but these cause many adverse side effects. Baclofen, which enhances the action of the inhibitory neurotransmitter gamma-amino butyric acid (GABA), is the agent of choice, because it causes relatively few adverse reactions. Recently a small implantable pump has been developed to infuse baclofen continuously into the subarachnoid space. The benzodiazepines diazepam and clonazepam, and dantrolene, a muscle relaxant, also help control spasticity. Surgery is a last resort (Gutierrez, et al., 1993).

[9] Autonomic Hyperreflexia

This condition usually occurs in patients with a lesion at T6 or higher. It involves an abnormal, exaggerated discharge by the sympathetic nervous system in response to a noxious stimuli—such as fecal impaction, urinary bladder distension or bedsores—below the lesion in the spinal cord. Autonomic hyperreflexia causes a severe increase in blood pressure that can be life-threatening because it involves a risk of cerebral hemorrhage. Symptoms include slow heartbeat, severe headache, nasal congestion, flushing and sweating below the level of the lesion.

Autonomic hyperreflexia is managed by first removing the noxious stimulus. This involves draining the bladder and checking the rectum for fecal impaction. The patient should be sat up in bed to decrease intracerebral pressure. If pressure remains elevated, the patient is given nifedipine, which is a coronary vasodilator, or hydralizine, an antihypertensive medication (Gutierrez, et al., 1993).

5.09 PSYCHOSOCIAL COMPLICATIONS

Spinal cord injury is a catastrophic trauma that has devastating psychological and social as well as physical effects. Patients' most common response is denial, followed by feelings of anger and then depression. Relatively few patients, however, experience a major depressive episode as defined by the American Psychiatric Association's *Diagnostic and Statistical Manual of Mental Disorders*. In one study, only 10 percent of patients with spinal cord injuries experienced major depression, while 20 percent had minor depression or mixed affective disorder (Malec, 1993). Many patients manage to confront their situation while still feeling fear about the future.

Patients who become depressed and those who had poor coping abilities before their injury are likely not to do well in rehabilitation and to develop medical complications. Those who adjust more effectively to their situation are more effective in rehabilitation and more likely to reach their maximum level of functional independence (Becker, 1988; Ahn, 1991).

The number of self-determined complications, such as substance abuse and suicide, has increased among spinal-cord-injury patients over the past 30 to 40 years. Approximately 5 to 10 percent of quadriplegics are estimated to attempt suicide. Almost all spinal-cord-injury patients experience severe emotional distress for as long as 2 years. The distress can manifest as overt anger or as indifference and withdrawal; both these reactions may be accompanied by self-neglect. The effects on family life are indicated by the fact that the divorce rate among these patients is twice the national average, with most divorces occurring in the second or third year after the injury (Marion and Clifton, 1991).

5.10   REHABILITATION

A patient's potential for regaining function during rehabilitation depends primarily on the level of the lesion and the patient's own motivation. The degree of support from the family, the home situation, the amount of financial support available and the patient's medical status are also factors (Ahn, 1991).

[1]   Rehabilitation Program

Comprehensive rehabilitation includes the following (Ahn, 1991; Chan, 1993):

- nursing and medical care;
- physical therapy;
- occupational therapy for training in carrying out activities of daily living, including driving and using a wheelchair or other adaptive equipment;
- psychological and vocational counseling; and
- social and recreational services.

Physical therapy covers the following (Ahn, 1991; Chan, 1993):

- passive range-of-motion exercises for the paralyzed extremities;
- active strengthening and range-of-motion exercises for muscles that retain some function;
- transfers from bed to wheelchair;
- use of braces; and
- wheelchair mobility.

[2] Prognosis

Once a patient survives the stay in the hospital, life expectancy is only about 10 percent less than that for the general population. However, such a patient requires lifelong medical care (Becker, 1988).

[a] Recovery of Function

The patient's Frankel class[6] serves as a prognostic indicator of functional recovery. Thus 94 percent of patients who present to the hospital in Frankel class A (complete injury) will still be in that class on discharge, despite all treatment. None of these patients will have a complete recovery. Among patients who present in Frankel class B, 62 percent will still be in that class at discharge. Fifty percent of those who present in Frankel C and 94 percent of those in Frankel D will also be unchanged at discharge (Gutierrez, et al., 1993).

[b] Rehabilitation Potential of Different Level Lesions

A quadriplegic with an injury above C4 is dependent on a respirator, though for some, an implanted phrenic nerve (nerve that innervates the diaphragm) pacemaker makes diaphragmatic breathing possible.

C4 quadriplegics can breathe and can drive a wheelchair, operate an environmental control unit and use a computer by means of a mouth-control unit. A C5 quadriplegic can self-feed, perform light grooming and drive a wheelchair using a cuff worn on a paralyzed hand. C6 quadriplegics can be self-sufficient with a wheelchair. C7 quadriplegics can perform activities of daily living independently.

T1 quadriplegics and T2 to T9 paraplegics are unable to walk. T10 paraplegics, however, are capable of limited ambulation using leg

---

[6] *See also* 5.04 [2] *supra.*

braces and crutches, although they require a wheelchair to carry out daily activities. T10 to L1 paraplegics require so much energy to swing their legs through crutches that they may be unable to ambulate functionally.

An L2 paraplegic is able to walk functionally with crutches or a walker and leg braces. Patients with injuries at L3 or a lower level are able to ambulate using ankle-foot supports and canes, crutches or a walker (Ahn, 1991).

5.11 EVALUATION OF IMPAIRMENT

The method for evaluating permanent impairment caused by injuries to the spinal cord and nerve roots that has been developed by the American Medical Association is based on the limitations imposed by the impairments of a person's ability to carry out activities of daily living (American Medical Association, 1993).

In addition to loss of motor function, sensory disturbances—including loss of perception of pain, temperature and vibration, as well as paresthesia and dysesthesia—and autonomic nervous system disturbances, for example, in regulation of circulation and temperature, are both rated according to the extent to which they impair specific functions. When more than one function is impaired, a chart is used to combine impairment estimates for all affected functions. The percentages given refer to impairment of the whole person.

[1] Spinal Cord

Impairments caused by spinal cord injuries are categorized into several functions.

[a] Station and Gait

The ability to stand and to walk is rated on a scale ranging from being able to stand up and walk but having difficulty with elevations, grades, stairs, deep chairs and distances (1 to 9 percent) to inability to stand without assistance from others, mechanical support and a prosthesis (40 to 60 percent).

[b] Use of Upper Extremities

As a rule, loss of use of the preferred or dominant upper extremity causes greater impairment than loss of use of the nonpreferred extremity. For example, a patient who can use the impaired limb for self-care, has difficulty grasping and holding objects, and has no digital dexterity would be rated as having a 10 to 24 percent impairment if the injury is to the preferred extremity but as having a 5 to 14 percent impairment if the nonpreferred extremity is affected. Such a patient should be re-evaluated periodically, however, since over time, the nonpreferred limb may develop as much functional ability as the preferred one had.

When both upper extremities are impaired, the total impairment is greater than a simple combination of the impairments of the two extremities. Thus a patient at the same level as the patient in the earlier example, but in whom both upper limbs are impaired, would receive a rating of 20 to 39 percent.

[c] Respiration

Impairment of the ability to breathe is rated from being able to breathe spontaneously but with difficulty when activities of daily living require exertion (5 to 19 percent) to having no capacity to breathe spontaneously (90+ percent).

[d] Bladder Function

The ability to control bladder emptying is rated from having some degree of voluntary control but being impaired by urgency or intermittent incontinence (1 to 9 percent) to having no voluntary or reflex control (40 to 60 percent).

[e] Anorectal Function

The ability to control anorectal emptying is rated from having reflex evacuation but limited voluntary control (1 to 9 percent) to no reflex regulation and no voluntary control (40 to 50 percent).

[f] Sexual Function

Awareness of sensation and (for men) ability to have an erection or to ejaculate are rated from being able to function sexually but having difficulty in achieving erection or ejaculating (in men) or lack of sensation and excitement (in men and women) (1 to 9 percent), to having no ability to function sexually and no awareness of sensation, in both sexes (20 percent).

[2]   Spinal Nerve Roots

Injury to nerve roots may cause muscle paralysis or weakness, or sensory deficit, pain or discomfort. Impairments may be partial, complete, bilateral or unilateral. Each of these characteristics is evaluated separately. In cases of bilateral involvement, the two unilateral impairments are rated, then combined by means of the chart to derive the whole-person impairment value.

[a]   Pain or Sensory Loss

This impairment is rated in five classes, ranging from no loss of sensation, abnormal sensation or pain (0 percent) to diminished sensation with severe pain or causalgia (a burning sensation or pain, especially in the palms and soles, caused by injury to the nerves that carry impulses from these parts). In some cases, the skin undergoes deteriorative changes preventing activity (81 to 95 percent).

[b]   Loss of Motor Function

This impairment is rated in six classes, ranging from ability to perform active movement against gravity with full resistance (0 percent) to no muscular contraction at all (100 percent).

5.100   BIBLIOGRAPHY

Reference Bibliography

Ahn, J. H.: General Considerations of Rehabilitation of Spinal Cord Injured Patients. In: Errico, T. J., et al. (Eds.): Spinal Trauma. Philadelphia: Lippincott, 1991.

American Medical Association: Guides to the Evaluation of Permanent Impairment, 4th ed. Chicago: American Medical Association, 1993.

Andrews, K. L. and Opitz, J. L.: Bladder Retraining. In: Sinaki, M. (Ed.): Basic Clinical Rehabilitation Medicine, 2nd ed. St. Louis: Mosby, 1993.

Becker, D. P.: Injury to the Head and Spine. In: Wyngaarden, J. B. and Smith, L. H., Jr. (Eds.): Cecil Textbook of Medicine, 18th ed. Philadelphia: Saunders, 1988.

Briggs, D.: Trauma and Emergencies in the Workplace. In: Zenz, C., et al. (Eds.): Occupational Medicine, 3rd ed. St. Louis: Mosby, 1994.

Chan, C. W.: Spinal Cord Injury. In: Sinaki, M. (Ed.): Basic Clinical Rehabilitation Medicine, 2nd ed. St. Louis: Mosby, 1993.

Ducker, T. B.: Treatment of Spinal-Cord Injury [editorial]. N. Engl. J. Med. 322(20):1459-1461, May 17, 1990.

Fowler, D. P.: Industrial Hygiene. In: LaDou, J.: Occupational Medicine. Norwalk, Conn.: Appleton and Lange, 1990.

Greenberg, J.: Neuroradiological Evaluation of Spinal Injury. In: Greenberg, J. (Ed.): Handbook of Head and Spine Trauma. New York: Marcel Dekker, 1993.

Gutierrez, P. A., et al.: Spinal Cord Injury: An Overview. Urol. Clin. North Am. 20(3):373-382, Aug. 1993.

Jellinger, K.: Pathology of Spinal Cord Trauma. In: Errico, T. J., et al. (Eds.): Spinal Trauma. Philadelphia: Lippincott, 1991.

Kirschner, K. L., et al.: Physical Medicine and Rehabilitation. J.A.M.A. 270(2):248-250, July 4, 1993.

Li, C., et al.: Somatosensory Evoked Potentials and Neurological Grades as Predictors of Outcome in Acute Spinal Cord Injury. J. Neurosurg. 72(4):600-609, Apr. 1990.

Malec, J. F.: Psychologic Aspects of Disability. In: Sinaki, M. (Ed.): Basic ClInical Rehabilitation Medicine, 2nd ed. St. Louis: Mosby, 1993.

Marion, D., and Clifton, G.: Injury to the Vertebrae and Spinal Cord. In: Moore, E. E., et al. (Eds.): Trauma, 2nd ed. Norwalk, Conn.: Appleton and Lange, 1991.

Martinez-Arizala, A. and Green, B. A.: Hypothermia in Spinal Cord Injury. J. Neurotrauma 9(Suppl.2):S497-505, May 1992.

Meyer, S.: Thoracic Spine Trauma. Semin. Roentgenol. 27(4):254-261, Oct. 1992.

Pasarin, G. A. and Green, B. A.: Emergency Room Assessment and Stabilization of Spinal Injury. In: Greenberg, J. (Ed.): Handbook of Head and Spine Trauma. New York: Marcel Dekker, 1993.

Preventing Illness and Injury in the Workplace. Washington, D.C.: U.S. Congress, Office of Technology Assessment, OTA-H-256, 1985.

Prieskop, F. G.: Occupational Safety. In: LaDou, J.: Occupational Medicine. Norwalk, Conn.: Appleton and Lange, 1990.

Rohe, D. E.: Sexuality and Disability. In: Sinaki, M. (Ed.): Basic Clinical Rehabilitation Medicine, 2nd ed. St. Louis: Mosby, 1993.

Rosenberg, N. L., et al.: Occupational Spinal Cord Injury: Demographic and Etiologic Differences from Non-Occupational Injuries. Neurology 43(7):1385-1388, July 1993.

Sommer, R. M., et al.: Clinical Physiologic Considerations and Anesthetic Management of Patients with Spinal Cord Injury. In: Errico, T. J., et al. (Eds.): Spinal Trauma. Philadelphia: Lippincott, 1991.

Sonntag, V. K. and Douglas, R. A.: Management of Cervical Spinal Cord Trauma. J. Neurotrauma 9(Suppl. 1):S385-396, Mar. 1992.

Spencer, D. D., et al.: Neurologic Surgery. In: Schwartz, S. I., et al. (Eds.): Principles of Surgery, 5th ed. New York: McGraw-Hill, 1989.

Trojaborg, W.: Clinical, Electrophysiological, and Myelographic Studies of 9 Patients with Cervical Spinal Root Avulsions: Discrepancies Between EMG and X-Ray Findings. Muscle Nerve 17(8):913-922, Aug. 1994.

Volle, E., et al.: Radicular Avulsion Resulting from Spinal Injury: Assessment of Diagnostic Modalities. Neuroradiology 34(3):235-240, 1992.

Wilberger, J. E., Jr.: Pharmacological Resuscitation After Spinal Cord Injury. In: Greenberg, J. (Ed.): Handbook of Head and Spine Trauma. New York: Marcel Dekker, 1993.

Additional Bibliography

Hamilton, M. G., et al.: Venous Thromboembolism in Neurosurgery and Neurology Patients: A Review. Neurosurgery 34(2):280-296, Feb. 1994.

Lewis, K. S. and Mueller, W. M.: Intrathecal Baclofen for Severe Spasticity Secondary to Spinal Cord Injury. Ann. Pharmacother. 27(6):767-774, June 1993.

Montgomery, J. L. and Mongomery, M. L.: Radiographic Evaluation of Cervical Spine Trauma. Procedures to Avoid Catastrophe. Postgrad. Med. 94(4):173, Mar. 1994.

Murphy, K. P., et al.: Cervical Fractures and Spinal Cord Injury: Outcome of Surgical and Nonsurgical Management. Mayo Clin. Proc. 65(7):949-959, July 1990.

Roth, E. J., et al.: Traumatic Central Cord Syndrome: Clinical Features and Functional Outcomes. Arch. Phys. Med. Rehabil. 71(1):18-23, Jan. 1990.

Segatore, M. and Way, C.: Methylprednisolone After Spinal Cord Injury. SCI Nurs. 10(1):8-14, Mar. 1993.

CHAPTER 6

Low Back Injuries

SCOPE

Occupational low back injuries are common complaints among young and middle-aged workers. Particularly affected are industrial workers, truck drivers, nurses, dancers and professional athletes. Sedentary workers are also at risk, including computer programmers, secretaries and attorneys. Actions that create hazards for the lower back include heavy lifting, repetitive motions, forceful motions, mechanical stresses, spinal vibration and static or awkward postures. In the majority of cases, the injury is self-resolving, usually within a six-week period. In a minority of cases, low back pain is caused by intervertebral disc disease; surgery may become the recommended treatment. Occasionally there is traumatic injury to the spine, but it may be a cumulative trauma rather than a sudden event. Many cases of low back pain require either computed tomography or magnetic resonance imaging to make a definitive diagnosis. Most low back injuries can be managed successfully by conservative methods, including short-term bed rest, heat, massage, pain medications and gentle aerobic exercise. Some workers with low back pain develop chronic symptoms and subsequent occupational disability.

SYNOPSIS

6.01   INTRODUCTION

Low back pain is one of the most common occupational health problems in the United States, perhaps affecting as much as 10 percent of the adult working population at any given time (Andersson, 1995). Among medical reasons for work absenteeism, low back pain is second only to upper respiratory infections. In addition, low back pain costs more than $16 billion in treatment and insurance compensation yearly. Low back pain is so prevalent that it will probably affect 80 percent of the working population some time during their occupational life (Andersson, 1995).

Low back pain can be caused by a variety of disorders, including inflammatory, degenerative (such as arthritis), neoplastic, gynecologic and metabolic difficulties. However, the great majority of low back pain is of unknown origin and is ultimately self-resolving (Andersson, 1995).

Back sprains and strains are perhaps the most common perceptible causes of low back pain. A *sprain* is defined as an injury to the ligaments, whereas a *strain* refers to muscle disruption caused by indirect trauma, such as excessive stretching (hyperflexion). In actual practice, these two terms are often used interchangeably.

Since there is currently no reliable method of distinguishing between a sprain and a strain injury, the conditions are often diagnosed by excluding other possible disease states. Other spinal disorders that may be investigated include spinal stenosis,[1] spinal instability,[2] facet syndrome,[3] internal disc disruption (herniation),[4] spondylolisthesis (slipped vertebrae),[5] spondylitis (degenerative arthritis)[6] and spondylolysis (a defect in the pars interarticularis, or space between the facet joints).[7]

Enlargement of the abdominal aorta with aneurysm formation may have an impact on the spinal nerve root, thus producing back pain and sciatic nerve radiation. In addition, certain infections of the spine or discs due to bloodstream infections may produce low back pain. Standard scans and blood tests can be used to diagnose these illnesses.

In reviewing worker's compensation records for back injury in a large teaching hospital over a two-year period, the American College

---

[1] *See also* 6.07[6] *infra.*

[2] *See also* 6.07[4] *infra.*

[3] *See also* 6.02[5] *infra.*

[4] *See also* 6.05[3] *infra.*

[5] *See also* 6.02[1][b] *infra.*

[6] *See also* 6.06[1] *infra.*

[7] *See also* 6.07[6][a] *infra.*

of Occupational and Environmental Medicine found that nurses' aides (who do a majority of lifting of patients) had a very high injury rate. Over three times as many nurses' aides lost time from work than did registered nurses and licensed practical nurses (Fuortes, et al., 1994).

The American College of Occupational and Environmental Medicine interviewed and observed almost 300 workers aged 25 to 60 whose work was assessed as sedentary (e.g., crane operators, drivers and office workers). The researchers' observations suggested that sustained sedentary work in a non-neutral trunk posture is a significant factor in the development of low back pain (Burdorf, 1993).

6.02 ANATOMY AND TERMINOLOGY

The anatomic structures that are most often affected by low back pain include the spine, the spinal cord and its nerves, the ligaments that support the spine and the muscles that permit mobility.

[1] The Spine

The spine, also known as the backbone or spinal column, is designed as a supporting rod for the head and trunk of the body. It is composed of a flexible chain of loosely linked bones called vertebrae. These vertebrae are linked by joints that allow movement in several directions.

Seen from the side (lateral view), the healthy spine resembles an S-shaped curve, bending toward the rear at the neck and toward the front at the lower back. *(See Figure 6-1.)* The spine is divided into five sections—cervical (neck), thoracic (also called dorsal; lower chest or rib cage), lumbar (lower back), sacral (the sacrum is a triangular bone that articulates with the pelvis at the level of the buttocks) and coccygeal (tailbone)—with the vertebrae in each section numbered accordingly.

The coccyx is the bottom-most tip of the spine. It is a vestigial structure resembling a bony finger. The focus of this chapter is the lumbar region of the spine. At the rear of the spine lie the spinous processes. These structures function as anchor points for the muscles, which keep the entire spine tensed and upright. *(See Figure 6-2.)*

[a] The Vertebrae

The lower back, or lumbar spine, is composed of five vertebrae that are labeled L1 through L5, top to bottom. The vertebrae have an outer

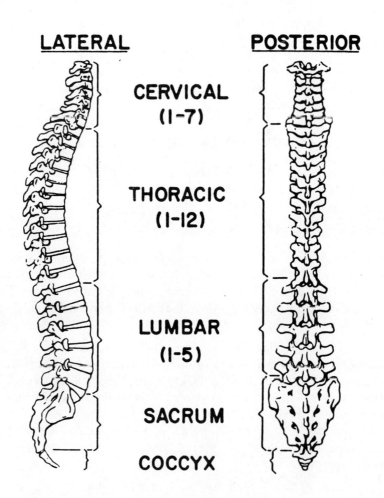

LATERAL   **POSTERIOR**

CERVICAL
(1-7)

THORACIC
(1-12)

LUMBAR
(1-5)

SACRUM

COCCYX

Fig. 6-1. Lateral (side) and posterior (rear) view of the vertebral column. Each vertebra is numbered according to the part of the spine it is in, e.g., the lumbar vertebrae are L1 through L5.

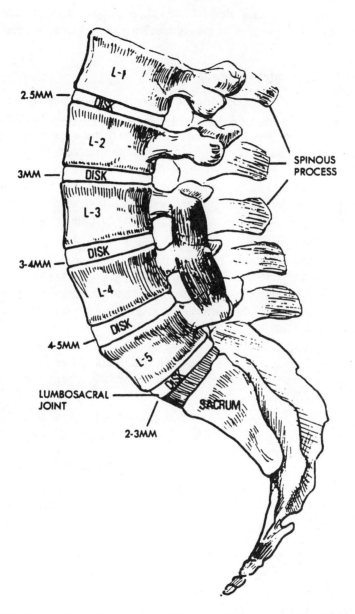

Fig. 6-2. The lumbar spine consists of five vertebrae separated by intervertebral discs. At the rear of the spine lie the spinous processes. These structures function as anchor points for the muscles, which keep the entire spine tensed and upright. The term *lumbosacral joint* refers to the disc that connects the fifth lumbar vertebra (L5) to the sacrum.

layer composed of hard, dense bone called compact bone. Inside each vertebra is a honeycomb of cancellous bone, which contains red bone marrow.

[b]   The Intervertebral Discs

Between the main parts, or central bodies, of each pair of vertebrae is a tough pad called the intervertebral disc. Each disc is composed of a hard, fibrous outer layer (anulus fibrosus) and a gelatinous center (nucleus pulposus). *(See Figure 6-3.)* These intervertebral discs act as shock absorbers for the jarring effects of twisting and bending that are part of everyday functioning. We are slightly taller in the morning than when we retire at night, because the discs, which are pressed together all day as we sit, stand, etc., expand to their normal thickness during restorative sleep.

As we age, the blood supply to the discs decreases over time and disappears completely at approximately 20 years of age (Ducreux, et al., 1995). After this time, the discs receive their nutrition through the process of osmosis (absorption of nutrients from body fluids). From about the age of 30, our intervertebral discs begin to degenerate, gradually losing water, becoming smaller and less springy and, consequently, less efficient as shock absorbers. After age 40, some people's discs become calcified, and in rare cases, a bony fusion forms across the affected disc.

Factors that compromise the normal functioning of the discs include repetitive vibration (as might be experienced by truck drivers and cab drivers) and smoking, which decreases the permeability of the discs (Kauppila, 1993), although the exact mechanism is uncertain. Pressure on a weakened disc caused by lifting something heavy without the muscle power to share the load can cause a disc to rupture, or herniate. *(See Figure 6-4.)* A herniated disc is sometimes erroneously referred to as a slipped disc. Actually there is no such thing as a slipped disc, because discs are attached by connective tissue to vertebrae above and below. As a disc herniates, the gelatinous center is forced out of the disc wall and may exert pressure on nearby nerves.

Once a disc has ruptured, it cannot repair itself. Therefore, injury to the disc may have lasting consequences, including pain and permanent disability.

Initial treatment may include a regimen of rest and simple pain medication, such as aspirin. The worker is taught good health practices,

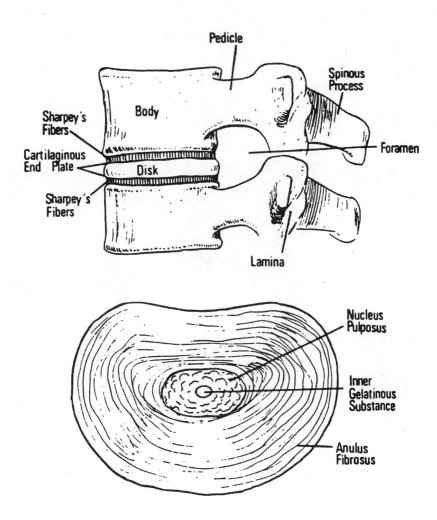

Fig. 6-3. (Top) Lateral view of the intra vertebral disc, showing the relationship of the disc to the adjacent vertebrae. (Bottom) Structure of the intervertebral disc.

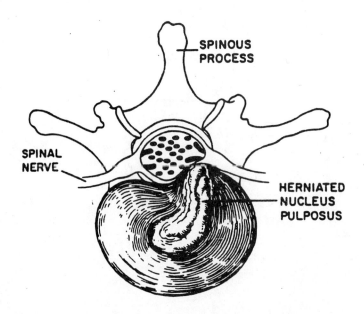

SPINOUS
PROCESS

SPINAL
NERVE

HERNIATED
NUCLEUS
PULPOSUS

Fig. 6-4. When material from a herniated disc compresses a nerve root, pain may result.

including proper bending, lifting and, later, back exercises. Adherence to this type of program will help cut down on the wear and tear on the discs. Normally most workers with disc degeneration will return to pain-free back functioning within two months of onset of symptoms.

Aerobic exercises and stretching can help the discs self-lubricate and stay healthy from the increased supply of blood to surrounding areas.

[2] The Spinal Cord

The spinal column houses the thick bundle of nerve fibers known as the spinal cord. These fibers transmit all the neurologic information required between the brain and the rest of the body for motion to occur and for sensory impulses to be felt. The spinal cord itself does not continue all the way to the base of the spinal column. At about the level of the first and second lumbar vertebrae, the cord divides into numerous individual nerves serving the lower part of the body.

[3]   The Ligaments

The spine is stabilized and supported by ligaments, muscles and tendons. Two tough bands of tissue (the infraspinous and supraspinous ligaments) run the entire length of the spine. These strong bands of tissue bind bones and other body parts together.

One potentially problematic ligament is the posterior longitudinal ligament, which runs down the length of the column behind the vertebral bodies. The fact that it is narrower at the level of the disc increases the danger that damage to this ligament may cause the disc to protrude back into the spinal canal, causing nerve irritation and subsequent pain.

Another potentially problematic ligament is the ligamentum flavum (yellow ligament), a large bunch of highly specialized fibers running along the back of the spine at the base of the spinous processes and connecting the bony back parts of the vertebrae (laminae). *(See Figure 6-5.)* The yellow ligament is the most elastic structure in the human body, but age unfortunately affects the elasticity. Ultimately the damaged ligament can bulge into the spinal canal. The result is a painful narrowing known as spinal stenosis.[8]

[4]   The Musculature

There are two primary muscle groups involved in low back pain: the extensors and the flexors. *(See Figure 6-6.)* The extensors lie in the middle of the back and enable humans to straighten and lift heavy objects. The flexors are in front and include all the abdominal muscles. The flexors enable us to bend forward and are crucial during lifting. The stomach muscles regulate the degree of arch or swayback (lordosis) in the lower spine. When the abdominal muscles are in poor shape, the abdominal contents can pull the trunk forward and out of proper anatomic alignment.

The abdominal muscles are composed of two to three layers of flat muscles covering the front and sides of the abdomen. The iliopsoas muscle runs along the front of the spine from the lumbar area to just below the hip joint. The erector spinae muscle runs down the back along both sides of the spine.

These muscles are sheathed in a fibrous tissue known as fascia. Some physicians have concentrated on the fascia as the actual source

---

[8] *See also* 6.07[6] *infra.*

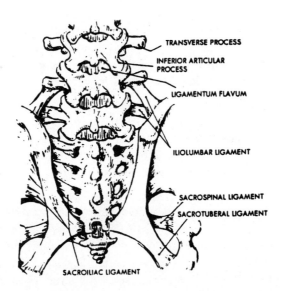

Fig. 6-5. The ligaments of the lower spine and pelvis. The ligamentum flavum runs along the back of the spine at the base of the spinous processes and connects the bony back parts of the vertebrae.

of low back pain. Surgeons in Japan have surgically removed portions of fascia in attempts to alleviate low back pain. Other physicians believe fibrositis and fibromyalgia are two related conditions that may be at the root of this type of lumbar distress.

Myofascial pain syndrome (MFPS) is one of the most frequent causes of soft tissue pain affecting the lumbar region of the spine. In this condition, pain increases after periods of immobility and becomes especially pronounced after prolonged sitting or upon first arising in the morning—a phenomenon known as gelation. MFPS can follow injury or occur without discernible cause. It is characterized by tender, painful areas within muscles.

[5]   The Facet Joints

On the other side of the spinous processes are the facet joints, which serve as hinges between the vertebra above and the one below. The function of each facet joint is to guide, direct and limit the movement of the spine.

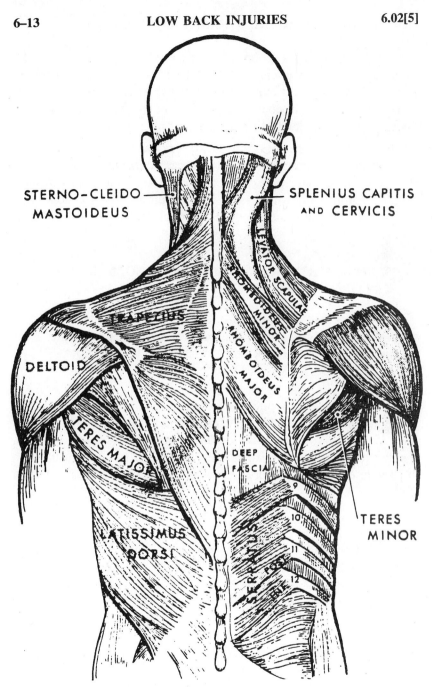

Fig. 6-6. Some of the muscles associated with the spine.

Each facet joint is surrounded by a capsule of connective tissue. This capsule secretes a lubricating substance called synovial fluid, the purpose of which is to reduce the friction between spinal structures and to permit smooth, coordinated movement. A series of ligaments keeps all the facet joints firmly in place.

The facet joints are not designed to carry excessive weight. Therefore, lifting or straining with an arched back puts enormous stress on the facets, which can in turn fracture or inflame the joint capsules. This condition is known as facet joint syndrome. Even excess body weight can seriously undermine the normal functioning of the facet joints.

6.03   RISK FACTORS FOR THE DEVELOPMENT OF LOW BACK PAIN

Risk factors for the development of low back pain include smoking, lifting heavy weights, vibration and, for women, pregnancy. Poor posture is also a risk factor.

[1]   Smoking

Nicotine appears to interfere with blood flow to the vertebral structures, including the discs. Therefore, smoking has been implicated as a contributing factor in the development of low back pain. Also, smokers often cough and suffer with bronchitis, a condition that can be severe enough to rupture intervertebral discs (Battié and Bigos, 1991).

Several possible explanations exist for the association between smoking and low back pain, including microfractures from decreased bone mineral content and osteoporosis (a condition involving thinning and weakening of the bones),[9] increased chest symptoms (coughing and intradiscal pressure) and changes in vertebral body blood flow affecting adequate discal metabolism.

[2]   Lifting

Lifting places significant mechanical stress on the anatomic structures of the lumbar spine, including the supportive muscles and ligaments. The force that must be counterbalanced varies, depending on the weight of the load, the degree of back flexion during the lift

---

[9] *See also* 6.07[1][a] *infra.*

and the distance between the load and the lifter's body. When a worker lifts with his or her back in a vertical stance, some of the load may be shifted to the legs, but only if that load is not too bulky (Waters, et al., 1993).

Any worker who does excessive manual lifting is more likely to suffer a spinal injury than his or her more sedentary co-workers, particularly when lifting has to be performed in a bent or twisted posture to accomplish the task. In addition, the more repetitive a task, the more chances there are for accidents to occur affecting the back. Back schools, when they are available, can instruct workers on safe lifting practices, but patient compliance is a big factor in the success or failure of this educational process. [10]

Sanitation workers represent a segment of the work force at very high risk of experiencing on-the-job back injury. The constant bending, lifting and then twisting with a load held away from the body is a most provocative set of motions for stressing the spine. Consequently it is estimated that 1 out of every 10 garbage collectors has suffered a work-related back injury. Fortunately, these workers also have very strong back muscles from the constant exercise associated with this work (Hochschuler, 1991).

[3] Vibration

Vibration, also called cyclic loading, is a well-known factor affecting fatigue and failure of low back structures. Workers who must drive long distances in the course of their work are subject to repetitive microtrauma to the spine (McLain and Weinstein, 1994). Over time, this condition becomes aggravated and may become a cumulative trauma disorder. To measure this type of cumulative trauma, an accelerometer has been developed for placement between the driver's buttocks and the vehicle's seat.

Since the closer the worker is to the source of the vibration, the more whole-body vibration he or she is exposed to, separation from the source and reduction of exposure levels are necessary. This can be accomplished through the use of vibration isolation and suspension systems imposed between the employee and the source of the vibration.

Truck driving, taxicab driving, bus driving and train conducting represent just a few of the occupations at particular risk for developing

---

[10] *See also* 6.15[2] *infra.*

this type of low back pain. Truck drivers are especially prone to intervertebral disc herniation. The constant vibration of the vehicle on rough roads over long periods of time, coupled with heavy lifting and unloading at the destination, makes truck drivers prime candidates for back trouble. These changes can include the development of spondylosis, spondylolisthesis, intraspongious disc herniation (Schmorl's nodes),[11] facet joint arthrosis, reduced disc height and retrolisthesis (posterior displacement of a vertebra in relation to the one below). Radiographic studies of these patients often reveal evidence of microtrauma to the spine (Andersson, 1991).

[4]   Pregnancy

With the pregnant worker's increase in girth comes a shift in her center of gravity forward. This action places considerable strain on the lumbar region of the spine. Also, the hormone relaxin is released during pregnancy. The purpose of this hormone is to loosen the pelvic ligaments for the upcoming birth process. Unfortunately, relaxin also interferes with the biomechanics of the sacroiliac and other joints. The accompanying decrease in abdominal muscle control also stresses the back, laying the groundwork for temporary or even chronic impairment.

To prevent low back pain in a pregnant employee, a regular regimen of adequate rest and exercise is recommended, including walking, swimming and biking. These aerobic exercises help maintain healthy muscle tone and good posture. A corset can also be worn for additional support to the weakened abdominal muscles.

A pregnant employee complaining of lumbar distress is thoroughly assessed, if only to rule out the presence of an actual disease process. To protect the developing fetus, x-rays are not permitted during the first trimester of pregnancy. The physician may recommend massage and the application of heat to alleviate some of the symptoms.

Female workers who are large-breasted are sometimes at an increased risk for developing low back pain. The additional weight tends to shift the center of gravity forward. This change in posture can result in lordosis (swayback) and may eventually compromise the worker's muscle control and balance. Some women also suffer from neck strain, headache and tingling in the fingers, and they may opt for breast reduction surgery.

---

[11] *See also* 6.08[1] *infra.*

6.04 CLASSIFICATION SYSTEM FOR BACK INJURIES

Although a variety of classification systems have been proposed to categorize low back pain over the years, one of the most comprehensive is that developed by the Quebec Task Force on Spinal Disorders. In this Canadian system, category 1 represents the majority of low back pain sufferers. In this group, back pain typically worsens as a result of mechanical activity and abates with rest. Low back sprain or strain is the usual diagnosis.

Category 2 represents those patients with moderate pain radiating to the proximal part of the leg (closer to the trunk). This symptom can indicate a problem in any number of low back structures, including muscles, bones, ligaments or the facet joints.

Category 3 represents patients with significant pain radiating distally (farther from the trunk) to one or both legs.

Category 4 represents patients with neurologic deficits, including loss or reduction of motor skills, reflexes or sensation. These symptoms are often consistent with the presence of lumbar disc herniation.

Category 5 represents patients with obvious spinal fractures. These fractures can cause severe compression of nerve roots or the cauda equina, potentially compromising the integrity of the spinal cord.

Category 6 represents patients with questionable diagnoses requiring imaging studies or electrodiagnostic tests for confirmation.

Category 7 refers to the most common cause of polyradiculopathy (abnormality of the sensory or motor nerve roots) and claudication (cramplike pain in the calves caused by poor circulation of the blood to the leg muscles)—spinal stenosis.[12]

Categories 8 and 9 represent patients who have previously undergone one or more surgeries without obtaining relief of their low back pain. This unfortunate condition is called failed back syndrome.[13] The separation of the postoperative period into one to six months is a significant distinction in this system. Normally, following simple disc surgery, healing occurs within six months, and the majority of patients have returned to their jobs within that time frame.

Category 10 refers to patients whose back pain has become chronic and for whom no anatomic cause has been diagnosed. At this juncture,

---

[12] *See also* 6.07[6] *infra.*

[13] *See also* 6.08[4] *infra.*

the physician may recommend counseling for this group of patients to address the psychological and psychosocial aspects of the problem (Andersson, 1995).

6.05 EPIDEMIOLOGY OF LOW BACK INJURIES

Low back injuries may be a result of a variety of causes, including infections, fractures and traumatic disc herniation.

[1] Infections

Infections of the lumbar spine are uncommon causes of low back pain. However, they must be considered during the diagnostic process, because the ultimate successful outcome depends on prompt recognition and treatment of the problem.

The clinical signs of spinal infection depend on the nature of the infecting organism. Many different microorganisms have been known to cause spinal infection. Systemic infections that can spread to the spine include tuberculosis, syphilis and fungal infections, especially blastomycosis (endemic to the southeastern and south central regions of the United States).

Bacterial infections can cause acute, toxic symptoms such as fever, pain and persistent weight loss. Fungal or tubercular infections may develop slowly, and they may be accompanied by little or no pain.

Most patients have pain in the involved region of the spine, with decreased mobility and muscular spasm. The normal laboratory tests tend to be nonspecific. Radiography may be helpful to demonstrate changes in the spine, but these changes commonly lag behind the infectious process.

The definitive diagnosis of spinal infection requires aspiration (removal through a hollow needle) or biopsy (removal of tissue, which is then examined under a microscope) of the infected area, with histologic (pertaining to cell structure) and microbiologic identification of the organism.

[2] Fractures

Fractures of the spine sometimes occur in the occupational setting, particularly in the construction industry, where falls from a great height are a constant hazard.

There are several types of spinal fractures. The most common, known as a compression fracture, results from a tremendous force acting on the spinal column to compress the vertebrae. This type of fracture usually results from a fall in a seated position, but it can also occur in the standing position. Compression is generally more severe in the anterior (front) portion of the vertebra, since this is the weakest portion of the structure.

If sufficient force is exerted on the vertebra, it may actually burst under the pressure. This is known as a bursting fracture and can represent a true medical emergency. During the burst, bone fragments may be dispersed into the spinal cord or cauda equina, resulting in neurologic injury. Occasionally this nerve damage can be extensive enough to result in total paralysis.

A third type of spinal injury, known as a fracture-dislocation, represents the complete disruption of the intervertebral and facet joints and their supportive ligaments. This injury usually results from a twisting mechanism and creates shearing. Damage to the spinal cord and cauda equina are common sequelae to this type of injury.

Given sufficient force, a direct blow can sometimes result in fracture of the vertebral arch process. This injury, which is fairly common in the mining industry, often results in intra-abdominal disruption as well.

Unless there is neurologic damage, most spinal fractures can be treated conservatively, and the injured worker can usually return to his or her former job at the same level of activity.

[3] Disc Herniation

Over the last decade, one of the most significant findings in spinal medicine has been the discovery that asymptomatic disc abnormalities are common in the adult spine. Recent studies indicate that up to a third of middle-aged individuals have a symptomless disc herniation in the lumbar spine (Jensen, et al., 1994). Some researchers have therefore suggested that the mere presence of a herniated disc is no longer necessarily an indication for treatment or concern.

In addition, similarly sized disc herniations may cause different symptoms, depending on the size of the spinal canal. For one individual, a large, bulging disc herniation may cause no pain or dysfunction, whereas for someone else, a small disc protrusion may result in significant neurologic symptoms, including motor weakness, reflex abnormalities and sensory deficits.

Disc herniations are classified into three groups:

- A *protruded* disc implies bulging with an intact anulus.

- An *extruded* disc implies that the anulus is disrupted while the posterior longitudinal segment remains intact.

- A *sequestered disc fragment* migrates through the posterior longitudinal ligament away from the disc space.

Herniation of a lumbar disc is usually considered to be a result of a degenerative process. The pathophysiology is related to biomechanical factors, including biochemical changes and abnormal mechanical stresses.

Over time, the discs suffer tears and defects in the anulus portion of the structure. These tears are often referred to as rim tears. As a disc ages, there may be a coalescence of these peripheral tears and delamination of the annular fibers. This slow attrition leads to the formation of fragments, reduction of tensile strength and eventual herniation of the disc material.

Usually damage to an intervertebral disc is a long, slow process with the final "traumatic" event merely the last in a long series of mechanical insults to the spine, although when there is deformation in the discs, it may be possible to sustain an acute injury. Generally, however, traumatic herniation of a healthy disc is a rare clinical event.

Disc herniation is sometimes seen in the younger work population, leading some researchers to suspect that there is a genetic component to this common illness. Degeneration may begin years before the actual onset of clinical symptoms. There may therefore exist a genetic predisposition that renders affected workers susceptible to this type of disc disease (Varlotta, et al., 1991).

6.06 RHEUMATOLOGIC CAUSES OF LOW BACK PAIN

Rheumatologic disorders are inflammatory diseases of the bones and joints that are frequently associated with systemic symptoms as well. These diseases often cause quantifiable serum (liquid portion of blood) antibody abnormalities, such as the presence of rheumatoid factor, which occurs in patients with rheumatoid arthritis. These changes are easily detected by laboratory tests. However, the rheumatologic diseases that most frequently involve the lumbar spine are not

associated with these serum anomalies and are referred to as seronegative. Collectively known as the seronegative spondyloarthropathies,
they include ankylosing spondylitis, Reiter's syndrome, psoriatic
arthritis and enteropathic arthritis.

Many factors are involved in the etiology of these diseases, but in
the case of the spondyloarthropathies, a genetic component is also
involved: Patients have a genetic predisposition but do not develop
the disease until some environmental event, such as infection or
trauma, triggers the onset. The genetic predisposition is associated with
the presence of a white blood cell antigen, HLA-B27, which can easily
be detected in laboratory testing.

[1]   Ankylosing Spondylitis

Ankylosing spondylitis is predominantly a disease of young men
aged 6 to 40. It is a chronic ailment in which there is a gradual onset
of back pain and stiffness. Typically the symptoms are worse in the
morning after a night of relative immobilization, and they improve
with activity.

The physical examination reveals tenderness of the sacroiliac joints
(the joints that join the sacrum to the ilium of the pelvis). Spinal
motion is progressively diminished in all directions.

The diagnosis is made by plain x-rays of the spine, although
abnormalities may not be evident early in the disease. Computed
tomography (CT)[14] and bone scans[15] are more sensitive in detecting
early manifestations. Laboratory findings include the presence of
HLA-B27 in up to 90 percent of patients.

[2]   Reiter's Syndrome

Reiter's syndrome is known as a triad, that is, a set of three groups
of associated symptoms. In this case, the constellation of signs
involves arthritis of the sacroiliac joints (those connecting the sacrum
to the ilium of the pelvis), conjunctivitis (commonly known as pink-
eye) and urethritis (inflammation of the lower urinary tract, with
attendant pain upon urination). Inflammation of the sacroiliac joints
(sacroilitis) often results in low back pain, reduced range of motion
and joint tenderness. Other symptoms may include fever, weight loss
and involvement of the spine and feet.

---

14 *See also* 6.10[3] *infra.*

15 *See also* 6.10[6] *infra.*

Reiter's syndrome often follows an infection of the urinary or intestinal tract. Microorganisms that can trigger the development of this syndrome include *Salmonella, Shigella, Campylobacter* and *Yersinia.*

[3]   Enteropathic Arthritis

Arthritis of the spine (spondylitis) may occur in patients with inflammatory bowel disease, such as ulcerative colitis (an inflammatory disease of the colon) or Crohn's disease (an ulcerative disease that may affect any part of the gastrointestinal tract). The signs, symptoms and x-ray findings of spinal involvement are similar to those in ankylosing spondylitis. There may be associated peripheral joint tenderness and other symptoms, such as skin lesions. The arthritis may commence before or after the onset of bowel symptoms.

[4]   Psoriatic Arthritis

Patients with psoriasis may develop a disabling arthritis that affects several joints, including the spine, sacroiliac joints and hands. There is no correlation between the severity of skin disease and the severity of the arthritis.

[5]   Other Rheumatologic Conditions

Two additional rheumatologic conditions are occasionally associated with low back pain. The first is *polymyalgia rheumatica,* a systemic inflammatory disease seen most often in elderly women. There may be pain in the back and other regions. Systemic symptoms are common, including fever, weight loss and general malaise.

Fibrositis, a condition of unknown origin that may be associated with back pain, is a syndrome involving pain in multiple regions, fatigue and stiffness. It is frequently associated with sleep disturbances and psychological abnormalities. Usually there is no objective evidence of disease on physical examination, although tenderness may be found at specific "trigger points"—zones that, when they are touched, initiate an attack of pain elsewhere. Occasionally tender nodules are found. X-rays and laboratory tests are normal. The existence of this syndrome as a distinct entity is as yet unclear.

Other arthritic diseases that are rarely associated with back pain include familial Mediterranean fever (an episodic disease of fever, peritonitis and arthritis), Behçet's syndrome (a chronic relapsing syndrome of oral and genital ulcers), vasculitis (inflammation of the blood vessels), meningoencephalitis (inflammation of the brain and its coverings, the meninges) and Whipple's disease (a rare inflammatory illness involving arthritis, intestinal malabsorption and diarrhea that probably has an infectious etiology).

Rheumatoid arthritis may affect the lumbar spine, although the disease is usually far advanced and widespread by the time lumbar involvement becomes evident.

6.07 MEDICAL CAUSES OF LOW BACK PAIN

Medical diseases are uncommon causes of low back pain. They include a variety of metabolic disorders, tumors and infections. In addition, pain from disease of the internal organs may be referred (felt in a location other than the site of origin) to the back.

[1] Metabolic Bone Disease

Several metabolic disorders, including osteoporosis, osteomalacia, parathyroid disease and acromegaly (overproduction of growth hormone), Paget's disease and others, may produce diffuse bone disease with low back pain. Of these, osteoporosis is the most common.

[a] Osteoporosis

Osteoporosis is characterized by bone loss in which there is equal loss of mineral (calcium) and bone matrix (the nonmineral elements). This is distinct from osteomalacia, in which more mineral than matrix is lost.

There are many causes of osteoporosis. It occurs normally in postmenopausal women but also is a consequence of a variety of diseases and is a side effect of certain medications, most notably corticosteroids. Smoking and excessive alcohol intake increase the risk.

Osteoporosis weakens the bone, predisposing the individual to fractures that include vertebral compression fracture, a major source of low back pain. In some cases, an obvious compression fracture cannot be found on x-ray, and very small microfractures are assumed to have occurred. The deformity that results from fractures places an excessive load on the soft tissues, which may exacerbate the back pain. The diagnosis is usually confirmed by x-ray. Laboratory test results are usually normal.

[b] Osteomalacia

Osteomalacia is a condition characterized by some bone loss, but there is more mineral loss. When this process occurs in childhood, rickets is the result; in adults, it is called osteomalacia. The causes include vitamin D deficiency (due to nutritional deficiency, kidney or bowel disease, or medications such as anticonvulsant drugs), phosphate deficiency, other medications and other etiologies.

Patients with osteomalacia experience bone tenderness and low back pain that is aggravated by physical activity. These patients sometimes develop deformities of the back. Laboratory abnormalities are common and variable, depending on the cause. The definitive diagnosis is made by bone biopsy.

[c] Paget's Disease

Paget's disease is usually classified as a metabolic disorder, but its origin is unknown. It is a disease in which bone cells dissolve at an increased rate, and the new bone that is laid down to replace it is abnormal and weak.

Paget's disease is very common in individuals over the age of 40, but it is usually asymptomatic. When symptoms appear, low back pain is common. The pain may be due to facet joint arthritis, vertebral fracture or nerve compression by bone overgrowth. The skull, pelvis and long bones of the legs are other common sites of involvement.

The physical examination may be yield no abnormal results, particularly early in the disease. With advanced disease, there may be bowing of the legs, spinal kyphosis (flexion deformity) and neurologic deficits from nerve compression.

Paget's disease is often diagnosed from an elevated level of serum alkaline phosphatase, an enzyme test that is routinely included in most blood test batteries. X-rays show a variety of abnormalities. Bone scans will demonstrate areas of active disease.

[2] Tumors

Tumors that produce low back pain may be located in the bone, the nerve tissue (as in spinal cord tumors) or the internal organs (such as the pancreas). Bone tumors may be primary (originating in the bone itself) or secondary (originating outside the bone; for example, breast cancer frequently metastasizes, spreading to the bone). Secondary tumors (also called skeletal metastases) are very much more common. These tumors are found with much more frequency in patients over the age of 50 years.

The list of primary tumors capable of producing back pain is extensive, but most are rare. Types of bone tumors include osteoblastoma, osteosarcoma, osteochondroma, giant cell tumor, chordomas and chondrosarcomas. Tumors of the spinal cord and its coverings may also produce back pain; these include meningiomas, neurofibromas and ependymomas. Lastly, multiple myeloma (a cancer of the bone marrow) and lymphoma (a malignancy of lymph node tissue) may result in back pain.

Tumors of the spine usually cause back pain, which is often attributed by the patient to a traumatic event such as a fall. The classic test for the existence of a spinal tumor is pain that increases when lying down. The pain also progresses and does not respond to the usual conservative measures used to treat mechanical back pain. It may be associated with tenderness over the affected area.

A bone tumor is usually first detected on x-ray. Many tumors are associated with characteristic changes. Magnetic resonance imaging (MRI) is also very helpful in identifying the type and location of a tumor and is considered the procedure of choice.[16] However, definitive diagnosis requires a biopsy.

[a]   Vertebral Hemangioma

Vertebral hemangioma, a lesion consisting of abnormal blood vessels, is a common primary tumor of bone affecting the spine. Although it is usually asymptomatic, it may be associated with low back pain. Neurologic involvement is rare.

Vertebral hemangiomas have a characteristic picture on x-ray and computed tomography (CT) scan that is diagnostic in most cases. This lesion is benign and seldom requires treatment.

[b]   Osteoid Osteoma

Osteoid osteoma is a benign tumor usually seen in young adults. When it occurs in the spine, it may produce back pain that is usually progressive. The lesion has a characteristic appearance on x-ray, although some cases may require CT scanning to adequately visualize the lesion. Definitive diagnosis requires a biopsy.

---

[16] *See also* 6.10[4] *infra.*

[c]   Multiple Myeloma

Multiple myeloma is a malignant tumor of the plasma cells (white blood cells responsible for the production of antibodies). These cells reside in the bone marrow, and thus the tumor can involve the bone. Low back pain may arise from bony involvement and may extend into the spinal canal, compressing the nerve tissue and producing neurologic symptoms. There are a variety of laboratory abnormalities, such as anemia, thrombocytopenia (low platelet count), high levels of abnormal immunoglobulins (antibodies) and hypercalcemia (high serum level of calcium). X-rays may reveal the bony lesion, except in early cases, in which CT scanning is probably more helpful. The diagnosis is confirmed by biopsy.

[d]   Secondary Tumors

The spine is a very common site for metastases of most common cancers, including breast, lung, colon, prostate and kidney. It is not uncommon for a cancer of one of these organs to present initially with symptoms referable to the spinal metastases.

The pain is usually progressive and may worsen at night. Neurologic symptoms may become apparent. There may be tenderness and limited range of motion on examination.

A variety of radiologic abnormalities may be seen, depending on the type of tumor and extent of spread. Lesions that may not be visible on x-ray may be detected by CT or bone scan. MRI is recommended for patients in whom metastatic cancer is suspected.

Laboratory abnormalities, such as anemia, increased levels of the enzyme alkaline phosphatase and hypercalcemia, are usually present.

[3]   Infections

Infections that can cause low back pain include vertebral osteomyelitis, intervertebral disc space infection, tuberculosis and brucellosis.

[a]   Vertebral Osteomyelitis

Vertebral osteomyelitis (inflammation of the vertebral bone and adjacent marrow) is a relatively uncommon infection that generally spreads from a primary infection in the urinary tract or elsewhere to the spine. It occurs with increased frequency among intravenous drug abusers and patients with diminished immunity, such as those with diabetes, sickle cell anemia and other chronic diseases. It may also follow spinal surgery. The disc may also be infected, and an abscess may develop.

The most common causative organisms are *Staphylococcus aureus,* a skin organism, and Gram-negative (organisms that do not take up Gram stain) intestinal bacteria. The latter probably set up infection in the urinary tract, which then spreads to the vertebrae. Two other causes of bacterial vertebral osteomyelitis are tuberculosis and brucellosis.

The predominant symptom is back pain, which frequently develops gradually over a period of two to three months before the diagnosis is made. Other symptoms usually associated with infection, such as fever, may be absent. Many patients report a history of recent infection or invasive medical procedures, such as cystoscopy (exploration of the bladder).

The diagnosis may be first suspected on laboratory testing, with an elevated erythrocyte sedimentation rate. This test, a nonspecific indicator of active inflammation in the body, is normally negative in patients with back pain from other causes. There may also be abnormalities in the white blood cell count. Routine spine x-rays[17] will show abnormalities in longstanding cases, although bone scans are more helpful in the early phases of the disease. The definitive diagnostic test is a blood culture or bone biopsy culture (growth of organisms from blood or bone specimens).

A spinal epidural abscess (infection in the epidural space, between the dura mater of the spinal cord and the membrane lining the canal of the vertebral column) may occur as a complication of vertebral infection. It is associated with back pain and neurologic deficits from compression of the local nerve tissue. This is the most serious of the spinal infections, because it can rapidly lead to paralysis and even death.

[b]   Intervertebral Disc Space Infection

Infection of the intervertebral disc space is uncommon. It may occur as a complication of disc surgery, or it may spread from an infection in the vertebrae or elsewhere in the body. There is low back pain, with tenderness and limited motion. Abnormalities in the sedimentation rate and white blood cell count are the major clues to the etiology

---

[17] *See also* 6.10[2] *infra.*

of the infection. Bone scans may also be useful in making the definitive diagnosis.

[c] Tuberculosis

Although the lung is the most common site of active infection, tuberculosis can infect many other organs. These infections are referred to collectively as extrapulmonary tuberculosis. The incidence of extrapulmonary tuberculosis has been rising in recent years, partly because individuals with human immunodeficiency viral (HIV) infections are prone to developing this form of the disease and may develop it long before full-blown AIDS (acquired immunodeficiency syndrome) appears.

The spine is the most common site of skeletal tuberculosis, where it may be referred to as Pott's disease, or tuberculous spondylitis. The disease usually originates in one vertebra, but it may spread to the adjacent structures, including the discs, soft tissues and spinal canal. In severe cases, spinal abscess or bony deformity may result.

The symptoms of vertebral tuberculosis are pain, which may radiate to the buttocks and thigh, low-grade fever and variable degrees of weight loss. The involved vertebrae are tender to palpation.

Spinal tuberculosis has a characteristic x-ray picture: Two adjacent vertebrae are wedged together, with loss of the disc space between them. The diagnosis is supported by positive skin testing for tuberculosis. Definitive diagnosis requires biopsy.

[d] Brucellosis

Brucellosis is a systemic bacterial infection that can be acquired occupationally by farmers, veterinarians, meat packers, slaughterhouse workers and livestock handlers who work with cattle. It may be acute or chronic and can affect virtually any organ system in the body. Bone involvement is relatively common, with disc space infection and vertebral osteomyelitis the most frequent forms.

Bones scans and spine x-rays demonstrate abnormalities. Blood tests may be positive for brucella agglutination titers (levels), but definitive diagnosis requires a biopsy.

[4] Spinal Instability

Spinal instability is usually triggered by minor mechanical overloading and is characterized by recurrent episodes of low back pain, sciatica or a combination of the two. Radiographic evidence of a shift in the alignment of the vertebrae confirms the diagnosis. If the vertebrae are fractured or impinged upon by tumor, the spinal instability can be diagnosed during the physical examination.

Infections can also cause such obvious deformity. In these patients, the flexion-extension tests can actually be harmful to nerve structures serving that portion of the spine.

[5] Scoliosis

Scoliosis is a condition in which the spine is curved sideways. From the side, the spine has a natural, slight S-shaped curvature. However, the spine should appear straight when it is viewed from the front or behind.

Except for infantile scoliosis, which is a very rare condition, scoliosis doesn't usually develop until the patient is approximately ten years old, the age that normally represents a significant growth spurt for the preadolescent. It may be that some people inherit a genetic predisposition for asymmetric growth and the resulting scoliosis.

This abnormal spinal development can first manifest itself as a walking problem, a posture problem or an actual hump in the person's back. Even a mild curve can sometimes be the cause of significant back pain, especially if the patient's occupation involves a lot of lifting, twisting, walking of stairs, etc.

Relatively few scoliosis patients require surgical intervention for treatment. Most back pain from mild scoliosis can be relieved with back-strengthening exercises.

[6] Spinal Stenosis

Spinal stenosis refers to a shrinking or narrowing of the spinal canal. This reduction in the size of the canal can be either congenital (present from birth) or developmental.

The causes of spinal stenosis include arthritis, injury, a failed surgery or even a change in posture. As the spinal canal narrows, there is less room for the spinal cord and related nerves to move without impingement. As a result, these structures can become irritated or inflamed, a situation that can lead to swelling and exacerbation of the problem. Symptoms known as neurologic claudication (pain and dysfunction of a limb) may be present; these are neurologic symptoms that are aggravated by exertion and relieved by sitting down. There may be neurologic deficits and, because multiple levels are often involved, the picture may be confusing. The straight leg raising test[18] is usually negative.

The diagnosis may be made with plain x-rays and confirmed by myelography with or without CT scanning. Spinal stenosis is difficult to treat with conservative methods, although sometimes surgery becomes the necessary course of treatment for increasing the size of the spinal canal. This is usually accomplished by removing the elements compressing the neural structures.

There are several types of stenotic lesions. Osteophytes (bone spurs) are the most common, followed by degenerative spondylolisthesis (forward slipping of a vertebra over the vertebra beneath) and diffuse idiopathic spinal hyperostosis (DISH), a proliferation of bone growth.

[a] Spondylolisthesis

Spondylolisthesis is a condition in which one vertebra slips forward on another (also called subluxation or displacement), often trapping the spinal nerve. There are five types of spondylolisthesis. The most common form is isthmic spondylolisthesis, which is caused by a defect in the neural arch at the pars interarticularis (one of the processes of the vertebral arch). *(See Figure 6-7.)* It is more common in males.

The defect may be congenital or acquired and is referred to as spondylolysis. This is more common in adolescent football players and female gymnasts, and it is thought to begin with a stress fracture. When the defect is severe, it slightly destabilizes the articulation between two vertebrae and leads to vertebral slipping or spondylolisthesis. Spondylolysis is seen in approximately 5 percent of the population over the age of 17; spondylolisthesis is also not uncommon in the asymptomatic population (Rothman, et al., 1989).

Spondylolysis appears to develop in adolescence, but the first symptoms may not occur until adulthood, when the onset is frequently attributed to a sudden twisting or lifting motion. Back pain aggravated by activity is the most common symptom. On physical examination, there is usually a palpable step at the site of the abnormality.

The diagnosis is usually evident on plain x-ray; bone scans may be used to further clarify when the diagnosis is unsure. Treatment is

---

18 *See also* 6.08[1] *infra.*

Fig. 6-7. In spondylolisthesis, a defect in the pars interarticularis causes anterior displacement of a vertebral body (arrow).

conservative and the same as for back pain in general. Patients cannot be expected to return to heavy work (Rothman, 1989).

Degenerative spondylolisthesis is quite common. In this disease, the facet joints degenerate to the point that they cannot maintain the vertebral position, and spondylolisthesis occurs. The usual site is the L4-L5 level. Women are more commonly affected, usually between the ages of 40 and 60.

[b] Idiopathic Vertebral Sclerosis

Idiopathic vertebral sclerosis is a disease of unknown etiology in which the disc space becomes narrowed and the anterior portion of the vertebral body develops sclerosis (hardening). The vertebra most commonly affected is L4. This disease occurs in women much more frequently than in men. The predominant symptom is severe back pain.

[c] Diffuse Idiopathic Skeletal Sclerosis (DISH)

This disease is characterized by diffuse new bone formation around the spine. Osteophytes (bony projections or spurs) extend to bridge multiple vertebrae. It is usually a benign, asymptomatic or minimally symptomatic condition that may be associated with metabolic disorders such as gout and diabetes.

The symptoms usually begin in individuals around the age of 40, with stiffness and pain that is usually mild. Difficulty swallowing may occur, thought to be related to osteophytes on the cervical (neck) vertebrae, which compress the esophagus.

The diagnosis is usually evident on x-ray.

[7] Other Medical Causes

Hematologic diseases such as sickle cell anemia and myelofibrosis may be associated with back pain. Pain may be referred to the back from several internal organs. Diseases commonly associated with back pain include pancreatic diseases (pancreatitis or cancer of the pancreas), abdominal aortic aneurysm (a dilatation and weakening of the wall of the abdominal section of the aorta) and diseases of the genitourinary tract (kidney, ureter, bladder and, in women, the uterus). Some gastrointestinal tract diseases may occasionally be associated with back pain, such as duodenal ulcers, gallbladder disease and diverticulitis.

Typically referred pain is not affected by activity. Other distinguishing characteristics depend on the nature of the underlying disease. When the disease is of gastrointestinal origin, the pain may be related to meals, or there may be associated nausea, vomiting or bowel symptoms. Kidney pain may be associated with urinary symptoms. In most cases of referred pain, the history and physical examination point to a visceral (pertaining to the abdominal organs) rather than a musculoskeletal origin.

6.08   LOW BACK PAIN SYNDROMES

Low back pain syndromes include sciatica, cauda equina syndrome and chronic low back pain.

[1]   Sciatica

Sciatica is a pain that radiates down to the buttocks and to the posterior part of the leg to below the knee. It is caused by compression of the nerve root, herniation of a disc or encroachment upon the spinal canal by a tumor or an infectious process. *(See Figure 6-8.)* However, herniated discs are the major cause. A definitive diagnosis can be made using radiologic techniques.

In 1926, Schmorl reported the existence of nodules originating from the disc tissue that protrude into other structures as a result of disc herniation. Schmorl's node is a nodule seen on spinal x-rays that results from intervertebral disc herniation. The ruptured nucleus pulposus protrudes into other structures, including adjacent vertebrae, the abdominal cavity or the spinal canal. In 1934, Mixter and Barr discovered a correlation between these intraspinal nodules and sciatica (Olmarker and Rydevik, 1991).

Another cause of sciatica is irritation due to compression or pressure on the sciatic nerve as it courses from the spine to the leg, for example, by a bulky wallet in the back pocket. This condition is known as hip-pocket sciatica. Neurologic deficits may be present at the physical examination, including numbness and sometimes weakness in the region of the affected nerve.

The main symptoms of sciatica include pain in the region of a specific nerve root and reproduction of symptoms during stretching of the nerve root. One of the tests used to detect sciatica is known as the straight leg raising (SLR) test. The test is usually performed

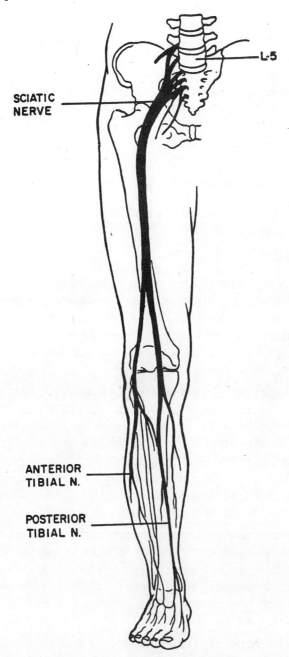

Fig. 6-8. The sciatic nerve and its divisions. In sciatica, impingement of an intervertebral disc or vertebra on the sciatic nerve at the L5 level causes pain and dysfunction along the nerve's distribution.

in the supine position (patient lying on the back). The physician raises the leg and straightens it, flexing the hip simultaneously. *(See Figure 6-9.)*

If this causes pain or muscle spasm in the back muscles of the thigh, the sign is considered positive, indicating irritation of the sciatic nerve or the roots of the lumbar nerves. If the pain experienced by the patient is in fact sciatica, then the positive test suggests a diagnosis of nerve root compression. If the patient feels the pain in the leg opposite from the one being lifted, then nerve root compression is even more definite.

The straight leg raising test is also performed with the patient seated. If true sciatica exists, then the symptoms produced in the seated position will be just as severe as those produced during the supine version of the test. If the pain created during the seated version varies from that produced during the supine version, the diagnosis of nerve root compression is abandoned.

Lasègue's sign is present in several abnormal conditions, including sciatica (pressure on the sciatic nerve due to a herniated disc between vertebrae) and meningitis (inflammation of the tissue covering the brain and spinal cord). In sciatica, flexion of the hip causes pain in

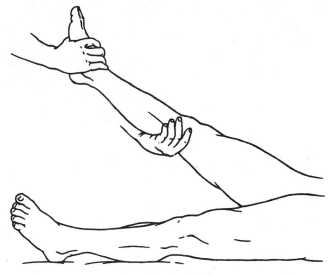

Fig. 6-9. The straight leg raising test is performed by lifting the patient's fully extended leg off the table so as to flex the hip. If the patient has a herniated disc, raising the leg is painful and motion is limited.

the muscles in the back of the thigh when the knee is extended and does not cause pain when the knee is flexed. This combination of symptoms is known as Lasègue's sign. This sign can help distinguish the disorder from diseases of the hip joint.

Several tests exist the results of which indicate a psychological rather than an anatomic cause for low back pain. In one, the physician presses on the patient's head (axial loading). This is a maneuver that does not normally produce low back pain by any known physiologic mechanism. A positive response to this manipulation may therefore have psychological relevance. In addition, inconsistent responses to tests that should produce pain are likewise indicative of a psychological component complicating the medical picture. Sensory deficits that do not correspond to any known nerve root abnormality are also noted.

Recovery from sciatica is slower than with low back pain only. However, at least half of sciatica patients recover within one month of symptom onset. Although the recurrence rate is high with sciatica, most patients recover from the acute symptoms with minimal residual impairment. Surgical intervention is necessary in only 5 or 10 percent of cases (Olmarker and Rydevik, 1991).

[2] Cauda Equina Syndrome

The spinal cord ends at the top of the lumbar spine. From there down, the spinal canal is filled with a bundle of nerves known as the cauda equina. These nerves control the muscles of the legs, the bladder, bowel function and sexual function. When the cauda equina's canal is encroached upon by any other structure, such as a disc, tumor or lesion—a condition known as spinal stenosis [19] —leg and low back pain may result.

The cauda equina syndrome is a set of symptoms resulting from compression of the cauda equina, the lumbar and sacral nerve roots. Its cause may be a centrally herniating intervertebral disc, a tumor or some other lesion. The most common symptom is sciatica radiating down both legs, and loss of bladder and bowel control. Although this syndrome is rare, its presence signals the need for prompt surgical intervention.

---

19 *See also* 6.07[6] *supra.*

[3] Chronic Low Back Pain

Patients who are still experiencing low back pain after a six-month rehabilitation period are generally considered to be chronic low back pain (CLBP) sufferers. Chronic low back pain has long been demonstrated to adversely affect work performance, social relationships and psychological health. Patients with chronic low back pain often manifest depression, anxiety and sometimes addiction to pain medication (Frost, et al., 1995). This dysfunction may exacerbate and perpetuate the pain, which may then increase the level of disability.

Screening devices can help physicians locate those patients who need a more detailed psychological evaluation and possible referral to a clinical therapist.

[4] Failed Back Syndrome

Failed back syndrome refers to a condition in which patients have endured multiple surgeries without resolution of their low back pain. Unfortunately, each successive operation appears to reduce the chance for a successful surgical outcome.

These deficits may be a result of many factors, including:

- inadequate rehabilitation;
- sedentary life-style;
- structural damage during surgery; or
- patient noncompliance with prescribed treatment.

Multimodal treatments are often recommended for patients with failed back syndrome, in order to reduce pain and inflammation. Medications such as aspirin or ibuprofen, physical therapy and sometimes injections of cortisone are administered in an attempt to restore normal back function and return the patient to his or her job.

6.09 CLINICAL APPROACH TO LOW BACK PAIN

For most patients with low back pain, the history and the physical examination provide the information basic to making the diagnosis.

[1] History

The patient's history should provide information relating to present symptoms, past symptoms, the presence of other significant medical conditions and the use of medications. The physician should ask about the onset of symptoms, especially if significant trauma has occurred. Pain is perhaps the most important symptom, and the physician must determine the site, the intensity and whether manipulation increases or alleviates the pain.

[2]   The Physical Examination

The physical examination is a critical element in properly diagnosing and treating low back pain. It consists of inspection, palpation, range of movement (ROM) testing, measurements and neurologic tests. The back and spine are inspected for abnormalities and deformities. The physician then observes the patient's posture, gait, and leg and back movements. Muscle strength is measured as well. The most important tests involve neurologic functioning, including sensory deficits, coordination and reflex tests.

There are several tests for evaluating nerve root irritation. The straight leg raising (SLR) test is perhaps the most well known. It is performed with the patient supine (on his or her back). The physician raises the leg, keeping the knee straight. If this reproduces the patient's pain, the examiner notes how far he or she had to raise the leg in order to elicit the pain. The test is considered positive when sciatica (posterior leg pain) occurs during the test.

[3]   Pain Assessment

A pain rating scale can be used to assess the level of intensity of the patient's perceived pain and to locate the source (Parker, et al., 1994). The pain rating scale evaluates the severity of the pain.

The pain drawing is another psychological screening device. The drawing can help distinguish between an emotional and an organic origin of the low back pain. The pain drawing consists of front and back outlines of a human form, on which the patient is required to indicate various unpleasant sensations he or she may be experiencing, including aches, pains, numbness, and pins and needles. Symbols are used to represent the type of pain, the intensity and the location (Parker, et al., 1994).

It is hypothesized that pain sufferers may produce unreal drawings with poor anatomic location and pain magnification (pain drawn outside the body or all over the body). Although a standardized method of scoring has yet to be agreed upon, the pain drawing is now being used as an indicator of psychological distress, as a method of differentiating between organic and nonorganic pain, and as a measure of physical impairment and disability.

6.10 DIAGNOSTIC TESTS

Diagnostic tests for low back pain include various laboratory analyses, x-rays, computed tomography, magnetic resonance imaging, discography, bone scans and various electrodiagnostic methods.

[1] Laboratory Tests

Low back pain can be caused by a variety of medical conditions, many of which result in abnormalities that can be quantified through laboratory testing. Inflammatory or rheumatologic diseases, such as ankylosing spondylitis (arthritis of the spine), psoriatic arthritis and Reiter's syndrome, may be accompanied by mild anemia (low blood level of iron) and a positive HLA-B27 test (human leukocyte antigen-B27). Polymyalgia rheumatica is often accompanied by an elevated erythrocyte sedimentation rate, a measure of how quickly blood settles at the bottom of a test tube after an anticoagulant is added. However, these tests are not specific for any particular disease process.

An elevated white blood cell count is often indicative of infection, and neoplastic disease (tumors) can produce higher than normal levels of calcium in the blood.

The majority of patients suffering from low back pain will not require these blood tests. The history and a thorough physical examination are usually sufficient to diagnose a medical rather than a mechanical back problem.

[2] Spinal X-rays

The simplest and most readily available diagnostic tests for back pain are the anteroposterior (front-to-back) and lateral (side view) roentgenograms (x-rays) of the involved spinal segment. These plain x-rays, which are also known as radiographs, are often used when the physician suspects the low back pain to be caused by fracture, infection, stenosis, tumor, a metabolic disorder such as osteoporosis, or rheumatologic disease such as arthritis.

Spinal x-rays can disclose age-related degeneration of the spine, but it is difficult to attribute low back pain to the aging process, since this kind of degeneration has also been observed in asymptomatic individuals (Frymoyer, 1991).

Unfortunately, standard x-rays cannot disclose the presence of disc herniation, ligamentous injury or muscular pathology. They are therefore not useful in assessing back pain caused by mechanical stresses.

[a] Myelography

Myelography is a radiologic test in which a radio-opaque medium is injected into the subarachnoid space around the spinal cord and the nerves that feed the lower spine. Then x-rays are taken of the area. This is often accomplished under fluoroscopic control to assure complete accuracy.

The contrast medium shows up on x-ray as a dense, white image. Anything that is pressing on the spinal cord or its surrounding nerves will look like an indentation in the column of dye. *(See Figure 6-10.)* The abnormality may be a bulging disc, a tumor, an infection or some other disease process.

Several agents have been used for this test, including air, oil and water-soluble varieties. Air contrast is used only in rare circumstances,

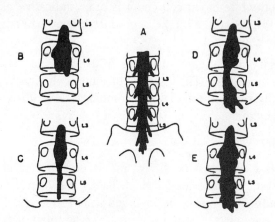

Fig. 6-10. Myelography patterns. A: Normal myelogram showing outline of spinal cord and nerves. B: Complete blockage of spinal canal at the L4-L5 level, by a space-occupying lesion such as a tumor. C: Filling defect between L4-L5. D: Large filling defect in thecal sac between L4 and L5. E: Depression of nerve root at L5-S1.

since x-ray resolution with this medium is of poor quality. However, if the myelography seems mandatory and the patient is highly allergic to contrast agents, this method can be used as an alternative. With oil contrast, the medium has to be removed following the test, as this agent cannot be absorbed by the body.

Unfortunately, allergic complications to contrast media are somewhat common and may include nausea, vomiting, confusion and seizures. Rare complications include stroke, paralysis or even death. Consequently, dosages are kept to the lowest possible levels.

Any patient found to be allergic to shellfish, iodine or a previously administered contrast medium is not an appropriate candidate for myelography. The risks involved include hypotension (low blood pressure), low back inflammation, brain tissue (meningeal) inflammation and, in rare cases, anaphylactic shock, an acute allergic reaction that is potentially fatal unless it is treated promptly.

[b] Venography

A venogram is a type of x-ray in which a contrast medium (dye) is injected into the lumbar spine, either through the spinous processes of the vertebrae or through a large vein in the thigh. The medium is then distributed to the veins in and around the spinal canal. If the physician detects an abnormal distribution of the dye, he or she may diagnose the presence of a herniated disc.

This test has several disadvantages, including substantial radiation exposure, a potential allergic reaction to the dye itself and the pain and tedium connected with the technique.

[3] Computed Tomography (CT) Scan

Helical or spiral computed tomography (CT) scan is a painless, noninvasive imaging modality capable of supplying detailed images of spinal injuries or disease. The data is derived as the patient moves through a tube that is rotating at a constant speed. The information can then be reformatted to recreate these images in two and three dimensions, enhancing the capability of detecting even the smallest spinal anomalies.

Computed tomography has several advantages over the plain x-ray (radiograph). CT is less impeded by overlying foreign matter, such as shock equipment or life support equipment. It is also extremely sensitive in defining soft tissue damage and in diagnosing subtle trauma or infection that may have been missed on the x-ray. CT is also rapid, requiring less patient compliance and repositioning than x-ray. Today specially designed CT trauma stretchers allow patient transition from the emergency room to the CT facility without physical transfer, reducing the discomfort, risk to the patient and time that elapses.

Computed tomography is becoming less expensive and is now more readily available, making it an appropriate modality for serial studies to assess responses to therapeutic measures. Major advances in the technology over the last decade have resulted in several other improvements, including thinner slice imagery and more refined image resolution. Unfortunately, CT does not reveal intraspinal tumors, and it cannot distinguish between a new disc herniation and old scar tissue.

[4]   Magnetic Resonance Imaging (MRI)

MRI is an imaging modality based on the interaction of a magnetic field, radiofrequency energy and the protons of molecules. Since hydrogen is present in all body tissues, the proton of the hydrogen atom is chosen more often than other possible options, such as carbon or magnesium. However, because the proton density of hydrogen in bone and calcified tissue is low, visualization of the spinal structures is not always accurate, and details can be missed on the scan.

The advantages of this modality include the ability to visualize intraspinal tumors, examine the entire spine and identify degenerative discs. MRI's advantage over CT scanning is that it does not require the patient to be exposed to ionizing radiation. Also, it is a much more sensitive diagnostic technique, allowing for the visualization of smaller lumbar structures and details. MRI is often used when surgery is being contemplated. MRI will not replace CT scanning, but it will probably remain an adjunctive confirmatory test.

The disadvantages of MRI include the necessity for specifically constructed facilities and expensive equipment. Also, the test requires specially trained personnel to interpret findings. Consequently MRI is currently available in only the larger urban hospital settings.

[5]   Discography

Discography is a controversial diagnostic technique that is both an objective imaging test and a subjective pain response test. A radiologist injects contrast medium into the nucleus of the disc and studies the dispersement of the medium to see if the internal architecture of the disc is intact. *(See Figure 6-11.)* This is known as determining the integrity of the disc containment status.

At the same time, a therapist records the patient's pain response to the injection to see if the injection recreates the patient's usual back and/or leg pain. Unfortunately, the test has a high level of false-positive responses, and there is a lack of conclusive scientific evidence that this test improves ultimate patient outcome (Fluke, 1995).

[6] Bone Scans (Scintigraphy)

Bone scanning (scintigraphy) is an x-ray technique that is capable of diagnosing recent fractures, tumors, infections and arthritis in the bones and joints of the spine. A radioactive material is injected into the bloodstream and settles in the bones. An instrument similar to a Geiger counter is used to detect the radiation emitted by the radioisotope. This radiation generates an image similar to an x-ray. Bones undergoing rapid cell growth, as with infection or fracture, then show up in the picture as a dense black area known as a hot spot.

One major advantage of this technique is that it emits only about a tenth the radiation of a routine spinal x-ray. Unfortunately, the test

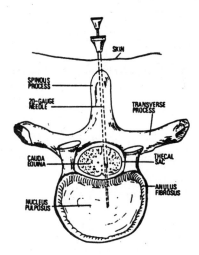

Fig. 6-11. In discography, dye is injected into an intervertebral disc. If the disc is herniated, the dye will leak from it and produce a telltale radiographic picture.

takes about four hours to complete and necessitates the patient's lying face down on an x-ray table for about one hour. This immobility can cause patients considerable discomfort.

[7]   Electrodiagnostic Tests

Electrodiagnostic tests include electromyography and dermatomal somatosensory evoked potentials (DSSEP).

[a]   Electromyography

Electromyography (EMG) is a test that is usually administered by a neurologist. It involves no radiation but has sometimes been known to cause moderate discomfort. Small pads are attached to the skin over the muscles. In some cases, very fine needles are inserted directly into the muscles. Once the pads or needles are correctly placed, the physician can study the pattern of electrical recordings created by nerve conduction.

Neural (nerve) pathology is diagnosed by changes in the electrical patterns and the speed of nerve conduction. Irritation of the nerve roots in the lower spine usually manifests as an abnormal electrical response. EMG is especially useful in diagnosing a disc encroaching on the nerves of the spinal canal.

[b]   Dermatomal Somatosensory Evoked Potentials (DSSEP)

Dermatomal somatosensory evoked potentials (DSSEP) is a recently developed electrical test used to help confirm the diagnosis of disc herniation.[20] In administering this test, the skin of the patient's foot is electrically stimulated, and the correspondingly evoked brain waves are recorded. An abnormal pattern suggests that a herniated disc is probably interfering with the signal being transmitted from the foot to the brain.

This test has yet to be proved to be completely reliable, however, and for now, the myelogram, CT scan and MRI are considered the more accurate modalities for diagnosing herniation of the disc.

---

[20] *See also* 6.05[3] *supra* for a discussion of disc herniation.

6.11 PSYCHOLOGICAL EVALUATION OF LOW BACK PAIN

Recent studies have demonstrated that a high rate of preinjury emotional trauma is associated with the subsequent development of chronic low back pain (Blair, et al., 1994). Some of the most severe childhood traumas reported include abandonment, battering, sexual molestation and emotional abuse. The stress caused by these early experiences may be a major factor in the future development of chronic low back pain.

One study concluded that low back injuries can be influenced by psychological factors. Researchers theorized that the apprehension of pain and the actual tolerance of pain were the most significant psychogenic factors affecting low back pain and dysfunction (Pope, et al., 1991). The study stressed the value of some type of psychological intervention. Psychotherapy and counseling can therefore play a major role in recovering from low back injuries.

Psychological tests and questionnaires have been developed to deal specifically with the emotional upheavals connected with low back pain. The SC2-90-R is a test designed to evaluate psychological stability. Nine major symptoms are included in the test. These include somatization (conversion of neuroses to physical ailments), obsessive-compulsive behavior, interpersonal sensitivity, depression, anxiety, hostility, phobic anxiety, paranoid ideation and psychosis. Disturbances in appetite and sleep patterns are also recorded (Moffroid, et al., 1994). Another well-known psychological test used to assess patient depression is the Beck Depression Inventory Symptom Check List (BDI) (Alaranta, et al., 1994).

The Treatment Outcome Patient Survey (TOPS) is another test designed to evaluate psychological disturbances (Blair, et al., 1994). It was developed as a screening tool to measure patients' perception of their physical health, emotional well-being, level of stress and degree of dissatisfaction with their work situations.

The McGill Pain Questionnaire (MPQ) is used in assessing the behavioral and emotional aspects of pain. The test consists of 20 word lists: 8 are indicative of pain intensity, 9 are related to the behavioral aspects of pain and 3 are associated with the psychological and emotional aspects of pain (Moffroid, et al., 1994).

As a predictive tool, the Vermont Low Back Pain Questionnaire (VLBPQ) attempts to identify which patients already suffering low back pain are likely to become occupationally disabled. The test takes between 10 and 15 minutes to complete and includes questions regarding employment history, job satisfaction, job requirements, personal interactions, educational level and socioeconomic status (Moffroid, et al., 1994).

In a recent study, psychological factors emerged as the most significant predictors of reported low back injury claims (Bigos, et al., 1991). Other than having current or recent low back pain, the next strongest predictor of future back problems involved perceptions of the workplace, especially low job task enjoyment. In fact, job dissatisfaction appeared to be a more significant predictor than physical markers, such as back muscle strength or spine flexibility (Alaranta, et al., 1994).

Similarly, other researchers concluded from their data that the presence of pain, unemployment and worker's compensation are significant factors in the psychological distress of workers with low back pain (Menard, et al., 1994).

In one study, a group of employees slated for disc surgery was given a questionnaire to complete. The purpose of the test was to determine worker profiles and to make predictions concerning low-back-pain-related disability (Cohen, et al., 1994). This group reported significant levels of occupational mental stress, depression, anxiety and job dissatisfaction. They also reported the perception of loss of control. As a group, these workers tended to be married rather than single and were not highly educated.

6.12   SURGICAL TREATMENT OF LOW BACK PAIN

The American Academy of Orthopedic Surgeons' criteria for surgical intervention in disc herniation stresses that surgery should not be considered unless there are serious neurologic complications or the patient has failed four to eight weeks of conservative therapy (bed rest, medication and isometric exercise). Analgesics and nonsteroidal anti-inflammatory drugs (NSAIDs) are the medications most commonly used to control low back pain.

[1] Pre-operative Screening Questionnaire

Recent research suggests that spending extra time on preoperative testing may substantially boost the success rate of spinal surgery and identify patients who might do better with a combination of conservative treatment and psychological support. A useful preoperative screening questionnaire might incorporate a structured interview, careful assessment of pain location and a psychological test to detect depression.

In this self-reporting system, the most significant predictors of poor outcome seem to be multiple pain locations, reduced physical mobility, duration of preoperative work disability and a high intensity of pain. Other significant factors include job status at the time of survey, past work history, job satisfaction (including satisfaction with medical benefits and retirement plans), workers' perception of whether the back injury was compensable and any previous hospitalizations (Lehmann, et al., 1993).

[2] Percutaneous Laser Disc Compression

There has recently been some success with a new, nonsurgical technique for herniated discs called percutaneous laser disc compression. This technique, which uses a laser to retract the herniated portion of the disc, shows great potential for reducing treatment costs and hospital stays.

Automated percutaneous lumbar discectomy (APLD) is a minimally invasive surgical procedure that was developed in the 1980s. It consists of inserting a thin, automated cutting instrument into the nucleus of the herniated disc to cut and suction out a small amount of nuclear material. The procedure is intended to debulk the disc and relieve compression of adjacent spinal nerves. Its advantages include short recovery periods and fewer complications than with more extensive surgical procedures. However, this technique's initial popularity has waned in more recent years, with anticipated results not living up to the initial expectations for it (Jensen, et al., 1994).

Other, less-invasive types of surgery include laser disc compression and chemonucleolysis. These procedures are all based on one principle—if you can decrease the volume of the disc centrally by removing nuclear tissue, then you can decrease the pressure and achieve an indirect decompression of the nerve root.

Diabetics suffering from lumbar disc disease or stenosis (narrowing of the spinal canal) cannot be expected to achieve the same clinical outcome as nondiabetics with these back problems. Among diabetic patients, there are higher rates of postoperative infections, prolonged hospitalizations and delayed healing. Also, individuals with diabetes sometimes contract microvascular disease, which can adversely affect the spinal nerve roots (Simpson, et al., 1993).

[3] Chemonucleolysis

Chemonucleolysis is a technique used to debulk a herniated disc by injecting a chemolytic agent—usually the enzyme chymopapain—into the nucleus. Studies indicate that the success rate of chemonucleolysis can approach that of open discectomy, especially with careful patient selection (Hoogland and Scheckenbach, 1995). The major, although rare, risk in administering chymopapain is a severe hypersensitivity reaction. Leakage of the material into the spinal canal can result in inflammation of the spinal cord, scarring around the lumbar dura and damage to surrounding nerves.

6.13 NONSURGICAL TREATMENT OF ACUTE LOW BACK PAIN

Therapeutic approaches for patients with low back pain include bed rest, medication, activity and exercise and other means.

[1] Bed Rest

In the past, prolonged bed rest was considered the treatment of choice for patients who were recovering from low back pain. More recently, the medical theory concerning bed rest has been modified. Now patients who are not exhibiting any neurologic abnormalities are advised to spend only two or three days in bed, gradually increasing their physical activities. In fact, the popular current opinion proposes that prolonged bed rest can actually result in muscle weakness and loss of bone mineral content (Moro, et al., 1995).

Researchers in Finland studied 186 city employees who visited Helsinki's occupational health centers because of low back pain (Malmivaara, et al., 1995). Sixty-seven patients were prescribed bed rest, 52 were taught back exercises and the remaining 67 were advised to take time off from work but to continue with their regular activity levels. This last group was considered the control group. The study concluded that the control group experienced fewer days of pain and returned to work sooner than either of the other two groups. This group also visited the clinic less often than the patients who exercised, for example.

[2] Medication

Pain management for acute low back pain most often involves the use of nonsteroidal anti-inflammatory drugs (NSAIDs) and aspirin. Muscle relaxants, tranquilizers and narcotic agents are also prescribed in more severe cases, but these drugs can have undesirable side effects, including addiction, mood alteration, sedation and constipation.

[3] Activity and Exercise

After two or three days of bed rest, increased activity and exercise are recommended. Some of the better workouts include walking, swimming and mild range of motion exercises (moderate degrees of flexion, extension and bending). Sitting is avoided (Arria and Staley, 1994).

Exercise programs designed to strengthen the back and abdominal muscles have been stressed (Malmivaara, et al., 1995). Aerobic exercises (those that raise the heart rate) are particularly effective in the treatment of low back pain.

Rehabilitative exercises for athletes recovering from low back injuries usually focus on slowly building strength and endurance. Progressive nonresistance exercise followed by light-resistance exercises may be the ideal program for recovering athletes.

[4] Physical Modalities

Some of the other modalities currently available for the therapeutic (nonsurgical) treatment of low back pain include the application of heat and cold, massage, ultrasound, biofeedback, acupuncture and transcutaneous electrical nerve stimulation (TENS). In addition, some physicians tout the efficacy of traction and spinal manipulation (chiropractic), especially when used in the early, acute phase following injury. However, other researchers believe the initial benefits of chiropractic manipulation are short-lived (Andersson and Frymoyer, 1991).

[5]   Chiropractic

Chiropractic treatment for low back pain usually involves manipulation and adjustment of the spinal column in order to restore proper anatomic alignment. Chiropractors believe that aligning the spine enhances its critical role in the efficient functioning of the nervous system.

In making diagnoses, doctors of chiropractic often use standard physical examinations, x-rays and laboratory tests. Studies have shown that chiropracty can relieve the painful symptoms of lumbar distress, especially when it is used in the early phase of the illness. Unfortunately, recurrence of pain is common, leading some to speculate on the short-lived nature of the treatment (Koes, et al., 1995).

6.14   NONSURGICAL TREATMENT OF CHRONIC LOW BACK PAIN

Chronic pain is defined as discomfort that lasts upward of six months. After that period of time, the difficulty takes on the special connotations of chronic pain.

[1]   Psychological Rehabilitation

The medical field has long recognized that psychological impairment can have a deleterious effect on a patient's recovery rate and can also impede his or her timely return to the workplace. During counseling sessions, patients are taught to cope with personal and family problems that may result from the protracted nature of their illness. Some pain centers also use behavior modification techniques to undermine the conditions that reinforce pain and disability.

[2]   Functional Restoration

Functional restoration is a multifaceted approach combining physical and psychological techniques. Endurance and overall conditioning are improved through patient involvement in sports and mild exercise. These programs also use occupational medicine and counseling to better prepare workers for their return to the occupational environment.

[3]   Work Hardening

Work hardening is a multidisciplinary, goal-oriented technique of returning the injured patient to his or her former job at the previous level of activity. This program is based on the theory that the gradual performance of tasks that simulate those on the specific job will ultimately allow the worker to fulfill the demands of that job. This is usually done in a protected, therapeutic environment.

Although work hardening can be quite helpful in returning the worker to employment productivity, success rates vary with different patient populations and varying degrees of patient compliance. Generally, programs treating workers with acute low back injuries will have more successful job re-entry rates than those treating patients suffering from chronic low back pain.

6.15　PREVENTION OF LOW BACK INJURIES

Employers are increasingly becoming aware of the benefits of prevention over treatment of low back injuries. The concept of "back school," for example, originated to educate workers who were already suffering from low back pain or who had recently recovered from such a condition. The idea was to instruct workers in all aspects of back care, including methods of safe lifting and physical fitness exercises. Now back schools are being utilized as a tool to increase workers' strength, in the hope of preventing the onset of low back pain among workers in high-risk occupations[21] (Andersson, 1995).

There are two types of approach to the prevention of occupational injuries: those that focus on the worker and those that focus on the workplace and equipment. Worker-oriented approaches involve screening to select those at risk for back injury, and education, particularly in lifting techniques. Once injury has occurred, disability prevention becomes a major issue. The workplace-oriented approach uses ergonomic principles to design chairs, tables, cranes and other equipment to minimize the stress on the back.

[1]　Pre-employment Screening

It has become evident that the majority of health care expenditures and compensation costs dealing with low back pain are derived from the small proportion of workers who will suffer for six months or more (Goel, et al., 1994). Therefore, the need becomes obvious for a preplacement screening program that will be predictive of work

---

[21] *See also* 6.15[2] *infra.*

absenteeism and chronic disability due to low back pain and dysfunction.

Pre-employment screening usually includes a medical history, physical examination and laboratory testing. The goal is to detect those workers at risk for future back pain. One problem with this approach is that it usually occurs in isolation from the occupational setting. The physician cannot evaluate a worker's fitness for a job without knowing the demands of the job itself.

The medical history is very useful in predicting future back pain if the worker reports a history of previous back problems. The magnitude of the risk can be estimated using knowledge of the details of previous back pain episodes (the length of time off work, a history of surgery, etc.). However, this information may not be reported. Also, back problems are so common that workers with this history cannot all be excluded from work.

In analyzing the predictive value of pre-employment screening tests for subsequent low back pain, one study found no useful relationship between performance values, the worker's estimate of the physical demands of the job relative to physical capacity, and later development of low back pain (Menard, et al., 1994). In fact, the most reliable predictor of future low back pain appeared to be a previous episode of lumbar distress.

[2]   Education

Education and training are used in an attempt both to prevent injury and to minimize disability once injury has occurred. Training in safe lifting procedures is very common, but its usefulness in preventing back injury has been the subject of some debate. Studies of its effectiveness have had conflicting results: The training itself is not always biomechanically sound, and compliance with the principles taught is poor under most circumstances (Andersson, 1995).

Strength and fitness training programs may have value in preventing back injury. Studies of the effects of such programs are not consistently positive, but the weight of the evidence is in their favor. It is not known if the physical exercise itself or its psychological benefits are responsible for the positive effect.

Back schools have been used as a form of treatment to minimize future problems in patients with back pain. Workers are taught about safe lifting and fitness, and they are also provided with a lot of information about the back, their individual problem and what to expect. The goal is to involve the patient in his or her own care. Back schools have met with considerable success when they are used as an intervention with patients who are symptomatic and have been symptomatic less than six months. The effectiveness of back schools used for prevention has yet to be adequately studied (Andersson, 1995).

A recent study in California evaluated the overall performance differences between a control group and those in a one-year back injury prevention program offering employees education, training, exercise and ergonomic improvements (Leiyu, 1993). The results indicated a modest overall decline in low back pain, with significant improvement in job satisfaction and reduction of risky behavior. This experiment demonstrates that health promotion in the workplace can reduce employee health risks, increase healthful behaviors and improve attitudes toward the employer organization. Whether such intervention will continue depends on maintenance of a favorable work environment and employee compliance with the behavior modification program.

[3] Disability Prevention

Recent efforts to address the problem of low back pain among industrial workers have begun to focus on disability prevention rather than on injury prevention. The goal is to channel the back-injured worker along the route that minimizes future disability, beginning with the very first contact between worker and health care professional. This involves training of company medical personnel and management in addition to workers. Management training is critically important in the area of work modification. Many back-injured patients could return to work if their jobs could be modified, even on a short-term basis.

In order to increase muscular performance capacity and flexibility of the spine, the Finnish program[22] was developed to provide both physical and psychological means of improvement.

_____

22 See also 6.15[4] infra.

[4]   Psychological Aspects

Employers have come to recognize that psychological and psycho-social work factors can adversely affect their workers and, ultimately, their productivity. Monotony has been identified as a key element in employee dissatisfaction and has been associated with the development of low back pain and subsequent absenteeism (Bigos and Battié, 1992).

Back schools provide education, passive physical therapy and a self-paced regimen of overall conditioning. Back strengthening exercises may be taught by a rehabilitation therapist, and back schools may also employ qualified psychotherapists to counsel patients in groups or on an individual basis.[23]

To improve an occupational handicap, it is not enough merely to treat the physical disability. Change must come from social legislation and labor market policy. Specific employer organizations and society in general must face the challenge of providing appropriate health care and emotional support to patients suffering from low back pain in order to minimize their occupational handicaps (Alaranta, et al., 1994).

The physician has a responsibility to patients, employers and health insurance carriers to provide a fair evaluation of functional disability without causing an unjustified reduction in the worker's occupational opportunities or personal sense of wellness. One psychological measure of self-esteem is sometimes referred to as locus of control or self-efficacy. A patient with an internal locus of control has sufficient self-esteem to believe that he or she can influence the good or bad events in life, including illness. An individual with an external locus of control believes he or she has no control over life's events. This latter situation can result in debilitating stress, which can in turn hinder or prolong recovery from a low back injury.

In Finland, where low back pain is the most common reason for disability pensions, a program known as AKSELI has been instituted to provide intensive physical and psychosocial training. In addition to physicians, the program also provides psychologists, social workers, physiotherapists, occupational therapists and work trainers. Cognitive behavioral disability management groups stress problem-focused discussions, including new decision-making skills, reconceptualizations of pain and labor problems (Alaranta, et al., 1994).

---

23 *See also* 6.15[2] *supra.*

[5] Ergonomics—Workplace Modifications

Ergonomics is the science that studies the relationship between human beings and their work environment. The underlying principle of ergonomics presupposes that some level of stress always exists between the worker and the workplace, and this stress can adversely affect the employee's health and ultimate productivity. This remains true for both active and sedentary occupations and for stresses that are both physical and psychological. Therefore, the goal of the ergonomist is to analyze and engineer solutions for alleviating the interfering physical and/or mental stresses inherent in the working environment.

In the past, ergonomists have designed chairs, desks, workstations and other work-related equipment to fit average-size males. In more recent years, ergonomists have begun to design equipment with recognition of the huge influx of women into the workforce and the requirements of a working population with highly individual needs.

One of the functions of an ergonomically designed workstation would be to prevent the postural stresses and awkward postures that can be responsible for cumulative trauma disorders. Biologically, when a muscle contracts, its blood vessels are compressed by adjacent contractile tissue. Vascular resistance increases with the level of muscle tension, and the blood supply to the working muscles decreases. If the muscle cannot relax periodically, the demand for metabolic nutrients exceeds the supply, and metabolic wastes accumulate in the tissues.

Sitting in a chair is a static posture that can create enormous strain on structures of the lower back, including muscles and discs. A person sitting in a slouched position is excessively flexing the back and overstretching the spinal ligaments. An ergonomically designed chair will support the lower back area. Elements to consider in a well-designed chair include the seat pad, the arm rests, the seat back and the seat frame.

Some of the ergonomic changes employers can make to prevent low back injuries include installing manual or power mechanical aids to assist with the movement of heavy weights (such as conveyors, hoists and articulating arms), providing an optimum work level to reduce unnecessary bending or stretching, and providing an adequate workplace layout that reduces unnecessary twisting or reaching.

6.16 PROGNOSIS

Low back pain usually resolves rapidly in over 90 percent of cases. Approximately 40 percent of patients will recover within one week, 80 percent within three weeks and 90 percent within six weeks (Levy and Wegman, 1995).

Unfortunately, the rate of recurrence is extremely high. One British study estimates that the probability of developing low back pain is almost four times greater in patients who have suffered a previous episode. In addition, the prognosis for full recovery decreases after prolonged work absences. It is estimated that if a worker has been off the job for more than six months, there is only a 50 percent probability of that worker's ever returning to gainful employment. Over one year, there may be only a 25 percent probability. Over two years, there is almost no probability (Levy and Wegman, 1995). Clearly, an early return to work is critical in preventing prolonged or permanent disability.

Returning injured workers to large companies may be easier, due to a greater opportunity to find light duty jobs for the patient, greater union support for the worker making it more difficult to abandon the injured worker, greater likelihood of being self-insured and thereby having greater control over financial work disincentives, and patient motivation to return to work to retain generally superior employment benefits afforded by the larger companies (Lehmann, et al., 1993).

6.17 EVALUATION OF IMPAIRMENT

In some occupational settings, judgments are made about the permissible type, intensity and schedule of work on the basis of dynamometry (measurement of the strength of a muscular contraction), because there is a prevalent belief that the probability of injury will be reduced if the estimated physical demands of the job in question do not exceed the worker's physical abilities, as measured by various techniques (Menard, et al., 1994). In some worker's compensation cases, arguments relating to the size of the award are made on the basis of dynamometry, because such measures are considered unbiased, and they accurately quantify an individual's maximal functional capacity.

Future function is difficult to predict from the results of dynamometry in patients with mechanical low back pain. The outcome is complicated to measure and is greatly influenced by a variety of biological, psychological and social factors that can change over a significant time span.

Evaluation may help identify those patients who will successfully resume their former overall level of activity, including work. During a typical physical examination, the physical activities of occupations may be simulated, including lifting, noting weight and height; carrying, noting weight borne, distance, horizontal pull with either arm, horizontal push with either arm, upward and downward pull and push with both arms. Also climbing, balancing, dexterity, talking, hearing, vision and coordination are noted. In one study, strength in each category was recorded using the Canadian Classification and Dictionary of Occupations ratings of sedentary, light, medium, heavy or very heavy (Menard, et al., 1994).

The National Institute for Occupational Safety and Health (NIOSH) has provided a test that measures such specific physical attributes as left and right hamstring length and lumbar mobility. A questionnaire is also administered that includes demographic data about age, gender, socioeconomic status, psychological perceptions, functional ability and self-reported low back pain levels (Moffroid, 1994).

The latest edition of the American Medical Association's *Guides to the Evaluation of Permanent Impairment* uses two approaches. One, the "Injury Model," assigns the patient to one of eight categories on the basis of objective clinical findings. The second approach involves measurements of range of motion and assigns impairment percentages according to limitations in motion. According to the *Guides,* patients with injuries that are listed in their Table 70, "Spine Impairment Categories for Cervicothoracic, Thoracolumbar, and Lumbosacral Regions," such as a herniated disk with evidence of nerve root irritation, are evaluated according to the Injury Model. If the patient's difficulties do not fall within the categories listed in that table, then the evaluation is made according to the Range of Motion Model, also described therein. As with all other AMA impairment evaluations, ratings are given in percentages for both the body part itself (e.g., lower extremity) and impairment of the whole person (American Medical Association, 1993).

6.100   BIBLIOGRAPHY

Reference Bibliography

Alaranta, H., et al.: Intensive Physical and Psychosocial Training Program for Patients with Chronic Low Back Pain: A Controlled Clinical Trial. Spine 19(12):1339-1349, 1994.

American Medical Association: Guides to the Evaluation of Permanent Impairment. Chicago: American Medical Association, 1993.

Andersson, G. B. J.: Low Back Pain. In: Levy, B. and Wegman, D. (Eds.): Occupational Health: Recognizing and Preventing Work-Related Disorders. Boston: Little Brown, 1995.

Andersson, G. B. J.: Epidemiology of Spinal Disorders. In: Frymoyer, J. W. (Ed.): The Adult Spine. New York: Raven Press, 1991.

Andersson, G. B. J. and Frymoyer, J. W.: Treatment of the Acutely Injured Worker. In: Pope, M. H., et al. (Eds.): Occupational Low Back Pain. St. Louis: Mosby-Year Book, 1991.

Arria, S. and Staley, C.: Preworkout Strategies for Low Back and Legs. Muscle and Fitness 55:62, Apr. 1994.

Battié, M. C. and Bigos, S. J.: Industrial Back Complaints. Orthop. Clin. N. Am. 22(2):273-282, Apr. 1991.

Bigos, S. J. and Battié, M. C.: Risk Factors for Industrial Back Problems. Semin. Spine Surg. 4:2-11, 1992.

Bigos, S. J., et al.: A Prospective Study of Work Perceptions and Psychosocial Factors Affecting the Report of a Back Injury. Spine 16(1):1-6, Jan. 1991.

Blair, J. A., et al.: Pre-injury Emotional Trauma and Chronic Back Pain: An Unexpected Finding. Spine 19(10):1144-1147, 1994.

Burdorf, A., et al.: Occupational Risk Factors for Low Back Pain Among Sedentary Workers. J. Occup. Med. 35:1213, Dec. 1993.

Cohen, J. E., et al.: Predicting Risk of Back Injuries, Work Absenteeism, and Chronic Disability. The Shortcomings of Preplacement Screening. J. Occup. Med. 36:1093, Oct. 1994.

Ducreux, D., et al.: Disk Herniation with Posterior Ring Apophysis Fracture in Young Adults. J. Radiol. 76(4):209-212, (Eng. Abstr.) Apr. 1995.

Fluke, M. M.: The Treatment of Lumbar Spine Pain Syndromes Diagnosed by Discography: Lumbar Arthrodesis [Letter]. Spine 20(4):501-504, Feb. 15, 1995.

Frost, H., et al.: Randomised Controlled Trial for Evaluation of Fitness Programme for Patients with Chronic Low Back Pain. B.M.J. 310(6973):151-154. Jan. 1995.

Fuortes, L. J., et al.: Epidemiology of Back Injury in University Hospital Nurses from Review of Worker's Compensation Records and a Case-Control Survey. J. Occup. Med. 5:1022, Sept. 1994.

Frymoyer, J.: The Adult Spine: Principles and Practice. New York: Raven Press, 1991.

Genaidy, A. M., et al.: Can Back Supports Relieve the Load on the Lumbar Spine for Employees Engaged in Industrial Operations? Ergonomics 38(5):996-1010, May 1995.

Goel, J. W., et al.: American College of Occupational and Environmental Medicine Preplacement Screening for Low Back Disability at the Workplace. J. Occup. Med. 7:1093, Oct. 1994.

Hochschuler, S.: Back in Shape. Boston: Houghton, Mifflin, 1991.

Hoogland, T. and Scheckenbach, C.: Percutaneous Nucleotomy an Effective Treatment for Low Back Pain Caused by Herniated Discs. J. Bone Joint Surg. 77(B):24, 1995.

Jensen, M. C., et al.: Leave Bulging Discs Alone. N. Eng. J. Med. 331(2):69-73, 1994.

Kauppila, L. I.: Prolonged Low Back Pain—A Sign of Poor Circulation? Duodecim. 109(21):1929-1933, 1993.

Lehmann, T. R., et al.: Predicting Long-Term Disability in Low Back Injured Workers Presenting to a Spine Consultant. Spine 18(8)1103-1112, 1993.

Leiyu, S.: A Cost-Benefit Analysis of a California County's Back Injury Prevention Program. Public Health Rep. 108:204, Mar.-Apr. 1993.

Levy, B. and Wegman, D. (Eds.): Occupational Health: Recognizing and Preventing Work-Related Disorders. Boston: Little Brown, 1995.

Malmivaara, A., et al.: The Treatment of Low Back Pain—Bed Rest, Exercises, or Ordinary Activity? N. Engl. J. Med. 332:351, Feb. 9, 1995.

McLain, R. F. and Weinstein, J. N.: Effects of Whole Body Vibration on Dorsal Root Ganglion Neurons: Changes in Neuronal Nuclei. Spine 19(13):1455-1461, 1994.

Menard, M. R., et al.: Pattern of Performance in Workers With Low Back Pain During a Comprehensive Motor Performance Evaluation. Spine 19(12):1359-1366, 1994.

Moffroid, M. T., ct al.: Distinguishable Groups of Musculoskeletal Low Back Pain Patients and Asymptomatic Control Subjects Based on Physical Measures of the NIOSH Low Back Atlas. Spine 19(12):1350-1358, 1994.

Moro, M., et al.: Failure Load of Thoracic Vertebrae Correlates with Bone Mineral Density Measured by DXA. Calcif. Tissue Int. 56(3):206-209, Mar. 1995.

Olmarker, K. and Rydevik, B.: Pathophysiology of Sciatica. Ortho. Clin. No. Amer. 22(2):223-232, Apr. 1991.

Parker, H., et al.: The Use of the Pain Drawing As a Screening Measure to Predict Psychological Distress in Chronic Low Back Pain. Spine 20(2):236-243, 1994.

Pope, M. H., et al. (Eds.): Occupational Low Back Pain. St. Louis: Mosby-Year Book, 1991.

Rothman, R. H., et al.: Anatomy and Pathophysiology of Low Back Pain. In: Wiesel, S. W., et al. (Eds.): Industrial Low Back Pain. Charlottesville, Vir.: Michie, 1989.

Simpson, J. M., et al.: The Results of Operations on the Lumbar Spine in Patients who Have Diabetes Mellitus. J. Bone Joint Surg. 75A(12):1823-1829, Dec. 1993.

Stocker, S. A.: Midday Recharger for Desk Jockeys. (Stretches to Relieve Muscle Fatigue Caused by Sitting). Prevention 47:118, July 1995.

Varlotta, G. P., et al.: Familial Predisposition for Herniation of a Lumbar Disc in Patients Who Are Less Than Twenty-one Years Old. J. Bone Joint Surg. 73A(1):124-127, Jan. 1991.

Waters, T. R., et al.: Revised NIOSH Equation for the Design and Evaluation of Manual Lifting Tasks. Ergonomics 36:749-776, 1993.

Additional References

American Academy of Orthopaedic Surgeons: Musculoskeletal Conditions in the United States. Park Ridge, Ill.: AAOS, 1992.

Andersson, G. B. J.: Low Back Pain. In: Levy, B. and Wegman, D. (Eds.): Occupational Health: Recognizing and Preventing Work-Related Disorders. Boston: Little, Brown, 1995.

Chatani, K., et al.: Characterization of Thermal Hyperalgesia, C-Fos Expression, and Alterations in Neuropeptides After Mechanical Irritation of the Dorsal Root Ganglion. Spine 20(3):277-289, Feb. 1, 1995.

Cherkin, D. C., et al.: An International Comparison of Back Surgery Rates. Spine 19:1201-1206, 1994.

Chodakiewitz, J. W.: Managing Chronic Intractable Pain. West. J. Med. 162:259, March 1995.

Cholewicki, J., et al.: Comparison of Muscle Forces and Joint Load from an Optimization and EMG Assisted Lumbar Spine Model: Towards Development of a Hybrid Approach. J. Biomech. 28(3):321-331, March 1995.

Coste, J., et al.: Clinical and Psychological Classification of Non-Specific Low-Back Pain. A New Study in Primary Care Practice. Rev. Epidemiol. Sante Publique 43(2):127-138, 1995.

Coste, J., et al.: Inter-and Intraobserver Variability in the Interpretation of Computed Tomography of the Lumbar Spine. J. Clin. Epidemiol. 47(4):375-381, Apr. 1994.

Devilee, R., et al.: Treatment of Fractures and Dislocations of the Thoracic and Lumbar Spine by Fusion and Harrington Instrumentation. Arch. Orthop. Trauma Surg. 114(2):100-102, 1995.

Dina, T. S., et al.: Lumbar Spine After Surgery for Herniated Disk: Imaging Findings in the Early Postoperative Period. A.J.R. Am. J. Roentgenol. 164(3):665-671, March 1995.

Donatelli, R. A. and Wooden, M. J. (Eds.): Orthopaedic Physical Therapy, 2nd ed. New York: Churchill Livingstone, 1994.

Dreyfuss, P. et al.: Positive Sacroiliac Screening Tests in Asymptomatic Adults. Spine 19(10):1138-1142, 1994.

Dvorák, J., et al.: Normal Motion of the Lumbar Spine as Related to Age and Gender. Eur. Spine J. 4(1):18-23, 1995.

Ferrari, S., et al.: Vitamin-D-Receptor-Gene Polymorphisms and Change in Lumbar-Spine Bone Mineral Density. Lancet 345(8947):423-424, Feb. 18, 1995.

Franck, L.: Seven Ways to Beat Lower Back Pain. Muscle and Fitness 55:192, Feb. 1994.

Fujimura, T., et al.: Work-Related Factors of Low Back Pain Among Nursing Aides in Nursing Homes for the Elderly. Sangyo Eiseigaku Zasshi 37(2):89-98, March 1995.

Gusta, A., et al.: [Pitfalls and Failures in Open Reduction and Stabilization of Thoracolumbar Fracture Using Harrington Rods] Chir. Narzadow Ruchu. Ortop. Pol. 60(1):19-22, (Eng. Abstr.) 1995.

Hilibrand, A. S., et al.: Acute Spondylolytic Spondylolisthesis. Risk of Progression and Neurological Complications. J. Bone Joint Surg. Am. 77(2):190-196, Feb. 1995.

Hoffman, K. L., et al.: Polyostotic Fibrous Dysplasia with Severe Pathologic Compression Fracture of L2. Skeletal. Radiol. 24(2):160-162, Feb. 1995.

Jensen, M.C., et al.: Leave Bulging Discs Alone. N. Engl. J. Med. 331(2):69-73, 1994.

Johns, R. E., Jr.: Chronic Recurrent Low Back Pain: A Methodology for Analyzing Fitness for Duty and Managing Risk Under the Americans with Disabilities Act. J.A.M.A. 272:512E, Aug. 17, 1994.

Joshi, G. P., et al.: Postoperative Analgesia After Lumbar Laminectomy: Epidural Fentanyl Infusion Versus Patient-Controlled Intravenous Morphine. Anesth. Analg. 80(3):511-514, Mar. 1995.

Keyserling, W. M.: Occupational Ergonomics: Promoting Safety and Health Through Work Design. In: Levy, B. and Wegman, D. (Eds.): Occupational Health: Recognizing and Preventing Work-Related Disorders. Boston: Little, Brown, 1995.

Koes, B. W., et al.: Methodological Quality of Randomized Clinical Trials on Treatment Efficacy in Low Back Pain. Spine 20(2):228-235, 1995.

Magid, D.: Computed Tomographic Imaging of the Musculoskeletal System: Current Status. Radiol. Clin. N. Am. 32(2):255-273, Mar. 1994.

Papp, T., et al.: Trefoil Configuration and Developmental Stenosis of the Lumbar Vertebral Canal. J. Bone Joint Surg. Br. 77(3):469-472, May 1995.

Quinn, M. M., et al.: Women and Work. In: Levy, B. and Wegman, D. (Eds.): Occupational Health: Recognizing and Preventing Work-Related Disorders. Boston: Little Brown, 1995.

Rozenberg, S., et al.: Clinical Significance of Heterogeneity of Vertebral Mineral Density. Maturitas 21(2):147-151, Feb. 1995.

Shekelle, P. G., et al: Comparing the Costs Between Provider Types of Episodes of Back Pain Care. Spine 20(2):221-227, 1995.

Susman, J.: Agency for Health Care Policy and Research (AHCPR): Guideline on Acute Low Back Problems (Editorial Comment), Am. Fam. Physician 51(2):334, Feb. 1, 1995.

Swanepoel, M. W., et al.: Human Lumbar Apophyseal Joint Damage and Intervertebral Disc Degeneration. Ann. Rheum. Dis. 54(3):182-188, March 1995.

Takahashi, K., et al.: Schmorl's Nodes and Low-Back Pain. Analysis of Magnetic Resonance Imaging Findings in Symptomatic and Asymptomatic Individuals. Eur. Spine J. 4(1):56-59, 1995.

Ulmer, J. L., et al.: Lumbar Spondylolysis: Reactive Marrow Changes Seen in Adjacent Pedicles on MR Images. A.J.R. Am. J. Roentgenol. 164(2):429-433, Feb. 1995.

van Doorn, J. W.: Low Back Disability Among Self-Employed Dentists, Veterinarians, Physicians and Physical Therapists in the Netherlands. A Retrospective Study Over a 13-Year Period (N = 1,119) and an Early Intervention Program with a 1-Year Follow-up (N = 134). Acta Orthop. Scand. Suppl. 263:1-64, June 1995.

Webster, B. S. and Snook, S. H.: The Cost of 1989 Workers' Compensation Low Back Pain Claims. Spine 19(10):1111-1116, 1994.

Zelko, J. R., et al.: Laparoscopic Lumbar Discectomy. Am. J. Surg. 169(5):496-498, May 1995.

CHAPTER 7

Muscle Strains and Tears

SCOPE

Muscle strains are common injuries. They occur especially in occupations that require static work, such as holding and carrying objects in the arms, working with a foot pedal and typing. Although few such injuries are serious, they may lead to disability if they become chronic. The back, neck and shoulder are the most common regions affected. Strains may arise during a sudden movement that exceeds the capacity of the muscle; these have an acute onset and are immediately recognized as injuries. In many cases of strain, particularly those involving the back, the diagnosis is presumed but not actually confirmed. Muscles may also be lacerated by external trauma or rupture due to excessive load. They may suffer cramps or undergo strain. Muscles may be torn when the demand placed on them is greater than they can withstand. Currently available diagnostic tests can only exclude other problems, such as bone or joint disease. The most useful test at present is the electromyogram, which records the electrical activity of the muscle at work or rest. Prevention involves education and training of the worker as well as modification of the workplace.

SYNOPSIS

7.01   INTRODUCTION

Problems related to muscles are extremely common in the workplace. Most involve nonspecific types of muscle pain, and few of these problems are serious. However, strains of the back and neck may lead to disability if they become chronic.

Muscle injury may arise in several different circumstances. In acute problems, muscles may be lacerated by external trauma or rupture due to excessive load. They may suffer cramps or undergo strain. Of all these, strain is by far the most common. In acute cases, strain is usually related to exertion, when a sudden demand that exceeds its capacity is placed on the muscle. In the attempt to meet the demand, the muscle is strained.

Chronic muscle problems are also common; these include chronic strain, tension neck and a variety of other regional pain syndromes that are thought to be largely of muscular origin and are usually related to posture. The posture most frequently associated with neck symptoms is sitting with the hands outstretched and engaged in fine motor movements of the wrist and fingers (such as working at a keyboard).[1] Shoulder symptoms are common in workers on assembly lines and in other occupations in which the hands are used at shoulder height or higher.[2]

Muscle injury may also result from damage to the muscle cells themselves, to nerves and, less frequently, to blood vessels. Disturbances in nerve function may produce paralysis and other abnormalities.

7.02　PHYSIOLOGY AND PATHOPHYSIOLOGY OF MUSCLE

The muscles comprise the largest single tissue of the body, accounting for approximately 40 percent of body weight. A single muscle is composed of several hundred thousand muscle fibers. Each fiber is enclosed in a membrane that tapers to a sinew at each end. These sinews combine at each end of the muscle to form a tough, fibrous tendon that attaches the muscle to bone.

[1]　Muscle Energy Sources

Muscle is a unique tissue that is capable of converting chemical energy (derived from food) into mechanical work. The chemical reactions in each muscle cell cause it to shorten; when this occurs in concert with all the other muscle cells in a single muscle, the muscle itself shortens, and the bones attached to each end of the muscle can move.

---

[1] See also ch. 8.

[2] See also ch. 2.

Muscles are activated by electrical impulses from nerves. These impulses travel down the muscle, eliciting a set of biochemical reactions that result in contraction. The electrical activity of the muscle may be recorded by a technique known as electromyography (EMG).[3]

In the absence of nerve input, muscles wither away (atrophy). This is commonplace after a stroke; the affected limb is paralyzed, becomes thin and loses its normal contour.

[2]   Muscle Biomechanics

Muscles do two kinds of work: dynamic work, which is associated with movement, and static work, which holds the body in a particular position.

[a]   Dynamic Work

Dynamic muscle work involves a rhythmic alternation between contraction and relaxation. During walking, for example, certain sets of muscles contract during the swing of the leg forward, others when the foot is planted down, and others when the foot pushes off. Each set of muscles contracts during one phase of the motion and relaxes during other phases.

One advantage of this rhythmic sequence is that it assists the flow of blood. Successive contractions and relaxations in the leg during walking act like a pump: Contractions squeeze the blood out, and relaxation effectively sucks it in. This enhances the flow of nutrients and oxygen into the tissue as well as the flow of waste products out of the muscle. This pumping effect plays a crucial role in efficient muscle function: Blood flow to active muscle is 10 to 20 times greater than such flow to resting muscle.

[b]   Static Work

Static muscular work is not rhythmic but involves the prolonged state of contraction required to maintain a specific posture: The muscle remains contracted and under tension for long periods. In reality, this does not necessarily mean continuous full contraction but continuous intermittent activity, without returning to full relaxation.

A major disadvantage of this type of activity is that effort must be expended in the absence of additional blood flow. In fact, continuous

---

[3] See 7.03[3] infra.

contraction can restrict blood flow into the muscle. There may well be insufficient nutrients for energy production, and eventually the muscle reverts to anaerobic metabolism (an energy manufacturing process that does not require oxygen). More important, waste products are not carried away by the blood but accumulate in the muscle; these are thought to be the source of the pain of muscular fatigue.

Because of these factors, static work is less efficient than dynamic work and requires more energy and a higher heart rate (Grandjean, 1988). It is, therefore, more strenuous.

Almost all occupations involve a certain degree of static work, some more than others. Holding and carrying objects in the arms, prolonged standing, manipulations that require the arms to be held out, standing while working a foot pedal and sitting while performing detailed hand movements (such as typing) all involve static work as a major component of the total work being done.

7.03 MECHANISMS OF MUSCLE INJURY

Muscle damage may occur directly as a result of overt trauma, such as a tear, fracture, crush injury or contusion (bruise). It may also result indirectly from nerve or blood vessel damage. The most common form of muscle trauma occurs as a result of excessive stretching, leading to a strain.

[1] Mechanical Trauma

One of the most significant kinds of injury to muscle is caused by mechanical trauma.

[a] Muscle Trauma

Muscles may be damaged by extrinsic or intrinsic forces. Extrinsic forces include those delivered by blunt trauma (causing a contusion or crush injury); laceration (severing a muscle); or fracture, which may be accompanied by tendon and ligament tears, significant bleeding from all structures into the muscle and piercing of the muscle by bone fragments.

[b] Tears

Muscle tears usually result from intrinsic forces, namely those that result from muscular work. These occur when demand is placed on the muscle to perform at levels higher than is possible.

Tears of an entire muscle are rare. These may also be called ruptures or severe strains. The term *strain,* however, is generally used to describe a lesser injury in which the damage is microscopic rather than involving a division of the whole muscle.

When exertion generates a force sufficient to rupture musculoskeletal structures, in most cases, the tendon will tear first rather than the muscle. The usual mechanism involves placing additional load on an already fully contracted muscle. The muscles in the shoulder area have been known to rupture when required to break a fall while already fully contracted.

[c] Strains

A strain has been defined as an indirect muscle injury caused by excessive stretch. Other terms used to describe the same phenomenon include *muscle pulls, tears* and *ruptures.*

Excessive stretch can produce muscle damage either through a macroscopic tear or, more frequently, through microscopic tears that alter the structure and function of the muscle cells. Damage on the cellular level is presumed to be the pathologic basis of strains, but it is not clearly understood.

There are two types of acute muscle pain: the strain, which is an acute painful event that occurs during exertion, and muscle soreness, which is pain that evolves after exercise without a single identifiable injury.

Evidence of muscle cell damage may be corroborated in some cases by the finding of elevated levels of muscle enzymes (e.g., creatine kinase) in the blood or in the urine (myoglobinuria). In some cases, there is bleeding and swelling in the muscle, and this may be visible on computed tomography (CT) scan. However, the vast majority of cases do not have such evidence; the diagnosis is presumed and never confirmed by testing.

Microscopic muscle damage has been reported in the workplace, and the risk is increased when a worker uses a heavy tool, performs strenuous work to which he or she is not accustomed or is required to assume an awkward posture. Heavy manual work of all types creates the possibility for this problem (Edwards, 1988). The upper extremity, neck and back are most commonly affected.

[d] Nerve Trauma

Mechanical trauma may also lacerate the nerves that stimulate a specific muscle. Cut nerves may be repaired, but it is never possible to reconnect each nerve fiber precisely, and the functional results of nerve repair are variable to poor. The more central the nerve injury, the worse the functional outcome. When a nerve to the hand is cut in the upper arm, for example, the prognosis for hand function is much worse (and covers a larger territory) than when the nerve is cut in the hand itself.[4]

Once the nerve supply to a muscle is cut off, the muscle cannot be stimulated to contract and is paralyzed. Since muscle bulk depends heavily on continued use, a muscle that is no longer in use undergoes wasting (atrophy).

[e] Arterial Trauma

If the blood supply to muscle is cut off, the muscle dies and is replaced by scar tissue. As part of the normal healing process, the scar shrinks or contracts as time passes. The result is a permanent muscle contracture that deforms the affected limb.

Much arterial trauma can be minimized by prompt attention to the lacerated or damaged arteries. In some cases, the arterial problem may be less evident; this is often the case in compartment syndrome, in which the pressure in a muscular compartment rises so high that it effectively cuts off the circulation. There are many causes of compartment syndrome, including swelling from any cause (such as thermal or electrical burns), crush injuries, hematoma formation (swelling due to bleeding in the muscle) and a variety of other injuries. A mild, chronic form of the compartment syndrome is also thought to be one cause of shin splints (pain along the front of the shinbone due to microscopic tears in the muscle).

[2] Cramp

A muscle cramp is a painful muscle contraction. It is described as electrically active, to distinguish it from other painful contractions (namely contractures), which are electrically silent. Cramps arise in some disease states, including electrolyte disturbances (imbalances of acid and ions such as calcium).

---

[4] See also ch. 1.

Writer's cramp, telegraphist's cramp and other such occupational hazards are thought to result from a disturbance of nerve input to muscle rather than a disturbance of the muscle itself.

[3] Fatigue

Muscle fatigue is thought to play a role in occupational muscle pain syndromes, but the scientific understanding of fatigue symptoms is poor. Physiologic muscle fatigue can be measured by electromyography (EMG). EMG is a diagnostic test that visually records the electrical changes in active muscles. It is obtained by tapping the electrical currents produced by muscular movement.

[4] Chronic Muscle Pain Syndromes

Several chronic pain syndromes are associated with occupational demands and are presumed to have a muscular basis, at least in part. These are largely problems related to posture. The myofascial pain syndrome is included here since it may be of muscular origin, is also referred to as a form of strain and is frequently on the diagnostic list in cases of chronic musculoskeletal pain.

[a] Posture

Painful syndromes have been associated with awkward postures or prolonged periods in a single posture. The origin is presumed to be muscular, but the pathogenesis of these syndromes is not clearly understood. The muscular theory of pathogenesis cites static loading as the causative factor.[5] The occupational cervicobrachial syndrome[6] is one example.

[b] Myofascial Pain Syndrome

The myofascial pain syndrome, also called fibrositis, fibromyalgia, fibromyositis and muscular rheumatism, is also included as a strain syndrome by some authors. Its pathophysiology is unclear, however, and its very existence as a distinct entity has been questioned. Patients with this syndrome complain of chronic, generalized aches and pains, with or without stiffness, involving three or more different anatomic sites. On examination, there are "trigger points" on the body that, when they are pressed, elicit pain.

---

[5] *See* 7.02[1][b] *supra.*

[6] *See* 7.06[2] *infra.*

This syndrome is thought by some to be due to a failure of postural muscles to properly relax, even during sleep. It has also been attributed to psychological disturbances.

[5] Psychological Influences

Psychological stress in the workplace has been investigated as a contributing factor in the reporting of muscle pain.[7] Control over the pace of work has been found to influence the impact of physical load. When workers have little or no control over their work environment, particularly the pace at which they must work, psychological stress has an important effect on the total load on the muscles (Ursin, et al., 1988).

A work task that demands considerable mental effort may also produce increased muscle tension. One study showed that shoulder muscle tension was increased in workers performing a complex task, compared with workers performing a simpler task (Waersted, et al., 1991).

Shift work may also increase the rate of muscle pain, in addition to other complaints. This may be due to disturbed sleep and rest cycles, creating a generalized disturbance in muscle relaxation (Ursin, et al., 1988).

7.04 CLINICAL APPROACH TO MUSCLE INJURIES

The clinical approach to muscle strain varies, depending on the mode of onset. Acute and chronic injuries present different problems; chronic injuries also need to be noted as part of the differential diagnosis.

[1] Acute Strains

An acute strain has a sudden onset. It must be distinguished from other acute injuries that might have occurred instead of or in addition to the muscle strain. This includes primarily fractures and damage to ligaments and tendons.

[a] History

The acute muscle strain injury is an event that occurs during exertion, usually a form of exertion that is not part of the usual daily

---

[7] *See also* ch. 13.

routine. Speed is a factor in many strain injuries; a sudden, forceful activity is more likely to lead to a strain than is a slower, more deliberate activity. The history of a strain injury may include sudden lifting (low back strain) or sudden movements to escape other injury (extremities) or break a fall (upper extremity).

[b] Physical Examination

The physical examination of strained muscles reveals painful, tender muscles, with pain exacerbated by both active and passive stretching. Some strained muscles are swollen, and in some cases, there is bruising, although this does not become evident until a few days after injury (it takes time for the blood to seep out of the muscle to the skin, where it appears as a bruise). Muscle weakness is also present in most cases.

Muscle strain is thought to be a major cause of low back pain,[8] although in most cases, a definitive diagnosis is not made. Because these muscles are deep, the typical signs (pain and tenderness) may not be evident.

In the case of a complete muscle tear, involving the entire muscle, the muscle contour is usually abnormal and the injury is plainly visible. In the case of a biceps tear, for example, where the biceps is normally a single muscle bulge in the upper arm, there will be two bulges, corresponding to the two ends of the torn muscle.

[c] Tests

In the case of acute injuries, tests are important to exclude injuries to other musculoskeletal tissues. X-rays evaluate bones, and in some cases, stress x-rays will reveal whether ligaments and other structures are intact. Magnetic resonance imaging (MRI; a technology in which the patient's body is placed in a magnetic field), has been used experimentally to study muscles and other musculoskeletal soft tissues, but it is not commonly used in the clinical setting for the evaluation of muscle strain.

In some experimental settings, muscle enzymes and electromyograms (visual recording of electrical changes in a muscle) have been used to study muscle injury, but these are not in routine clinical use. Thus the diagnosis of acute muscle strain is based on the history and physical examination.

---

[8] *See also* ch. 6.

[2] Chronic Muscle Injury

Most chronic muscle problems fall under the domain of repetitive motion or cumulative trauma disorders.[9] The repetitive event is often actually the maintenance of a particular posture, which places excessive demands on the postural muscles. The neck, back and shoulder are most frequently involved.

[a] History

The patient history focuses on the postural demands of both work and recreational habits. Past injuries, particularly automobile accidents (e.g., whiplash), may play a role in the evolution of the current symptoms. Chronic muscle injuries are diagnosed by excluding other entities, such as bony or disc pathology in the spine.

The difficulty of the diagnostic process is compounded by the fact that referred pain is common in the neck and shoulder region, as well as the back and hip region. Pain from more centrally located structures (the back or neck) is frequently referred to the extremities (hip or shoulder). This means that before a diagnosis of muscle pain in the shoulder can be made, problems in the neck should be excluded.

[b] Physical Examination

The physical examination must include the entire region. First, of course, the doctor examines the shoulder, looking for such problems as tendinitis, rotator cuff disorders and impingements,[10] as well as disorders of other soft tissue structures.

Patients with shoulder complaints also require a full neck examination, including a neurologic exam to rule out spinal problems.

In the case of the lower back, spinal nerve root irritation and disc herniation must be excluded, and specific maneuvers such as the straight leg raising test are helpful in this regard.[11]

[c] Tests

The goal of testing is to exclude other diagnoses; tests that confirm muscle injury are not in frequent clinical use. Ordinarily, if the patient's history and physical examination strongly suggest muscle

---

[9] *See also* ch. 8.

[10] *See also* ch. 2.

[11] *See also* ch. 6.

injury, testing is not done. This is especially true in the low back, where testing often reveals abnormalities that may be unrelated to the complaint but that instigate a costly diagnostic and therapeutic course that does not necessarily benefit the patient.

[3]   Treatment

A muscle that is completely disrupted will heal spontaneously by scar formation or may require surgical treatment, depending on the individual muscle and the patient's work demands.

Muscle strains are managed through the application of heat and cold, rest for short periods and graduated exercise. Early mobilization is important in muscle injury, to prevent joint stiffness and other problems. Nonsteroidal anti-inflammatory drugs (such as aspirin) are also recommended, particularly in acute injuries.

Chronic injuries may require changes in work posture on a temporary or permanent basis, depending on the severity of symptoms. Ergonomic measures designed to prevent postural problems are also helpful in treatment.[12]

7.05   REGIONAL MUSCLE STRAINS

Acute muscle strains are common in the extremities and the back (although acute back pain is only presumed to represent a muscle strain in many cases).[13] Chronic posture related muscle pain is particularly common in the neck and shoulder, with workers frequently complaining of symptoms in both areas. For this reason, the neck and shoulder will be considered together.

7.06   NECK AND SHOULDER

In the neck and shoulder, there are two frequent types of strain: the acute muscle strain and the postural muscle strain.

[1]   Acute Muscle Strains

Acute muscle strains of the neck and shoulder may occur in a variety of occupational situations, most of which involve a sudden, forceful movement of the neck or arm. Strains resulting from a single injury

---

[12] *See* 7.10 *infra* and ch. 8.

[13] *See also* ch. 6.

may occur during falling, slipping, over-reaching or sudden neck movements.

Whiplash injuries frequently combine muscle strains of varying severity with ligamentous sprain. These occur in the workplace, particularly in motor vehicle accidents, but they may also result from violent impact with moving machinery or from falling objects striking the worker on the forehead or the lower back. Whiplash injuries are frequently more severe than is clinically apparent and may result in prolonged pain.

[2] Postural Muscle Strains

Muscle pains that are either persistent over prolonged periods or recurrent are very common in the neck and shoulder region. The list of workers who are at increased risk is extensive and includes firefighters, assembly line workers, welders, painters, keyboard operators, word and data processors, cash register operators, operators of cranes and heavy machinery, hospital workers, shovelers and all workers who work with the arm maintained in a position above the shoulder level.

These individuals experience a number of shoulder and neck symptoms involving many of the muscles of the neck, upper back and shoulder, as well as tendons and other soft tissues of the region. The symptoms are often referred to collectively by terms such as the occupational cervicobrachial syndrome (a condition marked by pain in the shoulder, extending down the arm and/or the back of the neck), myofascial syndrome (irritation of the muscles and fibrous tissue of the back of the neck), neck-shoulder problems and shoulder girdle pain. These terms merely label a vague symptom complex; they do not constitute a pathologic entity.

[a] Risk Factors

Occupations that require the arms to be held in a position above the shoulders place workers at a particularly high risk for shoulder and neck problems. This risk may be further increased if the worker is unaccustomed to this position or if the hand must wield a heavy tool in this position. The weight of the tool must be counterbalanced by the shoulder muscles. Affected workers include individuals on automobile assembly lines, welders and painters.

[b] Pathology

There is some disagreement about the nature of occupational muscle disorders affecting the neck and shoulder. Some reports indicate that the muscles eventually become inflamed and then undergo fibrosis (scarring) in long-standing cases (Luck and Andersson, 1990).

The muscles most frequently studied include the trapezius (which fans out from the scapula, or shoulder blade, to the spine), infraspinatus (located posteriorly at the shoulder) and the deltoid (the muscle that forms the contour of the upper arm at the shoulder).

[c] Diagnosis

Pain in the neck and shoulder may arise from any of the structures in the region, including the spine, spinal nerves, peripheral nerves, bones, joints, ligaments, muscles or tendons. Furthermore, pain located in the shoulder does not necessarily reflect pathology in the shoulder; it may be referred from the neck. A thorough physical examination of both the shoulder and the neck usually points the examiner in the right direction.

The symptoms of occupational neck and shoulder muscle problems may be mimicked by cervical disc disease, cervical spondylosis (an abnormality of the cervical spine), thoracic outlet syndrome (compression of specific nerves and muscles in the chest), tendinitis, arthritis and rotator cuff pathology (which also may be occupational). The history and physical examination help distinguish some of these. For example, the pain of tendinitis may be produced by pressing on or manipulating the tendons; x-rays are helpful in the evaluation of arthritis and bony abnormalities.

The biggest diagnostic dilemma may arise in distinguishing occupational neck and shoulder muscle pain from thoracic outlet syndrome.

The diagnosis of occupational neck and shoulder symptoms is based on the clinical examination and the exclusion of other diseases. A variety of tests (such as x-rays and blood tests) may be helpful to rule out other pathology, but only one is considered to have potential for supporting the diagnosis: the electromyogram. This records on a graph the electrical activity of the muscle as it works and rests. In moderate and severe cases of occupational cervicobrachial syndrome, affected muscles show rapid fatigability (Luck and Andersson, 1990).

7.07 UPPER EXTREMITY

Muscle ruptures involving the upper extremity are rare. There are reports in the literature of ruptures of the pectoralis major, deltoid, biceps, triceps and, more rarely, other muscles. The numbers of cases is very low, however. The mechanism may be direct trauma or excessive stretch, as in a sudden motion of the arm to break a fall.

Muscle strains in the arm are common in individuals whose work involves intricate and forceful arm and hand movements. This can be a frequent problem for assembly line workers.

7.08 BACK

Low back pain is extremely common in industry. Most cases are thought to represent muscle strain, but there is little definitive proof. After disc, joint and bony pathology have been excluded, most patients are thought to have muscle strain as a source of their symptoms.[14]

Back strain may be related to posture; the back muscles are vital to the maintenance of all seated and standing postures. It may also be due to sudden exertion, most commonly, lifting. The back muscles must counterbalance both the motion and the weight being lifted; otherwise the body would topple in the direction of the movement. The position of the spine, the bulk of the load and the distance of the load from the center of the body all influence the demands placed on the back muscles.

The occupations at risk for back strain are numerous. Heavy lifting is a component of many industrial occupations and also affects nurses and health care workers, materials handlers, construction workers, miners, carpenters, mechanics and those who lift heavy equipment, such as firefighters. Truck drivers also have a very high rate of back problems, which may be due to the acute strain of loading and unloading, the postural demands of sitting and the effects of chronic vibration (called cyclic loading).

---

[14] *See also* ch. 6.

7.09 LOWER EXTREMITY

Muscle strains of the lower extremity are extremely common in those occupations that place demands on the legs. Those affected include waiters, cashiers and nurses.[15]

Lower extremity strains can also include shin splints. This entity is defined as pain in the anterior leg (the shin) of musculotendinous origin. The pathology may be inflammation of the tibialis posterior muscle or a chronic low grade compartment syndrome (a condition in which increased pressure in a confined space adversely affects circulation). The differential diagnosis includes a stress fracture of the tibia (shinbone), which may be ruled out by bone scan, or x-ray in more long-standing cases.

The cause of shin splints is overuse of the leg muscles, most commonly in running, but the condition may also occur with excessive walking.

7.10 PREVENTION

There are two approaches to the prevention of occupational injuries: those that focus on the worker and those directed at the workplace and the equipment. The worker-oriented approach involves education and training and, to a lesser extent, worker screening. Education in proper lifting techniques has been used to reduce the rate of muscle strain. The effectiveness of education is variable, however, since the methods taught are not always used.

The design of the workplace and of the equipment may help increase or decrease the rate of strains due to posture. The work method may also be altered, as, for example, with the institution of frequent rest periods to allow the worker's muscles to more completely relax.

A number of modifications can be made to the workplace to reduce the stress on the back, neck and shoulders. For example, the height of tables (and other work surfaces) and chairs can be adjusted to incorporate ergonomic principles and reduce the load on the postural muscles. The slope of the work surface can also be changed.

Tools can be designed to minimize the amount of work required to operate them; this includes the angle and size of the handle, the

---

[15] *See also* ch. 4.

weight of the tool and the use of tool balancers or slings for heavy tools.

7.100   BIBLIOGRAPHY

Reference Bibliography

Edwards, R. H. T.: Hypotheses of Peripheral and Central Mechanisms Underlying Occupational Muscle Pain and Injury. Eur. J. Appl. Physiol. 57:275–281, Feb. 1988.

Grandjean, E.: Fitting the Man to the Task. A Textbook of Occupational Ergonomics. Philadelphia: Taylor & Francis, 1988.

Luck, J. V. and Andersson, G. B. J.: Occupational Shoulder Disorders. In: Rockwood, C. Λ. and Matsen, F. A.: The Shoulder. Philadelphia: Saunders, 1990.

Ursin, H., et al.: Psychological Factors and Self-Reports of Muscle Pain. Eur. J. Appl. Physiol. 57:282–290, Feb. 1988.

Waersted, M., et al.: Shoulder Muscle Tension Induced by Two VDU-Based Tasks of Different Complexity. Ergonomics 34:137–150, Feb. 1991.

Additional References

Ayoub, M. A.: Ergonomic Deficiencies: III. Root Causes and their Correction. J. Occup. Med. 32:455–460, May 1990.

Bullock, M. I. (Ed.): Ergonomics. The Physiotherapist in the Workplace. New York: Churchill Livingstone, 1990.

Caughey, M. A. and Welsh, P.: Muscle Ruptures Affecting the Shoulder Girdle. In: Rockwood, C. A. and Matsen, F. A.: The Shoulder. Philadelphia: Saunders, 1990.

Garrett, W. E.: Muscle Strain Injuries: Clinical and Basic Aspects. Med. Sci. Sports Exercise 22:436–443, Aug. 1990.

Herring, S. A.: Rehabilitation of Muscle Injuries. Med. Sci. Sports Exercise 22:453–456, Aug. 1990.

Hoppmann, R. A. and Patrone, N. A.: Musculoskeletal Problems in Instrumental Musicians. In: Sataloff, R., et al. (Eds.): Textbook of Performing Arts Medicine. New York: Raven Press, 1991.

Kibler, W. B.: Clinical Aspects of Muscle Injury. Med. Sci. Sports Exercise 22:450–452, Aug. 1990.

Waersted, M. and Westgaard, R. H.: Working Hours as a Risk Factor in the Development of Musculoskeletal Complaints. Ergonomics 34:265–276, Mar. 1991.

CHAPTER 8

Repetitive Motion Disorders

SCOPE

Repetitive motion disorders comprise a variety of pain syndromes that develop during repeated performance of narrowly defined tasks over a long period. Nearly continuous repetition of some specific tasks is demanded in the modern workplace, leading to an overload of the body's adaptive abilities. The accumulation of injuries can lead to a major disorder that may affect the neck, shoulder, wrist, hand or other parts of the body. Tissue damage occurs in muscles, tendons, nerves or blood vessels. Included are such assorted injuries as carpal tunnel syndrome, tendinitis and thoracic outlet syndrome. The mechanisms of injury are understood for some disorders but not for others, and controversy exists about the degree to which many of them may be work-related.

8.01   INTRODUCTION

Repetitive motion disorders are pain syndromes that seem to result from repeated performance of stereotypic movements over a long period. The term encompasses many types of occupational injuries, the common feature of which is origin in repeated use of an area of the body. Although each repetition may cause little injury, the accumulation of multiple stresses over time may lead to major damage. Other terms for repetitive motion disorders include cumulative trauma disorders (CTDs), repetitive strain or stress injuries (RSIs), overuse syndromes and overuse injuries.

The incidence and causes of repetitive motion disorders are matters of controversy, with some investigators doubting a causal link between repetitive activities and tissue damage (Hadler, 1993). Others assert that the entire tempo of the modern workplace is at odds with natural physiologic rhythms (Dobyns, 1991; Rodahl, 1989). Today's form of required work is often intense and rapid, creating both musculoskeletal and mental stress. Awareness of this has led to research into ergonomics, a discipline that attempts to improve the physical environment in order to minimize the damage from repetitive movement.

Some experts believe that there are limits to the effectiveness of preventive measures and that the incidence of repetitive motion disorders will continue to increase (Rodahl, 1989). Others assert that these syndromes are due at least in part to media attention and the availability of worker's compensation and other types of disability insurance (Hadler, 1993).

8.02   MECHANISMS OF INJURY

Repetitive motion disorders can affect several different types of tissue. The general mechanism is not well understood but is thought to involve a combination of mechanical (compression, stretching and tearing), ischemic (lack of blood supply) and inflammatory processes (Dobyns, 1991; Leadbetter, 1992; Lundborg and Dahlin, 1989). Irritation of a muscle, tendon, blood vessel or nerve may occur as it is moved over or compressed by other structures. Within certain limits (which are not well defined), tissues may adapt to this stress. However, overuse, which overwhelms the adaptive response (Dobyns, 1991), may generate microtears in the stressed tissue. Over time, this leads to inflammation and accumulation of nonfunctional scar tissue. Inflammation may not only lead to loss of the affected tissue but may also increase the extent of damage by creating pressure on other structures.

[1]   Muscles

Overuse of a muscle or muscle group can lead to fatigue, inflammation and fibrosis (abnormal growth of fibrous tissue). Fortunately the process usually does not proceed beyond tenderness and stiffness to structural damage. However, accumulation of small injuries can lead to replacement of muscle by noncontractile (unable to contract and relax) scar tissue.

[2]   Tendons

Each time a muscle contracts, the tendon attaching it to the bone moves. Repetitive movements or forceful jerks can lead to irritation or tiny tears in the tendon. The resultant inflammation is known as tendinitis.[1]

Continued overuse of an inflamed tendon can lead to scarring and permanent damage.

---

[1] *See also* 8.06 *infra.*

Tenosynovitis[2] is inflammation of the membranous sheath covering the tendon of a joint. This can result from overuse (or infection) and can occur in the fingers, wrist or shoulder.

[3] Bursae

A bursa is a small membranous sac in a joint that acts as a friction-limiting cushion between bone and muscle or tendon. Bursitis is a painful inflammation of this sac. It usually results from repetitive or excessive motion of the involved joint. Bursitis can occur in the elbow, shoulder, knee or hip.[3]

[4] Nerves

Repetitive motion may lead to nerve irritation or compression. Of particular concern in the workplace are tunnel syndromes (entrapment neuropathies), in which nerves are damaged as a result of friction, stretching and compression as they pass through narrow openings on their way from origin to destination (Lundborg and Dahlin, 1989). Injury may be transient, but recurrent or chronic compression can result in long-term or permanent damage.[4]

[5] Blood Vessels

Damage to blood vessels often accompanies injury to other structures. Frequently nerve entrapment syndromes have a vascular component. This can decrease a tissue's nutrient and oxygen supply and lead to swelling from capillary leakage.

8.03 EPIDEMIOLOGY

Overuse disorders have long been recognized as a cause of occupational disability, but both awareness and prevalence have increased dramatically. The incidence of reported repetitive motion disorders and insurance claims has escalated over the last decade. Since 1989, more than 50 percent of occupational disorders that occur in the United States fall into the broad category of overuse syndrome (Rempel, et al., 1992). The cost to employer and worker, in terms of lost time, disability and medical expense, has become a matter of great concern

---

[2] *See also* 8.06 [4] *infra.*

[3] *See also* 8.07 and 8.12 *infra.*

[4] *See also* 8.08 *infra.*

to society (Louis, 1990; Williams and Westmorland, 1994). Of particular concern is the high number of injuries reported by white-collar workers using computer terminals.

[1]   Controversial Aspects of Repetitive Motion Disorders

Concern about the rising incidence of occupational musculoskeletal disorders has resulted in many articles about their prevention and treatment. At the same time, the increased number of cases has raised the question of whether the disorder itself is an epidemic or a fad (Felsenthal, 1994; Gerr, et al., 1991). Some experts think that the incidence of the disorder may be increased by worker's compensation availability (Dawson, et al., 1990; Hadler, 1993).

Epidemics of shoulder and neck pain among office workers in Japan from 1960 to 1980 and in Australia in the early 1980s aroused much controversy (Byrne, 1992; Cohen, et al., 1992; Gerr, et al., 1991). Many have argued that these epidemics stemmed more from political and psychosocial factors than from increases in occupational stress (Hadler, 1993). Recent studies (Byrne, 1992; Cohen, et al., 1992) have re-examined the Australian experience of so-called refractory cervicobrachial pain (repetitive strain injury in the shoulder-neck area) and found objective changes to explain the symptoms. Others, however, have contested their conclusions.

[2]   Current Studies

The evaluation and prevention of repetitive motion disorders has been complicated by multiple and often inexact names and definitions, lack of controlled clinical studies and difficulty in achieving a precise diagnosis of frequently vague symptoms (Dobyns, 1991; Gerr, et al., 1991; Rempel, et al., 1992). Current systematic efforts to define the nature and causes of these disorders include clinical evaluations, animal studies and occupational surveillance (Dobyns, 1991; Gerr, et al., 1991; Hanrahan and Moll, 1989; Higgs, et al., 1992; Matte, et al., 1989).

[3]   Etiology of Repetitive Motion Disorders

The increase in the incidence of repetitive motion disorders has been attributed to such workplace changes as computerized monitoring of worker productivity; new machinery that requires repetitive, fast, forceful movements; and division of jobs into small tasks that must be repeated many times per hour (Guidotti, 1992; Louis, 1990;

Williams and Westmorland, 1994). Enhanced awareness, diagnosis and reporting also play a large role.

Most frequently the upper extremity is affected. Key risk factors are repetition, high force, awkward positions, vibration, mechanical stress, frequent or prolonged pressure, temperature extremes and insufficient rest (Dobyns, 1991; Gerr, et al., 1991; Matte, et al., 1989; Rempel, et al., 1992).

8.04 DIAGNOSIS OF REPETITIVE MOTION DISORDERS

Diagnosis of repetitive motion disorders can be difficult. Symptoms may be vague, with an onset that is apparently unrelated to a definable cause. Radiologic (x-ray) assessment is often useful only for exclusion of other conditions. Electrophysiologic (pertaining to the conduction of impulses by nerve and muscle) tests, though they are promising, require specialized techniques and experienced interpretation.

[1] History

Diagnosis is based on a thorough history and physical examination. Occupation, hobbies and hand dominance, as well as immediate pain precipitants, are important aspects (Gupta and Kleinert, 1993). Coexistence of diseases that may affect healing or cause neuropathies, such as diabetes mellitus, arthritis and cardiovascular and neurologic problems, should be noted.

[2] Clinical Signs and Symptoms

Posture and limb position, both at rest and when active; skin characteristics; and muscle tone all provide important information. A variety of tests are used to assess nerve involvement (Botte and Gelberman, 1989; Gupta and Kleinert, 1993). Among the most common are Phalen's test, in which joint flexion (bending inward) elicits symptoms of tingling or numbness; Tinel's sign, which localizes tingling by tapping along the suspected nerve; various tests of sensory (related to perception) discrimination; and tests of dexterity and strength. Functional muscle assessment helps distinguish between sensory and motor (related to innervation of muscles) involvement.

It is important to test for both circulatory and muscular damage as well as neurologic changes. Absence or weakening of pulses, pallor or blanching can indicate vascular involvement and a need for appropriate circulatory tests, such as Doppler ultrasound studies (a form of ultrasonography in which continuous waves of ultrasound are used to detect motion; often, they produce an image on a screen as well as an audible output). *(See Figure 8-1.)*

[3]   Electrodiagnostic Studies

Neurophysiologic studies can help localize lesion sites but do not substitute for clinical examination (Ditmars, 1993; Iyer, 1993; Lieberman and Taylor, 1989; Sanders and Smith, 1991). They include both direct measurements of nerve response to various forms of stimulation and indirect assessment by electromyography (EMG), which measures muscle response to nerve input (Sanders and Smith, 1991). The patterns are compared to normal patterns and sometimes to the patient's normal side if the opposite side is unaffected (Szabo and Madison, 1992). In some cases, the usefulness of these tests is limited to exclusion of other diagnoses.

[a]   Nerve Conduction Studies

Nerve conduction studies measure velocity (the distance an impulse travels per unit of time) or latency (the time required for an impulse to travel from the stimulating to the recording electrode).

[b]   Electromyography

Electromyography (EMG) tests muscle response to nerve stimulus. In needle electromyography, a needle electrode is inserted into the muscle of interest, and the activity is measured at insertion, at rest and during contraction. *(See Figure 8-2.)* This can detect abnormalities in motor innervation and muscle fibers.

[4]   Radiographic Findings

Sufficient contrast seldom exists between injured and normal muscle, tendon or nerve to make radiographic evaluation feasible. However, standard x-ray views can rule out fracture, dislocation, arthritis and other skeletal pathology. Computed tomography is useful mainly to rule out the presence of tumors, fractures and vascular pathology (Botte and Gelberman, 1989). Magnetic resonance imaging (MRI) is based on water content and thus shows promise for distinguishing inflamed from normal tissue (Pope, 1992).

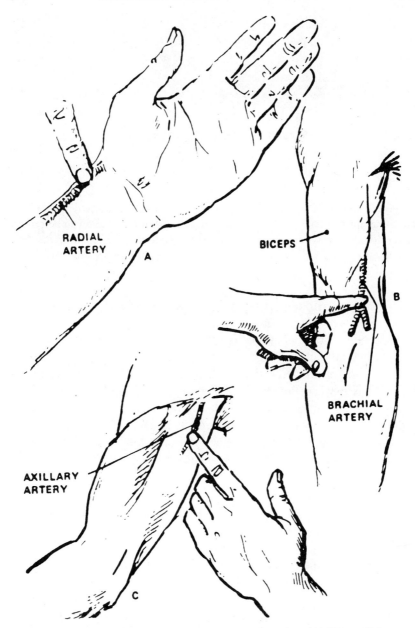

Fig. 8-1. Sites of arterial pulses in the upper extremity. (A) The radial artery is generally felt on the thumb side of the flexor surface of the wrist. (B) The brachial artery is felt in the groove between the biceps and triceps muscles on the medial surface of the upper arm. (C) The axillary artery can be felt in the armpit against the humerus.

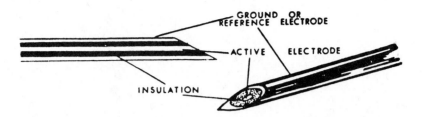

Fig. 8-2. In electromyography, a probe (an electrode or a needle) is inserted into the muscle, so the electrical potential of specific muscles can be relayed over connecting wires to a machine. The electrode is shielded or insulated at its tip, so localized recordings (limited hopefully to one muscle) can be picked up.

8.05 MUSCLE INJURIES IN THE UPPER EXTREMITY

Several theories of the pathogenesis of repetitive motion disorders emphasize muscular change (Dawson, et al., 1990). Sustained exertion can lead to generalized or localized muscle fatigue. Muscles exercised to exhaustion can degenerate, and muscular atrophy (wasting) can occur when nerve injury results in the cessation of innervation (Ditmars, 1993; Szabo and Madison, 1992). Disorders that are primarily muscular include tension neck syndrome (also known as occupational cervicobrachial disorder) and myofascial pain syndrome.

[1] Tension Neck Syndrome

The work-related shoulder and neck pain that occurred in epidemic-like outbreaks in Japan and Australia has been called occupational cervicobrachial disorder. This term refers to a pain syndrome localized around the scapula (shoulder blade), but it is not a well-defined entity. In some sources (Gerr, et al., 1991), the term comprises all work-related neck and shoulder disorders, including tension neck syndrome, cervical syndrome (pain due to degeneration of the cartilage pads between the vertebrae of the neck), tendinitis and thoracic outlet syndrome.[5] More commonly its use is restricted to neck torsion syndrome (also known as tension neck syndrome and tension myalgia).

---

[5] *See also* 8.08[1] [a] *infra.*

Tension neck syndrome involves painful spasms of the trapezius muscle, a large muscle attaching the upper limb girdle (the clavicle, or collarbone, and the scapula) to the skull and spine (Guidotti, 1992; Rempel, et al., 1992). This muscle is used in shrugging the shoulders and twisting the spine.

[a] Clinical Features

The primary symptom is a persistent aching, stiff neck, often with a headache (Guidotti, 1992). Pain may radiate down the arm or upper back. Range of motion is decreased, and neck movement is painful. Pain may persist at rest.

The differential diagnosis includes tendinitis, thoracic outlet syndrome, arthritis, cervical syndrome and spondylosis (stiffening of the vertebral column).

[b] Treatment

Treatment emphasizes work modification and exercise or physical therapy (Guidotti, 1992). Heat and massage may help.

[c] Prevalence and Work Association

The syndrome seems correlated with a forced working posture, repetitive movements and strain on the cervical (neck) spine. Workers at risk include automobile assemblers who work with their arms overhead, data entry personnel, switchboard operators, grocery checkers, bicycle couriers and those who carry a heavy load in one hand or on the shoulder (Williams and Westmorland, 1994).

Risk is increased by the previous occurrence of a neck or shoulder disorder or injury, or cervical disc disease. Other contributory factors are age, job satisfaction and posture (Rodahl, 1989).

Prevention involves the use of correctly designed chairs and desks, and instituting limitations on the weight of tools and materials that workers handle (Falkenburg and Schultz, 1993). Frequent work breaks also help. Maintaining good posture and performing strengthening exercises reduce the risk of this and other musculoskeletal disorders.

[2] Myofascial Pain Syndrome

Myofascial pain syndrome, sometimes considered a type of occupational cervicobrachial disorder, is characterized by pain that is localized in the neck, in the upper part of the trapezius muscle[6] and in

---

[6] See also 8.05[1] supra.

other muscles that are involved in head nodding and rotating. Pain is felt with pressure or twisting.

Causative actions include excessive reaching or twisting, carrying heavy loads and using the neck and shoulder to cradle a telephone (Gruskin, 1991). There seems to be an increased risk among secretaries whose switch from typewriters to computers leads them to stretch their heads forward to maintain the same eye distance to the computer screen that they had to the paper in the typewriter.

Prevention emphasizes good posture. Treatment involves work modification and exercise.

8.06   TENDON DISORDERS IN THE UPPER EXTREMITY

Two of the best-documented work-related disorders are tendinitis and tenosynovitis (Gerr, et al., 1991). Both are painful and disabling and play a role in nerve compression syndromes. Tendinitis—inflammation of the tendon (fibrous band connecting skeletal muscle to bone)—can affect any extremity, but in the workplace, it is most common in the wrist and fingers. Tenosynovitis is inflammation of the synovial sheath that encloses tendons running within fibro-osseous (having both connective tissue and bone) tunnels. The sheath's inner membrane secretes a viscous fluid that lubricates the joint, and this secretion increases during an inflammatory process.

Tendinitis, which is often accompanied or preceded by tenosynovitis, is common among people who perform repetitive work, especially when a tendon rubs against other structures as it passes through a fibro-osseous tunnel (Gupta and Kleinert, 1993). Occupational risk factors include repetitive tension and motion, bending and vibration. Risk increases with age, due to tendon stiffening (O'Brien, 1992).

Both the mechanism and the nomenclature of tendon injury are areas of active research, and disagreement exists about how repetitive stress damages a tendon (Leadbetter, 1992; Nirschl, 1992). Traditionally investigators have viewed tendinitis as an inflammatory process that occurs after mechanical microtrauma (Gellman, 1992; Thorson and Szabo, 1992). A newer view (Kibler, et al., 1992; Leadbetter, 1992; Nirschl, 1992) distinguishes tendinitis, defined as inflammation from injury, and tendinosis, defined as noninflammatory degeneration within the tendon due to vascular compromise, repetitive microtrauma or aging.

Tendinitis is diagnosed by tendon swelling found on physical examination, with localized pain on palpation or resisted movement. Common disorders are rotator cuff tendinitis, biceps tendinitis, lateral epicondylitis ("tennis elbow") and medial epicondylitis ("golfer's elbow") (Falkenburg and Schultz, 1993).

Tenosynovitis (also called tendovaginitis and tendosynovitis) is usually due to cumulative trauma, generally in the form of highly repetitive motions (Ditmars, 1993; Williams and Westmorland, 1994). It is frequently a coexisting condition or pathophysiologic cause in tunnel syndromes, in which the sheath's swelling compresses the nearby nerve.[7]

Stenosing tenosynovitis occurs when the inflamed sheath presses on the tendon. De Quervain's disorder, which affects the thumb, is considered a special case of this.

[1] Rotator Cuff Tendinitis

Rotator cuff tendinitis (supraspinatus tendinitis, subacromial pain syndrome) is a shoulder disorder characterized by inflammation of the supraspinatus tendon, which joins the supraspinatus muscle to the humerus (upper arm bone).

[a] Anatomy of the Shoulder and the Rotator Cuff

The shoulder joint is comprised of the scapula (shoulder blade) at the back, the clavicle (collarbone) in front and the humerus, whose rounded upper end fits into a socket (the glenoid cavity) of the scapula. *(See Figure 8-3.)* The joint is stabilized by the shoulder capsule, a large membranous sac that attaches to the scapula and to the neck (the narrow portion below the bone's rounded upper end) of the humerus. The rotator cuff, consisting of four tendons that fuse to form a cuff over the top of the shoulder joint, reinforces the capsule (Williams and Westmorland, 1994).

These tendons attach four muscles (the supraspinatus, infraspinatus, subscapularis and teres minor) to the head of the humerus. *(See Figure 8-4.)* These muscles stabilize the shoulder and rotate the humerus either medially (toward the axis of the body) or laterally (away from the axis of the body) and abduct (move away from the body) the arm. The supraspinatus tendon is cushioned by the subacromial bursa as

---

[7] *See also* 8.06[4] *infra.*

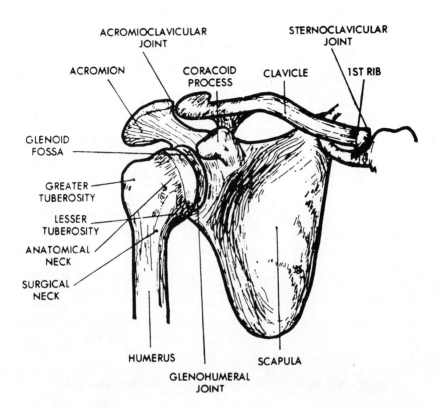

Fig. 8-3. The shoulder joint is comprised of the scapula (shoulder blade) at the back, the clavicle (collarbone) in front and the humerus, whose rounded upper end fits into a socket (the glenoid cavity) of the scapula.

it passes between the humerus and the acromion (a flattened projection of the scapula that overhangs the joint).

[b]   Mechanism of Injury

Rotator cuff tendinitis has several causes, which may be classed as extrinsic (due to mechanical impingement from outside the cuff) or intrinsic (due to changes within the cuff, such as aging or diminished vascular supply) (Fu, et al., 1991). In *primary mechanical impingement,* elevation of the arm leads to pressing of the supraspinatus tendon against the acromion. When this is repetitive or excessive (called shoulder impingement syndrome), the resulting irritation and ischemia (reduction in blood supply) lead to rotator cuff tendinitis (Fu, et al., 1991; Wolf, 1992).

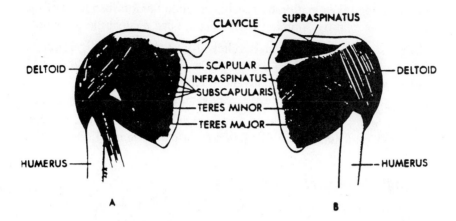

Fig. 8-4. The muscles of the shoulder: (A)anterior aspect, and (B) posterior aspect. The tendinous portions of the supraspinatus, infraspinatus, teres minor and subscapularis muscles form the rotator cuff.

Rotator cuff inflammation and weakness can result in *secondary impingement,* with the swollen tendon rubbing against the bony structures. Secondary impingement can also occur as a result of joint instability and a tendency for the shoulder to dislocate.

Most work related rotator cuff tendinitis appears to be caused by changes within the tendon from repetitive microtrauma (Fu, et al., 1991). In these instances, repetition prevents microtear healing, and as a result, inflammation, scarring and degeneration occur.

Inflammation of the subacromial bursa (bursitis) may accompany the tendinitis.

[c] Clinical Features and Diagnosis

The primary symptom of rotator cuff tendinitis is shoulder pain, sometimes radiating down the arm. Generally tendinitis pain is exacerbated by movement and relieved by rest, but it may occur at night also, especially if the cause is impingement. Movement may be limited by pain, stiffness or weakness.

A knowledge of the patient's history is important to establish the mechanism of injury and to determine whether it is work related. Pain with elevation of the arm from 70 to 100 degrees is a diagnostic sign

(Guidotti, 1992). Usually the affected tendon is swollen and painful on palpation (examination by touch). Forcible flexion (bending) of the arm causes pain by jamming the humerus head against the acromion.

Pain due to impingement is relieved by local anesthetic injection into the space below the acromion. Atrophy (wasting) of the rotator cuff muscles may occur in advanced cases.

Radiographic evaluation may include shoulder x-rays and magnetic resonance imaging. MRI can detect a range of conditions, but difficulties exist in distinguishing tendinitis from partial tears (Edelman and Warach, 1993; Pope, 1992).

[d]   Treatment and Prognosis

Treatment includes modification of the work setting and/or of worker behavior, rest, application of heat, physical therapy, range-of-motion exercises and nonsteroidal anti-inflammatory (NSAID) medication (Guidotti, 1992). Early diagnosis and treatment are key to the success of this therapy (Fu, et al., 1991). If conservative treatment fails or if tears are diagnosed, surgery may be necessary.

[e]   Prevalence and Work Association

Rotator cuff injuries are common among workers who perform repetitive tasks with their elbows above mid-torso height, particularly if their arms are raised overhead (Guidotti, 1992; Rempel, et al., 1992). Repetitive inward or outward shoulder rotation or arm abduction can irritate the tendons and cause inflammation (Falkenburg and Schultz, 1993). Use of heavy tools increases the load on shoulder muscles and strain on the tendons. Occupations involving risk include:

- overhead automobile assembly and repair;
- automobile body repair (particularly sanding, buffing and polishing);
- soldering, grinding, painting, welding, siding and awning installation, carpentry and other construction trades, punch press operation, meat packing, tree pruning, fruit picking, window washing, longshoring, grocery clerking and nursing (Guidotti, 1992; Williams and Westmorland, 1994).

[2]   Biceps Tendinitis

Biceps tendinitis may exist independently or with rotator cuff tendinitis (Guidotti, 1992; Wolf, 1992). The biceps, a large major flexor muscle of the upper arm, has two attachments at the shoulder: the short head and the long head. The bicipital tendon of the long head lies within a groove of the humerus and passes through the shoulder joint, under the acromion, before attaching to a projection of the scapula. Repetitive muscle tension can result in inflammation of the tendon, particularly in the groove. Biceps tendinitis occurs among workers who reach over their heads.[8] It is characterized by pain upon shoulder movement.

Treatment is similar to that for rotator cuff tendinitis, with the possible addition of corticosteroid injections (Wolf, 1992).

[3] Epicondylitis

Lateral and medial epicondylitis (tennis elbow and golfer's elbow, respectively) are pain syndromes involving the tendons that attach the forearm muscles to the distal (away from the center of the body) humerus (upper arm bone).

[a] Anatomy of the Elbow

The elbow is a hinge joint between the humerus and the radius and ulna (forearm bones). *(See Figure 8-5.)* The radius and ulna articulate (form a joint) in the proximal (nearer the central axis of the body) radioulnar joint, where the three bony surfaces move against one another in forearm rotation and bending.

The humerus has two projections where it widens just above the elbow: the lateral epicondyle on the outside and the medial epicondyle on the inside, toward the body. The tendons of the extensor-supinator muscles of the forearm (which straighten the wrist and fingers and rotate the forearm palm forward) attach to the lateral epicondyle. The tendons of the flexor-pronator group (which bend the wrist and rotate the forearm palm backward) attach to the medial epicondyle.

[b] Mechanism of Injury

Repetitive forearm rotation and wrist extension can irritate the tendons, leading to microtears and inflammation. In the limited elbow space, swollen tendons can cut off their own blood supply, leading to nutrient deprivation. Repetitive trauma often does not permit normal healing to take place, and a degenerative process occurs that leads to gray, swollen tissue (Gellman, 1992; Thorson and Szabo, 1992).

---

8 *See also* 8.02[2] *supra..*

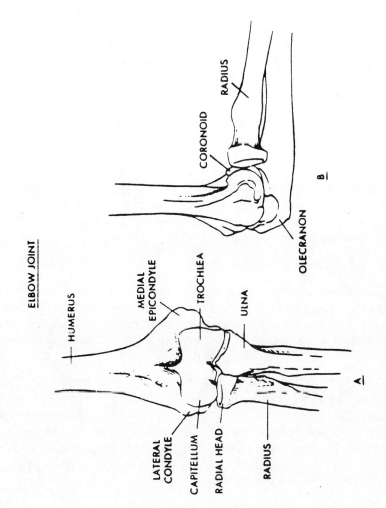

Fig. 8-5. (A) anterior and (B) lateral views of the right elbow joint.

[c]   Clinical Features and Diagnosis

The early symptom of epicondylitis is pain, especially after use. Usually pain is localized to the affected side of the elbow. There may be functional weakness.

In *lateral epicondylitis,* the patient feels pain along the outer aspect of the elbow, often radiating down the forearm. The pain is worsened by elbow or wrist extension, as in throwing. A diagnostic sign is pain when wrist extension is attempted against resistance while the forearm is pronated (Guidotti, 1992; Rempel, et al., 1992).

Pain occurs on the inner aspect of the elbow and forearm in *medial epicondylitis.* A diagnostic sign is pain when the wrist is flexed against resistance while it is supinated (palm rotated toward front, little finger toward the body) (Nirschl, 1992).

X-rays may show calcification and help rule out other problems (Nirschl, 1992). Magnetic resonance imaging is less useful in the elbow than in the shoulder, because of the smaller size of the tendons (Pope, 1992).

The differential diagnosis includes radial tunnel syndrome (dull tenderness, compared to the sharp pain of epicondylitis), posterior interosseous nerve entrapment[9] and thoracic outlet syndrome for lateral epicondylitis, and cubital tunnel syndrome[10] for medial epicondylitis.

[d]   Treatment and Prognosis

Conservative management comprises work modification, rest, non-steroidal anti-inflammatory medication, physical therapy and electrical stimulation. Failure to respond within a year may necessitate surgery (Gellman, 1992; Nirschl, 1992).

[e]   Prevalence and Work Association

Lateral epicondylitis, the most common occupational disorder of the elbow, is caused by repetitive or forceful wrist extension or forearm rotation. Workers at risk include welders, carpenters, bricklayers, grinders, polishers, small parts assemblers, meat packers and musicians (Guidotti, 1992; Williams and Westmorland, 1994).

---

[9] *See also* 8.08 [2] *infra.*

[10] *See also* 8.08[4] [a] *infra.*

Medial epicondylitis is much less common than tennis elbow. It is caused by repeated forearm rotation into the palm-down posture while bending the wrist (Johnson, 1993b). Workers at risk include telephone line workers and construction workers.

[4]   De Quervain's Tenosynovitis

De Quervain's tenosynovitis, the most common disorder with tendon sheath swelling, occurs in the abductor (moving away from the midline) and extensor tendons of the thumb. These tendons share a common sheath, and swelling can affect both. Impingement on the tendon by the swollen sheath and the production of excess synovial fluid can lead to loss of tendon function (Johnson, 1993b).

Symptoms include swelling, pain and tenderness at the base of the thumb. Pain is aggravated by attempts to extend the thumb. Flexion and adduction (movements bringing a limb or part close to the body) may produce a "trigger" effect or popping sensation. The differential diagnosis includes osteoarthritis, infection and systemic disease.

Treatment includes activity change, sometimes with splinting, heat/cold therapy and exercise. Severe continuing symptoms may require surgical decompression. Tool modification may also help.

De Quervain's tenosynovitis, which is commonly recognized as an occupational disorder, may be precipitated by forceful grasping and turning, particularly of hard objects such as pliers. Workers at risk include machinists, barbers, buffers, grinders, polishers, sanders, sawyers, ironers, carpenters, butchers and surgeons (Guidotti, 1992; Williams and Westmorland, 1994).

8.07   BURSITIS

Bursitis—inflammation of a bursa—is relatively uncommon. The type of bursitis most likely to be involved as a workplace disorder is that of the olecranon bursa at the tip of the elbow, which may become inflamed through leaning on the elbow or direct trauma.

Bursitis may be painful or asymptomatic (having no symptoms). Diagnosis is based on symptoms and aspiration of fluid (removal through a needle) to rule out such common causes as gout (a metabolic disease in which salts of uric acid deposit in the joints) or infection (Hadler, 1993).

Workers at risk are those who lean on their elbows, such as students, jewelers, carpenters and plumbers.

Treatment consists of avoiding compression of the bursa, possibly through the use of a cushion, and nonsteroidal anti-inflammatory or corticosteroid medication.

8.08   NERVE COMPRESSION SYNDROMES IN THE UPPER EXTREMITY

Whether nerve processes are within a tunnel or stretched over a bony protrusion en route from source to target, they are subject to compressive injury. Mild to moderate compression may result in reversible mild injury, in which the integrity of the axon (efferent, or outgoing, nerve process) is maintained, but conduction of the nerve impulse is blocked. This impairment of conduction may result from transient ischemia (decreased blood supply) or from localized damage to an axon or its myelin sheath (layered membrane wound around the outside of an axon, providing electrical insulation) (Schaumburg, et al., 1992). In the latter instance, recovery requires remyelination, a process that takes place over a period of several weeks.

Repeated compression, friction or stretching can result in permanent impairment. Chronic nerve entrapment can involve compression in a tunnel, where the space may be so narrow that any swelling leads to dangerous pressure on the nerve. It can also result from external forces or from angled stretching over joints or under ligaments (Schaumburg, et al., 1992).

The initial symptoms of a tunnel syndrome are usually sensory, because the sensory fibers are more sensitive to pressure than are motor fibers. If sensory fibers are compressed, pain may be sharp and burning and accompanied by a loss of some types of feeling. Pain from nerve compression is increased by motion but may be present continually, including during sleep. If motor nerves are compressed, pain is more likely to be deep and localized to a muscle or joint. Muscular weakness and atrophy can result from motor nerve involvement.

Treatment for nerve compression due to repetitive stress usually begins with a change of activity pattern and splinting or placing the limb in a sling, sometimes with ultrasound, heat and massage.

Nonsteroidal anti-inflammatory agents (these include aspirin and ibuprofen) are tried before resorting to corticosteroid injections.

Therapy that does not modify the causes of the problem may provide only temporary relief. A delay in diagnosis and treatment can result in progressive worsening and an increasing likelihood that damage will be permanent.

When conservative treatment fails, surgery may be used to remove the cause of compression. This is referred to as peripheral nerve decompression. A literature survey (Sanders and Shogan, 1991) of the results of surgical decompression at the wrist, elbow and cervical spine indicate that outcomes vary from failure to excellent, with best results occurring in patients with mild sensory (not motor) symptoms for less than a year.

Factors not related to activity per se that may predispose a person to development of an entrapment syndrome include vascular (blood vessel) problems, infection, tumors, arthritis, injury or edema (swelling due to accumulation of fluid) from hormonal changes of pregnancy, birth control pills, menstruation or menopause. Sometimes a space that is smaller than normal due to an anatomic anomaly may increase the risk that any pressure will lead to damage.

Nerve entrapment can occur at any point along the nerve where the surrounding anatomy makes compression possible. Upper extremity sites include the nerves of the neck or shoulders, the radial nerve, the median nerve and the ulnar nerve.

[1]   Nerve Compression in the Neck

Neck and shoulder symptoms are common in the workplace. These range from simple fatigue to paresthesia (abnormal sensations) and disabling pain. Areas affected include the brachial plexus (in thoracic outlet syndrome), cervical (neck) spinal cord roots, the suprascapular nerve and the long thoracic nerve.

[a]   Thoracic Outlet Syndrome

Thoracic outlet syndrome (cervicobrachial neurovascular, brachiocephalic or cervicothoracic syndrome) consists of upper extremity symptoms resulting from pressure on nerves or blood vessels between the base of the neck and the axilla (armpit). (See Figure 8-6.) The syndrome may involve any of several structures in the thoracic region, and symptoms make it difficult to distinguish the specific area.

This has resulted in controversy about diagnosis and treatment (Hadler, 1993; Sanders, 1991a; Toby and Koman, 1989).

Structures that are subject to compression are usually the nerves of the brachial plexus (the braid of nerve fibers formed by the anterior

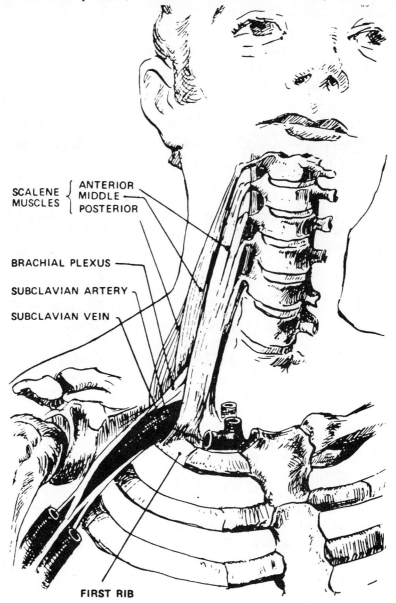

SCALENE
MUSCLES { ANTERIOR
MIDDLE
POSTERIOR

BRACHIAL PLEXUS

SUBCLAVIAN ARTERY

SUBCLAVIAN VEIN

FIRST RIB

Fig. 8-6. The major muscles, blood vessels and nerves of the thoracic outlet.

branches of cervical nerves C5-C8 and thoracic nerve T1; it begins in the base of the neck and extends into the axilla, where it divides into the major nerves of the arm). Less commonly (in fewer than 10 percent of cases), the subclavian artery or vein (major vessels to and from the arm) is compressed.

Normally the nerves of the plexus touch the scalene muscles of the neck while passing into the arm. Arm elevation can force the nerves against these muscles, resulting in irritation, particularly if the muscles are tight or inflamed. Bony features, such as an abnormal cervical rib, against which a nerve root may press can also predispose to thoracic outlet syndrome (Sanders, 1991b; Schaumburg, et al., 1992).

Symptoms include neck pain, arm weakness and numbness extending along the inner forearm into the medial two fingers (Karas, 1990), sometimes with headache (Sanders, 1991c). Symptoms may be precipitated or aggravated by postural changes, especially arm elevation. Vascular symptoms are aching or throbbing in the arms, coldness and periodic blanching of fingers.

Diagnosis is difficult because many physical signs are nonspecific (Toby and Koman, 1989). Tests based on neck or shoulder maneuvers are unreliable (Karas, 1990). Nerve conduction studies may show an absence of sensory impulses or lessened motor potentials (Sanders, 1991; Schaumburg, et al., 1992). The differential diagnosis involves ruling out cervical spondylosis, cervical disc disease, carpal tunnel syndrome, ulnar nerve entrapment and other brachial plexus disorders. Though it is relatively uncommon, vascular involvement should be ruled out by such tests as Doppler ultrasonography.

Any repetitive or prolonged arm extension above the head may cause thoracic outlet syndrome (Pecina, et al., 1991; Toby and Koman, 1989). A heavy load on the shoulders can exert downward pressure on the plexus, compressing it against the first rib. Persons at risk include assembly-line workers, auto mechanics, painters, plasterers, welders, slaughterhouse workers and others who work with their arms above their heads, particularly while holding heavy equipment or using vibrating tools (Sanders, 1991c). Workers who turn or flex the neck repetitively, such as computer operators and grocery checkout clerks, are also at risk. Hyperextension of the neck (extension beyond normal limits, for example, "whiplash" injury) in a previous accident may predispose a person to later thoracic outlet syndrome (Sanders, 1991c).

Conservative management is almost uniformly recommended for patients whose symptoms are neurologic (Voelkel, 1991). Emphasis is placed on exercises to improve posture, strengthen shoulder muscles and increase the neck's range of motion, and modification of activities to avoid elevation of the arms above the head.

Passive strengthening using electrical stimulation may also be beneficial. Nonsteroidal anti-inflammatory drugs, ultrasound, immobilization and corticosteroid injections may be used. Severe, persistent symptoms may require surgical decompression by removal of the muscular or bony structure that is causing the compression. Potential neurologic complications (Toby and Koman, 1989) and uncertainty of success (Sanders and Shogan, 1991) make this approach controversial.

[b]   Hyperabduction Syndrome

Sometimes classed as a cause or variant of thoracic outlet syndrome, hyperabduction syndrome involves compression of the neurovascular bundle of the axilla under the tendon of the pectoralis muscle and/or between the clavicle (collarbone) and first rib. Symptoms are paresthesias and pain in the fingers. This syndrome generally occurs with repetitive or continual stretching of the arms above the head, often with flexed elbows. The position is often used by bricklayers, masons, electricians and house painters (Pecina, et al., 1991).

Avoidance of hyperabduction is the best therapy.

[c]   Scapulocostal Syndrome

Pain and paresthesia in the shoulder, radiating into the neck and thorax, may be due to scapulocostal syndrome, in which, it is thought, nerves from the cervical roots are irritated. Poor posture, with the scapula at a contorted angle relative to the chest wall, may produce pain or dysfunction.

Such a posture may be found among truck drivers, surgeons and stenographers. The pain is not aggravated by shoulder or arm motion, and there is no objective sensory deficit or motor paralysis.

[d]   Suprascapular Nerve Syndrome

The suprascapular nerve arises from cervical nerve roots and passes within the scapular notch (on the scapula's superior surface) to innervate two of the muscles joining the scapula to the humerus. When the scapula moves, it is pulled against the notch by sudden, strong movements.

Individuals who work with their arms above their heads, such as electricians or house painters, may subject this nerve to chronic irritation from repeated stretching. Persons who carry heavy loads with a strap over the shoulder, such as mail carriers, cargo loaders and furniture movers, are also at risk.

Resultant shoulder pain can vary from sharp to blunt and may radiate down the arm (Pecina, et al., 1991). Even simple activities such as hair brushing can aggravate pain.

Treatment involves activity modification, followed by corticosteroid injection if needed. Surgical release of the transverse scapular ligament may be necessary if these fail.

[e] Long Thoracic Nerve Pathology

The long thoracic nerve originates from the lower cervical spinal branches and innervates the muscle that holds the scapula (shoulder blade) in place and helps move the arm outward and upward. It may be compressed by carrying heavy loads on the upper back (Narakas, 1989). Thus dock workers and furniture movers are at risk; it has also been diagnosed in miners, railway workers, tree cutters and smiths, who use heavy tools.

Symptoms include shoulder pain radiating to the axilla and arm. A winged appearance of the affected scapula when the arm is stretched in front of the body is diagnostic (Akesson, et al., 1990; Narakas, 1989). Recovery requires cessation of the cause of compression.

[2] Radial Nerve Compression

The radial nerve, which supplies most of the forearm muscles, is an extension of the posterior cord of the brachial plexus. (See Figure 8-7.) After crossing the axilla (armpit), it sends branches to the triceps muscle (which extends the elbow) and winds around the humerus (upper arm bone) in a spiral groove; here it is vulnerable to compression against the bone.

Branches of the radial nerve innervate the brachioradialis muscle, which forms the lateral border of the cubital fossa (anterior depression of elbow) and flexes the elbow. At the cubital fossa, the radial nerve divides into two branches: the superficial radial sensory nerve and the

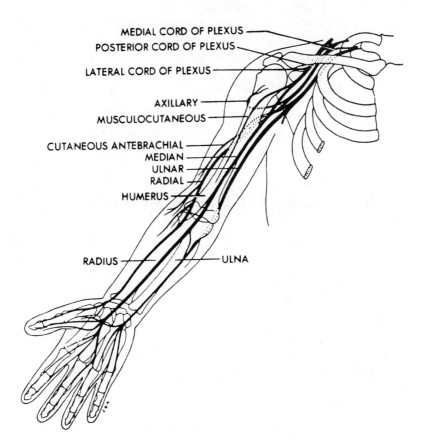

MEDIAL CORD OF PLEXUS
POSTERIOR CORD OF PLEXUS
LATERAL CORD OF PLEXUS
AXILLARY
MUSCULOCUTANEOUS
CUTANEOUS ANTEBRACHIAL
MEDIAN
ULNAR
RADIAL
HUMERUS
RADIUS   ULNA

Fig. 8-7. The radial nerve supplies most of the forearm muscles.

deep posterior interosseous nerve. The sensory nerve supplies the skin of the back of the hand and the last three fingers. The posterior interosseous supplies the forearm muscles, including the supinator muscle, which it enters through a space called the radial tunnel. (Supination is the rotation of the bones of the forearm to turn the palm upward/forward.) In the hand, it supplies the extensor muscles of the wrist and fingers.

Diagnosis of radial nerve injury may be complicated by the fact that most movements attributable to radial nerve innervation may be made by muscles that are innervated by other nerves (Schaumburg, et al., 1992). Injury may occur at any level from axilla (armpit) to wrist. Injury in the axilla results in interruption of the nerve supply to the triceps and consequent impairment of elbow extension, but most injuries occur below the axilla.

[a]   Wrist Drop Syndrome

Radial nerve damage in the upper arm usually results from compression against the humerus and leads to weakness or paralysis of the forearm extensor muscles, which extend, or raise, the back of the hand. When this occurs, the wrist drops and cannot be raised, and the thumb is flexed and cannot be moved outward. Finger movements and grip are relatively ineffective, because the wrist cannot be held in a functional position.

This syndrome may be caused by falling asleep with the upper arm draped over a chair edge or with another person's head resting against the inner surface of the upper arm. Occupations that require lifting heavy objects put their workers at risk for development of wrist drop (Posner, 1990).

Recovery sometimes occurs within a few weeks with no treatment. Usually it is aided by the use of a wrist splint to maintain wrist extension, together with specific strengthening exercises.

[b]   Radial Tunnel Syndrome

Radial tunnel syndrome (supinator syndrome) involves the posterior interosseous nerve as it passes through the radial tunnel in the supinator muscle (which wraps around the upper third of the radius) (Dawson, et al., 1990; Pecina, et al., 1991; Posner, 1990). Compression may occur at the edge or within the supinator muscle, or at the edge of a nearby muscle.

The most frequent symptom is dull, aching pain on the outside of the elbow or in the proximal (toward the body) lateral forearm, which is exacerbated by forearm pronation (rotation so that the radius "crosses" the ulna, the palm turning toward the back). Only in advanced cases is there muscular weakness (of wrist or fingers). Although compression of the posterior interosseous nerve at the elbow can have symptoms similar to tennis elbow, with which it can coexist, most authors recognize it as a separate clinical entity (Peimer and Wheeler, 1989).

Diagnosis depends on tenderness over the radial tunnel and pain on forearm supination against resistance (Dawson, et al., 1990; Posner, 1990). Electrodiagnosis may be useful.[11]

Conservative management includes avoidance of repetitive forearm motion, rest, splinting, anti-inflammatory medication and steroid injection. If these are unsuccessful, surgical decompression by release of the medial edge of the supinator may be required. The average surgical success rate in terms of relief of pain is 85 percent (Peimer and Wheeler, 1989).

Intermittent compression against the supinator edge during repeated forearm rotation with wrist flexion (as may occur when inserting a screw) may cause nerve compression and irritation. Workers at risk are carpenters, small-parts assemblers, conductors and violinists (Peimer and Wheeler, 1989).

[c] Superficial Radial Nerve Compression Syndrome

Entrapment of the sensory branch of the radial nerve (Wartenberg's syndrome) may be overlooked or misdiagnosed (Szabo, 1989). The superficial radial nerve descends near the surface of the lateral forearm. After crossing into the wrist, it divides into radial and ulnar branches, which innervate the dorsal (back) surfaces of the fingers.

The superficial (near the surface) location of this nerve makes it vulnerable to external compression. Above the wrist, it runs between tendons of the wrist flexor and extensor muscles and is subject to pressure from them when the forearm is pronated. Scar tissue from repetitive movement can entrap the nerve at the wrist so it cannot slide as the tendons change position. This leads to chronic irritation, edema (swelling) and fibrosis (formation of scar tissue).

Symptoms include numbness, tingling and pain over the dorsal radial aspect of the hand. They are exacerbated—and often brought on—by wrist motion or gripping with the thumb and index finger. Tapping along the course of the nerve elicits paresthesia (abnormal sensations, such as tingling). Conditions that may be confused with this syndrome are de Quervain's disease[12] and lateral antebrachial cutaneous nerve injury.[13]

---

[11] *See also* 8.04 [3] *supra.*

[12] *See also* 8.06 [4] *supra.*

[13] *See also* 8.08[5] *infra.*

Occupations at risk include those requiring repetitive forearm motions, such as using a screwdriver, writing or typing (Szabo, 1989).

If conservative management fails, surgical release of the nerve from the fascia (thin, tough layer of tissue) in the forearm has a high success rate.

[3]   Median Nerve Entrapment

Damage to the median nerve, as in carpal tunnel syndrome,[14] is common and is the most severely disabling of single nerve lesions (Schaumburg, et al., 1992).

The median nerve is vital to hand function, because it enables both precision and power grip. Precision grip depends on movements of the fingers against the thumb, and power movements are stabilized by the thumb. The median nerve supplies motor innervation to the thumb, enabling it to move outward (abduct), to flex and to oppose the other fingers. Thus damage can lead to loss of the use of the thumb. The median nerve also conducts sensory information from the palm and the palmar surfaces of the thumb, second and third fingers and part of the fourth. This provides the fine sensory input required for precision and speed in delicate movements.

The medial and lateral cords of the brachial plexus give rise to the roots of the median nerve, which innervates almost all the muscles of the anterior forearm as well as flexors of the wrist and fingers. The median nerve is in a superficial position just above the elbow, then may pass beneath a fibrous arch or a ligament as it enters the cubital fossa of the elbow. In the forearm, it divides into a deep motor branch, the anterior interosseous nerve (which supplies the flexors of the forearm), and a more superficial main branch. At the wrist, it lies among several tendons as it enters the carpal tunnel.

The median nerve is subject to compression at several sites. Its entrapment in the carpal tunnel at the wrist—a condition known as carpal tunnel syndrome—is the most common peripheral compression neuropathy (Szabo and Madison, 1992). Other sites include the elbow (pronator syndrome, anterior interosseous syndrome, supracondylar ligament entrapment) and the hand. Its superficial position above the elbow makes it vulnerable to external injury there.

---

14 *See also* 8.09 *infra.*

[a] Pronator Syndrome

The median nerve can be compressed at the elbow between the two heads of the pronator muscle (which turns the hand palm-down). Often this results from forearm muscle hypertrophy (enlargement) caused by repeated forearm rotation (Rosenbaum and Ochoa, 1993).

Symptoms are diffuse forearm aching and hand paresthesias (abnormal sensation), aggravated by activity and alleviated by rest (Johnson and Spinner, 1989). Forearm or thumb weakness may be present. Wrist and finger flexors are often affected.

Diagnostic signs include pain on forced wrist supination (rotation of the hand palm-forward) or extension, or on forced middle finger flexion (Schaumburg, et al., 1992). Sensory disturbances in the palm differentiate this from carpal tunnel syndrome.

Management involves avoidance of elbow flexion and pronation, limited forearm immobilization and prescription of nonsteroidal anti-inflammatory medication or corticosteroid injection.

Work requiring repetitive pronation and supination, such as carpentry, can lead to this syndrome. Occupations at risk include soldering, buffing, polishing, sanding, grinding, hammering, playing stringed instruments and switchboard operation (Dawson, et al., 1990; Dobyns, 1991; Williams and Westmorland, 1994).

[b] Anterior Interosseous Syndrome

The anterior interosseous nerve, which supplies the flexor (bending) muscles of the thumb and first two fingers, may be compressed by fibrous bands within the forearm muscles. This results in forearm pain with no sensory loss and weakness of the muscles responsible for flexion of distal (farther from the point of origin or trunk of the body) finger segments. Thumb abduction may be impaired; in advanced cases, the loss of pinching ability leads to problems with writing (Pecina, et al., 1991).

Compression may be found among workers who repeatedly flex and pronate their arms, such as assembly-line workers, carpenters, leather cutters, mechanics and butchers (Dawson, et al., 1990).

The results of conservative treatment are generally good if the cause of compression is removed.

[c] Median Nerve Injury in the Hand

The final sensory branches of the median nerve can be compressed in the hand, causing finger pain, sensitivity to cold and localized tenderness (Dawson, et al., 1990; Pecina, et al., 1991). Occupational activities at risk include using using scissors, staple guns or tools that press into the palm (sanders and screwdrivers), and carrying heavy objects with straps that cut into the palm or fingers (Dawson, et al., 1990).

[4] Ulnar Nerve Compression

The ulnar nerve supplies the flexor muscles of the forearm, muscles of the medial (toward the body's midline; here, the ring and little) fingers, and the skin of the medial fingers, palm and dorsum. It arises from the medial cord of the brachial plexus and winds around a groove in the posterior aspect of the medial epicondyle (projection of the lower end of the humerus) before entering the forearm. It lies deep until a few centimeters above the wrist. As it crosses into the hand, it is covered by fascia (sheet of fibrous tissue) that forms Guyon's canal with bones of the wrist (the hamate and the pisiform) on either side.

Entrapment of the ulnar nerve is the second most common entrapment disorder in the arm. It may be compressed in the axilla, elbow, cubital tunnel or Guyon's canal. Ulnar lesions lead to grip weakness, loss of the sense of hand position and impairment of precision of finger movements. The thumb is not affected as profoundly as by median nerve lesions (Schaumburg, et al., 1992).

[a] Cubital Tunnel Syndrome

The cubital tunnel by which the ulnar nerve enters the forearm is formed by the elbow's medial epicondyle, the heads of three forearm flexor muscles and associated ligaments and tendons. Elbow flexion or forearm rotation narrows the opening and may compress the nerve (Dawson, et al., 1990; Pecina, et al., 1991).

Early sensory symptoms, thought to be due to ischemia (Omer, 1989), include paresthesias and numbness or pain on the medial side of the upper forearm and in the fourth and fifth fingers. Pressure in the tunnel at night may cause nocturnal paresthesias. Symptoms may be precipitated by prolonged elbow flexion.

Continued compression results in thinning of myelin (the sheath covering some nerves), intraneural fibrosis (formation of abnormal fibrous tissue) and blood flow alterations. As nerve function is lost, muscles atrophy (waste), and dexterity for handling objects is lost.

The differential diagnosis includes cervical radiculopathy, in which pain tends to center in the neck and shoulder, and thoracic outlet syndrome.[15] Electrodiagnostic studies show slowed conduction across the elbow. The distribution of symptoms differs from that in carpal tunnel syndrome.

Treatment in patients with mild symptoms involves avoiding repeated elbow flexion and extension and other aggravating motions. The elbow may be splinted at night. Progression of sensory symptoms or motor involvement requires surgical intervention, frequently involving movement of the ulnar nerve away from the elbow into the muscle mass. The earlier the intervention, the better the recovery. The presence of symptoms for more than a year greatly diminishes the potential for full recovery.

Repetitive work involving the elbow may lead to cubital tunnel syndrome. Occupations at risk include carpentry (hammering), glass cutting, switchboard operation, sewing and playing stringed instruments, (Dawson, 1993; Rempel, et al., 1992). External compression from constant leaning on the elbow may occur in jewelers and students.

[b]   Compression in Guyon's Canal

The ulnar nerve may be compressed as it passes into the hand at Guyon's canal. Symptoms include sensory loss in the medial two fingers and/or muscle weakness (Dawson, et al., 1990). It is differentiated from entrapment at the elbow by the absence of forearm muscle weakness and by selective involvement of the little finger. Sensory symptoms are treated conservatively; motor symptoms or advanced sensory dysfunctions are treated surgically (Botte and Gelberman, 1989).

Compression may result from chronic repeated palmar trauma, as may occur in heavy manual labor or cycling. Other occupations at risk include carpentry, mechanics, bricklaying and playing musical instruments (Williams and Westmorland, 1994).

---

[15] *See also* 8.08[1] [a] *supra.*

[5] Musculocutaneous Nerve Compression

The musculocutaneous nerve arises from the lateral cord of the brachial plexus and supplies the biceps and brachialis muscles of the upper arm; its sensory branch, the lateral antebrachial cutaneous nerve, supplies the skin of the lateral forearm. Damage to the musculocutaneous nerve is rare, but compression of the lateral antebrachial cutaneous nerve can occur at the elbow, where only sensory fibers remain (Nunley and Howson, 1989).

Injury results in weakened elbow flexion and impaired sensation along the radial forearm. Symptoms are pain on motion, with burning or numbness in the radial forearm.

Supporting heavy objects at the elbow crease can compress this nerve. Acute compression can also result from repetitive, forceful exercise of the elbow in an extended position with the forearm twisted, as in carpentry (Pecina, et al., 1991).

If conservative management fails, surgical decompression by excision of a wedge of the biceps tendon resolves the problem.

8.09 CARPAL TUNNEL SYNDROME

Carpal tunnel syndrome is the most common nerve entrapment disorder (Dawson, et al., 1990). Symptoms result from compression of the median nerve as it passes through the wrist within the carpal tunnel, a narrow, confined space formed by the eight carpal bones and the transverse carpal ligament (a wide, thick fibrous band). *(See Figure 8-8.)* Within this limited space, swelling of any of the components can increase pressure in the tunnel. Because the median nerve provides both sensory (feeling) and motor (muscular movement) innervation to the thumb and middle three fingers, damage can result in pain and disability.

Although it has been extensively studied, carpal tunnel syndrome still remains a subject of controversy in terms of etiology, relation to work, diagnosis and treatment (Dawson, 1993; Hadler, 1993; Rempel, et al., 1992). However, its association with cumulative occupational trauma is becoming more generally accepted (Dawson, et al., 1990; Gerr, et al., 1991; Rosenbaum and Ochoa, 1993). The syndrome has been receiving increasing attention as it afflicts more and more management-level workers.

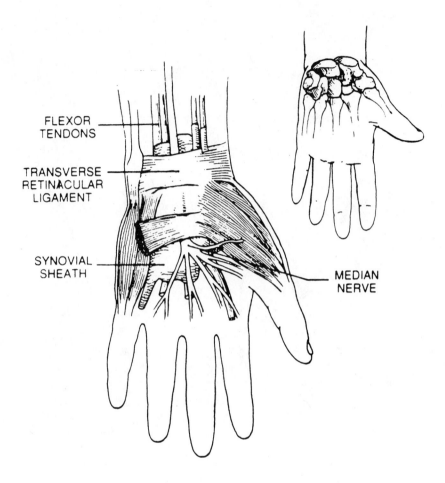

FLEXOR
TENDONS

TRANSVERSE
RETINACULAR
LIGAMENT

SYNOVIAL
SHEATH

MEDIAN
NERVE

Fig. 8-8. *Upper right:* The carpal tunnel is the archlike structure formed by the bones of the wrist. *Lower left:* It contains the flexor tendons of the fingers, held in place by the transverse retinacular ligament and enveloped by the synovial sheaths (lubricating membranes). The median nerve parallels the tendons but does not run as deeply.

[1] Anatomy of the Wrist and the Carpal Tunnel

The eight carpal bones of the wrist are arranged in two rows— four proximal (toward the body) and four distal (toward the hand). *(See Figure 8-9.)* Three articulate (form a joint) with the radius (large forearm bone on thumb side). All four distal bones articulate with the metacarpals (hand bones between the wrist and knuckles).

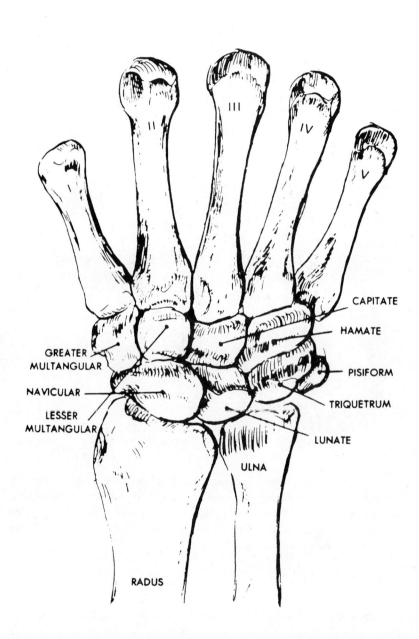

Fig. 8-9. The right wrist, viewed from the dorsal (top or back) surface. The carpal bones are arranged in two rows.

The carpal tunnel is a canal on the palmar (volar) surface, with the carpal bones toward the back (dorsal) and the transverse ligament (flexor retinaculum) forming the roof of the tunnel just under the skin. Within the tunnel lie the median nerve near the ligament and nine tendons for flexor (bending) muscles of the forearm. The tunnel is rigid and unable to expand.

[2] Mechanism of Injury

Carpal tunnel syndrome can result from any process that leads to increased pressure on the contents of the tunnel. The nerve is the most vulnerable component.

Nonspecific tenosynovitis (swelling of tendon sheaths) of the flexor tendons within the tunnel may be the most common cause of increased pressure. Wrist flexion can increase the pressure within the tunnel, even in the absence of other factors. Decreased capacity of the tunnel may result from prior fracture or dislocation of the hand or forearm, rheumatoid arthritis or congenital anomalies (Szabo, 1989).

Compression causes decreased blood flow, which may cause the early symptoms. Continued vascular insufficiency can lead to capillary damage and further edema (fluid accumulation). This can result in fibrosis (accumulation of fibroblast cells), which destroys the neural tissue.

Mechanical stress from compression can cause direct nerve injury (Dawson, 1993). Burning pain accompanies nerve regeneration if compression is relieved (Ditmars, 1993).

Neuropathies due to systemic conditions, such as diabetes and uremia, can predispose the median nerve to compressive injury. Carpal tunnel syndrome can also be caused by rheumatoid arthritis, osteoarthritis, pregnancy, myxedema, hemodialysis and many other less common conditions (Pecina, et al., 1991).

[3] Symptoms and Clinical Features

Early symptoms include numbness, painful tingling, and burning pain and weakness in the thumb and first three fingers (Dawson, 1993; Rosenbaum and Ochoa, 1993). These symptoms are often precipitated by repetitive hand or finger actions, but nocturnal symptoms that wake the patient are common. Shaking the hand may bring relief.

Sensory loss in the ring finger frequently occurs only on the lateral (away from the body) side. Numbness rarely radiates proximal to the wrist, but sometimes the forearm or shoulder aches. Typically the dominant hand is most affected, with involvement of the other hand being evident only upon electrodiagnostic studies (Schaumburg, et al., 1992).

Weakness eventually develops in the muscles that abduct and oppose the thumb. In advanced cases, the thumb cannot move properly in opposition to the other fingers, and the patient may drop objects.

Symptom progression can be insidious. In the early stages, the patient may complain of discomfort and fatigue, but no sensory deficit may be apparent on examination (Dawson, et al., 1990).

[4] Diagnosis

Clinical tests for carpal tunnel syndrome include Phalen's test and Tinel's sign[16] (Gupta and Kleinert, 1993). Testing of grip and pinch strength can help detect muscle involvement.

Electrodiagnostic testing[17] is frequently recommended for accurate diagnosis (Dawson, 1993; Rempel, et al., 1993), and it is one of the criteria accepted by the National Institute for Occupational Safety and Health (NIOSH) for carpal tunnel syndrome reporting (Matte, et al., 1989). Usually slowing of the rate of sensory nerve conduction is used, but often electromyography of the thenar (thumb) muscles is also done.

Other conditions from which carpal tunnel syndrome must be differentiated are cervical radiculopathy (compression of the cervical spinal roots), thoracic outlet syndrome[18] and proximal (closer to the body trunk) median nerve compression.

[5] Treatment and Prognosis

Treatment includes remedy of causative conditions, including avoidance of precipitating activities, therapy for systemic disorders and removal of space-occupying lesions. Splinting to maintain the wrist in a neutral position, particularly at night, is a useful first step but does not give permanent relief except with minimal injury.

Local injection of corticosteroid plus anesthetic, usually begun if symptoms persist after three to six weeks of splinting, often helps for a few months, but in many cases, effectiveness diminishes with each

---

16 *See also* 8.04 [2] *supra.*

17 *See also* 8.04 [3] *supra.*

18 *See also* 8.08[1] [a] *supra.*

subsequent injection, and no more than three or four should be administered (Schaumburg, et al., 1992). A claim that pyridoxine (vitamin B6) alleviates carpal tunnel syndrome (Ellis and Folkers, 1990) is not recognized as proven therapy (Rosenbaum and Ochoa, 1993).

Surgical decompression is needed when conservative management fails or when thenar weakness or atrophy is present. Transection (surgical cutting) of the flexor retinaculum often brings dramatic symptom abatement. Potential complications of this surgery include nerve transection, infection, scarring, neuroma (a tumorlike growth arising on the end of a cut nerve) formation and incomplete release (Szabo, 1989), but overall success rates are good (Dawson, 1993). Postoperative therapy includes ice packs, massage and phased range-of-motion and strengthening exercises.

Ergonomic design of workstations is often recommended, but it has rarely been studied in a systematic fashion.

[6] Prevalence and Work Association

The rise in attention to carpal tunnel syndrome has made it almost synonymous with repetitive motion disorder. Systematic study of the occupational causes of repetitive stress injuries is only beginning, but recognition is long-standing that some workers have an increased susceptibility to median nerve injury. Many early studies were not well designed, and the incidence of work-related disorders is a subject of continuing controversy (Dawson, 1993; Gerr, et al., 1991).

When workers' hands are flexed or extended for prolonged periods, the median nerve may be compressed for a length of time. The use of highly repetitive wrist movements with forceful movements or awkward positions seems to be correlated with the syndrome (Dawson, 1993).

Many occupations have been cited as carrying risk for carpal tunnel disorders, but most studies are flawed by lack of controls, unreliable diagnoses and faulty exposure assessments (Dobyns, 1991; Gerr, et al., 1991). Particularly high rates have been found in the meat-packing and shellfish-packing industries (reported to have a nearly 15 percent incidence, versus 1 percent in the general population) (Dawson, 1993; Szabo, 1989). The incidence is increased among workers using much hand force with frequent repetition, such as is done by automobile and electronic-parts assemblers, mechanics and machinists, auto body workers, electricians, carpenters, forestry workers and construction workers. Other workers who are at risk because of awkward hand positions include garment workers, painters, musicians, surgeons, dental hygienists and physical therapists.

Occupations that can cause nerve and tendon irritation by their demand for high-speed repetitive movements include grocery checkout, computer operation, typing, switchboard operation and packaging (Dawson, 1993; Dawson, et al., 1990; Guidotti, 1992; Rempel, et al., 1992; Williams and Westmorland, 1994). Vibration through use of power tools can also cause carpal tunnel syndrome and other disorders (Ditmars, 1993; Gupta and Kleinert, 1993).

8.10   VIBRATION-INDUCED DISORDERS

Vibration is a particular type of repetitive motion that can lead to such repetitive stress disorders as carpal tunnel syndrome (Szabo and Madison, 1992) or to a specific vibration induced disability known as vibration white finger (Ditmars, 1993; Falkenburg and Schultz, 1993; Gupta and Kleinert, 1993; Gupta and McCabe, 1993; Rodahl, 1989).

[1]   Effects of Whole-Body Vibration

The effects of whole-body vibration are difficult to assess, particularly since one of the primary complaints is fatigue (Rodahl, 1989). Other symptoms are headache, depression and weakness (Gupta and McCabe, 1993).

[2]   Vibration White Finger

Vibration white finger, which results from prolonged use of vibrating hand tools, has been recognized as an occupational disorder since 1966 in Japan and since 1985 in the United Kingdom (Gupta and McCabe, 1993). This condition, also known as vibration syndrome or hand-arm vibration syndrome, is classified as a traumatic vasospastic disease and affects the musculoskeletal, nervous and peripheral circulatory systems.

Hand symptoms include paresthesias, prolonged nerve conduction latencies[19] and reduced amplitude, joint pain, muscle weakness, loss

---

19 *See also* 8.04[3][a] *supra.*

of manual dexterity and development of Raynaud's phenomenon (a condition in which the fingers become white, stiff and painful upon exposure to cold). The development of symptoms is sometimes acute, but more often, it takes place over several years. In many cases, the symptoms are first precipitated by cold but then increase in frequency, intensity and extent.

Understanding of the mechanism of action of vibration is still incomplete, but it is known that the frequency (periodicity of the back-and-forth movement), velocity and acceleration of the vibratory movement determine its effects on the human body (Gupta and McCabe, 1993; Rodahl, 1989). The effect is greatest at a frequency in the 1 to 100 Hertz (Hz) range, because the human body is optimally tuned to vibration at this frequency. Other factors determining the type and extent of damage include direction of vibration in relation to the body, tool type and weight, hand posture, pattern and duration of exposure, and environmental conditions, such as temperature and noise.

Vibration has a variety of effects on body tissues. It reduces blood flow and may lead to vessel obstruction in small arteries, resulting in permanent damage (Ditmars, 1993; Gupta and McCabe, 1993). Changes in peripheral nerves include demyelination (loss of the insulating myelin sheath around nerve processes), axonal (relating to outgoing nerve process) degeneration and fibrosis (formation of abnormal fibrous tissue).

There is a direct deleterious effect on muscles and possibly on bone. Reports indicate that vibration can lead to the development of carpal tunnel syndrome, which is usually unresponsive to surgery (Ditmars, 1993; Gupta and McCabe, 1993). In addition, the force needed to hold a tool is greater when it is vibrating, and this increases the risk of other types of repetitive motion disorders (Rodahl, 1989).

Diagnosis depends on a history of exposure to vibration. Diagnostic tests include measurement of skin temperature and assessment of response to immersion in cold water; grip and pinch strength are also evaluated.

About a million workers in the United States are exposed to hand-arm vibration (Gupta and McCabe, 1993). Workers at risk include chain sawyers (most have symptoms after 1,000 hours of exposure, with functional changes after 5,000 to 8,000 hours), miners and stoneworkers (rock drillers have a 25 percent incidence of symptoms within one to five years), road workers, construction workers, hand grinders and polishers, riveters and dental technicians (Ditmars, 1993; Gupta and McCabe, 1993).

Occupational modifications include restrictions on the length of time of continuous operation, monitoring of received vibration level and frequency, job rotation and use of padded antivibration gloves. Tools may be modified to dampen vibration, improve balance, minimize required grip force and diminish noise (Falkenburg and Schultz, 1993; Gupta and McCabe, 1993; Johnson, 1993a). Many such preventive measures have become mandatory in industries around the world. Some experts advocate limitations on the age of workers using vibrating tools (Rodahl, 1989).

Treatment must first include cessation of exposure to vibration. In mild cases, tool modification and use of padded handles and gloves may permit the individual to continue working with power tools. Often it is necessary to retrain the worker for another job, however. Advanced cases in patients age 45 and over tend to be irreversible.

Palliative measures include heat hydrotherapy, biofeedback, non-steroidal anti-inflammatory medication and peripheral blood vessel dilators (alpha-receptor blockers and calcium channel blockers). Surgery is frequently ineffective, and symptoms tend to recur with renewed exposure.

8.11 NERVE COMPRESSION SYNDROMES OF THE LOWER EXTREMITY

Repetitive motion disorders of the leg and foot are common in recreation and professional sports but quite rare in the workplace. Among the exceptions are nerve compression syndromes due to prolonged sitting or kneeling, bursitis in the hip or knee, and repetitive-impact injury to the foot.

Nerve compression syndromes can affect the sciatic nerve, the lateral femoral cutaneous nerve, the common peroneal nerve and the posterior tibial nerve.

[1] Sciatic Nerve

The sciatic nerve arises from the lumbar and sacral sections of the spinal cord and innervates the knee flexors and all the muscles below the knee. *(See Figure 8-10.)* Prolonged sitting, especially on a small, hard surface, may compress the nerve in the thigh and buttocks and the blood vessels supplying it. Symptoms of injury can include loss of light touch perception, some paralysis and diminution of lower limb reflexes (Wagner, 1989).

[2]   Lateral Femoral Cutaneous Nerve

The lateral femoral cutaneous nerve crosses the iliac (hip) bones and passes under the inguinal ligament before reaching the skin of the anterolateral (front and side) thigh, which it innervates. In this path, it can be compressed or stretched by shifting of the legs or pelvis, leaning or increased abdominal muscle tension (in prolonged standing). It is a sensory nerve, and compression results in burning pain and paresthesia (abnormal sensation) on the outside of the upper thigh (Pecina, et al., 1991).

[3]   Common Peroneal Nerve (Foot Drop Syndrome)

The common peroneal nerve branches from the sciatic nerve near the knee, courses across the back of the knee (popliteal fossa) and winds around the head of the fibula (the smaller, outer bone of the lower leg). Prolonged kneeling, crouching or crossing the legs can compress the nerve against the fibula (Dawson, et al., 1990; Pecina, et al., 1991). Thus gardeners, vegetable pickers, shoe salespersons and plumbers are at risk.

The classic symptom is foot drop—a weakness in the muscles that raise the toes and front of the foot. Sensory loss may occur as well.

[4]   Posterior Tibial Nerve (Tarsal Tunnel Syndrome)

The posterior tibial nerve, which gives sensory innervation to the sole of the foot and motor innervation to the toes, may be compressed as it passes through the tarsal tunnel. This tunnel, located just below the medial malleolus (the lower projection of the tibia, the larger bone of the lower leg), is bounded by the bones and ligaments of the ankle.

Pressure on the nerve in this space can result in burning pain, numbness and tingling (Dawson, et al., 1990; Pecina, et al., 1991). There may also be muscle weakness.

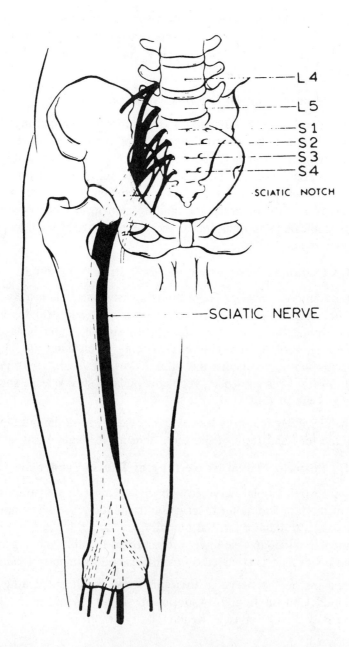

L 4
L 5
S 1
S 2
S 3
S 4

SCIATIC NOTCH

SCIATIC NERVE

Fig. 8-10. The sciatic nerve, which leaves the pelvis through the sciatic notch and runs down the leg, supplies the knee flexors and all the muscles below the knee. It is susceptible to injury from prolonged pressure.

8.12 HIP DISORDERS

The hip joint is basically stable, despite its wide range of motion, and repetitive motion disorders rarely affect it (Hadler,1993). However, prolonged sitting can cause bursitis (inflammation of a bursa).[20]

The hip has several bursae, two of which may cause hip pain. The ischiogluteal bursa is between the ischium (lower back part of the hipbone) and the gluteus maximus muscle of the buttocks. Ischiogluteal bursitis is also known as weaver's bottom; bicycle messengers may be at particular risk. The trochanteric bursa is over the greater trochanter (projection on the upper end of the femur, or thighbone). *(See Figure 8-11.)* Trochanteric bursitis is frequently diagnosed in bus drivers and others who sit for long periods, but its incidence may be overestimated (Hadler, 1993).

8.13 KNEE DISORDERS

Although occupational activities cause knee problems much less often than do athletic activities, prepatellar (between the skin and the patella or kneecap) bursitis or housemaid's knee can be found in workers who kneel for prolonged periods. These include floorers, carpet layers, tile setters and others. Inflammation may be present.

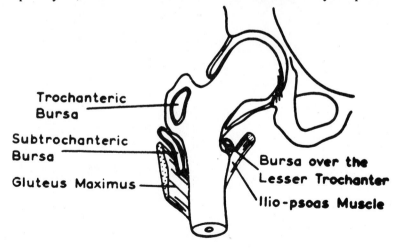

Fig. 8-11. The hip has several bursae. The trochanteric bursa lies over the greater trochanter (projection on the upper end of the femur, or thighbone).

---

[20] *See also* 8.02[3] *supra.*

8.14 FOOT DISORDERS

Prolonged standing or walking can lead to an inflammation of the connective tissue on the undersurface of the foot (plantar fasciitis). Overload of the bones and ligaments may produce this or pathology in some of the small bones of the foot.

8.100 BIBLIOGRAPHY

Reference Bibliography

Akesson, E. J., et al.: Thompson's Core Textbook of Anatomy, 2nd ed. Philadelphia: Lippincott, 1990.

Botte, M. J. and Gelberman, R. H.: Ulnar Nerve Compression at the Wrist. In: Szabo, R. M. (Ed.): Nerve Compression Syndromes: Diagnosis and Treatment. Thorofare, N.J.: Slack, 1989.

Byrne, E.: RSI Revisited (Commentary). Med. J. Aust. 156:372-373, 1992.

Cohen, M. L., et al.: In Search of the Pathogenesis of Refractory Cervicobrachial Pain Syndrome. A Deconstruction of the RSI Phenomenon. Med. J. Aust. 156:432-436, 1992.

Dawson, D. M.: Current Concepts: Entrapment Neuropathies of the Upper Extremities. N. Engl. J. Med. 329:2013-2028, 1993.

Dawson, D. M., et al.: Entrapment Neuropathies, 2nd ed. Boston: Little, Brown, 1990.

Ditmars, D. M., Jr.: Patterns of Carpal Tunnel Syndrome. Hand Clin. 9:241-252, 1993.

Dobyns, J. H.: Cumulative Trauma Disorder of the Upper Limb. Hand Clin. 7:587-595, 1991.

Edelman, R. R. and Warach, S.: Magnetic Resonance Imaging (Second of Two Parts). N. Engl. J. Med. 328:785-791, 1993.

Ellis, O. M. and Folkers, K.: Clinical Aspects of Treatment of Carpal Tunnel Syndrome with Vitamin B_6. Ann. N.Y. Acad. Sci. 585:302-320, 1990.

Falkenburg, S. A. and Schultz, D. J.: Ergonomics for the Upper Extremity. Hand Clin. 9:263-271, 1993.

Felsenthal, E.: Out of Hand: An Epidemic or a Fad. The Debate Heats up over Repetitive Stress. Wall St. Journal, July 14, 1994, pp. A1, A7.

Fu, F. H., et al.: Shoulder Impingement Syndrome. A Critical Review. Clin. Orthop. 269:162-173, 1991.

Gerr, F., et al: Upper-Extremity Musculoskeletal Disorders of Occupational Origin. Ann. Rev. Publ. Health 12:543-566, 1991.

Gellman, H.: Tennis Elbow (Lateral Epicondylitis). Orthop. Clin. N. Am. 23(1):75-82, 1992.

Gruskin, S. E.: Medical Management of Myofascial Pain Dysfunction. Clin. Phys. Ther. 25:319-328, 1991.

Guidotti, T. L.: Occupational Repetitive Strain Injury. Am. Fam. Phys. 45:585-592, 1992.

Gupta, A. and Kleinert, H. E.: Evaluating the Injured Hand. Hand Clin. 9:195-212, 1993.

Gupta, A. and McCabe, S. J.: Vibration White Finger. Hand Clin. 9:325-337, 1993.

Hadler, N. M.: Occupational Musculoskeletal Disorders. New York: Raven Press, 1993.

Hanrahan, L. P. and Moll, M. B.: Injury Surveillance. Am. J. Publ. Health (Suppl.) 79:38-45, 1989.

Higgs, P., et al.: Upper Extremity Impairment in Workers Performing Repetitive Tasks. Plast. Reconstr. Surg. 90:614-620, 1992.

Iyer, V. G.: Understanding Nerve Conduction and Electromyographic Studies. Hand Clin. 9:273-287, 1993.

Johnson, S. L.: Ergonomic Hand Tool Design. Hand Clin. 9:298-303, 1993a.

Johnson, S. L.: Therapy of the Occupationally Injured Hand and Upper Extremity. Hand Clin. 9:289-297, 1993b.

Johnson, R. K. and Spinner, M.: Median Nerve Compression in the Forearm: The Pronator Tunnel Syndrome. In: Szabo, R. M. (Ed.): Nerve Compression Syndromes: Diagnosis and Treatment. Thorofare, N.J.: Slack, 1989.

Karas, S. E.: Thoracic Outlet Syndrome. Clin. Sports Med. 9:297-310, 1990.

Larsson, L.-G.: Benefits and Disadvantages of Joint Hypermobility Among Musicians. N. Engl. J. Med. 329:1079-1082, 1993.

Leadbetter, W. B.: Cell-Matrix Response in Tendon Injury. Clin. Sports Med. 11:533-578, 1992.

Lieberman, J. S. and Taylor, R. G.: Electrodiagnosis in Upper Extremity Nerve Compression. In: Szabo, R. M. (Ed.): Nerve Compression Syndromes: Diagnosis and Treatment. Thorofare, N.J.: Slack, 1989.

Louis, D. S.: Evolving Concerns Relating to Occupational Disorders of the Upper Extremity. Clin. Orthop. 254:140-143, 1990.

Lundborg, G. and Dahlin, L. B.: Pathophysiology of Nerve Compression. In: Szabo, R. M. (Ed.): Nerve Compression Syndromes: Diagnosis and Treatment. Thorofare, N.J.: Slack, 1989.

Matte, T. D., et al.: The Selection and Definition of Targeted Work-Related Conditions for Surveillance under SENSOR. Am. J. Publ. Health (Suppl.) 79:21-25, 1989.

Nirschl, R. P.: Elbow Tendinosis/Tennis Elbow. Clin. Sports Med. 11:851-870, 1992.

Nunley, J. A. and Howson, P.: Lateral Antebrachial Cutaneous Nerve Compression. In: Szabo, R. M. (Ed.): Nerve Compression Syndromes: Diagnosis and Treatment. Thorofare, N.J.: Slack, 1989.

O'Brien, M.: Functional Anatomy and Physiology of Tendons. Clin. Sports Med. 11:505-520, 1992.

Omer, G. E.: The Cubital Tunnel Syndrome. In: Szabo, R. M. (Ed.): Nerve Compression Syndromes: Diagnosis and Treatment. Thorofare, N.J.: Slack, 1989.

Pecina, M. M., et al.: Tunnel Syndromes. Boca Raton, Fla.: CRC, 1991.

Peimer, C. A. and Wheeler, D. R.: Radial Tunnel Syndrome/Posterior Interosseous Nerve Compression. In: Szabo, R. M. (Ed.): The Compression Syndromes: Diagnosis and Treatment. Thorofare, N.J.: Slack, 1989.

Pope, C. F.: Radiologic Evaluation of Tendon Injuries. Clin. Sports Med. 11:579-599, 1992.

Posner, M. A.: Compressive Neuropathies of the Median and Radial Nerves. Clin. Sports Med. 9:343-363, 1990.

Rempel, D. M., et al.: Work-Related Cumulative Trauma Disorders of the Upper Extremity. J.A.M.A. 267:838-842, 1992.

Rodahl, K.: The Physiology of Work. New York: Taylor and Francis, 1989.

Rosenbaum, R. B. and Ochoa, J. L.: Carpal Tunnel Syndrome and Other Disorders of the Median Nerve. Boston: Butterworth-Heinemann, 1993.

Sanders, R. J.: History. In: Sanders, R. J. and Haug, C. E.: Thoracic Outlet Syndrome: A Common Sequela of Neck Injuries. Philadelphia: J. B. Lippincott Company, 1991a.

Sanders, R. J.: Etiology. In: Sanders, R. J. and Haug, C. E.: Thoracic Outlet Syndrome: A Common Sequela of Neck Injuries. Philadelphia: Lippincott, 1991b.

Sanders, R. J.: Clinical Presentation. In: Sanders, R. J. and Haug, C. E.: Thoracic Outlet Syndrome: A Common Sequela of Neck Injuries. Philadelphia: Lippincott, 1991c.

Sanders, R. J. and Shogan, S. H.: The Controversies Regarding Thoracic Outlet Syndrome. In: Sanders, R. J. and Haug, C. E.: Thoracic Outlet Syndrome: A Common Sequela of Neck Injuries. Philadelphia: Lippincott, 1991.

Sanders, R. J. and Smith, R.: Diagnostic Studies. In: Sanders, R. J. and Haug, C. E.: Thoracic Outlet Syndrome: A Common Sequela of Neck Injuries. Philadelphia: Lippincott, 1991.

Schaumburg, H. H., et al.: Disorders of Peripheral Nerves, 2nd ed. Philadelphia: Davis, 1992.

Szabo, R. M.: Superficial Radial Nerve Compression Syndrome. In: Szabo, R. M. (Ed.): Nerve Compression Syndromes: Diagnosis and Treatment. Thorofare, N.J.: Slack, 1989.

Szabo, R. M. and Madison, M.: Carpal Tunnel Syndrome. Orthop. Clin. N. Am. 23(1):103-109, 1992.

Thorson, E. and Szabo, R. M.: Common Tendinitis Problems in the Hand and Forearm. Orthop. Clin. N. Am. 23:65-74, 1992.

Toby, E. B. and Koman, L. A.: Thoracic Outlet Compression Syndrome. In: Szabo, R. M. (Ed.): Nerve Compression Syndromes: Diagnosis and Treatment. Thorofare, N.J.: Slack, 1989.

Voelkel, A.: Conservative Treatment. In: Sanders, R. J. and Haug, C. E.: Thoracic Outlet Syndrome: A Common Sequela of Neck Injuries. Philadelphia: Lippincott, 1991.

Wagner, F. C.: Compression of the Lumbosacral Plexus and the Sciatic Nerve. In: Szabo, R. M. (Ed.): Nerve Compression Syndromes: Diagnosis and Treatment. Thorofare, N.J.: Slack, 1989.

Williams, R. and Westmorland, M.: Occupational Cumulative Trauma Disorders of the Upper Extremity. Am. J. Occup. Ther. 48(5):411-420, 1994.

Wolf, W. B.: Shoulder Tendinoses. Clin. Sports Med. 11:871-890, 1992.

Additional References

Hodach, R. and Clark, E.: Carpal Tunnel Syndrome on CD-ROM (or CD-i). Milwaukee: MED. I. A., 1994.

Johnson, R. K.: Psychologic Assessment of Patients with Industrial Hand Injuries. Hand Clin. 9:221-229, 1993.

Larsson, L.-G.: Benefits and Disadvantages of Joint Hypermobility Among Musicians. N. Engl. J. Med. 329:1079-1082, 1993.

CHAPTER 9

Hernia

SCOPE

Most hernias occur in the groin area; ventral hernias occur in the umbilical and epigastric portions of the abdominal wall. Herniation of abdominal organs through the diaphragm into the chest may also occur after trauma. Ventral and inguinal hernia may be reducible, incarcerated or strangulated; strangulation represents a medical emergency that must be treated within several hours to prevent death. Genetic and acquired factors usually interact to trigger abdominal wall hernias, with heavy labor considered a contributing factor. Prevention of occupational hernia involves attention to worksite practices and conditions as well as routine physical examinations for potential victims. Diagnosis is made primarily through clinical examinations. Treatment is by operative repair, ideally on an elective basis as soon as the hernia is discovered. Operative mortality from repair of uncomplicated hernias is low, but the recurrence rate is high.

SYNOPSIS

9.01 INTRODUCTION

A hernia consists of the protrusion of a tissue or an organ through an abnormal opening in the body cavity that normally contains it. Most hernias occur in the abdominal wall, predominantly in the inguinal (groin) or femoral (thigh) areas. In older individuals, especially after abdominal surgery, herniation may occur directly through the abdominal wall (midline). Herniation of abdominal organs through the diaphragm into the chest may also occur, especially after a trauma that tears a hole in the diaphragm. (*See Figure 9–1.*) This chapter will cover both abdominal wall hernias and traumatic diaphragmatic hernias.

[1] History of Hernia Treatment

Attempts to manage abdominal hernias have been recorded since the first century A.D. In the nineteenth century, an Italian doctor (Bassini) devised a method of surgical repair that did not require the wearing of a truss (an appliance consisting of a pad attached to a belt

RIB CAGE

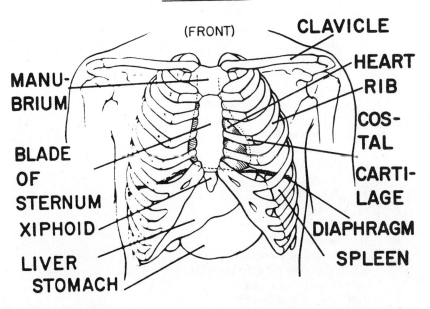

Fig. 9–1. Location of the diaphragm in relation to other structures.

held in place by a spring or straps) afterward. Between 1900 and the 1950s, various modifications were developed on this original operation. Since the mid–1950s, the so-called Shouldice technique has been widely used. It is favored both because of its excellent results and because it can be done as an outpatient procedure (Long and Sandler, 1990).

[2] Epidemiology

The true incidence of hernias is difficult to determine, but available figures indicate that it occurs in approximately 15 out of every 1000 persons (Nyhus, et al., 1991). Hernia is more than five times more likely in males than in females.

About half of all hernias are of the indirect inguinal type, and 25 percent are direct inguinal hernias.[1] In addition, umbilical hernias constitute 3 percent of the total; femoral hernias, 6 percent; and incisional and other ventral hernias, about 10 percent (Nyhus, et al., 1991).

---

[1] *See* 9.03[1] [a] *infra.*

A 1980 study found that 537,000 hernia repair operations were performed in one year in this country (Nyhus, et al., 1991). The U.S. Department of Health and Human Services has reported that disability due to hernias resulted in 40 million days of restricted activity per year, including 10 million days of lost work (Nyhus, et al., 1991). In addition, of 2 million abdominal incisions made in the United States every year, as many as 44 percent are made for hernia operations (Read, 1989).

9.02 DEFINITION OF ABDOMINAL HERNIAS

An abdominal wall hernia involves the protrusion of an abdominal viscus (interior organ) through a defect in the abdominal wall. This defect may be of congenital, acquired or, occasionally, traumatic origin. The herniated organ becomes enclosed within what is called a hernial sac, which is a pouch of the peritoneum (membrane lining the abdomen).

The omentum (a fold of peritoneum that hangs from the stomach) is the tissue that most often herniates. The hollow viscus that most often herniates is the intestine; however, every organ, except the pancreas and the duodenum, may push its way through a hole in the abdominal wall.

Hernias can be huge. There are reports of cases in which there were more organs in the hernial sac than were left inside the abdominal cavity.

Hernias are clinically classified into several categories: reducible, incarcerated, strangulated and sliding.

[1] Reducible Hernia

A reducible hernia is one in which the herniated material can be returned to its normal place. Such a hernia appears when the individual strains or coughs but disappears when the person lies down; only slight pressure is necessary to reduce such a hernia.

[2] Incarcerated Hernia

A hernia that cannot be reduced is said to be incarcerated. This occurs when a viscus becomes trapped by the opening through which it protrudes. The small intestine is the organ most frequently involved in an incarcerated hernia. (*See Figure 9–2.*)

An incarcerated hernia may be either acute and painful or chronic and asymptomatic, but as long as the organ's blood supply is not compromised, an incarcerated hernia does not constitute an immediate emergency (Nyhus, et al., 1991).

[3]   Strangulated Hernia

Should the blood flow to or from a herniated organ become compromised, the hernia is said to be strangulated. If it is not treated immediately, strangulation generally leads to intestinal obstruction and gangrene (tissue death and putrefaction), a potentially fatal condition; it therefore requires emergency surgery within five to six hours (Nyhus, et al., 1991).

[4]   Sliding Hernia

A sliding inguinal (pertaining to the groin area) hernia is present when part of the wall of the hernia sac is made up of the cecum (first part of the large intestine, on the right side) or the sigmoid colon (last part of the large intestine, on the left). (*See Figure 9–3.*) A sliding hernia results from a failure of two sections of the peritoneum to fuse where they cover the colon (Nyhus, et al., 1991).

9.03   ANATOMY OF ABDOMINAL HERNIAS

Abdominal hernias all involve the various layers of the abdominal wall. (*See Figure 9–4.*) Immediately beneath the skin lies a layer of fat. Below this layer lie the following three layers of muscle:

- the external oblique (obliquus externus abdominis);
- the internal oblique (obliquus internus abdominis); and
- the transverse (transversus abdominis).

These muscles are all bound together by sheets of connective tissue known as fascia and attached to the ribs, sternum and bones of the pelvis by flat, thin bands of fascia called aponeuroses. The rectus abdominis muscle runs longitudinally within layers of aponeurosis above the umbilicus and behind the aponeuroses below it. In any type of hernia, a defect or weakness in one of these abdominal wall layers is what allows protrusion of the hernia sac.

[1]   Inguinal Hernias

The internal inguinal ring is an opening in the transversalis fascia and transversus abdominis aponeurosis on each side of the body,

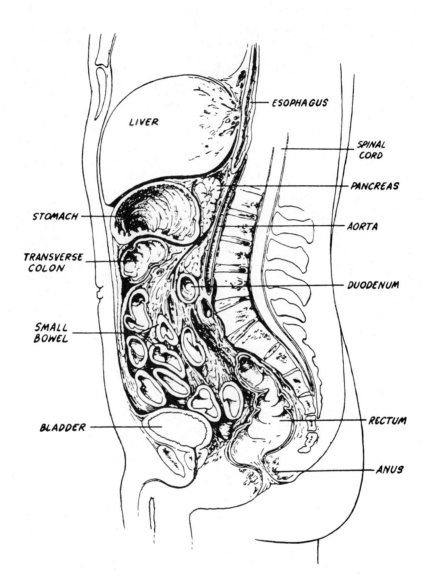

Fig. 9–2. Lateral view of the gastrointestinal tract. Note position of the abdominal viscera and other structures, including the small bowel (intestine).

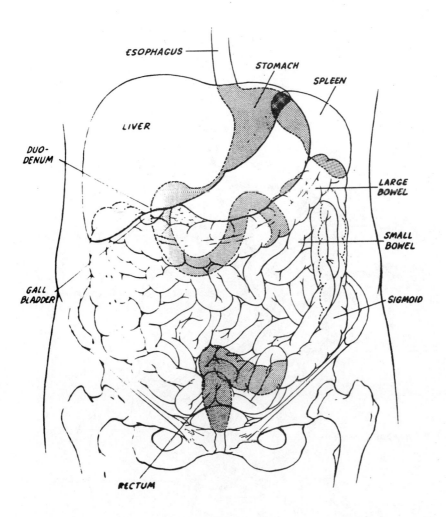

Fig. 9–3. Organs of the gastrointestinal system.

through which the spermatic cord in the male and the round ligament (one of a pair of cords arising from each side of the uterus) in the female pass out of the abdomen. These cords course through the inguinal canal, a passage about 1½ inches long, exiting it at the external inguinal ring.

[a] Indirect Inguinal Hernia

The processus vaginalis is a diverticulum (pouch or sac) of peritoneum that accompanies the testicle of the fetus as it descends to the

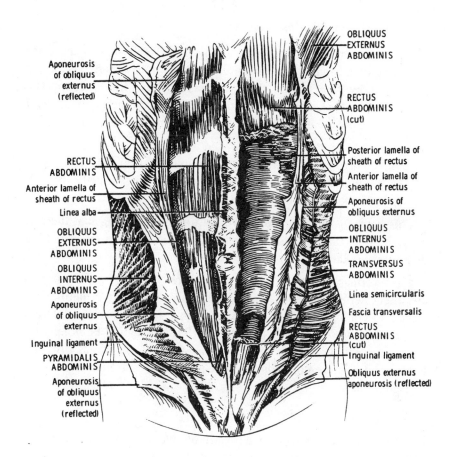

Fig. 9–4. Muscles of the abdomen, including the obliquus externus abdominis, the obliquus internus abdominis and the transversus abdominis.

scrotum during gestation. Normally the processus vaginalis obliterates completely by early infancy. Failure to obliterate constitutes a congenital anomaly the presence of which allows development of an indirect inguinal hernia (Nyhus, et al., 1991).

In an indirect inguinal hernia, the herniating organ leaves the abdomen through the internal inguinal ring, passes down the inguinal canal along with the spermatic cord and may protrude through the external inguinal ring or even into the scrotum. This hernia is of a type known as funicular, meaning that it protrudes through a tight ring of fibrous tissue and therefore has a tendency to become incarcerated and strangulated (Nyhus, et al., 1991).

[b] Direct Inguinal Hernia

The cause of a direct inguinal hernia is a weak area in the floor of the inguinal canal, which is made up of the transversalis fascia and reinforced by fibers from the transversus abdominis aponeurosis. When this reinforcement is incomplete, the floor of the inguinal canal is an area of potential weakness that can become thinner and stretched out or may even develop a tear.

A direct inguinal hernia enters the inguinal canal and, instead of exiting through the external inguinal ring, protrudes directly through the floor of the canal; the weakened fascia bulges outward.

This hernia is of the type known as diffuse, meaning that there is no tight ring that constricts the contents of the hernial sac. It is therefore unlikely to become incarcerated.

Most hernias that recur after repair of an indirect inguinal hernia are direct hernias. In such a case, the cause of the direct hernia is a failure to completely remove the processus vaginalis at the internal ring during the surgery (Nyhus, et al., 1991). It should be noted that direct inguinal hernias are uncommon in women, and the majority are bilateral. It is more common in older men with weakened abdominal musculature.

[2] Femoral Hernia

A femoral hernia is also a result of a congenital anomaly. Its development requires a weakness in the attachment of the transversalis fascia and the transversus abdominis aponeurosis to Cooper's ligament (a thick, strong, fibrous band that passes by the pubis).

The femoral hernia does not pass into the inguinal canal but rather under the inguinal ligament and through the femoral ring, the opening through which the femoral blood vessels enter the thigh. This space is small, so the resulting hernia will have a narrow neck, although it may become quite large within the loose connective tissue of the thigh. This hernia is therefore funicular in type (protrudes through a tight ring of fibrous tissue and therefore has a tendency to become incarcerated and strangulated).[2] Femoral hernia is more commonly observed in women, probably related to the wider femoral canal in women.

---

[2] *See* 9.03[1][a] *supra.*

[3] Ventral Hernia

Ventral hernias are those that occur in the abdominal wall elsewhere than at the groin. They include umbilical, epigastric and incisional hernias, as well as the more rare Spigelian and lumbar hernias. In adults, acquired umbilical hernia is really paraumbilical in origin.

[a] Umbilical Hernia

In umbilical hernia, there is protrusion of a viscus through a defect in the abdominal wall at the umbilicus, which has failed to close properly after birth. Such a hernia is fairly common in infants but may also develop in adults, most often in women after childbirth. In an adult, umbilical hernia poses a risk of incarceration and strangulation and therefore requires immediate treatment (Nyhus, et al., 1991).

[b] Epigastric Hernia

The epigastric hernia occurs at the midline of the abdomen, above the umbilicus. It is fairly common and has been found in about 5 percent of the population at autopsy; however, most epigastric hernias are small and asymptomatic and therefore are never diagnosed (Nyhus, et al., 1991). Such a hernia may consist only of a tag of omentum protruding through the linea alba (a vertical line between the two abdominis rectus muscles, formed by the intersecting attachments of the other abdominal muscles), or it may include viscera.

[c] Incisional Hernia

This type of hernia develops in the site of an earlier abdominal incision and is most often caused by wound infection. First the suture line separates; then the contents of the abdomen protrude. Small incisional hernias are funicular and liable to incarceration and strangulation.[3] However, they are usually large and diffuse (with no tight ring that constricts the contents of the hernial sac),[4] so although they become incarcerated fairly often, they rarely become strangulated.[5] A particularly severe complication is spontaneous rupture of the hernia, with evisceration. This event is more likely with incisional hernia than with other types because of the fragility of the overlying incisional scar.

---

[3] *See* 9.03[1][a] *supra.*

[4] *See* 9.03[1][b] *supra.*

[5] *See* 9.02 [3] *supra.*

Incisional hernia is much less likely to occur after transverse (crosswise) than after vertical abdominal incisions, since the lines of force exerted by the abdominal muscles are horizontal and tend to pull vertical incisions apart (Nyhus, et al., 1991).

Only about 50 percent of incisional hernias appear within a year of surgery; many appear as late as five years after the abdominal surgery. It is thought that a sawing motion of nonabsorbable sutures used to close the operative incision may be the mechanism responsible for the wound defect (Read, 1989).

Risk factors for incisional hernia include (Read, 1989):

- obesity;
- age over 60;
- smoking;
- alcoholism;
- trauma and other emergencies;
- male sex;
- cancer;
- wound infection;
- diabetes;
- more than one laparoscopy incision over 18 cm in length;
- vertical incisions; and
- surgery performed by individuals who are inexperienced in hernia correction.

[d]   Lumbar Hernia

The lumbar hernia is a relatively unusual type that develops in the abdominal wall on the side of the body, either in a surgical incision over the kidney or in an area known as Petit's lumbar triangle (i.e., trigonum lumbale, an area in the posterior abdominal wall bounded by the edges of the latissimus dorsi and external oblique muscles and the iliac crest), through a congenital weakness in the internal oblique muscle (Nyhus, et al., 1991).

[e]   Spigelian Hernia

Spigelian hernia is a rare type that protrudes through the spigelian fascia, a potentially weak area of the transversus abdominis aponeurosis. These hernias are small and therefore funicular, with a high incidence of incarceration and strangulation (Nyhus, et al., 1991).[6]

[4] Hernias in Women

Although 84 percent of femoral hernias occur in women, the overall incidence of femoral hernias is relatively low; as a result, the type of groin hernia most often found in women is the indirect inguinal. Since women have no spermatic cord and it is not necessary to preserve the round ligament, during repair, this ligament can be transected at the point where it leaves the internal ring, and the ring can be completely closed. In men, by contrast, the need to preserve the spermatic cord means that the internal ring cannot be completely closed. For this reason, women almost never experience recurrences of inguinal hernia (Nyhus, et al., 1991).[7]

In women, pregnancy, obesity and surgery are all associated with the development of hernia. When these three factors occur together in an individual woman, they often lead to femoral, umbilical or incisional hernia. Femoral and umbilical hernias often develop after multiple pregnancies; umbilical hernia is also associated with obesity.

The high incidence of incisional hernias in women may be related to hysterectomy. A sliding hernia in a woman may contain elements of the genital tract as well as part of the colon (Nyhus, et al., 1991).[8]

9.04 ETIOLOGY AND RELATION TO TRAUMA

Many factors play a role in the development of hernia, making it difficult to determine the specific role played by occupational factors or trauma. As a rule, physical effort or strain may reveal the presence of a hernia or exacerbate one already known to exist, but it is not the only cause.

[1] Predisposing and Precipitating Factors

Certain genetic, congenital and acquired factors can predispose to hernia development. Other factors, including sudden trauma or stresses, can precipitate the appearance of a hernia. Genetic and

---

[6] *See* 9.03[1][a] *supra.*

[7] *See* 9.03 *supra.*

[8] *See* 9.02[4] *supra.*

acquired factors interact to result in hernia; except for incisional and traumatic hernias,[9] some form of fascial or muscular abnormality must be present for a hernia to develop (Devlin, 1988).

[a] Congenital Variants

Groin hernias are believed to be a result of congenital anatomic variants, such as a preformed peritoneal sac; a weakness of the transverse abdominis aponeurosis, which renders it unable to prevent protrusion of abdominal contents through the internal inguinal ring; or an abnormal thinness of the fascial sheath of the rectus abdominis muscle near an inguinal hernia (Nyhus, et al., 1991). Such fascial or muscular anomalies may also result from acquired connective tissue disease. It seems, further, that abnormalities in the synthesis of collagen (a connective tissue protein) contribute to the development of hernia in adults. Studies have found decreased levels of collagen synthesis in hernia patients (Nyhus, et al., 1991).

Tissue defects in adult men with inguinal hernia have also been causally related to smoking, which is associated with increased levels of elastolytic enzyme (which aids in digestion of elastic tissue). This in turn is related to decreased collagen levels (Devlin, 1988). The significance of these observations to the cause of hernia is yet to be determined.

[b] Other Predisposing Factors

An important factor in hernia development is an increase in intra-abdominal pressure, which has the effect of helping force viscera through the defect in the abdominal wall. For this reason, conditions that tend to increase intra-abdominal pressure are predisposing factors. They include obesity, cardiac disease and pulmonary disease, as well as prostatism (obstruction of the urethra by an enlarged prostate gland), constipation and genitourinary disease. These cause voiding difficulties that lead patients to strain.

Pregnancy is also a factor in the development of femoral and umbilical hernias. Another factor is tissue atrophy due to aging.

[c] Precipitating Factors

Any factor that causes a sudden increase in intra-abdominal pressure, exerting force on an area in the abdominal wall that is weak due

---

[9] See 9.03[2] supra.

to a congenital or an acquired defect, can result in the sudden appearance of a hernia that is visible or palpable (detectable by manual examination). A sudden cough or sneeze or a strain caused by an attempt to lift a heavy weight may have this result.

Occasionally a hernia may result from severe trauma. More often, it develops slowly over years, not only in individuals who are engaged in heavy manual labor but also in those who are sedentary.

[2]   Traumatic Hernia

True traumatic hernias are rare. They occur after severe injury to the pelvis or lower abdomen and are classified into two categories, according to the mechanism of injury producing pelvic fracture. The diagnosis requires that there be immediate signs of soft-tissue injury in the area and early indication that a hernia is present.

In the first category, a powerful force acting on the pelvis from front to back tears the rectus abdominis from its origin on the pubic bone and results in the development of a broad-necked hernia. In the second, lateral (sideways) or lateral-vertical forces affecting the superior pubic ramus (a bar of bone projecting from the pubic bone near the hip joint) tear the fasciae and aponeuroses of the inguinofemoral area, and a direct inguinal hernia develops through the transversalis fascia just above the fracture line.

[3]   Effect of Trauma on Existing Hernia

Herniated organs are particularly vulnerable to trauma, because they are no longer protected by the layers of the abdominal wall. Because of the edema (swelling due to abnormal accumulation of fluid) that follows traumatic injury, trauma to a reducible hernia may lead to incarceration; trauma to an incarcerated hernia can result in strangulation.[10] Blunt abdominal trauma may cause rupture of an umbilical hernia, especially if the patient is pregnant or has cirrhosis with ascites (accumulation of abnormal fluid in the abdominal cavity) (Nyhus, et al., 1991).

9.05   HERNIA AND THE WORKPLACE

Since both genetic and acquired factors interact in causing hernia, it is often difficult to determine the relative role occupational factors

---

[10] *See* 9.02[3] *supra.*

play in its development. Frequently hernia development is related to age rather than occupation. Most often, a hernia develops slowly after many years of work. More rarely, a bulge appears as an immediate result of a strong effort made when the body is in an awkward position.

There is no evidence that vigorous physical activity causes hernia when no muscular or fascial abnormality is present: inguinal hernia is rare among weight-lifters (Devlin, 1988). However, heavy manual labor or an unusual strain at work is often considered a contributing factor to hernia development.

[1] Contributing Occupational Factors

It should be noted that hernia can be related not only to heavy labor but to sedentary work, since lack of exercise can result in a weak abdominal wall; then if the sedentary worker tries to perform an occasional heavy task, a hernia may appear. An example of this might be a bulldozer driver whose fatigued abdominal wall is subject to pressure from continual vibrational shocks.

A considerable variety of occupations have been associated with hernias. They include jobs that require lifting, carrying and moving heavy objects, such as that of porter, as well as jobs in such industries as mining, quarrying and metal manufacturing as well as that of all-terrain-vehicle driver. In sedentary workers, even a minor strain may produce a hernia.

[2] Prevention

Prevention of occupational hernia includes two approaches:

1. pre-employment and routine medical examinations; and

2. attention to conditions and practices in the workplace.

Thorough examination can discover a predisposition or enable early detection of a hernia that is already present. Workers who are known to be vulnerable or to have a hernia should not be placed in jobs involving jarring or straining in an abnormal position.

Certain workplace improvements can help avoid the adverse conditions that lead to hernia. These include mechanizing some jobs, for example, to eliminate manual handling, and training workers in effective stress-reducing skills for lifting and carrying. The use of ergonomic principles can improve other work practices as well.

9.06 DIAGNOSIS

Diagnosis of hernia is essentially clinical, depending on physical examination. Sometimes the hernia is asymptomatic and is only discovered during a routine physical.

[1] Physical Examination

The patient being examined for groin hernia stands before the examiner. For a male, the examiner inserts a finger into the inguinal canal through the external ring; if the hernia is not apparent, the patient is asked to strain by tensing the abdominal muscles. It is more difficult to discover a groin hernia in a female; she is asked to strain while the labia majora are examined. The patient being examined for a ventral hernia lies supine and raises the head and shoulders.

[2] Signs and Symptoms

The major symptom of a reducible hernia is pain, the nature and severity of which vary a great deal. The typical symptom of an inguinal hernia, for example, is an annoying feeling of heaviness and discomfort, usually when the patient strains or when a viscus temporarily enters the sac. However, if the hernia appears suddenly following an acute trauma, the pain may be severe at first, due to enlargement of the internal inguinal ring. If a loop of the small intestine enters the hernia sac, the patient may experience epigastric or umbilical pain due to stretching of the mesentery (part of the peritoneum attached to the intestine). The mass of an incarcerated hernia is tender.

The signs of a hernia depend on whether a viscus is present in the sac. If a viscus has entered the sac, it is difficult to discover. A solid organ can be felt as a movable, firm mass. The presence of a piece of intestine in the sac is indicated by crepitation (a crackling sound) on palpation (manual examination). A piece of omentum feels like a rubbery mass.

[3] Incarcerated or Strangulated Hernia

Because strangulation is potentially fatal, it is very important to recognize when this condition is imminent or actually exists.[11] Since it is difficult to distinguish an incarcerated hernia from one in which strangulation has begun, an incarcerated hernia should be treated as an emergency for which immediate surgery is indicated.

---

[11] See 9.02[3] supra.

Signs and symptoms of strangulation include pain in the area of the bulge and tenderness when it is touched. Other signs are the hernia suddenly becoming incarcerated (irreducible) and discoloration of the tissue over the bulge. Strangulated hernias also produce signs and symptoms of intestinal obstruction, including cramping and vomiting, a taut and distended abdomen, rapid pulse, shock, fever, low blood pressure and elevated white blood cell count. Patients with these signs should have a physical examination and herniography to search for possible hernia (Nyhus, et al., 1991).

[4]   Herniography

The term *herniography* refers to various x-ray studies of hernia. Both plain films and contrast x-rays may be helpful for certain patients. X-rays are useful with obese patients. A barium enema (x-ray of the colon after introduction of barium, a radiopaque contrast medium) has been used for elderly male patients with a history of bowel problems to detect the presence of a sliding hernia and thereby avoid colon injury during surgery.[12]

Contrast studies have also been used to diagnose incisional and umbilical hernias when the patient has symptoms but the hernia is small and the physical examination is inconclusive.

[5]   Groin Hernia

Indirect inguinal hernias usually cause little pain until they become incarcerated or strangulated--developments that may be signaled by sudden, severe pain. Usually diagnosis is simple, since the hernia protrudes into the scrotum as it develops. A direct inguinal hernia similarly causes little pain; it develops very slowly.

It is not necessary to differentiate between these two types of hernia preoperatively, since the surgical approach is the same for both. The femoral hernia does need to be differentiated, however, because it requires a different surgical approach. In femoral hernia, the bulge is located below the inguinal ligament.

[6]   Ventral Hernia

Umbilical hernias are generally easy to diagnose, since they cause a bulge instead of a depression at the navel. Although the degree of

---

[12] *See* 9.02[4] *supra.*

discomfort is usually mild, pregnant women may experience an increase in pain as the pregnancy progresses, then relief after birth.

Epigastric hernias can be difficult to diagnose if only omentum and no viscera have herniated. Upper abdominal pain unexplained by other causes, which is aggravated when the patient lies on the back, should raise a suspicion of epigastric hernia, particularly in obese patients. The aggravation of pain is thought to be due to stretching of the omentum. The diagnosis is confirmed by finding a small mass beneath the skin in the linea alba (Nyhus, et al., 1991).

Incisional hernias are easy to diagnose. When they are small, they can be very painful, with the pain decreasing as they grow.

9.07 TREATMENT

Except for some incisional hernias and in cases in which the patient is seriously ill and therefore a poor risk for surgery, the treatment of choice for hernia is operative repair as soon as possible, in order to avoid the serious complications of gangrene or intestinal obstruction secondary to strangulation.[13] Another possibility is the use of external support in the form of a truss to keep the hernia reduced. When they are used for groin hernias, however, these devices are not only expensive and a nuisance but generally unable to maintain proper reduction. For ventral hernias, on the other hand, particularly an incisional hernia whose repair will be difficult, use of a corset may be appropriate.

[1] Herniorrhaphy

Herniorrhaphy (hernia repair) is a frequently performed operation; however, the anatomy of the groin area is complicated, and controversy exists over which is the best procedure to follow. Repair of umbilical and epigastric hernia is simple, but incisional hernia can be difficult to repair, and the recurrence rate is high (Nyhus, et al., 1991).

Generally speaking, hernia repair consists of two steps:

   1. management of the hernia sac and the herniated organs; and

   2. repair of the defect in the fascia.

Management of a narrow-necked sac involves removing the sac and closing its neck. A broad-necked sac is not removed but simply

---

13 *See* 9.02[3] *supra.*

reduced beneath the fascia; the repaired fascia keeps it in place. Viscera attached to the sac by adhesions (scar tissue) must first be separated before reduction. If the hernia is a sliding type,[14] the portion of intestine that makes up part of the wall of the sac must be reduced before the sac is excised.

[a]   Groin Hernias

In repair of inguinal hernias, different techniques are required for different cases. The surgeon must devise an individualized approach during the procedure for each patient (Nyhus, et al., 1991).

It is with respect to the fascial repair of inguinal hernia that controversy exists. Proponents of the posterior approach, which involves overlapping of various layers of the transversalis fascia, hold that a distinction between deep and superficial layers of groin anatomy should be preserved. Proponents of the anterior approach do not make this distinction; they use superficial structures as supports in repairing deeper layers of the abdominal wall.

The first group maintains that this interconnection of layers causes strain at the suture line or the muscle attachment and may be responsible for recurrences. They acknowledge, however, that where the deeper layers do not provide enough tissue for the repair, use of superficial layers may be necessary (Nyhus, et al., 1991).

The most difficult inguinal hernias to repair are large indirect and direct hernias, since they require surgical reconstruction of the posterior inguinal wall and construction of a new internal inguinal ring. For this problem, McVay developed a repair using Cooper's ligament (also used for femoral hernia repair) (Nyhus, et al., 1991). Another technique used in inguinal hernia repair involves relaxing incisions placed in the rectus abdominis sheath that prevent tension on the suture line (Guarnieri, et al., 1992).

[b]   Ventral Hernias

Umbilical hernia requires the same emergency treatment as inguinal hernia because of its liability to incarceration and strangulation.[15] The preferred treatment for both umbilical and epigastric hernia is simple closure of the defect with sutures; recurrence is rare.

14 *See* 9.02 [4] *supra.*

15 *See* 9.02[3] *supra.*

Incisional hernia can present a difficult problem, however. Although the goal is simple closure of the defect, the same factors that caused the suture line to separate in the first place may still be present and disrupt the second suture line, enlarging the wound and making closure even more difficult. Some patients have suffered tissue loss due to infection or an increase in intra-abdominal pressure (for example, due to obesity) and therefore lack sufficient tissue to use in the repair (Nyhus, et al., 1991; Deysine, 1992).

Such a patient requires a preoperative regimen designed to remedy nutritional or metabolic problems that may hinder wound healing, to treat conditions that may increase intra-abdominal pressure and possibly to reduce weight.

Three types of surgical procedures have been developed for incisional hernias. Repair by simple closure, in which the edges of the wound are approximated (brought together) at the level of the transversalis fascia and above, is adequate for small incisional hernias and those occurring in vertical incisions. Since it seems that nonabsorbable sutures may contribute to incisional hernia development, it has been suggested that the use of synthetic, slowly absorbed monofilament sutures may reduce recurrences (Read, 1989).

Larger incisional hernias must be repaired using either autologous (from the individual) tissue grafts or prostheses. The major complication in the use of tissue grafts is infection of the graft, which may be reduced by the use of local and systemic antibiotics. However, if treatment of infection by debridement (removal of devitalized tissue) and antibiotics fails, a prosthesis may be necessary[16] (Nyhus, et al., 1991; Deysine, 1992).

[2] Management of Incarcerated and Strangulated Hernias

It is not possible to predict when an uncomplicated hernia will develop complications and require emergency treatment. To avoid this situation, elective repair while the hernia is still uncomplicated is preferable.

[a] Reduction of Incarcerated Hernia

When no systemic signs of strangulation are present, one attempt can be made by the physician to reduce a recently developed incarcerated indirect or direct hernia before the operation. The advantage of

---

16 *See* 9.03[3] [c] *supra.*

doing so is that within two or three days, edema (swelling due to accumulation of fluid) will subside, allowing the surgery to be anatomically more accurate and thus optimizing results.

Before performing the reduction, an ice bag may be applied to the area, and parenteral morphine (administered through a route other than the gastrointestinal system) is given if necessary. As the patient lies supine, the physician exerts gentle pressure on the hernia mass. If the hernia is difficult to reduce, it may be of the sliding variety.[17] Because the opening through which a femoral hernia protrudes is so narrow, no attempt should be made to reduce this type of hernia.

Two possible complications may result from too vigorous an effort to reduce the hernia. In reduction en masse, the herniated organ is reduced within the abdominal cavity but remains incarcerated within the sac. To ensure that this has not happened, the patient must be watched afterward for signs of intestinal obstruction. The second complication is reduction of a necrotic, strangulated piece of intestine within the abdominal cavity (Nyhus, et al., 1991).

[b]   Emergency Surgery for Strangulated Hernia

Before reduction of herniated strangulated viscera, the tissues must be examined to make sure that circulation has been restored. If it has, the organ can be reduced and fascial repair performed. If, on the other hand, the tissue is gangrenous, the necrotic sections must be excised and an anastomosis (opening created between two normally separate parts) constructed between the two viable sections of bowel at the ends of the excised part.

[3]   Management of Sliding Hernia

When a surgeon is operating on a sliding hernia, the major consideration is recognizing that such a hernia is present in order to exercise additional care to avoid injuring the intestine or its blood supply. The section of intestine forming part of the sac wall must be reduced before the sac itself is excised. The defect in the peritoneum and the fascial defect are then closed as usual (Nyhus, et al., 1991).

[4]   Management of Recurrences

Whereas prostheses are generally not used for primary repair of groin hernias, they have been recommended in cases of recurrence

---

[17] *See* 9.02[4] *supra.*

in which the repair is difficult. A variety of prosthetic materials have been used, including tissue grafts taken from fascia in the thigh and skin, ox fascia and synthetic meshes made of stainless steel, nylon, tantalum (a metallic element) and Marlex ® (polypropylene, a plastic). In difficult cases, such materials, used to reinforce the repair, have successfully prevented recurrences (Nyhus, et al., 1991).

Some synthetic materials, including stainless steel, tantalum and Marlex ®, have been found to develop fatigue fractures. Expanded polytetrafluoroethylene (e-PTFE) does not fracture when it is used to repair both primary and recurring groin hernias and ventral hernias (Deysine, 1992).

Prostheses have not always successfully prevented recurrence of incisional hernias. There may be protrusion around the edges of the prosthesis (Read, 1989). Another complication leading to recurrence of both groin and ventral hernias is graft infection. Prevention of infection requires meticulous infection control and use of local and systemic antibiotics. Once infection has developed, it is managed with debridement and antibiotics. If this treatment fails, the graft must be removed and a different prosthesis implanted (Deysine, 1992).

[5] Outpatient Procedures

About 50 percent of hernia operations are now performed on an outpatient basis, using a modified Shouldice technique (Nyhus, et al., 1991). The basis of the procedure is the use of multiple layers of fascia to double the thickness of the transversalis fascia layer. First the hernia sac is completely separated from the spermatic cord and the surrounding transversalis fascia. An indirect hernia sac is ligated (tied off); a direct one is obliterated. The transversalis fascia is then used to repair the posterior inguinal wall. If a femoral hernia is found, it is repaired by closing the femoral canal with sutures (Long and Sandler, 1990; Nyhus, et al., 1991).

The Shouldice repair is done under local anesthesia, enabling the patient to walk to and from the operating table and cooperate during the procedure, coughing or straining upon request to confirm closure of the fascial defect. The recurrence rate is reported to be under 1 percent. However, for this procedure, patients cannot be more than 10 percent overweight, except in emergency situations (Long and Sandler, 1990).

After a brief recovery period, the patient can be discharged the same day. Most patients can leave the hospital while the long-acting local anesthetic used during the procedure is still effective, and convalesce at home. After that, the patient can walk briskly up to an hour a day, resume sexual relations and begin driving the following day. Straining, calisthenics, jogging, aerobic exercise and lifting weights over 10 pounds must be avoided for four to six weeks.

Complications of the Shouldice procedure include allergic reaction to local anesthesia and an increase in scrotal swelling and ecchymosis (bruising), compared to hernia repairs carried out under general anesthesia. In addition, between 1 and 3 percent of patients who have had extensive dissection will develop some numbness in the upper thigh, which is generally said not to be annoying (Long and Sandler, 1990).

[6]   Laparoscopic Repair of Groin Hernias

The possibility of using laparoscopic procedures to repair groin hernias is currently under investigation. This type of repair may be suitable for use in correcting femoral hernias, which require only a minimal repair procedure, and indirect hernias with no or very little dilation of the internal inguinal ring.

At present, however, the considerations that usually favor laparoscopic procedures do not apply to hernia repair. Conventional hernias repair is done under local anesthetic with a small incision. Not only does laparoscopic repair require general anesthesia, but the total length of the three incisions this procedure requires is the same as that of the single conventional incision.

Further, the laparoscopic surgical instruments currently available do not enable surgeons to perform the fascia-to-fascia approximation required for direct, large indirect and recurrent hernias. It is possible that new instruments under development will eventually enable surgeons to repair all types of groin hernias laparoscopically (Nyhus, 1992).

9.08   TRAUMATIC DIAPHRAGMATIC HERNIA

Another type of herniation, related almost entirely to trauma, is protrusion of abdominal organs into the chest through a tear in the diaphragm caused by blunt or penetrating injury. Death caused by traumatic diaphragmatic hernia was reported as early as the sixteenth century (Bush and Margulies, 1990).

Diaphragmatic injuries can be extremely difficult to diagnose, especially when the tear is small, yet they can lead to serious sequelae and even death if they are left untreated.

[1] Epidemiology

The diaphragm is a dome-shaped structure composed of muscle and tendon that separates the abdominal and chest cavities, whose function is to assist respiration. The diaphragm contracts during inspiration, which pulls it downward and increases the volume of the chest cavity, thus allowing air to flow into the lungs. The diaphragm then relaxes during expiration, allowing the dome to rise, which pushes air out of the lungs.

Rupture of the diaphragm occurs in 3 to 8 percent of cases of blunt trauma that are serious enough to require laparotomy (surgical exploration of the abdomen), but blunt trauma causes only 10 to 30 percent of diaphragm injuries; the rest result from penetrating wounds. Young adults suffer a high incidence of these injuries (McHugh, 1991).

More than 95 percent of patients with diaphragmatic injury have serious associated abdominal, neurologic, thoracic and/or orthopedic injuries. The incidence of diaphragmatic injuries has increased since World War II, largely because there has been an increase in the number of motor vehicle accidents.

[2] Mechanisms of Injury

Blunt injuries that appear to have healed completely, as well as unimportant-seeming stab wounds of the diaphragm, can result in herniation of abdominal organs years later through an undiscovered defect.

[a] Blunt Trauma

Most blunt injuries of the diaphragm are caused by motor vehicle accidents (Pairolero, et al., 1989). Other causes include falls from considerable heights, blast injuries and crush injuries. It is thought that the mechanism of injury involves a sudden increase in pressure in the abdominal cavity relative to that in the chest cavity that is strong enough to rupture it. Most often the tear occurs radially (spreading outward from the center) along the posterolateral (behind and to the side) aspect of the diaphragm (Flint and Malangoni, 1987).

Blunt injuries occur predominantly on the left side of the diaphragm, partly because the right side is protected by the liver and partly because there is a weak area on the left that is the point of fusion of two embryonic components. Thus less pressure is required to rupture the left side than the right side. The diaphragm may also be torn from its attachments around the edge (Pairolero, et al., 1989).

[b] Penetrating Trauma

Penetrating wounds of the diaphragm are caused by stabbing or shooting or, in war, by other penetrating missiles. They may occur in any part of the diaphragm, but most are left-sided. This is both because most assailants are right-handed and because most are targeting the heart, which lies on the left side. Frequently the tear in the diaphragm is quite small (Pairolero, et al., 1989).

[c] Spontaneous Rupture

Heavy lifting, twisting or coughing combined with a valsalva maneuver (in which the individual forcibly exhales against a closed mouth and closed nostrils) can create enough intra-abdominal pressure to result in what is known as spontaneous rupture of the diaphragm (Pairolero, et al., 1989).

[d] Trauma and Pre-existing Hernia

Bochdalek's and Morgagni's hernias are two congenital types of diaphragmatic hernia that may already be present before an injury. They may be considerably enlarged by even a minor blunt trauma.

[3] Traumatic Diaphragmatic Hernia and the Workplace

The workplace presents a variety of hazards that can cause the types of injuries that may result in traumatic diaphragmatic hernia.[18]

[a] Causes of Injuries

Crush injuries, falls and explosions are the major causes of blunt diaphragmatic trauma. In the construction industry, hazards include collapse of structures and of trenches. In manufacturing industries, workers commonly fall from ladders or trestles or down stairs, or suffer

---

[18] *See also* ch. 5 for a discussion of injuries of the spinal cord and nerve roots.

projectile wounds. Foundry workers and those who handle flammable or explosive substances are at risk for blast injuries, which can eventually result in hernias.

[b] Prevention

Prevention of the hazards that can result in diaphragmatic injury is encompassed in the general set of measures that can be implemented to control workplace injuries. Two basic components of prevention are, first, safe design of the worksite and of machines and operations, and second, instituting an injury control program. Such a program trains workers to recognize and control hazards, sets company policies (such as instituting the requirement that certain safe work practices be followed) and implements these policies.

[4] Nature of Injury

The stomach is the organ that herniates most often through a diaphragmatic defect, with the colon next in frequency. On the left side, the small intestine, omentum and, less frequently, the left lobe of the liver may herniate. On the right, the liver, gallbladder and transverse colon may herniate. (*See Figure 9–5.*)

[a] Results of Herniation

Traumatic diaphragmatic hernia affects both cardiorespiratory function and the herniated organs themselves. The injury may paralyze the diaphragm by impairing the function of the phrenic nerve (arising from the cervical plexus, chiefly from the fourth cervical nerve, it is the main motor nerve of the diaphragm and imperative for proper respiration). The mass of herniated abdominal organs compresses the lungs, leading to hypoxemia (deficient oxygenation of the blood). However, the movement of these organs in and out of the chest in a paradoxic manner (at variance with the normal pattern) compromises ventilation (air exchange) in the alveoli (small air sacs in the lungs) and may result in pulmonary gas exchange defects leading to hypoxemia and even respiratory acidosis. This may be a very significant problem in patients with underlying cardiopulmonary disease. Continuing dilation of an incarcerated stomach may add to the respiratory impairment.

If the herniation is extensive, the chest organs are displaced to the contralateral (opposite) side and further compromise respiration and the return of venous blood to the heart. Rarely, abdominal contents

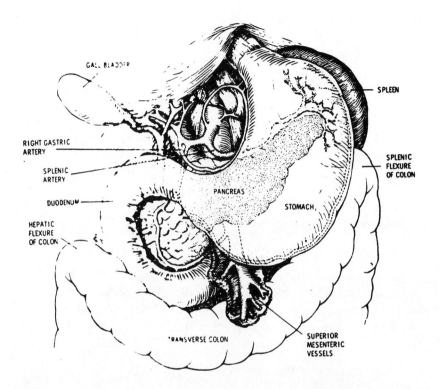

Fig. 9–5. Anterior view of the upper abdomen, including the transverse colon.

herniate into the pericardium (membrane covering the heart) and may compromise cardiac function. At the same time, the patient may be suffering other injuries involving blood loss and sepsis (Pairolero, et al., 1989; Flint and Malangoni, 1987).

The herniated viscera may themselves become incarcerated, obstructed and strangulated, progressing finally to gangrene. As with abdominal wall hernias, obstruction and strangulation represent a potentially fatal medical emergency (Pairolero, et al., 1989; Bush and Margulies, 1990).

Blunt trauma generally leads to a large tear in the diaphragm and acute herniation of abdominal viscera that, if not treated early, results in respiratory impairment. Penetrating injury that is not treated, on the other hand, will usually lead to herniation of a section of the gastrointestinal tract through a small tear, and consequent obstruction and strangulation. Because of the potential for strangulation, these small defects can be more dangerous than the larger injuries resulting from blunt trauma.

The pressure differential between the abdominal and thoracic cavities tends to cause such herniation when there is even a small tear in the diaphragm (Bush and Margulies, 1990). At first, only a tag of omentum may herniate; then, after a period that may last years, an increase in intra-abdominal pressure will cause herniation of a viscus. This mechanism explains why no case of a diaphragmatic injury healing spontaneously has ever been reported.

Cases have also been reported in which small penetrating wounds of the diaphragm, caused, for example, by stabbings, led to herniation of abdominal organs that did not become symptomatic until years later—in one case, 45 years later—when symptoms of intestinal obstruction led the individual to seek treatment (Bush and Margulies, 1990).

[b]   Sequence of Clinical Events

The presentation and clinical course of injuries resulting in traumatic diaphragmatic hernias is classified into three phases.

About 70 percent of cases of blunt trauma are first seen in the acute phase, with symptoms including dyspnea (breathlessness), vague abdominal pain, cyanosis (bluish color of the skin due to inadequate oxygenation of the blood), sometimes bowel sounds heard in the chest on auscultation (stethoscope examination) and decreased breath sounds in the chest. Frequently these patients have associated abdominal injuries, although there may be no external signs at all. However, these signs and symptoms do not reliably indicate that there is a diaphragmatic injury.

Small penetrating wounds generally cause no symptoms in the acute phase. This phase ends with the patient appearing to have recovered from the original injury (Bush and Margulies, 1990).

If the diaphragmatic injury is not discovered and treated at the time of injury, the latent phase follows. It may last for anywhere from a few days to many years. Symptoms that appear during this phase are predominantly gastrointestinal and vague enough to make diagnosis of diaphragmatic injury difficult. They include chronic pain in the left shoulder, vomiting, difficulty in belching and bloating after meals. These complaints resemble the symptoms of conditions such as peptic ulcer, gallstone disease and coronary artery disease. Their cause is believed to be sporadic entrapment of the herniated organs.

Patients may also have symptoms of acute respiratory distress or restrictive pulmonary disease. Between 17 and 51 percent of diaphragmatic injuries are diagnosed during the latent phase (Bush and Margulies, 1990).

The obstructive phase commences with the appearance of symptoms related to obstruction and strangulation of herniated organs. This happens within three years in 85 percent of patients. However, diagnosis can still be quite difficult. Severe pain may mimic coronary artery disease; colonic obstruction may lead to suspicion of colon cancer; or the diagnosis may be complicated by pregnancy.

If the strangulated organ ruptures, the result may be empyema (infection in the pleural space, that is, between the two layers of the membrane lining the lungs), hydropneumothorax (presence of fluid and air in the pleural space) or intra-abdominal abscess (infection). These complications may be misdiagnosed as being related to lung disease.

Further, the patient may not make the connection between these symptoms and an injury that occurred months or years earlier and therefore may fail to mention it to the physician. Another possibility is that the physician may fail to appreciate the significance of such a history. Specific questioning may be necessary to bring out the history of a long-ago injury (Bush and Margulies, 1990).

[5]   Diagnosis

Successful management of traumatic diaphragmatic hernia depends on early diagnosis and repair of the defect. In many cases, however, the diagnosis is missed, sometimes more than once. In acute cases, multiple associated injuries such as fractures and injuries to the spleen, stomach, liver and intestines may dominate the clinical picture. Frequently traumatic diaphragmatic hernia cannot be diagnosed until surgical exploration is carried out for other organ injuries (Pairolero, et al., 1989).

A critical factor in making the diagnosis is maintaining a high index of suspicion, particularly if there is a history of previous trauma and especially of penetrating injury between the fourth intracostal (between the ribs) space and the umbilicus (Bush and Margulies, 1990). Because of the difficulty of diagnosis, a large number of diagnostic modalities have been used.

[a] Signs and Symptoms

Diaphragmatic injury due to blunt trauma is usually associated with other injuries that require laparotomy; as a result, during surgery, the injury to the diaphragm is discovered and repaired. Otherwise, clinical examination is generally not useful, since physical findings are nonspecific and unreliable.

Early signs of acute herniation are dyspnea (difficulty breathing) and pain in the left side of the chest that may be referred to the shoulder. When the defect is small, there may be only a dull area heard on auscultation (stethoscope examination), with decreased breath sounds and decreased movement of the diaphragm, or no abnormal signs at all. However, acutely injured patients will also be splinting the injured side of the chest (holding the muscles rigid to avoid pain) and will have a hemothorax (blood in the pleural space), which tends to produce the same signs.

With larger degrees of herniation, the findings on percussion (striking short, sharp blows) will be a mixture of dullness and tympany (bell-like notes). Since initially peristalsis ceases after injury, bowel sounds are unlikely to be heard in the chest even if herniation has occurred. Further, the patient may require treatment for respiratory distress and perhaps shock that supersedes further attempts at diagnosis.

[b] Chest X-ray

Diagnosis is usually based on the chest x-ray, although the film may be normal in up to 37.5 percent of patients with diaphragmatic injuries (Bush and Margulies, 1990). In other cases, a hemothorax may obscure the indications of herniation. However, repeat films should indicate the diagnosis.

Radiographic signs suggesting diaphragmatic injury include a high diaphragm, mediastinal shift (organs of the mediastinum—that is, those between the lungs—shifted to one side) and radiolucent areas (that appear dark on the film) above the normal level of the diaphragm (Bush and Margulies, 1990). Typical multiple fluid levels suggesting the presence of bowel may be observed in the chest radiograph.

If the chest x-ray is abnormal and no surgery is planned for some other indication, the patient should have a contrast study to ensure that the diaphragm is not injured (Pairolero, et al., 1989).

It may also be useful to insert a nasogastric tube before taking an x-ray. The presence of the tube above the diaphragm, as seen on the film, will indicate herniation of the stomach or bowel (Harms, et al., 1987).

[c]   Contrast Studies

Contrast x-rays using barium administered either through a nasogastric tube or in an enema can demonstrate herniation of any part of the gastrointestinal tract. Injection of contrast material into the chest through a chest tube has also been used to diagnose traumatic diaphragmatic hernia. The path of the contrast medium as it passes from the pleural cavity into the peritoneal cavity is shown on the film. However, tube insertion poses a danger of empyema and development of a fistula (abnormal communication) between the colon and pleura (Bush and Margulies, 1990).

Contrast studies of the upper gastrointestinal tract should be performed before discharging a patient who has had severe chest and abdominal trauma that included the diaphragm (Pairolero, et al., 1989).

[d]   Endoscopy

Endoscopy is examination using a long, thin instrument called an endoscope that allows direct visualization of interior body spaces. Use of thoracoscopy (endoscopic examination of the chest) and laparoscopy (examination of the abdominal cavity) to establish a diagnosis in difficult cases has also been reported (Bush and Margulies, 1990).

[e]   Fluoroscopy

In fluoroscopy, the body is positioned between the x-ray machine and the fluoroscope, on the screen of which are projected the shadows of x-rays that pass through the body. Fluoroscopy of the diaphragm has been used for diagnosis, together with barium studies and the film of the chest x-ray (Bush and Margulies, 1990).

[f]   Computed Tomography

Although computed tomography (CT) has been used to diagnose traumatic diaphragmatic hernia, most experts agree that it is relatively insensitive and that since other methods are adequate, it is preferable to avoid the radiation exposure and cost of CT (Bush and Margulies, 1990; McHugh, 1991).

[g] Radionuclide Scanning

This procedure involves injecting a preparation of a radioactive isotope and then photographing the part in question with a gamma camera. A liver-spleen scan may be helpful for diagnosing traumatic diaphragmatic hernia when the liver has herniated into the right side of the chest or when the spleen has herniated into the left side. The scan may even reveal herniation of the colon as well (Bush and Margulies, 1990).

[h] Ultrasonography

Ultrasonography has been found to be of limited use in diagnosing traumatic diaphragmatic rupture (Bush and Margulies, 1990).

[i] Pneumoperitoneum

In this technique, air is introduced into the peritoneal cavity. If there is a defect in the diaphragm, the air will escape through it into the chest and be visible on x-rays taken with the patient upright.

Although some writers report that pneumoperitoneum is helpful for diagnosis of right-sided diaphragmatic injuries, others emphasize that it is unreliable if the peritoneum is intact or if there are adhesions (fibrous structures that cause body parts to adhere to each other abnormally) that prevent the air from escaping into the chest. Pneumoperitoneum also involves a risk of inducing a tension pneumothorax (air trapped in the pleural space) where none existed (Bush and Margulies, 1990).

[j] Laparotomy

Small penetrating wounds of the diaphragm may be discovered not because of acute herniation but during surgical exploration for the causes of other symptoms. For this reason, it is important to thoroughly examine the diaphragm during laparotomy for abdominal injuries. Although it is common practice to explore all penetrating wounds below the nipple, these small tears in the diaphragm are frequently missed.

[k]   Angiography

Angiography (contrast study of blood vessels) has been performed on the celiac and the hepatic artery to detect herniation of spleen on the left or the liver on the right. (*See Figure 9–6.*)

[6]   Treatment

Since injuries of the diaphragm do not heal spontaneously, treatment is always by surgical repair. In fact, traumatic diaphragmatic hernia and obstruction have been known to develop even in cases in which the tear in the diaphragm was sutured during laparotomy (Bush and Margulies, 1990).

In acute cases of herniation, immediate decompression of the stomach through a nasogastric tube can often relieve the breathing

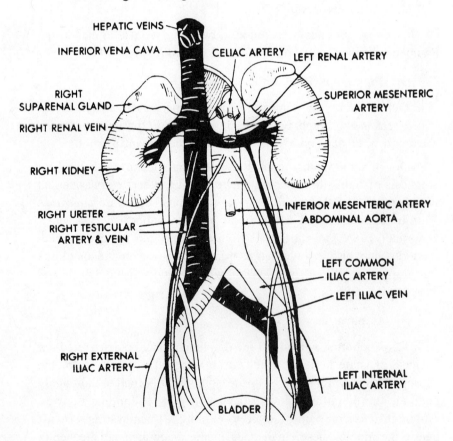

Fig. 9–6. The major blood vessels of the abdomen, including the celiac artery.

difficulty that accompanies hernias on the left side (Flint and Malan-goni, 1987).

Surgical repair of traumatic diaphragmatic hernia involves reduction of the herniated organs, followed by repair of the tear in the diaphragm. Acute injuries are generally repaired by an abdominal approach, unless there are associated chest injuries requiring thoracotomy. The abdominal approach allows repair of associated intra-abdominal injuries.

Delayed cases, however, usually require a chest incision, since when a hernia becomes chronic, the herniated organs become attached to other structures in the chest by adhesions that must be divided before the hernia can be reduced. Thoracotomy may also be preferred for hernias resulting from blunt trauma or if there have been earlier abdominal operations. If the hernia has become obstructed or strangu-lated, a combined thoracoabdominal incision may be necessary (Pairolero, et al., 1989).

Depending on the surgeon's preference, the defect is sutured in two layers or by imbrication (overlapping) of the torn edges. In rare cases, primary closure of the tear is not possible and a prosthetic material such as Marlex ® or Dacron ® has been used to close a gap or reinforce the suture line (Pairolero, et al., 1989).

Before the suture closure, a chest tube should be inserted for drainage in order to avoid pneumothorax (Flint and Malangoni, 1987).

[7] Prognosis

The mortality rate of traumatic diaphragmatic hernia ranges from 15 to 20 percent and for blunt injuries alone is between 14 and 25 percent (Flint and Malangoni, 1987). However, death in such cases is generally caused by the associated injuries, not the injury to the diaphragm itself.

Once a traumatic diaphragmatic hernia has become obstructed, there is a high risk of mortality. The mortality rate when strangulation develops and progresses to gangrene ranges from 20 to 80 percent (Bush and Margulies, 1990).

Repair of diaphragmatic injury has a favorable prognosis: Morbidity ranges from 60 to 80 percent, and mortality is 18 percent. Again, poor outcome is usually related to the nature of associated injuries as well as to delay in diagnosing traumatic diaphragmatic hernia (Pairolero, 1989).

9.09 PROGNOSIS

Uncomplicated hernia repairs have a very low operative mortality rate. However, mortality resulting from intestinal obstruction related to incarcerated or strangulated hernia remains high, although the rate has been decreasing as a result of improvements in surgical technique (Nyhus, et al., 1991).[19]

The incidence of strangulation could be reduced by greater awareness of the risk on the part of the general public and physicians, since many patients apparently put off telling a doctor when they notice a hernia, and physicians often do not promptly refer patients with hernias for surgery (McEntee, et al., 1989).

[1] Recurrence Rates

In general, the results of hernia repair are measured in terms of recurrence, and the rates are still relatively high: it is thought that 100,000 patients are at risk for groin hernia recurrence each year (Nyhus, et al., 1991). Indirect hernias have a lower rate of recurrence than direct or femoral hernias, and incisional hernias have a higher rate. Recurrence is frequent after a second repair of a hernia that has recurred once.

Factors related to recurrence include lack of understanding of subtle aspects of groin anatomy; poor operative technique (hernia repairs are often performed by inexperienced surgeons); and failure to follow up patients so that technical failings are not recognized (Nyhus, et al., 1991).

Since the recurrence rate reported for the Shouldice technique, as mentioned, is below 1 percent, rates for inguinal hernia repairs performed with an anterior approach[20] range from 5 to 20 percent (Nyhus, et al., 1991). Optimally it is possible to achieve a recurrence rate of 2 percent after repair of a recurrent hernia with a mesh implant (Nyhus, 1992).

The recurrence rate after primary repair of incisional hernia is 24.8 percent; after a second repair, the rate is 41 percent (Read, 1989).

---

[19] *See* 9.02[3] *supra.*

[20] *See* 9.07 [4] *supra.*

[2] Return to Work

Return to work after hernia repair depends on the nature of both the patient's job and the operation. After outpatient Shouldice repair, work restriction is minimal unless the job is strenuous or requires straining or heavy lifting, activities that should be avoided for four to six weeks (Long and Sandler, 1990). In one series of 283 patients, 95 percent returned to work within a week (Gilbert, 1987).

9.10 EVALUATION OF IMPAIRMENT

The effect of a hernia is to decrease an individual's ability to exert maximum effort, since he or she tends to avoid any strain that would increase intra-abdominal pressure. Clearly this would have more effect on job performance in an occupation involving vigorous physical effort than in a sedentary one. It is also possible that in a hazardous occupational environment, such a restraint on a worker's actions could increase the risk of injury.

The American Medical Association's system of evaluating abdominal wall impairment due to herniation is based on the extent of protrusion involved and the extent to which normal activity is limited by the discomfort or pain suffered by the individual. Procedures used to evaluate the hernia include physical examination and herniography.

Hernial impairment is categorized into three classes. The criterion common to all three is the presence of a palpable (detectable by manual examination) defect in the supporting structures of the abdominal wall.

[1] Class 1 Impairment

Class 1 impairment involves 0 to 5 percent impairment of the whole person. The criteria are the presence of a slight protrusion upon increased intra-abdominal pressure that is readily reducible, or occasional mild discomfort that does not prevent normal activity.

An example of Class 1 impairment would be a 60-year-old woman who developed an incisional hernia after cholecystectomy (gallbladder removal). When she rises after lying down, a light protrusion appears at one end of the scar, which she considers unattractive. She experiences no discomfort. She is considered to have 0 percent impairment.

[2] Class 2 Impairment

Class 2 impairment involves 10 to 15 percent impairment of the whole person. Criteria are protrusion that is frequent or persistent upon increased intra-abdominal pressure but remains manually reducible, or frequent discomfort that prevents heavy lifting but not normal activity.

An example of this class is a 50-year-old man who for several years has experienced recurring protrusion in the right groin area upon increased intra-abdominal pressure. The mass has increased in size and extended to the scrotum but can still be reduced without pain. The man, whose life-style is sedentary, prefers to accept his inability to lift heavy weights rather than have surgery, even though he was informed of the risks involved. He is considered to have a 10 percent impairment.

[3]   Class 3 Impairment

This class involves 20 to 30 percent impairment of the whole person. The criteria are a persistent, irreducible or irreparable protrusion and limitation of normal activity.

An example of Class 3 impairment is a 64-year-old man with bilateral groin hernias that recurred despite three repair attempts at repair. The hernias are partially reducible, and the man wears a truss. He has occasional discomfort and cannot do any lifting but is not willing to have more surgery. He is considered to have a 30 percent impairment (American Medical Association, 1993).

9.100 BIBLIOGRAPHY

Reference Bibliography

American Medical Association: Guides to the Evaluation of Permanent Impairment, 4th ed. Chicago: American Medical Association, 1993.

Bush, C. A. and Margulies, R.: Traumatic Diaphragmatic Hernia and Intestinal Obstruction Due to Penetrating Trunk Wounds. South. Med. J. 83(11):1347–1350, 1990.

Devlin, H. B.: Management of Abdominal Hernias. London: Butterworth, 1988.

Deysine, M.: Hernia Repair with Expanded Polytetrafluoroethylene. Am. J. Surg. 3:422, April 1992.

Flint, L. M. and Malangoni, M. A.: Abdominal Injuries. In: Richardson, J. D., et al. (Eds.): Trauma: Clinical Care and Pathophysiology. Chicago: Year Book Medical Publishers, 1987.

Gilbert, A. I.: Overnight Hernia Repair: Updated Considerations. South. Med. J. 80:191–195, 1987.

Guarnieri, A., et al.: A New Technique for Indirect Inguinal Hernia Repair. Am. J. Surg. 164(1):70–73, July 1992.

Long, T. D. and Sandler, J.: Outpatient Hernia Repair. The Shouldice Technique. A.O.R.N. J. 52:801, Oct. 1990.

McEntee, G. P., et al.: Timing of Strangulation in Adult Hernias. Br. J. Surg. 76(7):725–726, July 1989.

McHugh, K., et al.: Delayed Presentation of Traumatic Diaphragmatic Hernia. Clin. Radiol. 43(4):246–250, Apr. 1991.

Nyhus, L. M.: Laparoscopic Hernia Repair: A Point of View. Arch. Surg. 137(2):139, Feb. 1992.

Nyhus, L. M., et al.: Hernias. In: Sabiston, D. C., Jr. (Ed.): Textbook of Surgery: The Biological Basis of Modern Surgical Practice. Philadelphia: Saunders, 1991.

Pairolero, P. C., et al.: Esophagus and Diaphragmatic Hernias. In: Schwartz, S. I., et al. (Eds.): Principles of Surgery, 5th ed. New York: McGraw-Hill, 1989.

Additional References

Askew, G., et al.: Delayed Presentation and Misdiagnosis of Strangulated Hernia: Prospective Study. J.R. Coll. Surg. Edinb. 37(1):37–38, Feb. 1992.

Berliner, S. D., et al.: The Henry Operation for Incarcerated and Strangulated Femoral Hernias. Arch. Surg. 127(3):314–316, March 1992.

Gilbert, A. I.: Sutureless Repair of Inguinal Hernia. Am. J. Surg. 163(3):331–335, Mar. 1992.

Libman, E., et al.: Prostatectomy and Inguinal Hernia Repair: A Comparison of the Sexual Consequences. J. Sex Marital Ther. 17(11):27–34, Spring 1991.

Perez-Seoane, C., et al.: Endometriosis in an Inguinal Crural Hernia. Diagnosis by Fine Needle Aspiration Biopsy. Acta Cytol. 35(3):350–352, May-June 1991.

Sahdev, P., et al.: Traumatic Abdominal Hernia: Report of Three Cases and Review of the Literature. Am. J. Emerg. Med. 10(3):237–241, May 1992.

Yavetz, H., et al.: Fertility of the Male Following Inguinal Hernia Repair. Andrologia 23(6):443–446, Nov.-Dec. 1991.

CHAPTER 10

Noise-Induced Hearing Loss

SCOPE

Noise is one of the oldest known occupational hazards, but only recently has noise-induced hearing loss been seriously investigated. Hearing loss from noise now affects about ten million workers. The condition is not treatable by any surgical procedure; neither is it even well understood. Some accidental exposures cannot be avoided, but most noise-induced hearing loss is thoroughly preventable. Hearing loss from intense sounds of short duration is usually reversible. Far more serious is the irreversible loss associated with long periods of exposure to damaging noise levels. Such hearing loss is caused mainly by damage to the hair cells of the organ of Corti—specialized sensory cells that convert the mechanical effects of sound vibrations in the fluid of the ear into electrochemical nerve impulses. Tinnitus, or noises in the ear, frequently occurs among employees in a noisy workplace. Although effective noise control techniques exist, there is a great deal of noncompliance with protective guidelines. Although it is impossible to restore sensorineural hearing loss, a number of auditory rehabilitation programs have proved useful.

SYNOPSIS

10.01   INTRODUCTION AND CURRENT ISSUES

Noise is one of the oldest known occupational hazards. In the eighteenth century, it was noted that copper workers hammering metal suffered loss of hearing; similar observations were made of nineteenth-century blacksmiths and boiler makers (Polakoff, 1990). However, it is only recently that noise-induced hearing loss has been seriously investigated.

Loss of hearing from exposure to loud noise is not treatable by any medical or surgical procedure; neither is it even well understood. Some accidental exposures cannot be avoided, of course. However, with the use of hearing conservation measures, noise-induced hearing loss is generally preventable. Although effective noise control techniques do exist, occupational hearing loss remains a serious concern, largely due to a falling-off during the 1980s of enforcement of—and consequently compliance with—government regulations created in the early 1970s that established protective guidelines (Polakoff, 1990; Consensus Conference, 1990).

10.02   POPULATIONS AT RISK

About ten million people in the United States have hearing loss caused by noise exposure, mostly occupational (Consensus Conference, 1990). According to the National Institute for Occupational

Safety and Health (NIOSH), 1.7 million U.S. workers aged 50 to 59 have sustained compensable noise induced hearing loss. NIOSH estimates that 14 percent of all employees are exposed to work environments with noise levels over 90 dBA (distribution of frequencies).[1] In fact, more workers are exposed to hazardous noise levels than to any other important occupational hazard (Olishifski, 1988).

Since no comprehensive epidemiologic studies exist, more exact data is lacking on the number of workers who are exposed to damaging levels of noise. Some estimates put the number at eight to ten million employees in manufacturing industries; however, these estimates do not include an additional four million workers in industries such as construction, mining, transportation and agriculture who are also exposed to hazardous levels of noise (Polakoff, 1990).

10.03 MEASUREMENT OF NOISE

The term "sound" can refer both to the atmospheric pressure fluctuations (sound waves) that impinge upon the ear and to the subjective auditory sensations into which the ear converts this stimulation.

[1] Components of Sound

Sounds can be specified in terms of three components: amplitude, frequency and time.

[a] Amplitude

Amplitude refers to loudness. The most commonly used specification of loudness is known as sound level and is measured in units called decibels (dB). Speech at a normal conversational level has a sound level of about 50 to 65 dB; an air-cooled pressure motor one of 90 dB; a power saw, 110 dB; and a jet plane taking off, 120 to 145 dB. Sounds above 85 dB (some say 80 dB) are potentially damaging to hearing. Listeners begin to experience sounds as painful at 125 dB (Consensus Conference, 1990; Polakoff, 1990; Olishifski, 1988). Ordinarily the human ear can detect sound ranging from barely audible levels (0 dB) to levels as high as 120 or more dB (extremely loud and painful noise).

---

[1] *See* 10.03 *infra.*

The decibel scale is logarithmic. This means, for example, that a 20 dB sound is not twice as loud as a 10 dB sound but, rather, 100 times as loud. Awareness of this is an important component in the safety education of workers, who ought to understand that a noise increase of a small number of decibels will mean a significantly larger amount of noise (Polakoff, 1990).

[b]   Frequency

Frequency is equivalent to pitch, or number of sound waves per second. It is expressed in Hertz (Hz, or number of cycles per second). A normal young ear can hear frequencies ranging between 20 and 20,000 Hz. A pure tone consists of a very regular oscillation at one single frequency. A complex sound is comprised of a number of different frequencies. A sound's spectrum is the pattern of distribution of the frequencies it contains. In narrow-band noise, the frequencies largely fall within a narrow range; broad-band noises include a wide range of frequencies (Olishifski, 1988).

[c]   Time

This term refers to the time pattern over which a sound is heard. The term "continuous noise" denotes two things: (1) broad-band noise in which level and spectrum remain fairly constant, and (2) noise that is heard for 6 to 8 hours a day, 40 hours a week, 50 weeks a year. This is the type of noise environment to which most factory workers are exposed, and most regulations governing permissible levels of exposure are written for exposure to continuous noise.[2]

"Impulse" or "impact noise," on the other hand, is discontinuous. An example of impulse noise is a rifle shot; a drop forge creates impact noise. This type of noise is more difficult to measure (Olishifski, 1988; Consensus Conference, 1990).

[2]   Noise-Measuring Instruments

Often, employers ask a physician to evaluate the need for a hearing conservation program (HCP). The first step is to perform noise measurements, a procedure usually carried out on the doctor's behalf by an industrial hygienist. A variety of instruments are available to measure noise exposure (McCunney, 1988):

---

[2] *See* 10.10 *infra.*

- simple sound level meters;

- individual noise dosimeters, which integrate cumulative noise exposures over a typical work period; and

- octave-band analyzers, which break down overall noise into particular frequencies.

The most typical measurement in the workplace, obtained from either a sound level meter or a noise dosimeter, is the overall sound level.

The American Conference of Governmental Industrial Hygienists and the Occupational Safety and Health Administration (OSHA) recommend that the A scale be used for this measurement, since the distribution of frequencies in this scale approximates the way most people hear sound. Sound so measured is notated in dBA units (Olishifski, 1988; Consensus Conference, 1990).

Measurement of a worker's noise exposure includes two components: (1) making an adequate number of measurements over the course of one day or, preferably, several nonconsecutive days; and (2) taking the measurements at an appropriate location, preferably with the microphone no more than a few inches from the worker's ear (Olishifski, 1988).

[a]   Sound Level Meter

The sound level meter is the basic instrument used to measure loudness. In essence, it consists of the following components:

- a microphone;

- an amplifier that includes an attenuator adjustable in 10-dB intervals, to allow a wide range of sounds to be covered by the indicating needle;

- a set of frequency weighting networks, including an A-scale filter; and

- a meter to display the sound level in decibels.

Various types of sound level meters have been specified by the American National Standards Institute, ranging from highly precise instruments with several weighting networks to simpler, less accurate devices with only an A scale. Some of these instruments can perform an analysis showing how the sound energy is distributed across all audible frequencies, with loudness measured for different bands. This type of analysis is useful for determining the sources of noise (Olishifski, 1988).

[b] Dosimeter

The noise dosimeter is designed to electronically sum up exposure to noise levels. These vary as the worker moves toward and away from various sources of noise over a typical work period, thus producing a more accurate picture of individual exposure. The noise dose is an expression of this cumulative exposure. However, converting a series of decibel levels to an expression of actual exposure presents certain difficulties that limit the effectiveness of the dosimeter (Olishifski, 1988).

10.04 DEFINITION OF HEARING LOSS

Hearing loss due to noise exposure can occur to individuals at any age. It frequently results in difficulty understanding speech and in tinnitus (hearing ringing, buzzing or other noise in the ears). Extremely loud, brief sounds such as that produced by an explosion can result in immediate, permanent hearing loss. More often, hearing loss is gradual, a result of cumulative exposure to less intense noise (Consensus Conference, 1990).

Occupational hearing loss has been defined as "a partial or complete hearing loss in one or both ears arising in, or during the course of, and as the result of one's employment" (Olishifski, 1988). This term includes hearing loss caused by traumatic injury as well as that which is noise induced. Occasionally hearing loss can also be a result of exposure to toxic substances, such as heavy metals or solvents, in the workplace.

Occupational hearing loss caused by noise ranges from mild to profound. There are two types: acoustic trauma and noise-induced hearing loss.

[1] Acoustic Trauma

Sudden hearing loss due to intense sound of short duration is known as acoustic trauma. It can cause damage to all the ear structures, but particularly to the organ of Corti, the delicate sensory organ of hearing that is housed within the bony cochlea of the inner ear (Consensus Conference, 1990). (*See Figure 10–1.*)

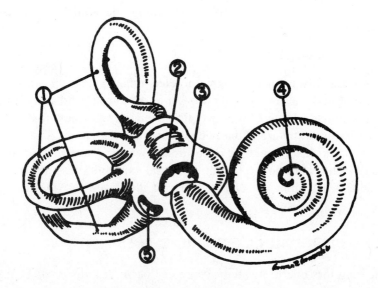

Figure 10–1. The bony inner ear. (1) three semicircular canals (2) vestibule (3) oval window (4) bony cochlea (5) round window

[2] Noise-Induced Hearing Loss

The term "noise-induced" is used specifically to denote the gradual, irreversible hearing loss associated with long periods of exposure to damaging levels of noise that are nevertheless below the level required to cause acoustic trauma. Usually noise-induced hearing loss affects both ears equally, but sometimes there is a difference in the degree that each ear is impaired. This can occur, for instance, when the noise always occurs on the same side, as in the case of sound generated by weapons (Olishifski, 1988; Consensus Conference, 1990).

[3] Temporary and Permanent Hearing Loss

There are two kinds of hearing loss: temporary and permanent. A temporary loss can be caused by transient exposure to dangerously high levels of noise. Such losses are called noise-induced temporary threshold shifts, or NITTS. NITTS may persist for minutes, hours or even days. The greater the length of the exposure, the greater the recovery time. With adequate rest, however, most people do recover. A person who experiences this kind of noise-induced damage notices hearing loss almost immediately. Audiometric examinations should be delayed until at least 14 hours after the offending episode.

Such temporary episodes can be dangerous, however. Day-to-day exposures to damaging levels of noise appear to be harmless. Their danger may be masked by the fact that hearing seems to recover completely before the following day's exposure. This recovery is pure illusion, however, because repeated episodes of NITTS will result in permanent damage, no matter how complete the recovery seems to be between exposures.

10.05 THRESHOLD SHIFT

The hearing threshold is the borderline of a person's hearing. It is defined as the loudness of a tone that a person can hear 50 percent of the time. Threshold shift is the increase in that threshold in reference to a previous measurement; that is, a decrease in hearing. Temporary threshold shift, or TTS, is a temporary loss of hearing that occurs after moderate exposure to damaging levels of noise. If the exposure does not continue, this effect is reversible, and hearing returns to normal. Continued exposure, however, will result in a permanent threshold shift (PTS) (Consensus Conference, 1990).

10.06 TYPES OF HEARING LOSS

There are various types of hearing loss due to occupational exposure. The most important type is noise-induced. However, hearing loss may occur with physical trauma to the ear or as a result of exposure to toxic substances in the workplace. Physical injury to the ear may produce damage to the conductive system (middle ear) or may involve sensorineural mechanisms. Occasionally tinnitus (noises within the ear) may be an associated symptom of any type of hearing loss.

The difference between these various types of hearing loss has implications for the differential diagnosis of occupational hearing loss.

[1] Sensorineural Hearing Loss

When sensorineural hearing loss is caused by noise exposure, it is thought to result from damage to the hair cells of the organ of Corti. These are specialized sensory cells that convert the mechanical effects of sound vibrations in the fluid that fills the cochlea (spiral-shaped canal of the inner ear) into electrochemical nerve impulses. These then travel along the acoustic nerve to the brain.

Animal experiments indicate that loud noises cause vascular, metabolic and chemical changes in the hair cells. Excess vibration may also result in direct mechanical damage to the hair cells or nerves. Initially these changes are reversible, but repeated exposure leads to increases in the number of damaged hair cells. Since such cells cannot regenerate, continued exposure causes increasingly severe hearing loss that is irreversible, since no medical treatment can restore them. When enough hair cells are damaged, the nerve cells supplying them begin to degenerate, leading to a corresponding degeneration in the central nervous system. It is not known, however, what role these nervous system changes play in noise-induced hearing loss (Polakoff, 1990; Hunter, 1987; Consensus Conference, 1990).

Sensorineural hearing loss involves an initial loss of sensitivity to higher frequencies—between 3000 and 6000 Hz. If the exposure is to high-frequency sound, usually only one area of the high-frequency area in the cochlea is injured.

This type of hearing loss characteristically involves difficulty in understanding speech. Although much of the sound energy of speech is low frequency, the information that enables the listener to distinguish sounds is in the high frequencies. Thus, if high-frequency damage is considerable, much speech becomes inaudible, especially against background noise (Consensus Conference, 1990).

[2]   Conductive Hearing Loss

Conductive hearing loss is due to a mechanical obstruction that blocks the transmission of sound through the outer or middle ear. Conductive hearing loss is most often associated with fractures that cause blood to accumulate in the external or middle ear, or with rupture of the eardrum or disruption of the bony ossicles that transmit sound to the organ of Corti.

[3]   Tinnitus

Tinnitus is a symptom the affected individual describes as a persistent, or occasionally intermittent, noise in one or both ears. It is ordinarily described as a ringing in the ear, but it may be perceived as a blowing or whistling sound. The occurrence of tinnitus is not considered a form of hearing loss but rather an early-warning signal of sensorineural hearing loss. It also causes additional debility in individuals who already have such loss. In one large study, 74 percent of patients with this condition reported that it was present more than 26 days a month. Among male patients with noise-induced hearing loss, 30 percent also had tinnitus; however, only 3 percent of women with noise-induced hearing loss also had tinnitus (Stouffer and Tyler, 1990).

However, severe tinnitus may also be present in persons with little or no hearing impairment. In the study just cited, 18 percent of the tinnitus patients had normal hearing or only mild impairment. Tinnitus is difficult to assess, because it is an entirely subjective phenomenon (Olishifski, 1988; Consensus Conference, 1990; Stouffer and Tyler, 1990).

10.07   SOUNDS THAT DAMAGE HEARING

Hazardous sounds are usually described in terms of sound level, frequency and duration. They must attain a certain loudness, include certain frequencies and last long enough to be damaging. Damage is caused by the amount of acoustic energy that reaches the ear and does not depend on the specific source of the sound. Thus a wide range of sounds encountered in all spheres of life can be hazardous.

[1]   Hazardous Sound Levels

Because of the individual variables involved,[3] it is not possible to make a clear distinction between safe and hazardous levels of noise. Experts generally agree that even high frequencies of sounds below 75 dBA will not cause permanent hearing loss. However, there is controversy over exactly where the line between harmless and harmful noise actually lies. Eight hours of exposure to 90 dBA will result in significant impairment to hearing in 1 out of 5 employees, and 1 in 20 will have serious enough impairment to be eligible for compensation (Polakoff, 1990).

Some current regulations, however, are based on the assumption that a worker can safely handle up to eight hours a day of exposure at 85 dBA. The current OSHA standard allows eight hours a day at up to 90 dBA.

Under some circumstances, OSHA allows workers to be exposed to even higher dBA levels. However, in these instances, OSHA requires shorter periods of exposure to the noise. This exchange is

---

[3] *See* 10.07[2] *infra.*

called the *trading ratio*. For example, if a worker is exposed to a 95-dBA machine, the length of such exposure must then be reduced by 50 percent. What really causes risk is the total exposure to sound energy.

The OSHA standard has been criticized from both sides. NIOSH, among others, believes it allows too high an exposure. By contrast, the International Standards Organization uses a lower 3-dBA trade-off rule (Consensus Conference, 1990). What is more, such criteria are based on exposure to continuous noise; it is not known whether they will also protect workers who are exposed intermittently to continuous noise or to impact or impulse noise (Polakoff, 1990; Olishifski, 1988; Consensus Conference, 1990).

Below approximately 140 dB, the time pattern of a sound does not affect the degree of hearing loss produced. Above 140 dB, however, impulse noise appears to be more harmful than other types (Consensus Conference, 1990).

Some less technical indications should lead a listener to suspect that a given sound may be harmful, for example, if it is considerably louder than conversation; if it makes communication difficult during exposure; and if it causes tinnitus or a muffling of sounds after exposure (Consensus Conference, 1990).

[2]   Sources of Hazardous Noise

Hazardous noise occurs in the home and workplace and during recreational pursuits, and it is also created by many forms of transportation. A diesel truck traveling 40 mph at a distance of 50 feet produces 80 dBA; a garbage disposal at a distance of 3 feet produces 80 dB and a food blender at 2 feet produces about 100 dB (Preventing Illness, 1985; Polakoff, 1990). Loud rock music (live or recorded), snowmobiles, small airplanes, lawn-care equipment, tools for woodworking, some toys, firecrackers and chain saws all operate at potentially hazardous sound levels. Hunting, motorcycling, auto racing and various spectator events also expose people to hazardous noise (Consensus Conference, 1990).

Workers in many industries—not only manufacturing but also forestry, mining, construction, transportation and agriculture, among others—are exposed to hazardous levels of noise.[4]

---

[4] *See* 10.09 *infra.*

10.08   FACTORS DETERMINING INDIVIDUAL SUSCEPTIBILITY

In addition to the characteristics of the hazardous sound, a number of factors determine how susceptible a given individual is to developing noise-induced hearing loss. People vary greatly in their sensitivity to noise, and this is one reason it is difficult to establish definitive criteria for safe levels. It is currently impossible to predict which people are most susceptible to noise-induced hearing loss (Olishifski, 1988; Consensus Conference, 1990).

[1]   Differences Among Individuals

Studies have shown individual variations in temporary threshold shift (TTS) and permanent threshold shift (PTS) as great as 50 dB after exposure to a specific noise. No known intrinsic biological factors can account for such variation, although differences in physiologic and anatomic characteristics of the inner ear may play a role. It is also possible that individuals who already have conductive hearing loss[5] may be less susceptible to sensorineural loss[6] because the attenuation (weakening) of sound caused by the mechanical obstruction protects the cochlea from loud noise.

Another suggestion is that dysfunctional middle ear muscles that are unable to contract to protect the inner ear may result in greater susceptibility. Several other factors—including pigmentation of the sensory receptors, eyes and skin, and reduced sensitivity due to pre-existing hearing loss—have been suggested as determining varying susceptibility, but none has been strongly supported by research (Consensus Conference, 1990).

[2]   Differences Within Individuals

Various factors can cause changes over time in the hearing of a particular individual.

[a]   Age

Progressive hearing loss that occurs with age, even in people with normal ears who have not been exposed to hazardous noise, is called *presbycusis*. Whether this loss is due to age alone or to noise exposure

---

[5] *See* 10.06 *supra.*

[6] *See* 10.06[1] *supra.*

other than occupational (called *sociocusis*) is a matter of controversy. However, the existence of presbycusis has led to the hypothesis that susceptibility to noise-induced hearing loss decreases with age. A recent study found that although 70-year-old men exposed to occupational noise had hearing 10 to 15 dB poorer than nonexposed men, this difference was no longer significant by the time both groups reached 79 (Rosenhall, et al., 1990).

The International Standards Organization has included the degree of presbycusis typical for each age in its Standard 1999.2, so that the proportion of hearing loss attributable to aging can be differentiated from that due to occupational noise (Consensus Conference, 1990; Olishifski, 1988).

[b] Drugs

Taking aspirin in large doses can result in tinnitus and temporary threshold shift, but the evidence does not indicate that it causes an increase in noise-induced hearing loss susceptibility. In animal studies, aminoglycosides (a group of antibiotic drugs, including streptomycin) have been found to be ototoxic (damaging to the ear or the auditory nerve), exacerbating the harmful effects of noise. This is especially true in patients with associated kidney dysfunction. It is prudent, therefore, for patients taking these medicines to avoid hazardous levels of noise (Consensus Conference, 1990).

[3] Gender

Young boys and girls do not differ significantly in hearing sensitivity. However, between ages 10 and 20, boys become less sensitive to high-frequency sounds than girls, and women retain better hearing than men throughout life. This difference is generally thought to be due not to intrinsic gender differences but to the fact that men are exposed to loud noise more than women are (Consensus Conference, 1990). However, one study (Rosenhall, et al., 1990) found that men who had not been exposed to occupational noise had poorer hearing than women of the same age who had also not been exposed. The study also found no differences in hearing between women exposed to noise and women not exposed to noise.

10.09 CAUSES IN THE WORKPLACE

Much hazardous occupational noise occurs in manufacturing industries, but many workers in other industries are also exposed daily to noise over 85 dBA.

[1] Manufacturing Industries

Manufacturing processes involving exposure to noise above 90 dBA include those producing petroleum and coal products, lumber and wood products, furniture, rubber and plastic, transportation equipment, chemicals, apparel, paper, ordnance, instruments, textiles, food, stone, clay and glass products, printed products and electrical and other types of machinery (Olishifski, 1988).

To take some specific examples, the power-feed planers used in woodworking, equipment used for welding and cutting metals, and the large machines used in hot-metal foundries all produce noise at levels that can damage hearing (Preventing Illness, 1985). In many cases, the loud noises produced by manufacturing machines are actually not necessary to their operation. Air flow from the ejectors of metal-stamping machines is one source of such noise; another is ejection of finished products by screw machines down a noisy metal chute. Pneumatic riveters, air hammers, drop forges, newspaper printing presses, bottling machinery, turbines and saws are other sources of hazardous noise (Olishifski, 1988; Consensus Conference, 1990).

[2] Other Industries

The saws used in commercial forestry are a significant source of hazardous noise. There is also evidence that the additional stress caused by the vibration of these tools creates enhanced susceptibility to hearing loss. Investigators have found that forest workers with vibration-induced white finger (a numb, mottled finger)[7] had noise-induced hearing losses that were greater and progressed more rapidly than hearing losses in subjects who did not have white finger. These results led to the suggestion that enhanced vasoconstriction or some other pathology that caused white finger could also enhance susceptibility to noise (Iki, et al., 1990).

Another group vulnerable to noise-induced hearing loss is professional divers. Diving exposes individuals not only to barotrauma

---

[7] See also ch. 8.

(injury due to air pressure imbalance) but to high levels of noise. Gas exchange during a helmeted dive produces 112 dB, while hyperbaric chambers used for divers who have the bends (sickness caused by an abrupt reduction in atmospheric pressure) produce 120 dB. A recent study found that at both initial testing and six-year follow-up, professional divers had higher hearing thresholds than normal controls and that the divers' hearing deteriorated faster than that of the nondivers (Molvaer and Albrektsen, 1990).

Among health care workers, operating room personnel may be exposed to noises as loud as 108 dB during a typical major operation, from sources such as suckers and alarms on anesthetic monitoring machines (Hodge and Thompson, 1990). Dental instruments may also operate at hazardous sound levels (Consensus Conference, 1990).

Other groups exposed to occupational hazardous noise are firefighters, police officers, agricultural workers, truck drivers, military personnel and construction workers (Consensus Conference, 1990).

10.10   HEARING CONSERVATION IN THE WORKPLACE

Although occupational noise-induced hearing loss is preventable, many workers are still exposed to hazardous levels of noise, since hearing conservation programs are often ineffective. Not all U.S. workers are covered by the OSHA standard, which currently applies to most, but not all, noisy industries. Although state regulations have been created to protect workers in other industries—except for agriculture—these rules are not uniform and are weaker than the OSHA standard (Polakoff, 1990; Consensus Conference, 1990).

10.11   OSHA STANDARD

The noise standard set by OSHA in 1971 requires that employers use engineering or administrative controls to keep workplace noise levels no higher than 90 dB. This standard includes the 5-dB tradeoff described earlier.[8]

[1]   Monitoring Noise Exposure

The amount of noise to which workers are exposed fluctuates over time. Therefore, codes that regulate exposure direct employers to add

---

[8] *See* 10.07[1] *supra.*

up all the exposures to which the workers are exposed. In 1983, the Hearing Conservation Amendment to the OSHA standard for manufacturing industries required employers to monitor employees' noise exposure and determine their eight-hour time-weighted average exposure. If the reduction to 90 dB cannot be maintained by engineering or administrative controls, employers must provide workers with hearing protectors to reduce exposure to below 90 dB and must ensure that these protectors are used (Preventing Illness, 1985; Olishifski, 1988).

OSHA further requires that workers who have impaired hearing must use hearing protectors when they are exposed to noise levels above 85 dB. These protectors must limit the workers' exposure to no more than 85 dB (Preventing Illness, 1985).

[2] Documenting Hearing Loss

Noise-induced hearing loss develops over time. Therefore, various documents gathered during a worker's span of employment can help establish cause and effect. Such documents include clinical records, noise surveys and audiometric monitorings. They also may include the calibration records of audiometers and other noise measurement devices, ambient noise levels as well as any worksite inspections of employees who were wearing ear protection equipment.

Those who are involved in recording clinical data have a duty to conserve documents in order to aid any hearing conservation program of a later date. When medical forms are filled out, all entries should be completed and the writing should be clear. Abbreviations, symbols and jargon are generally to be avoided.

Early evidence of noise-induced hearing loss can be provided by comparing old and new audiometric threshold readings. These are routinely obtained as part of an occupational monitoring program.

A comparison of the current with the baseline reading can be used to identify significant threshold shift (STS). Such comparisons are, in fact, required for OSHA compliance. Threshold shift is positive when the current audio level exceeds (i.e., is poorer than) the value recorded in the course of the baseline test. For OSHA, an STS is positive when the current examination equals or exceeds 10 dB at the audiometric frequencies of 2000, 3000 or 4000 Hz of either ear, compared to the baseline reading (McCunney, 1988).

10.12   HEARING CONSERVATION PROGRAMS

An effective hearing conservation program must have several components: identification of areas where noise levels are hazardous; administrative and engineering controls over noise levels; worker education; use of personal hearing protectors; and audiometric testing to monitor the effectiveness of the program.

[1]   Identification of Hazardous Noise

Sound surveys using sound level meters are necessary to assess the location and degree of hazardous sounds within a workplace (Preventing Illness, 1985).

[2]   Administrative and Engineering Controls

Administrative controls can reduce noise exposure by rescheduling workers. This can decrease the amount of time they spend in noisy areas. However, the most effective control measure is an engineering design that decreases the noise at the source. Engineering controls include redesigning machinery, muffling noisy parts, enclosing a machine or soundproofing the area where it is located (Preventing Illness, 1985).

For example, existing machinery can be modified by installing mufflers, dampers to reduce vibration or resilient mountings. Noise-reduction specifications can be applied before the purchase of new equipment. Effective maintenance can help avoid noise caused by worn gears or loose guards.

Another strategy is to substitute a different, less noisy process for one being used; for example, riveting could be replaced by flame welding.

Exposure can be reduced by enclosing a noisy machine or some especially noisy parts inside a sound-absorbing barrier (Olishifski, 1988). Noisy machinery can be walled off behind a soundproof partition or put in a different room, so that the noise affects only a relatively small number of operators. These workers then must wear effective hearing protectors.

[3]   Hearing Protectors

When noise cannot be reduced to an acceptable level, the provision and use of hearing protectors are essential to hearing conservation.

Several types are available, and it is important for employees to try a number of them until they find one comfortable enough that they are willing to wear it every day. Employees should be trained in the correct care and use of hearing protectors.

One difficulty with hearing protectors is that their effectiveness depends on creating a tight seal between the head or ear. Pressure is required to create the seal, and this pressure sometimes leads to pain (Consensus Conference, 1990; Preventing Illness, 1985).

[a] Types of Hearing Protectors

Inserts—These are earplugs made of a variety of materials, including rubber, neoprene, plastic, wax-impregnated cotton (dry cotton or wool provide no protection) and "Swedish wool," or very fine glass fiber. Expandable plugs are squeezed and placed in the ear canal, where they expand to fit its contours. Some inserts are custom molded. Whatever method is used, correct fit depends on a tight seal around the circumference of the ear canal (Olishifski, 1988; Sataloff and Sataloff, 1987).

Problems with earplugs include the possibility of infection in a dusty or dirty workplace, and discomfort that leads workers not to wear them (Preventing Illness, 1985).

Muffs—Earmuffs consist of cups of rubber or plastic held in place by a headband. The headband must maintain a sufficient degree of tension to create a proper seal. Muffs can be extremely uncomfortable in a hot, humid workplace and cannot be worn with eyeglasses (Preventing Illness, 1985; Sataloff and Sataloff, 1987).

Canal caps (ear caps)—These devices are made of soft rubber or plastic and held in place by a headband that maintains them at a proper angle to seal the external opening of the ear canal. Caps are best used for frequencies above 1000 Hz; they are less effective below 1000 Hz (Sataloff and Sataloff, 1987). Frequently workers must wear not only hearing protectors but also a respirator, a hard hat and protective eyewear as well. The headbands of ear caps can fit comfortably while accommodating these other devices (Eisma, 1990).

[b] Problems with Noise Reduction Ratings

All hearing protectors must be labeled with a number (the noise reduction rating, or NRR) that expresses the amount of noise attenuation the protector can provide. Appropriate protectors can then be selected according to the level of noise in the workplace.

Studies conducted by both the Environmental Protection Agency (EPA) and the National Institute for Occupational Safety and Health (NIOSH) found that existing noise reduction ratings on the package labels of various models of hearing protectors overstated the products' effectiveness (Preventing Illness, 1985). In the NIOSH study, 50 percent of 420 workers tested at their worksites received less than half the protection obtained in laboratory tests, which were the basis of the stated NRRs. Further, the EPA found that some laboratories consistently reported higher NRRs than others measuring the same devices, suggesting bias in the testing procedure. Eighty-five percent of the ratings reported by manufacturers of hearing protectors were based on results from the laboratory that reported the highest NRRs.

As of 1990, the accuracy of labeled ratings had not improved; due to budget cutbacks during the 1980s, the EPA, which is responsible for ensuring the accuracy of NRRs, was forced to discontinue its NRR program (Preventing Illness, 1985; Consensus Conference, 1990).

[4]   Worker Education and Compliance

The discomfort of hearing protectors is one reason workers sometimes ignore OSHA regulations and tend not to wear them. Another is that workers frequently do not realize the damaging effects of loud noise and simply accept it as a normal part of the job. For this reason, the hearing conservation program should include education of workers about the hearing process and why wearing hearing protectors is important. In one study, workers given hearing tests before and after their shifts were so impressed by the difference between the pre-and post-work results—whose meaning was explained by the testers—that five months later, the department had achieved 85 to 90 percent compliance. Another, equally noisy department in which workers received only a lecture about hearing conservation had only 10 percent compliance (Preventing Illness, 1985; Olishifski, 1988).

[5]   Audiometric Testing

Given the unreliability of NRRs (noise reduction ratings), audiometric evaluation of the effectiveness of workers' selection of hearing protection becomes critical. This testing detects hearing changes that occur if hearing protection is inadequate. Workers should be informed yearly of the results of their tests (Consensus Conference, 1990). Methods of audiometric testing are described in a later section.[9]

10.13 ASSESSMENT OF NOISE-INDUCED HEARING LOSS

It is crucial to determine what proportion of hearing loss in workers has been caused by occupational exposure. However, such a determination is often difficult, since people are exposed to so many recreational, domestic and other nonwork sources of noise.[10] When exposure to these other sources is low compared to that at the worksite, the hearing loss is generally considered to be compensable. Differentiating occupational hearing loss from that due to other causes, such as aging and disease, may also be difficult.

[1] Noise Measurements

Physicians are often asked to set up a hearing conservation program (HCP). The initial step is to perform noise measurements. Instruments for such an analysis include: (1) sound level meters; (2) individual noise dosimeters; and (3) octave band analyzers, which measure the overall noise according to frequency. Usually this involves first obtaining overall sound levels from either a sound level meter or a noise dosimeter.

First, area surveys are conducted, using a stationary sound level meter or noise dosimeter. The results of such surveys are used to identify the need for more detailed measurements. If noise exceeds 85 dB(A), additional measurements are taken. According to OSHA, the purpose of such area monitoring is to identify workers who should be enrolled in occupational hearing conservation programs; identify employees who need hearing protection; identify the amount of attenuation hearing protectors can provide; and educate employees and employers on the degree of hazard in the workplace.

Sometimes OSHA also requires the use of individual assessments, with the use of personal noise dosimeters. This, however, is both time consuming and subject to a great degree of variability (McCunney, 1988).

---

[9] See 10.15 infra.

[10] See 10.11 supra.

[2]   Complicating Factors

Demonstrating that there is a hazardous level of noise at the workplace supports the claim that a hearing loss is occupational. However, appropriate records of noise levels over the entire period of employment may not exist, and workplace noise levels may have changed due to replacement or rebuilding of machines. In such cases, current levels may not reflect earlier ones (Olishifski, 1988).

A final complicating factor is the time delay involved in the development of hearing impairment, which generally is not noticed until it is considerably advanced (Polakoff, 1990).

10.14   EARLY SIGNS

Early signs of hearing impairment include muffling of familiar sounds, difficulty in understanding speech against background noise, tinnitus (ringing in the ears), requests to others to speak more clearly or a need to be close to, or to look at, a speaker in order to understand speech (Olishifski, 1988).

10.15   AUDIOMETRIC TESTING

The only way to detect sensorineural hearing impairment is to measure hearing function at serial intervals. This is done by means of audiometric testing. In workers who will be exposed to significant noise levels, baseline audiometry is helpful in evaluating future hearing loss. Two functions are usually measured. *Pure-tone* audiometry measures sensitivity to pure tones at specified frequencies, and *speech* audiometry measures the ability to understand speech (Olishifski, 1988).

[1]   Precautions in Testing

Audiometry is an objective test that employs sounds of various frequencies to measure the ability of the individual to detect frequencies between 125 and 8000 Hz. For the audiometric results to be reliable, certain precautions must be taken: the audiometer must be maintained in perfect workng order and be accurately calibrated; background noise must be kept to a minimum, so that it does not interfere with the testing; and the examiner must be properly trained in standard audiometric testing procedures.

[2]   Goals of Testing

The goal of audiometric testing is to prevent hearing loss by identifying noise-induced changes in their early stages. Prevention depends on identifying and controlling dangerous noise levels and counseling subjects on the proper use of hearing protection.

[3]   Common Forms of Audiometric Tests

Since hearing losses can result from cumulative overexposures, it is necessary that audiometric testing be administered in sequence and then that the results be carefully compared. The most common kinds of audiometric examinations are:

- reference baseline examination, against which all follow-up examinations are compared. This is usually given 14 hours or more after the last exposure to a suspected noise source;

- initial follow-up for new workers assigned to noisy work areas. This is usually performed 90 days following placement;

- annual examinations performed routinely as part of a hearing conservation program;

- significant threshold shift (STS) validation audiograms, which are used to confirm findings before medical referral;

- close-scrutiny audiometric examination, which allows the physician to assure that further changes in hearing are not occurring among workers who have exhibited STS; and

- utility audiometric examinations, which are used to gain insight into the effectiveness of hearing protection and risk assessments. These can also be used to motivate workers.

Practitioners of occupational medicine have the ability to identify and eliminate the early changes that take place before the development of frank hearing impairment. Unfortunately, many cases of noise-induced hearing loss go undetected. This is because most affected individuals do not visit a clinician until their ability to hear and, especially, to understand speech has been permanently compromised (McCunney, 1988).

[4]   Pure-Tone Audiometry

An audiometer generates pure tones of specified levels at a series of frequencies in headphones worn by the subject. The lowest sound level at which each frequency can be heard is recorded on an audiogram that plots hearing threshold as a function of frequency. The subject's hearing level is expressed as the number of decibels above a standard zero reference point that is considered normal for each frequency.

A baseline audiogram made at the time of employment will help in determining whether any hearing loss was present before employment and will serve as a comparison point with future tests, in order to show impairment at an early stage. An audiometric test can show early losses well before the individual becomes aware of them (Olishifski, 1988).

[a] Bone-Conduction Threshold Test

The pure-tone audiogram measures sound conducted to the eardrum through the air; its result is called the air-conduction threshold. This result indicates whether there is a hearing loss but not whether it is conductive or sensorineural. The bone-conduction threshold test uses a vibrator held against the mastoid bone. The sound vibrations it generates are conducted through the bone directly to the inner ear. If the air-conduction test indicates a hearing loss but the bone-conduction threshold test shows normal hearing, then the loss is conductive and not caused by noise exposure (Olishifski, 1988).

[b] Real-Ear Attenuation at Threshold

This method of testing the effectiveness of hearing protectors involves using earphones to produce specified levels of noise at different frequencies. Next the worker puts on hearing protectors, and the audiometer generates the same noises. The difference in the sound levels with and without the protection measures the degree of attenuation the protectors afford (Preventing Illness, 1985).

[c] Accuracy of Pure-Tone Audiometry

Several factors may affect the accuracy of an audiogram, including the examiner's level of skill (especially in performing the bone-conduction threshold test), background noise in the room where the test is performed and the incentive created by the possibility of compensation (Olishifski, 1988).

In particular, audiometric tests may be affected by a temporary threshold shift (TTS) from which the worker has not yet recovered.

This TTS may have resulted from occupational or nonoccupational exposure. Experts differ as to how long it is necessary to wait after the last exposure to noise before administering the test; estimates range from 16 hours to 48 hours to 1 to 6 months (Olishifski, 1988).

It has been argued that once a baseline test has been made, subsequent audiometric tests should be made four to six hours after exposure, specifically to detect TTS. The presence of TTS would be a signal that hearing protection was inadequate. This procedure would make it possible to predict and prevent permanent hearing loss (Preventing Illness, 1985).

[5] Speech Audiometry

Although pure-tone audiometry methods have been standardized, it has not been possible to do so for speech testing, since many variables affect results, including vocabulary, education and intelligence as well as hearing level. Nevertheless, speech audiometry is useful for indicating the cause and nature of hearing loss. Two tests are generally used.

[a] Speech Reception Test

In this test, the subject hears a standardized list of two-syllable words spoken through headphones or loudspeakers. These words are recited at decreasing sound levels until a level is reached at which the subject can only hear the words 50 percent of the time. This test establishes the speech reception threshold, which should agree closely with the pure-tone threshold. If there is much difference, functional hearing loss should be suspected[11] (Olishifski, 1988).

[b] Speech Discrimination Test

This test is used when the speech reception threshold is high enough to indicate impairment. It uses lists of one-syllable words that test the listener's ability to differentiate consonants. The result is expressed as a percentage of the words the subject can understand (Olishifski, 1988).

10.16 DIFFERENTIAL DIAGNOSIS

Determining whether a hearing loss is occupational requires assessing a variety of factors, including the worker's medical and

---

[11] *See* 10.16[2] *infra.*

occupational history and the results of an audiogram and medical examination. A hearing loss may have more than one cause, and distinguishing what proportion of it is a result of occupational noise can be difficult.

[1] History and Clinical Examination

The patient history should include the worker's previous employment, experience in the military (where exposure to jet engine noise or gunfire often causes some hearing loss), past illness or injury such as blows to the head, family history of hearing loss and the use of drugs, including aminoglycosides and aspirin.

The examiner should inspect the external and middle ear, nose, throat and nasopharynx, as well as eye reflexes for abnormalities or signs of injury; nystagmus (rapid involuntary eyeball movements) should be noted. In addition to the audiometric tests described earlier[12] a test for recruitment (a sensation of loudness out of proportion to an actual increase in sound level) may be given. Even so, the results may be inconclusive, and diagnosis will depend on the examiner's judgment in weighing all the indications (Olishifski, 1988).

[2] Functional Hearing Loss

When an individual seems not to hear, but no organic pathology can be found, this is called *functional hearing loss*. This term covers both the person who is genuinely experiencing a loss of hearing and one who is malingering, or deliberately simulating or exaggerating such a loss.

Functional hearing loss may be due completely to emotional or psychological factors, may involve a functional loss superimposed on a minimal organic hearing loss (called a *functional* or *psychogenic overlay*) or may involve an attempt to exaggerate a hearing loss.

The person may actually have normal hearing underlying the functional loss. In such cases, there has often been an incident such as a family hearing loss or some allusion to deafness that triggered the individual's functional loss. Here the motivation is unconscious and may involve neurosis.

Psychological evaluation may be required to differentiate psychogenic loss from malingering (Sataloff and Sataloff, 1987; Olishifski, 1988).

---

[12] *See* 10.15 *supra.*

The best indication that a hearing loss is functional is a discrepancy of 15 dB or more between the results of the pure-tone audiogram and the speech reception test (Olishifski, 1988).

[3] Differentiation of Other Causes of Hearing Loss

Once hearing loss is determined to be sensorineural, there is no test that can rule out or confirm that noise is its single cause. The examiner must take into account the results of diagnostic tests in combination with possible nonoccupational causes suggested by the patient's history. Acoustic trauma, barotrauma (injury caused by an imbalance between the ambient pressure and that within the ear itself) and certain drugs can all impair hearing. So, too, can the effects of allergy on the upper respiratory tract, diseases including meningitis, tumors, vascular and neurologic illness, and many infectious diseases. Presbycusis, the loss of hearing due to aging, must also be taken into account.[13]

In general, when hearing loss is found to be conductive or of mixed conductive and sensorineural origin, the cause is something besides noise. Similarly, inconsistencies between different types of tests indicate functional loss (Olishifski, 1988).

10.17 CONSEQUENCES OF HEARING LOSS

Loss of hearing has its greatest impact on the ability to communicate, which means that even a small degree of impairment affects an individual's overall quality of life. In addition, hearing loss can have serious occupational consequences.

[1] Psychosocial Effects

Hearing loss has more severe consequences for the personality than any other physical impairment (Sataloff and Sataloff, 1987). The extra effort required to understand speech in noisy settings results in anxiety, irritability, fatigue and stress. The reaction of many hearing-impaired people is a tendency to withdraw from those social activities that are likely to involve embarrassment or frustration. A loss of interest in their environment might follow, as will decreased self-esteem. In the elderly, hearing loss has been associated with depression and may also involve cognitive impairment and dementia.

---

[13] *See* 10.08[2][a] *supra.*

These changes affect not only the hearing-impaired person but his or her family and friends. Inability to hear may make the person seem not to be paying attention, leading to family tension. Interestingly, the most severe consequences often accompany the mildest losses. This is probably because the person with a profound hearing loss is less able to deny that a problem exists and consequently can be helped (Consensus Conference, 1990; Sataloff and Sataloff, 1987; Polakoff, 1990).

[2]   Occupational Effects

Occupational consequences of noise-induced hearing loss may be either a real or an assumed impairment of performance. A hearing-impaired worker may have difficulty receiving messages in a noisy worksite, may be less able to notice important sound changes during the operation of machinery and may be endangered by an inability to hear warning signals.

At the same time, co-workers or supervisors may take the signs of hearing impairment to indicate a real reduction in job performance, so the employee may face job loss or transfer (Polakoff, 1990).

10.18   AUDITORY REHABILITATION

Although sensorineural hearing loss is presently irreversible, all persons who suffer it can be helped by various rehabilitative programs. Although it may be impossible to restore full hearing ability, the individual can be trained to hear better with the degree of hearing that remains. This may improve communication ability, thus changing negative attitudes and improving quality of life (Sataloff and Sataloff, 1987).

[1]   Auditory Rehabilitation Program Components

An auditory rehabilitation program is comprised of five steps:

1. Confusion and anxiety are relieved by informing hearing-impaired individuals that the problem is not in their mind but in their ears.

2. Patients are given explanations of how hearing loss can cause personality problems and are provided assistance in making psychological adjustments.

3. Individuals for whom a hearing aid is indicated are fitted with an appropriate device. Especially in cases of sensorineural loss, which involves difficulties of discrimination more than amplification, it is necessary to be sure a hearing aid will in fact be helpful.[14]

4. Auditory training helps people use their residual hearing as effectively as possible, both with and without a hearing aid. Techniques include training the individual to use intuition to sense the meaning of unheard parts of a conversation.

5. Patients learn speech reading, which involves looking with clear focus at other people's faces to pick up information that they cannot hear (Sataloff and Sataloff, 1987).

[2] Hearing Aids

The basic function of a hearing aid is to amplify sound; it does little to improve the ability to discriminate sounds. However, for persons with sensorineural hearing loss, the hearing aid may remove the strain of listening by compensating for loss of sound level, thereby improving the understanding of speech.

Modern hearing aids can be modified in many ways to adapt them to the needs of individual patients. For example, the loudness of just those frequencies in which the greatest loss has occurred can be enhanced. One special system, known as contralateral routing of signals (CROS), sends sounds from the deaf side to the good side by using a microphone on the deaf side and an amplifier and receiver on the other. BICROS, or bilateral contralateral routing of signals, is a system for people with bilateral hearing loss but only one ear that can be aided. It uses microphones on both sides and an amplifier on the aidable side (Sataloff and Sataloff, 1987).

[3] Cochlear Implant Surgery

This technique is used in cases of profound sensorineural hearing loss that cannot be aided by a conventional hearing aid. The cochlear implant is an instrument analogous to a hearing aid that is surgically positioned to directly stimulate the inner ear. However, it is only appropriate for carefully selected patients, who must undergo an intensive rehabilitation process to learn to use the implant (Sataloff and Sataloff, 1987).

---

[14] See 10.18[2] infra.

10.19 EVALUATION OF IMPAIRMENT

A variety of scales have been developed that use the results of pure-tone audiograms to predict the degree of impairment of speech understanding caused by a hearing loss. It should be noted, however, that there is no agreement among experts about the validity or usefulness of such scales in disability evaluations or even whether any estimate of speech understanding should be included. Neither is there consensus as to whether a patient's self-assessment should be part of such determinations (Consensus Conference, 1990).

One method of evaluation is employed by the American Medical Association (AMA). The AMA bases its evaluation on permanent binaural (relating to both ears) hearing impairment, which it defines as "the disadvantage caused by a binaural hearing impairment sufficient to affect efficiency in activities of daily living" (American Medical Association, 1993). The AMA evaluation makes its estimate of hearing level as the average of the hearing thresholds at the four frequencies at which the subject's hearing is to be tested by pure-tone audiometry: 500, 1000, 2000 and 3000 Hz. This test should be performed when the impairment is no longer progressing and after the maximum amount of rehabilitation has been obtained.

In evaluating monaural (relating to one ear) impairment, an average hearing level of 25 dB or below is taken to mean that no impairment exists. At the opposite extreme, an average over 91.7 dB is taken to mean that the impairment is 100 percent. Each decibel represents a 1.5 percent hearing impairment. A formula is then used to calculate binaural impairment from the results of the evaluation of monaural impairment.

The first step in the evaluation process is a pure-tone audiometric test of each ear separately at the specified frequencies. The four threshold levels thus obtained are totaled for each ear, and a percentage value for monaural impairment is obtained by consulting a chart. For example, total decibel values of 220 in the left ear and 140 in the right ear constitute 45 percent and 15 percent impairments, respectively.

Next the percentage of binaural impairment is determined from another chart. The values in the example given would equal a 20 percent binaural hearing impairment.

Finally, a third table is consulted to calculate impairment of the whole person. In this example, a 20 percent binaural impairment is equivalent to a 7 percent impairment of the whole person (American Medical Association, 1993).

10.100   BIBLIOGRAPHY

Reference Bibliography

American Medical Association: Guides to the Evaluation of Permanent Impairment, 4th ed. Chicago: AMA, 1993.

Consensus Conference: Noise and Hearing Loss. J.A.M.A. 263:3185–3190, 1990.

Eisma, T. L.: Manufacturers Develop Safety Gear for Worker Comfort, Style, Acceptance. Occup. Health Saf. 59:48–50, 1990.

Hodge, B. and Thompson, J. F.: Noise Pollution in the Operating Theatre. Lancet 335:891–894, 1990.

Hunter, D.: Hunter's Diseases of Occupations. London: Hodder and Staughton, 1987.

Iki, M., et al.: Vibration-Induced White Finger and Auditory Susceptibility to Noise Exposure. Kurume Med. J. 37 Suppl.: S33–44, 1990.

Molvaer, O. I. and Albrektsen, G.: Hearing Deterioration in Professional Divers: An Epidemiologic Study. Undersea Biomed. Res. 17:231–246, 1990.

Olishifski, J.: Occupational Hearing Loss, Noise, and Hearing Conservation. In: Zenz, C. (Ed.): Occupational Medicine: Principles and Practical Applications, 2nd ed. Chicago: Year Book Medical Publishers, 1988.

Polakoff, P. L.: Problems Arising from Noise Exposure Plague Workers: Many Need Protection. Occup. Health Saf. 59:37, 1990.

Preventing Illness and Injury in the Workplace. Washington, D.C.: U.S. Congress, Office of Technology Assessment, OTA-H–256, 1985.

Rosenhall, U., et al.: Presbycusis and Noise-Induced Hearing Loss. Ear Hear. 11:257–263, 1990.

Sataloff, R. T.and Sataloff, J.: Occupational Hearing Loss. New York: Marcel Dekker, 1987.

Stouffer, J. L. and Tyler, R. S.: Characterization of Tinnitus by Tinnitus Patients. J. Speech Hear. Res. 55:439–453, 1990.

Additional References

Allonen-Allie, N., and Florentine, M.: Hearing Conservation Programs in Massachusetts' Vocational/Technical Schools. Ear Hear. 11:237–240, 1990.

Bergström, B., et al.: Development of Hearing Loss During Long-Term Exposure to Occupational Noise. A 20-Year Follow-Up Study. Scand. Audiol. 15:227–234, 1986.

Custard, G.: Personal Protective Devices. Ear Protectors—Do They Really Work? Occup. Health (Lond.) 41:273–275, 1989.

Gasaway, D. C.: OSHA 1910.95 Advances OHCPs: Changes, Updates Continue Today. Occup. Health Saf. 59:59–61, 1990.

Lewis, P., et al.: Operating Room Noise. Can. J. Anaesth. 37:579, 1990.

Liberman, M. C.: Quantitative Assessment of Inner Ear Pathology Following Ototoxic Drugs or Acoustic Trauma. Toxicol. Pathol. 18:138–148, 1990.

Murata, K., et al.: Central and Peripheral Nervous System Effects of Hand-Arm Vibrating Tool Operation. A Study of Brainstem Auditory-Evoked Potential and Peripheral Nerve Conduction. Int. Arch. Occup. Environ. Health 62:183–187, 1990.

Reynolds, J. L., et al.: Hearing Conservation Programs (HCPs): The Effectiveness of One Company's HCP in a 12-Hr Work Shift Environment. Am. Ind. Hyg. Assoc. J. 51:437–446, 1990.

Smoorenburg, G. F.: On the Limited Transfer of Information with Noise-Induced Hearing Loss. Acta Otolaryngol. Suppl. (Stockh) 469:38–46, 1990.

CHAPTER 11

Cerebral Deficits Following Head Injury

SCOPE

Occupational head injury generally results from acceleration-deceleration or direct tissue damage, acquired through a fall or an external force impacting on the head. The most serious consequence of head injury is brain damage. Prevention of head injury on the worksite requires safe plant and equipment design, safe construction, and proper maintenance and use of protective headwear. Head injury is evaluated using a variety of scales and tests of motor, cognitive, behavioral and psychological function. Recovery occurs in stages, although the greatest amount of improvement occurs within the first six months. The extent and nature of permanent impairment depend on a variety of factors, the most important being the amount of brain tissue destroyed and the patient's age. Alterations in intellectual function are more devastating to patients and their families than physical disabilities. Long-term rehabilitation is often required. The ultimate outcome of head injury depends on factors ranging from the extent of physical damage to the patient's inherent characteristics to the quality of social support. However, in the great majority of severe injuries, the individual is unable to return to work.

11.01 INTRODUCTION

Head injuries are the third most important cause of neurologic impairment in the nation and the foremost cause of death and disability in persons under the age of 35. Each year 500,000 people sustain head injury, of whom 100,000 die. Among the survivors, between 50,000 and 100,000 sustain severe impairments that leave them unable to live independently, and over 200,000 experience some residual effects that impair their daily activities (Jacobs, 1988). Head injury is most common among young people and the elderly.

The most serious consequence of head injury is damage to the brain. Injury or destruction of brain tissue leads to mental changes, which, in turn, cause emotional reactions to the social and occupational effects of mental impairment. The long-term effects on both patients and their families can be devastating.

According to one estimate, 325,000 cases of head injury each year can be classified as mild (Wolpow, 1991). Although the seriousness of severe head injury is generally easily apparent, mild injuries often seem unimportant. Yet even mild injury may lead to up to a year of subtle impairment of mental function, the effects of which are exacerbated by the failure of employers and families to recognize that subsequent changes in the injured person's personality or ability to handle work tasks are caused by the injury and not by "craziness" or malingering (Wolpow, 1991).

11.02   GENERAL CAUSES OF INJURY

Head injury is caused by motor vehicle accidents (which result in 35 percent of such injuries), accidental falls (28 percent), industrial accidents (11 percent), assaults (6 percent) and other causes (20 percent) (Carlton and Stephenson, 1990).

11.03   MECHANISMS OF INJURY

Brain injuries are categorized as primary or secondary, and as focal (occurring in one local site) or diffuse (occurring in a number of loci scattered throughout).

[1]   Primary Brain Injury

Primary brain injury is that which occurs at the moment of impact; it may be diffuse or focal, and it may result from any of several mechanisms of injury. Primary brain trauma includes coup injuries (in which the brain tissue lying directly underneath the site of the blow is damaged) and contrecoup injuries (in which tissue at the opposite side of the head is affected).

[a]   Acceleration-Deceleration Injury

This is the most common type of brain injury. In an acceleration injury, the skull is suddenly jerked into motion (as when one boxer hits another) while the brain, remaining stationary, strikes the moving skull. In a deceleration injury, the rapidly moving skull is suddenly stopped (as by the impact of an automobile collision), while the brain continues to move for a fraction of a second and strikes the skull.

In both cases, injury occurs as the elastic brain is deformed by the impact, resulting in diffuse injury to nerve cells. There may or may not be contusion (bruising involving rupture of blood vessels). In the most severe injuries, there may be hematoma (localized collection of blood) as well as contusion, resulting in severe neurologic impairment, since the mass of the hematoma exerts pressure on brain tissue (Becker, 1988).

Acceleration-deceleration mechanisms may also result in a shearing type of injury that damages blood vessels and nerve cells by stretching and tearing them (Derechin, 1987).

[b]   Direct Tissue Injury

This type of injury is focal (occurring in one local site) and, by definition, large enough to be seen with the naked eye. It involves contusion and hematoma, and it may result in destruction of a large area of the brain. However, the victim may remain conscious unless the brain stem is also affected (Becker, 1988).

[2]   Secondary Brain Injury

Secondary injury is that which results from pathophysiologic sequelae after the original impact. Once the brain has been injured, its vulnerability to additional injury is enhanced. Thus postinjury complications such as ischemia (decreased blood supply to a body part), increased intracranial pressure due to an expanding hematoma or cerebral edema (swelling due to abnormal accumulation of fluid), and accumulation of toxic metabolic products due to the breakdown of cell membranes can all increase the ultimate neurologic impairment suffered by the patient (Becker, 1988; Derechin, 1987).

11.04   NATURE OF INJURY

Most often, a brain injury results in some alteration in level of consciousness. This change can range from a brief visual effect ("seeing stars") and a feeling of being stunned or disoriented to a period of unconsciousness that lasts for days or weeks (Becker, 1988).

Loss of consciousness results from dysfunction of the brain stem and diencephalon (a subcortical division of the brain that includes the hypothalamus) or of both cerebral hemispheres. An example of the first type of lesion is compression of the brain stem (which includes the reticular activating system, the area of the brain that is concerned with arousal and awakeness) caused by a mass lesion after a focal injury; an example of the second is diffuse injury that causes neural damage throughout both cerebral hemispheres.

[1]   Mild Brain Injury

This category of brain injury, generally known as concussion, ranges from an experience of "seeing stars," with a brief period (up to several minutes) of feeling dazed and stunned, to a reaction involving an immediate, though brief, period of unconsciousness. Within a few minutes, the patient comes to and seems normal.

Patients who sustain mild injury typically do not experience retrograde amnesia (in which the person cannot recall events immediately prior to the injury), but they often cannot remember the impact itself or events occurring up to 10 minutes afterward (post-traumatic amnesia).

The hallmark of concussion is that clinical and x-ray examination reveals no evidence of lasting structural damage. However, this type of injury may involve damage to the axons (long message-carrying neural fibers, which form the brain's white matter) of the nerve cells. It is this damage that leads to what is known as postconcussion syndrome (Becker, 1988; Wolpow, 1991).[1]

[2] Moderate Brain Injury

In moderate injury, the period of unconsciousness lasts five minutes or longer, and the injured person typically remains in a confused, stuporous state upon awakening. Normal alertness is regained within a few days. In the meantime, the patient may be fractious and restless, and speak only in short sentences or phrases. There may be temporary hemiparesis (muscular weakness or partial paralysis affecting one side of the body) or a temporary deficit in the visual field. During this period, the brain is vulnerable to secondary injury (Becker, 1988).[2]

[3] Severe Brain Injury

Severe injury is characterized by a period of unconsciousness that lasts 20 minutes or, frequently, far longer. Patients are unable to speak recognizable words or comprehend commands, and they often show signs of serious neurologic damage, including decerebrate motor posturing (rigid extension of the body, indicating damage to upper parts of the brain stem) and decorticate motor posturing (rigid flexion, or bending, and outward turning of the arms and hands, indicating damage to cortical function). Many of these patients die (Becker, 1988).

Patients who remain unconscious for days or weeks are confused upon awakening and experience extended periods of retrograde and

---

[1] *See* 11.08[3] *infra.*

[2] *See* 11.03 [2] *supra.*

post-traumatic amnesia. Impairment of cognitive function and of personality ranges from mild to severe, though some patients can make a satisfactory recovery.

Although some patients who show decerebrate motor posturing can also recover fairly well, most of the survivors of severe injury are left with serious cognitive and physical disabilities or may even remain in a vegetative state with no cognitive function (Becker, 1988).

11.05　HEAD INJURY IN THE WORKPLACE

Although head injuries constitute only 6 percent of workplace injuries, they have been considered first in importance; this is because injuries that seem minor, since they involve only brief losses of consciousness, can have long-lasting though subtle effects.[3]

[1]　Causes of Head Injury

Head injury in the workplace may be caused by the worker being projected (as out of a motor vehicle or by a fall) and landing on the head, or by an external force hitting the head (such as a falling brick) (Briggs, 1988). Falls on a work surface are the most frequent cause of workplace injuries in general, and the danger of being hit by falling objects is present in a number of industries (Preventing Illness, 1985).

[a]　Construction Industry

Because of the constantly changing conditions at worksites, the construction industry is particularly hazardous. Dangers posed to construction workers include falls from heights, being hit by falling or swinging objects, and collapse of buildings or trenches. Workers may be hit by falling bricks, or they may fall from scaffolds, from ladders that are improperly constructed or not manufactured to code, or through insufficiently blocked holes in floors or roofs. Structure collapse during concrete pouring, which can be caused by improper pouring or failure to allow enough curing time, can kill and injure many workers. Similarly, inadequately shored trenches can collapse on top of workers (Preventing Illness, 1985).

[b]　Other Industries

In manufacturing industries, falls from trestles can occur if walkways are not wide enough or sufficiently well lit. Falls can also occur

---

[3] *See* 11.01 *supra.*

from ladders and stairs during maintenance procedures, or into uncovered pits or bins. Workers can be struck by crane loads or by falling objects in shipping and receiving areas.

Foundries that do hot-metal work pose a high risk of head injury. Massive machinery handling heavy, hot materials, such as moving ladles, can strike workers.

Miners are at risk from roof collapse in underground mines and from falling objects in surface mines (Preventing Illness, 1985).

[c] Motor Vehicle Accidents

Motor vehicle accidents are the most common cause of head injury in general.[4] They are also among the five top causes of work-related injuries, accounting for some 30 to 40 percent of occupational fatalities (Preventing Illness, 1985).

Occupational motor vehicle accidents can occur on construction sites and in and around factories, as well as on the open road, and may involve vehicles used for employee transport.

[2] Prevention of Head Injury

Prevention of head injury is included in the general set of techniques used to control workplace hazards. Control of the transfer of destructive energy can be applied at three points: at the source of energy (e.g., securing bricks on a construction site so they do not fall on workers); at the point of transmission of energy (building overhead barriers so falling bricks do not strike workers); and at the worker (issuing hard hats).

Preventing injury at the source involves initial safe design of sites, plants, equipment and construction processes. Companies may also set up formal injury prevention programs. The notion that workplace injuries are primarily caused by unsafe behavior on the part of workers has often impeded the institution of safe design (Preventing Illness, 1985).

[a] Falls

At construction sites, falls can be prevented by the use of appropriately constructed ladders and railings that are strong and high enough, proper erection of temporary scaffolding and stairs, and adequate

---

[4] *See* 11.02 *supra.*

blocking of openings in elevator shafts, roofs and floors. In manufacturing plants, providing walkways that are wide enough and adequately lit (according to specific codes available for designers) may prevent falls. Provision of gratings and other covers, as well as sufficient lighting, may avoid falls into pits or bins. Stairs should be adequately lit and designed with nonslip treads.

[b] Other Injuries

Safe design at the planning stage can prevent building collapse during construction. Proper maintenance of plant structures, including checking for and repairing settling footings and cracked foundations, settling walls, defective joists and beams, and rotted roofs or floors, will also prevent collapse. Shoring of trenches and sloping trench sides will prevent collapse. Mine roofs can be bolted or timbered to prevent collapse.

Designing construction sites so that workers do not need to enter areas where there are flying objects will avoid injury, as will using earth-moving equipment that is fitted with cages around the driver's seat to protect the worker from falling and from swinging objects.

In plants, cranes with swinging loads can be sited away from work areas. Shipping and receiving docks can be designed so that they are isolated from workers, thus avoiding the hazard of falling objects. Hot-metal-work equipment can be fitted with automatic safety locks or brakes, as well as devices that warn when ladles are being moved.

[c] Motor Vehicle Accidents

Prevention of motor vehicle accidents depends on proper training of drivers; provision of adequate braking systems on trucks, earth-moving equipment and tractor trailers; and meeting of other safety standards such as adequate emergency exits on vehicles used for employee transport.

[d] Protective Headgear

Construction workers, miners, firefighters and workers in other industries depend on protective headgear for immediate protection from injury. However, workers have suffered injury even when wearing these devices.

[i]   Types of Protective Headgear

Protective headgear is designed to protect the wearer against impact. Some models are also meant to protect against transmission of electricity, to varying degrees. *Hard hats,* or industrial helmets, are classified A, B and C, with Class B providing the greatest electrical protection, Class A less electrical protection and Class C none at all.

Miners' helmets, which miners must wear in underground mines and in surface mines where there is a risk of injury from falling objects, are mostly industrial helmets to which a lamp has been added, and are classified A, B and C.

Firefighters' helmets must be self-extinguishing as well as provide protection against impact.

[ii]   NIOSH Tests

Since there is no government certification of protective headgear, purchasers must rely on manufacturers' assertions that equipment conforms to ANSI standards. In the mid–1970s, the National Institute for Occupational Safety and Health (NIOSH) tested a number of models of protective headgear to determine whether they met American National Standards Institute (ANSI) criteria, as the manufacturers claimed they did. NIOSH found significant variations from these standards, especially among Class B (providing the most electrical protection) hard hats. What is more, certain types of tests were not performed, such as nonvertical impact resistance and, for firefighters' helmets, an impact resistance test made at 300 degrees C. to reflect actual working conditions. The results of the NIOSH tests suggest, therefore, that many of these devices may not perform as claimed (Preventing Illness, 1985).

[iii]   Bureau of Labor Statistics Study

A study of injuries sustained by workers wearing hard hats, carried out by the Bureau of Labor Statistics (BLS), also indicated a high failure rate of these devices. The shells of 37 percent of the helmets broke under impact, and the suspensions of 17 percent failed. The study showed that the helmet does not have to break under impact for the worker to be injured; injury can occur if a strong force pushes the shell down onto the worker's head.

The study also showed why some workers did not wear hard hats: Most employees were not issued the helmets, were not required to wear them or did not know they were necessary. Fewer than 20 percent said they did not wear the helmets because these devices were uncomfortable or interfered with work. At the same time, 95 percent of the workers who did wear hard hats did so because they were required to (Preventing Illness, 1985).

[e] Injury Control Programs

One major component of an injury-control program is worker training and education. Other elements of such a program include establishing company policies for injury prevention (such as the requirement of wearing protective headgear); incorporating safety considerations into new plant design or modifications of existing plants; investigating injuries that do occur in order to avoid others in the future; maintaining accurate records of causes of injury; and placing workers in jobs suitable to their physical abilities (Preventing Illness, 1985).

11.06 EVALUATION OF HEAD INJURY

The initial observations made by the occupational physician who provides immediate emergency care provide a baseline for later observations by other caretakers (Briggs, 1988). Subsequently a number of rating scales and other types of tests are used to assess the motor, behavioral, cognitive and psychological condition of the patient with head injury.

[1] Emergency Management and Evaluation

Control of the airway is the first step in managing a head-injured patient. This is essential for providing adequate ventilation and oxygenation, since oxygen transport to the brain may be compromised by the injury. In addition, severe brain injury may compromise respiration. Hence, airway control may require intubation and oxygen therapy or even artificial ventilation.

The physician observes the patient's vital signs, pupil size and reactivity, and degree of motor activity, and notes whether the patient can verbalize normally, respond to painful stimulation or make purposeful movements. Pupils that are either dilated and fixed or small and fixed are associated with serious injury and poor outcome. These observations should be recorded at 15- to 30-minute intervals until the patient is hospitalized and/or referred to a neurosurgeon (Briggs, 1988).

[2] Rating Scales

Although in general, the greatest cognitive deficits are associated with the severest injuries, no definitive relationship has been demonstrated between the results on rating scale tests and the actual outcome in a given case (Dikmen, et al., 1987).

Some experts believe that all patients with head injury should have a formal neuropsychological examination, since the subtle impairments that may remain after a person seems to have recovered can cause real handicaps in daily living. Since such problems are most apparent in the early stages of recovery, testing should begin then and continue during rehabilitation (Gensemer, et al., 1989).

[a] Glasgow Coma Scale

The initial evaluation of all patients with head injury includes ranking their level of consciousness on the Glasgow Coma Scale. Scores range from 3, meaning deeply comatose, to 15, indicating normal neurologic status. Coma is assessed by observation of neurologic function, as indicated by eye opening and motor and verbal responses to verbal commands or a painful stimulus (Gensemer, et al., 1989).

[b] Assessment of Memory

Difficulty in remembering new information is the impairment most commonly reported by patients with head injury (Dikmen, et al., 1987). Instruments used to assess memory include the Selective Reminding Procedure and the Wechsler Memory Scale.

[i] Selective Reminding Procedure

This multiple-trial, free-recall procedure evaluates the patient's ability to store, retain and then retrieve new verbal information, such as word lists (Dikmen, et al., 1987).

[ii] Wechsler Memory Scale

This scale measures the patient's awareness of general and personal information and orientation as to time and place, as well as his or her ability to count backward and by threes, recite the alphabet, learn pairs of words, retain details of short passages, and remember and draw geometric figures (Dikmen, et al., 1987).

[c] Halstead Impairment Index

This instrument consists of five tasks that involve abstract reasoning, distinguishing patterns of tones, placing blocks in differently shaped slots in a board, speed of finger tapping and recognizing a nonsense sound printed on paper when it is heard. The test takes between three and four hours to complete (Gensemer, et al., 1989).

[d] Western Neuro Sensory Stimulation Profile

This test, which consists of 32 items, is used to assess cognitive function in patients with severe injuries and to monitor changes in those who are slow to recover. It measures arousal/attention, expressive communication and responses to tactile, visual, auditory and olfactory stimuli (Ansell and Keenan, 1989).

11.07 STAGES OF RECOVERY

Exactly how recovery of brain tissue occurs is not known. More than 90 percent of patients achieve their final level of recovery within six months after injury, although some may have a reduced rate of additional improvement for up to 18 months (Guentz, 1987; Becker, 1988).

Cognitive skills return in an order that parallels the developmental sequence of a child. Thus alertness returns first, followed by attention; ability to differentiate between self and environment; ability to determine the sequence of steps in an activity; ability to meaningfully categorize persons, objects and other phenomena; ability to organize objects and actions appropriately to carry out a task; and ability to integrate new and old information and adjust oneself accordingly (Guentz, 1987).

Recovery occurs in three general stages.

[1] Stage 1: Coma

In this stage, the patient remains in a coma and requires intensive physical care (Bond, 1984).

[2] Stage 2: Disorientation

Stage 2 covers the period of post-traumatic amnesia, before the patient's memory for day-to-day events returns. Patients show three different types of behavior, all involving disorientation as to time, place and person, and changes in cognition, mood and behavior.

Most commonly, patients in this stage are noisy and aggressive, with impaired attention, and they are usually unable to recognize family, friends and staff. Alternatively, they may be quiet but confused and continue to have cognitive impairments after prolonged post-traumatic amnesia. Least frequently, patients display delusions, illusions or visual hallucinations (Bond, 1984).

[3] Stage 3: First Two Years

In this stage, consciousness is re-established as post-traumatic amnesia ends. Orientation, with full memory for daily events, is restored, along with normal sleep patterns, and attention improves.

At this point, the nature of the patient's permanent impairments emerges, such as slowness of cognitive processing and memory deficits. As these deficits appear, their manifestation is influenced by the patient's emotional reactions to them. Depending on pretrauma personality traits and external circumstances, patients may develop either adaptive or maladaptive behaviors in response to their disabilities.

Thus patients may show irritability due to an inability to tolerate frustration. They may become anxious and depressed, as acknowledgment of their disabilities alternates with denial. They may also develop transient psychiatric syndromes, including hypomania (grandiosity and loss of inhibitions), paranoid delusions, hyperaggressiveness and frontal lobe syndrome.[5]

[4] Levels of Cognitive Functioning Rating Scale

The Levels of Cognitive Functioning is a rating scale used by health-care professionals and patients' families to assess patients' progress during recovery, in order to coordinate treatment, select appropriate techniques and adjust expectations. Developed at Rancho Los Amigos Hospital in California and referred to as the Rancho levels, the scale

---

[5] *See* 11.08[4] *infra.*

has eight levels that correlate the patient's behavioral responses with cognitive abilities (Guentz, 1987).

The levels range from I, "no response," at which the patient is in a deep coma; to III, "localized response," at which the patient responds to specific stimuli (e.g., withdraws from pain), though inconsistently; to VI, "confused, appropriate," at which the patient's responses are appropriate to the situation but he or she remains somewhat disoriented; to VIII, "purposeful and appropriate," at which the patient is alert, oriented and functional but—relative to his or her pretrauma status—may still have deficits in such abilities as abstract reasoning and tolerance of stress (Guentz, 1987).

11.08   RESIDUAL IMPAIRMENTS

Cognitive and behavioral deficits and changes are the most common sequelae of head injury, but this type of trauma can also result in physical deficits as well. However, alterations in intellectual function are more devastating in their effects for both patients and their families, because such permanent deficits can profoundly change patients' lives, preventing them from working or even living independently (Jacobs, 1988; Becker, 1988; Guentz, 1987).

The mental effects of head injury derive from a combination of diffuse and focal injuries to brain tissue. As a rule, the more tissue damage there is, the greater the mental disabilities, although their ultimate nature also depends on the location of the damage (Becker, 1988).

Patients with mild injuries may suffer subtle disruption of brain function lasting up to a year (Wolpow, 1991).[6] Patients with moderate injury usually recover to a satisfactory level of functioning, although they often suffer subjective symptoms for two years or more, and some continue to have a degree of mental impairment. Those with severe injuries rarely recover their full capacities and may be left with severe deficits (Becker, 1988).

[1]   Cognitive and Perceptual Impairments

Cognition involves the ability to understand one's environment correctly, retain selected important information and respond in a way that furthers one's intentions (Guentz, 1987). Impaired cognition

---

6 *See* 11.08[3] *infra.*

therefore involves difficulties with memory, processing information, learning, planning activities in the proper sequence and carrying them out, paying attention and concentrating (Grinspun, 1987).

In practical terms, this means that patients have trouble with reading, writing, speaking clearly, using numbers, remembering appointments, communicating and finding their way when going someplace (Jacobs, 1988).

Cognitive function can be affected not only by damage to brain tissue but also by the neurobehavioral effects of this damage, such as fatigue and restlessness (Grinspun, 1987).

A longitudinal study suggests that head injury in early adulthood exacerbates cognitive decline in later life. Eighty-four World War II veterans who survived penetrating head injury were examined in the 1950s and again in the 1980s; they differed from controls on all tests used of cognitive functions. The investigators hypothesized that the additional reduction of cognitive capacities in the head-injured group resulted from a combination of head injury as a young adult, secondary effects of the injury over time, stress resulting from a compromised brain having to function over decades and changes in the brain related to aging (Corkin, et al., 1989).

[a] Memory Problems

Most head injury involves amnesias (memory deficits), which represent a significant component of disability. There are three types of amnesia: *retrograde* amnesia or long-term memory deficits (lack of memory for events or information existing before the injury); *post-traumatic* amnesia or recent memory deficits (lack of memory for new information from one hour to the next or one day to the next); and *immediate memory deficits* (inability to remember information from minute to minute) (Guentz, 1987).

[b] Attention Deficits

Although memory and learning deficits are the most prominent sequelae of head injury, problems with attention and mental slowness can be severe (Brooks, 1984). It appears, in fact, that head-injured patients' problems with attention may be a result of a slowing of the normal rate of information processing in their brains. This slowness causes attention deficits by making people unable to handle the amount of information required to perform a task in the normal time.

The increased difficulty such an individual experiences in dealing with activities of daily living requires a compensatory increase in effort. It has been hypothesized that over time, such extra effort may produce symptoms similar to those of chronic stress. Thus symptoms that may appear to others to be neurotic may actually be a consequence of the original head injury.

[2] Communication Impairments

Deficits in communication may result directly from the head injury or be secondary to cognitive impairment, such as mental slowness or the ability to think abstractly. These deficits may also result from neurobehavioral conditions, such as fatigue and restlessness.

The patient whose speech and language skills are affected may be unable to speak clearly or fluently due to apraxia (inability to perform the movements necessary for speaking), aphasia (inability to understand and use words) or dysarthria (inability to articulate clearly) (Grinspun, 1987).

[3] Postconcussion Syndrome

Patients often experience a complex of annoying symptoms following head trauma that may last as long as a year or, in some cases, several years. Those with mild injury are more likely to experience the syndrome, since they, unlike the severely injured, are subject to expectations that they should be able to function at their premorbid capacity (Becker, 1988).

A prominent component of postconcussion syndrome (also known as post-traumatic syndrome) is headache, usually the muscle-tension type. In addition, patients who have a damaged nerve under the scalp will experience neuralgic pain over the area this nerve supplies. Others may suffer a series of migraines that can last for months.

The inability to handle more than one kind of information at a time lies behind typical intellectual deficits similar to those described earlier,[7] but more subtle. Memory problems, which prevent people from learning new information, are connected to a decrease in creativity and reduced motivation. Fatigue—emotional and intellectual as well as physical—prevents patients from completing tasks they take on. Since the effects are subtle, they are most disturbing in people

---

[7] See 11.08 [1] supra.

whose work is intellectually demanding. At the same time, the patient is likely to have lost some insight and does not realize that he or she is not ready to resume normal activities.

Another aspect of the syndrome is personality change. Many patients become more assertive than they were, and because this change involves interactions with those around them, it may be less reversible than the other symptoms (Wolpow, 1991).

Although it has been suggested that at least one cause of postconcussion syndrome is the existence of a claim for compensation, it seems clear from the frequency of the syndrome and the consistency of the complaints that it has a biological foundation (Becker, 1988). Many writers, therefore, stress that postconcussion syndrome has nothing to do with neurosis or malingering (Wolpow, 1991).

[4] Behavioral and Emotional Changes

Behavioral and emotional changes after injury include depression, fatigue, anxiety, increase in general tension, mood swings, irritability, lack of insight, lack of spontaneity, hyperactivity, impulsiveness, aggressiveness and emotional regression. Patients who lose the capacity for abstract thinking develop an egocentricity that alienates family and friends. Patients who lack insight or awareness may need supervision in order to avoid either dangerous situations or wandering (Jacobs, 1988; Grinspun, 1987; Stavros, 1987).

Secondary changes brought on by loss of the ability to work and by other disabilities, as well as by the social alienation resulting from personality changes, include lowered self-esteem, despair and paranoia. Patients are likely to deny the true level of their disability as a protective mechanism and have unrealistic expectations of recovery. The resulting feelings of frustration may lead an individual to act out and be labeled violent. Anger may be projected onto relatives or an employer believed to be responsible for the accident that caused the injury. Other patients may become suicidal (Stavros, 1987). One study reported a high incidence of violence against relatives and criminal convictions among patients with head injury (Rappaport, et al., 1989).

Certain specific psychiatric disorders may follow severe injury, including frontal lobe syndrome, dissociative disorders and other disorders.

[a] Frontal Lobe Syndrome

This syndrome follows damage to the frontal lobes (front part of the brain), which results in the loss of impulse control, problem-solving ability and sensitivity to others (Guentz, 1987). Thus the syndrome is associated primarily with behavioral and emotional changes. It appears at the point that consciousness is regained, taking the form of extremes of mood and behavior. Patients lack insight and are disinhibited, euphoric and irresponsible; they manifest an aimless drive. They seem childish and egocentric and have no tact or concern for others. Except in the very severely injured, previous personality characteristics tend to be magnified.

Although some patients become apathetic and inert, in others, the loss of inhibition leads to heightened aggressiveness and inappropriate, uncontrolled sexual behavior, both of which can be extremely troubling to families. Because they lack insight, patients may engage in unacceptable attempts at physical intimacy, expose themselves or make offensive comments. Aggressiveness involves violent reactions out of proportion to the triggering event.

The more insight has been lost, the more severe the syndrome tends to be. In all but the worst injuries, however, it decreases in severity over the course of many months, because the patient either spontaneously develops or is taught the ability to control himself or herself, or because external restraints are applied (Bond, 1984; Wood, 1984).

[b] Dissociative Disorders

A group of symptoms including amnesia, motor paralysis, anesthesias and other sensory disturbances constitute the dissociative disorders. These involve a defect of mental integration, in which certain mental processes split off from normal consciousness and function on their own. Another example is fugue, in which an amnesic patient physically flees his or her normal surroundings.

Dissociative disorders usually manifest in the early postinjury period, but they may also be associated with depression that develops later. These patients are likely to thwart and obstruct their own rehabilitation process.

[c] Other Disorders

Injury to the brain stem may lead to *arousal disorders,* in which the patient completely lacks interest in his or her environment and remains lethargic and drowsy.

Patients with *motivational disorders* lack drive, or the ability to move from an interest in something to actual physical participation.

Attention seeking, which occurs infrequently, can involve shouting, breaking windows or injury to self, such as banging the head against a wall. These may be learned behaviors engaged in as an attempt to avoid difficult, stressful situations. They can be very difficult to manage.

[5]   Occupational Effects

Follow-up studies of patients with severe head injuries report that the great majority were unable to work after their injuries. A study of 142 families of persons with severe traumatic head injury, contacted between one and six years after the injury, found that 70 percent of those who were previously employed left their jobs because of the injury. An additional 10 percent lost their jobs, while only 2.2 percent continued working without interruption (Jacobs, 1988).

Another study of 63 severely injured patients who were contacted up to ten years after the head injury found that although none had been previously unemployed (they either had a job, cared for a household or were in school), 61 percent were unemployed five to ten years later. Among these, 23 percent fewer were in blue-collar jobs than had been in such jobs before, while none of the 11 percent who had been in professional jobs could resume them (Rappaport, et al., 1989).

The group with the highest prevalence of head injury is young adults, for whom the ability to work is an important basis of their sense of self-worth. Thus it is notable that head-injured young adults tend to go back to work before they resume leisure or social activities; many return to work before they achieve their premorbid level of functioning. The speed of returning to work appears to be determined more by physical disability than by mental deficits (Carlton and Stephenson, 1990).

Ability to work is affected by personality and cognitive deficits as well as by physical impairment. Thus any of several contributing factors may lie behind a given individual's failure to return to work. Some people may be injured while they are adolescents, before acquiring any occupational skills or training. Others may already have skills but suffer physical and/or cognitive deficits that prevent them from working. For others, residual emotional or behavioral impairments may interfere with their ability to do the work. Finally, disability payments may function as a disincentive that pushes people into dependency. Each of these factors calls for a different form of treatment (Jacobs, 1988).

[6]   Social Problems

Problems with communication and changes in behavior frequently interfere with social interactions, especially when the patient had neurotic or psychopathic characteristics before the injury (Jacobs, 1988). Patients often are unable to deal with everyday social situations, especially in the early postinjury period (Grinspun, 1987). They experience difficulty with assertiveness and with social interaction outside the home, and they tend to become socially isolated— apparently more so than can be explained by their physical limitations.

Severe personality changes lead to fewer and more superficial social contacts. Even minor changes, such as irritability, while they may not disrupt social life, can create frictions within the family. Patients are frequently apathetic about engaging in leisure activities (more so than with respect to work), and this increases their social isolation; this social isolation is an extremely devastating effect of head injury.

These problems may be exacerbated by well-meaning but mistaken family members who either deny the impairments that do exist and encourage the patient toward unrealistic goals or take the opposite course and become overprotective, influencing the patient to be passive.

[7]   Family Problems

The fact that services to meet the considerable long term needs of head-injury survivors are generally lacking means that tremendous emotional, financial and other caretaking burdens fall on the families of these patients. A study of 142 families[8] reports that "the hidden financial, physical, and emotional costs associated with caring for a head injured survivor often impair or destroy the family unit." Many of these families "were on the verge of breaking up, putting the person in an institution, or taking some other drastic action" (Jacobs, 1988).

---

[8] See 11.08[5] supra.

[a] Emotional Issues

The families of head-injury survivors must undergo a grieving process for both the patient's loss and their own. They must also assume the emotional burdens imposed by the need for caretaking, which often brings major life-style changes, including shifts in roles among family members. Families are subject to stresses affecting marital, sibling and parent-child relationships; changes in daily routines; and the need to adjust previous long term goals (Jacobs, 1988; Stavros, 1987).

Initial denial associated with hope as the patient awakens from coma becomes despair as time passes and the patient does not regain his or her previous level of functioning. The patient's parents may feel guilt or depression, while siblings or children may feel neglected and also guilty; children may experience sleep disturbances, bedwetting, headaches and other symptoms. Adults may develop anxiety disorders or mood disturbances (Stavros, 1987).

In general, families have more difficulty accepting and coping with "invisible" changes, such as cognitive deficits and personality changes, which betoken the fact that the survivor is no longer the same person, than they have dealing with obvious physical impairments (Grinspun, 1987; Jacobs, 1988).

[b] Financial Issues

Families often experience financial difficulties due to the cost of medical care and rehabilitation for the patient with head injury, especially when the patient was the family's financial support or when other members must give up jobs to take care of him or her (Jacobs, 1988).

[8] Physical Impairments Affecting Mental State

Certain physical impairments resulting from head injury have a particular impact on the patient's mental recovery.

[a] Post-traumatic Epilepsy

Post-traumatic epilepsy involves recurring psychomotor fits (seizures during which the patient suffers impairment of consciousness and performs semi-purposeful movements, with loss of memory for the entire episode) due to temporal lobe (situated below the frontal lobe) seizures resulting from neural damage inflicted by the injury.

The seizures may result in increased aggressiveness, or they may appear only as subtle emotional and behavioral changes that may not be noticed for months, although the family may find them difficult to cope with.

Failure to recognize the cause of these changes may result in inappropriate treatment. When the condition is recognized, the patient requires medication to control the seizures, since further seizures can damage more brain tissue. However, most antiepileptic drugs dull mental functioning and thus delay cognitive recovery (Guentz, 1987).

[b]   Hearing and Visual Impairments

Focal damage will result in specific neurologic deficits that also retard recovery. Injury to the eye, optic nerve (the second cranial nerve, which carries visual impulses from the retina toward the brain) or occiput (back part of the skull) can cause total blindness or partial visual deficits that affect functional ability. Similarly a reduction in hearing can prevent the patient from correctly interpreting his or her environment, extending the stage of confusion and making the patient more prone to distrust and suspicion (Guentz, 1987).

11.09   REHABILITATION

Rehabilitation of individuals with head injury is both physical and mental. The goals are to bring the patient to the highest level of functioning of which he or she is capable, to bring the patient back into relations with family and community while maximizing quality of life, and to minimize the cost of long-term care (Guentz, 1987).

There are three stages of treatment for patients with severe injury: acute care in an intensive care or neurosurgical unit in the hospital; acute rehabilitation in an inpatient rehabilitation unit; and long-term rehabilitation either at home or in a long-term facility. Typically the rehabilitation team includes a neuropsychologist, clinical nurse specialist, primary nurse, home care coordinator, dietitian, occupational therapist, physical therapist, recreational therapist, social worker, physiatrist (physician specializing in rehabilitation and physical medicine) and speech-language pathologist (Grinspun, 1987).

Head-injured patients generally require long-term case management that provides a variety of services, ranging from transportation to home health care to constant supervision. Under such a plan, a case manager (for example, a nurse or social worker) is hired by a third-party payer such as an insurance company or by workers' compensation to monitor the patient's progress, evaluate and coordinate services and provide support for the family. The problem is that in many cases, funds and needed services are unavailable (Stavros, 1987; Jacobs, 1988).

Rehabilitation of mental deficits involves both cognitive and behavioral techniques.

[1] Cognitive Techniques

Since the greatest proportion of recovery occurs within six months of injury, rehabilitation should begin as soon as possible to maximize the patient's potential for regaining function. There are two approaches to cognitive remediation: cognitive and behavioral.

[a] Cognitive Approach

This technique uses a vivid image as a mnemonic (memory aid) by associating it with the first word on a numbered list. Although use of this system helps patients remember more items, it does not improve memory function itself; when the system is not used, memory remains impaired.

[b] Behavioral Approach

This approach uses aids such as a printed activity schedule and a timer set for five minutes before an appointment. Patients receive praise for being prompt and are ignored when they are not on time.

[2] Behavioral Techniques

These techniques are used to manage behavioral disorders that retard rehabilitation. One type of procedure is designed to evoke desirable behavior; the other, to decrease undesired behavior. Behavioral management works less well for patients with significant frontal lobe damage and for those who lack drive. It is not effective at all for those with dissociative disorders[9] and has been reported to make them worse. However, considerable success has been reported with other types of severely injured patients who were difficult to manage.

---

[9] *See* 11.08[4][b] *supra.*

[a] Positive Reinforcement

This procedure is based on rewarding desired behavior to elicit more of it. A token economy system is used, in which plastic tokens given out for good behavior can be redeemed for candy, cigarettes or even just praise, encouragement or additional attention.

[b] Negative Reinforcement

This more controversial technique may become necessary with patients who lack motivation, for whom positive reinforcement may be ineffective. It takes two forms: Negative punishment involves taking away meals or privileges, such as free movement, or even locking disruptive individuals in a room for five minutes.

Positive punishment is highly controversial, because it has involved using electric shock, although a less violent way to administer a noxious stimulus is to pass a bottle of aromatic ammonia under a patient's nose. Inhaling the vapor disrupts the undesired behavior (Wood, 1984).

[3] Skills Training

Patients with head injury often lack a wide range of skills, ranging from basic self-care to higher order skills, such as speech and writing. In some cases, life-style changes made necessary by the injury require the patient also to acquire new skills, such as performing household tasks so that the spouse can go to work. Patients may also need to learn how to contact and deal with service-providing agencies (Jacobs, 1988).

In addition, traditional techniques of improving social skills have been reported to be successful in improving behavior deficits in patients with severe brain injury. Such a program involves instruction in the reasons behavior should be changed; modeling the new behaviors to be learned; rehearsing them; providing feedback using videotapes; and social reinforcement of correctly learned behaviors (Brotherton, et al., 1988).

11.10 PROGNOSIS

The outcome for survivors of head injury depends on a variety of factors, ranging from the extent of actual physical damage to the availability of treatment to the quality of the patient's social support.

[1]   Factors Inherent in the Patient

Recovery is influenced by the patient's age and general condition before the injury.

[a]   Age

Age seems to be second only to severity of injury in determining whether a person with head injury can return to work. In one study, among patients who had been unconscious over 24 hours, 70 percent of those under the age of 20 returned to work, but only 30 percent of those over 50 could do so (Oddy, 1984). In older persons, damage to brain tissue has a considerably greater effect than in the young, producing a disproportionately more severe mental deficit.

[b]   Physical Condition

Patients with organic brain syndrome (impairment of brain tissue function) due to substance abuse or who have had previous significant head injuries have a poorer prognosis than others (Guentz, 1987).

[c]   Mental Condition

The patient's pretraumatic personality and social competence will affect her or his recovery, in particular, by shaping whatever adaptive or maladaptive behaviors emerge after the injury[10] as she or he attempts to cope with the new circumstances obtaining after the injury. Patients with a history of chronic psychiatric disorders will have fewer coping skills to begin with, and once their mental abilities are diminished by the injury, they usually are unable to handle daily living. Neuroses or psychopathic characteristics are also likely to handicap adjustment and disturb relationships with others (Guentz, 1987).

[d]   Social Support

The presence of support from family or other individuals—or the absence of such support—has a tremendous influence on outcome. Given the lack of services available for many individuals with head injury, the family becomes the most important element in treatment after the acute stage. Thus it is rare for survivors to achieve optimum recovery without caring involvement on the part of their families (Guentz, 1987).

---

[10] See 11.10 [3] infra.

[2]   Factors Acquired at Time of Injury

The major factor affecting outcome is the severity of the injury; as a rule, the more brain tissue that is lost, the greater are the mental impairments suffered. In severe injury, the prognosis depends largely on the extent of damage to the brain stem (Becker, 1988).

Specific neurologic deficits can retard recovery or make it impossible. Patients who suffer total blindness in addition to cognitive and memory deficits have a poor prognosis. Partial hearing and visual impairment results in additional confusion in a patient with mental deficits, since these impairments make it more difficult to interpret the environment correctly.

Problems with language retard recovery; frontal lobe damage results in difficulty with re-establishing occupational activities and social relationships. Prolonged retrograde amnesia (in which the person cannot recall events immediately prior to the injury) directly affects recovery of other forms of memory; the longer the period for which long-term memory is lost, the poorer the prognosis for recovering recent memory (Guentz, 1987).

The length of time during which post-traumatic amnesia lasts is frequently used to predict outcome, although because investigators have used varying criteria for post-traumatic amnesia, the reliability of this measure is not definitively established (Brooks, 1984).

[3]   Factors Acquired Postinjury

As cognitive skills reappear, the patient may develop behaviors, such as aggressiveness or attention seeking, that are maladaptive but may nevertheless be encouraged by the family or medical staff, who are happy to see any behavior at all. Unless these behaviors are corrected by behavioral modification techniques, they become obstacles to recovery and, in the worst cases, become ingrained and require sedation or institutionalization.

The need to medicate for control of post-traumatic epilepsy also slows recovery because of the dulling effect of the medication (Guentz, 1987).

Finally, it appears that another significant factor is lapse of time between the injury and the beginning of rehabilitation. Early admission to an intensive hospital rehabilitation program seems to have a significant positive effect on both short-term and long-term outcome (Rappaport, et al., 1989).

[4]   Reported Outcomes

Although reports vary, it is clear that severe brain injury profoundly disables the great majority of victims.

One study indicated that 50 percent of all survivors of brain injury could expect a good recovery if they received a full range of services; 30 percent would remain moderately impaired, requiring case management for the rest of their lives (which often includes full-time supervision); 15 percent would remain severely impaired and need total care in the home or an institution; and 4 to 5 percent would remain comatose (Stavros, 1987).

A long-term study of 63 survivors of severe injury found that most of these patients could be expected to survive indefinitely, since they did not have life-threatening medical conditions. However, most survived with impairments that made continuing care a necessity. Among patients in this group, 76 percent showed improvement at follow-up, 5 percent showed little or no improvement and 19 percent were worse; of these last, 13 percent died. Among those who improved, 36.5 percent had good improvement, 36.5 percent had fair improvement and 25 percent had a poor outcome (Rappaport, et al., 1989).

Further, whereas 72 percent had received their income from a full-time job before injury, only 9 percent did so afterward. The rest were dependent for income on social security, disability payments, local welfare and/or family (Rappaport, et al., 1989).

11.11   EVALUATION OF IMPAIRMENT

According to the system of evaluation developed by the American Medical Association (1993), deficits caused by brain damage are categorized in terms of limitations in the patient's ability to carry out activities of daily living, taking into account associated mental, emotional and personality mechanisms as well. Four categories are relevant to cerebral deficits following traumatic head injury. All percentages given are for impairment of the whole person.

[1]   Language Disturbances

This category is concerned with the brain's function of comprehending, storing and producing language. The four established criteria reflect disturbances in the ability both to understand and to produce language in situations of daily living.

Minimal disturbance is rated at between 0 and 9 percent, and moderate impairment, at 10 to 24 percent. Complete inability to understand language resulting in "unintelligible or inappropriate production of language for daily living" is rated at 25 to 39 percent. Complete inability either to comprehend or produce language is rated at 40 to 60 percent.

[2]   Complex, Integrated Cerebral Functions

This category includes deficits with respect to orientation, abstract thinking, memory, planning and carrying out activities, and acceptable social behavior.

Ability to perform most activities at the same level as before injury although with some impairment of complex integrated functions is rated at between 1 and 14 percent. Impairment of complex functions such that performing daily activities requires some level of supervision or instruction is rated at 15 to 29 percent. Impairment that requires daily activities to be performed at home or in another facility under direction is rated at 30 to 49 percent. Severe impairment that prevents any form of self-care is rated at 50 to 70 percent.

[3]   Emotional Disturbances

This category ranges from an extreme of aggression to lack of normal response. It includes euphoria, irritability, mood swings, depression and impairment of the ability to interact normally with other people.

Mild limitation of daily social and interpersonal functioning is rated at 0 to 14 percent. Moderate limitation of some but not all daily living functions in a social setting is rated at 15 to 29 percent. Severe disturbance that impedes useful action in almost all instances is rated at 30 to 49 percent; severe limition of all daily activities, requiring care by another person, is rated at 50 to 70 percent impairment of the whole person.

[4]   Disturbances of Consciousness

This category includes confusion (hyperactivity or hypoactivity), stupor (poorly organized response to painful stimuli) and coma. Mild change in consciousness is rated at 0 to 14 percent; long-lasting alteration of state of consciousness, lessening capabilities in personal care and other activities of daily living is rated at 15 to 29 percent; a state of semi-coma with complete dependency is rated at 30 to 49 percent; and persistent vegetative state is rated at 50 to 90 percent impairment of the whole person.

[5] Calculation of Impairment

When an injury results in several impairments that fall into more than one category, impairment is calculated not by adding all the values together but by taking the largest value to represent all the types of impairment. For example, an individual with a 15 percent complex function impairment, a 35 percent communication impairment, an emotional disturbance constituting a 30 percent impairment and a consciousness disturbance rated at 5 percent would be considered to have a brain function impairment rating of 35 percent of the whole person.

11.00 BIBLIOGRAPHY

Reference Bibliography

American Medical Association: Guides to the Evaluation of Permanent Impairment, 4th ed. Chicago: American Medical Association, 1993.

Ansell, B. J. and Keenan, J. E.: The Western Neuro Sensory Stimulation Profile: A Tool for Assessing Slow-to-Recover Head-Injured Patients. Arch. Phys. Med. Rehabil. 70(2):104–108, Feb. 1989.

Becker, D. P.: Head Injuries. In: Wyngaarden, J. B. and Smith, L. H., Jr. (Eds.): Cecil Textbook of Medicine, 18th ed. Philadelphia: Saunders, 1988.

Bond, M.: The Psychiatry of Closed Head Injury. In: Brooks, N. (Ed.): Closed Head Injury: Psychological, Social, and Family Consequences. New York: Oxford University Press, 1984.

Briggs, D.: Trauma. In: Zenz, C. (Ed.): Occupational Medicine: Principles and Practical Applications, 2nd ed. Chicago: Year Book Medical Publishers, 1988.

Brooks, N.: Cognitive Deficits After Head Injury. In: Brooks, N. (Ed.): Closed Head Injury: Psychological, Social, and Family Consequences. New York: Oxford University Press, 1984.

Brotherton, F. A., et al.: Social Skills Training in the Rehabilitation of Patients with Traumatic Closed Head Injury. Arch. Phys. Med. Rehabil. 69(10):827–832, Oct. 1988.

Carlton, T. O. and Stephenson, M. D.: Social Work and the Management of Severe Head Injury. Soc. Sci. Med. 31(1):5–11, 1990.

Corkin, S., et al.: Penetrating Head Injury in Young Adulthood Exacerbates Cognitive Decline in Later Years. J. Neurosci. 9(11):3876–3883, Nov. 1989.

Derechin, M. E.: Pediatric Head Injury. Crit. Care. Nurs. Q. 10(3):12–24, Dec. 1987.

Dikmen, S., et al.: Memory and Head Injury Severity. J. Neurol. Neurosurg. Psychiatry 50(12):1613–1618, Dec. 1987.

Gensemer, I. B., et al.: Psychological Consequences of Blunt Head Trauma and Relation to Other Indices of Severity of Injury. Ann. Emerg. Med. 18(1):9–12, Jan. 1989.

Grinspun, D.: Teaching Families of Traumatic Brain-Injured Adults. Crit. Care Nurs. Q. 10(3):61–72, 1987.

Guentz, S. J.: Cognitive Rehabilitation of the Head-Injured Patient. Crit. Care. Nurs. Q. 10(3):51–60, Dec. 1987.

Jacobs, H. E.: The Los Angeles Head Injury Survey: Procedures and Initial Findings. Arch. Phys. Med. Rehabil. 69(6):425–431, June 1988.

Oddy, M.: Head Injury and Social Adjustment. In: Brooks, N. (Ed.): Closed Head Injury: Psychological, Social, and Family Consequences. New York: Oxford University Press, 1984.

Preventing Illness and Injury in the Workplace. Washington, D.C.: U.S. Congress, Office of Technology Assessment, OTA-H–256, 1985.

Rappaport, M., et al.: Head Injury Outcome Up to Ten Years Later. Arch. Phys. Med. Rehabil. 70(13):885–892, 1989.

Stavros, M. K.: Family Issues in Moderate to Severe Head Injury. Crit. Care Nurs. Q. 10(3):73–82, Dec. 1987.

Wolpow, E. R.: After the Fall: Mild Head Injury. Harvard Health Letter 16(6):1–3, April 1991.

Wood, R. L.: Behavior Disorders Following Severe Brain Injury: Their Presentation and Psychological Management. In: Brooks, N. (Ed.): Closed Head Injury: Psychological, Social, and Family Consequences. New York: Oxford University Press, 1984.

Additional References

Adamovich, B. B.: Information Processing, Cognition, Attention, and Communication Following Closed-Head Injury. Folia Phoniatr. (Basel) 42(1):11–23, 1990.

Kaplan, C. P.: Differential Reading Recovery in Patients with Severe to Moderate Closed Head Injury. Am. J. Phys. Med. Rehabil. 69(6):297–301, Dec. 1990.

Mattson, A. J. and Levin, H. S.: Frontal Lobe Dysfunction Following Closed Head Injury. A Review of the Literature. J. Nerv. Ment. Dis. 178(5):282–291, May 1990.

Prigatano, G. P. and Altman, I. M.: Impaired Awareness of Behavioral Limitations After Traumatic Brain Injury. Arch. Phys. Med. Rehabil. 71(13):1058–1064, Dec. 1990.

Siegel, T.: Six Months As a Brain Injury Patient. Rehabil. Nurs. 15(5):268–269, Sept.-Oct. 1990.

CHAPTER 12

Heart Disease

SCOPE

Heart disease is the leading cause of death in the United States and a major cause of illness and disability. The most prevalent form of heart disease is myocardial infarction (heart attack), which affects nearly 1.5 million people in the United States each year. Myocardial infarction is usually (but not always) characterized by a crushing pain in the chest or arm. X-rays, electrocardiograms and enzyme tests are useful in the diagnosis of this condition. Emergency treatment is centered around increasing the oxygen supply to the heart, decreasing the pain and reassuring the patient. In an occupational setting, heart disease must be evaluated with a view to both background and precipitating factors. Background factors include cigarette smoking, family history, abnormalities of fat metabolism, diabetes and hypertension. Precipitating factors include noise, heat and cold, shift work, sedentary work and emotional stress. The heart may also be damaged by toxic substances. However, it is not clear to what extent chronic exposure to chemicals at relatively low dosages damages the heart. The question is made more difficult by the many factors—physical, emotional and mental—that affect overall heart health.

SYNOPSIS

12.01 HEART DISEASE

Heart disease is the leading cause of death in the United States. It is also a major cause of illness and disability. In any particular case, identifying the precipitating cause of heart failure is crucial. Such causes must be distinguished from the background factors that predispose to the disease.

[1] Background Factors

Various epidemiologic factors have been shown to contribute to the development of heart disease. Occupation is one of these factors that can influence an individual's risk of developing chronic heart disease, but it is not believed to be a prominent one in comparison to cigarette smoking, high blood pressure and elevated serum lipid and cholesterol levels (Petronio, 1988; Theriault, 1988). Job-related exposures that may influence the risk for cardiovascular disease include noise, heat and cold, shift work, sedentary work and emotional stress.

Some chemicals that occur in the workplace have also been identified as causes of acute cardiotoxicity (heart damage), but the role of chronic low level occupational exposures in the development of heart disease is not well understood.

[2] Precipitating Factors

The underlying causes of heart disease may exist for many years without producing any recognizable symptoms or disability. But work-related stress and exertion may precipitate this underlying condition. Precipitating factors can include physical overexertion, excessive environmental heat or humidity, and emotional crises. The causal link between these factors and heart disease has been recognized by many medical experts.

In each particular case, a distinction must be drawn between background factors and precipitating causes. Background factors such as diabetes and lipid abnormalities lead directly to coronary atherogenesis (arteriosclerosis) and can cause a major coronary event without any known precipitating cause.

[3] Screening

Employers may provide screening in the workplace for preventable but nonoccupational cardiovascular risk factors, such as blood pressure and serum cholesterol elevations. Some employers are also concerned with the evaluation of workers' fitness to return to strenuous jobs after an episode of cardiac illness, as well as the medical screening of workers, such as firefighters, drivers or pilots, who could endanger others if they had a heart attack on the job.

12.02   EPIDEMIOLOGY OF HEART DISEASE

An estimated six million Americans have ischemic heart disease, as defined by a history of angina and/or a previous myocardial infarction. Coronary heart disease is the leading cause of death in the United States, having caused more than 500,000 deaths in 1988. About 1,500,000 Americans suffer a myocardial infarction each year; thus a third of all heart attacks are fatal. Some 5 percent of heart attacks occur in people under the age of 40, and 45 percent occur in people under age 65 (American Heart Association, 1991).

In the United States, death rates from ischemic heart disease increased markedly between 1940 and 1963, after which they showed an equally dramatic decline. Epidemiologists have not identified a single cause for the decline, but it is believed that improved treatment of myocardial infarctions and reductions in cigarette smoking and dietary fat consumption all contributed. More effective treatment of hypertension (high blood pressure) is also considered a factor (Biehrman, 1991).

With the rare exception of certain hereditary disorders, a single cause for ischemic heart disease is virtually never identifiable in an individual patient. Instead, epidemiologists have studied large populations of healthy persons to identify factors that are associated with the risk of developing heart disease over a period of time. Major risk factors are those that are also clearly associated with a significant increase in the risk of ischemic heart disease.

These major risk factors, in turn, are grouped as either modifiable or not modifiable. The unmodifiable factors are being a male, increasing age and heredity. The major modifiable risk factors are cigarette smoking, elevated serum cholesterol levels and high blood pressure (hypertension) (American Heart Association, 1991). Although none of these major risk factors is directly work related, occupational exposures to noise[1] and to certain chemicals[2] may be associated with blood pressure increases (Rosenman, 1990).

Contributing risk factors also include coexistence of diabetes, obesity, physical inactivity and emotional stress (American Heart Association, 1991).

---

[1] See 12.05[1] *infra.*

[2] See 12.04 *infra.*

Most occupational exposures are regarded as contributing risk factors or factors of unproved or hypothetic significance. Some workplace exposures increase the risk or accelerate the development of atherosclerotic heart disease (caused by irregularly distributed lipid deposits in the arteries); others increase the risk of an event such as myocardial infarction or sudden death in workers who already have coronary atherosclerosis. Still others induce acute cardiac events in previously healthy workers. There is good evidence, for example, of a relationship between heart disease or heart attacks and occupational exposure to carbon monoxide, carbon disulfide and nitrates. The evidence for stress, noise, lead and arsenic as risk factors is limited.[3]

Anecdotal accounts and individual studies suggest that cold and heat, electromagnetic radiation, cadmium and certain solvents may increase the risk for ischemic heart disease. Organic solvents and certain pesticides have been implicated as direct causes, rather than risk factors, in cardiac muscle damage, cardiac arrhythmia and sudden cardiac death (Rosenman, 1990).[4]

12.03　TYPES OF HEART DISEASE

There are various forms of heart disease. Most of these are ultimately related to the formation of hardened plaques on the insides of the major arteries.

[1]　Atherosclerotic Heart Disease

Atherosclerotic heart disease is caused by the accumulation of cholesterol and other material in the walls of the coronary arteries, which supply blood to the heart. This process, called atherosclerosis, affects most people as they age, but in only a fraction of people does it cause heart disease. Atherosclerotic heart disease is also called coronary heart disease or coronary artery disease (because it affects the coronary arteries) and ischemic heart disease (deprivation of oxygen in the tissues, resulting from an insufficient blood supply).

Atherosclerosis begins as early as age ten, when fatty streaks begin to develop in the walls of some blood vessels. Virtually everyone develops fatty streaks in the coronary arteries, but two other types of

---

[3] *See* 12.04 and 12.05 *infra.*

[4] *See* 12.04 and 12.05 *infra.*

atherosclerotic lesions—fibrous plaques and complicated lesions—affect only some people and are associated with symptoms of atherosclerotic heart disease.

[a] Fibrous Plaques

Fibrous plaques are raised lesions that bulge into the interior (lumen) of the coronary arteries, narrowing the arteries and obstructing blood flow.

[b] Complicated Lesions

Complicated lesions are associated with changes such as ulceration, calcification, hemorrhage and thrombi (clots), all of which may result in complete blockage of the arteries.

[2] Cardiac Ischemia

Cardiac ischemia results in the symptom of angina, or chest pain. Certain electrocardiographic (EKG) abnormalities are hallmarks of ischemia (insufficient blood supply). These EKG changes may sometimes be observed in patients who do not experience the symptom of chest pain—a condition called silent ischemia. Because exercise increases the amount of oxygen the heart needs to pump blood, patients with ischemic heart disease have a reduced capacity to exercise before chest pain and/or EKG abnormalities develop. Exercise EKG testing is frequently used to detect and monitor ischemic heart disease.

[3] Myocardial Infarction

A second consequence of cardiac ischemia is myocardial infarction (heart attack). This is permanent damage to the heart muscle (myocardium) resulting from an episode of coronary artery blockage. (*See Figure 12–1* and *Figure 12–2.*) Myocardial infarction is the number-one killer in the United States today. Of the 1.5 million heart attacks that are identified and treated each year, about a third are fatal. However, about 80 percent of patients who survive a myocardial infarction can return to work within three months (American Heart Association, 1991).

Chest pain usually heralds the onset of a myocardial infarction, though about 15 to 20 percent of infarctions are painless (Pasternak and Braunwald, 1991).

It is not uncommon for evidence of a previous, unrecognized myocardial infarction to be discovered in a patient who is being

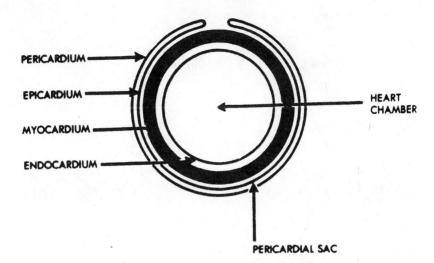

PERICARDIUM

EPICARDIUM

MYOCARDIUM

ENDOCARDIUM

HEART CHAMBER

PERICARDIAL SAC

Fig. 12-1. Diagrammatic cross section of the heart shows the pericardium, epicardium, myocardium and endocardium, all of which surround the heart chamber.

evaluated for ischemic heart disease. The pain of a myocardial infarction is typically described as similar to the sensations of angina[5] but more intense and longer lasting, and pain may radiate to the arms or to other locations.

Patients who may be experiencing a heart attack should be transported immediately to the nearest hospital that can provide emergency cardiac care. Medical intervention is more likely to be successful the earlier it is instituted. Treatment has two main goals: preventing life-threatening arrhythmias (irregularities of the heartbeat) and minimizing the amount of heart tissue that is infarcted (irreversibly damaged as a result of ischemia, i.e., insufficient blood supply). To maintain oxygenation of the heart, patients are given oxygen-enriched air, and myocardial oxygen demand is reduced by such anxiety-relieving measures as rest, sedation and analgesic drugs.

[a] Precipitating Factors

Various factors can lead to the development of a heart attack. These include atherosclerosis ("hardening of the arteries"), which is characterized by fatty deposits, called plaques, on the arterial walls

---

[5] *See* 12.03 [2] *supra.*

SMOKE INHALATION INJURY

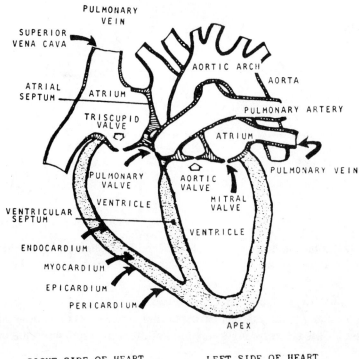

RIGHT SIDE OF HEART   LEFT SIDE OF HEART

Fig. 12-2. Schematic cross section of the heart shows, among other things, the myocardium (heart muscle). This is the section of the heart that is damaged in cases of myocardial infarction.

(Biehrman, 1991). When a thrombus attaches itself to a plaque, it can cut off circulation to heart tissue.

In addition, other factors can predispose an individual toward myocardial infarctions. These include physical and emotional stress, hyperlipidemia (high blood levels of cholesterol and other fats), diabetes, hypertension (high blood pressure), genetic factors, obesity and a sedentary life-style.

[b] Diagnosis

The classic symptom of myocardial infarction is a crushing or squeezing chest pain, which may radiate down one or both arms, up into the neck or jaw, or into the back. Chest pain may be accompanied by sweating, nausea, vomiting or dyspnea (shortness of breath).

Such symptoms are by no means universal, however. Some people, especially diabetics and the elderly, have what is called a silent MI. In such cases, there is no pain, but the patient suffers definite changes in the electrical activity of the heart muscle and complains of faintness, shortness of breath or various symptoms of blood circulation problems.

About 25 percent of people who have heart attacks have had no previous symptoms, despite the fact that they had extensive coronary artery disease.

The diagnosis of myocardial infarction cannot be definitively confirmed until laboratory tests are reviewed and a series of electrocardiograms (EKGs) are obtained. A chest x-ray also contributes to the picture, because it shows fluid in the lungs (indicative of heart failure). Radioactive scanning can document the size and position of an infarction, particularly if other tests are not clearly diagnostic; however, it is usually not a first-line test.

[c]   History and Physical Examination

Twenty to 40 percent of patients with a first myocardial infarction have experienced a period of unstable angina (attacks of chest pain) before the heart attack.

The patient suffering a myocardial infarction may have mild to severe chest pain.[6] This discomfort is usually described as crushing, squeezing or viselike. It may radiate to one arm (usually the left), the neck, jaw, teeth or the back. The patient, especially if elderly or diabetic, may not experience any pain at all, however. Blood pressure may be normal, high or low. A heart murmur is sometimes detectable in such patients.

[d]   Chest X-ray

Some degree of heart failure is usually visible on chest x-ray. For this reason, a chest film is a routine part of the cardiac workup. An unusual bulge in the heart suggests a ventricular aneurysm (weakened portion that balloons out under pressure). Enlargement of the heart is also visible on x-ray. Acute congestive heart failure is also visible as a near "white-out" of the lung field.

---

[6] *See* 12.03[3] [b] *supra.*

[e]   Electrocardiogram

An electrocardiogram (EKG) is a tracing or graph that represents the electric currents generated by the heart muscle as it contracts. This is the most commonly used procedure for evaluating cardiac status and detecting the presence and location of a myocardial infarction. Arrhythmias (abnormal heartbeats), which can originate from any cell in the myocardium, are also common. Continuous cardiac monitoring is a cornerstone of acute coronary care.

[f]   Laboratory Studies

When heart muscle is damaged, it releases several characteristic enzymes into the bloodstream. These enzymes can be measured and used to help diagnose and determine the size of an infarct. Creatine kinase (CK) is the most sensitive of the cardiac enzymes. Lactate dehydrogenase (LD) is another enzyme the level of which rises after myocardial infarction. Serum glutamic oxaloacetic transaminase (SGOT) level is elevated within 8 to 12 hours after a myocardial infarction and peaks in 18 to 72 hours. However, this enzyme is not specific to cardiac muscle; it is also released by the liver and skeletal muscles, and so it is not a sensitive test for myocardial injury.

[g]   Other Tests

In addition, a number of other tests are useful in the diagnosis of myocardial infarction. Primary among these is cardiac catheterization, an invasive test in which radiopaque (visible on x-ray) dye is injected into the coronary arteries through a catheter (slender tube) and then into the heart. Cardiac catheterization is a diagnostic technique to evaluate coronary blood flow in someone who has angina or valvular disease. It can also document hemodynamic (relating to the physical aspects of blood circulation) abnormalities resulting from impaired myocardial function.

Another test is radionuclide imaging, including radioactive scanning (scintigraphy) with thallium–201. (Thallium is a metallic element that is a physiologic analogue of potassium. It concentrates in normal and ischemic heart muscle cells, but not in necrotic tissue.) Thallium–201 is used to evaluate myocardial scarring and to locate and determine the size of an acute or a chronic myocardial infarction. It is quite sensitive within the first six hours of the heart attack.

[h] Treatment

When a person who is suspected of having a myocardial infarction enters the emergency medical system, care is aimed at decreasing the heart muscle's oxygen demands and increasing the oxygen supply. Special attention is given to decreasing pain, because pain indicates that the myocardium is ischemic (in need of increased blood supply).

[i] Immediate Care

Cardiac arrest and sudden death are two disastrous but common complications during the early hours of a myocardial infarction. Immediate treatment involves cardiopulmonary resuscitation (CPR) and defibrillation (restoring normal heart contraction by passing an electric current through the heart muscle). Access to a vein is secured, and a continuous cardiac monitor is also put in place to identify cardiac rhythms and note any changes induced by resuscitative drugs.

If the patient reaches the hospital within three hours of the initial infarction, thrombolytic therapy may be attempted. This consists of injecting an agent such as streptokinase or tissue plasminogen activator (TPA), both of which can dissolve a clot (thrombus) that is blocking a coronary artery. If the patient continues to have angina or if imaging studies show continuing artery blockage, revascularization[7] may be carried out with either percutaneous transluminal coronary angioplasty (PTCA) or a bypass operation as soon as possible (Pasternak and Braunwald, 1991).

Every effort should be made in all phases of cardiac care to provide reassurance and emotional support to the patient. This should be done not only for humane reasons but because calm, confident care helps reduce the patient's anxiety and thus his or her myocardial oxygen consumption.

[j] Ventricular Fibrillation

Ventricular fibrillation is the rapid, uncontrolled cardiac arrhythmia that precedes sudden cardiac death. It usually develops within the first few hours of an infarction but may be prevented by giving an antiadrenergic drug or treatment with a defibrillator (any agent or measure, e.g., an electric shock, that arrests fibrillation of the ventricular muscle and restores the normal beat).[8]

---

[7] See 12.06[2] infra.

[8] See 12.03[4] infra.

In the specialized medical setting, oxygen is administered, and the tachycardia (an abnormally rapid beating of the heart) is treated with a defibrillator, a device that uses two paddles placed on the chest to transmit electrical impulses that normalize the heart rhythm (Myerburg and Castellanos, 1991).

[4]   Cardiac Arrhythmia

A third consequence of ischemia is cardiac arrhythmia, a disruption of the heart's normal rhythm. (*See Figure 12–3.*) There are several kinds of cardiac rhythm disturbances, which vary in severity and may or may not be associated with ischemic heart disease. *Ventricular tachycardia* is usually associated with ischemic heart disease and a present or previous myocardial infarction; the most severe type of ventricular tachycardia, *ventricular fibrillation,* is also associated with sudden cardiac death. The vast majority of people who die suddenly from a cardiac arrhythmia had pre-existing atherosclerosis or a myocardial infarction, but these conditions are not a necessary requirement for severe arrhythmia to develop.

Ventricular fibrillation may also occur in the absence of a myocardial infarction. These arrhythmias rapidly result in collapse, loss of consciousness and death, usually within an hour of the onset of symptoms. In the patient who loses consciousness as a result of probable cardiac arrest, cardiopulmonary resuscitation should be administered immediately, if possible.

[5]   Sudden Cardiac Death

Sudden cardiac death is defined as a heart-related death that occurs within one hour of the onset of symptoms, or the death of a person who loses consciousness within one hour of the onset of symptoms, though life may be prolonged for a longer period by medical intervention without the patient recovering consciousness. Although ventricular fibrillation is the usual underlying event in sudden cardiac death, patients may survive ventricular fibrillation; hence the term "sudden cardiac death" is not synonymous with "collapse due to ventricular fibrillation," though it is sometimes incorrectly used in that way. Patients who suffer a sudden cardiac death may have been known to have pre-existing heart disease, but the unexpected time and nature of their death is a feature of the definition. About half of all cardiac deaths are sudden and unexpected (Myerburg and Castellanos, 1991).

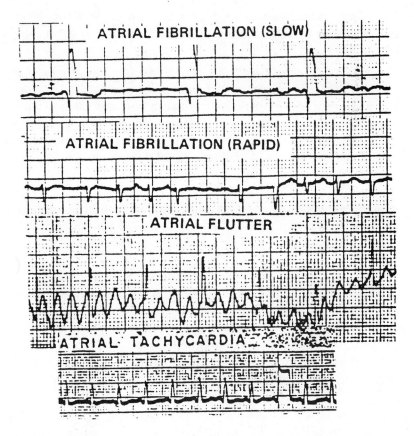

Fig. 12-3. EKG tracings of one type of abnormality: atrial fibrillation. The several kinds of cardiac rhythm disturbances vary in severity and may or may not be associated with ischemic heart disease. They are often associated with sudden cardiac death.

12.04　CARDIOTOXIC CHEMICALS

The acute cardiac effects of exposure to carbon monoxide, certain organic solvents and some pesticides, as well as withdrawal from occupational exposure to organic nitrate, are well accepted. However, it has been difficult to evaluate the link between chronic, low-dose exposure to workplace chemicals and heart disease risk. The major known nonoccupational risk factors account for about 50 percent of the incidence of coronary heart disease, with the remaining 50 percent thought to be due to chance or as-yet unidentified factors (Petronio,

1988). This variability has made it harder to perceive the comparatively small contribution that occupational exposure to chemicals is likely to have.

In many cases, it has been impossible to directly measure exposure and dose-disease relationships for workplace chemicals. Epidemiologic studies support a relationship between coronary atherosclerosis and carbon disulfide, arsenic and perhaps nitrates. They also indicate a possible, but unproved, relationship between hypertension and occupational exposure to cadmium or lead.[9]

[1] Carbon Monoxide

Carbon monoxide is the most frequently encountered cardiotoxic substance in the workplace (Benowitz, 1990). Carbon monoxide exposure may occur in any setting where workers are exposed to combustion engines and other combustion processes. The risk is especially high when ventilation is poor. Occupational groups that are at risk for carbon monoxide exposure include firefighters, police officers, toll collectors, garage workers, motor vehicle inspectors, bridge and tunnel officers, and foundry and blast furnace workers (Kristensen, 1989b). Carbon monoxide is also an environmental pollutant, and cigarette smoking is an important nonoccupational source of carbon monoxide.

When it is inhaled, carbon monoxide binds to the hemoglobin molecule on red blood cells, which ordinarily transports oxygen to the tissues. This binding results in the formation of carboxyhemoglobin and a reduction in the delivery of oxygen to body tissues by the blood. In healthy individuals, the heart responds to carboxyhemoglobin formation by increasing its output, so that blood flow to the tissues is increased. In people with coronary heart disease, elevated carboxyhemoglobin in the blood, combined with exercise, may precipitate angina or even a myocardial infarction.[10]

Reduced exercise thresholds for angina have been observed in persons with blood carboxyhemoglobin levels as low as 2.7 percent, which is lower than the average blood level observed in nonsmokers working in foundries, auto repair shops and garages (Benowitz, 1990). Smoking two packs of cigarettes a day results in markedly higher levels.

---

[9] *See* 12.04[6] *infra.*

[10] *See* 12.03[3] *supra.*

Cardiotoxicity is part of the clinical picture of acute carbon monoxide poisoning. Acute exposure to high levels of carbon monoxide has been reported to precipitate sudden death in workers with pre-existing coronary artery disease (Atkins and Baker, 1985). Elevated carboxyhemoglobin levels are also associated with transient electrocardiogram (EKG) abnormalities[11] and with greater vulnerability for cardiac rhythm disturbances (Rosenman, 1990).

Chronic exposure to carbon monoxide has been associated with accelerated atherosclerosis in cigarette smokers and in laboratory animals, but the effect of workplace exposures on atherosclerosis has not been studied extensively. Some evidence suggests that firefighters, toll collectors and motor vehicle inspectors have an elevated risk for heart disease and that their risk declines after carbon monoxide exposure ends (Rosenman, 1990). However, the evidence of a relationship between occupational carbon monoxide exposure and atherosclerosis remains inconclusive (Kristensen, 1989b).

Carbon monoxide exposure can also lower the threshold for symptoms of occlusive arterial disease in the legs. In this syndrome, called *intermittent claudication,* pain and weakness occur upon walking as a result of diminished blood supply due to atherosclerosis of the arteries in the legs. These symptoms are produced at a lower level of effort if the worker has elevated carboxyhemoglobin levels.

[2] Carbon Disulfide

Carbon disulfide, a solvent used in rayon manufacture and in the rubber, chemical and pharmaceutical industries, is another well-documented cause of cardiac disease. Prolonged exposure to carbon disulfide is associated with accelerated coronary atherosclerosis and an increased incidence of coronary heart disease, as well as atherosclerosis of the cerebral and peripheral arteries. Sometimes the renal (kidney) arteries are also affected. The mechanism for this effect has not been fully explained, but it is suggested that carbon disulfide exposure may elevate blood pressure or serum cholesterol levels (Benowitz, 1990; Rosenman, 1990).

Workers in rayon viscose manufacture are exposed to carbon disulfide. A frequently cited Swedish study showed that after five years of follow-up, rayon viscose workers had a greater than fivefold

---

[11] *See* 12.03[2] *supra.*

elevation in coronary deaths, compared to another group of nonexposed workers. When measures were instituted to reduce exposure, the risk of cardiac death in rayon workers returned to background levels after an additional eight years (Nurminen and Hernberg, 1985).

Acute carbon disulfide poisoning results mainly in central nervous system toxicity. An early sign of chronic exposure is alterations in the small blood vessels of the retina of the eye, a finding that is fairly specific for carbon disulfide exposure in workers who do not have diabetes. Periodic examination of the eye to detect these changes can be useful in detecting the early development of atherosclerosis. Carbon disulfide levels cannot be measured routinely in blood or other body fluids.

Discontinuation of excessive exposure may reverse the vascular alterations associated with prolonged carbon disulfide exposure. The Occupational Safety and Health Administration (OSHA) has recommended that levels of carbon disulfide in workplace air be limited to an average of 4 parts per million (ppm) (Benowitz, 1990).

[3] Organic Nitrates

Nitrates are used in the manufacture of dynamite and in drugs used to treat angina. Nitroglycerin is the best known, but ethylene glycol dinitrate, an organic nitrate that is more volatile and more toxic than nitroglycerin, is also used in explosives. Nitrates owe their efficacy in controlling the symptoms of heart disease to their ability to dilate the blood vessels, resulting in lowered blood pressure and a reduction in the heart's need for oxygen.

These effects partially explain the cardiotoxicity of nitrates. Workers who are exposed to nitroglycerin and other nitrates may at first experience symptoms due to vasodilation (increase in the caliber of blood vessels), such as facial flushing, headache and dizziness. After about one to four years, workers become accustomed to nitroglycerin exposure by developing compensatory vasoconstriction (decrease in the caliber of blood vessels). When these workers are no longer exposed to nitroglycerin and the effects wear off—which occurs within one to three days—they may experience the cardiac symptoms associated with vasoconstriction, including angina, coronary spasm, myocardial infarction, cardiac arrhythmia and even sudden cardiac death. The terms "Monday morning angina" and "Monday morning death" have been coined to describe these consequences of nitrate withdrawal.

These symptoms may affect workers who do not have coronary artery disease; however, those with coronary atherosclerosis may suffer these effects earlier and with increased intensity (Petronio, 1988).

Workers who are exposed to nitroglycerin include manufacturers of explosives, users of explosives (such as road builders, construction workers and the military) and pharmaceutical manufacturers. Recent epidemiologic evidence suggests that cardiovascular risk may remain elevated in nitrate workers for longer periods that can be explained by short-term withdrawal effects.

Early studies of Swedish explosives workers showed a twofold to threefold elevation in rates of coronary artery disease after 20 years of exposure to nitroglycerin and ethylene glycol dinitrate (Hogstedt and Davidson, 1980). These results have since been repeated by other investigators, in a study that also confirms that ethylene glycol dinitrate is the more toxic of the two nitrates (Craig, et al., 1985). In the Swedish workers, the increase in disease rates occurred despite reductions in workplace exposures to nitrates that occurred during the 20 years of exposure. A majority of deaths in these workers occurred months to years after exposure ceased. These observations suggest that nitrate exposure increases disease risk by a mechanism other than habituation and withdrawal; elevation of blood pressure is a possible explanation.

Nitrates, especially ethylene glycol dinitrate, are volatile and can be inhaled or absorbed through the skin. Automation of explosives manufacturing processes and workplace engineering controls have reduced workers' exposure to nitroglycerin. Most dynamite manufacturing processes using ethylene glycol dinitrate are now performed under remote control. Ventilation of the workplace and hand protection are other preventive measures. OSHA recommends a maximum workplace nitroglycerin concentration of 0.2 parts per million (ppm) in air (Benowitz, 1990).

"Monday morning angina"[12] usually resolves itself gradually after nitrate exposure is discontinued, but symptoms may persist or recur for weeks or months. Nitrate withdrawal may be treated with pharmaceutical nitrate preparations or with calcium-channel blockers, another category of drugs that prevents coronary artery spasm.

---

12 *See* 12.04[3] *supra.*

[4] Organic Solvents and Chlorofluorocarbons

Poisoning with organic solvents may cause arrhythmia and sudden cardiac death; chronic low-level exposure to these substances is not reported to contribute to atherosclerotic heart disease.[13] At low levels of exposure, these chemicals increase the sensitivity of the heart to stimuli that induce arrhythmia. Higher exposures may result in a slowed heartbeat or cardiac arrest (Benowitz, 1990). (*See Figure 12–4.*) Work situations that have been associated with sudden death have usually involved either the use of solvents in confined spaces or accidental spills (Rosenman, 1990).

Halogenated hydrocarbon solvents are used in many jobs and industrial processes, including dry cleaning, painting and chemical manufacture. These substances include tetrachloroethylene, trichloroethylene and trichloroethane. Nonhalogenated solvents such as chlorinated fluorocarbons (CFCs) and benzene may also be associated with cardiac arrhythmia, though the risks are not as well described. CFCs are used as solvents, refrigerants and propellants for aerosol sprays.

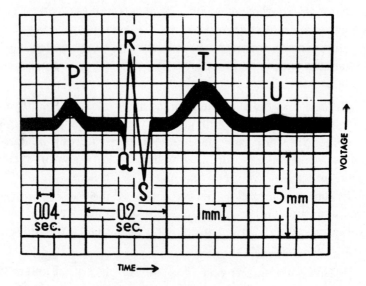

Fig. 12-4. Normal electrocardiographic representation of a single heartbeat. High levels of exposure to certain chemicals may result in a slowed heartbeat or even in cardiac arrest.

---

[13] *See* 12.03[1] *supra.*

Acute poisoning with solvents may result in dizziness, headaches, cardiac palpitations and fainting. Exposure to large concentrations may result in convulsions, coma or cardiac arrest. Cardiac arrhythmias stop after exposure to the toxic solvent is discontinued. Exposure to solvents should be minimized by adequate ventilation of the workplace, proper handling of the substances and sometimes by the use of a respirator. Workers with heart disease should not have jobs in which they may be exposed to organic solvents or CFCs (Rosenman, 1990).

[5] Pesticides

Organophosphate and carbamate pesticides, widely used in agriculture, can affect the heart as a result of acute poisoning. These pesticides interfere with the production of a neurohormone, acetylcholinesterase, that transmits impulses between nerve cells. The cardiac effects of poisoning are a rapid heartbeat and mild hypertension, followed by a slow heartbeat and hypotension. Cardiac rhythm abnormalities may also occur. Severe poisoning results in muscle paralysis, respiratory failure and coma.

Treatment consists of decontaminating the patient and providing cardiac and respiratory support. Patients should have cardiac monitoring for several days after the acute poisoning, as arrhythmias (heartbeat irregularities) may develop during recovery. To prevent poisoning, agricultural workers who are exposed to these pesticides should wear protective clothing and respirators, and biological monitoring should be performed routinely (Benowitz, 1990). The development of heart disease has not been described as a consequence of chronic low level exposures to these pesticides.

[6] Heavy Metals

Acute lead poisoning causes widespread vasoconstriction and particularly affects the circulation in the kidneys, though cardiac arrhythmia has been observed in patients with lead poisoning. The possible role of chronic lead exposure in the development of ischemic heart disease has been studied and discussed extensively. If lead exposure does increase ischemic heart disease risk, it does so through the medium of blood pressure elevation.

In one comprehensive review of 63 studies of the relationship between occupational lead exposure and blood pressure, the author concluded that low-level lead exposure (corresponding to blood levels of 30 μg/dL) are associated with increases in blood pressure. The incidence of cerebrovascular disease (stroke and related events) was shown to be elevated in workers who were exposed to lead, but the incidence of ischemic heart disease (hypertension is also a risk factor for stroke) was not. Somewhat higher levels of lead exposure have also been associated with death from stroke and other cerebrovascular causes in lead workers and in workers with a history of lead poisoning, but these studies did not show an excess of deaths from heart disease (Kristensen, 1989b).

Elevated rates of death from ischemic heart disease were observed in several groups of copper smelter workers, who are exposed to arsenic on the job. This association has been given weight by reports of heart disease in persons exposed to arsenic in drinking water and in people who became ill after an accidental contamination of beer with arsenic in Manchester, England, in 1900. Of the 70 people who died and 6,000 who became ill after drinking the contaminated beer, almost all had cardiovascular disease. Cardiac arrhythmias and EKG abnormalities have been observed in patients with acute arsenic poisoning (Benowitz, 1990; Kristensen, 1989b).

Cadmium causes hypertension in animals, and there has been some epidemiologic evidence linking cadmium with hypertension in humans, but the relationship has been debated for years. The quality of the epidemiologic evidence in these studies is not good, and to many scientists, a relationship seems unlikely (Benowitz, 1990; Kristensen, 1989b). Heart disease has occurred as a result of another episode of beer contamination, this time with cobalt, but cardiac sequelae in workers exposed to cobalt has not been widely studied (Kristensen, 1989b).

12.05   NONCHEMICAL RISK FACTORS

Nonchemical exposures that have been investigated for their role in cardiovascular disease include a range of physical and emotional stressors. For the most part, these stressors have been associated with the chronic development of heart disease or other cardiovascular endpoints; only one—vigorous physical activity, has been associated with immediate cardiac effects (Kristensen, 1989a).

[1]　Noise

The relationship of noise to cardiovascular disease has been extensively studied, with at least 100 epidemiologic studies published and an equal number of experimental investigations in human subjects and animals (Kristensen, 1989a). Millions of workers are exposed to either constant or intermittent noise on the job. Exposures are high in the electric utility industry and in most factories, mines and smelters (Theriault, 1988).

In the workplace, sound is measured with a portable sound level meter and expressed as dBA, a measurement of decibels that is balanced against the A scale, which reflects the ear's sensitivity to noise.[14] To prevent job-related hearing loss, the U.S. Occupational Safety and Health Administration (OSHA) has adopted the maximum exposure standard of an average 85 dBA over an 8–hour work day, with a maximum upper limit of 115 dBA for 15 minutes or less (Hamernik and Davis, 1988).

In practice, many workers are exposed to sound levels of greater than 85 dBA for varying time durations during the workday, and exposures as low as 90 to 100 dBA have been associated with transient increases in blood pressure. These increases usually subside after the worker becomes accustomed to the noise.

Noise produces hormonal and neurologic hyperarousal (excitation) characteristic of the stress response. These changes result in elevations in blood pressure, heart rate and serum cholesterol level, as well as alterations in the peripheral blood vessels (Theriault, 1988). Many factors in addition to loudness can increase the stressful impact of noise, including unpredictability, lack of worker control and lack of meaningfulness of the noise (Kristensen, 1989a).

Epidemiologic studies on the long-term effects of noise have varied in quality as well as in their results. However, the preponderance of evidence suggests that chronic exposure to noise on the job is a risk factor for cardiovascular disease. Most of the published studies use blood pressure elevation as their endpoint, and there is a lack of evidence about other types of cardiovascular disease. More evidence is also needed concerning the aspects of noise that result in cardiovascular disease; that is, the relative contribution of loudness itself versus the other stress inducing aspects of noise (Kristensen, 1989a).

---

[14] *See also* ch. 10.

[2] Temperature Extremes

Exposure to extremes of heat and cold have been associated with an increased incidence of angina attacks and cardiovascular mortality. Nonoccupational studies have shown that cardiovascular disease mortality is increased on days when outdoor temperatures are particularly hot or cold. However, epidemiologic studies have not answered the question of whether these effects are acute or chronic. Heat and cold may increase the risk of myocardial ischemia and heart attacks in workers who already have ischemic heart disease, but it is not known whether temperature extremes actually predispose healthy workers to developing heart disease. Frequently pre-employment medical screening results in the disqualification of workers with pre-existing heart disease for jobs that would expose them to extremes of heat and cold. Naturally this leads to a reduced incidence of heart disease endpoints in epidemiologic studies of such workers, irrespective of the effects of heat or cold (Kristensen, 1989a).

Workers adjust to a new job in a hot environment by a physiologic process called acclimatization, one element of which is an increase in cardiac output. Although healthy workers may have no difficulty making this adjustment, in workers with heart disease, the circulation may not be able to supply the increased oxygen required by the heart to increase its output. The result may be a myocardial infarction or worsening of heart failure (Kristensen, 1989b).

Substantial evidence is not abundant for the long-term effects on cardiac health of jobs that are performed in the presence of heat. A few studies suggest that prolonged exposures to high temperatures may result in increases in blood pressure, but more evidence is needed regarding this and, especially, other cardiovascular endpoints (Kristensen, 1989b).

Even less is known about the chronic effects on the heart of work in a cold environment. However, it is clear that cold does increase the likelihood of angina attacks and myocardial infarction in people who already have ischemic heart disease (Kristensen, 1989b).

[3] Nonionizing Radiation

Low-frequency electromagnetic fields include those generated by radiofrequency radiation and microwaves. These frequencies, located on the spectrum between ionizing radiation and audible sound waves, are used in television, radar and other telecommunications applications as well as in industrial processes, such as metal working and the sealing of wood and plastic. An estimated 21 million workers are exposed to these frequencies on the job (Hu, 1988).

Excess rates of ischemic heart disease have been observed in people who live near sources of electromagnetic radiation, such as buried power lines. However, studies of occupational exposure to nonionizing radiation have been inconclusive. Rates of cardiac disease were not elevated in military recruits or workers at electrical facilities. Most studies that show increased rates of heart disease in exposed workers are from Eastern Europe and are difficult to evaluate in terms of Western measures of exposure. However, some evidence from experiments in animals and small studies of humans in occupational groups suggests that there is at least a basis to pursue further research in this area (Kristensen, 1989b).

Microwaves and high-power radio waves can interfere with the operation of cardiac pacemakers. Pacemaker malfunction has been observed near microwave ovens, radar and communications systems, gasoline ignition systems and other sources of this type of radiation. Shielding of the source of radiation is effective in preventing adverse effects in workers who have cardiac pacemakers (Hu, 1988).

[4]   Passive Smoking

The effect of passive cigarette smoking on heart disease has been studied mostly in the nonsmoking spouses and the children of smokers. This research is very recent, and little is known about occupational cardiac risks from passive smoking.

Exposure to cigarette smoke lowers the threshold for angina in people who have ischemic heart disease. This is probably a result of exposure to carbon monoxide, which is a product of cigarette combustion (Kristensen, 1989b).

[5]   Physical Fitness, Activity and Inactivity

Jobs are becoming increasingly sedentary as a result of technologic innovations and other developments. On the basis of epidemiologic studies of the general population, there is general agreement that a sedentary life-style increases cardiovascular disease risk by about twofold (Kristensen, 1989b). However, the application of this data to the occupational setting is not clear cut. Several physically active jobs, such as forestry, unskilled construction work, manual labor, mining and quarrying, have been associated with higher-than-average rates of cardiovascular mortality (Karvonen, 1984).

Physical fitness has many positive effects on risk factors for cardiovascular disease, including reducing serum cholesterol levels and weight. Life-style choices such as diet and cigarette smoking also affect risk levels. Persons who choose active jobs are likely to have a higher level of physical fitness than those who choose sedentary jobs; on the other hand, many sedentary workers exercise in their leisure time. The relationship between physical activity on the job and heart disease risk may be confounded by the association between heart disease risk and low socioeconomic status; teachers and administrators, for example, have a lower heart disease risk than laborers and miners (Karvonen, 1984).

Sudden cardiac deaths during vigorous physical activity have been described in men pursuing leisure activities. Sudden deaths on the job have been observed in firefighters, but carbon monoxide inhalation is probably a contributing factor in such deaths (Robinson, et al., 1988). The protective effect of physical fitness gained on a physically active job may outweigh the risks of sudden, vigorous activity. Lower-than-average rates of cardiac mortality have been reported in some groups of active workers, including farmers, fishermen, construction carpenters, paper and printing workers, and electrical workers.

[6] Job Stress

Stressful jobs are generally regarded as those in which high demands are placed on the worker, but over which he or she has little control. A "job strain" model that incorporates both these features of stressful work has been important in epidemiologic research in the past decade (Kristensen, 1989a). Other factors that may make work stressful include overstimulation and understimulation, job insecurity, lack of meaning, lack of predictability and conflict (Kristensen, 1989a).

Other possible stressors include physically hazardous work, jobs requiring constant vigilance and jobs in which failure can produce dire consequences. Air traffic control, which is associated with high blood pressure, is the classic example of this type of stressful work. Stress due to the presence of ambient noise is another factor.[15]

---

[15] See 12.05[1] supra.

Although shift work is viewed as stressful, long hours per se are not, unless the total number of hours worked per week is extremely high—in the range of 70 hours or more.

Stress can affect cardiovascular health by either physiologic or behavioral mechanisms. Stress results in a state of physiologic hyperarousal that may cause high blood pressure, elevations in levels of serum cholesterol and ischemic heart disease. Stress may also predispose the worker to counterproductive behavior such as cigarette smoking, poor eating habits and possibly type A behavior, a fairly common behavior pattern that has been identified as a risk factor for coronary artery disease.[16]

The type A behavior pattern comprises traits of hostility, competitiveness and time urgency, a pattern that was at first thought to be inherent in the individual and not subject to alteration. More recently, researchers have shown that type A behavior can be modified by training or by making situational changes. This finding suggests that certain jobs are more likely than others to aggravate type A behavior and its consequences.

Several epidemiologic studies have confirmed the validity of the "strain" model as a predictor of cardiovascular disease risk. Other studies have shown the importance of aspects of stress as cardiovascular disease risk factors in specific jobs: for example, in sea pilots (great responsibility, long and irregular work hours), construction workers (strenuous, repetitive, demanding work) and bank employees (job insecurity, frustration and competition) (Kristensen, 1989a). Boring jobs, as well as jobs that involve hectic, monotonous repetition of tasks and no learning, are also associated with ischemic heart disease risk.

The role of shift work as a cardiovascular risk factor has been a subject of controversy. Of several studies that have addressed the topic, the better-designed ones tend to show that a relationship does exist. A number of studies from Scandinavia showed that shift work was associated with a modest increase in rates of cardiovascular disease of about 1.4 times background levels, with rates further increased in workers who were exposed for longer periods and in jobs involving monotony or noise (Kristensen, 1989a).

---

[16] *See also* ch. 13.

12.06   DIAGNOSIS AND TREATMENT OF CARDIOVASCULAR DISEASE

The chronic heart conditions that may be associated with occupational exposure are hypertension and ischemic heart disease. Acute myocardial infarction and ventricular fibrillation are also associated with such conditions.

Cardiac arrhythmias, which may occur after poisoning with organic solvents, pesticides, lead or arsenic, are transient and resolve with discontinuance of the exposure and elimination of the toxin from the body. In some cases, an antiarrhythmic drug, such as lidocaine, or a beta-adrenergic blocking agent, may be administered to help control arrhythmias. Certain antiarrhythmic agents should be avoided in the treatment of patients who are poisoned with organic pesticides, because such agents may aggravate the cardiac rhythm disturbances that occur with these toxins (Benowitz, 1990).

[1]   Hypertension

Blood pressure elevations are usually asymptomatic and discovered during routine medical screening or physical examination. There is no biologically obvious distinction between normal and high blood pressure; instead, cutoff values of mild, moderate and severe hypertension have been established empirically on the basis of the known consequences of these elevations.

Blood pressure is expressed as systolic over diastolic pressure, as measured against a column of mercury, for example, 120/80 mm Hg. Systolic pressure is the blood pressure when the heart beats, and diastolic pressure is the pressure between heartbeats. Isolated systolic hypertension is less common than diastolic hypertension (particularly in working populations, as opposed to the elderly). Diastolic pressure between 90 and 104 mm Hg is considered mild hypertension, 105 to 114 mm Hg is moderate and over 115 mm Hg is severe hypertension (Williams, 1991).

Although more than 60 million Americans are believed to be either undiagnosed hypertensives or undergoing treatment for hypertension, the condition by itself is rarely fatal (American Heart Association, 1991). Instead, hypertension is treated because it may cause heart failure (a gradually developing condition of cardiac enlargement and weakening caused by the heart having to work harder to pump blood) and because hypertension increases the rate of coronary atherosclerosis[17] and the onset of myocardial ischemia.[18]

Even mild elevations of blood pressure are associated with an increased risk of developing cardiac disease. Certain nondrug treatments are recommended for all patients with hypertension, and in those with mild blood pressure elevations, these may be sufficient to reduce blood pressure to normal. These modifications include reduction of calories, salt and fat in the diet; smoking cessation; regular exercise and the avoidance of stress.

Drug treatment is used for patients with moderate to severe blood pressure elevations and sometimes for those whose mild elevations persist. A large variety of drugs have been developed to control hypertension, with different modes of action and differing indications, contraindications and side effects. The main classes of antihypertensive drugs are diuretics (which reduce blood volume), vasodilators (which dilate the blood vessels), antiadrenergic agents (which block neurologic hyperactivity that contributes to blood pressure elevation), calcium channel blockers (which prevent coronary spasm) and angiotensin converting enzyme (ACE) inhibitors (which block the production by the kidneys of a hormone that increases blood pressure).

Physicians treat hypertension aggressively, so that if a patient does not respond to one drug, another one or a combination is tried.

[2] Ischemic Heart Disease

Angina is the usual presenting sign of ischemic heart disease. The typical patient with angina is a middle-aged man (only 20 percent of patients with angina are women) who complains of transient sensations in the chest, such as squeezing, pressure, heaviness, smothering or choking. These sensations are rarely described as pain. Many people—as many as three to four million Americans—may have silent ischemia (episodes of cardiac muscle oxygen deprivation that are not accompanied by symptoms) (American Heart Association, 1991). These silent episodes can only be detected by tests such as an exercise EKG or 24–hour Holter monitoring (wearing a portable EKG device while carrying out usual daily activities for 24 hours).

The exercise EKG is also used to investigate patients who complain of symptoms of chest discomfort. In this test, patients perform

---

[17] *See* 12.03[1] *supra.*

[18] *See* 12.05[2] *supra.*

progressively harder exercise (usually walking on a treadmill) while their blood pressure and EKG are monitored. The appearance of symptoms, certain EKG abnormalities, ventricular arrhythmia or a failure of the blood pressure to increase in response to exercise all signal a high likelihood of coronary artery disease.

Additional tests such as echocardiography or imaging with injected radioactive contrast agents can increase the accuracy of the diagnosis. Coronary angiography (also called coronary arteriography), an imaging technique in which dye is inserted into the coronary arteries through a catheter and observed with a high-speed x-ray camera, is used to evaluate more severely affected patients, including those who may be candidates for revascularization procedures (the process of restoring an adequate blood supply to a structure).

Patients with ischemic heart disease are advised to modify their risk factors by such measures as weight reduction, smoking cessation and adoption of a low-fat diet. Patients whose jobs involve strenuous activity may be advised to change jobs or to pace themselves more slowly. Nitrates are the mainstay of drug treatment for angina; these drugs act by dilating the blood vessels, which increases blood flow and reduces the workload of the heart. Antiadrenergic drugs (that counteract the effects of impulses of the sympathetic nervous system) and calcium channel blockers (that inhibit the movement of calcium ions across the cell membrane) may also be given.

For patients who do not respond to medical treatment, an invasive revascularization procedure may be the next step. Revascularization may be accomplished by percutaneous transluminal coronary angioplasty (PTCA), in which a balloon is inserted into the coronary arteries through a catheter and is inflated, causing the plaque to rupture.

In coronary artery bypass grafting, the other widely used revascularization procedure, an occluded artery is removed and replaced with another blood vessel from the patient, usually a vein taken from the leg or an artery from the chest.

12.07 WORKER FITNESS EVALUATION

Because cardiac disease is very common, the health care provider in industrial settings is frequently concerned with evaluating the ability of workers with cardiac disease to perform jobs that require physical effort. In addition, asymptomatic workers in certain public safety occupations may be investigated for unsuspected heart disease. Work-related disability evaluation for heart disease is sometimes a concern, although unless a work-related accidental exposure or exertion can be directly implicated, cardiac disease is generally viewed as a personal rather than an occupational disease (Theriault, 1988).

[1] Screening of Asymptomatic Employees

Workplace risk factor screening, smoking cessation programs and exercise facilities are becoming increasingly common as employee benefits. These programs are generally viewed as beneficial, as long as they are not offered in a coercive manner and appropriate intervention is provided for workers who are identified as being at risk.

Programs to evaluate asymptomatic workers with exercise EKG tests [19] if they are in strenuous jobs or potentially exposed to low levels of carbon monoxide are more controversial. Although they have some scientific validity in detecting unsuspected ischemic heart disease, these tests are not completely reliable in detecting or ruling out coronary heart disease. Some writers have expressed concerns that the identification of cardiac disease may lead to "defensive medicine" in the workplace and to discrimination in hiring or promoting, or to unnecessary work restriction (McCormick, 1991; Theriault, 1988).

The American Heart Association and American College of Cardiology jointly recommend routine evaluation for silent coronary ischemia in previously sedentary men over the age of 40 who are beginning a strenuous job, as well as for all workers over the age of 40 in certain public safety occupations (police officers, firefighters and pilots) (Temte, 1988). Workers who could endanger others if they have a heart attack on the job also include security guards, drivers of ground transportation, military personnel, seamen and electricians (Bruce and Fisher, 1989).

Although fewer than 1 percent of aviation accidents are a result of sudden pilot illness (Froom, et al., 1988), pilots have been the focus of special regulatory concern. Since 1959, the Federal Aviation Administration's "Age 60 Rule" has been in effect: Captains and first officers on regulated flights must retire from flying by age 60. Age discrimination rules prohibit mandatory early retirement of healthy workers at age 55, but these regulations do not apply to firefighters and police officers.

---

[19] *See* 12.06[2] *supra.*

These broad-brush age-related strategies of risk reduction are viewed by many experts as imprecise, unnecessarily restricting the employment of many healthy, highly experienced older workers while paying insufficient attention to younger workers who may be at risk. Alternatives for evaluating cardiac risk in public safety occupations are being investigated, but for the present, they have not replaced the age-based rules.

[2] The Worker with Ischemic Heart Disease

Regular physical exertion may be beneficial for workers with ischemic heart disease and workers who have had a myocardial infarction (Temte, 1988). However, the physical and emotional demands of a job should not exceed the worker's capacities. Evaluation of the fitness of a worker with ischemic heart disease should begin with a complete medical history, including the patient's current level of activity and the factors that are likely to induce symptoms. Aspects of the job that should be considered include not only the level of exertion but also its timing and duration, whether the exercise is static or dynamic, and the psychosocial stressors involved.

Dynamic exercise increases cardiovascular conditioning and may be beneficial for workers with heart disease. Static or isometric exercise increases muscle strength but does not improve cardiovascular fitness and can be hazardous for patients with cardiovascular disease. Resting, exercise or 24–hour EKG testing[20] may help identify ischemia in patients who are being evaluated for a strenuous job (Temte, 1988).

The energy requirements of different job activities are sometimes expressed as METs, a unit of measure that expresses multiples of basal oxygen consumption at rest. For example, welding is associated with expenditure of 3 to 4 METs, sawing hardwood as 7 to 8 METs and firefighting as 10 METs or more. The maximum energy expenditure of which a worker is capable can be measured objectively with exercise testing. Patients with symptomatic ischemic heart disease may work at 6 METs or less before curtailment by angina or EKG abnormalities, while active healthy men may achieve levels of 12 to 15 METs. This method is useful for matching tasks to workers who are returning to their jobs after a myocardial infarction and for

---

[20] See 12.06 [2] supra.

increasing workers' confidence that they can perform these activities safely (Temte, 1988).

Workers who have suffered a myocardial infarction are generally encouraged to return to work as soon as they can without jeopardizing their health. The healing period after a myocardial infarction is six to eight weeks (Theriault, 1988).

Workers may be advised to begin part-time at first, perhaps with lighter tasks than usual or longer rest periods. A worker with a job that affects public safety does not continue in this job after a myocardial infarction; on a case-by-case basis, workers with strenuous jobs or jobs in which they are isolated from emergency medical care may also be reassigned (Temte, 1988).

Workers who have had a coronary artery bypass operation are encouraged to return to work within three months. People who have had these operations are usually capable of doing strenuous work, and most can do so without taking medication. However, patients who have had these operations tend to do no better than patients who are maintained on medications (Temte, 1988).

For any worker who has been on leave for heart disease, prompt rehabilitation and the avoidance of unnecessary disability are important concerns. Many patients are not rehabilitated to their full capabilities, which results in huge costs in lost wages and productivity (Temte, 1988).

[3] Disability Evaluation

In its *Guides to the Evaluation of Impairment,* the American Medical Association recommends exercise EKG testing[21] as an objective measurement of cardiac impairment in patients with ischemic heart disease. Clinical observation and information about the ability to carry out ordinary physical activity are important as well. The AMA has formulated the following guidelines for evaluating disability in workers with ischemic heart disease (American Medical Association, 1993):

> ● Class 1—Impairment of Whole Person, 0 to 9 percent: In the absence of a clear history of angina or other evidence of disease, coronary angiography has been performed and coronary artery stenosis (narrowing) of less than 50 percent has been detected.

---

[21] *See* 12.06[2] *supra.*

- Class 2—Impairment of Whole Person, 10 percent to 29 percent: The patient has laboratory-confirmed angina or a past myocardial infarction but is asymptomatic while performing ordinary daily activities or even moderately heavy exertion. He or she can exercise to 90 percent of predicted heart rate without developing significant EKG abnormalities.

- Class 3—Impairment of Whole Person, 30 percent to 49 percent: The patient has a past myocardial infarction or angina combined with objective evidence of ischemia; or the patient has angiographically demonstrated coronary artery narrowing of at least 50 percent. The patient may be free of angina symptoms due to drugs or dietary modifications, but may develop angina during moderately heavy exertion. Alternatively, the patient may have recovered from a revascularization procedure but continue to receive treatment and to have symptoms during moderately heavy exercise.

- Class 4—Impairment of Whole Person, 50 percent to 100 percent: The patient has a documented previous myocardial infarction or angina with strong evidence of ischemia; or the patient has angiographically documented coronary artery narrowing of at least 50 percent. In addition, despite medication and/or dietary adjustment, the patient experiences symptoms at ordinary levels of exertion or there is laboratory evidence of cardiac enlargement or abnormal ventricular function. Patients in Class 4 may have undergone a revascularization procedure, but they continue to receive treatment and to experience symptoms while carrying out ordinary daily activities.

12.100 BIBLIOGRAPHY

Reference Bibliography

American Heart Association: 1991 Heart and Stroke Facts. Dallas: American Heart Association, 1991.

American Medical Association: Guides to the Evaluation of Permanent Impairment, 4th ed. Chicago: American Medical Association, 1993.

Atkins, E. H. and Baker, E. L.: Exacerbation of Coronary Artery Disease by Occupational Carbon Monoxide Exposure: A Report of Two Fatalities and a Review of the Literature. Am. J. Ind. Med. 7:73–79, 1985.

Benowitz, N. L.: Cardiovascular Toxicology. In: LaDou, J. (Ed.): Occupational Medicine. Norwalk, Conn.: Appleton & Lange, 1990.

Biehrman, E. L.: Atherosclerosis and Other Forms of Arteriosclerosis. In: Wilson, J. D., et al. (Eds.): Harrison's Principles of Internal Medicine. New York: McGraw-Hill, 1991.

Bruce, R. A. and Fisher, L. D.: Strategies for Risk Evaluation of Sudden Cardiac Incapacitation in Men in Occupations Affecting Public Safety. J. Occup. Med. 31:124–133, Feb. 1989.

Craig, R., et al.: Sixteen-Year Follow-Up of Workers in an Explosives Factory. J. Soc. Occup. Med. 35:107–110, Winter 1985.

Froom, P., et al.: Air Accidents, Pilot Experience, and Disease-related In-Flight Sudden Incapacitation. Aviat. Space Environ. Med. 59:278–281, Mar. 1988.

Hamernik, R. P. and Davis, R. I.: Noise and Hearing Impairment. In: Levy, B. S. and Wegman, D. H. (Eds.): Occupational Health. Recognizing and Preventing Work-Related Disease. Boston: Little, Brown, 1988.

Hogstedt, C. and Davidson, B.: Nitroglycol and Nitroglycerine Exposure in a Dynamite Industry 1958–1978. Am. Ind. Hyg. Assoc. J. 41:373–375, 1980.

Hu, H.: Other Physical Hazards and Their Effects. In: Levy, B. S. and Wegman, D. H. (Eds.): Occupational Health. Recognizing and Preventing Work-Related Disease. Boston: Little, Brown, 1988.

Karvonen, M. J.: Physical Activity and Cardiovascular Morbidity. Scand. J. Work Environ. Health 10:389–395, Dec. 1984.

Kristensen, T. S.: Cardiovascular Diseases and the Work Environment. A Critical Review of the Epidemiologic Literature on Nonchemical Factors. Scand. J. Work Environ. Health 15(3):165–179, June 1989a.

Kristensen, T. S.: Cardiovascular Diseases and the Work Environment. A Critical Review of the Epidemiologic Literature on Chemical Factors. Scand. J. Work Environ. Health 15:245–264, Aug. 1989b.

McCormick, J. S.: Looking for Cardiovascular Risk Factors in Employees. J. Soc. Occup. Med. 41:64–5, 67–72, Summer 1991.

Myerburg, R. J. and Castellanos, A.: Cardiovascular Collapse, Cardiac Arrest, and Sudden Death. In: Wilson, J. D., et al. (Eds.): Harrison's Principles of Internal Medicine. New York: McGraw-Hill, 1991.

Nurminen, M. and Hernberg, S.: Effects of Intervention on the Cardiovascular Mortality of Workers Exposed to Carbon Disulfide: A 15 Year Follow-Up. Br. J. Ind. Med. 42:32–35, 1985.

Pasternak, R. C. and Braunwald, E.: Acute Myocardial Infarction. In: Wilson, J. D., et al. (Eds.): Harrison's Principles of Internal Medicine. New York: McGraw-Hill, 1991.

Petronio, L.: Chemical and Physical Agents of Work-Related Cardiovascular Diseases. Eur. Heart. J. 9(Suppl.):26–34, Nov. 1988.

Robinson, C. C., et al.: An Epidemiologic Study of Sudden Death at Work in an Industrial County, 1979–1982. Am. J. Epidemiol. 128(4):806–820, Oct. 1988.

Rosenman, K. D.: Environmentally Related Disorders of the Cardiovascular System. Med. Clin. North Am. 74:361–375, 1990.

Temte, J. V.: Cardiovascular Conditions and Worker Fitness and Risk. Occup. Med. 3:241–254, Apr.-June 1988.

Theriault, G. P.: Cardiovascular Disorders. In: Levy, B. S. and Wegman, D. H. (Eds.): Occupational Health. Recognizing and Preventing Work-Related Disease. Boston: Little, Brown, 1988.

Williams, G. H.: Hypertensive Vascular Disease. In: Wilson, J. D., et al. (Eds.): Harrison's Principles of Internal Medicine. New York: McGraw-Hill, 1991.

CHAPTER 13

Mental Stress Disorders

SCOPE

Occupational stress has been associated with depression, anxiety, neurosis and substance abuse, as well as with specific stress-related mental disorders. Stressors may arise from forced-pace work, repetitiveness, toxic exposures, danger, lack of control, lack of social support, role conflict or ambiguity, conflict in interpersonal relationships, harassment, lack of job security, de-skilling of jobs and unemployment. Clinical manifestations include nonspecific symptoms, such as memory disturbance, difficulty making decisions, anxiety, boredom, irritability, depression and hopelessness, and behavioral changes, such as substance abuse, sleep disorders and disturbed relationships. Specific stress-related mental disorders include posttraumatic stress disorder, mass psychogenic illness and burnout. It is rarely possible to determine to what degree a mental disorder is caused by occupational stress, since many factors contribute, all of which the clinician must consider. The most effective treatment is to reorganize the work environment to reduce or eliminate sources of stress. Workers may also receive individual and group counseling or psychotherapy and stress management training. Prevention of stress requires monitoring the work environment to identify potential stressors, educating workers to recognize and cope effectively with stress, and redesigning jobs to increase worker control and provide a more supportive environment.

SYNOPSIS

13.01 INTRODUCTION

Studies of occupational stress have emphasized physical rather than mental illness. However, it is generally recognized today that stress in the workplace affects psychological and emotional as well as physical functioning. Occupational stress has been associated with depression, anxiety, neurosis and substance abuse, as well as with specific stress-related disorders. These conditions diminish the worker's effectiveness and result in considerable morbidity, disability and mortality.

Evidence indicates that modern production technologies and global economic trade mechanisms are increasing the risks for occupational stress, through changes in individual jobs, organizational structures and labor markets that diminish the skill levels of jobs and decrease job security (Baker and Karasek, 1995; Baker and Schottenfeld, 1995). Evaluating psychosocial factors related to occupational stress is difficult, however, and has been the subject of much disagreement. Many factors must be taken into consideration, including the worker's individual psychological profile, his or her subjective perceptions, interpersonal relationships with supervisors and co-workers, the nature of the specific tasks and other physical factors, such as levels of noise and toxic exposures (Elo, 1994).

[1] Stress

The term *stress* has a variety of meanings. It can refer to an environmental event or condition, a person's appraisal of the environmental condition, a response to the condition or an inability to meet the demands placed on the individual by the environment. More generally, *stress* also refers to the body's entire adaptive process, including the experience of stressors (noxious stimuli that cause stress), through the stress response, to the long-term effects on health. The term *strain* refers to a short-term reaction to a stressor (Baker and Karasek, 1995). Responses to stress occur on a range of levels, from physiologic to behavioral to psychological.

[2] Types of Stressors

Stressors may be physical, such as an injury or a chronic illness, or psychosocial, such as interpersonal conflict or the death of a loved one. They may be acute, like accidents, or chronic, like unsatisfactory relationships. Change is a common feature of all types of stressors.

For this reason, major life events are stressors, and individuals who experience a number of such events appear to be at an increased risk of developing stress-related illness.

Life events include divorce, marriage, retirement, change of residence, birth of a child and loss of employment. As indicated by this list, positive events as well as negative ones can be sources of stress (Holland, 1994). Lack of change may also be stressful, as occurs in extremely monotonous jobs, especially when a desired change does not occur.

[3]   Epidemiology of Occupational Mental Stress

Psychological disorders are a leading category of occupational health problems. Mental stress first became recognized as being eligible for worker's compensation in the 1960s and 1970s. By the mid-1980s, occupational stress was cited in 75 percent of claims in which absenteeism was primarily due to mental stress. Of these, 90 percent were caused by cumulative psychic trauma in the workplace (as opposed to single traumatic events) (deCarteret, 1994).

Mental-stress-related disorders are now the fastest-growing category of workers' compensation claims (deCarteret, 1994). In 1985, 15 percent of all claims for occupational disease were related to stress. Currently about 25 percent of American workers experience some type of mental health problem caused by stress (deCarteret, 1994). Over 10 percent of the workforce reports experiencing high, as opposed to moderate or mild, levels of stress. This means that stress is the second most prevalent occupational hazard, after loud noise[1] (Baker and Schottenfeld, 1995).

13.02   The Stress Response

Early stress research conceptualized stress as an entirely physiologic process. In the physiologic paradigm, stress can be either positive (eustress) or negative (distress), depending on whether the adaptive response is successful (Baker and Karasek, 1995). More recently, stress has been viewed as being psychophysiologic in nature. That is, it has emotional and psychological as well as physiologic components, all of which interact to produce the stress response (Peterson, 1994).

---

[1] *See also* ch. 10 for a discussion of noise-induced hearing loss.

[1] Physiologic Basis of Stress

The earliest definition of the stress response was Hans Selye's description of the general adaptation syndrome in 1936. He described a three-stage, nonspecific physiologic response of the body to a stressor that disrupted the body's homeostasis (ability to maintain a stable state).

This acute stress response involves activation of the sympathetic nervous system to make possible "fight or flight." Stimulation of the adrenal medulla (inner portion of the adrenal gland) in response to a stressor results in increased secretion of the hormone epinephrine and increases in heart rate, respiratory rate and blood pressure. This response is associated with time pressure, danger and stressful social situations (Holland, 1994; Baker and Karasek, 1995).

In chronic stress, secretion of corticotropin-releasing factor and other mediators stimulates the adrenal cortex (outer portion of the adrenal gland) to secrete corticosteroids (hormones) and raises the heart rate and the blood pressure. This reaction may also impair the immune response. This chronic response is not a "fight" reaction but one of withdrawal or "flight," presumably in a situation in which the individual has no control over the stressor (Holland, 1994; Baker and Karasek, 1995).

[2] Stress As a Psychosocial Response

Stress has been defined as "a (perceived) substantial imbalance between demand and response capability, under conditions where failure to meet demand has important (perceived) consequences." In this perspective, stress includes both the environment and the individual's own perceptions of the stressor. In particular, the individual's appraisal of the situation and his or her style of coping with it are important in determining the physiologic response and the resulting development of a stress-related disorder (Baker and Karasek, 1994; Peterson, 1994).

The way stress becomes manifest in an individual worker is a function of a variety of factors, including that person's physiologic and psychological constitution and the type of support provided by the social environment. Because of this complex etiology, it is often difficult to determine whether a stress reaction such as depression or anxiety constitutes a disease or is work related.

[3] Mediating Factors

Mediating factors, or modifiers, are individual or environmental characteristics that act to vary the individual's response at each stage of the stress response.

[a] Individual Factors

Individual modifiers may be psychological and/or physiologic. Age, general state of health and sex are physiologic modifiers that affect an individual's ability to tolerate stress. Psychological modifiers include emotional stability, behavioral style, need for achievement, effectiveness of coping skills, flexibility or rigidity, and conformity or inner-directedness.

The way in which a person develops a new response or uses an old response to handle a stressful situation is referred to as his or her coping style. Successful handling of stress depends on effective coping strategies, and training in such strategies is one component of stress prevention programs[2] (Baker and Schottenfeld, 1995; Baker and Karasek, 1995).

[b] Environmental Factors

A number of studies have demonstrated that the most important modifier alleviating the stress response is social support. This support can involve providing clear and effective information, providing appropriate instructions and tools for performing tasks, and providing emotional support. A supportive environment helps workers cope with emotional distress, although investigators disagree over whether support reduces stress directly or simply buffers the effects of stressors.

By contrast, an unsupportive environment of social unrest—such as labor-management disputes, racial disputes or other community conflicts—can intensify the adverse effects of stress. For these reasons, an important component of stress management involves encouraging the development of social support networks in the workplace (Baker and Schottenfeld, 1995; Baker and Karasek, 1995).

13.03 OCCUPATIONAL SOURCES OF MENTAL STRESS

A variety of stressors exist in the workplace. They may be physical, related to the way work is organized or psychosocial. It is therefore

---

2 *See also* 13.07 and 13.08 *infra.*

difficult to draw a clear line of causation from a given stressor to a specific health effect, as can be done, for example, when a toxic chemical causes a specific physical sign. In addition, several causes of occupational stress may act together to produce one health effect or, conversely, one stressor can cause a variety of responses.

In evaluating occupational stress, therefore, this complexity must be kept in mind. In particular, the organizational and economic aspects of stress must be taken into consideration. Many researchers emphasize the importance of recognizing objective environmental factors that cause stress, as opposed to focusing only on the subjective, individual characteristics of the worker (Baker and Karasek, 1995; Quinn, et al., 1995).

[1] Models of Occupational Stress

A variety of models have been developed to describe how occupational stress is caused. Some focus on environmental factors, such as overtime, shift work, role conflict or ambiguity, and unemployment. Others describe general characteristics of stressful work, such as chronicity and external pacing. However, these models are unable to describe the actual process by which stress develops.

Still other models attempt to integrate the components of stress, in order to predict what elements of work will be stressful. The most widely studied of these models are the person-environment fit model and the job demand–control model (Baker and Karasek, 1995).

[a] Cognitive Models

Cognitive stress models analyze stress in terms of the amount of information the worker must process in order to perform the job. In this view, stress results from an overload of information that the worker cannot handle. Other cognitive models focus in addition on underutilization of the worker's skills or abilities as a source of stress.

Overload and underload of the worker's capacities are both seen as being basic to mental stress, since after a period of time, performing extremely simple jobs becomes just as stressful as performing extremely demanding ones. Overload and underload may be quantitative, involving too much or too little to do, or qualitative, involving work that is too difficult or too easy (Baker and Karasek, 1995; Peterson, 1994; Elo, 1994).

The cognitive models emphasize the worker's interpretation of the stressful situation more than the objective external stressors that may be present. Interventions based on cognitive models focus on reducing stress by helping the worker reinterpret the stressful situation to make it less threatening, for example, by reinterpreting the behavior of a supervisor or co-worker. However, these models do not allow for stressors that do not involve information overload, such as deadlines and interpersonal conflict (Baker and Karasek, 1995).

[b]   Physiologic Models

The physiologic models are based on the physiologic "fight or flight" response and chronic withdrawal stress responses.[3] These responses arise in the limbic areas of the brain, which mediate motivation, emotional response and reaction to social interactions. The physiologic models thus address emotional responses, such as anxiety and depression, to time pressure, job insecurity and difficult psychosocial relationships, which the cognitive models leave out (Baker and Karasek, 1995).

[c]   Person-Environment Fit Model

This model takes into consideration the fit between, on one hand, the demands of the job and the worker's ability to meet them, and on the other, the worker's motivation and the job's ability to satisfy it. Stress results when demands such as job complexity or workload are too great for the worker, or when the job supplies too little income or too little challenge to satisfy the worker's motivations for working.

The person-environment fit model usefully emphasizes the need for job design to accommodate individual differences among workers. However, the model does not clarify the relationship between the two types of possible misfits it describes. Neither has it been found effective in predicting what types of work conditions will cause stress (Baker and Karasek, 1995).

[d]   Job Demand–Control Model

Unlike the other models, the job demand–control model focuses primarily on external constraints created by the work rather than the worker's perceptions as the source of stress. It states that high job demands alone do not cause stress. They cause stress in combination

---

[3] *See also* 13.02[1] *supra.*

with a low level of ability to exert control over how the individual's skills are utilized to perform the work. Control involves such factors as pacing the work, choosing a work method and participating in some decisions within the organization. The level of control is referred to as *decision latitude.*

This model describes jobs in terms of demand and control. Jobs with high demands and low control—such as waiter, video display terminal operator and assembly-line worker—will have adverse effects on mental health. Jobs with high demands and high levels of control, however, create motivation in the worker instead of strain.

Studies using this model indicate that control is a major factor in the development of stress. Jobs with too little decision latitude result in the most mental health problems, regardless of how high the level of demand is. Workers performing machine-paced jobs, for example, had increased levels of the stress-associated hormones adrenaline, noradrenaline and cortisol. Work conditions that encouraged them to exert control reduced their neuroendocrine stress response and increased their feelings of satisfaction with the job and of well-being. In women, depression was a major outcome of low-control jobs (Peterson, 1994; Baker and Karasek, 1995).

[2] Types of Occupational Stressors

Occupational stressors may be categorized as those deriving from the nature of a given job, those deriving from the nature of the organization in which the individual works and those arising from outside the organization.

[a] Job-Related Stressors

One group of job-related stressors involves time-related demands, such as forced-pace work (as on an assembly line), required overtime work, piecework (in which pay is determined by the number of products produced) and shift work.

Forced-paced work is controlled by some factor external to the worker, such as an assembly-line machine or a computer. There are many different types, but generally forced pacing involves many demands made at brief intervals without any control by the worker. Frequently such jobs also involve haste, having much work to accomplish within a set time period, often while attending to one or several machines (Elo, 1994).

Shift work disturbs the normal pattern of biological and social functioning. When it involves permanent displacement of the work schedule to nighttime or a rotating shift schedule, shift work is especially likely to result in physical and nervous disturbances (Akerstedt and Knutsson, 1995; Baker and Karasek, 1995). Workers vary greatly in their susceptibility to adverse reactions to shift work, although generally they grow more vulnerable as they age. About 25 percent of shift workers are thought to experience serious problems on the job, in the family and in social life (Holland, 1994).

Another type of stressful work requires the worker to make precise discriminations regarding a product's shape, color, sound, etc. This requirement occurs in quality-control jobs and those employing visual display units. This type of work is particularly stressful when an error can result in a large loss of money (Elo, 1994).

Physically dangerous or unpleasant conditions, such as high noise levels, hazards from potential exposure to toxic materials, inadequate facilities for performing the work or an unsanitary or badly lighted worksite, are another cause of stress. For example, a study of nursing homes found that not having enough staff per shift, lifting heavy patients and shortage of essential resources were sources of stress among staff (Dunn, et al., 1994).

A third type of job-related stressor involves psychosocial aspects of the job, relating to how authority is allocated and how tasks are divided. An example is structural restraints that define and monitor the work process in detail and allow the worker little or no freedom in carrying out tasks. Such restraints are a feature of repetitive work and also of some highly skilled jobs, such as aircraft maintenance done according to a checklist and bookkeeping.

Social isolation, in which the task must be performed without the chance to converse with other people, causes strain. Such isolation occurs in jobs in which the worker encountering difficulties cannot obtain assistance from co-workers or supervisors, such as surveillance or guard duty, and when there is constant loud noise, such as in a factory. Being able to see the other workers does not relieve the stress of isolation if it is impossible to speak to them.

Responsibility for safety is a stress factor if the job entails taking care in order to avoid harming people. Vehicle and crane operators, airline pilots and workers handling explosives and dangerous chemicals encounter this type of stress. Similarly, responsibility for other people's welfare, as in health care, education and social service jobs, also creates stress.

Another type of psychosocial stress is burdensome contacts, which involve interactions about difficult issues (as in dealing with an angry or impatient customer) or having to deal with another person's negative emotions (such as caring for an ill, frightened person) (Elo, 1994; Baker and Karasek, 1995).

[b] Organizational Stressors

This type of stressor is related to the structure of the organization as a whole, the individual's role in it and interpersonal relationships. Role ambiguity occurs when the worker's specific duties, goals or scope are unclear, as when a supervisor gives instructions that are vague or contradictory. Between 35 and 60 percent of workers are said to experience role ambiguity (Baker and Karasek, 1995).

In role conflict, the worker is torn between the demands of different entities within the organization (such as supervisors versus subordinates) or is required to do work the worker does not think fits his or her role. One study suggested that 48 percent of workers experience role conflict (Baker and Karasek, 1995). Another type of role conflict occurs between the demands of work and of family, as when a child is sick (Dunn, et al., 1994).

Conflict in interpersonal relationships, arising from competition, lack of trust, lack of support from supervisors or other workers, and poor cooperation, is another source of stress. Most studies have found that workers see job factors such as role conflict and poor employer-employee relationships as more stressful than their work itself (Rogers, et al., 1991; Dunn, et al., 1994; Baker and Karasek, 1995).

[c] Extra-Organizational Stressors

Extra-organizational stressors are those that arise outside the immediate work setting but affect employment. A major stressor in this category is lack of job security, which has become particularly acute due to the development of global patterns of production and trade. These global market trends have reduced skill levels and decreased decision latitude in individual jobs, while also increasing competition for jobs. Job insecurity has become a particularly widespread concern as U.S. companies have laid off large numbers of white-collar as well as blue-collar workers (Baker and Karasek, 1995; Phelan, et al., 1991).

Other stressors deriving from these economic trends include under-promotion, fear of obsolescence and unemployment. Since employment is an important source of self-esteem and social status as well as of income, loss of employment is associated with anxiety, depression, anger and increased rates of suicide and psychiatric hospitalization.

The effects of unemployment are most pronounced among young people. Unemployed youth have developed high rates of alcohol abuse (Baker and Karasek, 1995; Baker and Schottenfeld, 1995).

[3]   The Stress Process

Models of the actual stress process generally begin with the stressor, then move to the worker's subjective response to it, the way this response is affected by mediators, the short-term outcome (strain) and, finally, to chronic outcomes, such as mental or behavioral disturbances.

Much research on occupational stress among large populations shows that a causal relationship exists between psychosocial factors in the work environment and psychological responses. However, it is not possible to establish cause-and-effect relationships between specific stressors and their effects on the health of an individual worker or a small group. The relationship between stressors and an individual worker's response is interactive, and psychological reactions are always the product of more than one cause (Elo, 1994; Baker and Karasek, 1995).

[4]   Employment Groupings

Certain types of employment are particularly stressful. Among them are high-demand, low-control jobs such as machine-paced manufacturing jobs or those involving quality control of products made by high-capacity machines. In the latter, the need to maintain alertness in the face of repetitive tasks is an added source of stress. Although these stressful characteristics are usually associated with factory assembly lines, modern offices dependent on computer technology now also share these same features.

Occupations in which failure to fulfill the demands of the job has severe consequences in terms of money, valuable materials or equipment, or people's lives are also highly stressful. Examples include foremen and managers, air traffic controllers, sea pilots and the uniformed professions, such as police officers (Elo, 1994; Baker and Karasek, 1995).

The health care professions are also particularly stressful, with dentistry considered the most stressful (Freeman, et al., 1995). In one study, health care providers working with terminally ill people reported the intensity of the job as a stressor (Walcott-McQuigg, 1994).

As predicted by the demand-control model, stressors have greater impact on workers in occupations of low socioeconomic status, who have little control over their work. This occupational category includes garment and electronics manufacturing, poultry processing and various types of home work paid by piece rates (Quinn, et al., 1995). In one study, blue-collar workers reported more stress than those at higher socioeconomic levels (Peterson, 1994).

[5] Employee Groupings

Gender, race and ethnic group are other factors that affect levels of occupational stress. A number of common occupational and domestic stressors are unique to women. In particular, women continue to experience the double burden of paid employment and family responsibilities to a greater degree than men. They also tend to have lower-status and less remunerative jobs than men (Kushnir and Kasan, 1992-1993).

Employers' increasing use of part-time and temporary workers also affects women, since women are more likely to take these jobs either because of their flexible hours or because they are the only jobs available. The insecurity of these jobs, their low pay and lack of benefits, and the need for additional overtime (since such jobs are often added during deadline periods when extra work is needed) contribute to the workers' stress.

Home work, also typically done by women, may involve clerical work, garment work or other types of manufacturing, such as semiconductor manufacturing. It is usually paid at piece rates.

A final stressor that primarily affects women is sexual harassment in the workplace. Between 40 and 80 percent of women have experienced some kind of sexual harassment, which in some cases has been associated with psychological reactions, such as depression (Quinn, et al., 1995).

The increased presence in the workforce of racial minorities exposes them to occupational stress arising from racism. Thus, for example, a study of a culturally diverse group of middle-income women reported that black and Latina women, in addition to stressors experienced by all women, were also targets of racism, manifested as insubordination, inappropriate comments and lack of promotion (Walcott-McQuigg, 1994).

13.04   GENERAL MANIFESTATIONS OF MENTAL STRESS

Workers' compensation claims suggest that chronic mental disorders related to stress are a significant problem among American workers. In many parts of the country, compensation is awarded for "gradual mental stress," which is stress caused by the cumulative effects of normal employment, as opposed to individual traumatic events (Baker and Karasek, 1995).

Occupational mental stress has been clearly documented to result in short-term situational responses. The evidence for an association between occupational stress and chronic mental illness is not as clear, although some specific stress-related disorders have been described.[4] In general, stress is one of a number of factors that combine to cause the health effects described in this section.

[1]   Short-term Responses

The short-term psychological effects of stress include cognitive changes, low self-esteem and emotional reactions. Typical cognitive deficits are difficulty concentrating, decreased perceptiveness, memory disturbances, difficulty making decisions and diminished creativity. Emotional responses include job dissatisfaction, anxiety, boredom, guilt, tension, irritability, depression and hopelessness (Elo, 1994).

[2]   Behavioral Responses

Short-term behavioral responses to stress include excessive use of alcohol and other drugs, increase in cigarette smoking, sleep disorders and disruptions in personal relationships. Alcohol and drug use may be responsible for absenteeism, poor job performance and accidents. The worker may become withdrawn, unusually aggressive or hypersensitive, which can lead to uncooperativeness or other attitudes that cause friction with co-workers. All these factors decrease productivity (Elo, 1994; Lucas, 1992; Baker and Karasek, 1995).

---

[4] *See also* 13.05 *infra.*

A long-term behavioral manifestation of occupational stress that occurs among workers with low-control jobs is learned helplessness. In this condition, the individual has essentially given up control over his or her life and becomes passive, withdrawing from participation in family and community activities (Baker and Karasek, 1995).

13.05 SPECIFIC STRESS-RELATED DISORDERS

Stress is considered the major causative factor for the disorders described in this section.

[1] Post-traumatic Stress Disorder

Extremely traumatic events can cause a delayed psychological reaction that is known as post-traumatic stress disorder (PTSD) and classified as an anxiety disorder.

[a] Causes

The type of traumatic event that causes PTSD is one most people would find severely upsetting or terrifying. In the workplace, such an event might be a life-threatening injury, chemical exposure or illness, or seeing another worker severely injured or killed.

Repeated episodes of exposure to danger can also cause PTSD. Serious traumas cause the most severe reactions, but less intense injuries, exposures or illnesses may also result in adjustment disorders that may be manifested as anxiety, depression or physical symptoms. The incidence rates of PTSD after a traumatic event depend upon its severity, with the highest rates following the most severe trauma (Baker and Schottenfeld, 1995; Baker and Karasek, 1995).

[b] Manifestations of PTSD

The cardinal sign of PTSD is re-experiencing of the traumatic event, which may occur through recurrent waking recollections or dreams. Such re-experiencing is triggered by a stimulus that reminds the individual of the event. Workers who suffer toxic exposures may in addition come to think that they are allergic to many substances.

Other symptoms of PTSD are decreased emotional responsiveness, detachment from the external world, difficulty concentrating, sleep disturbances and survivor guilt if others have died in the event. These reactions can be severe enough to be disabling (Baker and Karasek, 1995).

[c]   Atypical PTSD

A subtype of PTSD described as atypical PTSD occurs in workers who are exposed to toxic substances that are known to cause specific symptoms. These workers may subsequently experience recurrent anxiety or specific symptoms after exposure to harmless substances or very small amounts of the toxic substances.

Atypical PTSD is quite similar to a somatoform disorder, in which the patient has physical symptoms indicating a physical disorder, but no organic basis for them can be identified (Holland, 1994).

[2]   Mass Psychogenic Illness

Mass psychogenic illness is an outbreak among a group of people of collective physical symptoms, together with beliefs about the cause of these symptoms, but without any identifiable physical cause. This type of outbreak has occurred since the Middle Ages.

In the modern worksite, mass psychogenic illness generally occurs among workforces composed of mostly female workers performing boring, repetitive jobs under conditions of physical and/or emotional stress. Typically an outbreak of illness among a number of workers follows a "trigger stimulus," often a bad smell. Cases of illness spread among workers who speak to or see each other, increasing the general anxiety level. Their symptoms tend to be vague and nonspecific, including headache, dizziness, weakness and nausea. Symptoms are likely to be transitory but also recurrent.

Mass psychogenic illness is generally viewed as a psychophysiologic response to a stressful work environment. The fact that women are affected more than men has been explained with reference to the fact that women traditionally are more likely to do boring, repetitive jobs than men. For these reasons, it is preferable to focus on improving the work environment rather than attempting to identify susceptible workers (Baker and Schottenfeld, 1995; Holland, 1994).

[3]   Burnout

Burnout has been discussed mostly among professionals, but it can occur in any type of worker. Often the individual begins as an overachiever and performs so well that he or she is given increasing responsibility until reaching a point at which the worker can no longer perform. The individual is tired, has trouble sleeping and becomes depressed. Other typical symptoms are shortness of breath and intestinal problems. The worker loses interest in the work, may become suspicious and irritable and, off the job, may be unable to relax or enjoy other activities. To escape these feelings, the person may take refuge in narcotics, tranquilizers or alcohol, which may lead to addiction (Baker and Karasek, 1995).

13.05 DIAGNOSIS

Determining precisely to what extent the etiology of a mental disorder is related to occupational stress is practically impossible, since so many factors contribute to the stress process and no single, definitive instrument for measuring them exists. Certain general approaches are possible, however.

[1] Measuring Stress Reactions

There are a number of instruments for assessing stress reactions. Physiologic tests include measuring galvanic skin response (reaction of the skin to certain stimuli, as measured by changes in its resistance to the passage of galvanic current) or metabolites of catecholamines (products of the breakdown of substances that mimic the action of the sympathetic nervous system, for example, constricting arteries and raising blood pressure) in the urine. Psychological tests are generally in the form of structured interviews. However, these instruments tend to be impractical for use in the work setting.

The clinician therefore must rely on observation of a number of more available, though nonspecific, indicators. These include (Baker and Karasek, 1995):

- general symptoms the worker complains of;
- level of motivation for work;
- substance abuse and other behavioral reactions;
- the presence of anxiety, depression and other emotional responses;
- the results of cognitive tests and job performance evaluations;
- physiologic indications, such as heart rate, serum cholesterol level and blood pressure;
- the presence of illness that may be stress related; and
- other factors, such as the nature of social support, that can influence an individual's vulnerability to stress.

[2] Diagnosis of Occupational Stress

In determining whether an illness is stress related, the clinician must take into account all of the following (Baker and Karasek, 1995):

- stress factors that can be identified, both on and off the job;
- the worker's physical and psychological state of health;
- the presence of other factors that could cause the health effects;
- factors influencing vulnerability to stress; and
- whether other workers manifest similar health effects.

Complete psychiatric evaluation is indicated in only a few situations, for example, when there has been severe trauma, such as toxic exposure, illness or injury; when disability is prolonged; or when disability or symptoms are disproportionate to what might be expected given the patient's medical condition (Baker and Schottenfeld, 1995).

13.07 TREATMENT

This section discusses the treatment of stress reactions in individual workers and methods of reducing workers' susceptibility to stress. However, individual treatment is only one aspect of stress management as a whole, which also includes prevention of stress through improvements in the work environment.[5]

[1] Individual Treatment for Stress

Specific stress reactions, such as hypertension (high blood pressure), depression and anxiety, are treated according to standard medical practice with appropriate drugs. Individual treatment may also include counseling or psychotherapy and substance abuse treatment through employee assistance programs, which provide assessment and referrals for workers with stress-related problems (Baker and Karasek, 1995).

The recommendations formulated by the National Institute of Occupational Safety and Health (NIOSH) for preventing occupational psychological disorders include enrichment of psychological health services for workers. Unfortunately a recent trend toward reducing or discontinuing insurance coverage for psychological disorders and

---

[5] *See also* 13.08 *infra.*

substance abuse is likely to make such services less available in the future (Baker and Schottenfeld, 1995).

Stress disorders related to shift work may be prevented by the use of appropriately timed exposure to bright lights and darkness and by redesigning work schedules to make physiologic adaptation easier (Baker and Schottenfeld, 1995).

[2] Minimizing Individual Vulnerability

A variety of individual and group programs provide counseling, training and general support to decrease the workers' susceptibility to stress. Such programs teach workers how to identify particular stressors and avoid unnecessary ones. They also teach stress management techniques, such as relaxation training, biofeedback and time management, and they educate workers in more effective styles of coping. Assertiveness training makes workers more capable of controlling stressful situations. In addition, general support is provided through exercise and recreational programs that help workers expand their sources of self-esteem as well as other outlets for their abilities (Holland, 1994; Baker and Karasek, 1995).

13.08 PREVENTION

Long-term success in preventing stress is most likely when both employer and health care provider take part in the stress management program. This approach assumes that workers have some responsibility to take self-help measures to control stress, while the employer has a responsibility to reduce stressors present at the worksite and to provide stress-management support for the workers (Baker and Karasek, 1995).

Labor unions may also provide a variety of interventions to reduce stress at all stages of the stress process. These range from educational and employee assistance programs, to stress surveys and medical studies, to collective bargaining and other advocacy measures to induce employers to reform the work environment (Landsbergis and Cahill, 1994).

[1] Assessment of Potential Stressors

The key measure in a stress-control program is monitoring the worksite to identify potential stressors. Traditionally the physical and chemical risk factors and the physical burden of the work have been assessed. Assessment of psychosocial factors is more difficult, because it involves the workers' subjective experience, but it is also essential.

As part of this assessment, it is important to include a questionnaire surveying workers about their perceptions of stressful aspects of their jobs. The questionnaire can be used in combination with objective descriptions by evaluators of the tasks involved and of how the job fits into the larger organizational structure.

The assessment of each job should consider its content and conditions as a whole, independent of who performs it, since many jobs are performed by different workers on different shifts. Overall, the assessment should include the intensity and duration of each stressor and note its importance relative to other stressors, since some stressors can be compensated for by control over the work situation (Elo, 1994).

[2]   Employee Assistance Programs

Employee assistance programs can help prevent stress reactions as well as assist in managing them once they occur. Group counseling, workshops and other educational programs teach workers about stress and its adverse effects. Workers learn self-awareness and problem analysis to enable them to tell when they are experiencing stress and to detect the stressors that cause it (Holland, 1994; Baker and Karasek, 1995).

[3]   Work Reorganization Programs

Stress reduction through improvement of working conditions is the second major focus of the NIOSH recommendations for protecting workers' psychological health. Reorganizing work is more effective in reducing stress-related problems than employee assistance programs focused on promoting health.

One study of 1,523 professional and managerial corporation employees found that individual interventions carried out through employee assistance programs were not optimally successful in reducing either employees' psychological problems or the cost of treatment for mental health problems. The researchers concluded that such interventions had to be accompanied by changes in the psychosocial aspects of the work environment itself (Phelan, et al., 1991).

NIOSH recommends improving work conditions by redesigning jobs. Recommendations for good job design include:

- a schedule compatible with the worker's other roles outside the job;

- a workload commensurate with the worker's abilities;

- meaningful and stimulating content;

- opportunities for control and input;

- well-defined roles and responsibilities;

- supportive social environment; and

- job security with the chance for advancement.

Implementing a work reorganization program starts with the assessment of workplace stressors. The second step involves developing interventions, such as changing schedules, restructuring jobs and improving communications, as well as implementing various strategies for increasing social support. In this stage, worker participation enhances the success of the program. The third stage is evaluation of the results with follow-up surveys (Baker and Karasek, 1995).

Unfortunately, the current economic climate, in which increased competitiveness leads employers to require greater productivity from workers, is not likely to produce the suggested changes. The available data indicate that present-day economic and technologic trends are likely to result in increasing levels of occupational stress in the future (Baker and Schottenfeld, 1995).

13.09   EVALUATION OF IMPAIRMENT

Frequently it is very difficult to determine the precise degree of a permanent mental impairment, and often there is no certainty that such an impairment is even present. In making such a determination, it must also be remembered that the extent of impairment may not be related to the patient's diagnosis. For this reason, the evaluation must include specific descriptions of functional limitations.

The American Medical Association (AMA) system for evaluating mental disorders is based partly on the Social Security Administration's (SSA) "Listing" for mental disorders. The SSA requires that there must be a medically determinable impairment, that the impairment must make the individual unable to work and that the impairment is expected to last at least a year (American Medical Association, 1993).

[1]   Principles of Assessment

The AMA describes three critical principles for assessing mental impairment.

1. The diagnosis must be taken into consideration in determining the severity of impairment, but it is not the only criterion. The patient may have an impairment without meeting the criteria for a mental disorder specified in the American Psychiatric Association's *Diagnostic and Statistical Manual of Mental Disorders*, 4th edition (1994), known as the DSM-IV, or the *International Classification of Diseases,* 9th revision, Clinical Modification (ICD-9-CM; developed by the World Health Organization).

2. The patient's motivation to get better may be central in determining outcome.

3. The assessment should include a review of the patient's history, treatment and efforts at rehabilitation.

[2]   Assessing Severity of Impairment

To determine the severity of impairment, the SSA system assesses the following four aspects of functional limitation:

1. Activities of daily living, including capacity for self-care, hygiene, ambulation, communication, sexual function, sleep, and social and recreational activities. The evaluator assesses not only how many activities are limited but the overall level of limitation.

2. Social functioning, including appropriate interaction and effective communication with others. What is significant is the way in which the mental disorder interferes with overall functioning; for example, a person who is hostile or uncooperative may be able to shop but will be unable to work.

3. Concentration, persistence and pace, which refer to a person's ability to sustain attention adequately to accomplish tasks required in work settings.

4. Deterioration in work settings, which means a repeated inability to adapt to the stresses typical of a work environment. These stresses include decision making, attendance, social interactions and completing tasks on time.

[3] Further Considerations

Certain special circumstances must also be taken into consideration. Highly structured and supportive settings, such as hospitals, halfway houses or board-and-care facilities, minimize the stress their residents must cope with. People living in these supportive situations may show few overt indications of mental disorder while residing in the facility but be unable to function outside it.

The evaluator must also note functional limitations that persist even though the patient is taking psychoactive medications. The side effects of such medications, such as a decrease in activity level, must also be considered in judging the overall severity of impairment.

Finally, the effects of rehabilitation must be weighed, since rehabilitation can often help an individual decrease his or her degree of impairment.

[4] Special Categories of Impairment

Some categories of mental disorders are subject to controversy regarding whether they should in fact be considered causes of mental impairment. These include the following:

- Substance abuse. Current SSA policy accepts a substance addiction disorder as a disabling impairment, with the degree of disability depending on the severity of the functional limitations. Proposed rules provide for evaluating substance abuse disorders in the same way as other mental disorders, requiring that two of four DSM-IV criteria be met.

- Personality disorders. Proposed SSA rules would evaluate personality disorders according to whether the disorder caused marked difficulties in at least two of the four aspects of functional limitation.[6]

- Pain is relevant to mental impairment, since mental illness may change the perception of pain, for example, making it the object of an obsession or a somatic (bodily) expression of an emotional problem. However, it can be extremely difficult to determine whether pain is a symptom of a mental impairment. Usually a multidisciplinary approach is required.

- Malingering is rare but may be seen with mental disorders. It can be suspected when the symptoms are vague,

---

[6] See also 13.09[2] supra.

inconsistent, exaggerated and do not conform with the known signs and symptoms of the patient's complaint.

● Motivation. Evaluating motivation is difficult, because it can be hard to differentiate lack of motivation from mental impairment. In some cases, the question of secondary gain (a psychological or social advantage gained from a symptom of illness) arises, and lack of motivation appears to be a major reason for a continued inability to function.

[5]   Method of Evaluation

The AMA system of evaluating mental impairment consists of a five-category scale used to rate mental impairment in each of the four functional areas. No percentages of impairment of the whole person are assigned to these categories, since no precise measures of impairment in mental disorders are available.

● Class 1: no impairment.

● Class 2: mild impairment. Any impairment that exists still permits most useful functioning.

● Class 3: moderate impairment. The impairment enables the individual to carry out some, but not all, useful functioning.

● Class 4: marked impairment. This level of impairment significantly prevents useful functioning.

● Class 5: extreme impairment. The impairment prevents any useful functioning.

For most people, class 5 impairment in one area of functioning would be likely to prevent any form of work. Marked limitation in two or more areas would probably make work impossible without special support, as in a structured setting. Moderate and mild limitations do not preclude the performance of complex tasks.

13.100 BIBLIOGRAPHY

Reference Bibliography

Akerstedt, T. and Knutsson, A.: Shiftwork. In Levy, B. S. and Wegman, D. H. (Eds.): Occupational Health: Recognizing and Preventing Work-Related Disease, 3rd ed. Boston: Little, Brown, 1995.

American Medical Association: Guides to the Evaluation of Permanent Impairment, 4th ed. Chicago: American Medical Association, 1993.

American Psychiatric Association: Diagnostic and Statistical Manual of Mental Disorders, 4th ed. Washington, D.C.: American Psychiatric Association, 1994.

Baker, D. B. and Karasek, R. A.: Occupational Stress. In: Levy, B. S. and Wegman, D. H. (Eds.): Occupational Health: Recognizing and Preventing Work-Related Disease, 3rd ed. Boston: Little, Brown, 1995.

Baker, E. L., Jr. and Schottenfeld, R.: Disorders of the Nervous System. In: Levy, B. S. and Wegman, D. H. (Eds.): Occupational Health: Recognizing and Preventing Work-Related Disease, 3rd ed. Boston: Little, Brown, 1995.

deCarteret, J. C.: Occupational Stress Claims: Effects on Workers' Compensation. A.A.O.H.N. J. 42(10):494-498, Oct. 1994.

Dunn, L. A., et al.: Occupational Stress Amongst Care Staff Working in Nursing Homes: An Empirical Investigation. J. Clin. Nurs. 3(3):177-183, May 1994.

Elo, A.-L.: Assessment of Mental Stress Factors at Work. In: Zenz, C., et al. (Eds.): Occupational Medicine, 3rd ed. St. Louis: Mosby, 1994.

Freeman, R., et al.: Occupational Stress and Dentistry: Theory and Practice. Part I. Recognition. Br. Dent. J. 178(6):214-217, Mar. 25, 1995.

Holland, P. J.: Psychiatric Aspects of Occupational Medicine. In: McCunney, R. J. (Ed.): A Practical Approach to Occupational and Environmental Medicine, 2nd ed. Boston: Little, Brown, 1994.

Kushnir, T. and Kasan, R.: Major Sources of Stress among Women Managers, Clerical Workers, and Working Single Mothers: Demands vs. Resources. Public Health Rev. 20(3-4):215-229, 1992-93.

Landsbergis, P. A., and Cahill, J.: Labor Union Programs to Reduce or Prevent Occupational Stress in the United States. Int. J. Health Serv. 24(1):105-129, 1994.

Lucas, G.: Stress and Mental Health. Practitioner 236(1514):511-516, May 1992.

Peterson, C. L.: Work Factors and Stress: A Critical Review. Int. J. Health Serv. 24(3):495-519, 1994.

Phelan, J., et al.: Work Stress, Family Stress, and Depression in Professional and Managerial Employees. Psychol. Med. 21(4):999-1012, Nov. 1991.

Quinn, M. M., et al.: Women and Work. In: Levy, B. S. and Wegman, D. H. (Eds.): Occupational Health: Recognizing and Preventing Work-Related Disease, 3rd ed. Boston: Little, Brown, 1995.

Rogers, J. M., et al.: The Occupational Stress of Judges. Can. J. Psychiatry 36(5):317-322, June 1991.

Walcott-McQuigg, J. A.: Worksite Stress: Gender and Cultural Diversity Issues. A.A.O.H.N. J. 42(11):528-533, Nov. 1994.

Additional References

Basson, C. J. and van der Merwe, T.: Occupational Stress and Coping in a Sample of Student Nurses. Curationis 17(4):35-43, Dec. 1994.

Carayon, P.: Stressful Jobs and Non-Stressful Jobs: A Cluster Analysis of Office Jobs. Ergonomics 37(2):311-23, February 1994.

Eells, T. D. and Showalter, C. R.: Work-Related Stress in American Trial Judges. Bull. Am. Acad. Psychiatry Law 22(1):71-83, 1994.

Evans, G. W.: Working on the Hot Seat: Urban Bus Operators. Accid. Anal. Prev. 26(2):181-193, Apr. 1994.

Ezoe, S. and Morimoto, K.: Behavioral Lifestyle and Mental Health Status of Japanese Factory Workers. Prev. Med. 23(1):98-105, Jan. 1994.

Fairburn, J.: OH Management Model. Part 3: Approach to Stress. Occup. Health (Lond.) 46(6):196-198, June 1994.

Flett, R., et al.: A Perspective on Occupational Concerns of Rehabilitation Service Providers. Disabil. Rehabil. 17(2):76-82, Feb.-Mar. 1995.

Freeman, R., et al.: Occupational Stress and Dentistry: Theory and Practice. Part II. Assessment and Control. Br. Dent. J. 178(6):218-222, Mar. 25, 1995.

Kushnir, T., et al.: Teaching Stress Management Skills to Occupational and Environmental Health Physicians and Practitioners. A Graduate-Level Practicum. J. Occup. Med. 36(12):1335-1340, Dec. 1994.

Leary, J., et al.: Stress and Coping Strategies in Community Psychiatric Nurses: A Q-Methodological Study. J. Adv. Nurs. 21(2):230-237, Feb. 1995.

Pithers, R. T. and Fogarty, G. J.: Symposium on Teacher Stress. Occupational Stress Among Vocational Teachers. Br. J. Educ. Psychol. 65 (Pt. 1):3-14, Mar. 1995.

Scott, M. J. and Stradling, S. G.: Post-Traumatic Stress Disorder without the Trauma. Br. J. Clin. Psychol. 33(Pt. 1):71-74, Feb. 1994.

Trent, J. T., et al.: Telecommuting: Stress and Social Support. Psychol. Rep. 74(3 Pt. 2):1312-1314, June 1994.

Tyler, P. A. and Ellison, R. N.: Sources of Stress and Psychological Well-Being in High-Dependency Nursing. J. Adv. Nurs. 19(3):469-476, Mar. 1994.

Vines, S. W.: Relaxation with Guided Imagery: Effects on Employees' Psychological Distress and Health Seeking Behaviors. A.A.O.H.N. J. 42(5):206-213, May 1994.

Zeier, H.: Workload and Psychophysiological Stress Reactions in Air Traffic Controllers. Ergonomics 37(3):525-539, Mar. 1994.

CHAPTER 14

Reproductive Disorders and Birth Defects

SCOPE

Workplace causes of adverse effects on reproductive and developmental health include exposure to chemicals, physical agents and infectious organisms. Only a few agents of reproductive or developmental toxicity in humans are well identified by sufficient epidemiologic, exposure and experimental animal studies. Men, women and the conceptus are vulnerable to specific occupational health hazards at various reproductive end points, which may result in infertility, birth defects, spontaneous abortion (miscarriage), stillbirth, prematurity, low birth weight, toxicity from breast milk and childhood cancer. Few chemicals causing reproductive effects are subject to control by workplace standards. Reproductive toxicity from known workplace agents can be diagnosed by physical examination, blood and semen analysis, and exposure history. Employers should advise workers about possible exposures to occupational chemicals possessing potential reproductive or developmental toxicity.

SYNOPSIS

14.01   INTRODUCTION AND DEFINITIONS

Occupationally caused reproductive and developmental disorders are of interest today, among other reasons, because of the increasing number of pregnant women in the work force. Both men and women, however, may encounter potentially harmful workplace factors. These agents may act from the period before sperm and egg formation through lactation. Of the more than 104,000 chemical and physical agents in the workplace, only 5 percent have been assessed for reproductive effects (Gold, et al., 1994). One in five human couples are involuntarily sterile, and about 15 percent of pregnancies end in spontaneous abortions. About 3 percent of surviving fetuses have developmental defects at birth; this number doubles with increasing age and identification of more defects (Thomas, 1991).

Reproductive toxicity refers to adverse effects on male or female reproductive structure or function, the conceptus or lactation, interfering with the normal reproductive and behavioral development of the offspring. Within this definition, *teratogenicity* is the ability of an agent to cause gross structural malformations in the developing fetus. *Behavioral teratogenicity* is the ability to affect the developing fetus and cause abnormal intellectual development or behavior after birth; the toxic effects may occur in utero or through the milk. *Developmental toxicity* is a term used to define abnormal structural or functional development of children following exposure of women during pregnancy or lactation. Classically, abnormal development includes malformation, death, growth retardation and functional defects.

Epidemiology is the branch of science that studies the distribution and determinants of a disease or condition among human populations, associating manifestations with possible causes. In the assessment of occupational exposures causing reproductive effects, epidemiologic studies are examined more frequently than animal experiments.

14.02 REPRODUCTIVE BIOLOGY AND WORKPLACE EXPOSURE

Men, women and the fetus have various reproductive targets that are vulnerable to occupational reproductive hazards. Workplace hazards for men are poorly recognized. In one study in Massachusetts, for example, women were restricted from 58 hazardous work areas because of exposure to known reproductive toxicants, while only one restriction applied to male workers whose partner was trying to conceive (Grajewski and Schnorr, 1992).

In both males and females, the gonads have a dual function: secretion of sex hormones and production of gametes (germ cells for ova and sperm). These functions depend on the hormones secreted by the pituitary gland (hypophysis; also called the master gland, reflecting its status as the most important endocrine gland of the body): follicle stimulating hormone (FSH) and luteinizing hormone (LH).

[1]   Male Anatomy and Effects

The male reproductive system consists of the scrotum, containing the testes and epididymis, which is connected to efferent ducts that enter the urethra and penis after passing various accessory glands.

[a]   Testes

In the testes (gonads), the male reproductive system produces the sex hormones and gametes (spermatogonia) that mature into sperm (spermatozoa) during the process known as spermatogenesis. The spermatozoa go through a process of cell division that produces one set of chromosomes, which contain the genes. Mutations of the chromosomal genes may be produced by exposure to toxic agents, such as lead or mercury, during spermatogenesis, sometimes resulting in birth defects (Thomas, 1991).

Occupational exposure to damaging substances can affect the maturing sperm cells at several stages, causing changes in production or quality, e.g., low numbers or lack of sperm, decreased sperm motility, chromosomal aberrations, mutated cells or malformed cells. After removal of the toxin, normal numbers of spermatozoa may be produced. Mutated sperm deoxyribonucleic acid (DNA; the genetic material that is passed on to offspring) may pass damaged genes to future generations, causing spontaneous abortion or birth defects. The gonads are affected by compounds such as antineoplastic drugs (used in treating cancer) and alkylating agents. The effects may be indirect, e.g., phthalates may lower zinc levels and produce testicular damage (Thomas, 1991).

Stem cells in the testes produce millions of immature sperm per day. The maturing sperm move away from the testes through ducts, the seminiferous tubules, where they enter a testicular fluid. Another cell in the tubules, the Sertoli cell, also produces hormones, including small amounts of estrogen, and enzymatic proteins required for spermatogenesis; some toxic chemicals act indirectly on sperm through effects on Sertoli cells. These include dibromochloropropane (DBCP), an important agricultural chemical, and monoethyl phthalate (MEHP), an industrial chemical (Thomas, 1991). In addition, toxic damage to the tissue covering the testes or exposure to heat may have a prolonged effect on sperm production.

[b] Semen

The immature sperm leave the testes through tubules to go to the epididymis for maturation and storage; the epididymis has important fluids that are part of the seminal fluid and that can be perturbed by environmental chemicals.

Various accessory organs contribute to the sperm fluid, known as the seminal plasma (or semen); these are the prostate gland, the seminal vesicles and the urethral and Cowper's glands. The quality of the semen is affected by abnormal function of these glands. For example, metals and androgens affect the animal prostate gland (Thomas, 1991), and semen is affected by toxic chemicals, such as glycol ethers (Ratcliffe, et al., 1993) and ethylene dibromide (Grajewski and Schnorr, 1992).

At the time of erection and emission, the sperm move from the end of the epididymis to the urethra; nerve stimulation causes ejaculation, moving sperm out of the urethra. Erection and ejaculation may be affected by psychotropic, hypotensive and narcotic drugs, hormones, pesticides and chemicals acting on the autonomic part of the central nervous system; they are also affected by psychological factors (Thomas, 1991).

[c] Hormones

The semen and sperm production are influenced by hormones, including testosterone and small amounts of other androgens, produced by special cells in the testes, the Leydig cells. Production is influenced by luteinizing hormone (LH) from the pituitary system. Androgens also are required for the growth of the accessory sex organs, body masculinization and other characteristics. Toxins such as the insecticide kepone have an estrogenlike effect on testosterone production, which is especially vulnerable at certain critical periods of testicular differentiation. Chemicals affecting male hormones may cause loss of sex drive, poor sperm production and impotence. For example, hormonelike toxins, such as stilbene, may affect libido and potency (Quinn, et al., 1990). Stilbestrol and diethylstilbestrol (DES) cause genital tract abnormalities in the male and female offspring of exposed women, produce reduced sperm in males and lower fertility in females.

Exposure to hundreds of types of environmental agents have been associated with reproductive dysfunction in men, including exposure to the following (Thomas, 1991):

- industrial chemicals: ethylene glycol, monoethyl ether, hexane, inorganic and organic lead, mercury, trace chemicals, vinyl chloride, acrylamide, phthalates;

- pesticides: carbon disulfide, chlordecone (kepone), ethylene dibromide and DBCP;

- sterilants such as ethylene oxide;

- various consumer products, such as food additives;

- physical factors: heat, light, oxygen, radiation; and

- pharmaceutical agents.

[2] Reproductive Effects in Women

The female reproductive system is less vulnerable than the male, but it can be affected by many toxic elements from the time of ovulation through nursing.

[a] Anatomy and Physiology

The female reproductive system contains two ovaries in the abdominal cavity, located near the fallopian tubes, the horn-shaped portion of the uterus. The ovaries contain a central medulla and an outer cortex. The uterus is continuous with the vagina and lined by the endometrium. The mouth of the uterus is called the cervix.

The ovarian cortex contains follicles in various stages of development. A follicle consists of an oocyte (developing egg cell; gamete) surrounded by follicle cells. The oocyte, like the male gamete, divides to form one set of chromosomes. A lifetime complement of several hundred thousand follicles is present at birth in each ovary. Most degenerate due to the process of atresia (involution), but about 400 develop into mature ova released by the mature follicle, usually one by one, during ovulation. The mature ovum enters the end of the uterine tube and changes into an enriched form. It forms a zygote with the sperm, begins multiplying, and the developing embryo migrates, enters the fallopian tube and becomes implanted in the uterus. The placental circulation is established, and the cells of the embryo begin to differentiate into different types of tissues. If the ovum is not fertilized and embedded in the uterine wall, the endometrial sloughing known as menstruation occurs.

The ovaries may be affected by toxicants, resulting in early menopause or ovarian disease. Oocytes are especially sensitive to ionizing radiation. Some examples of foreign agents known to cause oocyte toxicity in animal experiments are:

- polycyclic aromatic hydrocarbons;

- antineoplastic (chemotherapeutic) agents; and

- antiestrogens.

The follicle may be destroyed, or ovulation may be blocked by other drugs. The DNA in the oocyte or follicle can undergo mutation, but the body sometimes can repair some DNA damage by special mechanisms (Manson and Kang, 1994).

Like sperm, the development of gametes into mature ova is under hormonal influence. The ovaries secrete large amounts of estrogens and progesterone, a hormone preparing the uterus for pregnancy; they also make small amounts of androgens. The additional female sex hormones, follicle-stimulating hormone (FSH) and luteinizing hormone (LH), are synthesized in the pituitary gland. Chemicals affecting endocrine function include (Thomas, 1991):

- endogenous (native) hormones;

- nonphysiologic estrogenlike compounds, such as DES, kepone, DDT, methoxychlor and environmental chemicals such as dioxins and PCBs in food (Birnbaum, 1994);

- triphenylethylene drugs (e.g., naloxidone, tamoxifen);

- drugs acting on the central nervous system (e.g., marijuana, barbiturates, narcotics);

- toxic compounds such as formaldehyde;

- dimethyl benz[a]anthracene (DMBA);

- polyaminohydrocarbons (PAHs);

- polychlorinated biphenyls (PCBs); and

- certain plant and mushroom toxins.

Toxic compounds can affect the corpus luteum and female hormones or cause sterility or loss of sexual drive (libido). The vaginal fluid and flora are also affected by external factors, such as hormones and microorganisms. The female libido is affected by (Ratcliffe, et al., 1993):

- carbon disulfide;

- oral contraceptives and cyproterone acetate, an antiandrogen;

- tranquilizers, monoamine oxidase inhibitors and drugs of abuse;

- cytotoxic drugs;

- danazol (used to treat endometriosis); and

- fenfluramine (an antiobesity drug).

Other environmental chemicals associated with reproductive dysfunction in women include (Thomas, 1991):

- anesthetic gases (operating room personnel);

- aniline, benzene and toluene;

- pesticides: carbon disulfide, chloroprene;

- sterilants: ethylene oxide and formaldehyde; and

- industrial chemicals: glycol ethers, lead and smelter emissions, methyl mercury, phthalic acid esters, polychlorinated biphenyls (PCBs) and vinyl chloride.

[b]   Fertilization

After copulation, the sperm enter the vagina and the uterus, making their way to the oviduct. If an ovum is present in the tube, fertilization may occur. The union of sperm and ovum that forms the zygote results in a new assortment of the parental chromosomes that convey characteristics such as brown or black hair color. The two sets of chromosomes—23 from the female and 23 from the male sex cells—may not go correctly through the sorting process (meiosis) to form the one set of 46 chromosomes in the fertilized zygote; for example, parts of chromosomes may cross over to other chromosomes. Various types of chromosomal abnormalities or aberrations may occur (e.g., changes in appearance, length or number). Also, the chromosomal genes may possess earlier DNA mutations.

Both chemicals and drugs may influence fertilization. Germ cell formation, maturation and union are complex events that are influenced by many foreign substances.

14.03 EFFECTS ON THE EMBRYO, FETUS AND CHILD

Many external conditions may influence the implantation of the zygote in the uterus and cause a failed pregnancy. In addition to genetic damage to either sperm or ovum, the developing embryo or fetus may be exposed to toxic substances. Although the placental barrier may afford some protection, certain periods during organogenesis (organ development) are especially sensitive. Well-known examples of prenatal exposure causing congenital deformations include rubella (German measles) and the drug thalidomide.

[1] The Embryo and Fetus

The developing embryo (the conceptus from the period of implantation to the eighth week) continues to divide in the uterus, according to a genetically programmed schedule. Circulation is established through the placenta. The embryo or fetus (from eight weeks after conception until birth) can be affected by various factors. The cells undergo highly ordered changes and differentiate into three basic cell layers that become the embryonic organs. Toxic alterations that occur in certain genes from the father or mother can cause spatial and temporal changes in the differentiation pattern, producing malformations in the progeny and sometimes in future generations.

Toxic developmental changes may be mediated by sperm from exposed males. In animal studies, fetal malformations have been shown to result from the father's exposure to methadone, thalidomide, lead and narcotics. These problems may also be due to exposure to toxic chemicals, such as formaldehyde, benzene, toluene and pesticides (Schrag and Dixon, 1985), and there are many other possible causes.

[a] Spontaneous Abortion (Miscarriage) and Stillbirth

Exposures are less likely to be lethal the later they occur in pregnancy. The embryo is more susceptible to damage from teratogens than the fetus, in part because most of the organ systems are formed during the embryonic stage. The fetal phase is one of growth and maturation of existing organ systems; exposure during this phase can result in intrauterine (within the uterus) growth retardation or functional abnormality of a specific system.

The terms "spontaneous abortion" and "miscarriage" usually refer to the loss of an early pregnancy; typically this point is defined as the twenty-eighth week of gestation. Spontaneous abortions (miscarriages) occur at a frequency of 10 to 20 per 100 pregnancies; 30 to 40 percent have chromosomal aberrations (Manson and Wise, 1991). Studies in India indicate that the wives of men who were exposed to pesticides in cotton fields had significant increases in the rate of abortion, stillbirth, neonatal death and congenital defects, compared to controls (Rupa, et al., 1991). A higher rate of spontaneous abortion has been found among women exposed to aliphatic hydrocarbon solvents directly or in graphics work, compared to unexposed control pregnancies (Lindbohm, et al., 1992). A high association between solvent use and spontaneous abortion was also found among women employed in the electronics industry (Lipscomb, et al., 1991).

[b] Birth Defects

A teratogen causes structural or functional alteration (reversible or irreversible) due to damage to the fertilized egg or zygote (the conceptus) before its implantation or prior to the embryo starting organ formation. The conceptus is vulnerable to environmental chemicals, since its cells are undergoing rapid division, especially at certain times in the programmed sequence of differentiation. Furthermore, the human immune surveillance system is absent or immature in the developing embryo or fetus; thus it does not recognize foreign chemicals or lesions and destroy them.

Teratogenicity may develop in the postembryonic fetus or the neonate (newborn), but it may not be manifested until sexual maturity. Defects encompass death, frank structural malformations, functional deficits and developmental delays, and they may be quantitative or qualitative. The examples of deformities caused by maternal exposure to the drug thalidomide and the rubella virus are well known.

Exposure to many substances has been associated with malformation to varying degrees. Certain compounds and occupations are categorized according to risk:

- high risk—exposure to ethanol, methylmercury, PCBs and products used in chemicophysical laboratory work;

- limited risk—exposure to anesthetic gases and carbon monoxide; and

- low risk—exposure to hexachlorophene, lysergic acid diethylamide (LSD), nitrous oxide; smelter work and tobacco work.

Ethanol- and PCB-caused malformations in laboratory animals are similar to those in humans, while methyl mercury-caused malformations in test animals differed (Hemmincki and Vineis, 1985). Congenital malformations can result from exposure to:

- radiation;
- sex hormones;
- retinoids;
- hexachlorophene;
- codeine; and
- certain dietary deficiencies.

Occupational chemicals such as DBCP and toluene are also associated with teratogenicity (Baker, 1994).

Various malformations and structural variations seen in animal studies have been associated with maternal toxicity from foreign compounds. Pregnancy itself causes changes in skin and lung absorption, blood and plasma distribution, binding of free compound, metabolism and excretion (Manson and Kang, 1994).

14.04 POSTNATAL PROBLEMS

Postnatal problems from maternal exposure to drugs, microorganisms and toxins include prematurity, low birth weight and delayed effects. Reproductive toxicity can continue beyond the actual live birth; adverse reactions, such as behavioral toxicity and childhood cancer, may take years to become evident. Postnatal cardiovascular and kidney effects may occur.

[1] Prematurity and Low Birth Weight

"Prematurity" is defined as the birth of a live infant before 36 or 37 weeks of gestation. Premature infants are at risk for death or permanent impairment, because the organs that carry out certain vital functions—the lungs, central nervous system and gastrointestinal tract, for example—may not be fully developed.

Low birth weight is a separate but related issue. It is defined as a weight at birth of less than 2,500 grams, or 5½ pounds. Low birth weight may be a result of prematurity, intrauterine growth retardation or a combination of the two. Babies who suffer intrauterine growth retardation are small for their gestational age. Their organs and systems may be developmentally normal for their gestational age, but the same factors responsible for their small size may place them at risk for birth complications or other poor outcomes.

Normally about 7 percent of live human babies have low birth weight. Toxic chemicals are one cause of both prematurity and low birth weight. For example, both maternal and paternal lead exposures are associated with low birth weight of children, the degree depending upon the parental dose, as demonstrated by blood levels (Lockitch, 1993; Hertz-Picciotta and Neutra, 1994). Associated maternal exposures may include formaldehyde, benzene, toluene or pesticides. In the workplace, interactions may occur that indirectly affect neonatal weight, such as exposure to smoke in a smelting plant or to chemicals that are capable of inducing maternal occupational asthma.[1]

The role of cigarette smoking has been investigated in terms of preterm delivery and low birth weight. Cigarette smoking has been shown to increase the risk of low birth weight by several times. It has been suggested that nicotine and carbon monoxide contribute to the problems of prematurity and low birth weight (Rom, 1992).

[2] Problems in Infants and Children

The neonate may be affected by toxic exposures in utero (in the uterus; in the period before birth), during labor or ingested in breast milk. Maternal exposure to the insecticides mirex and kepone, aspirin and the pesticide product ethylene thiourea (ETU) have been shown to cause neonatal cardiovascular toxicity and perinatal (immediately before, during or after the time of birth) death in animal experiments (Grabowski, 1988). Cardiac dysrhythmia also occurs in humans.

[a] Breast Milk

The placental barrier prevents or decreases the entry of many compounds, but the neonate has less ability to eliminate drugs and chemicals by metabolizing and excreting them. Toxic chemicals absorbed by lactating women can be secreted into the breast milk, and the impact of exposure of breast-feeding infants to these chemicals is currently being investigated.

Although there are unquestionable benefits to breast-feeding, the nursing mother may inadvertently pass on drugs or environmental and

---

[1] *See also* ch. 17 for a complete discussion of occupational asthma.

occupational chemicals to the newborn. With chronic exposure, these may have potentially serious effects, depending upon the physico-chemical characteristics of the compound. These chemicals may pass through the milk and then have adverse effects on the newborn. Harmful industrial chemicals such as hexachlorophane and mercury have been inadvertently ingested in food (Peters, et al., 1993).

[b] Behavioral Toxicity

Neonatal behavioral toxicity may be evidenced by neurobehavioral changes, withdrawal or altered mental ability. In animal experiments, for example, a rat is tested for its righting reflex, swimming or navigating a water maze, using a positive control (a substance known to produce the effect being evaluated) such as vitamin A (Saillenfait and Vannier, 1988). In humans, highly probable occupational influences on the developing central nervous system include lead, mercury and ionizing radiation. Possible influences are parental occupational exposure to cadmium, organic solvents, anesthetics and pesticides (Roeleveld, et al., 1990).

[c] Childhood Cancers

Childhood cancer is being explored as a possible late-appearing effect of genetic mutations related to the occupation of either parent. Since genetic mutations and chromosomal changes due to environmental agents cause both teratogenic changes and cancer, this area is poorly defined. The oncogenes (causes of tumors) producing malignancies must be better understood.

Several childhood cancers are associated with inheritance, congenital disorders, malformations or other conditions. These include:

- Wilms' tumor, hepatoblastoma, adrenocortical carcinoma;
- Ewing's sarcoma, nephroblastoma, neuroblastoma, testicular carcinoma;
- melanoma;
- basal cell carcinoma, medulloblastoma, rhabdomyosarcoma;
- leukemia, retinoblastoma, gastrointestinal carcinoma;
- Epstein-Barr-virus-associated B-lymphocyte lymphoma;
- osteosarcoma;
- squamous cell carcinoadenomas in multiple endocrine neoplasia syndromes; and

- tumors in neurofibromatosis (von Recklinghausen's syndrome).

Responsible agents include ionizing radiation, stilbestrol, androgen, iron, tyrosine, monosaccharides, Epstein-Barr virus and papillomavirus type 5 (Pizzo, et al., 1989). Solvents and hydrocarbons have been associated with childhood cancers and leukemia (Giacoia, 1992). Prenatal exposure to certain drugs (e.g., alcohol, DES) causes a heightened risk of developing cancer later in life.

14.05   INFERTILITY

Infertility is the inability to conceive after a year or more of unprotected coitus. Many occupational hazards can cause infertility. In both men and women, infertility has many causes besides exposure to toxic chemicals, drugs or occupational hazards. For example, anatomic problems may exist.

[1]   Male Infertility

Occupational exposure to toxic chemicals can affect male fertility. For example, in a Dutch study, fruit growers who were exposed to high levels of pesticides had fertility problems during the spraying season, compared to workers with lower exposure levels (deCock, et al., 1994). In studies of Belgian and Chinese workers exposed to lead, fertility and levels of sperm decreased, compared to other workers (Gennart, et al., 1992; Hu, et al., 1992; Xuezhi, et al., 1992). An infertile male exposed to mercury in a chemical factory had mercury in the tissue of his testes, in contrast to a control patient (Keck, et al., 1993). New methods are being used to identify causes of infertility and assess male fecundity (Schrader, 1992; Taskinen, 1992; Thompson, 1993).

Many studies associate exposure to ethylene glycol ethers with male infertility (Wess, 1992; Veulemans, et al., 1993). These glycol ethers are absorbed through the skin and found in the urine of chronically exposed workers in German varnish production and in ceramics (Sohnlein, et al., 1993).

External factors causing male infertility can often be identified and corrected. Mechanical or epigenetic (not affecting DNA) sperm damage may occur, e.g., from exposure to high temperature (Agnew, et al., 1991). The semen may contain harmful metabolites (breakdown products from the process of metabolism). Toxins such as kepone may affect the developing testes.

[2] Female Infertility

Reduced female fertility results from exposure to chemicals such as diethystilbestrol (DES). In a careful epidemiologic study, reduced fertility was demonstrated among women exposed to organic solvents, based on number of reproductive cycles before attaining pregnancy (Sallman, et al., 1995). Occupational exposure of women to mercury decreases fertility (Rowland, et al., 1995). Radiation in magnetic resonance workers (Evans, et al., 1993) and nitrous oxide exposure (Wynn, 1993; Meskin, 1993) are other potential causes of female infertility. Stress and overexertion in exercise result in delayed ovarian cycles in young athletes.

14.06 INDIVIDUAL AGENTS CAUSING WORKPLACE REPRODUCTIVE HAZARD

Although studies involving humans clearly demonstrate reproductive effects and/or teratogenicity from exposure to methyl mercury, lead, certain viruses and ionizing radiation, controversies exist about epidemiologic reports suggesting that nitrous oxide or video display terminals (VDTs) cause reproductive harm, spontaneous abortion or malformations (Eger, 1991). Studies are not consistent in showing reproductive effects from anesthesia, mixed pesticides and solvents. In addition to laboratory and health care work, occupational exposures strongly suspected of causing reproductive damage include:

- industrial chemicals: vinyl chloride, rubber chemicals and plastics;
- arsenicals;
- carbon monoxide;
- halogenated hydrocarbons;
- paint;
- chemicals used in boot and shoe repair; and
- chemicals used in iron and steel foundry work.

The cause of reproductive problems among rubber workers is unknown, but rubber production includes potentially neoplastic and genotoxic chemicals, e.g., the animal carcinogen dibenzothiazyl disulfide (MBTS) (Ema, et al., 1989). Ethylene thiourea (ETU), a metabolite of ethylene bisdithiocarbamate, a rubber chemical and pesticide, is a recognized animal teratogen. The major teratologic effects of ETU in rats and mice are hydrocephalus (swelling of the brain due to accumulation of fluid), other central nervous system defects and thyroid effects (Frakes, 1988). Data on some well-known exposures causing reproductive and developmental toxicity are given here, beginning with the generally accepted toxic agents.

[1] Lead

Lead is known to cause miscarriage, uterine death, premature birth and low birth weight, slow behavioral development, high infant mortality and behavioral problems. Well-controlled epidemiologic studies throughout the world have demonstrated neurotoxic reproductive and developmental changes from prenatal or early postnatal exposure to high levels of lead (Lindbohm, et al., 1992; Bellinger, et al., 1991, 1994; Andrews, et al., 1994; Kristensen, et al., 1993; Xuezhi, et al., 1992; Tabacova and Balabaeva, 1993; Lockitch, 1993; Rothenberg, et al., 1994).

The adverse health effects of lead are being identified at levels below most acceptable occupational environmental exposures. These effects include preterm delivery, congenital abnormalities and decreased growth. Maternal exposure before conception may play a role in blood levels during pregnancy. Paternal exposure before pregnancy may affect the fetus. Since removal of a pregnant woman from the workplace may be of little value, the acceptable level of workplace exposure to lead is being progressively decreased in many countries (O'Halloran and Spickett, 1992-1993; Needleman, 1990).

[2] Methyl Mercury

Mercury exposure may cause adverse reproductive effects. Reproductive problems (spontaneous abortion, birth defects, stillbirth) correlate with high mercury levels in hair and the total exposure of women dentists and dental assistants in the dental office (Sikorsky, et al., 1987). High-level exposure to inorganic mercury or mercury vapors produced a decrease in fertility in dental assistants, compared to low-exposed and unexposed control workers (Rowland, et al., 1995). Low-level exposure to methyl mercury produces prenatal toxicity, and all forms of mercury cross the placenta from mother to fetus (Goyer, 1986).

A review of 39 studies of male occupational exposure and elevated risk of spontaneous abortion implicated mercury strongly, based on quantitative exposure estimates (Savitz, et al., 1994). Animal studies show that transplacental metallic mercury is toxic to sperm and is mutagenic, and produces developmental changes in the fetus (Goyer, 1986).

Whether parental exposure to heavy metals other than lead and mercury has an effect on reproduction is uncertain (Lauwerys, et al., 1995; Fagher, et al., 1993).

[3]   Ionizing Radiation

Radiation may cause genetic mutations and chromosomal changes in both regular and genetic cells; thus progeny from parents exposed to radiation may exhibit birth defects. Cancer therapy with ionizing radiation is well accepted as a cause of male infertility, and women develop ovarian dysfunction (amenorrhea) after irradiation, depending upon dose and age (Sherins and Mulvihill, 1989).

[4]   Infectious Agents

Certain viruses and the toxoplasmosis parasite are common causes of reproductive toxicity and birth defects, often causing death or severe malformations (Murray, et al., 1994).

[a]   Viruses

Various viruses affect pregnant women, cause congenital disease or affect newborns. These include cytomegalovirus (CMV), herpes simplex virus (HSV) and rubella virus. No viral vaccine or drug is yet available for them (Murray, et al., 1994).

CMV is the most common cause of congenital defects, affecting 0.5 percent to 2.5 percent of all newborns. Ten percent of these show clinical disease such as microcephaly (small head size), enlarged spleen, hearing loss and mental retardation. Prevalent in low socioeconomic conditions, the disease may be transmitted to health care personnel by blood, urine, saliva and other body fluids.

The danger from rubella and congenital rubella syndrome has been largely eliminated by vaccination programs. In 1964 to 1965, over 12 million rubella cases occurred, causing 2,160 deaths and 20,000 cases of congenital rubella syndrome, characterized by cataracts, heart defects, deafness, growth retardation, microcephaly and mental retardation. The virus is spread by respiratory secretions, especially in crowded conditions; teachers and health care personnel are at special risk.

Herpes simplex virus (HSV) may be transmitted in utero or in passage through the birth canal. A usually fatal, devastating disease in the newborn, it results from contact with saliva, vaginal secretions and other fluids. Medical personnel are at special risk, especially if gloves are not used. No vaccines are available, but antiviral drugs and gamma globulin are used for control.

Other viruses, such as the parvovirus B19, may affect the fetus in utero; Coxsackie and echo viruses may affect the newborn soon after birth. Hepatitis E virus has a high mortality rate for pregnant women (20 percent) and may occur as asymptomatic viral shedding (through blood and secretions), possibly endangering health care personnel.

The AIDS virus affects newborns of HIV-positive mothers; few health care workers, however, have acquired this disease from needle sticks or other exposure to contaminated blood. Infants born with AIDS are prone to other diseases and cancers.[2]

[b] Toxoplasmosis

The parasite *Toxoplasma gondii* usually causes a benign infection in healthy individuals. A severe congenital infection may result, however, if the mother is infected during pregnancy. If infection occurs in the first trimester, spontaneous abortion or stillbirth may occur. Infants who are infected may subsequently acquire manifestations such as epilepsy, microcephaly (small head), mental retardation, blindness and hearing loss. Mothers may acquire the infection from ingesting or contacting improperly cooked meat and meat juices or by exposure to products contaminated by cat feces. Restaurant, grocery and domestic workers may be at risk.

[5] Carbon Monoxide

Carbon monoxide (CO) poisoning is common in the United States. Fetal malformations and neurologic damage occur in progeny of firefighters exposed to carbon monoxide and in workers from poorly ventilated factories; observable changes occur in the carbon monoxide

---

[2] *See also* ch. 19 for a discussion of AIDS.

level in blood and expired air (Norman and Halton, 1990). In pregnant women, especially in the first trimester, accidental CO poisoning causes central nervous system disorders and delayed sequelae for both mother and fetus, especially at high levels of exposure (Seger and Welch, 1995; Koren, et al., 1991). Acute workplace exposure has caused fetal deaths and toxic effects, including congenital malformations and functional abnormalities (Norman and Halton, 1990; Woody and Brewster, 1990).

[6] Solvents and Halogenated Hydrocarbons

A solvent is any compound in which other substances can be dissolved; organic solvents are a large group of chemicals, and diverse results are not surprising among studies that do not identify components.

Occupational solvents include aliphatic hydrocarbons (linear carbons) and aromatic hydrocarbons (carbons in a ring). A well-controlled Finnish study of about 1,000 workers suggests that maternal exposure to the solvents tetrachloroethylene, methylene chloride and aliphatic hydrocarbons increased the number of spontaneous abortions in this group. However, another Finnish study of infants with birth defects could not explain increased risk by solvent exposure (Nurminen, et al., 1995). Increased time to pregnancy (significantly reduced fecundity) occurred among women workers exposed to organic solvents in shoe factories, dry-cleaning and the metals industry (Sallman, et al., 1995).

Aromatic hydrocarbons caused low birth weight and birth defects in children of persons exposed to laboratory reagents, paint thinners and antifreeze, along with an increased rate of spontaneous abortions (Giacoa, 1992). Paternal exposure to the common solvent toluene increased the spontaneous abortion rate (Lindbohm, et al., 1992). Exposure to toluene and orthocresol have been associated with low birth weight and birth defects, but toluene was not embryotoxic, fetotoxic or teratogenic in rabbits (Klimisch, et al., 1992).

The solvent ethylene glycol monoethyl ether and its acetate are widely distributed in industry and accepted as reproductive hazards by the Occupational Safety and Health Act (OSHA). Workers exposed to these solvents during paint stripping and painting or in varnish and ceramic production had high concentrations in urine and blood, with high skin absorption (Vincent, et al., 1994; Sohnlein, et al., 1993).

The polyhalogenated hydrocarbons (PBBs and PCBs) are toxic solvents with important industrial uses, such as electrical insulation and flame retardation; they were associated with male and female reproductive changes, including increased infant mortality and menstrual changes. Neurodevelopmental damage from high doses was observed in chemical and oil workers and persons exposed through industrial accidents. Studies of oil, chemical and atomic workers indicate a higher frequency of cancer and infant mortality among exposed workers, but no change in fertility, fetal loss, low birth weight or congenital malformations (Savitz, et al., 1984). Animal studies indicate that exposure of rats, rabbits and mice to these vapors causes reproductive and developmental hazards, including effects on the male, pregnant female and fetus (Wess, 1992).

[7]   Anesthesia

Occupational exposure to anesthetics was one of the first reported reproductive workplace hazards, but the data are not consistent. Nitrous oxide (NO) is associated with fetal injury and abortion in many studies, especially in operating room and dental personnel (Donaldson and Meechan, 1995). It causes reproductive, neural and muscle toxicity by interfering with normal biochemical mechanisms (Louis-Ferdinand, 1994). Occupational exposure of medical and dental personnel during normal low level use of NO as an anesthetic is not likely to produce adverse reproductive effects, except in individuals who are deficient in vitamin B_{12} or who are engaged in prolonged or repetitive use. Thus the results of epidemiologic and occupational studies are not always clear (Erickson and Kallen, 1986; Eger, 1991; Florack and Zielhuis, 1990). Scavengers have been developed to remove NO oxide traces (News, 1992), and vitamin B_{12} supplements can reverse some NO effects or serve as a protective agent (Ostreicher, 1994).

Data on human exposure to ethylene oxide is scarce and inconsistent. In some studies, exposure to ethylene oxide is associated with fetal toxicity and abnormalities (Florack and Zielhuis, 1990). Male occupational exposure has been associated with spontaneous abortion in several studies (Savitz, et al., 1994).

[8]   Video Display Terminals (VDTs) and Other Nonionizing Radiation

The cathode ray tubes in video display terminals (VDTs) emit several types of radiation, including visible light and radiofrequency waves, which are presumed to be harmless. The tubes also produce internal x-rays, most of which are filtered out by the screen. The very low levels that escape are well within commonly accepted industrial standards.

The role of VDT radiation in causing reproductive effects is uncertain. In some studies, exposure has been correlated with preterm birth, spontaneous abortion and infant mortality (Nielsen and Brandt, 1992), but most studies conclude that no association exists (Schnorr, 1990). Correlation of reproductive effects with exposure to VDTs is difficult because of frequency variations and differences in operator distance from the terminals (Haes and Fitzgerald, 1995).

[9] Pesticides and Specific Agricultural Chemicals

Certain pesticides, such as 1,2-dibromochloropropane (DBCP), the metabolite ethylene thiourea (ETU) and oryzalin, possess reproductive toxicity (Dixon, 1986), but variable results have been obtained for other compounds. The differing results may be due to the specific chemical exposure, which is not always defined. In a large Finnish study examining maternal toxicity in 1,306 pairs of infants with birth defects and matched controls, a somewhat increased rate of defects was found with maternal exposure to agricultural chemicals; a higher ratio was found for orofacial clefts (Nurminen, et al., 1995; Gordon and Shy, 1981).

In a study of almost 50,000 pregnancies of employed women in Canada, an increased odds ratio for congenital defects was found for women in agriculture and horticulture (McDonald, et al., 1988). A New Brunswick report describes a potential association between stillbirths and exposure to agricultural chemicals during the second trimester of pregnancy, especially for spina bifida and other major anomalies (White, et al., 1988). An Indian study examined 1,016 couples in which the males were directly exposed to pesticides, compared to 1,016 unexposed males, and found that the number of spontaneous abortions, stillbirths, neonatal complications and congenital defects increased, and fertility and the frequency of live births decreased (Rupa, et al., 1991).

However, in a California study of women exposed to agricultural chemicals, no difference was found between exposed and unexposed workers for spontaneous abortion, low birth weight, preterm birth or toxemia (Willis, et al., 1993). Similarly, in a Colombian study, no significant birth defects occurred in children of workers exposed to pesticides in floriculture, compared to random controls (Restrepo, et al., 1990).

[10]   Physical Factors

Various physical hazards may cause reproductive toxicity. Non-chemical hazards may include radiation, hyperthermia, heat, noise, hyperbaric or hypobaric environments, vibrations and overexertion. High temperature is especially related to loss of sperm viability. Standing and stress were linked with prematurity in a group of 1,470 pregnant nurses, especially in women who had previously given birth to a premature baby (Luke, et al., 1995). Any reproductive effects of maternal exercise appear to be related to individual physiologic factors in the mother and fetus (Ratcliffe, et al., 1993).

[11]   Occupations Associated with Specific Workplace Hazard

Some studies suggest the association of certain occupations with high reproductive risk; the agents are not always defined. In addition to exposure to radiation, anesthetics, stressful exertion and infectious agents, health care workers are exposed to harmful pharmaceutical agents causing reproductive and developmental toxicity, such as cytotoxic or neoplastic drugs used to treat cancer (Fishbein, 1991; Deitchman and Wall, 1994; Parillo, 1994; Skov, 1993; Niewag, et al., 1994). Exposure to alkylating antineoplastic drugs produces increased risk for miscarriages, malformations and leukemia, as shown in humans and experimental studies of animals. Five European countries have guidelines for the safe handling of antineoplastic drugs, but these lack uniformity with OSHA regulations (Skov, 1993). No reliable screening tests have been developed (Parillo, 1994).

Firefighters are exposed to potential teratogens, such as (Winder, 1990; McDiarmid, et al., 1991):

- benzene;
- cadmium;
- aldehydes;
- chloroform;
- hydrogen cyanide;
- nitrogen oxide;

- PCBs;

- sulfur dioxide;

- toluene;

- vinyl chloride;

- carbon monoxide; and

- physical factors.

14.07 STEPS TO REDUCE HAZARD

Steps to reduce occupational reproductive hazards include identifying dangerous exposures, monitoring regulatory requirements based on animal or epidemiologic studies, reducing use, developing remedial procedures, giving precautionary warnings to pregnant women and parents who wish to conceive, and preventing exposure by moving the worker elsewhere or providing salaries for home maintenance during the first trimester of pregnancy.

[1] Evaluation Programs

Evaluation of workplace chemicals is needed to provide workers with accurate information about potential reproductive hazards. Occupational health nurses may reduce worker exposures by noting trends and by providing education programs for employees (Snow, 1994).

[2] Measurement

Adverse reproductive and developmental effects are measured through epidemiologic methods and by experimental animal studies. Most countries require testing of new drugs in animals in order to determine their toxicity and teratogenicity, and some countries test pesticides and food additives as well. Few tests involve inhalation or skin exposure, however, and reproductive and developmental toxicity have not been evaluated for most mutagenic (capable of causing genetic alteration) occupational chemicals.

Experimental studies assist in assigning a mechanism to the effect of a reproductive or developmental toxin. Some toxins act directly on one target; others act on several targets and at several levels; some act indirectly or require chemical activation by certain compounds or body metabolites, including complex organic compounds such as polyaromatic hydrocarbons (PAHs) or polychlorinated biphenyls

(PCBs). The metabolites also may act to detoxify and remove the foreign compound from the body (Ratcliffe, et al., 1993). Toxins such as PCBs have several mechanisms of action.

Few reports correlate the results of laboratory animal or in vitro (test tube culture) tests with epidemiologic studies showing reproductive or developmental toxicity from exposure to occupational chemicals; few reports critique the flaws in laboratory studies or the methodologic reasons for the disparate results of epidemiologic studies. Thorough review should permit informed decisions about the hazard of potential exposures, enabling individuals to exercise precaution and free choice.

[a] Epidemiology

The epidemiologic demonstration of reproductive and developmental effects from workplace exposure is complex, with many confounding variables and requirements for consideration of statistic aspects, such as sample size. Studies may be retrospective or prospective. Ideally, in a prospective study, epidemiologists collect exposure data (e.g., presence of paint, lead in blood) before the actual pregnancy or birth, so that they are not influenced by the outcome (i.e., healthiness of fetus). Focal clusters of cases having reproductive or developmental toxicity may be examined retrospectively to look for a common cause at an occupational location, or they may be matched with control subjects by age, sex or other factors to examine differences. Epidemiologic studies also may use census information or large groups (cohorts) such as worker registries to examine disease patterns among persons with common exposures. They may link occupational exposure levels with health records of reproductive outcome.

Reviews or pooled epidemiologic meta-analyses may show very diverse results. They should be based on rigid criteria, comparing factors such as quantity (dose), distance, frequency and duration of exposures. Potential pitfalls include the use of such approximate measures as retrospective time to pregnancy to estimate fertility, exposure estimates based on occupational titles and failure to consider socioeconomic factors (Weinberg, et al., 1993; Dula, et al., 1993; Katz, et al., 1994).

[b] Animal Studies

Test results from animal teratogenicity and reproductive studies often serve as a guide indicating when human studies are needed.

Analyses may begin with the data base of genotoxic occupational carcinogens.[3] Tests to show reproductive effects in animals often use a tier or stepwise system, testing the various potential reproductive effects in diverse species. Animal studies best show visible malformations and death at the late fetal stage; they may miss other forms of developmental toxicity, such as functional deficits.

In general, the higher the animal species, the more reliable the study for predicting human developmental effects, i.e., studies in a mouse or dog are generally more reliable than those using a chick embryo, bacteria or an invertebrate. Some tests strongly correlating with human teratogenicity are based on the frog embryo, however (Vismara, et al., 1993), or on in vitro tissue cultures. An effect demonstrated in several species is more convincing than a reproductive effect in a single species. For example, ethylene glycol monomethyl ether, ethylene glycol monethyl ether and their acetates were shown to produce multiple reproductive effects in the mouse, rat, rabbit, dog and monkey (Wess, 1992), resulting in an occupational standard for human exposure. Many animal tests or effects do not, however, correlate with adverse reproductive effects in humans. For example, the mouse and rat are resistant to the important teratogen thalidomide, but certain strains of other animals respond (Manson and Wise, 1991).

[c] Exposure End Points in Humans

In general, exposure to solvents can be measured by chemicals in expired air, blood or urine. In female animals, tests measure ovarian organ weight, structure, oocyte count, ovulation and other factors. These include hypothalamus, pituitary, oviduct, uterus and vaginal structure and function, fertility and in vitro fertilization. For women, the effects of exposure also can be measured by observation of the menstrual cycle, hormone levels and reports of libido. The fertility of a couple may be measured by birth rate, time to pregnancy and teratogenicity.

Useful tests for determining male reproductive toxicity in humans and animals include:

- examination of testes and hormone level;
- analysis of semen (total sperm, morphology, motility); and

---

[3] *See also* ch. 15 for a discussion of occupational cancer.

- reports on libido and impotence.

Models exist for the extrapolation of animal data to humans (Meistrich, 1989).

[3] Regulatory Requirements for Reproductive Hazard Evaluation in Animals

U.S. agencies use standard reproductive toxicity testing programs for drugs, pesticides and direct and indirect food additives. The Food and Drug Administration (FDA) uses a series of experimental animal tests for ingested substances. These tests measure fertility and reproductive function in males and females, developmental toxicology and teratology, perinatal and postnatal toxicity, and the effect of drugs over three generations. The tests require a year to complete and are very expensive.

Methods exist to extrapolate the results of well-validated animal models to therapeutic regimens in humans. The Environmental Protection Agency measures compounds such as pesticides over two generations. The National Toxicology Program tests compounds according to the Fertility Assessment by Continuous Breeding (FACB) protocol (Thomas, 1991). The relevance of these animal tests to humans and especially to the human occupational setting is not always certain, but valuable predictions have included the reproductive toxicity of vinyl chloride and DBCP (1,2-dibromochloropropane).

The FDA does not examine the teratogenicity and reproductive toxicity of compounds used on the skin, although skin absorption is measured. Occupational comparison of standard tests requires dose extrapolation and consideration of exposure route (e.g., inhalation or skin). The Occupational Safety and Health Act (OSHA) sets standards for exposure to pesticides, lead, ethylene oxide, ionizing radiation and glycol ethers, but these are not based upon reproductive toxicity per se (Giacoia, 1992).

[4] Prevention and Use Reduction

Reduction of exposure to reproductive toxins may be attained by substituting new compounds or practices for hazardous ones, by lowering occupational exposures and by facilitating temporary removal of especially susceptible persons.

[a] Use Reduction

The technique of chemical hazard management by reduction of toxic substance use has emerged recently in at least nine states (Geiser, 1993) and includes reduction of reproductive and developmental toxicants. This "pollution preventive approach" tries to remove exposure to toxic and hazardous wastes at the beginning of the process rather than at the end. Some examples of reducing common reproductive or developmental toxins include:

- phasing out lead in gasoline, paint and copper tubing;
- replacing mercury in paint and dry cell batteries;
- replacing chlorinated solvents in industrial degreasing and cleaning operations with alkaline-or aqueous-based cleaning agents;
- replacing ethylene oxide in hospital sterilization;
- replacing DDT, chlordane, heptachlor and kepone with other pest management agents;
- phasing out PCBs from all but contained electrical equipment;
- replacing ethylene glycol ethers in semiconductors with polypropylene-based products;
- replacing epoxy resins with substitutes; and
- using glycol ether de-icing alternatives.

[b] Remedial Methods

Among the remedial methods that have been developed for dealing with reproductive toxins are:

- using scavengers (substances added to consume or inactivate traces of impurities) for ethylene oxide or for formaldehyde (Feinman, 1988);
- administering folinic acid or methionine with nitrous oxide (Louis-Ferdnand, 1994); and
- using vitamin B_{12} to counter some of the effects of nitrous oxide (Ostreicher, 1994).

[c] Precautionary Warnings

In the Netherlands and other European countries, a precautionary occupational exposure limit (OEL) is applied to substances suspected of causing reproductive toxicity, based on previous levels, animal inhalation data or using 0.1 mg/m^3 as the OEL. Much lower levels than 0.1 mg/m^3 are given for compounds such as pesticides, carbon monoxide, diethyl ether and formaldehyde (Stijkel and Reijnders, 1995). Maternal alcohol and/or drug abuse are significant factors in the causation of prematurity and low birth weight.

[d]   Preventive Measures

In Denmark, pregnant women can receive maintenance allowances if they work in an environment that is potentially hazardous to the fetus. Many women take advantage of this opportunity during the first trimester of pregnancy (Larsen, et al., 1992).

14.08   JUDICIAL ASPECTS

In 1991, the Supreme Court barred corporate fetal protection policies (*Automobile Workers v. Johnson Controls,* 499 U.S. 187, 1991). Excluding fertile or pregnant women from the workplace because of alleged health concerns constitutes illegal sex discrimination.

Since males can also influence reproduction, companies must develop new ways of protecting both male and female employees from exposure to compounds that affect fertility or pregnancy. Possibilities include prevention of hazardous exposure by changing practices; allowing transfer to departments with less or no exposure; income protection (in some countries, the government or the employer provides partial salaries to workers who stay home during the critical periods of pregnancy); private lawsuits; and allowing employees to make the decision of whether to be exposed, following education on potential risks provided by the employer (Graham, et al., 1993; Clauss, et al., 1993, Daniels, et al., 1990).

14.100   BIBLIOGRAPHY

Reference Bibliography

Agnew, J., et al.: Reproductive Hazards of Fire Fighting. I. Non-chemical Hazards. Am. J. Ind. Med. 19(4):433-445, 1991.

Andrews, K. W., et al.: Prenatal Lead Exposure in Relation to Gestational Age and Birth Weight: A Review of Epidemiologic Studies. Am. J. Ind. Med. 26(1):13-32, July 1994.

Baker, E. L.: A Review of Recent Research on Health Effects of Human Occupational Exposure to Organic Solvents. A Critical Review. J. Occup. Med. 36(10):1079-1092, 1994.

Bellinger, D., et al.: Pre-and Postnatal Lead Exposure and Behavior Problems in School-agedChildren. Environ. Res. 66(1):12-30, July 1994.

Bellinger, D., et al.: Weight Gain and Maturity in Fetuses Exposed to Low Levels of Lead. Environ. Res. 54(2):151-158, Apr. 1991.

Birnbaum, L. S.: Endocrine Effects of Prenatal Exposure to PCBs, Dioxins, and Other Xenobiotics: Implications for Policy and Future Research. Environ. Health Perspect. 102(8):676-679, Aug. 1994.

Clauss, C. A., et al.: Litigating Reproductive and Developmental Health in the Aftermath of UAW versus Johnson Controls. Environ. Health Perspect. 101 Suppl.2:205-220, July 1993.

Daniels, C. R., et al.: Health, Equity, and Reproductive Risks in the Workplace. J. Public Health Policy 11(4):449-462, Winter 1990.

de Cock, J., et al.: Time to Pregnancy and Occupational Exposure to Pesticides in Fruit Growers in the Netherlands. Occup. Environ. Med. 51(10):693-699, 1994.

Deitchman, S. and Wall, D.: Health Hazard Evaluation Report. Florida Hospital, Orlando, FL. Hazard Evaluation and Technical Assistance 89-034302348 (NIOSH), Government Reports Announcements and Index (Dept. of Commerce), Issue 7, 1994.

Dixon, R. L.: Toxic Responses in the Reproductive System, Ch. 16. In: Klaasen, C.D., et al.: Casarett and Doull's Toxicology, 3rd ed. New York: Macmillan, 1986.

Donaldson, D. and Meechan, J. G.: The Hazards of Chronic Exposure to Nitrous Oxide: An Update. Br. Dent. J. 178(3):95-100, Feb. 11, 1995.

Dula, A., et al.: Occupational and Environmental Reproductive Hazards Education and Resources for Communities of Color. Environ. Health Perspect. 101 Suppl 2:181-189, July 1993.

Eger, E. I. II: Fetal Injury and Abortion Associated with Occupational Exposure to Inhaled Anesthetics. Am. Assoc. Nurse Anesthet. J. 59(4):309-312, Aug. 1991.

Ema, M., et al.: Evaluation of the Teratogenic Potential of the Rubber Accelerator Dibenzthiazyl Disulfide in Rats. J. Appl. Toxicol. 9(6):413-417, Dec. 1989.

Erickson, A. and Kallen, B.: An Epidemiological Study of Work with Video Screens and Pregnancy Outcome. I. A Registry Study. Am. J. Ind. Med. 9:447, 1986.

Evans, J. A., et al.: Infertility and Pregnancy Outcome among Magnetic Resonance Imaging Workers. J. Occup. Med. 35(12):1191-1195, Dec. 1993.

Fagher, U., et al.: The Relationship between Cadmium and Lead Burdens and Preterm Labor. Int. J. Gynaecol. Obstet. 40(2):109-114, Feb. 1993.

Feinman, S.: Formaldehyde Toxicity and Hypersensitivity. Boca Raton, Fla.: CRC Press, 1988.

Fishbein, L.: Chemicals Used in the Rubber Industry. Sci. Total Environ. 101(1-2):33-43, 1991.

Florack, E. I. and Zielhuis, G. A.: Occupational Ethylene Oxide Exposure and Reproduction. Int. Arch. Occup. Environ. Health 62(4):273-277, 1990.

Frakes, R. A.: Drinking Water Guideline for Ethylene Thiourea, a Metabolite of Ethylene Bisdithiocarbamate Fungicides. Regul. Toxicol. Pharmacol. 8(2):207-218, Jun. 1988.

Geiser, K.: Protecting Reproductive Health and the Environment: Toxics Use Reduction. Environ. Health Perspect. 101 Suppl.2:221-225, 1993.

Gennart, J. P., et al.: Fertility of Male Workers Exposed to Cadmium, Lead, or Manganese. Am. J. Epidemiol. 135(11):1208-1219, June 1, 1992.

Giacoia, G. P.: Reproductive Hazards in the Workplace. Obstet. Gyn. Survey 447(10):679-687, 1992.

Gold, E., et al.: Introduction: Rationale for an Update. Reproductive Hazards. Occup. Med. 9(3):363-372, July-Sept. 1994.

Gordon, J. E. and Shy, C. M.: Agricultural Chemical Use and Congenital Cleft Lip and/or Palate. Arch. Environ. Health 36(5):213-221, Sept.-Oct. 1981.

Goyer, R. A.: Toxic Effects of Metals, Ch. 19. In: Klaasen, C.D., et al.: Casarett and Doull's Toxicology, 3rd ed. New York: Macmillan, 1986.

Grabowski, C. T.: Postnatal Cardiovascular Effects. Handout at Teratology Society Meeting, Department of Biology, University of Miami, Coral Gables, Fla., 1988.

Graham, T., et al.: A Labor Perspective on Workplace Reproductive Hazards: Past History, Current Concerns, and Positive Directions. Environ. Health Perspect. 101 Suppl. 2:199-204, July 1993.

Grajewski, B. A. and Schnorr, T. M.: Epidemiologic studies of Adverse Reproduction Outcomes in Working Populations. Scand. J. Work Environ. Health 18 (Supp. 2):40-42, 1992.

Haes, D. L., Jr., and Fitzgerald, M. R.: Video Display Terminal Very Low Frequency Measurements: The Need for Protocols in Assessing VDT User Dose. Health Phys. 68(4):572-578, Apr. 1995.

Hemminki, K. and Vineis, P.: Extrapolation of the Evidence on Teratogenicity of Chemicals Between Humans and Experimental Animals: Chemicals Other Than Drugs. Teratogenesis Carcinog. Mutagen. 5(4):251-318, 1985.

Hertz-Picciotto, I. and Neutra, R. R.: Resolving Discrepancies Among Studies: The Influence of Dose on Effect Size. Epidemiology 5(2):156-163, Mar. 1994.

Hu, W. Y., et al.: A Toxicological and Epidemiological Study of Reproductive Functions of Male Workers Exposed to Lead. J. Hyg. Epidemiol. Microbiol. Immunol. 36(1):25-30, 1992.

Katz, E. A., et al.: Exposure Assessment in Epidemiologic Studies of Birth Defects By Industrial Hygiene Review of Maternal Interviews. Am. J. Ind. Med. 26(1):1-11, July 1994.

Keck, C., et al.: Autometallographic Detection of Mercury in Testicular Tissue of an Infertile Man Exposed to Mercury Vapor. Reprod. Toxicol. 7(5):469-475, Sept.-Oct. 1993.

Klimisch, H. J., et al.: Studies on the Prenatal Toxicity of Toluene in Rabbits Following Inhalation Exposure and Proposal of a Pregnancy Guidance Value. Arch. Toxicol.66(6):373-381, 1992.

Koren, G., et al.: A Multicenter Prospective Study of Fetal Outcome Following Accidental Carbon Monoxide Poisoning in Pregnancy. Reprod. Toxicol. 5(5):397-403, 1991.

Kristensen, P., et al.: Perinatal Outcome Among Children of Men Exposed to Lead and Organic Solvents in the Printing Industry. Am. J. Epidemiol. 137(2):134-144, Jan. 15, 1993.

Larsen, A. I., et al.: Management of Occupational Risk to Reproduction in a Danish County. Scand. J. Soc. Med. 20(1):25-30, Mar. 1992.

Lauwerys, R. R., et al.: Health Risk Assessment of Long-Term Exposure to Non-genotoxic Chemicals: Application of Biological Indices. Toxicol. Lett. 77(1-3):39-44, May 1995.

Lindbohm, M. L., et al.: Effects of Parental Occupational Exposure to Solvents and Lead on Spontaneous Abortion. Scand. J. Work Environ. Health 18 Suppl. 2:37-39, 1992.

Lipscomb, J. A., et al.: Pregnancy Outcomes in Women Potentially Exposed to Occupational Solvents and Women Working in the Electronics Industry. J. Occup. Med. 33(5):597-604, May 1991.

Lockitch, G.: Perspectives on Lead Toxicity. Clin. Biochem. 26(5):371-381, Oct. 1993.

Louis-Ferdinand, R. T.: Myelotoxic, Neurotoxic, and Reproductive Adverse Effects of Nitrous Oxide. Adverse Drug React. Toxicol. Rev. 13(4):193-206, Winter 1994.

Luke, S., et al.: The Association between Occupational Factors and Preterm Birth. A United States Nursing Study. Am. J. Amer. Obstet. Gynecol. 173(3):849-862, Sept. 1995.

Manson, J. M. and Kang, Y. J.: Test Methods for Assessing Female Reproductive and Developmental Toxicology, Ch. 28. In: Hayes, A. W. (Ed.): Principles and Methods of Toxicology, 3rd ed. New York: Raven Press, 1994.

Manson, J. M. and Wise, L. D.: Teratogens, Ch. 7. In: De Vita, V. T., et al.: Cancer. Principles and Practice of Oncology, 3rd ed. Philadelphia: Lippincott, 1989.

McDiarmid, M. A., et al.: Reproductive Hazards of Fire Fighting II. Chemical Hazards. Amer. J. Ind. Med. 19:447-472, 1991.

McDonald, A. D., et al.: Prematurity and Work in Pregnancy. Br. J. Ind. Med. 45:56-62, 1988.

Meistrich. M. L.: Evaluation of Reproductive Toxicity by Testicular Spermhead Counts. J. Am Coll. Toxicol. 8:551-567, 1989.

Meskin, L. H.: No Laughing Matter [Editorial]. J. Am. Dent. Assoc. 124(1):8, Jan. 11, 1993.

Murray, P. R., et al.: Medical Microbiology. St. Louis: Mosby-Year Book, 1994.

Needleman, H. L.: What Can the Study of Lead Teach Us About Other Toxicants? Environ. Health Perspect. 86:183-189, June 1990.

News: Scavenging Equipment Prevents Nitrous Oxide Fertility Threat. J. Am. Dent. Assoc. 123(12):18, Dec. 1992.

Nielsen, C. V. and Brandt, L. P.: Fetal Growth, Preterm Growth and Infant Mortality in Relation to Work with Video Display Terminals during Pregnancy. Scand. J. Work Environ. Health 18(6):3346-3350, Dec. 1992.

Niewag, R. M., et al.: Safe Handling of Antineoplastic Drugs. Results of a Survey. Cancer Nurs. 17(6):501-511, Dec. 1994.

Norman, C. A. and Halton, D. M.: Is Carbon Monoxide a Workplace Teratogen? A Review and Evaluation of the Literature. Ann. Occup. Hyg. 34(4):335-347, Aug. 1990.

Nurminen, T., et al.: Agricultural Work during Pregnancy and Selected Structural Malformation in Finland. Epidemiology 6(1):23-30, Jan. 1995.

O'Halloran, K. and Spickett, J. T.: The Interaction of Lead Exposure and Pregnancy. Asia Pac. J. Pub. Health 6(2):35-39, 1992-1993.

Ostreicher, D. S.: Vitamin B_{12} Supplements as Protection against Nitrous Oxide Inhalation. N. Y. State Dental J..60(3): 47-49, Mar. 1994.

Parillo, V. L.: Documentation Forms for Monitoring Occupational Surveillance of Healthcare Workers Who Handle Cytotoxic Drugs. Oncol. Nurs. Forum, 21(1):115-120, Jan.-Feb. 1994.

Peters, P. W., et al.: Drugs of Choice in Pregnancy: Primary Prevention of Birth Defects. Reprod. Toxicol. 7(5):399-404, Sept.-Oct. 1993.

Pizzo, P. A., et al.: Solid Tumors of Childhood, Ch. 47. In: De Vita, V. T., et al.: Cancer. Principles and Practice of Oncology, 3rd ed. Philadelphia: Lippincott, 1989.

Quinn, M. M., et al.: Investigation of Reports of Sexual Dysfunction among Male Chemical Workers Manufacturing Stilbene Derivatives. Am. J. Ind. Med. 18(1):55-68, 1990.

Ratcliffe, J. M., et al.: Reproductive Toxicity, Ch. 43. In: Richardson, M.: Reproductive Toxicology. Weinheim, New York: VCH, 1993.

Restrepo, M., et al.: Birth Defects among Children Born to a Population Occupationally Exposed to Pesticides in Colombia. Scand. J. Work Environ. Health 16(4):239-246, Aug. 1990.

Roeleveld, N., et al.: Occupational Exposure and Defects of the Central Nervous System in Offspring. Review. Br. J. Ind. Med. 47(9):580-588, 1990.

Rom, W. (Ed.): Smoking and Low Birth Weight. In: Rom, W.: Environmental and Occupational Medicine, 2nd ed. Boston: Little Brown, 1992.

Rothenberg, S. J., et al.: Prenatal and Perinatal Low Level Lead Exposure alters Brainstem Auditory Evoked Responses in Infants. Neurotoxicology 15(3):695-699, Fall 1994.

Rowland, A. S., et al.: Nitrous Oxide and Spontaneous Abortion in Female Dental Assistants. Am. J. Epidemiol. 141(6):531-538, Mar. 15, 1995.

Rupa, D. S., et al.: Reproductive Performance in Population Exposed to Pesticides in Cotton Fields in India. Environ. Res. 55(2):123-128, Aug. 1991.

Saillenfait, A. M. and Vannier, B.: Methodological Proposal in Behavioral Teratogenicity Testing: Assessment of Propoxyphene, Chlorpromazine, and Vitamin A as Positive Controls. Teratology 37(3):185-199, Mar. 1988.

Sallman, M., et al.: Reduced Fertility among Women Exposed to Organic Solvents. Am. J. Ind. Med. 27(5):699-713, 1995.

Savitz, D. A., et al.: Review of Epidemiologic Studies of Paternal Occupational Exposure and Spontaneous Abortion. Am. J. Ind. Med. 25(3):361-383, Mar. 1994.

Savitz, D. A., et al.: Survey of Reproductive Hazards among Oil, Chemical, and Atomic Workers Exposed to Halogenated Hydrocarbons. Am. J. Ind. Med. 6(4):253-264, 1984.

Schnorr, T. M.: The NIOSH Study of Reproductive Outcomes among Video Display TerminalOperators. Reprod. Toxicol. 4(1):61-65, 1990.

Schrader, S. M.: Data Gaps and New Methodologies in the Assessment of Male Fecundity in Occupational Field Studies. Scand. J. Work Environ. Health 18 (Suppl 2):30-32, 1992.

Schrag, S. D. and Dixon, R. L.: Occupation Exposure associated with Male Reproductive Dysfunction. Ann. Rev. Pharmacol. Toxicol. 25:567-592, 1985.

Seger, D. and Welch, L.: Carbon Monoxide Controversies: Neuropsychological Testing, Mechanism of Toxicity, and Hyperbaric Oxygen. Ann. Emerg. Med. 24(2):242-248, Aug. 1995.

Sherins, R. J. and Mulvihill, J. J.: Adverse Effects of Treatment, Ch. 60. Section 5: Gonadal Dysfunction. In: DeVita, V. T., et al.: Cancer. Principles and Practice of Oncology, 3rd ed. Philadelphia: Lippincott, 1989.

Sikorski, R., et al.: Women in Dental Surgeries: Reproductive Hazards in Occupational Exposure to Metallic Mercury. Int. Arch. Occup. Environ. Health 59:551-557, 1987.

Skov, T.: Handling Antineoplastic Drugs in the European Community Countries. Eur. J. Cancer Prev. 2(1):43-46, Jan. 1993.

Snow, J. E.: Occupational Exposure to Glycol Ethers: Implications for Occupational Health Nurses. Am. Assoc. Occup. Health Nurs. J. 42(9):413-419, Sept. 1994.

Sohnlein, B., et al.: Occupational Chronic Exposure to Organic Solvents. XIV. Examinations Concerning the Evaluation of a Limit Value for 2-Ethoxyethanol and 2-Ethoxyethyl Acetate and the Genotoxic Effects of These Glycol Ethers. Int. Arch. Occup. Environ. Health 64(7):479-484, 1993.

Stijkel, A and Reijnders, L.: Implementation of the Precautionary Principle in Standards for the Workplace. Occup. Environ. Med. 52:304-312, 1995.

Tabacova, S. and Balabaeva, L.: Environmental Pollutants in Relation to Complications of Pregnancy. Environ. Health Perspect. 101 (Suppl. 2):27-31, 1993.

Taskinen, H.: Prevention of Reproductive Health Hazards at Work. Scand. J. Work Environ. Health 18 (Suppl. 2):27-29, 1992.

Thomas, J. A.: Toxic Responses of the Reproductive System, Ch. 16 In: Amdur, M. O.: Casarett and Doull's Toxicology, 4th ed. New York: Pergamon Press, 1991.

Thompson, S. T.: Preventable Causes of Male Infertility. World J. Urol. 11(2):11-19, 1993.

Veulemans, H., et al.: Exposure to Ethylene Glycol Ethers and Spermatogenic Disorders in Man: A Case-Control Study. Br. J. Ind. Med. 50(1):71-78, Jan. 1993.

Vincent, R., et al.: Occupational Exposure to Organic Solvents during Paint Stripping and Painting Operations in the Aeronautical Industry. Int. Arch. Occup. Environ. Health 65(6):377-380, 1994.

Vismara, C., et al.: The Use of In Vitro Fertilization in the Frog Embryo Teratogenesis Assay in Xenopus (FETAX) and its Application to Ecotoxicology. Sci. Total Environ. Supp. Part 1:787-790, 1993.

Weinberg, C. R., et al.: Pitfalls Inherent in Retrospective Time-to-Event Studies: The Example of Time to Pregnancy. Stat. Med. 12(9):867-879, May 15, 1993.

Wess, J. A.: Reproductive Toxicity of Ethylene Glycol Monomethyl Ether, Ethylene Glycol Monoethyl Ether, and their Acetates. Scand. J. Work Environ. Health 18 (Suppl. 2):43-45, 1992.

White, F. M., et al.: Chemicals, Birth Defects and Stillbirths in New Brunswick: Associations with Agricultural Activity. Can. Med. Assoc. J. 138(2):117-124, Jan. 15, 1988.

Willis, W. O., et al.: Pregnancy Outcome among Women Exposed to Pesticides through Work or Residence in an Agricultural Area. J. Occup. Med. 35(9):943-949, 1993.

Winder, C.: Reproductive Hazards at Work. Teratology 42(3):324, Sept. 1990.

Woody, R. C. and Brewster, M. A.: Telencephalic Dysgenesis Associated with Presumptive Maternal Carbon Monoxide Intoxication in the First Trimester of Pregnancy. J. Toxicol. Clin. Toxicol. 28(4):467-475, 1990.

Wynn, R. L.: Nitrous Oxide and Fertility. Gen. Dent. 41(2):122-123, Mar.-Apr. 1993.

Xuezhi, J., et al.: Studies of Lead Exposure on Reproductive System: A Review of Work in China. Biomed. Environ. Sci. 5(3):266-275, Sept. 1992.

Additional References

Davis, J. R., et al.: Family Pesticide Use and Childhood Brain Cancer. Arch. Environ. Contam. Toxicol.24(1): 87-92, 1993.

Dellpizzo, F.: Epidemiological Studies of Work with Video Display Terminals and Adverse Pregnancy Outcomes (1984-1992). Am. J. Indust. Med. 26(4):465-480, 1994.

Figa-Talamanca, I. and Hatch, M. C.: Reproduction and the Workplace: What we Know and Where We Go from Here. Int. J. Occup. Med. Toxicol., 3(3):279-303, 1994.

Hass, U. and Jakobsen, B.M.: Prenatal Toxicity of Xylene Inhalation in the Rat: A Teratogenicity and Postnatal Study. Pharmacol. Toxicol. 73(1):20-23, July 1993.

Langman, J. M.: Xylene: Its Toxicity, Measurement of Exposure Levels, Absorption, Metabolism, and Clearance. Pathology 26(3):301-309, July 1994.

Lundsberg, L. S., et al.: Occupationally related Magnetic Field Exposure and Male Subfertility. Fertil. Steril. 63(2):384-391, Feb. 1995.

Roe, F. J.: Styrene: Toxicity Studies—What do they Show? Crit. Rev. Toxicol. 24 Suppl:S117-125, 1994.

Roman, B. L., et al.: In Utero and Lactational Exposure of the Male Rat to 2,3,7,8 Tetrachlorodibenzo-p-dioxin: Impaired Prostate Growth and Development without Inhibited Androgen Production. Toxicol. Appl. Pharmacol. 134:241-250, 1995.

Whorton, D., et al.: Reproductive Effects of Inorganic Borates on Male Employees: Birth Rate Assessment. Environ. Health Perspect. 102 (Suppl. 7):129-132, Nov. 1994.

CHAPTER 15

Occupational Cancer

SCOPE

Exposure to carcinogens in the workplace can contribute significantly to the development of a variety of cancers. Lung cancer is associated with chronic exposure to carcinogens inhaled in the workplace. These take the form of fibers, gases and particles and include asbestos, benzene, vinyl chloride, the chloromethyl ethers and radon. Other respiratory cancers include cancers of the nasal sinuses and larynx, and mesothelioma, a highly malignant disease that affects the pleural lining of the chest cavity and is associated exclusively with exposure to asbestos. Certain cancers of the gastrointestinal tract, including those affecting the esophagus, stomach, intestines, rectum, pancreas, liver and gallbladder, are associated with particular occupations. For example, the risk of esophageal cancer is higher among asbestos workers, and stomach cancer incidence is higher than average among workers in mining, shipyards, insulation manufacture and plumbing. Carcinogens also commonly affect the organs of the genitourinary tract, such as the bladder, kidneys and prostate. These include a number of soots, tars and oils, and are associated with occupations such as boot and shoe repair, the rubber industry, auto industry and various manufacturing processes. Nonmelanotic skin cancers are associated with several occupations that involve continual exposure to ultraviolet radiation. Brain tumors correlate strongly with exposure to vinyl chloride, as does non-Hodgkin's lymphoma, a condition also associated with exposure to arsenic, asbestos and chemicals used in rubber production. In order to minimize occupational cancers, preventive steps are needed to make the workplace safer. These include providing employees with respirators and protective clothing as well as complying with federal standards for workplace safety.

SYNOPSIS

[g] Benzidine and Related Compounds
[h] 4–Aminobiphenyl
[i] Cadmium
[j] Polycyclic Aromatic Hydrocarbons
[k] Soots, Tars and Oils
[l] Dusts
[m] Ultraviolet Radiation
[n] Ionizing Radiation

15.100   BIBLIOGRAPHY

15.01   INCIDENCE OF OCCUPATIONAL CANCER

During the 1960s, 1970s and early 1980s, the magnitude of cancer risk from all environmental exposures (including occupational carcinogens) was evaluated. Estimates of the percentage of cancers associated with environmental exposures ranged from 60 to 90 percent or more. Today these estimates are regarded as excessive (Swanson, 1988).

For a variety of reasons, it is difficult to identify the precise contribution of occupational factors to the incidence of cancer. Foremost among them is that the exact cause of a particular case of cancer rarely can be determined. Unlike most other occupational illnesses, occupational cancer does not differ in clinical presentation from cancer that arises spontaneously or is caused by other factors. Persons who develop cancer after exposure to an occupational carcinogen may have additional risk factors that are unrelated to their jobs, such as cigarette smoking, exposure to carcinogens in the home or outdoor environment, or a genetic predisposition. Furthermore, most people have been employed at more than one occupation in their lifetime, making it difficult to attribute cancer with any certainty to a given job.

Latency is another phenomenon that makes it difficult to identify occupational causes of cancer. Because cancer does not usually develop until after a prolonged period following initial exposure to a carcinogen (typically 20 or more years), it is too soon to report whether most chemicals introduced into the workplace in the past 20 years are carcinogenic in humans.

Despite these difficulties, many attempts have been made to assess the proportion of cancer cases attributable to occupational factors. One widely accepted estimate in the 1980s was that of Doll and Peto (1981), who placed the percentage of occupational cancer in the United

States at 4 percent. According to their epidemiologic findings, occupational exposures cause 17,000 cancer deaths in the United States each year.

15.02 MECHANISMS OF CANCER

Cancer occurs when the normal replicative function of a cell is disrupted and the cell begins to grow and divide in an uncontrolled manner. Cancer usually arises from a single cell, which changes through a process called malignant transformation so that it is no longer regulated by the physical or biochemical mechanisms that normally control cell growth. The population of cancer cells that is formed in this manner becomes undifferentiated; that is, the cells lose the distinctive characteristics that once enabled them to fulfill their normal role in the body. Cancer cells may migrate to regional lymph nodes and/or directly enter the bloodstream, from which they can establish new colonies (metastases) in distant parts of the body. In general, the more undifferentiated the tumor cells and the more widely the disease metastasizes, the worse the prognosis.

Cancer causes illness and death by three major mechanisms:

- growth of tumors that encroach physically on organs in the body (*see Figure 15–1*);

- invasion of tissues and disruption of their normal function; and

- production by the tumor itself of substances that are toxic to body tissues.

[1] Carcinogenesis

Carcinogenesis refers to the process by which chemical and other carcinogens enter the nucleus of the cell and produce a mutation or change in the DNA (genetic material of the cell transmitted from the cell to its progeny). Under ordinary circumstances, the cells of the body are bombarded regularly by chemical and other mutagens; thus mutation is a fairly common event. Usually the affected cell dies or the mutation is repaired by enzymes within the cell before it can become permanently established. If exposure to the carcinogen is great or prolonged, though, a cell carrying a mutation may survive to establish a colony of cancer cells through the process of malignant transformation.

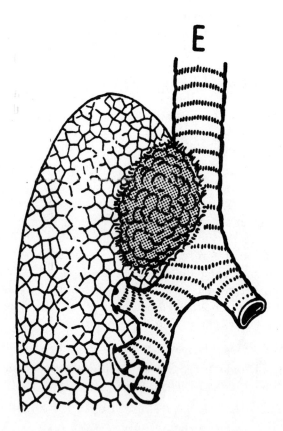

Fig. 15-1. A tumor of the lung encroaching on the trachea.

Carcinogens that act by inducing malignant transformation are called *cancer initiators.* A second group of carcinogenic substances, *cancer promoters,* act at a later stage of cancer development through mechanisms that are less well defined. (Hormones are examples of cancer promoters; cigarette smoke is both an initiator and a promoter.)

Still other factors, known generically as *risk factors,* increase an individual's risk for cancer (often through poorly understood mechanisms) but cannot themselves be called carcinogenic. This group includes "life-style" risk factors, such as an excess of saturated fat in the diet, dietary fiber deficiency and age at first pregnancy. Most persons who develop cancer (similar to those who do not) have been exposed to multiple known carcinogens, cancer promoters and risk factors during their lives, and this makes it difficult to attribute their cancer to a particular cause.

[2] Dose-Response Relationship

Known carcinogens can interact in different ways. In a population at risk, they can have an additive effect (the risk is increased by adding the proportion of cancers known to be caused by each agent), a multiplicative effect (in which the attributable risks are multiplied), an effect that falls somewhere between these two or something less. Most carcinogens, however, demonstrate a dose-response relationship. In other words, the greater the exposure, the greater the risk of cancer.

The importance of a threshold effect in occupational carcinogenesis has long been debated. It is apparent that at very low levels of exposure (i.e., below a certain threshold), carcinogens have a negligible impact on cancer risk in a normal population. However, it is not possible to say with certainty that low exposures have absolutely no effect on cancer risk. Some researchers and regulators take the view that it is safer to presume there is no threshold below which exposure to a carcinogen is safe (Howard, 1987).

15.03 CARCINOGENS IN THE WORKPLACE

The lungs are the main portal of entry for occupational carcinogens, including those that affect other organs, such as the bladder. Substances that can be inhaled include gases, fumes, vapors and particulates. For some carcinogenic substances, such as benzidine, the primary route of exposure is absorption through the skin. The third portal of entry for carcinogens, ingestion by mouth, is not thought to be important for occupational carcinogens. Some carcinogens may enter the body through more than one portal.

Estimates of the number of chemicals that are manufactured or present in the workplace vary widely. Tens of thousands of chemicals are in daily use or production in the United States, and the number of new chemicals added to the list each year may exceed 1,000 (Fishbein, 1982). Only a small proportion of these chemicals have been evaluated for possible carcinogenicity. New chemicals are not tested routinely for carcinogenicity when they are introduced; rather, observers usually wait for retrospective evidence that cancer has occurred before suspected carcinogens are evaluated.

[1] Epidemiologic Studies

Epidemiology is the systematic observation of the occurrence of a disease in human populations. Epidemiologic studies have been useful for identifying unsuspected occupational carcinogens through unusual patterns of cancer occurrence in groups of workers. The identification of a high-risk occupational category—for example, woodworkers or copper smelters—can suggest an entire range of chemicals that should be evaluated for possible carcinogenicity. Most of the known carcinogens have been identified through epidemiologic observation of workers and confirmed with subsequent animal studies.

Epidemiologists begin to suspect that a workplace exposure is carcinogenic when the rate of cancer in a group of workers increases above that expected in a group of people who are comparable with regard to age, sex, general health, smoking history and other risk factors. The observation of excess risk does not take place until the latency period for occupational carcinogenesis has elapsed. For example, the excess risk of cancer among asbestos workers was not observed until at least 20 years after asbestos began to be used widely in the workplace (Fraumeni and Blot, 1982). It is therefore difficult to detect excess cancer risk in working populations without decades of follow-up, particularly if the workers are young enough to be at low risk for cancer. It is also difficult for epidemiologic studies to show numerically small cancer risks that are associated with low exposures to carcinogens.

[2]   Animal Studies

Because of the long latency period for cancer in humans, studies of laboratory animals have become the predominant method for investigating suspected carcinogenesis. The typical test method is to administer the chemical to laboratory rodents and rabbits by mouth, skin inoculation or inhalation for their entire lives. The development of cancer, and particularly the same type of cancer at the same site as that observed in humans, is taken as evidence (although not proof) of carcinogenicity.

Animal studies are not foolproof. Their results can be difficult to interpret. Also, it has been found that many substances that cause cancer in animals do not do so in humans, although the reverse is rarely the case. Some substances that cause cancer in animals do so in only one of several species tested or only in newborn animals. Laboratory rats and mice are prone to develop cancer even in the absence of external stimuli, and carcinogens may be given to animals in doses that do not realistically reflect human exposures.

[3] Rapid Screens

Animal studies are too expensive and time consuming to use to screen large numbers of chemicals for carcinogenicity or mutagenicity. Thus, tests of mutagenicity in organisms such as yeast or bacteria are carried out to screen large numbers of chemicals rapidly. The most widely used such test is the Ames test, which is performed on *Salmonella* bacteria. The Ames test has been useful for identifying mutations that occur in health care workers who are involved in the preparation of cancer chemotherapy agents.

Tests may also be carried out on cell lines obtained from mammals, including humans. Typically, cell cultures are incubated with the test chemical, and observers note any cellular DNA damage and whether the cultured cells can repair themselves in the presence of the test chemical. Because single tests are not highly predictive of an agent's mutagenicity, multiple tests should be conducted on different cell systems. If a suspected carcinogen is found to be mutagenic in several different test systems, further evidence should be obtained by testing it in living animals (Tamburro, et al., 1982).[1]

15.04 LUNG CANCER

Lung cancer, the leading cause of cancer death in the United States, affects some 100,000 men and 50,000 women each year. It is highly malignant, with the majority of patients dying within one year after its diagnosis (Minna, 1991).

Only 20 percent of patients with lung cancer are diagnosed at an early stage, when the tumor is localized and definitive treatment possible. However, even for these patients, the prognosis is poor. In most cases, lung cancer is not diagnosed until the disease has spread to the lymph nodes (25 percent) or distant sites in the body (55 percent) (Minna, 1991).

[1] Etiology

A very high proportion of lung cancers are preventable if proper steps are taken to limit exposure to carcinogens. Cigarette smoking is by far the leading cause of lung cancer, but occupational exposures also make an important contribution. One estimate implicates occupational exposure to carcinogens in 15 percent of cases of lung cancer

---

[1] *See* 15.03[2] *supra.*

in men and 5 percent in women. The figure is lower in women because they are less likely to have occupations that involve exposure to the major pulmonary carcinogens (Doll and Peto, 1981). According to epidemiologic findings, occupational exposures cause 11,000 deaths from lung cancer in the United States each year.

In contrast, cigarette smoking is thought to contribute to 80 percent of cases of lung cancer in men and 40 percent in women (Fraumeni and Blot, 1982). The incidence of lung cancer in women has risen with the increase in the number of women who smoke. Cigarette smoking increases the risk of lung cancer in workers who are exposed to other carcinogens and markedly exacerbates the effects of certain occupational carcinogens, such as asbestos and radon.

Epidemiologic studies have shown an elevated incidence of lung cancer in various occupational groups, including auto workers, foundry workers, hairdressers, miners, printers and woodworkers (Raffle, et al., 1987). In some cases, cancers have been associated with exposure to known carcinogens; in others, the presumed association either has not yet been confirmed by additional testing or has been confirmed only by animal studies (Kilburn, 1986).

An elevated risk of lung cancer also has been observed consistently in some occupations in which there is no documented exposure to a known carcinogen. In these cases, the risk may be related to exposure to substances that have not yet been identified as carcinogens.

Benign lung neoplasms (tumors) make up a very small proportion of all tumors affecting the lung and are not known to be associated with occupational exposures (Green and Vallyathan, 1986).

[a] Asbestos and Other Mineral Fibers

Asbestos is a naturally occurring fibrous mineral that is mined and processed into materials that insulate against heat, cold, fire and electricity. It is incorporated into a host of widely used products, including building insulation materials, fire-resistant textiles, brake linings, cement and filters. Asbestos exposure contributes to cancer at many other sites in the body in addition to the lungs.[2] Because it is such a potent carcinogen and is used so widely in industry, it has long been considered by some to be the most important cause of occupational cancer (Fraumeni and Blot, 1982).

---

[2] *See also* ch. 16.

The risk of asbestos-related lung cancer is elevated in workers who mine or mill asbestos and in workers in the textile, insulation, shipyard, railroad, construction, cement and automobile brake industries. There is a dose-response relationship between asbestos exposure and lung cancer incidence; that is, the rate of lung cancer increases in asbestos workers in direct proportion to the duration and the concentration of their exposure.[3] However, the risk is elevated even in workers who are exposed for short periods; for example, in men who were exposed to asbestos while holding temporary jobs in shipyards during World War II, the present-day risk of lung cancer is elevated by 60 to 70 percent over those who had no such exposure (Fraumeni and Blot, 1982).

The risk of lung cancer begins to increase above background levels within 10 years after initial occupational exposure to asbestos. However, the average latency period between the initial exposure and the development of cancer—and thus the peak rate of lung cancer in exposed workers—may range from 20 to 35 years after they begin working with asbestos.

Cigarette smoking may increase the risk of lung cancer as much as tenfold in workers exposed to asbestos (Fraumeni and Blot, 1982; McDonald, 1990). The relationship between the carcinogenic effects of asbestos and cigarette smoking demonstrates an important principle: that some carcinogens, when they are working synergistically (in tandem), can have a multiplicative rather than additive effect on cancer incidence.

As the evidence of cancer risk has mounted since the 1970s, the asbestos industry has gone into a steep decline. However, because of its long latency, asbestos-related lung cancer is still a significant problem. Initially, manufactured mineral fibers such as mineral or rock wool and glass fibers that were used as substitutes for asbestos were thought to be safe. However, early in the 1980s, observers reported that these substances, too, could cause lung cancer. The carcinogenicity of manufactured mineral fibers has been less well studied than asbestos, and it is not clear whether these substances pose an equal risk to workers (McDonald, 1990).[4]

---

[3] See 15.02[2] *supra.*

[4] See 15.12[4] [a] *infra* for information on the prevention of occupational exposure to asbestos.

[b] Polycyclic Aromatic Hydrocarbons

Elevated rates of lung cancer have been observed in workers who are exposed to polycyclic aromatic hydrocarbons, which are formed by combustion or other processes involving coal or petroleum products. Excess lung cancer risk has been reported in coke oven workers (in the steel industry) and in workers who are exposed to carbon black, which is used in the manufacture of rubber.

Workers who are exposed to volatile organic solvents may also be at elevated risk; for example, printers exposed to both solvents and carbon black have an excess risk of lung cancer. Roofers, who may inhale benzo [a]pyrene given off by hot asphalt, also are at risk (Frank, 1987). Workers in the aluminum industry are exposed to carbon monoxide, coal tar pitch volatiles and other organic and inorganic carcinogens (Lemen, 1986). Diesel exhaust is a suspected pulmonary carcinogen in groups including underground miners who are exposed to the exhaust in a closed environment for long periods of time (Raffle, et al., 1987).[5]

[c] Radon

Radon (specifically radon–222) is a radioactive gas that is a naturally occurring decay product of radium, which is in turn a decay product of uranium. Radon is ubiquitous in soil and rock, and a small number of radon molecules constantly enter air and water from these sources. As a result, radon is found everywhere in both indoor and outdoor air, though its concentration varies tremendously. Exposure to radon in the natural environment is thought to be the cause of about 20 percent of the cases of lung cancer that occur in nonsmokers (Voelz, 1988).

Radon produces two decay products, polonium–214 and polonium–218. These products, which are called *radon daughters* or *radon progeny,* are the actual cause of lung cancer. They occur as small radioactive particles that enter the lung, where they emit radiation that damage the DNA of the cells lining the lungs.[6]

Workers in some underground mines, and particularly in uranium mines, are at excess risk of developing lung cancer as a result of radon

---

[5] *See* 15.12 [4] [j] *infra* for information on the prevention of occupational exposure to polycyclic aromatic hydrocarbons.

[6] *See* 15.02[1] *supra.*

exposure. A high incidence of lung cancer has been observed in several studies of uranium miners in Europe, Canada and the western United States (Axelson, 1990). Less commonly, lung cancer resulting from radon exposure has been reported in miners of iron, tin and fluorspar. In these studies, the risk of radon-exposed miners developing lung cancer has ranged from 1.5 to 15 times that of comparable groups that were not exposed to radon (Axelson, 1990).

The relationship between radon and cigarette smoking is complicated. On the one hand, cigarette smoke is a potent co-carcinogen with radon, with the two probably having a synergistic effect on cancer incidence. Since radon daughters attach themselves to airborne dust and smoke particles, a high level of smoke would also increase the concentration of radon progeny in the air. On the other hand, radon progeny attached to airborne particles are less likely to enter the lungs. The total effect of the combination of smoking and radon exposure on cancer risk has been difficult to determine, not least because the great majority of radon-exposed miners are smokers as well. According to one estimate, average lung cancer latency may be longer in nonsmokers or light smokers (19 years) than in heavy smokers (13 years) (Lemen, 1986).

Exposures to radon are measured in several ways. The working level (WL) was developed to describe a certain level of radioactivity to which miners may be exposed. The working level month (WLM) describes exposure to one WL for 170 hours, or one working month. In the 1970s, 4 WLM was established as the maximum allowable lifetime radon exposure for mine workers in several countries, including the United States. Before these standards took effect, some miners were exposed to as much as 3,720 WLM (Axelson, 1990). Since the 1950s, occupational exposure to radon has been reduced drastically.

The concentration of radon in air is also measured in picocuries per liter (pCi/L). One pCi/L equals about 0.005 WL. This measurement is most often used to describe radon levels indoors. Radon exposures are also measured in International System (SI) units, which can be used to describe both radon concentrations in air (like pCi/L and WL) and cumulative radon exposure (like WLM).[7]

---

[7] See 15.12[4] [d] *infra* for information on the prevention of occupational exposure to radon.

[d] Other Carcinogenic Substances

The list of other proved or suspected carcinogens that affect the lungs is long. The National Institute for Occupational Safety and Health (NIOSH) classifies arsenicals as carcinogens, and exposure to arsenic has been associated with lung cancer in copper smelters, manufacturers of pesticides and herbicides and vineyard workers who handle arsenic-containing pesticides (Frank, 1987; Lemen, 1986). Hemangiosarcomas of the liver also have been attributed to arsenic exposure.[8]

Chloromethyl ethers are volatile chemicals used in various industrial processes, including the synthesis of organic chemicals, textile finishing and the manufacture of some resins, dyestuffs, solvents and bactericides. Chloromethyl methyl ether (CMME) and particularly bis(chloromethyl) ether (BCME) are potent pulmonary carcinogens (Lemen, 1986). Also carcinogenic are chromium and other chromates, used in the production of pigments and alloys and in other processes (Frank, 1987).[9]

Nickel exposure can cause lung cancer, though the risk has been largely eliminated by improved engineering of nickel refineries (Fraumeni and Blot, 1982). Mustard gas, a poison gas manufactured for use during World War I, is mainly of historic interest as an occupational carcinogen. Other known or suspected occupational pulmonary carcinogens include beryllium, vinyl chloride (a gas emitted in the manufacture of polyvinyl chloride) and various vegetable dusts to which furniture makers may be exposed (Frank, 1987; Fraumeni and Blot, 1982). Cobalt, which is present in certain mining operations, also has come under suspicion as a possible lung carcinogen.

Several studies of lung cancer in nonsmokers who were involuntarily exposed to cigarette smoke on the job suggest that the occupational exposure may contribute minimally to cancer risk, but the evidence is not yet conclusive (Tager, 1989).

---

[8] See 15.12[4] [c] infra for information on the prevention of occupational exposure to arsenic.

[9] See 15.12[4] [b] infra for information on the prevention of occupational exposure to chloromethyl ethers.

[2] Diagnosis

Lung cancer is sometimes detected in asymptomatic persons when they receive routine chest x-rays, but more often, patients are evaluated after they seek medical care for symptoms suggestive of lung cancer. Screening programs of cigarette smokers and workers exposed on the job can often detect lung cancer while it is still asymptomatic and therefore less advanced; however, it is uncertain whether earlier discovery has an impact on the survival of individuals with lung cancer. Once lung cancer is diagnosed, the cell type is determined and the tumor staged to establish the prognosis and the best course of treatment.

[a] Clinical Presentation

The symptoms of lung cancer vary with the location of the tumor, its size and whether the cancer has spread (metastasized) to affect other organs. Specific symptoms such as coughing, hemoptysis (bloody sputum), dyspnea (shortness of breath) and pneumonitis (pulmonary obstruction secondary to bronchial obstruction by tumor, which results in fever and productive cough), are local disease effects. Tumors that have grown very large or metastasized to other structures in the chest may result in shortness of breath, chest pain, difficulty swallowing, hoarseness, radiating shoulder pain and cardiac abnormalities such as arrhythmia or heart failure.

Lung cancer most often metastasizes to the brain, liver and bone, and the clinical presentation of metastatic lung cancer can include symptoms related to these or any other affected organs. Brain metastasis may result in neurologic abnormalities; bone metastasis, pathologic fractures and spinal cord compression syndromes; and metastasis to the liver may result in pain, loss of appetite and elevated liver enzyme levels observed in blood tests.

Advanced lung cancer also may produce different *paraneoplastic syndromes,* so called because they are not directly related to the local effect of the tumor or to tumor metastasis. In some cases these syndromes result from the secretion of hormone by the tumor, but in most cases, the cause is unknown. For some patients, a paraneoplastic syndrome is among the symptoms of the disease. Generalized symptoms often include fatigue, weight loss, appetite loss, weakness, fever and suppressed immune system function. Manifestations of less common paraneoplastic syndromes include abnormal blood chemistry resulting from hormonal secretion by the tumor, and a syndrome that affects the bones and connective tissues to produce clubbing of the extremities, bone pain and tenderness. Hypercalcemia may occur as a complication of lung cancer and result in kidney failure and neurologic-type symptoms.

[b] Screening

Screening (testing for disease in asymptomatic persons) is an accepted part of the preventive approach in occupational settings with known exposure to carcinogens. The goal of screening is to detect disease at an early stage, when treatment would result in a better outcome. However, though screening detects disease more often and at an earlier stage than would otherwise occur, it has not been shown to reduce lung cancer mortality (Minna, 1991; Sepulveda, 1986).[10]

Screening is carried out using chest x-rays alone or in combination with sputum cytology (analysis of expectorate for the presence of cancer cells). X-ray is the more sensitive of the two tests—that is, it detects a higher proportion of existing lung cancers—but it is still not as highly sensitive as an ideal screening test would be. X-rays cannot detect lung lesions smaller than 1 cm. Sputum cytology is more specific than x-rays for detecting lung cancer; that is, a specific abnormality identified by sputum cytology is more likely to represent lung cancer than to be a "false-positive" finding. However, cytologic detection of cancer cells in the sputum requires an excellent sample and a highly experienced cytologist in order for the test to have validity.

Because these two tests tend to detect different types of lung cancers, combining them increases the yield of lung cancer screening (Sepulveda, 1986).

[c] Tissue Diagnosis

Tissue (or histologic) diagnosis is carried out to confirm that a lesion is malignant and to determine the cell type of the tumor. Histologic diagnosis can be performed on cytologic samples obtained by lavage (washing with fluids) or by needle aspiration (removed from the body through a fine needle), but other methods of obtaining a tissue sample are preferable, as they produce more accurate evaluations. Tissue may be obtained by a bronchoscopic biopsy of the lesion itself, of an

---

[10] *See* 15.12[3] *infra.*

affected lymph node or of a metastatic lesion. The cell type of the lesion can be determined using samples obtained at the time of surgical resection.

Lung cancer may arise as several different cell types. The four major cell (or histologic) types, which account for approximately 85 to 95 percent of lung cancer, are squamous (or epidermoid) carcinoma, small cell (or oat cell) carcinoma, adenocarcinoma and large cell carcinoma. In diagnosing lung cancer, it is important to identify the cell type, because small cell carcinoma is treated differently and has a poorer prognosis than other types.[11]

Certain histologic types are associated with different occupational exposures. However, this association is difficult to evaluate because cigarette smoking, age at diagnosis and the method of diagnosis also influence the observed frequency of different cell types. Thus, cell type is of limited usefulness as evidence that lung cancer in a particular individual is related to occupational exposure. The frequency of adenocarcinoma is increased in workers exposed to asbestos, and that of small cell carcinoma is higher in workers exposed to radon or to chloromethyl ether. Less pronounced associations have been observed in copper smelters between arsenic exposure and adenocarcinoma; these workers may also have a higher-than-expected frequency of poorly differentiated squamous cell carcinoma (Green and Vallyathan, 1986).[12]

[d] Staging

Cancer staging systems have been established to describe the severity of disease in a uniform manner. Staging is useful both for planning treatment and establishing a prognosis for individual patients and to make valid comparisons in studies.

Lung cancer staging is carried out on the basis of a complete patient history and physical examination, chest x-rays, tumor biopsy or other tissue sampling, bone marrow aspiration to detect metastasis and computed tomography (CT) scans of the chest and of other sites of suspected metastasis. Anatomic staging establishes the location and extent of the tumor. Physiologic staging, which is based on evidence of cardiac function, pulmonary function, smoking status and other

---

11 *See* 15.04[4] *infra.*

12 *See* 15.04 [1] *supra* for information on the association of cancer with exposure to these and other chemical carcinogens.

variables, takes additional factors into account to determine whether the patient can tolerate aggressive tumor treatment.

Non-small-cell lung cancer is staged anatomically using the TNM system, which serves as an international standard. *T* describes the tumor size, *N* the degree of lymph node involvement and *M* the presence or absence of metastatic disease. For example, "T2–N0–M0" describes a tumor that is greater than 3 cm in size but that has not metastasized to regional lymph nodes or distant organs. The numerous TNM categories are then grouped into stages (0 to IV) that reflect the overall severity of disease.

Small cell lung cancer is categorized into a simple two-stage system: limited and extensive stage disease. About 30 percent of patients with small cell cancer have limited stage disease at diagnosis, with disease confined to one side of the chest and sometimes the regional lymph nodes. Extensive stage disease is disease of any greater extent (Minna, 1991).

[3] Investigation of Occupational Exposure

Rarely, if ever, can lung cancer be definitively attributed to occupational carcinogen exposure. Even if the patient does not smoke, a certain amount of lung cancer arises spontaneously in nonsmokers. To determine whether an occupational exposure can be implicated in the development of lung cancer, two conditions must be met: the lung cancer must be the primary cancer (not a metastasis from a primary tumor arising at another site), and there must be adequate evidence that the patient has been exposed to a specific carcinogen on the job (Chase, et al., 1985).[13]

Evaluations of the likelihood that an occupational carcinogen contributed to cancer in an individual patient are new, rapidly evolving and highly imprecise. Evidence used to make such determinations may include the worker's history of exposure to the carcinogen, his or her smoking history and epidemiologic evidence about the risks of lung cancer in exposed and unexposed individuals.

[4] Treatment and Prognosis

The prognosis for lung cancer is poor and has not improved in recent years, despite many treatment developments. Only about 10 percent

---

[13] *See* 15.12 *infra* for information on the reduction of occupational exposures to carcinogens.

of patients are alive five years after lung cancer is diagnosed (Hodous and Melius, 1986). Even in patients with localized disease, five-year survival is only 30 percent in men and 50 percent in women (Minna, 1991).

[a]   Non-Small-Cell Carcinoma

Surgical resection is the primary treatment of non-small-cell carcinoma, but surgery is only carried out in the minority of patients who stand a reasonable chance to benefit by it. Surgical resection is confined to patients with stage I or II disease (tumors that have not spread outside the lung), and some with stage III disease (local spread within the chest, but no involvement of other major organs in the chest and no lymph node or distant metastases). Reduced lung function or cardiac abnormalities may contraindicate surgery even in patients with nonmetastatic disease.

Patients may be treated with either pneumonectomy (excision of the entire lung) or lobectomy (removal of one of the three lobes of the lung). Unless the tumor is small and well localized, surgery may be followed by radiotherapy. Radiotherapy alone is used to treat certain patients whose lung cancer is too far advanced for surgery. Patients with distant metastases may receive radiation or chemotherapy to treat the metastatic disease.

Fewer than half of the patients with lung cancer undergo surgery; the operation is judged to be definitive (to have removed all disease) in about three fourths of these patients. Nevertheless, the majority of patients thought to have "definitive" treatment die of metastatic disease, most within 2 years of the operation. About 30 percent survive for 5 years and 15 percent for 10 years (Minna, 1991).

Some patients develop occult (hidden) lung cancer, in which neoplastic cells are observed in the sputum sample but no disease is apparent on chest x-ray. Thorough examination of the lungs with a bronchoscope and sampling of the tissue will usually reveal the location of the lesion. These cancers are treated conservatively, with removal of the lesion and sparing of as much lung tissue as possible. The five-year survival rate for occult lung cancer is 60 percent (Minna, 1991).

[b]   Small Cell Carcinoma

Small cell carcinoma is highly lethal; without treatment, patients survive an average of 6 to 17 weeks after diagnosis (Minna, 1991).

However, small cell carcinoma is responsive to chemotherapy and radiotherapy. Patients are treated with relatively high dose multiagent induction chemotherapy, and those who respond to induction undergo cycles of maintenance chemotherapy. Chest radiotherapy may also be used, alone or in combination with chemotherapy, if the disease is localized to the chest. Patients with brain metastases, which are very common in small cell carcinoma, receive high-dose brain irradiation. The brain may also be irradiated prophylactically, to prevent the development of a metastasis. Such aggressive combination therapy may increase the duration of survival to a year or more.

15.05   MESOTHELIOMA

Mesothelioma is cancer of the mesothelium, a layer of epithelial cells covering several membranes that line the major body cavities. Mesothelioma is nearly always caused by exposure to asbestos, either in the workplace or the environment. Although the condition is occasionally benign, the form associated with asbestos exposure is among the most highly malignant of cancers.[14]

Mesothelial tissue covers the pericardium, a membrane that surrounds the heart, as well as the peritoneum, a membrane that lines the walls of the abdominal and pelvic cavities and is interspersed between the organs. Mesothelioma can develop at either of these sites, but it is most common in the pleural mesothelium, which affects the membrane that lines the thoracic cavity and encloses the lungs. (*See Figure 15–2.*)

[1]   Occupational Mesothelioma

An estimated 80 percent of cases of mesothelioma are thought to be caused by direct occupational exposure to asbestos (Speizer, 1991). When it is not directly related to occupation, mesothelioma results from asbestos exposures that are indirectly related to occupation, such as background levels of airborne asbestos in cities with large shipyards, or small amounts of asbestos that workers unwittingly introduce into their homes. The background incidence of mesothelioma (the number of cases not associated with asbestos exposure) is extremely low. Cigarette smoking does not contribute to the incidence of mesothelioma.

---

[14] *See also* ch. 16.

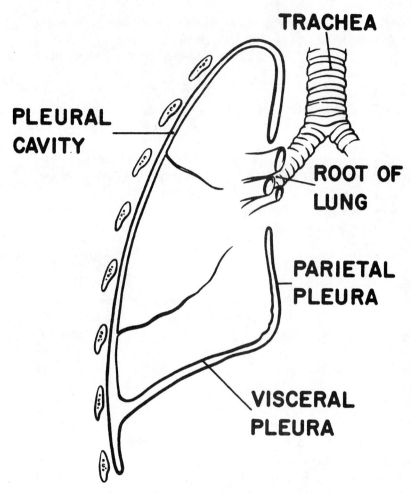

Fig. 15-2. The pleura lines the walls of the thoracic cavity. The portion that covers the lungs is referred to as the visceral pleura, and the portion that covers the chest wall is the parietal pleura.

The risk of mesothelioma is highest among individuals who work directly with asbestos, including miners, those who mill asbestos or work in factories where asbestos products are made, installers of insulation, shipbuilders and others who routinely inhale asbestos dust. The risk of mesothelioma increases with the level and duration of asbestos exposure. There has been some suggestion that higher exposures are related to the risk for peritoneal rather than pleural mesothelioma, though this association is uncertain (Fraumeni and Blot, 1982).[15]

The relationship between asbestos and mesothelioma is not a simple dose-response curve. Rather, mesothelioma can develop after very brief exposures to low levels of asbestos and has been reported among workers such as auto mechanics, drywall tapers and handlers of drywall cement, all of whom have only incidental contact with the material. This phenomenon also explains the "bystander effect": mesothelioma in persons who do not work with asbestos but merely near it, such as carpenters and painters in shipyards, maintenance workers in chemical plants and even automobile salespeople who supervise repair work. There have been numerous reports of mesothelioma in family members of asbestos workers, and the incidence of mesothelioma is increased among people who live within a 1-mile radius of an asbestos plant, shipyard or other source of contamination (Lilis, 1986).

The annual incidence of mesothelioma in the United States is 9 per million among white men and 3 per million in white women. The rates are lower in black men and women but difficult to determine precisely because so few cases occur. The incidence of mesothelioma is higher in places near sources of environmental contamination. In Washington, D.C., and coastal Virginia, where shipbuilding is a major industry, the annual rate surpasses 25 per million in men (Fraumeni and Blot, 1982).

The incidence of mesothelioma has been increasing since the condition was first observed some 30 years ago. Because of its long latency of 30 to 50 years, mesothelioma has its peak incidence in people at or near retirement age. It is often difficult to pinpoint past asbestos exposure in a person who develops mesothelioma, since he or she may have been exposed long ago during a temporary job. The development of mesothelioma in people who worked in shipyards for a few years during World War II has been established as a common scenario (Fraumeni and Blot, 1982).

[2] Diagnosis, Treatment and Prognosis

Malignant mesothelioma produces symptoms that include rapidly worsening unilateral chest pain and shortness of breath, weight loss,

---

[15] *See* 15.12[4] [a] *infra* for information on the prevention of occupational exposure to asbestos.

appetite loss, fatigue and sometimes cough or fever. Clear or bloody pleural effusions (leakage of fluid into the space enclosed by the membrane lining the lung) are often present. Mesothelioma is associated with two characteristic changes seen on x-ray: unilateral pleural effusion (congestion) and opacities protruding from the pleura into the lung tissue.

On rare occasions, mesothelioma can be definitively diagnosed by cytologic examination of pleural fluid obtained by aspiration. Mesothelioma can be diagnosed more easily with a pleural biopsy or by analysis of the tissues obtained on thoracotomy, an operation in which the chest is opened to obtain tissue to make the diagnosis. However, these procedures are dangerous, since tumor often grows along the track left by the needle or the surgical scar. Often the condition is not diagnosed until autopsy.

Mesothelioma is usually widespread by the time it becomes symptomatic, growing along the lining of the body cavities and eventually engulfing the enclosed organs. Pleural mesothelioma can spread to contiguous structures in the chest, such as the lung, liver, diaphragm or contralateral pleura. Lymph node involvement is also fairly common. Mesothelioma occasionally metastasizes to distant sites, including the brain, kidney, thyroid, adrenal glands and other organs. The disease progresses rapidly and is usually fatal within a year after diagnosis. No treatment is known to be effective.

Evaluating patients with mesothelioma for compensation is fairly straightforward. In virtually every case in which occupational asbestos exposure can be documented, the entire risk of cancer is assigned to the exposure, even if there is some small background environmental exposure (Chase, et al., 1985).

15.06 CANCERS OF THE UPPER RESPIRATORY TRACT

The upper respiratory tract includes the nasal passages, the oral cavity, the pharynx and the larynx. Some occupational carcinogens are known to affect the nasal passages and larynx.

[1] Nasal Carcinoma

Cancers of the nasal cavity and sinuses are uncommon and have their peak incidence in the sixth and seventh decades of life. Smoking increases the risk for these cancers, but not to the degree that it does for other respiratory malignancies (Calcaterra and Juillard, 1990b).[16]

[a]   Occupational Exposures

Cancer of the nasal passages or sinuses has been associated with occupational exposure to isopropyl alcohol, particularly among workers who manufacture isopropyl alcohol by a method called the strong acid process (Monson, 1990). There have been several reports of excess cases of nasal cancer in workers who are exposed to leather in the boot and shoe industry, and the risk of disease is elevated in persons who are exposed to wood dust, such as furniture makers and makers of wood patterns used in the automotive industry. Cases of nasal cancer have also been observed in several groups of workers in nickel refineries, though the cause is thought to be the exposure to furnace dust and fumes and not nickel itself, which is carcinogenic (Raffle, et al., 1987).

[b]   Diagnosis, Treatment and Prognosis

Tumors of the nasal cavity usually cause nasal airway obstruction and a runny nose, occasionally with bloody streaking of the nasal mucus. Because most tumors of the nasal sinuses are not detected until they are relatively large, symptoms are usually related to their size and include sinusitis (caused by blocking sinus drainage), facial pain and regional sensations of fullness, eye symptoms and symptoms related to the tumor's impingement on the cranial nerves.

Tumors of the nasal cavity may be examined directly through the nasal openings. Tumors of the sinuses usually are evaluated with x-rays and CT scan. A biopsy is performed to determine whether the tumor is malignant.

Tumors of the nasal cavity may be treated with either surgery or radiotherapy. With either method of treatment, the five-year survival rate is about 50 percent. Tumors of the nasal sinuses have a poorer prognosis, and for those involving the most internal of the sinuses, long-term survival is rare (Calcaterra and Juillard, 1990b). These tumors are treated with some combination of surgery and radiotherapy; chemotherapy may be employed as an adjunct. After treatment, many

---

[16] *See* 15.04 [1] *supra.*

patients wear a prosthetic device to restore a more normal appearance to the face.[17]

[2] Laryngeal Carcinoma

Cancer of the larynx is relatively common, representing about 1 percent of all cancer diagnosed in the United States. It has its peak incidence in men ages 60 to 65 (Calcaterra and Juillard, 1990a).

[a] Occupational Exposures

Carcinogens that predominantly affect the larynx are found in alcohol and tobacco. In retrospective studies, asbestos has been linked to laryngeal cancer, although this finding is still disputed. Elevated rates of laryngeal cancer have also been observed in several occupational groups for which it is difficult to pinpoint a carcinogen, including dock workers, sailors, meat cutters and sales clerks (Austin, 1982; Raffle, et al., 1987). Risk is also thought to be greater for workers who manufacture ethyl or isopropyl alcohol by the strong acid process (Monson, 1990).[18]

[b] Diagnosis, Treatment and Prognosis

Hoarseness is the predominant symptom of cancer of the larynx. Pain and difficulty swallowing may also be present. Tumors of the larynx are examined by palpating (examining manually) the larynx and viewing the tumor indirectly with a mirror. The extent of the lesion may be evaluated with CT or magnetic resonance imaging (MRI). A biopsy sample is obtained using a laryngoscope (a fiberoptic viewing device inserted into the throat under general or local anesthesia). Cancer of the larynx is staged with a "TNM" system reflecting the size and extent of the tumor, lymph node involvement and distant metastases.[19]

Combinations of surgery and radiotherapy are employed in treating cancers of the larynx. The prognosis depends to a great degree on the location of the tumor. Tumors of the glottis (the vocal cords) grow slowly and are unlikely to metastasize; when they are irradiated, the

---

[17] See 15.12[4] [1] infra for information regarding the reduction of occupational exposure to dusts.

[18] See 15.04 [1] supra for information regarding the carcinogenicity of these and other agents capable of producing cancer of the respiratory tract.

[19] See 15.04[2][d] supra.

five-year survival rate is 90 percent. Reconstructive surgery may be carried out to prevent future choking, ensure an open airway and aid in rehabilitation of the voice. Other laryngeal tumors have a poorer prognosis: their five-year survival rate ranges from about 50 percent to as low as 5 percent (Calcaterra and Juillard, 1990a).[20]

15.07   CANCERS OF THE GASTROINTESTINAL TRACT

Gastrointestinal (GI) cancers affect not only the GI tract itself—the esophagus, stomach, intestines and rectum—but also the other organs involved in digestion: the liver, pancreas and gallbladder. (*See Figure 15–3.*) Cancers of the gastrointestinal tract account for a fourth of all malignancies diagnosed in the United States and a third of all cancer deaths (Neugut and Wylie, 1987).

Because the incidence of gastrointestinal cancers varies widely among nations and population groups, it is believed that life-style, heredity and disposition as well as occupational and other environmental exposures play an important role in their development. Certain types of gastrointestinal cancer have definitely been associated with particular occupations and/or carcinogens. For other types, an association with occupation is only suspected or inconclusively established.

[1]   Esophageal Cancer

Cancer of the esophagus in the United States is relatively uncommon, but it is highly lethal. In the United States, this disease was diagnosed in about 10,000 individuals in 1989 and resulted in 9,400 deaths. In the United States and western Europe, esophageal cancer is more common in men than in women and far more common among blacks than whites. Most often, it appears in people over the age of 50 and is commonly associated with poverty (Mayer, 1991a).

Most epidemiologists believe that occupational exposures make only a small contribution to the incidence of esophageal cancer. In the United States, the vast majority of this type of cancer is believed to be caused by cigarette smoking, the consumption of alcoholic beverages and the interaction of the two. Physical damage to the esophagus, caused by consumption of hot foods or liquids, or by exposure to therapeutic irradiation, also increases the risk. Other

---

[20] *See* 15.12 *infra* for information regarding the reduction of occupational exposure to carcinogens implicated in laryngeal cancer.

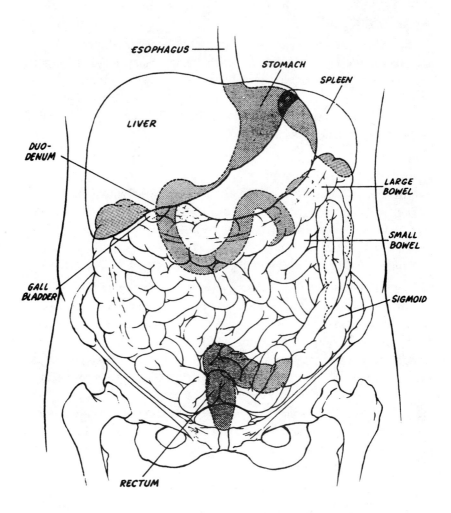

Fig. 15-3. Lateral view of the abdominal organs.

contributing causes include heredity, a deficiency of certain vitamins or minerals and smoked opium (Alderson, 1986; Mayer, 1991a).

[a] Occupational Exposures

Esophageal cancer has not been conclusively associated with any particular job category, occupational process or carcinogen. The low incidence of this type of cancer in general, combined with the overwhelming contribution of nonoccupational risk factors, makes the epidemiologic investigation of possible occupational associations extremely difficult.

The evidence is strongest for a link with asbestos. Studies of the association of asbestos exposure with esophageal cancer—and, in fact, with all gastrointestinal cancers—have had inconsistent results, however. There is no clear causal relationship, but it has been suggested that asbestos fibers present in food and drinking water may be a factor in the development of such cancers.[21]

In the workplace, asbestos is primarily an airborne contaminant. It is assumed, however, that the main portal of entry for asbestos as a gastrointestinal carcinogen is by mouth. Presumably, without adequate worker protection, airborne carcinogens can contaminate food, the sputum or the hands, and then may be ingested inadvertently. However, ingested asbestos has not been shown consistently to cause gastrointestinal cancer in experimental animals (Levine, 1985).

Some studies of asbestos workers have shown that there is no excess risk of esophageal cancer, while others have shown esophageal cancer death rates several times as high as in the general population (Levine, 1985). There is some evidence that of all the sites within the gastrointestinal tract that are exposed to ingested asbestos, the esophagus is the most vulnerable to its carcinogenic effects. Since it is possible that the risk of stomach and colorectal cancer in asbestos workers is elevated, it seems reasonable to assume that there are elevated risks for esophageal cancer as well (Neugut and Wylie, 1987). The latency period for gastrointestinal cancer may be as long as 20 to 40 years after the initial asbestos exposure (Levine, 1985).[22]

Some, but not all, workers in the rubber industry are at excess risk of developing esophageal cancer. Vulcanization workers are probably at increased risk, though the responsible carcinogenic substance has not been identified. It has been suggested that excess risk of esophageal cancer may occur in some jobs that are associated with a high rate of alcohol consumption and among workers in occupations involving metal work, such as plumbers, brass and bronze workers and electrical apparatus makers (Day and Munoz, 1982). Members of other job categories for which evidence of excess esophageal cancer risk is still

---

[21] *See also* ch. 16 *supra.*

[22] *See* 15.03 *supra.*

inconclusive include painters, woodworkers, laborers, roofers and some manufacturing jobs (Neugut and Wylie, 1987).[23]

[b] Diagnosis, Treatment and Prognosis

The first symptom of esophageal cancer is usually dysphagia—a painful difficulty in swallowing food. Dysphagia is a result of a narrowing of the esophagus due to tumor growth and usually results in a loss of appetite, with consequent weight loss. As the tumor grows, the symptoms become progressively worse, until the patient cannot swallow even liquids. The pain on swallowing radiates to the chest or back. Dysphagia usually does not occur until the tumor is quite advanced; hence, early diagnosis of esophageal cancer is uncommon. In any case, treatment is difficult and the prognosis poor. Fewer than 5 percent of all patients with esophageal cancer are alive five years after diagnosis, and the survival rate for patients whose tumors can be surgically resected is still under 20 percent (Mayer, 1991a).

If esophageal cancer is suspected, further investigations include routine contrast x-rays to localize the lesion. Because tumors that are small enough to be surgically resected can be difficult to see on x-ray, esophagoscopy (visualization through a fiberoptic viewing tube) should be carried out. The esophagoscope can also be used to obtain a small sample of tissue from the lesion for histologic examination to confirm malignancy. Since esophageal tumors often spread to neighboring regions of the gastrointestinal tract, these structures should be examined through an endoscope as well.

A minority of patients have esophageal tumors small enough for surgical resection, but these operations are associated with a postoperative death rate of about 20 percent. Patients who are poor surgical risks receive initial radiotherapy, sometimes combined with chemotherapy. Although such treatments are rarely curative, they may shrink the tumor, palliate symptoms and prolong life somewhat (Mayer, 1991a).

[2] Stomach Cancer

For unknown reasons, the worldwide incidence of stomach cancer has decreased markedly since the early twentieth century, when it was by far the leading cause of cancer in American men. In 1989, 20,000

---

[23] *See* 15.12[4] [a] *infra* for information on the prevention of occupational exposure to asbestos.

cases were diagnosed and 13,900 deaths were attributed to gastric cancer (Mayer, 1991a).

The risk of gastric cancer is elevated among the poor. Other risk factors include familial susceptibility, a diet low in fresh fruits and vegetables, and possibly cigarette smoking as well (Alderson, 1986). Also implicated is the long-term consumption of foods that are preserved by such means as salting, smoking or drying, which give foods a high nitrite content (Mayer, 1991a).

[a] Occupational Exposures

A number of substances in the workplace have been associated with stomach cancer risk, including asbestos and dust particles. Several studies have documented excess risk among asbestos-exposed workers employed in mining, shipyards, insulation manufacture and installation as well as plumbing and pipefitting (Neugut and Wylie, 1987).

Excess stomach cancer rates have been reported in several occupational groups that have a high exposure to airborne dust, such as underground miners, though the association of gastric cancer with poverty may also account for some of its excess incidence among miners. Dust can be ingested in two ways: directly by way of the hands or the food itself, or after it has been inhaled by being coughed up and inadvertently swallowed (Wright, et al., 1988).

Other occupational dusts associated with stomach cancer risk include wood dust (in woodworkers and particularly pattern makers, who construct wood prototypes for mass-produced machinery such as automobiles), silica (in stonecutters), talc, alumina and silica carbide (in jewelers and manufacturers of synthetic abrasives) and nickel dust (in refinery workers). Although it is assumed that the "dirty" quality of the air, as opposed to the characteristics of individual dusts, is responsible for the excess stomach cancer risk (Neugut and Wylie, 1987), at least one study suggests that metallic dusts are more potent carcinogens than other dusts (Wright, et al., 1988).

Exposure to chemicals may also increase the risk for stomach cancer, though the association is less clear than for dusts. Occupational groups that may be at increased risk from chemical exposure include petroleum refinery workers, printers (who are exposed to solvents, dyes and inks) and workers who are exposed to cutting oils (Neugut and Wylie, 1987).[24]

---

[24] *See* 15.12[4][a], 15.12[4] [k] and 15.12[4] [l] *infra* for information regarding the reduction of occupational exposure to asbestos and carcinogenic oils and dusts.

[b]   Diagnosis, Treatment and Prognosis

Stomach cancers typically are not symptomatic until well advanced. The initial symptom of stomach cancer is usually an abdominal sensation that may range from discomfort after meals to constant, severe pain. Patients eventually develop anorexia, a wasting syndrome that includes loss of appetite and loss of weight. Nausea, vomiting and dysphagia (difficulty swallowing) sometimes occur. A palpable abdominal mass does not develop until the cancer is far advanced. Stomach cancer is diagnosed with a contrast x-ray, and gastroscopy (examination through a viewing device extended through the mouth and esophagus) may be carried out to confirm the diagnosis.

The optimal treatment for stomach cancer is resection of the tumor and the lymph nodes adjacent to the stomach. If the tumor is proximal—located in the upper stomach near the esophagus—the resection involves a total or near-total gastrectomy (surgical removal of the stomach); however, for distal tumors, a partial gastrectomy may be adequate. Only about 25 to 30 percent of patients have their cancer diagnosed while it can still be surgically resected. Patients who are treated surgically have a five-year survival rate of about 25 percent for distal tumors and 10 percent for proximal (Mayer, 1991a).

The prognosis is very poor for patients with unresectable gastric tumors. Radiation therapy is generally ineffective, and patients' responses to chemotherapy are partial and transient.

[3]   Colorectal Cancer

Tumors of the small intestine are relatively uncommon and not associated with occupational exposures. By contrast, cancer of the large intestine—called colorectal cancer—is one of the most common malignancies and probably involves some occupational risk factors. Second only to lung cancer as a cause of cancer mortality, colorectal cancer was diagnosed in an estimated 150,000 Americans in 1989 and resulted in over 61,000 deaths (Mayer, 1991b).

Colorectal cancer has been the subject of much research concerning causation and risk, prevention and early detection. The two major risk factors for colorectal cancer appear to be diet and hereditary predisposition. The association of the disease with higher socioeconomic status, its greater incidence in urban than in rural areas and its low incidence among Mormons and Seventh-Day Adventists may all be associated with different dietary patterns in these populations. Colorectal cancer is associated with the so-called typical Western diet, though it is not known exactly which nutrients contribute to risk and by what mechanisms.

Diets that are high in animal fats and low in fiber— the menu that has been adopted in most affluent industrialized countries— are thought to be the predominant cause of colorectal cancer. Calcium supplementation of the diet reduces risk for the disease. Heredity, the second major risk factor, is implicated in up to 25 percent of patients with colorectal cancer (Mayer, 1991b).

[a] Occupational Exposures

Although the occurrence of colorectal cancer is not thought to be heavily influenced by occupational factors, researchers have identified that some exposures, when they are combined with a low level of physical activity and a high level of stress on the job, predispose individuals to disease (Mayer, 1991b).

Several studies have shown that persons in physically active jobs— for example, farmers and foresters—have lower rates of colorectal cancer than people in sedentary white-collar positions such as administrators, clerical workers, bankers and professionals (Neugut and Wylie, 1987). It has been suggested that people who are active all day have increased bowel activity, which may be the mechanism by which risk is reduced. In active workers who are exposed to high levels of carcinogens, physical activity may have a protective effect (Fredriksson, et al., 1989).

One large population-based study of American workers showed that colorectal cancer was associated with stressful jobs (those that placed high demands on the worker, but over which the worker had little control). Other stressful aspects of work that were associated with colorectal cancer included job insecurity, a heavy work load and frequent conflicts (Spiegelman and Wegman, 1985).

Asbestos is widely (although not universally) accepted as a colorectal carcinogen. The authoritative International Association for Research on Cancer (IARC) lists asbestos as a Group 1 colorectal carcinogen (indicating that there is ample evidence of carcinogenicity in both animals and humans)[25] (Swanson, 1988), but some authors find the evidence inconclusive (Neugut and Wylie, 1987; Weiss,

---

[25] *See* 15.12 *infra.*

1990). The body of research is flawed, because many studies involve only small numbers of patients and group all gastrointestinal cancers together rather than separating them by site within the GI tract. Some studies of asbestos-exposed workers are confounded by the protective effect of physical activity, or include cases of peritoneal mesothelioma (a rare cancer derived from the cells of the lining of the abdominal cavity, associated with asbestos exposure) that are misdiagnosed as gastrointestinal cancer.

Excess risk for colorectal cancer has been observed in people who work with wood or metal, in occupations such as abrasives manufacture, metal works, machinists, millwrights, copper smelters, and wood pattern and model makers. These workers may be exposed to carcinogenic cutting and lubricating oils, metal or wood dusts, solvents and abrasives (Neugut and Wylie, 1987). Textile and leather workers appear to be at increased risk as a result of exposure to dyes, solvents and metallic compounds. One chemical used to produce synthetic fibers, acrylonitrile, is a proven gastrointestinal carcinogen in animals, and there is limited evidence of its carcinogenicity in humans (Schottenfeld and Winawer, 1982; Swanson, 1988). Some studies have suggested that rubber and chemical workers are also at increased risk for colorectal cancer, but the evidence is not conclusive; neither has the role of dusts or fibers been firmly established (Neugut and Wylie, 1987).[26]

[b] Diagnosis, Treatment and Prognosis

Colorectal cancer often does not produce noticeable symptoms until it is advanced. However, it is possible to screen for colorectal cancer in asymptomatic individuals.

Because the peak incidence of colorectal cancer occurs in people over the age of 50, screening tests are recommended at periodic intervals in asymptomatic middle-aged and older persons. Screening guidelines vary, but one typical recommendation is for the physician to conduct a digital rectal examination as part of the regular medical examination of all persons over 40 years of age (Mayer, 1991b). Cancer screening may also be carried out by testing a stool sample to determine whether the patient is bleeding rectally, or by using a

---

[26] See 15.12[4] [a], 15.12[4] [k] and 15.12[4] [l] infra for information regarding the reduction of occupational exposure to asbestos and carcinogenic oils and dusts.

proctoscope or sigmoidoscope to visualize as much of the inner surface of the bowel as can be seen.

If screening examinations do not detect cancer, they may still detect polyps—small protrusions growing from the bowel wall. Although it is believed that most colorectal cancers develop from polyps, the reverse is not necessarily true: Thirty percent of all middle-aged or elderly persons develop polyps, but only rarely do these lesions become malignant (Mayer, 1991b). Nevertheless, the presence of polyps may indicate a need for more frequent screening or a biopsy.

Finally, screening for colorectal cancer is recommended in some occupational settings.[27] Yet for all the discussion about screening for colorectal cancer, it has not been conclusively demonstrated that screening results in an increase in the cure rate for patients with colorectal cancer. Thus the optimal screening schedule—and screening itself—remain a matter of controversy (Mayer, 1991b).

If colorectal cancer is not detected by screening, the first symptom a patient notices may be bleeding from the rectum, altered bowel habits, abdominal cramping or a narrowing in the caliber of the stool caused by bowel obstruction. Since patients may bleed into the stool a great deal without noticing it, anemia may be the first sign of colorectal cancer.

The diagnosis of colorectal cancer is made by barium enema—in which the empty bowel is infused with contrast material and an x-ray is made—and by colonoscopy, during which the tumor is viewed and a tissue biopsy sample is taken for analysis. The regional lymph nodes are sampled during the operation in which the tumor is resected. The presence of nodal or distant disease also influences the disease stage determination and the prognosis.

The prognosis is good for patients whose tumor growth is limited to the mucosa and submucosa (the most superficial layers of the bowel lining), with five-year survival rates greater than 90 percent. In patients with lymph node involvement, the five-year-survival rate ranges from 30 percent to 60 percent, depending in part on how many lymph nodes are affected. Survival of five years is uncommon in patients who have metastatic disease. The liver is the main initial site of cancer metastasis from the bowel (Mayer, 1991b).[28]

---

27 *See* 15.12 [3] *infra.*

28 *See* 15.07[4] *infra.*

Complete surgical resection of the tumor is carried out as the primary treatment whenever possible, even in patients with metastatic disease. Since colorectal cancer may recur even after what appears to be complete surgical resection, patients may receive radiation therapy either before or after the operation to reduce the likelihood of a recurrence. Patients who appear to be cured by surgery receive frequent physical examinations and other tests in the years following treatment to find any early recurrences. Chemotherapy is not uniformly beneficial for patients with colorectal cancer, but it may benefit some subgroups.

[c] Medical Screening for Colorectal Cancer in the Workplace

Colorectal cancer screening is carried out in some occupational settings where the risk of cancer is known to be increased, even in the absence of known exposure to a clearly documented carcinogen. Cancer screening of pattern makers in the automotive industry is one well studied example of a program that was instituted in response to requests from union members (Bang, et al., 1986; Hoar, et al., 1986).

Fecal occult (hidden) blood tests, digital rectal examinations and flexible sigmoidoscopy are the main tests used to screen for colorectal cancer. Though it is widely advocated, the value of fecal occult blood testing remains controversial. In one study of pattern makers, fecal occult blood testing was found to be inadequately sensitive; that is, it missed a substantial number of cancers that were detected by sigmoidoscopy (Bang, et al., 1986). Occult blood in the feces is associated with colorectal cancer in fewer than 10 percent of asymptomatic people; thus positive test results may lead to expensive and uncomfortable additional tests in many people who do not have cancer (Mayer, 1991b). However, other authors believe fecal blood testing to be an excellent screening test for colorectal cancer, as it is easy to use, inexpensive and specific (not likely to be falsely positive if there is no blood in the stool) (Haskell, et al., 1990).

Another serious shortcoming of fecal blood testing is that, according to several studies, only a third of those who are advised to use the tests comply with this advice (Haskell, et al., 1990). Patients must sample their own stool on three successive days, using specially treated paper, and the samples are sent to a laboratory for analysis. The result can be positive for patients who have failed to follow the instructions to avoid eating red meat during the days immediately preceding the test. Patients who are positive for fecal occult blood usually repeat the test after they have been on a special diet, and a second positive test indicates the need for additional studies.

Digital rectal examinations and sigmoidoscopy are screening examinations that are carried out in the physician's office. The digital examination, which is simple to carry out and can detect other conditions as well as rectal masses, is recommended as a routine part of the annual medical examination in persons over age 40. The limitation of this technique, of course, is that its range is limited to pathology of the rectum. Sigmoidoscopy allows the physician to view the inside surface of the first 60 cm of the bowel, using a flexible fiberoptic instrument.

[4]   Liver Cancer

Liver cancer is relatively uncommon, accounting for between 1 and 2 percent of malignant tumors. The prognosis, however, is grim: Most patients die within three to six months of diagnosis (Isselbacher and Wands, 1991). Risk factors for liver cancer include heavy alcohol consumption, any type of chronic liver disease (such as cirrhosis or some metabolic diseases) and infection with the hepatitis B virus.

[a]   Occupational Exposures

The liver is one of two main routes for excretion of carcinogens that enter the circulation (the other is the kidney), and it is the main route for excretion of carcinogens that enter the circulation by means of the digestive tract. Thus the liver is exposed to many systemic carcinogens.

A marked excess of a relatively rare type of liver cancer, hepatic angiosarcoma, has been observed in workers who were exposed to vinyl chloride. These workers may have four times the risk of liver cancer of comparable unexposed groups (Alderson, 1986). The International Association for Research on Cancer (IARC) classifies vinyl chloride as a Group 1 carcinogen, which means there is ample evidence of carcinogenicity in both animals and humans.[29] Various investigators have identified the latency period for vinyl-chloride-induced liver cancer. It may begin 10 to 15 years after the initial exposure but take as long as 28 years to express itself (Neugut, et al., 1987).

---

29 *See* 15.12 *infra.*

Occupational exposure to arsenic (which is mined, used in smelting and incorporated into pesticides) may also increase the risk for liver cancer. Farmers and agricultural workers may have an elevated rate of liver cancer due to arsenic exposure, though the data is not conclusive.

There is limited evidence that liver cancer is associated with exposure to solvents, various chemicals used in woodworking, formaldehyde and cutting oils. For unknown reasons, the risk may be elevated for workers in the rubber industry. Evidence concerning asbestos exposure is inconclusive (Neugut, et al., 1987). Occupations involved with the manufacture or sale of alcoholic beverages are also associated with an increased risk of liver cancer, perhaps as a result of alcohol consumption (Alderson, 1986; Neugut, et al., 1987).

Health care workers may be exposed to the hepatitis B virus, which is a risk factor for liver cancer. Hepatitis B is an infectious disease that can be acquired by means of exposure to blood, tissues and body fluids infected with the hepatitis B virus. A minority of people who are infected with this virus become asymptomatic carriers: They continue to appear healthy but are chronically infected and can transmit the virus to others. It is these chronically infected carriers who are at risk of developing liver cancer. According to one report, 1 percent of health care workers may be chronic carriers of the hepatitis B virus (Dienstag, et al., 1991). Occupational groups at increased risk include surgeons, pathologists, medical technologists who draw or work with blood, hemodialysis personnel and any others who are frequently exposed to blood (Dienstag, et al., 1991).

[b]   Diagnosis, Treatment and Prognosis

The prognosis for liver cancer is extremely poor. Some patients with the disease die before it is diagnosed, because they have another liver condition, such as cirrhosis (progressive disease of the liver, with overgrowth and impairment of function and structure), which is also fatal and has symptoms similar to liver cancer.

Hepatomegaly (a palpable enlargement of the liver) with pain or tenderness or a mass in the liver may be the first sign of liver cancer. Usually these signs do not appear until the disease is too far advanced for treatment to have any effect. In patients with other conditions that place them at risk for liver cancer, screening tests may help identify early disease. These include ultrasound imaging and blood tests for alpha-fetoprotein or elevated alkaline phosphatase, two biochemical markers that suggest the presence of liver cancer.

When a person is suspected of having liver cancer, the physician can utilize a variety of imaging techniques, such as ultrasound, magnetic resonance imaging (MRI), computed tomography (CT) scanning or hepatic artery angiography (imaging the major blood vessels of the liver after injecting contrast material into them). A biopsy can be helpful, but it may sometimes fail to locate the tumor. In some patients, the diagnosis is made by means of an open liver biopsy.

If the patient has a single, small tumor, surgical resection may be attempted, but few patients have operable tumors, and the likelihood of prolonged survival even after resection is low. Liver transplants have been attempted in some patients with liver cancer, but these have had limited success because the tumors often recur or metastasize (spread to distant sites) (Isselbacher and Wands, 1991).[30]

[5] Cancer of the Biliary Tract

The gallbladder and the various ducts through which bile is conducted make up the biliary tract. The gallbladder is a small organ located on the rear surface of the liver. It acts as a reservoir for bile, a yellowish green or brown fluid secreted by the liver and used in the digestion and absorption of nutrients in the small intestine.

Cancers of the biliary tract account for a small percentage of all malignancies in the United States, with an annual incidence of about 6,500 cases of gallbladder cancer and a far lower incidence of cancers affecting other structures of the biliary tract. Gallbladder cancer affects four times as many women as men. The average age of onset is 70 years (Greenberger and Isselbacher, 1991; Neugut, et al., 1987). Most patients with cancers of the biliary tract die within the first year after diagnosis.

[a] Occupational Exposures

There has been relatively little research into occupational risk factors for biliary tract cancer, in part because these tumors are uncommon. Since the disease occurs primarily in elderly women, the relationship to occupation is obscure. However, since the gallbladder

---

[30] *See also* 15.12[4][c], 15.12[4] [e] and 15.12[4] [k] *infra* for information regarding the reduction of occupational exposure to arsenic, vinyl chloride and cutting oils.

and its ducts are exposed to systemic carcinogens during their excretion, it is reasonable to suppose that these structures are at risk from such exposure.

A few surveys have shown that rubber, auto, chemical and asbestos workers all have increased risks of biliary cancer. Similarly, elevated rates of gallbladder cancer are seen in the rubber, chemical, auto, textile, metal fabricating, petroleum, paper and shoe industries. The risk for bile duct cancer may be increased for workers in the asbestos, aircraft, automotive, chemical, rubber and wood finishing industries. Cancer of the ampulla of Vater, a structure that joins the biliary tract to the digestive tract, is associated with employment in the chemical and rubber industries (Neugut, et al., 1987).

Experimental studies in animals have identified several chemicals that are capable of causing cancer in the biliary tract. However, little is known about the nature of specific exposures that may occur in different occupations.

[b]   Diagnosis, Treatment and Prognosis

The most common initial signs of gallbladder cancer are abdominal pain associated with weight loss, jaundice (yellow appearance caused by deposition of bile pigment in the skin) and a palpable abdominal mass. Once these symptoms have appeared, it is likely that the disease has spread beyond the gallbladder. Unless the tumor is discovered incidentally during an abdominal operation for another reason, the likelihood of long-term survival is negligible. Three fourths of patients have inoperable cancer at the time of diagnosis, and 95 percent of them die within the year. Of all patients, including those with operable tumors, only 5 percent survive for five years. Chemotherapy and radiation therapy offer no benefit in the treatment of gallbladder cancer (Greenberger and Isselbacher, 1991).

Patients with cancer of the bile ducts (called cholangiocarcinoma) have biliary obstruction, jaundice, weight loss and sometimes vague abdominal pain. They may have a palpably enlarged liver or gallbladder. These tumors are diagnosed by cholangiography, a procedure in which dye is injected endoscopically into the bile ducts, which are then visualized radiographically. The prognosis for this tumor is very poor, though chemotherapy and radiotherapy are sometimes used in an attempt to ameliorate symptoms.

Jaundice is the main presenting symptom of cancer of the ampulla of Vater, which is also diagnosed by endoscopic cholangiography. These cancers are treated by surgical excision. If the disease is localized, as many as 40 percent of patients may survive for five years, but if lymph node metastases are present, the prognosis is much worse (Greenberger and Isselbacher, 1991).[31]

[6]   Pancreatic Cancer

The pancreas, which is located behind the stomach, secretes digestive enzymes into the upper small intestine and manufactures insulin, a regulator of carbohydrate metabolism. Any failure of this organ, whether it is caused by cancer or another disease, is rapidly fatal except for the rare instances when the cancer can be surgically resected. Pancreatic cancer is the fifth most common cause of cancer mortality in the United States, responsible for about 25,000 deaths a year (Mayer, 1991c).

Compared to other cancers, little is known about the causes of pancreatic cancer. Cigarette smoking is the only well established risk factor. Dietary studies suggest that the risk for pancreatic cancer may be increased by heavy consumption of alcohol, fats and some meats. On the other hand, a diet high in fresh fruits and vegetables may have a protective effect. However, none of these associations is firmly established (Fontham and Correa, 1989).

[a]   Occupational Exposures

Many studies have explored possible associations between occupation and the occurrence of pancreatic cancer, but there have been few, if any, consistent results. Several occupational groups have been shown to be at increased risk for pancreatic cancer, but not in any pattern that could be interpreted in a logical way or that points to any particular workplace carcinogen. The only group mentioned as being at risk in a large number of surveys is the job category of "stationary engineer." Individuals in this position, who have only a small excess risk of pancreatic cancer, are employed watching over power plants in factories. However, it is not clear to what particular hazardous activity or carcinogen these workers are exposed. Other employment categories that may be associated with an elevated risk for pancreatic

---

[31] *See* 15.12 *infra* for information regarding the reduction of occupational exposures to carcinogens.

cancer include managers and administrators, paper workers, metal workers, timber workers, dentists, chemists and electrical workers (Mack, 1982).

[b] Diagnosis, Treatment and Prognosis

Jaundice is usually the initial presenting symptom of pancreatic cancer, followed within a short time by abdominal pain, loss of appetite and weight loss. Noninvasive diagnostic procedures, such as blood tests and imaging, often fail to detect or confirm pancreatic cancer, and the diagnosis must often await a surgical biopsy. Complete surgical resection of the tumor, the only treatment that offers hope of long-term survival, is possible in only 10 to 15 percent of patients. Patients whose tumors cannot be resected survive an average of five months after the diagnosis is made; those who can undergo surgical resection have a five-year survival rate of 10 percent (Mayer, 1991c).[32]

15.08 CANCERS OF THE GENITOURINARY TRACT

The urinary tract is one of the two primary routes by which systemic carcinogens are cleared from the body. (The other is the liver.[33]) The urinary tract is commonly exposed to certain carcinogens, and the bladder is the third most common site of occupational cancer, after the lungs and skin.

Several occupational bladder carcinogens were documented in the last decade (Schulte, et al., 1987). Elevated rates of kidney cancer are also associated with certain occupations, though the role of specific carcinogenic substances in the kidney is less well established. Occupational associations have been described for cancer of the prostate.[34] Other male reproductive organs and the female reproductive system do not seem to be at risk for cancer from occupational exposures.

[1] Bladder Cancer

Each year cancer of the urinary bladder is diagnosed in 40,000 people in the United States and accounts for 11,000 deaths. Bladder

---

[32] *See* 15.12 *infra* for information regarding the reduction of occupational exposures to carcinogens.

[33] *See* 15.07[4] *supra.*

[34] *See* 15.08[3] *infra.*

cancer affects three times as many men as women and usually occurs after the age of 40 (Garnick and Brenner, 1991). Cigarette smoking may increase the risk of bladder cancer two- to four-fold (Alderson, 1986).

[a] Occupational Exposures

Occupational exposures contribute significantly to the incidence of bladder cancer. Estimates of the proportion of bladder cancers attributable to job exposures are variable, ranging from as low as 0 to 3 percent to as high as 24 percent in different populations, depending in part on their respective frequency of exposure to bladder carcinogens (Vineis and Simonato, 1991). About 10 percent of all bladder cancer in the United States may be attributable to occupational exposures (Doll and Peto, 1981).

Bladder cancer was among the earliest occupational cancers to be recognized when it was reported in 1895. This was approximately 20 years after the widespread introduction of aromatic amines into the synthetic dye industry, a period consistent with the known latency of bladder cancers (Schulte, et al., 1987). Subsequent epidemiologic studies have shown bladder cancer risk to be increased among workers who are exposed to the aromatic amines 2–naphthylamine, magenta, benzidine and auramine (Alderson, 1986).

The International Association for Research on Cancer (IARC) lists four bladder carcinogens among the substances it says show strong evidence of carcinogenicity in humans: 4–aminobiphenyl, benzidine, 2–naphthylamine and the group of soots, tars and oils. In addition, among its list of occupations definitely associated with cancer risk at specific body sites, the IARC lists auramine manufacture, boot and shoe repair, and the rubber industry as associated with bladder cancer (Swanson, 1988).

Epidemiologic studies have shown bladder cancer risk to be elevated among workers who are involved in the manufacture of dyes using aromatic amines but not among workers who use these dyes once they are manufactured unless the use involves some unusual process, such as drying or grinding the dyes (Schulte, et al., 1987). Bladder cancer risk may be elevated among rubber industry workers as a result of exposure to these dyes (Morrison and Cole, 1982).

MDA (4,4′-methyline-dianiline), a chemical that is structurally similar to benzidine, may also be associated with a threefold increase in bladder cancer risk in exposed workers (Schulte, et al., 1987). MDA is used primarily in the manufacture of polyurethane foam. MOCA (4,4′-methylenebis(2–chloroaniline)), another aromatic amine, can cause bladder cancer in animals and is a suspected bladder carcinogen in humans. MOCA has not been manufactured in the United States since 1979, but workers in the polyurethane industry may still be exposed to this substance (Schulte, et al., 1987).

The excess risk of bladder cancer in the boot and shoe industry and in other jobs involving work with leather may be associated with the dusty environment in which these jobs are carried out (Morrison and Cole, 1982). The risk of bladder cancer is elevated among truck drivers and, variably, other workers who are exposed to motor vehicle exhausts, implicating polycyclic aromatic hydrocarbons (PAHs) as the cause (Risch, et al., 1988).

A large study involving Italian workers found bladder cancer risk to be associated with exposure to dyes or paints, chemicals, herbicides and gases or fumes (la Vecchia, et al., 1990). A similar study involving American workers confirmed that bladder cancer risk was high in several previously suspect occupational categories, including truck mechanics, petroleum refinery workers, hairdressers, barbers and metal workers (Silverman, et al., 1989). Hairdressers exposed to hair dyes may have an increased risk of bladder cancer (Steineck, et al., 1990). Pesticide exposure may be associated with bladder cancer in pesticide manufacturers, crop sprayers and nursery workers (Zahm, et al., 1987).

Numerous epidemiologic studies suggest that the latency period for occupational bladder cancer may be extremely variable, perhaps because of the varying potency of different carcinogens. Studies have shown average latency periods as short as 18 years and as long as 45 years. The incidence of occupational bladder cancer in a group of exposed workers may begin to rise above background levels as early as 2 years after exposure begins (Morrison and Cole, 1982).

[b] Diagnosis, Treatment and Prognosis

Hematuria (blood in the urine) is the most common presenting symptom of bladder cancer and may be noticed either visibly by the person or microscopically in a urine sample. Other persons with bladder cancer may complain initially of pain on urination or the frequent, urgent need to urinate. Bladder cancer can be detected by screening of asymptomatic individuals.[15]

---

[15] *See* 15.12 [3] *infra.*

If cancer is suspected, urinary cytology—microscopic examination for the presence of abnormal cells—is carried out on a urine sample or a bladder washing. Intravenous pyelography (IVP), a diagnostic test in which contrast material is injected into the blood and passes rapidly into the urine, allows x-ray visualization of the kidneys, ureter and bladder. Cystoscopy allows the insertion of a fiberoptic viewing device into the bladder for direct viewing to obtain tissue samples for analysis. If cancer is present, abdominal or pelvic CT scanning may be carried out to assess the extent of disease. (*See Figure 15–4.*)

Patients whose bladder tumors are localized may be treated very simply and have an excellent likelihood of long-term survival. Tumors that are localized to the inner layer of the bladder wall may be resected through an endoscope inserted through the urethra, the tube via which urine leaves the body. After localized lesions are resected, patients must continue to undergo cystoscopy at intervals to detect any disease

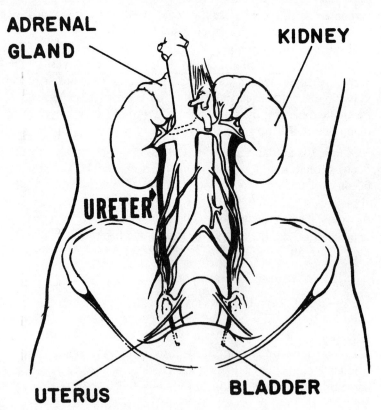

ADRENAL
GLAND

KIDNEY

URETER

UTERUS

BLADDER

Fig. 15-4. Frontal view of the female genitourinary tract.

recurrences, which occur in more than half of patients. Disease recurrences usually appear within a year and are similar in invasiveness to the original tumor (Whitmore, 1990). Superficial recurrences are treated with a second endoscopic resection, as well as intravesical (within the bladder) chemotherapy or immunotherapy. Only about 12 percent of patients treated in this way go on to develop invasive disease (Garnick and Brenner, 1991).

Patients with disease that invades the muscle of the bladder itself or the surrounding fat are treated with cystectomy, an operation in which affected portions of the bladder and disease-free margins are removed. Although cystectomy is often radical, surgeons may try to use less aggressive procedures that allow the patient to continue to urinate normally, if this can be done without compromising survival. If bladder-sparing surgery is not possible, the patient must wear an external ostomy appliance to collect and dispose of urine. Patients may receive radiation therapy either before or after cystectomy, and chemotherapy is sometimes offered as well.

About 45 percent of patients with invasive bladder cancer survive for five years. Patients who present with or who develop metastatic disease undergo chemotherapy, but prolonged responses are rare. Most patients with metastatic disease die within two years (Garnick and Brenner, 1991).

[c] Medical Screening for Bladder Cancer in Industry

Bladder cancer is fairly common. Certain occupations are known to contribute significantly to bladder cancer incidence, and specific bladder carcinogens and high-risk jobs have been identified. These factors, combined with the bladder's relatively easy access for medical evaluation, would appear to make bladder cancer screening widely accepted and practiced in industry. However, a national consensus conference on the subject held in 1989 showed that although acceptance is growing, several important questions about screening remain to be answered (Schulte, 1990).

Few employees in high-risk jobs are offered active surveillance for bladder cancer, and many do not even know that they are at increased risk. Among the categories of workers who are consistently shown to be at increased risk for bladder cancer are painters, truck drivers and machinists. The number of American workers who are potentially exposed on a full-time basis to animal bladder carcinogens (substances that cause bladder cancer in test animals) increased from 60,000 in the 1970s to 700,000 in the 1980s. Because of the average 20-year latency period of bladder cancer, workers who were exposed during these decades are still at risk for cancer (Ruder, et al., 1990).

One reason specific recommendations for screening programs have not been made is a lack of studies investigating the clinical impact of screening. It is not known whether screening and early detection actually decrease bladder cancer mortality, although there is some evidence suggesting that early detection does improve survival. Neither is it known which test or combination of screening tests is the most effective and efficient. To be sufficiently sensitive to detect bladder cancer, screening protocols should use a battery of different tests. However, such an approach would result in many false-positive results, identifying a high proportion of patients who do not have bladder cancer, but who would nevertheless undergo additional invasive studies (Geller, et al., 1990).

Bladder cancer screening protocols usually involve several noninvasive tests designed to detect hematuria (blood in the urine) or abnormal, cancerous cells in the urine. These tests include urine cytology, urinalysis, home dipstick testing of urine for hematuria and quantitative fluorescence imaging analysis, a new technique to analyze abnormal cells in the urine. Patients with positive results would then be evaluated with intravenous pyelography (IVP), a test in which contrast material is injected into the blood, and cystoscopy, a technique in which a flexible fiberoptic viewing device is inserted into the bladder.[36]

[2] Kidney Cancer

There are two main types of kidney cancer—renal cell carcinoma (also called cancer of the renal parenchyma) and cancer of the renal pelvis. Each has different epidemiologic characteristics and occupational correlates.

The renal parenchyma makes up the functioning body of the kidney. Cancers of the renal parenchyma (renal cell cancer) account for about 85 percent of all kidney cancers. These malignancies are diagnosed in about 18,000 Americans each year and cause 8,000 deaths (Garnick and Brenner, 1991). Renal cell cancers affect twice as many men as

---

[36] *See* 15.12[4] [g] and 15.12[4] [h] *infra* for information on the reduction of occupational exposures to carcinogens that cause bladder cancer.

women and have a peak age of onset of 55 to 60 years. Tobacco smoking is the only well-documented "life-style" risk factor for renal cell carcinoma (Morrison and Cole, 1982), although some dietary risk factors are suspected. The risk of renal cell carcinoma is also increased in people with hereditary factors and in patients who are on dialysis for kidney failure.

The renal pelvis is the channel by which the kidneys join the ureters (tubes that carry urine to the bladder). Cancer of the renal pelvis accounts for about 10 percent of all cases of kidney cancer. The renal pelvis is susceptible to the same carcinogens and carcinogenic risk factors as the bladder.[37]

[a] Occupational Exposures

Many studies of occupational kidney cancer do not distinguish between the two main types of tumor—renal cell cancer and cancer of the renal pelvis—though it is believed that different carcinogens are probably implicated for each type. Aromatic amines are the primary carcinogens affecting the renal pelvis, but soot, natural gas and oils are also implicated (McLaughlin, et al., 1983; Schulte, et al., 1987). Carcinogens that affect the renal parenchyma are more difficult to identify, but probably include cadmium (Schulte, et al., 1987).

Occupational associations with renal (kidney) cancer have been difficult to identify, in part because these cancers are relatively uncommon. Coke oven workers and dry cleaners seem to be at consistently increased risk for renal cancer. Other occupational associations with renal cancer have been observed in some studies but not across the board. Few studies of occupational kidney cancer were carried out before the 1970s, and only recently has knowledge about occupations at risk begun to accumulate (Schulte, et al., 1987).

Besides cadmium, asbestos is the only specific occupational carcinogen that evidence suggests may be associated with kidney cancer. Asbestos is primarily a pulmonary and gastrointestinal carcinogen, entering the body via inhalation and ingestion and having its effects on local tissues. Some doubt exists as to whether asbestos can enter the circulation and act as a renal carcinogen. Autopsies show that asbestos fibers can reach the kidneys in humans, but these do not provide evidence of renal carcinogenicity. Ingested asbestos was

---

[37] See 15.08[1][a] *supra.*

observed to cause kidney cancer in laboratory animals. Some epidemiologic studies have found no excess cases of kidney cancer in asbestos workers, but a few studies with enough subjects to produce statistically valid results have shown elevated kidney cancer rates in asbestos-exposed insulation workers, shipyard workers and manufacturers of asbestos products (Smith, et al., 1989).

[b]   Diagnosis, Treatment and Prognosis

About 60 percent of the time, blood in the urine (hematuria) is the first sign of renal cell carcinoma. However, because this hematuria is usually microscopic, it is not detected unless the patient happens to undergo a urinary evaluation. Gross hematuria—blood that is visible to the naked eye—is usually not evident until the tumor is large, by which time other symptoms related to the tumor's size may be present, including pain in the flank and a palpable renal mass.

In many patients, the first indication of renal cell carcinoma may be the systemic symptoms of fatigue, weight loss and cachexia (wasting). Other early signs may be fever, anemia or hematologic or hormonal abnormalities that show up on blood tests.

The diagnosis of renal cell carcinoma is made by intravenous pyelography, with nephrotomography (a special technique to x-ray the kidney) and ultrasonography (a method of visualizing foreign bodies or deep structures by using ultrasonic waves) to help determine whether an identified lesion is a tumor or merely a cyst. If the nature of the lesion is not resolved by these tests, computed tomography (CT) or magnetic resonance imaging (MRI) may be employed.

If the cancer is localized to the kidney and there is no evidence of metastatic disease, the kidney is removed surgically (radical nephrectomy). Some surgeons also sample the regional lymph nodes during the operation to determine whether disease has spread. The disease is assigned a stage on the basis of the results of this operation.

Patients with localized disease do not receive radiation or chemotherapy after radical nephrectomy. Those who have metastatic disease may undergo chemotherapy, hormonal therapy or immunologic therapy, though these treatments are under study at present and not likely to be of marked benefit (Garnick and Brenner, 1991).

Most patients with cancer of the renal pelvis seek medical attention with gross hematuria. These patients may be investigated with IVP (intravenous pyelography) and/or urinary cytology, but the diagnosis is made with the more sensitive techniques of cystoscopy (examination of the interior of the bladder by looking through a tubelike instrument) and retrograde pyelography (in which contrast material for x-ray studies is injected via the bladder and ureter).

For low-stage, low-grade tumors, the tumor may be excised locally and the kidney preserved. For more advanced disease, a radical nephrectomy is carried out, and the surgeon also removes the ureter and the cuff by which the ureter attaches to the bladder (otherwise this cuff is a likely site of disease recurrence). Patients must undergo follow-up evaluations, since they are at risk to develop cancer of the bladder or of the remaining renal pelvis. Reported five-year survival rates for cancer of the renal pelvis range from 10 to 50 percent (Garnick and Brenner, 1991).[38]

[3] Cancer of the Prostate

The prostate is a walnut-sized gland located below the bladder in men, which contributes certain substances to the seminal fluid. (*See Figure 15–5.*) Cancer of this gland is the second most common malignancy among American men, with 96,000 cases diagnosed in 1987. It is also the third leading cause of cancer mortality in men over the age of 55 (after lung and colorectal cancer), accounting for over 26,000 deaths in 1987 alone (Sagalowsky and Wilson, 1991).

The incidence of prostate cancer is higher among blacks than whites, increases with age and is elevated in men with blood group type A. Aside from these characteristics, risk factors for prostate cancer have not been identified with any consistency (Sagalowsky and Wilson, 1991).

In most men, the prostate enlarges with age, a condition called benign prostatic hypertrophy. This condition may or may not indicate risk for prostate cancer. Some studies have shown no relationship, while others have shown as much as a fourfold increased incidence of prostate cancer among men who first developed prostatic hypertrophy (Alderson, 1986; Greenwald, 1982). Other potential risk factors with variable associations with prostate cancer include circumcision and various indicators of increased sexual activity (such as age at first intercourse or number of sexual partners). These reports appear

---

[38] *See* 15.12[4][a] and 15.12[4] [i] *infra* for information on the reduction of occupational exposures to carcinogens that cause cancer of the kidney.

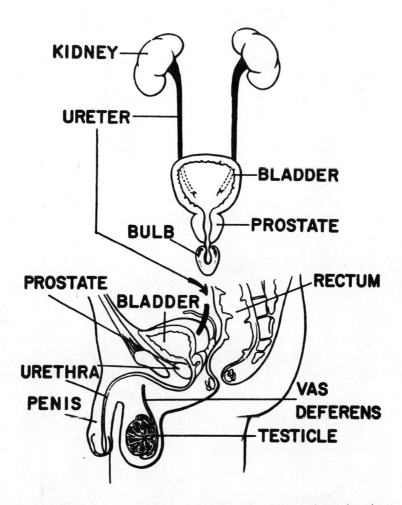

Fig. 15-5. Frontal (top) and lateral (bottom) view of the male genitourinary tract.

consistent enough to suggest that sexual activity may be a risk factor for prostate cancer, although the mechanism by which this might occur remains unknown. It is possible that a history of sexually transmitted disease is a risk factor (Alderson, 1986; Checkoway, et al., 1987).

[a]   Occupational Exposures

Epidemiologists have found increased rates of prostate cancer among workers in several occupations, although in many job categories, a specific carcinogen has not been implicated. Occupations that involve exposure to cadmium, such as cadmium production workers, welders, electroplaters and manufacturers of alkaline batteries, are associated with increased risk (Greenwald, 1982).

Other workers with elevated prostate cancer risk that may be due to cadmium exposure include those employed in manufacturing processes involving paint, metals, motor vehicles and aircrafts. The risk may also be elevated among auto repair workers and mechanics, suggesting that exposure to exhaust fumes, solvents or fuel oils may induce prostate cancer, and farm workers who are exposed to pesticides that may contain carcinogens, including cadmium (Brownson, et al., 1988).[39]

Among workers in other occupations for which an excess risk of prostate cancer has been reported, it has not been possible to identify a potential carcinogen exposure. These include rubber workers (with only a small excess prostate cancer incidence), bookkeepers, shipping and receiving clerks, compositors and typesetters, ministers, retailers, coal miners, motor vehicle dealers and many others who seem to have little in common with one another (Greenwald, 1982).

Some of these occupations probably do involve exposure to an as-yet-unidentified prostate carcinogen, while in others, the excess incidence of prostate cancer may have occurred by chance. There has been some suggestion that prostate cancer risk is elevated in men of higher socioeconomic status, which may explain its association with some of the white-collar jobs in this group (Brownson, et al., 1988).

[b]   Diagnosis, Treatment and Prognosis

Prostate cancer may exist for long periods without causing any symptoms that lead to medical evaluation. Autopsy studies have shown that only about a third of cases of prostate cancer ever become clinically evident.

Prostate cancer is frequently asymptomatic at the time it is diagnosed and often discovered only by palpating the gland during routine medical examinations. Because it is so often asymptomatic, more than 80 percent of patients have locally invasive disease or metastatic disease at the time of diagnosis (Sagalowsky and Wilson, 1991). Prostate cancer may be diagnosed by histologic analysis of prostate

---

[39] *See* 15.14 [4] [i] *infra* for information on reducing occupational exposure to cadmium.

tissue removed during surgery for benign prostatic hypertrophy; in fact, this is the only way short of autopsy that stage A (prepalpable) disease is identified.

When it is symptomatic, prostate cancer may produce symptoms of dysuria (pain on urination), difficulty urinating, increased urinary frequency or complete urinary retention. Other symptoms include back or hip pain and hematuria (blood in the urine).

Palpation of the prostate during the digital rectal examination is very important in the detection of early disease and is recommended as part of the routine physical examination of middle-aged and older men. In this examination, the physician, extending a finger into the patient's rectum, can palpate the posterior surface of the prostate gland, where cancer usually begins, as well as the nearby seminal vesicles, into which a locally invasive tumor may extend.

Suspect lesions may be visualized using ultrasonography, magnetic resonance imaging or computed tomography. These imaging tests are not diagnostic, but they may be helpful in localizing a lesion more precisely for biopsy. Fine-needle aspiration, in which a needle is inserted through the scrotal skin into the lesion to obtain a sample by aspiration, is the usual means of biopsy. Blood tests, such as the prostatic acid phosphatase and prostatic cancer antigen tests, also are useful for following and diagnosing suspected cases of prostatic cancer.

Treatment of prostate cancer depends on the extent of the disease. Prostate cancer is evaluated using the Whitmore staging system, in which stage A disease is that discovered by analysis of tissue obtained during operations for benign prostatic hypertrophy. For most patients with Stage A prostate cancer, that operation is enough to cure the disease; however, radical prostatectomy (removal of the entire prostate) has been recommended when stage A disease involves the gland more extensively.

Radical prostatectomy is also the treatment for stage B cancer, in which the tumor is palpable but disease remains confined to the prostate. The role of surgery is debatable in stage C (locally invasive) disease and it has no benefit in stage D (metastatic) disease. Damage to surrounding nerves during radical prostatectomy may result in impotence or urinary incontinence, but improvements in surgical technique have reduced the likelihood of these complications (Sagalowsky and Wilson, 1991).

Because of the risk of these complications, radiotherapy was developed as an alternative to radical surgery. Some patients receive traditional external radiation therapy. Others (mainly those with small, localized prostate cancers) may have "seeds" of radioactive material surgically implanted in the prostate. It is not clear whether radiotherapy is more effective in prolonging life than radical surgery, but there is some evidence that it may not be (Sagalowsky and Wilson, 1991). Chemotherapy is not highly effective in treating prostate cancer, and its role is mainly confined to palliation for patients with metastatic disease.

15.09 SKIN CANCER

The skin is an important site of occupationally related cancers. Exposure on the job to sunlight, ionizing radiation and certain chemicals is thought to make a major contribution to nonmelanotic skin cancer, accounting for perhaps 10 percent of these common and relatively easy to treat neoplasms (Doll and Peto, 1981). Workers in several job categories are thought to be at increased risk for melanoma—the more serious type of skin cancer—but the mechanism that places them at risk remains poorly defined.

[1] Nonmelanotic Skin Cancer

Nonmelanotic skin cancer is the most common type of cancer in the United States, affecting more than 500,000 Americans each year (Swanson, 1991). In most cases, nonmelanotic skin cancer is limited in extent when it is discovered, and with the proper treatment, it is cured more than 95 percent of the time. Only 1 percent of cases of nonmelanotic skin cancer are fatal (Scotto and Fraumeni, 1982). Nonmelanotic skin cancer is so common and curable that it is not included in the official cancer tallies.

There are two predominant types of nonmelanotic skin cancer. The first is *squamous cell carcinoma,* which affects the cells that form the outer layers of skin. This cancer accounts for about three fourths of the relatively rare skin cancer deaths. *Basal cell carcinoma,* the second type, is more common but even less likely to be fatal. These cancers affect the cells that form the lower layers of epidermis, the glands and other structures in the skin (Scotto and Fraumeni, 1982).

Cumulative exposure to ultraviolet (UV) radiation from the sun is the main risk factor for nonmelanotic skin cancer. Thus, outdoor work, such as farming and maritime occupations, is considered a high-risk category for this type of disease. Continuing depletion of the ozone layer, which acts as a screen against solar UV rays, is expected to result in an increase in the incidence of skin cancer in the future.

Skin cancer occurs more commonly in caucasian than in dark-skinned persons and is more common in equatorial regions than at latitudes that receive less sun. Most skin cancer occurs on the head and neck—the body parts that receive the greatest sun exposure. In several epidemiologic studies, the total amount of time spent in work outdoors was directly associated with risk for nonmelanotic skin cancer.

Skin cancer risk is also associated with xeroderma pigmentosum, a disease in which sun-induced damage to the DNA of the skin is not repaired. The risk is increased among people who have fair skin that freckles or sunburns easily (Emmett, 1987).

[a]   Occupational Exposures

The incidence of skin cancer is elevated among outdoor workers, such as farmers and people who fish, who have prolonged exposure to sunlight. Ultraviolet light is also generated by UV lasers and by high-temperature arcs such as germicidal and black-light lamps, welding torches and laboratory equipment. Workers who are exposed to UV light from these sources include welders, lamp testers, food and tobacco irradiators, film projectionists, physicians, dentists, optometrists, chemists and many others (Moss, et al., 1987).

Workers who are exposed to ionizing radiation may also be at increased risk for skin cancer. Excess rates of skin cancer have been observed among uranium miners and radiologists, with latency periods of 25 to 30 years (Scotto and Fraumeni, 1982). Skin cancers usually arise in areas of skin that have first developed chronic radiation dermatitis (skin ulcers that result from local damage by repeated small doses of ionizing radiation). Skin cancer arising from radiodermatitis has been described in the numerous health care workers who in the past were inadvertently exposed while operating x-ray equipment (Mathias, 1988). Nuclear industry workers also incur potential exposure of the skin to ionizing radiation. The latency of skin cancers induced by ionizing radiation depends on the total dose received; it reportedly ranges from as little as 7 weeks to 56 years, with a mean of 25 to 30 years (Emmett, 1975).[40]

Skin cancers are among the many kinds of cancer that can also be induced by polycyclic aromatic hydrocarbons (PAHs). It has been suggested on the basis of studies involving animals that PAHs can potentiate the carcinogenic effects of UV radiation (Emmett, 1987). Polycyclic aromatic hydrocarbon (PAH) exposure was probably responsible for the very first type of occupational cancer to be described in the late eighteenth century—scrotal cancer in chimney sweeps. The skin of the scrotum seems to be more permeable to externally applied substances than the skin of other body areas. In fact, as recently as the mid-1980s, chimney sweeps were seen to have an elevated incidence of scrotal squamous cell cancer (Alderson, 1986).[41]

Arsenic can cause both squamous and basal cell carcinoma, as well as some kinds of premalignant skin lesions. Unlike other carcinogens, which work externally on the skin, arsenic does its damage after being accidentally inhaled, ingested or injected. Arsenic-induced skin tumors are usually multiple and affect areas of the body that are not ordinarily exposed to the sun. Workers who are exposed to arsenic include miners and copper smelters, as well as pesticide and herbicide manufacturers and users (Emmett, 1987; Emmett, 1975).[42]

[b] Diagnosis, Treatment and Prognosis

Actinic keratoses are sun-induced lesions that arise on the head, neck, forearms and hands. These thickened, scaly lesions are considered precancerous; an unknown but probably small proportion develop into skin cancer. Actinic keratoses should be examined periodically for thickening, crusting or ulceration that may signal transformation into skin cancer. They may be treated with cryosurgery (freezing with liquid nitrogen) or by topical application of the chemotherapeutic agent 5–fluorouracil (5–FU) to improve appearance and prevent the development of skin cancer.

Basal cell carcinomas usually occur as single lesions arising *de novo* on sun-exposed skin. There are five different histologic types, which

---

[40] *See* 15.12[4] [m] *infra* for information regarding reduction of occupational exposure to ultraviolet radiation.

[41] *See* 15.12[4] [j] *infra* for information regarding reduction of occupational exposure to polycyclic aromatic hydrocarbons.

[42] *See* 15.12[4] [c] *infra* for information regarding reduction of occupational exposure to arsenic.

have different clinical appearances as well as somewhat different prognoses. Basal cell carcinomas may be raised, red or scaly, pigmented or plaquelike. Squamous cell carcinoma may arise in sun-damaged skin or pre-existing lesions such as radiodermatitis, scars or chronic ulcers. It may appear as a nodule or an ulcer, with or without pigmentation.

Small lesions that are suspected skin cancers may be treated with an excisional biopsy (removal of the entire lesion with a margin of normal tissue). The diagnosis is then confirmed by a pathologist's analysis of the excised tissue.

If the lesion is too large to be treated adequately with an excisional biopsy, the diagnosis should be confirmed with an incisional biopsy before more extensive surgery is carried out. Except for very large lesions, most skin cancers can be excised on an outpatient basis, under local anesthesia. Cure rates after surgical excision are well over 90 percent (Strick, 1985).

For large lesions, alternative approaches to surgical excision include electrodesiccation (destruction of small growths by electrical sparks) and curettage (a process of scraping off growths by means of a spoonlike instrument called a curet), radiation therapy (use of an ionizing beam to destroy cancer cells), cryosurgery (freezing with liquid nitrogen to destroy tumors) and Moh's chemosurgery. The latter technique, used for large, recurrent or otherwise difficult to treat skin cancers, involves excising the tumor, stiffening the surrounding tissues with a chemical and then removing the tissue in very thin slices. Each slice is then analyzed for tumor cells before the next layer is removed. This technique often has better cosmetic results than extensive surgery for large lesions, and cure rates in the hands of expert dermatologic surgeons have been greater than 95 percent (Strick, 1985).

Clinical staging is not used for basal cell or squamous cell carcinoma. A minuscule proportion of basal cell carcinomas are metastatic at diagnosis. Although only 2 percent of squamous cell cancers are metastatic, the five-year survival rate for patients with metastases to the regional lymph nodes or to distant sites is less than 50 percent (Strick, 1985).

[2] Melanoma

Melanoma is a type of cancer that arises from the melanocytes, cells contained within the outer layers of the skin. Melanocytes are the repositories for melanin, the pigment that gives the skin its dark color and helps protect it from sun damage. Melanoma usually arises from pigmented nevi, or birthmarks, which contain very large numbers of melanocytes.

The peak incidence of melanoma is in the middle-aged and elderly. The disease is diagnosed in about 28,000 Americans and causes 5,800 deaths in this country each year (Sober and Koh, 1991).

Although it seems likely that melanoma risk is related to exposure to ultraviolet rays from the sun, this association is not universally accepted. Evidence against the role of solar radiation includes findings that melanoma risk is higher in indoor white-collar workers than in outdoor workers and that, unlike nonmelanotic skin cancer, body sites that are exposed to the sun are not affected more often than unexposed sites (IARC Monograph No. 40, 1986).

The incidence of melanoma has increased markedly since the 1940s, perhaps as a result of an increase in sun exposure. Increased exposure to chemicals has been suggested as an alternative explanation (Emmett, 1987).

The incidence of melanoma is higher in lower-latitude geographic locations and among people who were exposed as children to lower-latitude sunlight, regardless of where they spent their adult years. Melanoma is more likely to affect light-skinned Caucasians than dark-skinned Caucasians, Asians or persons of African descent. People whose skin is especially sensitive to sunlight, who are pale and who freckle or sunburn easily are at greatest risk.

Melanoma risk is associated with (Alderson, 1986; Sober and Koh, 1991):

- higher socioeconomic status;
- family history of the disease;
- xeroderma pigmentosum, a rare skin disease in which damage to the DNA of cells is not repaired; and
- certain types of nevi, or moles.

A specialized form of highly malignant melanoma is observed in immunocompromised individuals, such as those with acquired immunodeficiency syndrome (AIDS).

[a]   Occupational Exposures

Although sun exposure is related to risk for melanoma in the general public, outdoor workers do not seem to be at increased risk compared to persons who work indoors. This may be because of selection bias (i.e., people with sun-sensitive skin are more likely to choose indoor occupations) (Lee, 1991). Another explanation is that the risk may be lower in people who are continually exposed to the sun and gradually develop a protective suntan, as opposed to those who experience only intermittent exposures (Emmett, 1987).[43]

Several studies have shown that white-collar and professional workers are at increased risk for melanoma, among them physicians, dentists, pharmacists, airline pilots, university teachers, chemists, accountants and insurance brokers (Vagero, et al., 1990; Vagero, et al., 1986; Gallagher, et al., 1986). In several studies, increased melanoma risk among white-collar workers was observed only for those anatomic sites that are usually covered by clothing (Vagero, et al., 1986). Researchers have proposed several theories to account for this perplexing association of melanoma with high-status indoor work. Exposure to fluorescent lights is one theory, although it remains unsubstantiated. Another possible explanation is that the higher-status workers in offices are also more likely to take long vacations, to spend holidays in tropical climates, to have only intermittent sun exposure on weekends or to have a history of sunburns as children (Emmett, 1987; Gallagher, et al., 1986; Vagero, et al., 1986).

The overall picture remains confusing. For example, several American studies have shown a high incidence of melanoma among people who live in counties where petrochemical industries are located. However, since most of these counties are located in the South, a confounding effect of sunlight cannot be ruled out. A large cluster of melanoma cases was observed in employees of the Lawrence Livermore Radiation Laboratory in California (Austin, et al., 1981), but in general, melanoma has not been associated with exposure to ionizing radiation (Lee, 1982).

[b]   Diagnosis, Treatment and Prognosis

Melanoma is detected by visual examination of the skin. Any pigmented nevus (mole) that changes in size or appearance or that

---

43 *See* 15.12[4] [m] *infra* for information regarding reduction of occupational exposure to ultraviolet radiation.

contains pigment of different hues is suspect. Any small nevus that resembles melanoma should be removed through full-thickness excisional biopsy. In addition to providing the diagnosis (as well as all the treatment that may be required for a superficial melanoma), the excisional biopsy allows the physician to determine the depth of the lesion—an important prognostic factor. If the tumor is too large to permit excisional biopsy, an incisional biopsy sample can be taken through either the center or the darkest part of the lesion.

The majority of melanomas are diagnosed while they are confined to the skin, in what is called clinical stage I. About 85 percent of patients diagnosed with stage I melanoma survive for five years, and of those with superficial lesions (less than 0.76 mm thick), 96 to 99 percent are cured. Stage II disease is associated with lymph nodes that are palpable as a result of disease involvement. The five-year survival rate is 50 percent if only a single node is involved, but it is only 15 to 20 percent if four or more nodes are involved. Finally, only about 5 percent of patients with metastatic (stage III) disease survive for five years (Sober and Koh, 1991).

At the time of diagnosis, patients with melanoma should be examined closely from head to toe under good illumination, since there is a good chance that they have additional melanomas or precursor lesions. Aside from the biopsy, diagnostic tests are generally not carried out unless there is evidence that the disease is metastatic. Stage I disease is surgically excised, usually with a wide margin of tumor-free tissue around the lesion. However, wide excisions on the face can be disfiguring,and those on the hands or feet, disabling. Different surgeons have different opinions on the optimal margin for these excisions (Sober and Koh, 1991).

Surgical excision of the lymph nodes is usually carried out if they are affected. A single distant metastasis may also be removed surgically, but it is more often the case that melanoma has multiple metastases. Chemotherapy and radiation therapy may be palliative for some patients. Metastatic melanoma has been the focus of much active research recently; experimental treatments such as immunotherapy (stimulation of the immune system to combat disease), high-dose chemotherapy with bone marrow transplantation (grafting of bone marrow tissue to fight cancer) and antibody-targeted drugs (drugs combined with immune proteins) show some promise.

15.10   BRAIN TUMORS

The incidence of brain tumors is known to be elevated among workers in several occupations, but except for those who are exposed to vinyl chloride, the mechanism of increased brain tumor risk remains unexplained.

Tumors of the brain, the meningeal covering of the brain and the spinal cord—the structures that make up the central nervous system—cause some 90,000 deaths in the United States each year (Hochberg and Pruitt, 1991). The brain is by far the most common site of central nervous system cancer. Only about a fourth of all brain tumors are primary; the rest arise as metastases from cancer at other sites in the body.

Overall, primary brain tumors are relatively uncommon in adults, but they are often rapidly fatal. Those between the ages of 60 and 70 are at greatest risk for brain tumors (Jones, 1986). In the United States and several other industrialized countries, the incidence of brain tumors has increased in recent decades—an increase that is thought to be real rather than an artifact of improved ability to detect the tumors (Davis, et al., 1990). In most industrialized countries, the incidence of brain tumors is significantly higher and has been increasing more steeply in men than in women, particularly those aged 45 to 65 (Kessler and Brandt-Rauf, 1987). These observations, together with studies of cancer induction in animal experiments, have led investigators to suspect that occupational exposures may be involved in some primary brain tumors.

Many other potential risk factors for brain tumors have been studied. These epidemiologic investigations are made more difficult by the fact that there are many different kinds of cells and tissues within the brain, all of which can become cancerous. It is likely that different kinds of brain cancer are associated with different exposures, risk factors, latency periods and other possible findings. The relatively low incidence of brain tumors also increases the difficulty of identifying possible risk factors.

Brain tumors occasionally occur in familial clusters and have been associated with a few relatively uncommon diseases, including tuberous sclerosis (characterized by seizures, mental retardation and skin nodules). The incidence of brain tumor is increased for persons who were exposed to therapeutic scalp irradiation as children for tinea capitis (ringworm of the scalp), a treatment that is no longer used. A few investigators have reported single cases or a small number of cases in which brain tumors developed years after the individual received a traumatic head injury, but this association has not been proved (Alderson, 1986; Schoenberg, 1982).

[1] Occupational Exposures

More than 30 chemicals have been identified as capable of producing brain tumors in experimental animals, but only one of them, vinyl chloride, has been confirmed as a human central nervous system carcinogen.

Vinyl chloride is a gas used in the manufacture of polyvinyl chloride. Several studies have shown that workers involved in polyvinyl chloride production may be three to four times as likely to die of brain tumors as comparable groups of unexposed workers. Glioblastoma multiforme, a highly malignant type of brain tumor, may also occur more frequently in polyvinyl chloride workers than in comparable groups (Kessler and Brandt-Rauf, 1987). Brain tumors have been observed to develop in polyvinyl chloride workers after an average latency period of 21 years. It has been suggested that workers in this industry today probably do not receive vinyl chloride exposures high enough to increase their risk for brain tumors (Moss, 1985).[44]

It has also been suggested that acrylonitrile, a chemical used as a pesticide and in various manufacturing processes, may be a central nervous system carcinogen. However, exposures to this highly toxic chemical are already greatly restricted, and the exposures received by workers today are so low that an association with brain tumors may never be proven (Jones, 1986).[45]

Epidemiologic studies have shown the risk of brain cancer to be elevated in several occupations in which a specific chemical exposure has not been identified. Predominant among these are rubber manufacture and the petrochemical industry. The studies that showed an excess incidence of brain tumors in rubber workers mainly involved workers employed in the tire industry before 1930 or 1940, however. More recent studies have not shown the same excess incidence, which

---

[44] *See* 15.12[4] [e] *infra* for information regarding reduction of occupational exposure to vinyl chloride.

[45] *See* 15.12[4] [f] *infra* for information regarding reduction of occupational exposure to acrylonitrile.

suggests that workers in the modern rubber manufacturing industry may be exposed to fewer central nervous system carcinogens (Kessler and Brandt-Rauf, 1987). Employment in the nuclear fuels and weapons industries is of concern to occupational epidemiologists because of these workers' exposure to low levels of ionizing radiation. Several other occupational groups have been shown in more than one study to have an increased incidence of brain tumors, for reasons that are as yet unknown. These include farmers, who are exposed to pesticides, and professional and white-collar workers, who have no known chemical exposures (Kessler and Brandt-Rauf, 1987; Reif, et al., 1989). Recently some have suggested that use of cellular phones may be a cause, but investigation has not verified this supposition.

[2]   Diagnosis, Treatment and Prognosis

There are no screening tests for brain tumors. Instead, the tumors are diagnosed after symptoms appear. Symptoms result from infiltration of brain tissue by the tumor, the compression of tissues and organs in the head by the tumor, elevated intracranial pressure or cerebral edema (swelling).

Headache is the most common first symptom of brain tumor. The tumor may also cause altered mental function, which can appear as either generalized mental slowness or specific disturbances in speech, memory or gait. Tumors in some areas of the brain may result in syndromes that resemble mental illness, with hallucinations, abrupt mood changes and altered behavior. Tumors in other areas may cause seizures. Patients with malignant astrocytoma (a well-differentiated type of brain cancer), the type of brain tumor that has been most often associated with occupation, are more likely to first exhibit seizures and personality changes than other symptoms (Hochberg and Pruitt, 1991).

In a patient with symptoms that suggest a brain tumor, the physician first carries out physical and neurologic examinations. The neurologic examination is a specific routine in which the physician questions the patient to determine whether any intellectual, memory or personality abnormalities are present and then carries out tests for signs of neurologic damage and for impairments caused by elevated intracranial pressure. Imaging studies are also carried out, usually computed tomography (CT) scans and magnetic resonance imaging (MRI).

The histologic type of the tumor may be determined with a biopsy or at the time of surgical resection. Brain tumors are classified on the basis of the types of cells or structures they affect. Although certain tumor types are identified as benign or malignant, the distinction is less important than for other types of cancer, because both benign and malignant tumors are often lethal due to their expansion within the skull and disruption of bodily functions controlled by the brain. Glioma, the most common type of brain tumor in adults, affects the glial cells that make up the matrix of the brain. Among the subtypes of glioma are astrocytomas, which include the highly malignant glioblastoma multiforme. This subtype has been observed to occur with greater-than-expected frequency among polyvinyl chloride workers and perhaps workers in other occupational groups as well.

Glioblastomas and other malignant astrocytomas have a poor prognosis. If these tumors are operable, surgery is carried out in an attempt to remove as much of the tumor as possible while minimizing impairment of the patient's mental functions. This is a difficult task, since the margins of these tumors are closely interwoven with normal brain tissue. Patients who are successfully treated with surgery usually have recurrent symptoms within an average of six months, followed soon by progressive neurologic deterioration, coma and death. Radiation therapy and chemotherapy can prolong survival somewhat. However, even in a subgroup of young patients with a relatively favorable prognosis, the survival rate was only 20 percent following radiotherapy and chemotherapy (Hochberg and Pruitt, 1991).

15.11 LYMPHOMA

Lymphomas are cancers that affect the lymphocytes—cells that are found mainly in the lymphoid system and the blood. Lymphocytes are the cells that function as the body's immune system, attacking or producing antibodies or antigens (substances capable of producing an immune response) to any foreign organisms. The lymphomas are a diverse group of cancers, with three main types—Hodgkin's, non-Hodgkin's and Burkitt's lymphomas—each of which is an entirely distinct disease.

Burkitt's lymphoma has not been associated with any occupational exposures.

Non-Hodgkin's lymphoma comprises several different disorders, probably with somewhat different epidemiologic characteristics and risk factors. About 30,000 cases of non-Hodgkin's lymphoma are diagnosed in the United States each year (Nadler, 1991). The risk is greater for persons with disorders of immune system function, whether the disorder is associated with familial factors, immunosuppressive medical treatment or a disease linked with immune dysfunction, such as rheumatoid arthritis, lupus erythematosus, hypothyroidism or AIDS (Heath, 1985).

Hodgkin's disease, which is diagnosed in about 7,500 Americans each year, has been increasing in incidence in recent years, particularly among young adults. There is one peak in incidence among 20– to 30-year-olds and a second among people over the age of 50. The risk for Hodgkin's disease is increased for individuals in families that have an inherited susceptibility to the disease. Evidence also suggests that the risk may be increased for persons who were infected with the Epstein-Barr virus, which causes infectious mononucleosis (Heath, 1985; Nadler, 1991).

[1]   Occupational Exposures

An excess incidence of non-Hodgkin's lymphoma has been observed, though not consistently, among vinyl chloride workers and among anesthesiologists. Epidemiologic evidence also suggests that non-Hodgkin's lymphoma incidence is increased among workers who are exposed to phenoxyl herbicides, chemicals used in rubber production, arsenic and asbestos. Chemists and farmers may also have an increased incidence of non-Hodgkin's lymphoma, though suspected carcinogens among workers in these occupations have not been identified (Heath, 1985). Other groups with a high incidence of non-Hodgkin's lymphoma include sales, clerical and postal workers; insurance and real estate brokers; engineers; stationary engineers; electrical workers; mechanics and machinists (Greene, 1982).

The association of Hodgkin's disease with occupational exposure is more tenuous. Woodworkers are the only occupational group in whom an excess incidence of Hodgkin's disease has been consistently observed. The excess risk in woodworkers is small and does not appear to justify medical screening or special protection (Grufferman, 1982). Evidence suggests that the risk may also be increased among chemical workers and rubber workers (Heath, 1985).[46]

---

[46] *See* 15.12[4] [e] *infra* for information regarding reduction of occupational exposures to vinyl chloride.

[2] Diagnosis, Treatment and Prognosis

Over half of the patients with Hodgkin's disease are first seen with few symptoms other than a tumor mass or palpable lymph nodes. A large minority are first seen with nonspecific systemic symptoms, such as fever or night sweats. The diagnosis is confirmed by biopsy of the affected site. Patients then undergo a series of diagnostic tests for staging, including physical examination, pathologic examination of the blood, biochemical blood tests, bone marrow biopsy, chest x-rays and CT scans. Exploratory abdominal surgery and liver biopsy are often employed.

Patients with Hodgkin's disease are treated with radiotherapy, chemotherapy or a combination of the two. Those with low-stage, localized disease receive radiotherapy; chemotherapy is administered only in the event of a relapse. About 80 percent of patients with Hodgkin's disease are cured by radiotherapy alone. Patients with more advanced stages of disease receive a carefully selected protocol consisting of combination therapy or chemotherapy alone, depending on disease stage. Chemotherapy may result in a cure in 50 percent of patients with widespread disease (Nadler, 1991).

Most patients with non-Hodgkin's lymphoma are first seen with a persistent painless enlargement of the lymph nodes, called lymphadenopathy. Their first symptoms are rarely systemic. The diagnosis of non-Hodgkin's lymphoma is confirmed by a biopsy, and patients then undergo a series of diagnostic tests for staging, including physical examination, pathologic examination of the blood, biochemical blood tests, bone marrow biopsy, chest x-rays and CT scans.

Radiation has a limited role in the primary treatment of non-Hodgkin's lymphoma and is reserved for patients whose disease can be confirmed as being limited in extent. About 60 to 80 percent of patients who receive radiotherapy alone are cured. Patients with more advanced disease undergo chemotherapy. Cure rates with chemotherapy approach 80 percent, but the aggressive chemotherapy regimens used in non-Hodgkin's lymphoma are themselves highly toxic. Some patients receive bone marrow transplants to enable them to tolerate very high dose chemotherapy regimens (Nadler, 1991).

15.12 PREVENTING OCCUPATIONAL CANCER

Two approaches are used in the attempt to prevent occupational cancer. *Primary prevention,* which aims to prevent the development of cancer, involves efforts to reduce worker exposure to carcinogens through engineering of the workplace or personal protective measures. These efforts are based on standards set forth by state and federal government regulatory bodies, primarily the Occupational Safety and Health Administration (OSHA).

Secondary prevention, which is undertaken with the objective of identifying cancers that are present but not yet symptomatic, involves screening exposed workers to detect cancer at an earlier stage, when treatment could possibly improve the prognosis.

[1] Identification and Regulation of Workplace Carcinogens

The International Agency for Research on Cancer (IARC), the worldwide authority on cancer causation, periodically publishes monographs on the carcinogenicity of different substances. These reports, considered to be comprehensive and authoritative, are consulted by national governments seeking to regulate industrial carcinogens. IARC reviews the evidence for different substances or groups of related substances, classifies them into four categories and identifies industrial processes that are associated with risk for cancer.

Group 1 (substances or processes known to be carcinogenic in humans) is comprised of 23 substances and 7 industrial processes. (*See Table 15–1.*) Group 2 includes substances or processes that are reasonably suspected to be carcinogenic on the basis of "limited evidence" in humans or "sufficient evidence" in animals. Group 3 lists the other substances that have been evaluated but that cannot be classified as carcinogenic. Group 4 lists substances for which evidence militates against carcinogenicity. Some of the carcinogens listed by IARC are not used in industry.

Table 15–1
Group 1 Carcinogens with Occupational Exposures

I. INDUSTRIAL PROCESS	SITE
Auramine manufacture	Bladder
Boot and shoe manufacture and repair (certain occupations)	Nasal cavity, bladder
Furniture manufacture	Nasal cavity
Isopropyl alcohol manufacture (strong acid process)	Sinuses, nasal cavity, possibly larynx
Nickel refining	Lung, nasal cavity

Rubber industry (certain occupations)	Bladder, leukemia, stomach, prostate, brain, others
Underground iron mining (with radon exposure)	Lung
II. CHEMICAL	SITE
4–Aminobiphenyl	Bladder
Arsenic and arsenic compounds	Skin, lung
Asbestos	Lung, larynx, mesothelioma, larynx, colon, rectum, esophagus
Benzene	Leukemia
Benzidine	Bladder
BCME and CMME	Lung
Chromium	Lung
Mustard gas	Bladder
2–Naphthylamine	Bladder
Soots, tars, and oils	Skin, lung, bladder, stomach
Vinyl chloride	Liver, brain, lung

———

In the United States, lists of carcinogenic substances are published by the National Institute for Occupational Safety and Health (NIOSH) and the Occupational Safety and Health Administration (OSHA), the National Toxicology Program, the American Conference of Governmental Industrial Hygienists (ACGIH) and the Environmental Protection Agency (EPA). These lists are compiled by a variety of methods, and they may be comprehensive or cover only a select group of carcinogens.

OSHA is the primary agency charged with regulating worker exposure to carcinogens on the job. OSHA cannot require a manufacturer to prove that a newly used chemical or process does not cause cancer, but it may regulate exposure to substances that are already known to be carcinogenic.

In the 1970s, OSHA promulgated threshold limit values (TLVs) for 14 carcinogens, including the pulmonary carcinogens arsenic, asbestos, coke oven emissions and nickel, as well as soots, tar and mineral oils. These TLVs are sometimes regarded as inadequate, having been based on limited information available at the time; however, some remain in effect (Ashford, 1988). Subsequently OSHA revised or renegotiated acceptable exposure standards for asbestos, arsenic, coke oven emissions and several other carcinogens. In 1980, OSHA set forth a generic carcinogen standard under which suspect workplace carcinogens could be treated in a uniform way. However, it has not yet applied this standard to any new substances. Most of the 20 or so carcinogens that are regulated by OSHA are regulated under the old "14 carcinogens" standard or other legal agreements that were individually established.

In addition to OSHA, agencies or organizations such as NIOSH, the American Conference of Governmental Industrial Hygienists (ACGIH), the American National Standards Institute (ANSI), the American Industrial Hygiene Association (AIHA), the National Academy of Sciences–National Research Council and the Mine Safety and Health Administration have promulgated recommendations about tolerable exposures to chemicals and other cancer hazards in the workplace. In the cases of some carcinogens—for example, asbestos—NIOSH has suggested revisions of the OSHA standards. The ACGIH has also published suggested revisions of some of the OSHA standards. The Mine Safety and Health Administration sets exposure standards for underground and above-ground miners that cover (among other carcinogens) asbestos and radon.

[2] Primary Prevention: Reducing Exposures

Primary prevention of occupational cancer depends on efforts to reduce employees' exposure to carcinogens to within permissible limits. This may be accomplished by engineering control of the workplace environment to reduce levels of contaminants in the air and by providing workers with personal protective clothing and equipment. The latter is considered less than ideal and is only recommended if engineering measures cannot reduce exposures to permissible levels.

[a] Engineering Controls

The optimal way to engineer for reduced exposures to carcinogens is to include safety measures in the design of plants or when a new manufacturing process is being implemented in an existing plant. Controls built into the system are more reliable than those that depend on administrative activities, such as scheduling or worker training. A variety of standards and recommendations have been established and should be consulted when planning a new plant or a new process.

Once a new facility or new process is in place, periodic sampling should be carried out to determine whether the engineering controls are adequately protecting workers. Substances to be sampled include general room air, air in the vicinity of workers, industrial raw materials, dusts and biological samples (such as blood and urine) collected from the worker. Samples may be obtained using a great diversity of techniques, schedules and sampling schemes. One author recommends that the sample should be obtained and analyzed using the same procedures employed by OSHA and the ACGIH in setting their standards (Powell, 1979).

The level of airborne carcinogens in the workplace may be reduced by the following methods:

- Substitution of a less hazardous material in the manufacturing process (for example, using an insulating material other than asbestos).

- Use of general ventilation, or dilution ventilation, which keeps air flowing through the workplace to reduce the concentration of airborne contaminants. Dilution ventilation is achieved through the use of exhaust fans, open windows and design of the workplace to maximize air flow. This method is not thought to be suitable for dangerous substances that must be filtered out of the air before it is discharged outdoors. General ventilation may be used to lower the level of radon in underground mines.

- Use of exhaust ventilation, which captures the air given off at the source and filters it to remove particulate material. Exhaust ventilation may be used to reduce levels of asbestos fibers or polycyclic aromatic hydrocarbons arising from a particular process.

- Improving design of the manufacturing environment, process and equipment to minimize exposures. These measures include having all work with dangerous substances carried out in an enclosed area apart from the majority of workers, scheduling risky jobs for a time when most workers are not in the plant, automation of jobs involving carcinogenic chemicals and providing equipment (such as glass-enclosed glove boxes) that physically isolate the worker from the process.

● Use of wet manufacturing methods, which can be as simple as keeping the floor wet and working with moistened materials to keep dust levels low.

[b] Personal Protective Equipment

Personal protective equipment is considered a secondary method of exposure reduction, because it does not directly address the problem. A worker might unknowingly be exposed to carcinogens if he or she wears defective or improperly fitted equipment. Also, many workers find protective gear uncomfortable and do not like to wear it.

Protective clothing is made of various materials, depending on the nature of the protection that is needed; for example, sometimes clothing must be impervious to a particular chemical, but at other times, a lesser degree of protection is deemed adequate. The clothing can include a helmet or hood, special boots and gloves, and goggles to protect the eyes. Clothing should be cleaned and maintained by the employer, should not be worn on successive days without cleaning and should not be worn outside the workplace. Workers are often required to shower before changing back into their street clothes after a shift.

Some respirators are simply gas or dust masks provided to filter out airborne chemicals or dusts. Others are entire breathing devices that supply clean air. Different types of respirators are manufactured for different substances and work settings, and each must meet rigid specifications set forth by OSHA. It is important to make sure that the respirator is adequately fitted to the worker's face, since contaminants can enter around the sides of an improperly fitted device.

[3] Secondary Prevention: Health Screening

In addition to screening or examination for occupationally related cancers, pre-employment history and physical examination should be carried out to determine whether a worker is already at increased risk for cancer as a result of cigarette smoking, family history, previous occupational exposure or some other factor. Such examinations cannot be used to deny employment to a healthy worker, but they may be useful in guiding a worker who is already at high risk to a job with less exposure to a carcinogen. It should be recognized that the pre-employment history is not a highly reliable source of information, since human memory is fallible, and a person may deny previous exposures for fear of not getting a job.

Once on the job, workers are examined at regular intervals, depending on their job category and estimated exposure to a carcinogen. Often a known or suspected carcinogen produces other symptoms of target organ damage at a lower dose than would result in cancer; organ function studies (for example, studies of liver enzyme levels or pulmonary function) may detect this early damage. If the worker is exposed to a known carcinogen, screening tests for cancer of the target organ should be part of the routine examination. In the case of lung cancer, these tests include chest x-rays and cytologic studies.

[4] Control of Exposure to Specific Carcinogens

Engineering controls are preferable to the use of personal protective clothing and respirators in limiting exposures to toxic chemicals. When carcinogens are involved, both types of protection may be required. In addition, periodic medical examination of exposed workers is mandatory.

[a] Asbestos

Asbestos is linked with cancer of the esophagus, stomach, bowel and kidney,[47] but it is primarily considered a pulmonary carcinogen and a cause of lung cancer[48] and mesothelioma.[49]

According to NIOSH, the permissible level of asbestos exposure in the workplace should be set at the lowest level measurable in air by existing technology (Sittig, 1985). There appears to be no threshold level below which exposure to asbestos does not increase cancer risk; rather, federal guidelines are set that protect against the noncarcinogenic effects of asbestos on the lung. No standard has been established that is regarded as providing complete protection against cancer.

The American Conference of Government Industrial Hygienists (ACGIH) set exposure guidelines for asbestos and other workplace chemical exposures in 1983/1984. In 1983, OSHA also proposed an "emergency standard" for asbestos exposure that still stands. The OSHA standard is 0.5 asbestos fibers per cc of air for an eight-hour

---

[47] See 15.07 supra.

[48] See 15.04[1] [a] supra.

[49] See 15.05 supra.

period. The ACGIH standard is a complicated formula with different exposure levels for different sizes of each of the four types of asbestos fiber (Sittig, 1985).[50] Smaller fibers are thought to be more potent than large ones for producing cancer.

Periodic surveillance of workers with chest x-rays and lung function tests is required in all industries in which asbestos exposure occurs. These tests should be performed every two years, and more often in workers who have had more than ten years exposure or who already show signs of deteriorating lung function. Workers also must receive medical examinations before they are employed, periodically during employment and when their employment is ended. These examinations should include questions about smoking habits and past exposures to asbestos and other dusts, as well as physical examinations for evidence of lung, heart and gastrointestinal disease.

When the level of asbestos dust in the air cannot be controlled by improving ventilation, workers should be supplied with protective clothing and respirators. Protective clothing should be vacuumed before it is removed.

[b]   Chloromethyl Ethers

There is no safe standard for exposure to the pulmonary carcinogens bis(chloromethyl) ether (BCME) or chloromethyl methyl ether (CMME).[51] These chemicals enter the body via inhalation of vapors and, to a lesser degree, through the skin. All contact with or inhalation of these substances should be avoided. In addition to engineering controls designed to minimize the level in air and water, exposure to the chloromethyl ethers is minimized when workers wear full-body protective clothing (with goggles) and use chemical cartridge respirators. After work, workers should shower before changing to street clothes. Pre-employment and ongoing medical screening should include examination of the skin and lungs, x-rays and possibly sputum cytology.

[c]   Arsenic

Arsenic, a suspected liver and skin carcinogen, is also known to be a pulmonary carcinogen that can be controlled in the workplace.[52]

---

[50] *See also* ch. 16 for a discussion of asbestosis and related cancers.

[51] *See* 15.04[1][d] *supra.*

[52] *See* 15.04[1] [d], 15.07 [4] and 15.09[1][a] *supra.*

NIOSH has set a maximum exposure limit for arsenic of 10 micrograms/cubic meter of air, using an eight-hour average. Arsenic has many toxic effects in addition to cancer causation, and chest x-rays and sputum cytology are only two of many surveillance tests that are carried out periodically on exposed workers. Workers should wear protective clothing and respirators; impervious clothing should be worn by workers who handle liquid arsenic preparations.

[d] Radon

Exposure to the pulmonary carcinogen radon usually is controlled by ventilating the mine where it is found. Sufficient air must be exchanged each hour to prevent buildup of radon and radon progeny to a significant level. Sometimes measures are also taken to reduce the amount of radon released into the air, either by pressurizing the air in the mine, closing off unused sections of the mine or covering the mine walls with a sealant. Radon particles are sometimes removed from the air by filters or electrostatic precipitators. Respirators are effective for removing radon progeny, but not radon itself, from inhaled air. Respirators are not generally used except for special jobs involving short, high-intensity exposures (Voelz, 1988).[53]

[e] Vinyl Chloride

Vinyl chloride, a gas used as a solvent and also as an ingredient in the manufacture of polyvinyl chloride, is classified as a carcinogen by the International Association for Research on Cancer (IARC) and by the American Conference of Government and Industrial Hygienists (ACGIH). It is suspected of being a brain, lymphatic and gastrointestinal carcinogen.[54] Several million workers are involved in industrial processes in which vinyl chloride is used. The federal exposure limit for vinyl chloride is 1 part per million (ppm) in air over an 8-hour day and a peak of no more than 5 ppm averaged over a 15–minute period.

Inhalation is the main route of entry for vinyl chloride. If engineering controls cannot reduce air concentrations to permissible levels, workers are required to wear respirators with an air supply. If levels are less than 25 ppm, a gas mask may be worn instead. Workers should also wear protective clothing, since vinyl chloride is a skin irritant.

---

[53] *See* 15.04[1][c] *supra.*

[54] *See* 15.10[1], 15.11 [1] and 15.07[4][a] *supra.*

Pre-employment and periodic physical examinations should include palpation of the liver and liver function tests. The latter are blood tests that can detect elevated levels of liver enzymes, which can be signs of liver damage. The pre-employment and ongoing medical patient histories should include detailed information about exposures that could harm the liver, including alcohol intake, hepatitis and exposure to hepatotoxic (toxic to liver cells) drugs or chemicals. Periodic liver scans or ultrasonography (a method of outlining or visualizing body parts by means of ultrasonic waves) may be carried out to detect liver cancer (Sittig, 1985).

[f]   Acrylonitrile

Acrylonitrile is classified as a carcinogen by the Environmental Protection Agency (EPA) and as a probable carcinogen by the International Association for Research on Cancer (IARC). In addition to the colon, it also affects the lungs and the prostate.[55] Acrylonitrile is used as a pesticide and in the manufacture of various plastics, synthetic fibers, chemicals and other substances. Both the federal time weighted average exposure and the American Conference of Government and Industrial Hygienists (ACGIH) threshold limit value are 2 ppm in air.

Acrylonitrile can be inhaled or absorbed through the skin. It can enter the body from contaminated rubber or leather and may sometimes be ingested or absorbed by the eye or through skin contact. Exposed workers should wear respirators, clothing (not leather) to protect the skin and eye protection. Medical surveillance should include attention to organs in which acrylonitrile may be carcinogenic, including the liver and lungs.

[g]   Benzidine and Related Compounds

Benzidine and other aromatic amines are considered carcinogenic and have been implicated in bladder cancer.[56] As a result, their use in industry has been either abandoned or reduced to a minimum. Benzidine is used primarily in dye manufacture, but other industrial processes in which it may be used include the manufacture of rubber and of plastic films and in various medical and other laboratory processes. The National Institute for Occupational Safety and Health

---

[55] *See* 15.03[7][a], 15.04[1] [d] and 15.08[3][a] *supra.*

[56] *See* 15.08[1][a] *supra.*

(NIOSH) has estimated that very few American workers are in jobs that involve benzidine exposure (Sittig, 1985).

Formerly used in dye and rubber manufacture, 2–naphthylamine is no longer made in the United States and is used in research only. Auramine is still used in the manufacture of dyes for textiles, leather and paper, but NIOSH estimates that only a few thousand workers are in jobs that involve potential exposure to auramine. People who work with the finished products dyed with auramine dyes are not considered at risk (Sittig, 1985). MOCA (4,4'-methylenebis(2–chloroaniline)) is used in the production of solid elastomeric parts, as a cure for epoxy resins and in the manufacture of urethane foams.

All these substances are classified as carcinogens, and there are no permissible workplace exposure levels. Workers who must handle aromatic amines are required to wear protective clothing, gloves and, in some situations, respirators with an air supply. Workers must shower before leaving the workplace after each shift, and the protective clothing should be placed in special containers for disposal or decontamination.

[h] 4–Aminobiphenyl

Another substance classified by the International Association for Research on Cancer (IARC) as a Class 1 bladder carcinogen is 4–aminobiphenyl.[57] This substance, formerly used in rubber and dye manufacture, is no longer manufactured in the United States, but it is still used in research. It is regulated by OSHA as a carcinogen, with no permissible exposure levels.

In workplaces where 4–aminobiphenyl is present, stringent engineering controls should be in effect to prevent airborne contamination. Workers who must handle 4–aminobiphenyl should wear full-body protective clothing, gloves and a respirator with an air supply. Workers should shower upon removing protective garments after the work shift. Medical screening of workers should focus on previous and concurrent exposure to other carcinogens and on screening for bladder cancer.

[i] Cadmium

Cadmium, a natural mineral, is a suspected kidney and prostate carcinogen and is classified as carcinogenic and a hazardous substance

---

[57] See 15.08 [1][a] supra.

by the Environmental Protection Agency (EPA).[58] The general population ingests a certain amount of cadmium that occurs naturally in food or that enters the water supply from metal pipes. Cadmium is also a component of tobacco smoke.

In industry, cadmium is used as a protective coating for metals and as a component of various alloys. It is used in the electrodes of alkaline batteries, in nuclear power generation, as a component of polyvinyl chloride plastics, in nickel plating and in many other processes. It is used as an amalgam in dentistry. Cadmium compounds are found in poisons used in agriculture; in pigments, paints and glass; and in chemicals used in photo processing.

Regulators have set the following exposure limits: for cadmium dust 0.2 mg/m^3 in air, with a ceiling of 0.6 mg/m^3 (NIOSH) or 0.05 mg/m^3 (American Conference of Government and Industrial Hygienists); for cadmium fumes 0.1 mg/m^3 in air, with a ceiling of 0.03 mg/m^3 (NIOSH) or 0.05 mg/m^3 (ACGIH) (NIOSH Pocket Guide to Chemical Hazards, 1985). Workers who are exposed to higher levels of cadmium dusts or fumes should wear a respirator, and those who are exposed to cadmium dust should also wear eye protection. An evaluation for kidney disease should be part of the pre-employment medical examination, and subsequent blood tests are advised to detect early signs of kidney dysfunction (Sittig, 1985).

[j] Polycyclic Aromatic Hydrocarbons

Polynuclear aromatic hydrocarbons (PAHs) are associated with skin and respiratory cancer.[59] They include the known carcinogen benzo [a]pyrene, other compounds that may be carcinogenic and still others that probably are not. Few attempts have been made to set uniform exposure standards to PAHs (Sittig, 1985). The ACGIH recommends a threshold limit value of 0.2 mg/cubic meter for benzene solubles. OSHA, NIOSH and ACGIH also have promulgated a mosaic of exposure standards covering employees in several different industries (such as coke oven workers) and based on different methods of assaying exposure.

PAHs enter the body through the lungs. Therefore, emission controls are used to reduce PAH exposure in the workplace. Most occupations no longer involve potentially carcinogenic exposures of the skin to

---

[58] *See* 15.08[2][a] and 15.08[3] [a] *supra.*

[59] *See* 15.04[1] [b] and 15.09[1] [a] *supra.*

PAHs. Workers whose skin may be exposed to PAHs should keep contact with these substances to a minimum, wash their hands and face after potential exposures and avoid simultaneous exposure to UV radiation (Emmett, 1975).[60] Pre-employment and ongoing periodic medical examinations are recommended for workers who handle these substances.

[k]   Soots, Tars and Oils

Soots, tars and mineral oils are a group of substances also listed as Class 1 bladder carcinogens by the IARC.[61] These substances are largely given off as wastes or occur as contaminants or by-products of industrial processes. Exposure to coal tar, coal soot and fumes as well as other coal wastes is believed to cause cancer of the bladder, skin, lungs and gastrointestinal tract.[62] Polycyclic aromatic hydrocarbons (PAHs) are the suspected carcinogens in these substances. Because soots, tars and oils contain variable amounts of PAHs, no exposure limits to these substances have been set (Sittig, 1985).

Various fluids used as cutting oils are employed in drilling, grinding and other machining operations. Although research has indicated that cutting oils and fluids may play a role in stomach and liver cancer etiology, standards of maximum workplace exposure have not been promulgated.[63] Some synthetic cutting fluids contain nitrosamines, which have been shown to be carcinogenic in animals. Cutting fluids that do not contain nitrosamines should be substituted whenever possible. Other methods of worker protection include ventilation of the work area, isolation of the process, protective clothing, and on a temporary basis the use of a respirator (Sittig, 1985).

[l]   Dusts

The American Conference of Government and Industrial Hygienists (ACGIH) sets threshold limit values (TLVs) for different kinds of toxic and nontoxic dusts. For example, the TLV for hardwood dust is 1 mg/m^3, for grain dust 4 mg/m^3 and for softwood dust 5 mg/m^3 (Sittig, 1985). Regulation of some inorganic dusts which are pulmonary carcinogens is also of potential importance.[64]

---

[60] See 15.12[4][m] *infra.*

[61] See 15.12[1] *supra.*

[62] See 15.08[1], 15.09[1] [a], 15.04[1][b] and 15.07 *supra.*

[63] See 15.07[2] and 15.07 [4] *supra.*

[64] See 15.04[1] [d], 15.05 [1] and 15.06[1][a] *supra.*

Despite their epidemiologic association with gastric cancer, organic and many inorganic dusts are not identified or regulated by any official body as carcinogens.[65] It is their other effects on worker health that usually form the basis of regulation. For example, silica is primarily regulated because it causes silicosis, a nonmalignant lung disease, rather than cancer.

Dust control measures in the workplace include the full range of ventilation strategies and wet manufacturing methods. If these measures are not fully effective, workers should wear respirators with filters, when necessary.

[m] Ultraviolet Radiation

The avoidance of exposure to ultraviolet (UV) radiation decreases the risk of basal and squamous cell skin cancers and probably of melanoma as well.[66] Wearing hats with brims and tightly knit clothing with long sleeves can protect the skin from UV radiation, but protective clothing can be uncomfortable when it is worn outdoors in hot weather. Sunscreens are the most effective way to prevent sun-induced skin damage. Outdoor workers should use sunscreens with a solar protection factor (SPF) of at least 15 that protect the skin from a wide range of ultraviolet wavelengths (most commercially available sunscreens only screen out ultraviolet B radiation, one portion of the UV spectrum). The sunscreen should be resistant to perspiration and should be re-applied several times every day.

Workers should avoid exposures to chemicals that may augment the carcinogenic effects of solar radiation. These substances include polycyclic aromatic hydrocarbons[67] and other known carcinogens, some pharmaceuticals that increase the skin's sensitivity to the sun, skin irritants and immunosuppressive drugs (Emmett, 1987). Outdoor workers should receive periodic dermatologic examinations, especially if they have fair, sun-sensitive skin.

Personal protection is recommended for welders and other workers who are exposed to high-intensity ultraviolet (UV) radiation from a manufactured source. These workers should wear goggles, face shields and masks to protect their eyes. Protective clothing and barrier creams can shield the skin from exposure. Shiny surfaces that reflect UV

---

[65] See 15.07[2] [a] *supra.*

[66] See 15.09 *supra.*

[67] See 15.12[4] [j] *infra.*

radiation should be covered or removed from the workplace. Operations that produce high levels of UV radiation should be carried out behind barriers that shield other workers (Moss, 1977).

[n]   Ionizing Radiation

Nuclear energy and weapons industry workers and health care workers are at risk for skin cancer and radiodermatitis from ionizing radiation.[68] Skin cancer can be induced by ionizing radiation in cumulative dose equivalents of 30,000 rem (Emmett, 1975). The current recommendation regarding occupational radiation exposure was set by the National Council on Radiation Protection and Measurement, a body appointed by Congress. This council recommended that radiation doses in industry be kept "as low as reasonably possible," a recommendation that often results in exposures lower than the established numeric limits. The current exposure limit for the skin of the whole body is set at $7\frac{1}{2}$ rem per calendar quarter, and for the hands, forearms, feet and ankles, at $18\frac{3}{4}$ rem per quarter (Voelz, 1988).

Shielding is the most effective way to limit workers' exposure to ionizing radiation. X-ray machines, both those used in industry and in medical diagnosis, are designed to shield their operators from exposure. Radiologists, dentists and x-ray technicians operate x-ray equipment remotely from outside the room. Nuclear industry workers may wear full-body protective clothing with gloves and respirators or may work with radioactive materials enclosed in glove boxes. Nuclear industry plants are designed to sequester processes involving radioactive materials away from where most employees work (Voelz, 1988).

Workers who are accidentally exposed to large amounts of radiation undergo decontamination. In the case of skin exposure, this usually involves washing the skin repeatedly over several days with water and a mild detergent, taking care not to abrade the skin.

Prospective employees in an industry with risk of cutaneous exposure to ionizing radiation should be questioned about their past exposures to ionizing radiation, not only at work but also as part of medical treatment. Any history of skin disease should be noted. The symptom triad of skin atrophy, hyperkeratosis (skin thickening) and telangiectasia (reddish lesions caused by dilated blood vessels) indicates chronic radiodermatitis and suggests a past exposure to ionizing radiation (Voelz, 1988).

---

[68] *See* 15.09[1][a] *supra.*

The skin should be examined as part of the periodic medical evaluation that is recommended for all workers who are potentially exposed to ionizing radiation. Areas of chronic radiodermatitis should be watched for the development of skin cancer, and certain types of skin lesions with a high risk of becoming cancerous should be surgically excised (Voelz, 1988).

15.100 BIBLIOGRAPHY

Reference Bibliography

Alderson, M.: Occupational Cancer. London: Butterworths, 1986.

Ashford, N. A.: Federal Regulation of Occupational Health and Safety in the Workplace. In: Levy, B. S. and Wegman, D. H. (Eds.): Occupational Health. Recognizing and Preventing Work-Related Disease. Boston: Little Brown, 1988.

Austin, D. F.: Larynx. In: Schottenfeld, D. and Fraumeni, J. F.: Cancer Epidemiology and Prevention. Philadelphia: Saunders, 1982.

Austin, D. F., et al.: Malignant Melanoma Among Employees of Lawrence Livermore National Laboratory. Lancet 2:712–716, Oct. 3, 1981.

Axelson, O.: Cancer Risks from Exposure to Radon Progeny in Mines and Dwellings. Rec. Res. Cancer Res. 120:146–165, 1990.

Bang, K. M., et al.: Sensitivity of Fecal Hemoccult Testing and Flexible Sigmoidoscopy for Colorectal Cancer Screening. J. Occup. Med. 28:709–13, Aug. 1986.

Brownson, R. C., et al.: Occupational Risk of Prostate Cancer: A Cancer Registry–Based Study. J. Occup. Med. 30:523–526, June 1988.

Calcaterra, T. C. and Juillard, G. J. F.: Larynx and Hypopharynx. In: Haskell, C. M. (Ed.): Cancer Treatment, 3d ed. Philadelphia: Saunders, 1990a.

Calcaterra, T. C. and Juillard, G. J. F.: Nasal Cavity and Paranasal Sinuses. In: Haskell, C. M. (Ed.): Cancer Treatment, 3d ed. Philadelphia: Saunders, 1990b.

Chase, G. R., et al.: Evaluation for Compensation of Asbestos-Exposed Individuals. II. Apportionment of Risk for Lung Cancer and Mesothelioma. J. Occup. Med. 27:189–198, Mar. 1985.

Checkoway, H., et al.: Medical, Lifestyle, and Occupational Risk Factors for Prostate Cancer. Prostate 10:79–88, 1987.

Davis, D. L., et al.: Is Brain Cancer Mortality Increasing in Industrial Countries? Ann. N.Y. Acad. Sci. 609:191–204, 1990.

Day, N. E. and Munoz, N.: Esophagus. In: Schottenfeld, D. and Fraumeni, J. F., Jr. (Eds.): Cancer Epidemiology and Prevention. Philadelphia: Saunders, 1982.

Dienstag, J. L., et al.: Acute Hepatitis. In: Wilson, J. D., et al. (Eds.): Harrison's Principles of Internal Medicine, 12th ed. New York: McGraw-Hill, 1991.

Doll, R. and Peto, R.: The Causes of Cancer: Quantitative Estimates of the Avoidable Risks of Cancer in the United States Today. J. Natl. Cancer Inst. 66:1193–1308, June 1981.

Emmett, E. A.: Occupational Skin Cancers. Occup. Med. 2:165–177, Jan.-Mar. 1987.

Emmett, E. A.: Occupational Skin Cancer: A Review. J. Occup. Med. 17.44–49, Jan. 1975.

Fishbein, L.: Overview of Mutagens and Carcinogens in the Environment. In: Sugimura, T., et al. (Eds.): Environmental Mutagens and Carcinogens. Proceedings of the 3d International Conference on Environmental Mutagens. New York: Alan R. Liss, 1982.

Fontham, E. T. and Correa, P.: Epidemiology of Pancreatic Cancer. Surg. Clin. North Am. 69:551–567, June 1989.

Frank, A. L.: Occupational Cancers of the Respiratory Tract. Occup. Med. 2:71–83, Jan.-Mar. 1987.

Fraumeni, J. F., Jr. and Blot, W. J.: Lung and Pleura. In: Schottenfeld, D. and Fraumeni, J. F. (Eds.): Cancer Epidemiology and Prevention. Philadelphia: Saunders, 1982.

Fredriksson, M., et al.: Colon Cancer, Physical Activity, and Occupational Exposures. A Case-Control Study. Cancer 63:1838–1842, May 1, 1989.

Gallagher, R. P., et al.: Occupation and Risk of Cutaneous Melanoma. Am. J. Ind. Med. 9:289–294, 1986.

Garnick, M. B. and Brenner, B. M.: Tumors of the Urinary Tract. In: Wilson, J. D., et al. (Eds.): Harrison's Principles of Internal Medicine, 12th ed. New York: McGraw-Hill, 1991.

Geller, A. C., et al.: Advances in Screening Protocols for the Detection of Early Bladder Cancer. J. Occup. Med. 32:929–935, Sept. 1990.

Green, F. H. Y. and Vallyathan, V.: Pathology of Occupational Lung Cancer. In: Merchant, J. A. (Ed.): Occupational Respiratory Diseases. Rockville, Md.: U.S. Department of Health and Human Services, Sept. 1986.

Greenberger, N. J. and Isselbacher, K. J.: Diseases of the Gallbladder and Bile Ducts. In: Wilson, J. D., et al. (Eds.): Harrison's

Principles of Internal Medicine, 12th ed. New York: McGraw-Hill, 1991.

Greene, M. H.: Non-Hodgkin's Lymphoma and Mycosis Fungoides. In: Schottenfeld, D. and Fraumeni, J. F., Jr. (Eds.): Cancer Epidemiology and Prevention. Philadelphia: Saunders, 1982.

Greenwald, P.: Prostate. In: Schottenfeld, D. and Fraumeni, J. F., Jr. (Eds.): Cancer Epidemiology and Prevention. Philadelphia: Saunders, 1982.

Grufferman, S.: Hodgkin's Disease. In: Schottenfeld, D. and Fraumeni, J. F., Jr. (Eds.): Cancer Epidemiology and Prevention. Philadelphia: Saunders, 1982.

Haskell, C. M., et al.: Colon and Rectum. In: Haskell, C. M. (Ed.): Cancer Treatment, 3d ed. Philadelphia: Saunders, 1990.

Heath, C. W., Jr.: Epidemiology and Hereditary Aspects of Malignant Lymphoma Including Hodgkin's Disease. In: Wiernik, P. H., et al. (Eds.): Neoplastic Diseases of the Blood. New York: Churchill Livingstone, 1985.

Hoar, S. K., et al.: Screening for Colorectal Cancer and Polyps Among Pattern Makers. J. Occup. Med. 28:704–8, Aug. 1986.

Hochberg, F. and Pruitt, A.: Neoplastic Diseases of the Central Nervous System. In: Wilson, J. D., et al. (Eds.): Harrison's Principles of Internal Medicine, 12th ed. New York: McGraw-Hill, 1991.

Hodous, T. K. and Melius, J. M.: Clinical Presentation. In: Merchant, J. A. (Ed.): Occupational Respiratory Diseases. Rockville, Md.: U.S. Department of Health and Human Services, Sept. 1986.

Howard, J. K.: Occupationally Related Cancer. In: Howard, J. K. and Tyrer, F. H. (Eds.): Textbook of Occupational Medicine. New York: Churchill-Livingstone, 1987.

International Association for Research on Cancer: Ultraviolet Radiation (Monogr.). Eval. Carcinog. Risk Chem. Hum. 40:379–415, 1986.

Isselbacher, K. J. and Wands, J. R.: Neoplasms of the Liver. In: Wilson, J. D., et al. (Eds.): Harrison's Principles of Internal Medicine, 12th ed. New York: McGraw-Hill, 1991.

Jones, R. D.: Epidemiology of Brain Tumours in Man and Their Relationship with Chemical Agents. Food Chem. Toxicol. 24:99–103, Feb. 1986.

Kessler, E. and Brandt-Rauf, P. W.: Occupational Cancers of the Brain and Bone. Occup. Med.: State Art Rev. 2:155–63, 1987.

Kilburn, K. H.: Medical Screening for Lung Cancer: Perspective and Strategy. J. Occup. Med. 28:714–718, Aug. 1986.

La Vecchia, C., et al.: Occupation and the Risk of Bladder Cancer. Int. J. Epidemiol. 19:264–268, June 1990.

Lee, J. A. H.: Melanoma. In: Schottenfeld, D. and Fraumeni, J. F., Jr. (Eds.): Cancer Epidemiology and Prevention. Philadelphia: Saunders, 1982.

Lemen, R. A.: Occupationally Induced Lung Cancer Epidemiology. In: Merchant, J. A. (Ed.): Occupational Respiratory Diseases. Rockville, Md.: U.S. Department of Health and Human Services, Sept. 1986.

Levine, D. S.: Does Asbestos Exposure Cause Gastrointestinal Cancer? Dig. Dis. Sci. 30:1189–1198, Dec. 1985.

Lilis, R.: Mesothelioma. In: Merchant, J. A. (Ed.): Occupational Respiratory Diseases. Rockville, Md.: U.S. Department of Health and Human Services, Sept. 1986.

McDonald, J. C.: Cancer Risks Due to Asbestos and Man-Made Fibers. Rec. Res. Cancer Res. 120:122–131, 1990.

Mack, T. M.: Pancreas. In: Schottenfeld, D. and Fraumeni, J. F., Jr. (Eds.): Cancer Epidemiology and Prevention. Philadelphia: Saunders, 1982.

McLaughlin, J. K., et al.: Etiology of Cancer of the Renal Pelvis. J. Natl. Cancer Inst. 71:287–291, Aug. 1983.

Mathias, C. G. T.: Occupational Dermatoses. In: Zenz, C.: Occupational Medicine. Principles and Practical Applications, 2d ed. Chicago: Year Book Medical Publishers, 1988.

Mayer, R. J.: Neoplasms of the Esophagus and Stomach. In: Wilson, J. D., et al. (Eds.): Harrison's Principles of Internal Medicine, 12th ed. New York: McGraw-Hill, 1991a.

Mayer, R. J.: Tumors of the Large and Small Intestine. In: Wilson, J. D., et al. (Eds.): Harrison's Principles of Internal Medicine, 12th ed. New York: McGraw-Hill, 1991b.

Mayer, R. J.: Pancreatic Cancer. In: Wilson, J. D., et al. (Eds.): Harrison's Principles of Internal Medicine, 12th ed. New York: McGraw-Hill, 1991c.

Minna, J. D.: Neoplasms of the Lung. In: Wilson, J. D., et al. (Eds.): Harrison's Principles of Internal Medicine, 12th ed. New York: McGraw-Hill, 1991.

Monson, R. R.: Occupational Epidemiology. Boca Raton, Fla.: CRC Press, 1990.

Morrison, A. S. and Cole, P.: Urinary Tract. In: Schottenfeld, D. and Fraumeni, J. F., Jr. (Eds.): Cancer Epidemiology and Prevention. Philadelphia: Saunders, 1982.

Moss, A. R.: Occupational Exposure and Brain Tumors. J. Toxicol. Environ. Health 16:703–711, 1985.

Moss, E., et al.: Radiation. In: Occupational Diseases: A Guide to Their Recognition. Rockville, Md.: U.S. Department of Health, Education, and Welfare, National Institute for Occupational Safety and Health, 1977.

Nadler, L. M.: The Malignant Lymphomas. In: Wilson, J. D., et al. (Eds.): Harrison's Principles of Internal Medicine, 12th ed. New York: McGraw-Hill, 1991.

Neugut, A. I. and Wylie, P.: Occupational Cancers of the Gastrointestinal Tract. I. Colon, Stomach, and Esophagus. Occup. Med.: State Art Rev. 2:109–135, 1987.

Neugut, A. I., et al.: Occupational Cancers of the Gastrointestinal Tract. II. Pancreas, Liver, and Biliary Tract. Occup. Med.: State Art Rev. 2:137–153, 1987.

NIOSH Pocket Guide to Chemical Hazards. Fifth Printing. Washington, D.C.: U.S. Department of Health and Human Services, DHEW (NIOSH) Publication No. 78–210, Sept. 1985.

Powell, C. H.: Evaluation of Exposure to Chemical Agents. In: Cralley, L. V. and Cralley, L. J. (Eds.): Patty's Industrial Hygiene and Toxicology. Volume III: Theory and Rationale of Industrial Hygiene Practice. New York: Wiley, 1979.

Raffle. P. A. B., et al. (Eds.): Hunter's Diseases of Occupations. Boston: Little Brown, 1987.

Reif, J. S., et al.: Occupational Risks for Brain Cancer: A New Zealand Cancer Registry-Based Study. J. Occup. Med. 31:863–867, Oct. 1989.

Risch, H. A., et al.: Occupational Factors and the Incidence of Cancer of the Bladder in Canada. Br. J. Ind. Med. 45:361–367, June 1988.

Ruder, A. M., et al.: National Estimates of Occupational Exposure to Animal Bladder Tumorigens. J. Occup. Med. 32:797–805, Sept. 1990.

Sagalowsky, A. I. and Wilson, J. D.: Hyperplasia and Carcinoma of the Prostate. In: Wilson, J. D., et al. (Eds.): Harrison's Principles of Internal Medicine, 12th ed. New York: McGraw-Hill, 1991.

Schoenberg, B. S.: Nervous System. In: Schottenfeld, D. and Fraumeni, J. F., Jr. (Eds.): Cancer Epidemiology and Prevention. Philadelphia: Saunders, 1982.

Schottenfeld, D. and Winawer, S. J.: Large Intestine. In: Schottenfeld, D. and Fraumeni, J. F., Jr. (Eds.): Cancer Epidemiology and Prevention. Philadelphia: Saunders, 1982.

Schulte, P. A.: Screening for Bladder Cancer in High-Risk Groups: Delineation of the Problem. J. Occup. Med. 32:789–792, Sept. 1990.

Schulte, P. A., et al.: Occupational Cancer of the Urinary Tract. Occup. Med.: State Art Rev. 2:85–107, 1987.

Scotto, J. and Fraumeni, J. F., Jr.: Skin (Other Than Melanoma). In: Schottenfeld, D. and Fraumeni, J. F., Jr. (Eds.): Cancer Epidemiology and Prevention. Philadelphia: Saunders, 1982.

Sepulveda, M. J.: Screening. In: Merchant, J. A. (Ed.): Occupational Respiratory Diseases. Rockville, Md.: U.S. Dept. of Health and Human Services, Sept. 1986.

Silverman, D. T., et al.: Occupational Risks of Bladder Cancer in the United States. I. White Men. J. Natl. Cancer Inst. 81:1472–8180, Oct. 4, 1989.

Sittig, M.: Handbook of Toxic and Hazardous Chemicals and Carcinogens. Park Ridge, N.J.: Noyes Publications, 1985.

Smith, A. H., et al.: Asbestos and Kidney Cancer: The Evidence Supports a Causal Association. Am. J. Ind. Med. 16:159–166, 1989.

Sober, A. J. and Koh, H. K.: Melanoma and Other Pigmented Skin Lesions. In: Wilson, J. D., et al. (Eds.): Harrison's Principles of Internal Medicine, 12th ed. New York: McGraw-Hill, 1991.

Speizer, F. E.: Environmental Lung Diseases. In: Wilson, J. D., et al. (Eds.): Harrison's Principles of Internal Medicine, 12th ed. New York: McGraw-Hill, 1991.

Spiegelman, D. and Wegman, D. H.: Occupation-Related Risks for Colorectal Cancer. J. Natl. Cancer Inst. 75:813–821, Nov. 1985.

Steineck, G., et al.: Urothelial Cancer and Some Industry-Related Chemicals: An Evaluation of the Epidemiologic Literature. Am. J. Ind. Med. 17:371–391, 1990.

Strick, R. A.: Skin Cancer. In: Haskell, C. M. (Ed.): Cancer Treatment, 2d ed. Philadelphia: Saunders, 1985.

Swanson, N. A.: Skin Cancer. In: Wilson, J. D., et al. (Eds.): Harrison's Principles of Internal Medicine, 12th ed. New York: McGraw-Hill, 1991.

Swanson, G. M.: Cancer Prevention in the Workplace and Natural Environment. A Review of Etiology, Research Design, and Methods of Risk Reduction. Cancer 62:1725–1746, 1988.

Tager, I. B.: Health Effects of Involuntary Smoking in the Workplace. N.Y. State J. Med. 89:27–31, Jan. 1989.

Tamburro, C. H., et al.: Approaches to Occupational Cancer. In: Alderman, M. H. and Hanley, M. J.: Clinical Medicine for the Occupational Physician. New York: Marcel Dekker, 1982.

Vagero, D., et al.: Occupation and Malignant Melanoma: A Study Based on Cancer Registration Data in England and Wales and in Sweden. Br. J. Ind. Med. 47:317–324, May 1990.

Vagero, D., et al.: Melanoma and Other Tumors of the Skin Among Office, Other Indoor and Outdoor Workers in Sweden 1961–1979. Br. J. Cancer 53:507–512, Apr. 1986.

Vineis, P. and Simonato, L.: Proportion of Lung and Bladder Cancers in Males Resulting from Occupation: A Systematic Approach. Arch. Env. Health 46:6–15, 1991.

Voelz, G. L.: Ionizing Radiation. In: Zenz, C. (Ed.): Occupational Medicine. Principles and Practical Applications. Chicago: Year Book Medical Publishers, 1988.

Weiss, W.: Asbestos and Colorectal Cancer. Gastroenterology 99:876–884, Sept. 1990.

Whitmore, W. F., Jr.: Current Therapy of Bladder Cancer. J. Occup. Med. 32:921–925, Sept. 1990.

Wright, W. E., et al.: Adenocarcinoma of the Stomach and Exposure to Occupational Dust. Am. J. Epidemiol. 128:64–73, July 1988.

Zahm, S. H., et al.: The National Bladder Cancer Study: Employment in the Chemical Industry. J. Natl. Cancer Inst. 79:217–222, Aug. 1987.

Additional References

Alavanja, M. C., et al.: Cancer Mortality in the U.S. Flour Industry. J. Natl. Cancer Inst. 82:840–848, May 6, 1990.

Albin, M., et al.: Mortality and Cancer Morbidity in Cohorts of Asbestos Cement Workers and Referents. Br. J. Ind. Med. 47:602–610, Sept. 1990.

ATSDR (Agency for Toxic Substances and Disease Registry) Case Studies in Environmental Medicine. Vinyl Chloride Toxicity. J. Toxicol. Clin. Toxicol. 28:267–286, 1990.

Bethwaite, P. B., et al.: Cancer Risks in Painters: Study Based on the New Zealand Cancer Registry. Br. J. Ind. Med. 47:742–746, Nov. 1990.

Checkoway, H., et al.: Latency Analysis in Occupational Epidemiology. Arch. Environ. Health 45:95–100, Mar.-Apr. 1990.

Coggon, D., et al.: Stomach Cancer and Work in Dusty Industries. Br. J. Ind. Med. 47:298–301, May 1990. Cooke, M.: Cancer of the Skin. Occup. Health (Lond.) 42:262–264, Sept. 1990.

Eide, I.: A Review of Exposure Conditions and Possible Health Effects Associated with Aerosol and Vapour from Low-Aromatic Oil-Based Drilling Fluids. Ann. Occup. Hyg. 34:149–157, Apr. 1990.

Fleisher, J. M.: Occupational and Nonoccupational Risk Factors in Relation to an Excess of Primary Liver Cancer Observed Among Residents of Brooklyn, New York. Cancer 65:180–185, Jan. 1, 1990.

Fluorescent Lighting and Malignant Melanoma. International Non-ionizing Radiation Committee of the International Radiation Protection Association. Health Phys 58:111–112, Jan. 1990.

Frumin, E., et al.: Occupational Bladder Cancer in Textile Dyeing and Printing Workers: Six Cases and Their Significance for Screening Programs. J. Occup. Med 32:887–890, Sept. 1990.

Gibbs, A. R.: Role of Asbestos and Other Fibres in the Development of Diffuse Malignant Mesothelioma. Thorax 45:649–654, Sept. 1990.

Gibbs, G. W.: Colorectal Cancer and Polypropylene Exposure: How Good is the Evidence? [Letter.] J. Occup. Med. 32:1143–1145, Nov. 1990.

Haguenoer, J. M., et al.: Occupational Risk Factors for Upper Respiratory Tract and Upper Digestive Tract Cancers. Br. J. Ind. Med. 47:380–383, June 1990.

Hartge, P., et al.: Unexplained Excess Risk of Bladder Cancer in Men. J. Natl. Cancer Inst. 82:1636–1640, Oct. 17, 1990.

Hemstreet III, G. P., et al.: Quantitative Fluorescence Image Analysis in Bladder Cancer Screening. J. Occup. Med. 32:822–828, Sept. 1990.

Hulka, B. S.: Principles of Bladder Cancer Screening in an Intervention Trial. J. Occup. Med. 32:812–816, Sept. 1990.

Hurst, R. E., et al.: Molecular and Cellular Biological Approaches and Techniques in the Detection of Bladder Cancer and Enhanced Risk for Bladder Cancer in High-Risk Groups. J. Occup. Med. 32:854–862, Sept. 1990.

Johnson, E. S.: Association Between Soft Tissue Sarcomas, Malignant Lymphomas, and Phenoxy Herbicides/Chlorophenols: Evidence from Occupational Cohort Studies. Fundam. Appl. Toxicol. 14:219–234, Feb. 1990.

Kelly, S. J. and Guidotti, T. L.: Phenoxyacetic Acid Herbicides and Chlorophenols and the Etiology of Lymphoma and Soft-Tissue Neoplasms. Public Health Rev. 17:1–37, 1989–1990.

Kurokawa, Y., et al.: Toxicity and Carcinogenicity of Potassium Bromate—A New Renal Carcinogen. Environ. Health Perspect. 87:309–335, July 1990.

Lippmann, M.: Man-Made Mineral Fibers (MMMF): Human Exposures and Health Risk Assessment. Toxicol. Ind. Health 6:225–246, Mar. 1990.

Loomis, D. P. and Savitz, D. A.: Mortality from Brain Cancer and Leukaemia Among Electrical Workers. Br. J. Ind. Med. 47:633–638, Sept. 1990.

Marsh, G. M., et al.: A Protocol for Bladder Cancer Screening and Medical Surveillance Among High-Risk Groups: The Drake Health Registry Experience. J. Occup. Med. 32:881–886, Sept. 1990.

Mason, T. J. and Vogler, W. J.: Bladder Cancer Screening at the DuPont Chambers Works: A New Initiative. J. Occup. Med. 32:874–877, Sept. 1990.

Messing, E. M. and Vaillancourt, A.: Hematuria Screening for Bladder Cancer. J. Occup. Med. 32:838–845, Sept. 1990.

Mumford, J. L., et al.: Human Lung Cancer Risks Due to Complex Organic Mixtures of Combustion Emissions. Rec. Res. Cancer Res. 120:181–189, 1990.

Neuberger, M. and Kundi, M.: Occupational Dust Exposure and Cancer Mortality—Results of a Prospective Cohort Study. IARC Sci. Publ. 65–73, 1990.

Park, R. M., et al.: Brain Cancer Mortality at a Manufacturer of Aerospace Electromechanical Systems. Am. J. Ind. Med. 17:537–552, 1990.

Pietri, F., et al.: Occupational Risk Factors for Cancer of the Pancreas: A Case-Control Study. Br. J. Ind. Med. 47:425–428, June 1990.

Piolatto, G., et al.: Bladder Cancer Mortality of Workers Exposed to Aromatic Amines: An Updated Analysis. Br. J. Cancer 63:457–459, March 1991.

Prout, G. R., Jr.: Historical and Modern Role of Cystoscopy and Bladder Mucosal Biopsy in Detecting Bladder Cancer in a High-Risk Population. J. Occup. Med. 32:834–837, Sept. 1990.

Report of the International Committee on Nickel Carcinogenesis in Man. Scand. J. Work. Environ. Health 16:1–82, Feb. 1990.

Sama, S. R., et al.: Cancer Incidence Among Massachusetts Firefighters, 1982–1986. Am. J. Ind. Med. 18:47–54, 1990.

Samet, J. M. and Hornung, R. W.: Review of Radon and Lung Cancer Risk. Risk Anal. 10:65–75, Mar. 1990.

Sankila, R. J., et al.: Relationship Between Occupation and Lung Cancer as Analyzed by Age and Histologic Type. Cancer 65:1651–1656, Apr. 1, 1990.

Seidman, H. and Selikoff, I. J.: Decline in Death Rates Among Asbestos Insulation Workers 1967–1986 Associated with Diminution of Work Exposure to Asbestos. Ann. N.Y. Acad. Sci. 609:300–318, 1990.

Siemiatycki, J.: Discovering Occupational Carcinogens in Population-Based Case-Control Studies: Review of Findings from an

Exposure-Based Approach and a Methodologic Comparison of Alternative Data Collection Strategies. Rec. Res. Cancer Res. 120:26–38, 1990.

Silverman, D. T., et al.: Occupational Risks of Bladder Cancer Among White Women in the United States. Am. J. Epidemiol. 132:453–61, Sept. 1990.

Smart, C. R.: Bladder Cancer Survival Statistics. J. Occup. Med. 32:926–928, Sept. 1990.

Smith, A. H., et al.: Epidemiological Evidence Indicates Asbestos Causes Laryngeal Cancer. J. Occup. Med. 32:499–507, June 1990.

Sorahan, T. and Sole, G.: Coarse Fishing and Urothelial Cancer: A Regional Case-Control Study. Br. J. Cancer 62:138–141, July 1990.

Teta, M. J., et al.: An Update of Mortality Due to Brain Neoplasms and Other Causes Among Employees of a Petrochemical Facility. J. Occup. Med. 33:45–51, Jan. 1991.

Theriault, G.: Cancer Risks due to Exposure to Electromagnetic Fields. Rec. Res. Cancer Res. 120:166–180, 1990.

Theriault, G. P., et al.: Bladder Cancer Screening Among Primary Aluminum Production Workers in Quebec. J. Occup. Med. 32:869–872, Sept. 1990.

Vineis, P. and Simonato, L.: Proportion of Lung and Bladder Cancers in Males Resulting from Occupation: A Systematic Approach. Arch. Environ. Health 46:6–15, Jan.-Feb. 1991.

Vitasa, B. C., et al.: Association of Nonmelanoma Skin Cancer and Actinic Keratosis with Cumulative Solar Ultraviolet Exposure in Maryland Watermen. Cancer 65:2811–2817, June 15, 1990.

Wald, P. H. and Schneider, J. S.: Medical Surveillance for Melanoma at the Lawrence Livermore National Laboratory. Occup. Med. 5:607–616, July-Sept. 1990.

Ward, E., et al.: Excess Number of Bladder Cancers in Workers Exposed to Ortho-Toluidine and Aniline. J. Natl. Cancer Inst. 83:501–506, Apr. 3, 1991.

Ward, E., et al.: Screening Workers Exposed to 4,4'-methylenebis(2–chloroaniline) for Bladder Cancer by Cystoscopy. J. Occup. Med. 32:865–8, Sept. 1990.

Woodward, S. D. and Winstanley, M. H.: Lung Cancer and Passive
   Smoking at Work: The Carroll Case. Med. J. Aust. 153:682–684,
   Dec. 3–17, 1990.

CHAPTER 16

Asbestosis and Related Cancers

SCOPE

Asbestos is a potent source of injury to lung tissue, causing both fibrosis of the lung interstitium and cancers of the lung and other organs. Widespread industrial use of asbestos has caused considerable exposure among workers, with effects that become manifest 30 years later in an increased incidence of asbestosis and lung cancer. Factors determining whether asbestos will cause lung disease include the toxicity of the dust, the intensity and duration of the exposure, and individual susceptibility. Although new use of asbestos has dropped, continued exposure occurs during demolition or renovation of structures containing asbestos, as well as among workers in maintenance and repair of automotive brakes and among families of exposed workers. Restrictive lung disease caused by asbestos involves decreased lung volume, impaired gas exchange and diminished compliance. This results in cough, difficulty breathing and increased vulnerability to pulmonary infection. Smoking both exacerbates asbestosis and acts as a co-carcinogen in causing lung cancer, increasing the risk substantially. Prevention depends on protecting all workers from any level of exposure to asbestos dust that might cause disease. This involves both substitution of less toxic materials and exposure control practices in the workplace.

SYNOPSIS

16.01 INTRODUCTION

The lung is the site of the most extensive interface between humans and their environment. Since toxic materials are generally present in the highest concentrations at worksites, most environmentally induced lung disease is caused by occupational exposure (Sheppard, 1988). Occupational lung disease is the leading work related disease in the United States (Preventing Illness, 1985).

[1] History of Asbestos Disease

Asbestos is a particularly potent source of injury to lung tissue, causing a range of disorders affecting not only the tissue of the lung itself but the pleura, peritoneum and other organs. Concern about asbestos-related diseases has increased in recent years, due to widespread occupational exposure to this mineral during and after World War II. Because of the long latency period of asbestos-related disease, the health effects of this exposure have only recently become apparent through epidemiologic studies.

[2] Definition of Asbestosis

Asbestosis is a pneumoconiosis, a disease that results from the deposit of considerable amounts of dust in the lungs. The term *asbestosis* itself refers to nonmalignant lung disease resulting from inhalation of asbestos fibers. More specifically, this term is restricted to fibrosis (formation of fibrous tissue) of the pulmonary interstitium (supporting tissue of the lung) (American Thoracic Society, 1986).

Inhaled asbestos also causes fibrosis and other nonmalignant abnormalities of the pleura (membrane covering the lungs), as well as several types of neoplasms, most significantly lung cancer and mesothelioma, a tumor occurring in the pleura or peritoneum (membrane lining the abdominal cavity). (*See Figure 16–1.*)

16.02 ASBESTOS MINERALS

The broad category called "asbestos" is actually several different fibrous minerals. Its physical properties make it extremely useful for industry. However, the fibrous nature of asbestos is also responsible for its detrimental effects on the human body. Its ability to cause lung disease is largely dependent on the size and type of the particular mineral fibers of which it is composed.

[1] Properties of Asbestos

The term *asbestos* refers not to a single substance but to a group of six different fibrous minerals—that is, minerals that break up into fibers instead of dust when they are crushed. Of these, chrysotile or white asbestos represents 95 percent of the asbestos produced in the world; its long, strong fibers can be made into fabrics. The fibers of

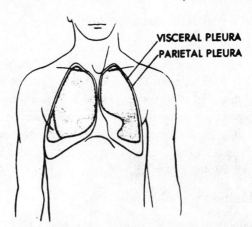

Fig. 16–1. The visceral pleura surrounds the lung; the parietal pleura lines the inner surface of the chest. In an intact chest wall, the two layers are separated only by a thin layer of lubricating fluid.

crocidolite (blue asbestos) and amosite (brown asbestos) are resistant to heat and acid (Levy, 1988).

These qualities make asbestos extremely useful in industry, and production and use grew considerably after its introduction in the late nineteenth century. Asbestos was used in shipbuilding and construction as well as in the manufacture of brakes, textiles and insulation. Although since the late 1970s the use of asbestos has dropped dramatically, at least in the United States, exposure to asbestos already in place in ships and buildings, as well as in remaining industrial uses, is still of concern (Sheppard, 1988; American Thoracic Society, 1986).

[2] Asbestos in the Lung

The gross asbestos fibers that can be seen with the naked eye consist of bundles of fibrils. These fibrils are so small they can be visualized only with an electron microscope. This fact has implications for both diagnosis and environmental exposure standards, since regulatory agencies and pathology laboratories may not have such a microscope readily available.

The ability of asbestos fibers to penetrate into lung tissue depends on their diameter, not their length; as a rule, fibers with a diameter over 5 microns cannot penetrate into the smaller recesses of the lung tissue. When fibers smaller than this enter the lung, they break up into fibrils, which, although they are tiny, have a large surface area in relation to their mass. This means that very small amounts of asbestos in the lung can result in a great amount of tissue reactivity. What is more, asbestos fibers can remain in the lung for many years without being degraded, thus continuing to stimulate an inflammatory reaction (Sheppard, 1988).

16.03 HISTORY OF ASBESTOS-ASSOCIATED DISEASE

Evidence that asbestos dust could cause fibrotic lung disease was described as early as 1906 in Britain; in this country, the Prudential Insurance Company stated in 1918 that it would not issue life insurance policies to asbestos workers because of the adverse health effects of asbestos. Nevertheless, the ability of this mineral to cause pulmonary fibrosis was not fully recognized by the medical community until a series of studies was carried out during the 1930s (Selikoff, 1986).

Even so, it was not until 1960 that a maximum exposure standard was mandated by law. That standard covered only employees of some companies doing business with the government. Not until 1971 was an industry-wide standard established, and the exposure level it permitted was one that is still likely to result in the development of asbestos-related disease in ensuing decades.

There was a similar delay in recognizing the carcinogenicity of asbestos.[1] The first case report associating lung cancer with asbestos exposure was published in 1935, but it was not until studies performed in the 1950s and 1960s provided considerable additional evidence that the association was accepted and the need for exposure control recognized. There was a similar, though shorter, lag between the initial identification of the association between asbestos exposure and mesothelioma (tumor occurring in the membranes lining the lung and abdominal cavity) and the full recognition of the importance of the problem (Selikoff, 1986).

According to a recent historical study, one factor in the failure to identify asbestos as an occupational carcinogen was the systematic development and then suppression of evidence on the cancer-causing potential of asbestos by the asbestos industry itself. The result was exposure of millions of workers (Lilienfeld, 1991).

16.04 EPIDEMIOLOGY

It has been estimated that between 1940 and 1979, 27.5 million workers were exposed to asbestos (American Thoracic Society, 1986). Even in the late 1980s, about 50,000 workers were involved in manufacturing products that contain asbestos. Forty thousand insulation workers were directly exposed to asbestos. In addition, also exposure of about 3.5 million workers continued in buildings and construction, among employees who handled asbestos-containing products. Of the insulation workers, over 70 percent were found to have abnormal chest x-rays after 20 to 30 years of exposure (Levy, 1988).

[1] Asbestosis and Cancer

Asbestosis is the most common asbestos-associated disease, although cancers cause more asbestos-related deaths. In the earliest days of asbestos use, when workers might be surrounded by clouds of dust, exposure was so intense that individuals were likely to die of asbestosis

---

[1] *See* 16.04[1] *infra.*

before lung cancer had time to develop. Now, however, studies show that the relative proportion of deaths due to cancer and asbestosis depends on the extent of exposure.[2]

In one study of 17,800 asbestos insulation workers between 1967 and 1976, the cause of death was asbestosis in 7 percent of cases and lung cancer in 20 percent. However, in a study of miners and millers who experienced intense exposure, 15 percent of deaths were caused by asbestosis (Selikoff, 1986).[3] Scientists have extrapolated from such studies and calculated that between 1 and 3 percent of cancer deaths in the United States are caused by asbestos (Preventing Illness, 1985).

[2] Prevalence of Pleural Abnormalities

Chest x-rays of between 20 and 60 percent of workers who experienced intense exposure to asbestos show evidence of pleural fibrosis (formation of fibrous tissue in the lining of the lung). Pleural effusion (fluid in the pleural space) is now a recognized complication, as well. The prevalence of pleural fibrosis caused either by environmental exposure or household contact ranges from 2 to 17 percent; this prevalence is expected to increase in the next 15 to 20 years (Schwartz, 1991).

[3] Disease Through Family Contact

Estimates of the number of workers exposed to asbestos do not include the members of their families. However, there is evidence that asbestos workers—and even workers who did not themselves use asbestos but worked with others who did—are themselves a sufficient source of exposure for their family members to develop asbestosis (Selikoff, 1986; Kilburn, 1986b). Mortality rates of family contacts of asbestos workers are under study.[4]

Mortality from asbestos-related disease is also related to smoking, although in a complicated way.[5]

---

[2] See 16.08[1] infra.

[3] See 16.08[2] infra.

[4] See 16.06[5] infra.

[5] See 16.08[4] [c] and 16.09[1][b] infra.

16.05   DETERMINANTS OF DISEASE

These factors determine whether a given individual will develop lung disease in response to the inhalation of particulates:

- toxicity of the material;
- dimensions of the asbestos fiber;
- intensity and duration of exposure; and
- the individual's susceptibility.

[1]   Toxicity

Both the site at which the asbestos fiber is deposited in the lung and its chemical properties affect the lung's reaction to it. Particles are deposited in the lung based on size; the small diameter of asbestos fibers (even the relatively long ones) means that they are capable of reaching the alveoli, or air cells of the lung (Levy, 1988). (*See Figure 16–2.*) Fibers have also been found in the pleura (membrane enveloping the lung), peritoneum (lining of the abdominal cavity), lymph nodes in the chest, spleen, liver, gastric wall and in abdominal tumors (Schwartz, 1991).

[2]   Asbestosis

The exact mechanism by which asbestos causes the tissue injury that develops into asbestosis is not known, although it is thought that the fibers stimulate the release of cytotoxic (harmful to cells) substances, with an inflammatory reaction and development of fibrosis (Sheppard, 1988).

[3]   Neoplasms

Asbestos is a powerful mutagen (agent that induces mutations, or changes in genetic material). Although the mechanism by which asbestos causes cancer is not known, evidence indicates that the dimensions of the asbestos fiber are more important to its carcinogenicity than are its chemical properties. Rather than being a chemical carcinogen itself, asbestos seems to act as a tumor promoter. Different kinds of fibers have different carcinogenic potentials, presumably according to their varying physical properties (Levy, 1988).

[4]   Dose and Duration of Exposure

The risk of developing asbestos-related disease involves a dose-response relationship. That is, the extent of risk in a given case depends

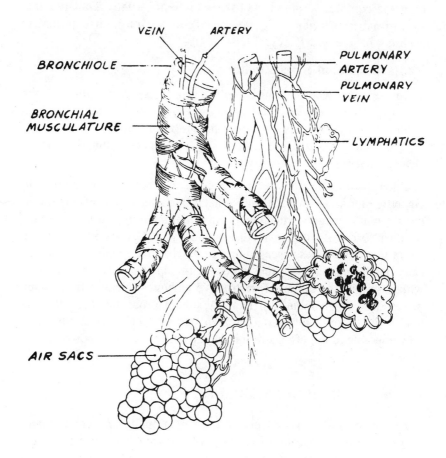

VEIN   ARTERY

BRONCHIOLE

PULMONARY ARTERY

PULMONARY VEIN

BRONCHIAL MUSCULATURE

LYMPHATICS

AIR SACS

Fig. 16–2. The alveoli—tiny air sacs at the end of the bronchioles—are surrounded by connective tissue called the interstitium.

on the intensity of exposure multiplied by itsduration. This means that a brief but heavy exposure can result in asbestosis and pleural disease.

The effective intensity of exposure to asbestos depends both on the actual number of fibers that are present in the lung (total lung fiber burden) and on the duration of the time period since the first exposure occurred (Sheppard, 1988). This is because asbestos exposure is not only cumulative but persistent. That is, each day's dose of inhaled fibers is added to the previous day's, and all the fibers remain in the lung and continue to affect the tissues (Selikoff, 1986). Thus progression of asbestosis has been shown on x-rays even after exposure to asbestos has ceased (Levy, 1988).

[5]   Individual Susceptibility

Since people who have received the same doses vary greatly in the severity of the disease they develop, it seems clear that individual host factors play a role in disease development. However, host susceptibility is difficult to assess, except in the case of cigarette smoking, which clearly increases susceptibility.[6]

Other factors thought to influence susceptibility (in addition to cigarette smoking) include individual variations in the efficiency of the alveolar mechanism that clears dust from the lung, and the presence of other forms of pulmonary disease (Levy, 1988). Another possible factor that determines susceptibility to inhaled irritants is a genetically caused deficiency in a protein called serum alpha–1 antitrypsin (SAT), which inhibits the action of destructive enzymes released from tissue in response to an inhaled irritant. A simple procedure for detecting SAT, which could be used to screen potential employees who may be vulnerable to the effects of inhaled dusts, has been proposed (Levy, 1988).

16.06   SOURCES OF EXPOSURE

Exposure to asbestos occurs both occupationally and environmentally. There is a spectrum of intensity of exposure ranging from direct to indirect occupational exposure, to family contact with persons occupationally exposed and to various levels of environmental exposure.

[1]   Occupational Exposure

Most risk of exposure to asbestos occurs in mining, manufacture of asbestos textiles and among workers who install and remove asbestos insulation around furnaces and steam pipes. The risk is greater in milling operations and industries that use the finished asbestos products, where fine particles float in the air, than in the mines.

Many other industries also present an exposure risk, since asbestos is also used in automotive brake and clutch linings, tile, shingles, paint

---

6 *See* 16.08[4][c] and 16.09[1][b] *infra.*

filler, electric wire insulation and plastics. Employees who work with these products are exposed to asbestos (Levy, 1988).

In the past, asbestos was widely used in building construction and shipbuilding, but such use has virtually ended in the United States. However, exposure continues to occur when buildings and ships containing asbestos are demolished or renovated (Sheppard, 1988).

Since the 1960s, awareness has grown that there is also a risk to workers who are not classified as "asbestos workers" but who might inhale asbestos as they work alongside asbestos workers. These include shipyard workers, building maintenance and repair workers, and brake repair and maintenance workers.

[a]   Shipyard Workers

Large numbers of people were employed in shipyards in the United States during World War II, and approximately 200,000 have continued to work in shipyards since then. Although very few actually worked directly with asbestos, workers in other trades experienced indirect exposure.

Studies of these workers have found that over half of those examined who were employed for at least 30 years demonstrate abnormalities on x-ray that are typical of asbestosis. Malignant mesothelioma (a tumor occurring in the membranes lining the pleura and abdominal cavity) is common among them, and cases of lung cancer seem to be increasing (Selikoff, 1986). Although the total risk among these workers and their families is still unknown, one study of shipyard workers and their families in Los Angeles found an asbestosis prevalence rate of 11 percent in wives, 8 percent in sons and 2 percent in daughters. Most of these workers themselves received only indirect exposure (Kilburn, et al., 1986b).

[b]   Building Maintenance and Repair Workers

Much of the asbestos used as insulation in factories, power plants, homes and refineries between 1890 and 1970 is still present in those structures. Asbestos was also used for decoration and acoustic finishes in nightclubs, schools, restaurants and hotels; and tons of asbestos-containing fireproofing material was sprayed on steel beams in high-rise buildings between 1960 and 1969. This material is friable (capable of being crumbled or reduced to powder by hand pressure), and when it deteriorates, asbestos particles are released into the air.

Maintenance workers in these buildings are at risk of developing disease; this has already been demonstrated in the chemical industry. Repair and removal of these asbestos materials presents a significant exposure risk to workers carrying out these tasks, as well as a major control problem (Selikoff, 1988). Asbestos abatement programs are now in place in many cities, so that many building owners have undertaken removal of the asbestos from these buildings.

[c]   Brake Repair and Maintenance Workers

The large number of cars and trucks used in this country presents a risk of asbestos exposure both to workers who repair and replace brake linings and to the public at large, since maintenance and repair work releases dust into the air. However, the extent of risk is not known, since little data exists about these workers. Some studies have reported both x-ray signs of asbestosis and cases of mesothelioma. By the mid–1980s, brakes made without asbestos were available (Selikoff, 1986).

[2]   Nonoccupational Exposure

Recognition of the risk posed by asbestos has resulted in considerable public concern about the effects of asbestos that is present in the environment. Asbestos contamination has become so widespread that many city residents have some asbestos fibers in their lungs.

Although "there is no evidence that casual or indirect exposure, such as occurs in the general population, causes asbestosis" (American Thoracic Society, 1986), there are reports of asbestosis-related disease in the families of workers who have been exposed to asbestos. These family members had no exposure other than their household contact with the workers.[7]

To date, epidemiologic studies of the risk of lung cancer have focused on occupational exposures (Selikoff, 1986).

[a]   Mining and Quarrying

Asbestos is often present in minerals that are extracted for other industrial uses, such as iron ore. In such locations, mining operations may result in contamination of air and public water supplies. In 1977, for instance, it was discovered that the use of crushed stone from a quarry in Maryland in roads in the Washington, D.C., area had resulted

---

[7] See 16.04 [3] supra.

in relatively high levels of airborne asbestos along roads and in parking lots (Selikoff, 1986).

[b] Consumer Products

Asbestos has been present in some consumer products in forms that create a possibility of its being released into the air. Some of these products are spackling compounds used in home repair, which release dust when they are mixed and sanded, asbestos cement products, papier-mâché products, the fabric used in some coats as well as commercial and hand-held hair dryers (Selikoff, 1986).

[c] Schools

Considerable contamination of construction sites and their environs occurred during the 1960s, when asbestos materials were sprayed onto steel building skeletons. Subsequently damaged or deteriorating asbestos surfaces were found to be releasing dust into the air. Although the exposure levels that were measured varied, in some cases, they were considerably higher than in the air outside the buildings.

Although the hazard posed by these exposure levels is not known, the reports of asbestos-related disease in families of asbestos workers suggest that higher levels do indeed present some risk of disease (Selikoff, 1986).

16.07 DIAGNOSTIC MODALITIES

Diagnosis of asbestos-related disease depends primarily on the history, radiography (x-rays) and pulmonary function testing, although diagnostic procedures such as computed tomography and gallium lung scan may also be used.

[1] History

A history of the patient's occupational life is the most important element in diagnosing asbestos-related disease. It must include a complete history of all jobs the person has held, with descriptions of actual activities, what materials were handled and the patient's location in relation to other workers. It also should include the use and effectiveness of exposure controls such as exhaust ventilation, respirators and special work clothes.

In addition, the history should cover hobbies (e.g., home repair work involving the use of products containing asbestos may result in exposure),[8] whether the patient ever smoked and how much, and any information that might also suggest a nonoccupational cause of disease (Sheppard, 1988).

[2]   Radiography

Chest x-rays are essential in diagnosing asbestosis and pleural abnormalities, and they are also used for surveillance of workers at risk to detect lung changes before any clinical manifestations are evident.

A classification system developed by the International Labor Office (ILO) to standardize the interpretation of chest films for pneumoconioses (chronic diseases of the lung marked by an overgrowth of connective tissue) is used to express the results. (*See Figures 16–3a, 16–3b and 16–4.*)

The first ILO classification of radiographs was established in 1930. It was revised in 1958, and in the next decade or so, several other classification systems were proposed to deal with the problems of x-ray-assisted diagnosis. In 1971, at a meeting of the Medical Research Council Pneumoconiosis Unit in Penarth, Wales, the various systems were united into one international standard. This was accepted by the ILO, and it is this system that is now accepted all over the world. The ILO system has improved accurate epidemiologic work and has improved individual diagnosis of the disease.

The primary purpose of the system is the codification of the x-ray changes associated with pneumoconiosis. By providing a uniform key for identifying and quantifying the type and extent of disease, the classification system contributes to a more accurate medical approach. It includes not only pneumoconiosis from asbestos but also disease associated with other types of dust particles, including coal dust, silica, carbon and beryllium.

The system describes the typical opacities seen on the films by shape, size and profusion. It permits physicians to assess an individual patient's prognosis (Sheppard, 1988). However, although the chest x-ray can detect radiographic signs typical of asbestosis, it does not indicate the presence or degree of respiratory impairment (Levy, 1988).

---

[8] *See* 16.06[2][a] *supra.*

FEATURE		CODE		DEFINITION
Small Opacities				
Rounded				
Type				The nodules are classified according to the approximate diameter of the predominant opacities.
	p	q(m)	r(n)	p = rounded opacities up to about 1.5 mm in diameter.
				q(m) = rounded opacities exceeding about 1.5 mm and up to about 3 mm in diameter.
				r(n) = rounded opacities exceeding about 3 mm and up to about 10 mm in diameter.
Profusion				The category of profusion is based on assessment of the concentration (profusion) of opacities in the affected zones. The standard radiographs define the midcategories (1/1, 2/2, 3/3).
	0/-	0/0	0/1	Category 0 = small rounded opacities absent or less profuse than in category 1.
	1/0	1/1	1/2	Category 1 = small rounded opacities definitely present, but few in number. The normal lung markings are usually visible.
	2/1	2/2	2/3	Category 2 = small rounded opacities, numerous. The normal lung markings are usually still visible.
	3/2	3/3	3/4	Category 3 = small rounded opacities, very numerous. The normal lung markings are partly or totally obscured.
Extent	RU LU	RM LM	RL LL	The zones in which the opacities are seen are recorded. Each lung is divided into three zones — upper, middle, and lower.
Irregular				
Type				As the opacities are irregular, the dimensions used for rounded opacities cannot be used, but they can be roughly divided into three types.
	s	t	u	s = fine irregular, or linear, opacities.
				t = medium irregular opacities.
				u = coarse (blotchy) irregular opacities.
Profusion				The category of profusion is based on assessment of the concentration (profusion) of opacities in the affected zones. The standard radiographs define the midcategories (1/1, 2/2, 3/3).
	0/-	0/0	0/1	Category 0 = small irregular opacities absent or less profuse than in category 1.
	1/0	1/1	1/2	Category 1 = small irregular opacities definitely present, but few in number. The normal lung markings are usually visible.
	2/1	2/2	2/3	Category 2 = small irregular opacities, numerous. The normal lung markings are usually partly obscured.
	3/2	3/3	3/4	Category 3 = small irregular opacities, very numerous. The normal lung markings are usually totally obscured.
Extent	RU LU	RM LM	RL LL	The zones in which the opacities are seen are recorded. Each lung is divided into three zones — upper, middle, and lower — as for rounded opacities.
Combined profusion	1/0 2/1 3/2	1/1 2/2 3/3	1/2 2/3 3/4	When both rounded and irregular small opacities are present, record the profusion of each separately and then record the combined profusion as though all the small opacities were of one type, i.e., either rounded or irregular. This is an optional feature of the classification, but it is strongly recommended.
Large Opacities				
Size	A	B	C	Category A = an opacity with greatest diameter between 1 cm and 5 cm, or several such opacities the sum of whose greatest diameters does not exceed 5 cm.
				Category B = one or more opacities larger or more numerous than in category A whose combined areas do not exceed the equivalent of the right upper zone.
				Category C = one or more opacities whose combined areas exceed the equivalent of the right upper zone
Type		wd	id	In addition to the letter A, B, or C, the abbreviation "wd" or "id" should be used to indicate whether the opacities are well defined or ill defined.

Fig. 16–3a. ILO U/C 1971 International Classification of Radiographs of the Pneumoconioses.

FEATURE	CODE	DEFINITION
Pleural Thickening		
Costophrenic angle	R L	Obliteration of the costophrenic angle is recorded separately from thickening over other sites. A lower limit standard radiograph is provided.
Chest wall and diaphragm		
Site	R L	
Width	a b c	Grade a = up to about 5 mm thick at the widest part of any pleural shadow.
		Grade b = over about 5 mm and up to about 10 mm thick at the widest part of any pleural shadow.
		Grade c = over about 10 mm at the widest part of any pleural shadow.
Extent	0 1 2	Grade 0 = not present or less than grade 1.
		Grade 1 = definite pleural thickening in one or more places such that the total length does not exceed one-half of the projection of one lateral wall. The standard radiograph defines the lower limit of grade 1.
		Grade 2 = pleural thickening greater than grade 1.
Ill-Defined Diaphragm	R L	The lower limit is one-third of the affected hemidiaphragm. A lower limit standard radiograph is provided.
Ill-Defined Cardiac Outline (Shagginess)	0 1 2 3	Grade 0 = absent or up to one-third of the length of the left cardiac border or equivalent.
		Grade 1 = above one-third and up to two-thirds of the length of the left cardiac border or equivalent.
		Grade 2 = above two-thirds and up to the whole length of the left cardiac border or equivalent.
		Grade 3 = more than the whole length of the left cardiac border or equivalent.
Pleural Calcification		
Site	Wall Diaphragm Other R L	
Extent	0 1 2 3	Grade 0 = no pleural calcification.
		Grade 1 = one or more areas of pleural calcification the sum of whose greatest diameters does not exceed about 2 cm.
		Grade 2 = one or more areas of pleural calcification the sum of whose greatest diameters exceeds about 2 cm but not above 10 cm.
		Grade 3 = one or more areas of pleural calcification the sum of whose greatest diameters exceeds about 10 cm.
Additional Symbols	ax cp es pq bu cv hi px ca di ho rl cn ef k tba co em od tbu	ax = coalescence of small rounded pneumoconiotic opacities bu = bullae ca = cancer of lung or pleura cn = calcification in small pneumoconiotic opacities co = abnormality of cardiac size or shape cp = cor pulmonale cv = cavity di = marked distortion of intrathoracic organs ef = effusion em = marked emphysema es = eggshell calcification of hilar or mediastinal lymph nodes hi = enlargement of hilar or mediastinal lymph nodes ho = honeycomb lung k = septal (Kerley) lines od = other significant disease. This includes disease not related to dust exposure, e.g., surgical or traumatic damage to chest walls, bronchiectasis, etc. pq = pleural plaque (uncalcified) px = pneumothorax rl = rheumatoid pneumoconiosis (Caplan's syndrome) tba = tuberculosis, probably active tbu = tuberculosis, activity uncertain

Fig. 16–3b. ILO U/C 1971 International Classification of Radiographs of the Pneumoconioses—Continued.

SHORT CLASSIFICATION				COMPLETE CLASSIFICATION				
Feature	*ILO U/C 1971*			*Feature*	*Complete ILO U/C 1971*			
No Pneumoconiosis	0			No Pneumoconiosis (Small opacities, rounded or irregular)	0/−	0/0	0/1	
Suspect Pneumoconiosis	−							
Pneumoconiosis				Pneumoconiosis				
SMALL OPACITIES				SMALL OPACITIES				
Rounded				Rounded				
Type	p	q(m)	r(n)	Type	p	q(m)	r(n)	
Profusion	1	2	3	Profusion	1/0 2/1 3/2	1/1 2/2 3/3	1/2 2/3 3/4	
Extent	−			Extent	RU LU	RM LM	RL LL	
Irregular								
Type	s	t	u	Irregular				
Profusion	1	2	3	Type	s	t	u	
Extent	−			Profusion	1/0 2/1 3/2	1/1 2/2 3/3	1/2 2/3 3/4	
Combined profusion (Optional, but strongly recommended)	1	2	3	Extent	RU LU	RM LM	RL LL	
LARGE OPACITIES				Combined profusion (Optional, but strongly recommended)	1/0 2/1 3/2	1/1 2/2 3/3	1/2 2/3 3/4	
Size	A	B	C	LARGE OPACITIES				
Type	−			Size	A	B	C	
PLEURAL THICKENING				Type	wd (well defined) id (ill defined)			
Costophrenic angle	−			PLEURAL THICKENING				
Chest wall and diaphragm				Costophrenic angle	R (Right)	L (Left)		
Site	pl			Chest wall and diaphragm				
Width	−			Site	R (Right)	L (Left)		
Extent	−			Width	a	b	c	
ILL-DEFINED DIAPHRAGM	−			Extent	0	1	2	
ILL-DEFINED CARDIAC OUTLINE	−			ILL-DEFINED DIAPHRAGM				
PLEURAL CALCIFICATION Site	plc			Site	R (Right)	L (Left)		
Extent	−			ILL-DEFINED CARDIAC OUTLINE				
ADDITIONAL SYMBOLS	All obligatory ax cp es pq bu cv hi px ca di ho rl cn ef k tba co em od tbu			Extent	0	1	2	3
				PLEURAL CALCIFICATION				
				Site	Wall Diaphragm Other R (Right) L (Left)			
				Extent	0	1	2	3
				Additional Symbols	All obligatory ax cp es pq bu cv hi px ca di ho rl cn ef k tba co em od tbu			

Fig. 16–4. Short and Complete ILO U/C 1971 International Classifications.

[3]   Computed Tomography

This technique produces a cross-sectional view of a selected plane of the body by means of a series of scans taken at minute intervals, then synthesized into an image by a computer. It is more accurate than standard x-rays for detecting pleural disease. High-resolution computed tomography (CT) has been found to be more sensitive than conventional CT in detecting both pulmonary and pleural fibrosis (Aberle, et al., 1989).

[4]   Gallium Lung Scan

This technique uses radioactive gallium, a metal, to detect pulmonary inflammation. A dose of radioactive gallium is administered intravenously, and images of the chest are recorded by a gamma camera. The gallium accumulates and is retained in the inflammatory lesions. Abnormal results of gallium scans have been recorded in individuals whose chest x-rays show no abnormal changes (Hayes, 1989).

[5]   Pulmonary Function Testing

Pulmonary function tests measure disorders of lung mechanics, gas exchange and ventilation. They may be used to test both static and dynamic function of the lung. Abnormal results show the nature of lung dysfunction, but not its cause. Since values representing normal lung function vary considerably among healthy individuals, it is important to perform serial evaluations on workers during the course of employment to determine whether changes occur in relation to a baseline value (Sheppard, 1988).

The basic instrument of pulmonary function testing in industry is the spirometer. The patient breathes into the mouthpiece of this device, which measures several parameters of respiratory function.

Vital capacity (VC) is the maximum amount of air the patient can exhale after the largest possible inhalation. When the exhalation is done forcefully, this value is called the forced vital capacity (FVC). The forced expiratory volume (FEV_1) is the volume of air exhaled during the first second. A decrease in the forced vital capacity (FVC) is a nonspecific abnormality that may reflect, among other things, disease of the airways, the parenchyma (functional tissue) of the lung or respiratory muscle function. The ratio of forced expiratory volume in one second (FEV_1) to the FVC is helpful in distinguishing between restrictive abnormalities (e.g., asbestosis) and obstructive abnormalities (e.g., small airways disease).

The residual volume (RV) is the amount of air remaining in the lungs after an exhalation. It is determined by measuring the dilution of helium in the spirometer after 7 minutes of breathing. The residual volume added to the vital capacity equals the total lung capacity (TLC). Reduction in both vital capacity and total lung capacity represents a restrictive ventilatory impairment.

The pulmonary diffusing capacity is a useful test when carefully performed to estimate the amount of the lung surface that is available for gas exchange. It is usually reduced in fibrosis of the lung such as that due to asbestosis (Levy, 1988).

[6] Exercise Testing

These tests are performed while the patient is exercising on a bicycle ergometer or a treadmill. The total amount of air expelled per minute and the oxygen consumption are measured. Exercise testing can determine whether breathlessness is due to cardiovascular or pulmonary impairment (Levy, 1988; Sheppard, 1988).

[7] Bronchoalveolar Lavage

This procedure is performed under local anesthesia, using a fiberoptic bronchoscope whose tip is inserted into a small bronchus. Saline solution is instilled into the lung and then aspirated into a bottle. The fluid is then centrifuged, and the cells are counted.

Bronchoalveolar lavage is used to detect, quantify and characterize pulmonary inflammation, the presence of which is indicated by abnormal increases in the numbers of various types of leukocytes (white blood cells) and alveolar macrophages (scavenger cells) (Hayes, 1989).

16.08 ASBESTOSIS AND OTHER NONMALIGNANT DISEASES

Asbestosis and the other nonmalignant diseases resulting from asbestos inhalation result in restrictive lung impairment. Restrictive diseases are those that affect the interstitium (space between tissues or organs), rendering it stiffer and thus reducing the volume of air that can be inhaled and exhaled.

[1]   Pathology

Pathologic changes in asbestos-related disease result in the development of stiff fibrous tissue, which decreases compliance (elasticity) of the lung and pleura.

[2]   Asbestosis

Asbestosis is defined as a fibrosis (overgrowth of fibrous tissue) of the pulmonary parenchyma (active tissue of the lungs) in which asbestos fibers are present. Asbestos fibers are taken up by macrophages (cells that engulf and consume foreign bodies), which stimulates the production of fibrous tissue (Levy, 1988). The lungs become stiff and smaller in volume.[9]

Under the microscope, the lung tissue is seen to contain asbestos fibers and asbestos bodies. Asbestos bodies are formed from a small number of longer fibers, which become coated with a protein-type material and are visible under the light microscope as brown or black fibers. Visualizing the more numerous short, uncoated fibers requires an electron microscope (Sheppard, 1988; Levy, 1988; American Thoracic Society, 1986).

[3]   Pleural Disease

In addition to asbestosis, several pleural abnormalities are associated with asbestos:

- pleural plaques;
- pleural thickening; and
- pleural effusion.

Plaques are localized patches of fibrosis; pleural thickening is a diffuse fibrotic reaction. Pleural effusion is an exudate (fluid that has escaped from blood vessels, usually due to inflammation) containing inflammatory cells (American Thoracic Society, 1986).

Pleural plaques and thickening are the most common abnormalities found on x-rays; they often appear when there is no x-ray sign of interstitial fibrosis (Levy, 1988).

[4]   Clinical Manifestations

Although histologic study (dealing with the examination of minute structures of tissue) of biopsied lung tissue can confirm a diagnosis

---

[9] *See* 16.04[1] *supra.*

of asbestosis by documenting asbestos fibers in the lung, lung biopsy is usually not performed. This is because in most cases, the risk to the patient would outweigh any possible benefit (Sheppard, 1988). Thus the diagnosis is generally based on clinical examination.

[a]   Signs and Symptoms

Symptoms of asbestosis generally do not appear until 20 to 30 years after the initial exposure (Levy, 1988). The first symptoms are most often cough and dyspnea (difficulty breathing) that initially is most noticeable during exertion. Typically dyspnea is due to decreased forced vital capacity (FVC) and lung volumes, impaired gas exchange and diminished compliance (Selikoff, 1986). Pleural fibrosis can also reduce vital capacity and impair diffusion independently of interstitial fibrosis, and it can be severe enough to cause death from pulmonary insufficiency (Levy, 1988; Schwartz, 1991).

As the disease progresses, cough and dyspnea become more severe. Auscultation (examination with a stethoscope) may reveal rales (abnormal respiratory sounds). There may be cyanosis (bluish tinge of the skin due to insufficient oxygen in the blood) and clubbing of the fingers (proliferation of the soft tissue at the tips).

Pulmonary function tests show reductions in lung volumes and diffusing capacity and a reduced flow of air, but not airway obstruction, unless the patient smokes (Sheppard, 1988). (*See Figure 16–5.*)

[b]   Management of Patients with Asbestosis

Since asbestos exposures are now generally lower, workers with asbestosis now have less lung scarring than those in the past, and they rarely die because of progression of the fibrosis itself. Rather, their diminished reserve makes them more vulnerable to pulmonary infection such as pneumonia, which can cause death due to cor pulmonale (heart disease with pulmonary hypertension caused by lung disease).

For this reason, such individuals must restrict their activities during bad weather to avoid infection, and they should be given antibiotics at any sign of pulmonary infection (Selikoff, 1986).

There is no effective treatment for asbestosis; for this reason, the focus must be on prevention.

[c]   Relation to Smoking

People with asbestosis are strongly advised not to smoke. Since cigarette smoking also causes lung disease, it adds an extra burden

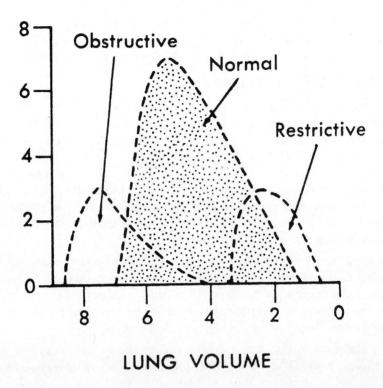

Fig. 16–5. Flow-volume curves show obstructive, restrictive and normal patterns. Lung volume is given in liters; the vertical scale refers to flow rate, in liters/second.

to the lung, in the form of bronchitis and emphysema. One study found that death from asbestosis was 2.8 times as frequent among smokers in a group of subjects than among nonsmokers (Selikoff, 1986).

Another study found that cigarette smoking in itself did not lead to pulmonary fibrosis in a general population or enhance it among families of shipyard workers exposed to asbestos. However, cigarette smoking and asbestos appeared to have a synergistic effect among the workers themselves; workers who smoked had more pulmonary fibrosis than nonsmoking workers (Kilburn, et al., 1986a).

Pleural plaques[10] are related to cigarette smoking as well as to the cumulative dose of asbestos. Smoking does not cause a decrease in

---

[10] *See* 16.08 [3] *supra.*

total lung capacity (TLC), but its effect can combine with that of asbestos to cause decreased flow and diffusing capacity. Impaired diffusing capacity is apparently related more to smoking than to intensity of asbestos exposure (Sheppard, 1988; Levy, 1988). When restrictive lung disease coexists with obstructive lung disease, it may be virtually impossible to determine the relative weight of asbestosis and cigarette smoking in the etiology (American Thoracic Society, 1986).

[d]   Establishing the Diagnosis

Pleural plaques are the most common sign indicating asbestos exposure, although patients who have no involvement of the interstitium are usually asymptomatic (Sheppard, 1988). According to an official statement of the American Thoracic Society, the diagnosis of asbestosis requires six findings:

- a history of exposure;

- an appropriate time period between exposure and diagnosis;

- x-ray abnormalities;

- pulmonary function tests that show restrictive impairment;

- impaired diffusing capacity; and

- bilateral crackles heard on auscultation (listening to the sounds of the body, usually by means of a stethoscope) (American Thoracic Society, 1986).

A difficulty in diagnosis is that the symptoms of asbestosis—for example, dyspnea and clubbing (enlargement of the ends of the fingers)—are nonspecific and are also typical of unrelated diseases, such as chronic obstructive pulmonary disease or congestive heart failure. However, if there is a clear history of exposure combined with diffuse interstitial fibrosis on the x-ray, asbestosis can be presumed (American Thoracic Society, 1986).

[5]   Correlation Among X-ray Findings, Pulmonary Function Tests and Disability

Although the principles of diagnosis as described[11] apply generally, the results of diagnostic studies frequently do not correlate with patients' subjective experiences. Many individuals whose x-rays are

---

[11] See 16.08[4] supra.

abnormal have few symptoms and no impairment in functioning, while others (up to 10 percent of patients) have normal x-rays but suffer respiratory distress (Selikoff, 1986; Sheppard, 1988). Interstitial fibrosis has been demonstrated when tissue was examined microscopically even though x-rays were normal (Levy, 1988).

The corollary is that radiographic documentation of a limited amount of asbestosis does not necessarily mean that disability is present or will develop (Selikoff, 1986; American Thoracic Society, 1986).

16.09 RELATED CANCERS

It has been difficult in most cases to identify specific materials encountered occupationally as carcinogens because of the long latency periods, the high incidence of lung cancer among the general population and the confounding factor of smoking habits. However, asbestos is one of the few substances definitely proved to cause cancer in humans.

Cancers caused by asbestos are similar to cancers due to other causes and are of all cell types (Sheppard, 1988).

[1] Lung Cancer

Lung cancer is the most common neoplasm caused by asbestos. Like lung cancer due to other causes, it has a very poor prognosis—one that is possibly even worse for asbestos workers, since the presence of respiratory impairment and asbestosis may make surgery impossible (Selikoff, 1986). As with asbestosis, the focus must be on prevention.

[a] Risk

Lung cancer has a latency period of at least 10 to 14 years from the onset of exposure; its incidence peaks at 30 to 35 years. It can occur at excess rates among asbestos-exposed workers who have no signs of asbestosis on x-rays (Selikoff, 1986). Rates of lung cancer are five times greater in nonsmoking workers exposed to asbestos than in comparable nonsmokers not so exposed (Levy, 1988).

Evidence indicates that this greater incidence requires exposure intensities similar to those that cause asbestosis (Sheppard, 1988). The prevalence is highest in the asbestos textile industry, presumably because exposure to dust is more intense in that industry (Levy, 1988).

Although a dose-response relationship exists for the development of lung cancer among workers, the effects of less intense environmental exposures are not known. No evidence exists of any risk of malignancy from exposure to less than 100 fibers per year. However, there is no threshold below which a carcinogen is no longer carcinogenic; it is possible that the presence of even a few fibers in the lung can be detrimental, especially when other factors, such as cigarette smoking, are present (Selikoff, 1986).

[b] Relation to Smoking

Smoking acts synergistically with asbestos to cause lung cancer, which means that the risk of lung cancer among asbestos workers in part depends on their smoking habits. Although asbestos exposure increases the lung cancer risk even among nonsmokers, the risk goes up dramatically when the factor of cigarette smoking is added. Studies have reported lung cancer risks between 30 and 90 times greater for asbestos workers who smoke than for nonsmokers who were not exposed to asbestos (Sheppard, 1988). Similarly, death rates due to lung cancer for asbestos workers who smoke are 10 times higher than for asbestos workers who do not smoke (Levy, 1988).

Less information is available regarding pipe and cigar smoking. The data indicates that there is an interaction between these forms of smoking and asbestos exposure, but information is insufficient to construct specific risk estimates (Selikoff, 1986).

[c] Establishing the Diagnosis

The basis of a diagnosis of lung cancer caused by asbestos is a history of intense exposure. Asbestosis and pleural disease resulting from asbestos inhalation frequently produce a restrictive pattern of lung impairment. In some instances, small airways disease may result from asbestos inhalation, and this will produce an obstructive lung function pattern. The airways disease is more prominent in smokers. If possible, the diagnosis should be confirmed by counting the asbestos fibers found in tissue samples after biopsy or autopsy. The presence of coexisting pulmonary fibrosis is not necessary to confirm the diagnosis (Sheppard, 1988).[12]

---

[12] *See also* ch. 15.

[d] Management

Studies have demonstrated that if workers exposed to asbestos stop smoking, their risk of death from lung cancer decreases considerably—in one study, by a third (Selikoff, 1986). Thus, one aspect of public health and individual management is informing exposed workers not to smoke or to stop if they are smokers. However, though this measure is important, it does not replace controlling exposure to dust, especially since cigarette smoking is not related to the development of other cancers associated with asbestos (Selikoff, 1986).[13]

[2] Mesothelioma

Mesothelioma is a tumor that develops in the pleura (membrane enveloping the lungs) or peritoneum (lining of the abdominal cavity) and spreads over the surfaces of the chest and abdominal cavities. It generally has a latency period of at least 20 years, but there have been instances in which the time period between exposure to asbestos and death from mesothelioma was only 3½ years (Selikoff, 1986; Levy, 1988).

Mesothelioma was formerly quite rare and has only become more common as asbestos exposure has increased. It is therefore considered a "signal" neoplasm, the appearance of which indicates that asbestos exposure has occurred. It seems that incidence rates vary depending on the type of exposure; for example, mesothelioma may be more common than lung cancer or asbestosis among family members of asbestos workers. It also appears that lower exposures can cause mesothelioma than are necessary to cause asbestosis (Selikoff, 1986).[14]

Pleural thickening on one side only on the chest x-ray suggests mesothelioma. The patient may experience pleuritic chest pain as early as ten years before the tumor develops (Sheppard, 1988; Levy, 1988). There is no effective treatment for this tumor, and patients most often die within a year after it is diagnosed (Selikoff, 1986).

[3] Other Cancers

Several other types of cancer have been found to have an increased incidence among asbestos workers: cancers of the esophagus, stomach,

---

[13] See 16.03 supra.

[14] See also ch. 15.

colon, rectum, kidney, larynx and oropharynx (the part of the pharynx below the soft palate). Among these, cancers of the esophagus, oropharynx and larynx have appeared in excess numbers only among asbestos workers who smoked; the others did not show this concentration. Other types of cancers have been found among asbestos workers at higher than expected rates,[15] but not at statistically significant levels (Selikoff, 1986).

Some evidence indicates that asbestos fibers migrate through the mucosa of the gastrointestinal tract (Levy, 1988). It seems also that fibers reach the kidney through the bloodstream after they have been either inhaled or ingested, raising general public health implications for asbestos-contaminated water supplies (Selikoff, 1986).[16]

16.10 PREVENTION

Since it is difficult to identify predisposing factors (other than cigarette smoking) that would make a given individual susceptible to developing asbestos-related disease, prevention depends on protecting all workers from any level of exposure that might cause disease to any of them. The difficulty lies in determining that level.

Standard-setting by government tends to lag behind the emergence of new scientific data on the dose-response relationship. As a result, "physicians cannot assume that a given occupational exposure is not responsible for causing a disease, even if the exposure level was below the current standard" (Sheppard, 1988).

[1] Regulatory Standards

The approach taken to setting standards for asbestos exposure is based on the principle of controlling rather than banning the use of hazardous materials. The strictness of controls is determined by considerations of cost effectiveness as well as the risk to workers' health. In the case of asbestos, "this approach has not worked well," according to Selikoff (1986).

The first standard for occupational exposure was set in 1960; it has been lowered several times since. Nevertheless, the scientific data indicate that these standards have not been effective in protecting workers. For example, one calculation of the potential risk to workers

---

[15] See also ch. 15.

[16] See also ch. 15.

who were exposed for 10 years to asbestos at a concentration of 0.5 fibers per mL of air estimated that there would be 82 lifetime excess cancers per 10,000 exposed workers (Hughes and Weill, 1986).

However, the still lower standard recommended by the National Institute for Occupational Safety and Health (NIOSH) in 1976 (Selikoff, 1986) had still not been promulgated by the Occupational Safety and Health Administration (OSHA) as of 1991.

[2]   OSHA Standard for Asbestos Exposure

The current Occupational Safety and Health Administration (OSHA) standard sets a permissible exposure level of 0.2 fibers per mL of air. This standard is set for fibers greater than 5 microns in length, for an eight-hour average airborne concentration.

Based on data showing that this exposure level would not protect workers against cancer, and probably not against asbestosis either, NIOSH has recommended to OSHA a new standard of 0.1 fiber per mL for industrial exposure. NIOSH has also recommended a standard setting a peak concentration of 0.5 fibers per mL of air for a 15–minute period (Selikoff, 1986).

Even this recommended standard would probably not prevent all cases of asbestos-induced cancer, but it would most likely decrease the incidence of cases. However, NIOSH's recommendation (Levy, 1988; Selikoff, 1986) has so far not been implemented by OSHA.

It should be noted that the OSHA standard refers only to fibers longer than 5 microns. It does not cover the larger number of smaller fibers that are also present. Thus, even if the 0.1 fiber/mL standard were adopted, workers would still be subjected to some exposure, and since fibers are retained in the lungs, their lung burden of asbestos would still increase.

[3]   Measuring Exposure Levels

In order to comply with an exposure standard, it is necessary to measure actual exposure levels at a worksite. OSHA recommends collecting asbestos dust with a sampling pump and counting the fibers at 400 to 450 magnification, using a phase contrast microscope (a type of light microscope) (Levy, 1988). However, many smaller fibers are present that cannot be seen except with an electron microscope (Selikoff, 1986).

16.11 CONTROL OF EXPOSURE

Preventing exposure to asbestos has two basic components. The first is substituting alternative, less toxic materials to eliminate the use of new asbestos. The second is minimizing the exposure that occurs when working with asbestos that is currently in place. Exposure control involves improving the following (Sheppard, 1988):

- engineering controls;
- administrative measures;
- work practices; and
- public education.

[1] Engineering and Administrative Controls

Engineering controls installed to reduce exposure include general exhaust ventilation systems in mills and local exhaust systems placed next to hand-powered tools in other industries (Levy, 1988). The most effective control measures are those based on engineering design (Olishifski and Zenz, 1988).

Administrative controls implement protective standards and safety procedures for workers to follow. OSHA requires employers to provide medical surveillance programs for employees who are exposed to asbestos, including preplacement, annual and termination examinations (involving a history, chest x-ray and pulmonary function test) and retention of records for at least 30 years (Schumacher, 1988).

[2] Work Practices

Appropriate work practices can minimize the amount of asbestos that is released into the environment while it is being handled. Particularly important is the use of wet methods to reduce the generation of dust at mines and quarries, roadways, storage piles and waste dumps (Levy, 1988). In abatement projects involving removal of asbestos from buildings, wet removal techniques are generally employed (Schumacher, 1988).

Asbestos cement, plaster and similar materials should be mixed in closed containers. Asbestos-containing waste materials must be collected and disposed of in sealed containers, such as thick, sealed plastic bags or drums, and tagged with a warning label (Schumacher, 1988).

Good housekeeping practices involve removal of dust from ledges and floors by vacuum cleaners and use of wet cleaning methods in mills (Olishifski and Zenz, 1988; Levy, 1988).

[3] Personal Protective Devices

Personal protective devices include both respirators and disposable overalls to prevent contamination of the workers' own clothes that will be worn home (Levy, 1988). OSHA specifies that respirators cannot be used to meet the exposure standard. They are only permitted during the period required to implement controls and work practices that will reduce exposure levels to the permissible limit (Schumacher, 1988).

[a] Types of Respirators

Respirators are used when work must be done in areas of high dust concentration. The most widely used respirators are dust masks or air-purifying respirators, which consist of a soft facepiece to which a filter is attached. As the worker breathes in, air is drawn through the filter. Most masks include a check valve that prevents the exhaled air from passing back through the filter.

Atmosphere-supplying respirators use a motor to draw contaminated air from the workplace into a filter and blow pure air into a facepiece or helmet. Air is supplied from a tank worn by the worker or from a hose connected to an air source. This type is more likely to be accepted and used by workers.

OSHA requires that employers provide respirators; clean, inspect and repair them; and make sure that employees wear them properly (Olishifski and Zenz, 1988). Deficiencies in respirator programs have been found in 40 to 70 percent of inspections of worksites where overexposure has occurred (Preventing Illness, 1985).

[b] Problems with Respirator Use

Problems with respirators involve fit, worker compliance and reliability of equipment. The different sizes and shapes of faces among workers, the wearing of glasses and the presence of beards and mustaches as well as stubble on men who do not shave daily all can interfere with achieving an airtight seal, which is critical for adequate protection. If the seal is not airtight, contaminated air can leak in at the sides, especially in air-purifying respirators, since the negative pressure inside the mask tends to draw outside air in.

The restriction of vision and of speech caused by most respirators causes discomfort. Breathing may also become difficult when strenuous physical effort is necessary. These, too, affect worker compliance in wearing respirators. For this reason, the respirator program must include components that will ensure the workers' cooperation. First, it should be clear that respirators are being used only after every possible measure has been taken to reduce exposure levels. Second, respirators should be properly fitted. Third, workers should be educated as to why the respirator is necessary and trained in its proper use (Olishifski and Zenz, 1988; Preventing Illness, 1985).

Laboratory studies of respirator effectiveness have shown that the motorized air-supplying type provide better protection than the air-purifying type. The results of field testing of respirators indicate that the amount of protection provided under conditions of normal use is frequently much lower than that achieved in the laboratory.

This occurs both because workers wear the devices only intermittently, due to discomfort, and because of deficiencies in respirator programs, including poor fitting, poor maintenance, poor worker training and inadequate supervision during use (Preventing Illness, 1985).

[4] Public Education

Public education campaigns directed at individuals who have been occupationally exposed to asbestos in factories, brake repair, shipyard, insulation and construction work as well as building maintenance have been carried out by the National Cancer Institute, trade unions, asbestos manufacturers and other groups. In 1978, the U.S. Surgeon General's office sent a mailing describing the asbestos hazard to every physician in the country. The Social Security Administration also mailed a description of the cancer hazard from asbestos to every Social Security recipient. People were advised not to smoke or to stop as soon as possible if they did smoke (Selikoff, 1986).

16.12 EVALUATION OF IMPAIRMENT

The classification scheme used by the American Medical Association for evaluation of impairment due to respiratory disease is based on criteria developed by the American Thoracic Society (American Medical Association, 1988). The scheme describes four classes of impairment.

[1] History and Physical Examination

The history should include detailed information about the patient's employment, including dates of exposure to asbestos as well as smoking history. The severity of dyspnea (difficulty breathing) is evaluated on a scale of mild, moderate or severe, although severity of dyspnea in itself is not a criterion for determining impairment.

The physical examination includes blood pressure and heart and respiratory rates after a 5-minute rest, as well as pulmonary function tests. Exercise testing is done when the patient's complaint of dyspnea is more severe than spirometry (pulmonary measurements with a gas-measuring device) or diffusing capacity values indicate.[17]

[2] Criteria Used in Evaluation

Five values are used in determining respiratory impairment: forced vital capacity (FVC), forced expiratory volume in the first second (FEV_1), FEV_1/FVC ratio, diffusing capacity of carbon monoxide (D_{co}) and measured exercise capacity (VO_2 max).

The VO_2 max is used to determine whether dyspnea is caused by respiratory disease or some other condition. It does not provide a hard and fast criterion; a moderate decrease in this value may still represent severe impairment if it leaves the worker unable to meet the requirements of occupational activity during an eight-hour period.

In the case of pneumoconiosis, impairment that is not directly related to lung function is not quantifiable by the tests described; such evaluation depends on the judgment of a physician expert in lung disease.

[3] Classes of Impairment

In the American Medical Association's *Guides to the Evaluation of Permanent Impairment* (1993), Class 1 represents no impairment (0 percent) of the whole person. Criteria for Class 1 are values of FVC, FEV_1, and D_{co} all ≥ 80 percent of the predicted value, and FEV_1/FVC ≥ 70 percent of predicted, or VO_2 max > 25 mL/(kg × min).

Class 2 represents mild (10 to 25 percent) impairment of the whole person. Values constituting a Class 2 impairment are FVC between 60 and 79 percent of predicted, or FEV_1 between 60 and 79 percent

---

[17] *See* 16.12 [2] *infra.*

of predicted, or D_{co} between 60 and 69 percent of predicted, or VO_2 max between 20 and 25 mL/(kg $\times$ min).

An example of Class 2 is a 58–year-old man with a six-year history of cough and slowly progressing dyspnea during exertion. For a period of 5 years that ended 15 years prior to his examination, he had sprayed asbestos insulation on building walls. Chest x-rays showed diminished volumes, pleural plaques[18] and interstitial fibrosis.[19] Examination disclosed crackles at the bases of both lungs. He was diagnosed with asbestosis and found to have a 25 percent impairment of the whole person, although it was recognized that as the disease progressed, over time, his impairment could increase.

Class 3 represents moderate (26 to 50 percent) impairment of the whole person. Values are FVC between 51 and 59 percent of predicted, or FEV_1 between 41 and 59 percent, or D_{co} between 41 and 59 percent, or VO_2 max between 15 and 20 mL/(kg $\times$ min).

Class 4 represents severe (51 to 100 percent) impairment of the whole person. Values are FVC $\leq$ 50 percent of predicted, or FEV_1 $\leq$ 40 percent of predicted, or D_{co} $\leq$ 40 percent of predicted, or VO_2 max $\leq$ 15 mL/(kg $\times$ min).

An example of Class 4 is a 60–year-old man who had been an insulator for 40 years and had intense asbestos exposure during 5 years. He was also a heavy smoker. For 10 years before examination, he had noticed increasing shortness of breath and fatigue. Examination disclosed clubbing (enlargement of the ends of the fingers), cyanosis (condition in which the skin turns blue) and rales (crackles) in both lungs as well as pleural thickening and fibrosis seen on the chest x-ray. He was diagnosed with asbestosis and pulmonary emphysema, and found to have a 70 percent impairment of the whole person.

---

18 *See* 16.08[3] *supra.*

19 *See* 16.01[2] *supra.*

16.100 BIBLIOGRAPHY

Reference Bibliography

Aberle, D. R., et al.: Asbestos-Related Pleural and Parenchymal Fibrosis: Detection with High-Resolution CT. Radiology 166:729–734, Mar. 1988.

American Medical Association: Guides to the Evaluation of Permanent Impairment, 4th ed. Chicago: American Medical Association, 1993.

American Medical Association: Guides to the Evaluation of Permanent Impairment, 3rd ed. Chicago: American Medical Association, 1988.

American Thoracic Society, Medical Section of the American Lung Association: The Diagnosis of Non-Malignant Diseases Related to Asbestos. Am. Rev. Respir. Dis. 134:363–368, Aug. 1986.

Hayes, A. A., et al.: Gallium Lung Scanning and Bronchoalveolar Lavage in Crocidolite-Exposed Workers. Chest 96:22–26, July 1989.

Hughes, J. M. and Weill, H.: Asbestos Exposure—Quantitative Assessment of Risk. Am. Rev. Respir. Dis. 133:5–13, Jan. 1986.

Kilburn, K. H., et al.: Interaction of Asbestos, Age, and Cigarette Smoking in Producing Radiographic Evidence of Diffuse Pulmonary Fibrosis. Am. J. Med. 80:377–381, Mar. 1986a.

Kilburn, K. H., et al.: Asbestos Diseases and Pulmonary Symptoms and Signs in Shipyard Workers and Their Families in Los Angeles. Arch. Intern. Med. 146:2213–2220, Nov. 1986b.

Levy, S. A.: An Overview of Occupational Pulmonary Disorders. In: Zenz, C. (Ed.): Occupational Medicine: Principles and Practical Applications, 2d ed. Chicago: Year Book Medical Publishers, 1988.

Lilienfeld, D. E.: The Silence: The Asbestos Industry and Early Occupational Cancer Research—A Case Study. Am. J. Public Health 81:791–800, June 1991.

Olishifski, J. B. and Zenz, C.: Elements of Respiratory Protection. In: Zenz, C. (Ed.): Occupational Medicine: Principles and Practical Applications, 2d ed. Chicago: Year Book Medical Publishers, 1988.

Preventing Illness and Injury in the Workplace. Washington, D.C.: U.S. Congress, Office of Technology Assessment, OTA-H–256, 1985.

Schumacher, A.: A Guide to Hazardous Materials Management: Physical Characteristics, Federal Regulations, and Response Alternatives. New York: Quorum Books, 1988.

Schwartz, D. A.: New Developments in Asbestos-Induced Pleural Disease. Chest 99:191–198, Jan. 1991.

Selikoff, I. J.: Asbestos-Associated Disease. In: Last, J. M. (Ed.): Maxcy-Rosenau Public Health and Preventive Medicine, 12th ed. Norwalk, CT: Appleton-Century-Crofts, 1986.

Sheppard, D.: Occupational Pulmonary Disorders. In: Wyngaarden, J. B. and Smith, L. H., Jr. (Eds.): Cecil Textbook of Medicine, 18th ed. Philadelphia: Saunders, 1988.

Additional References

Bourbeau, J., et al.: The Relationship Between Respiratory Impairment and Asbestos-Related Pleural Abnormality in an Active Work Force. Am. Rev. Respir. Dis. 142:837–842, October 1990.

Frumkin, H., et al.: Radiologic Detection of Pleural Thickening. Am. Rev. Respir. Dis. 142:1325–1330, Dec. 1990.

Kilburn, K. H. and Warshaw, R. H.: Effects of Individually Motivating Smoking Cessation in Male Blue Collar Workers. Am. J. Public Health 80:1334–1337, 1990.

Reifsnyder, A. C., et Al.: Malignant Fibrous Histiocytoma of the Lung in a Patient with a History of Asbestos Exposure. Am. J. Roentgenol. 154:65–66, Jan. 1990.

CHAPTER 17

Occupational Asthma

SCOPE

Occupational asthma is a disease of usually reversible airway obstruction caused by exposure to agents in the workplace. It is the most common compensable form of occupational lung disease today and has been associated with over 200 different causative agents. The risk depends on the industry, and within industries at risk, cigarette smoking and the allergic tendencies of the workers may affect the likelihood of developing symptoms. The diagnosis of occupational asthma is based on a thorough patient history, identification of specific agents and careful documentation with objective pulmonary function testing. The treatment is to remove the worker from the worksite where exposure occurs. However, this does not lead to complete recovery in most cases; the majority of affected workers continue to have symptoms, sometimes for years.

17.01 INTRODUCTION

Asthma is a common disease of the lungs in which the bronchial tubes become obstructed, reducing the flow of air through them. This produces difficulty in breathing, as well as coughing and wheezing. The obstruction is generally episodic and reversible, but in severe cases as well as in patients whose disease persists for many years, the constriction can become chronic.

A wide variety of physical and chemical stimuli can precipitate acute episodes in patients with asthma. These stimuli include exercise, breathing cold air, respiratory infections and exposure to airborne pollutants such as dilute sulfuric acid (sulfur dioxide) and ozone. Several specific agents may also precipitate an attack, some through well-defined allergic mechanisms and others through mechanisms that are not yet well understood. Because these stimuli do not ordinarily elicit such a bronchial response in normal individuals, the airways of patients with asthma are termed hyper-reactive.

Specifically, occupational asthma is asthma that is precipitated by agents found in the workplace. It may develop in workers who already have hyper-reactive airways, that is, in individuals with previously diagnosed asthma. When it develops in a worker without previous lung problems, it may sensitize the bronchial tubes so that they eventually react to nonspecific stimuli.

[1] Anatomy

To understand the onset of asthma, and specifically occupational asthma, it is necessary to understand the anatomy of the organs involved, particularly the lungs. The lungs are composed of an extensive network of tubes arranged like an inverted tree. The trachea (windpipe) can be visualized as the trunk of the tree. It divides into two large branches, called the right and left main bronchi. (*See Figure 17–1.*) Each of these divides, in turn, into smaller branches, which again divide into yet smaller branches. The smallest branches are called bronchioles, which in this analogy represent the twigs of the tree. (*See Figure 17–2.*)

Up to this point, the major function of the branches of this tree is air transport. For this reason, the branches of the bronchial tree are collectively called the airways. The movements of the diaphragm and rib cage expand the lungs, sucking air through all the branches of the

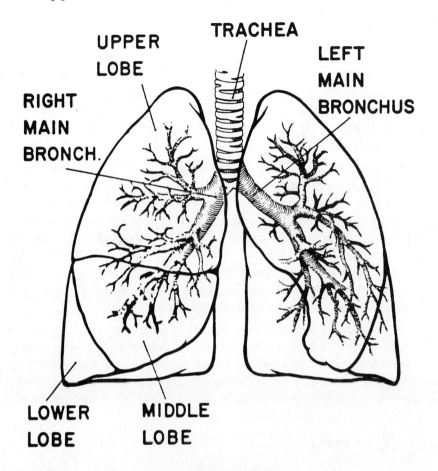

Fig. 17–1. The lungs, the trachea (windpipe) and the two main bronchi (branches of the windpipe). Asthma is a common disease in which these bronchial tubes become obstructed, reducing airflow.

tree, down to the bronchioles. (*See Figure 17–3.*) At the end of the bronchiole are the alveoli (air sacs), where gas exchange takes place. If the analogy were exact, these would be the leaves of the tree. But the alveoli in fact are more like delicate sacs that sit like a clump of bubbles at the end of each bronchiole. Altogether, there are some 300 million of them. Their walls are so thin that oxygen and carbon dioxide pass easily through them. The alveolar walls are lined with tiny blood vessels called capillaries, which have equally thin walls.

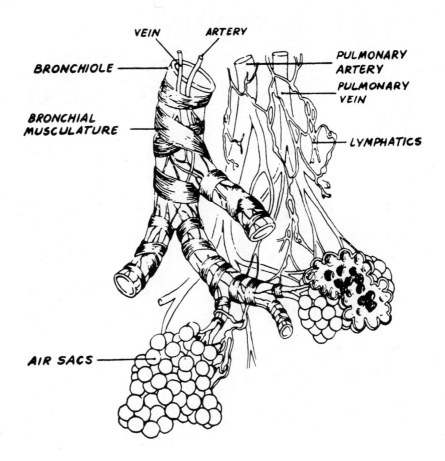

Fig. 17–2. The bronchioles are the smallest branches of the bronchial "tree." The bronchioles end in the air sacs (alveoli).

Oxygen passes from the air in the alveolus into the capillary, where it is picked up by hemoglobin (oxygen-carrying protein) molecules in the red blood cells. Carbon dioxide, a major metabolic waste product, passes from the blood into the alveolus and exits the lungs with the expired air.

[2] Functional Properties of the Airways

The airways are not just inert tubes. Their walls are lined with cells whose surfaces are covered with cilia, tiny hairs that sweep particulate matter back toward the throat, where it can be swallowed or coughed

RIB CAGE

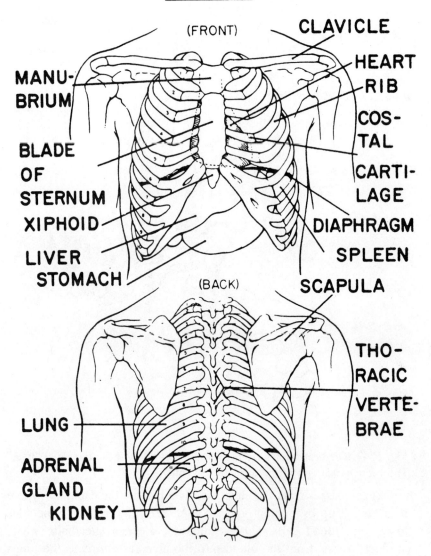

Fig. 17–3. Front and rear views of the rib cage and nearby structures and organs. Movement of the rib cage, as well as the diaphragm, is responsible for the expansion of the lungs in breathing.

out. The lining also contains cells that secrete the mucus that coats the inside of the airways and helps trap unwanted particulate matter.

The walls of the bronchial tubes also contain smooth muscles that are capable of contracting and narrowing the diameter of the airway. This muscle is supplied (innervated) by nerves of the autonomic nervous system (the part of the nervous system that works in an automatic and involuntary way).

There are, in fact, two types of autonomic innervation: sympathetic and parasympathetic. In the lung, parasympathetic nerves cause contraction of the bronchial smooth muscle, constricting the airway. Histamine and other substances can also constrict the muscle, resulting in narrower airways.

The principal sympathetic innervation to the airways is called the beta adrenergic system. It has receptors for agents called beta adrenergic agonists, which induce bronchial airway relaxation and dilation.[1]

[3] Terminology and Definitions

Asthma has been defined in several ways:

- a condition of intermittent airway obstruction;
- an inflammatory disorder of the bronchioles; and
- a condition of increased bronchial responsiveness to a variety of stimuli.

Two similar terms, *asthma* and *hyper-reactivity,* are usually (but not always) considered to be two distinct entities. Other features of asthma may also be included in the definition, such as the increased number of eosinophils (a type of white blood cell) found in the blood of some asthma patients.[2]

In general, asthma and hyper-reactivity can each be considered to represent a separate spectrum of clinical and pathologic conditions, with considerable overlap between them. Asthmatics are usually thought of as having hyper-reactive airways, in addition to other characteristics (e.g., inflammation). Although airway hyper-reactivity is a major feature of asthma, this term also encompasses a much more general condition that may occur in normal individuals, for example,

---

[1] See 17.06 *infra.*

[2] *See* 17.05 *infra.*

following a respiratory infection or inhalation of certain substances, such as ozone.

[4]   Epidemiology of Asthma

Asthma is a common problem. It is much less common in adults than in children, as many children appear to outgrow the illness. It has been estimated that asthma affects approximately 5 percent of all adults in the United States and approximately 7 to 10 percent of American children (McFadden, 1991). In the majority of cases, the disease begins in childhood or early adulthood.

[5]   Pathophysiology of Asthma

The focal characteristic of asthma is reversible airway obstruction, which in turn is caused by agents to which the airways have become hyper-reactive. Asthma is increasingly thought of as primarily an inflammatory disease, with hyper-reactivity resulting from the inflammation. The sequence of events is as follows: Hyper-reactivity triggers bronchial constriction due to muscular contraction (bronchospasm) and inflammation, which leads to swelling of the bronchial wall and excessive mucus production. (*See Figure 17–4.*) These processes result in an obstruction of the bronchial tubes.

For many years, the role of muscular contraction was emphasized and was the focus of treatment.[3] Currently, however, the role of inflammation is receiving much more attention, to the point that some consider asthma to be essentially an inflammatory disease.

The clinical results of airway constriction are the following:

- difficulty breathing (dyspnea);
- coughing; and
- wheezing. A wheeze is a high-pitched musical sound that is produced by the passage of air through a narrow tube, in this case, the small airways. This is considered the hallmark of bronchospasm (bronchial constriction).

[a]   Bronchial Constriction

The lungs are supplied with nerves (innervated) from the autonomic nervous system. This is the part of the nervous system that runs the internal organs; it can be thought of as the "automatic" nervous system,

---

[3] *See* 17.06 *infra.*

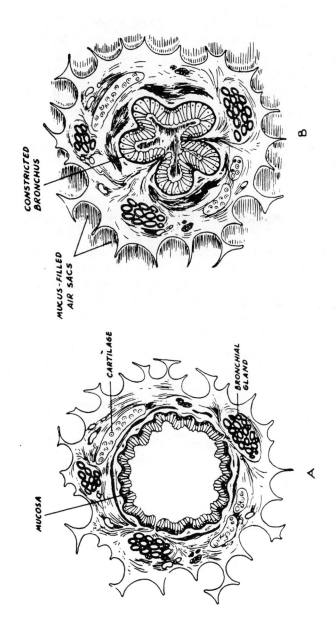

Fig. 17–4. Hyperreactivity triggers bronchospasm, swelling of the bronchial wall and excessive mucus production. (A) Cross section of a normal small bronchus (bronchiole). (B) Cross section of a similar vessel constricted by mucus. Air sacs are shown also filled with mucus.

because it functions without input from the conscious brain. There are two components of the autonomic nervous system—the sympathetic and parasympathetic nervous systems—and they usually have opposing actions.

The sympathetic nervous system has two different types of receptors, called alpha and beta, and these usually have different actions. In the lungs, stimulation of the beta receptors produces dilation of the bronchi, while stimulation of the alpha receptors causes constriction. It is not clear, however, what role the alpha system has in human airways. The parasympathetic input to the bronchi produces constriction, also.

The major neurotransmitter of the sympathetic nervous system is epinephrine, also called adrenaline. The sympathetic receptors are often referred to as either beta-adrenergic or alpha-adrenergic (activated by epinephrine) receptors. The major neurotransmitter of the parasympathetic system is acetylcholine; parasympathetic receptors may be referred to as cholinergic.

[b] Inflammation

Inflammation is a process by which tissues respond to injury. When injury occurs, the mechanisms of inflammation are set in motion. Initially the tiny blood vessels in the tissue become leaky, and fluid and cells that normally flow in the blood leak out into the tissue. This causes the tissue to become swollen, among other reactions.

Injury also stimulates cells to release of a number of chemicals, called mediators, that initiate and modulate the chain of events that constitutes inflammation. Histamine is one of these mediators (hence the use of antihistamines in allergy and cold remedies). Mediators have been shown to cause blood vessel leakiness, stimulate bronchoconstriction through muscular contraction, stimulate mucus secretion and activate inflammatory cells (white blood cells and others).

The biological function of inflammation is to:

- clean up the damage created by an injury;
- destroy microbial invaders;
- remove damaged tissue; and
- set the stage for cellular repair.

By necessity, this process of inflammation involves some powerful cells, which are capable of digesting tissues, as well as some potent mediators. Most of the time, this works to the advantage of the human host, but in asthma (and in other so-called inflammatory diseases), this is not the case. The inflammatory process may, in fact, damage the airway lining, and this damage is thought to contribute to maintaining airway hyper-reactivity (Lopez and Salvaggio, 1987).

[c] Allergy and the Immune System

Allergy refers to variations in individual responsiveness to certain substances in the environment. When people are exposed to plant pollens, for example, some individuals develop asthma or rhinitis (inflammation of the nasal passages). This reaction is mediated by the immune system and is commonly referred to as hay fever (an allergy to pollen).

Certain individuals have a genetic predisposition of the immune system to react to environmental agents such as pollen. During the initial exposures to pollen, their immune system makes a specific type of antibody called IgE (immunoglobulin, type E).[4] Once the IgE is formed, the individual is "sensitized." Upon subsequent exposures, IgE is immediately released, whereupon it triggers all the inflammatory events of an allergic reaction.

The substances that trigger specific antibody (Ig) reactions are referred to as *antigens*. Bacteria, viruses and many chemicals can be considered to be antigens. In allergic reactions, the antigen may be referred to as an *allergen*. Allergens induce IgE, as opposed to IgG or other Ig responses, which are involved in the immune response to such illnesses as measles, hepatitis and poliomyelitis.

Studies have shown that asthma is mediated by immune mechanisms in many, but by no means all, cases. This is particularly true for occupational asthma. Some occupational asthma is clearly mediated by the IgE and is usually (but not always) associated with a genetic predisposition to allergy. In other cases, however, the mechanism is less clear. Different immune system reactions may be involved (namely, mechanisms not involving IgE), or, in some cases, the airway inflammation of asthma may be triggered by some direct toxic effect.

[d] Atopy

An individual with atopy has a history of childhood allergic reactions, e.g., eczema. An atopic person who is asthmatic may

---

[4] *See* 17.05[2] [b] *infra.*

develop symptoms due to exposure to known allergens. These individuals, however, may demonstrate antibodies (IgE) to a variety of allergens that may or may not be causal for their asthma (Bernstein, 1992). The respiratory symptoms may involve the upper (nose and throat) or lower (lungs) respiratory tract. The skin test produces a local reaction on the skin to the application (by scratch or prick) of specific allergens. Other definitions of atopy include skin rashes also (such as eczema).

Atopic individuals are predisposed to developing a variety of IgE-mediated allergic reactions, including eczema (a skin rash, also called atopic dermatitis), allergic rhinitis (nasal inflammation, e.g., hay fever) and asthma.

Atopy is very common in the general population, although it is more common in children and can diminish or disappear with age. It has been shown to be a risk factor not only for asthma but also for asymptomatic airway hyper-reactivity (Clark, 1990).

Because it is so common, atopy is frequently a compounding factor in the investigation of occupational asthma. The evaluation of a worker with newly developed asthma requires that the investigator take a thorough history of the patient, going back to childhood to search for possible atopic reactions.

[e] Antigens and Haptens

An antigen is a substance that is capable of reacting with a specific antibody to initiate an immune system reaction. Some substances cannot trigger this reaction alone but can do so when they are combined with some human tissue protein. The agent makes contact with the bronchial lining and complexes (unites) with a specific protein in the tissue. This complex then behaves like an antigen. Such substances are called *haptens*. Some forms of occupational asthma are caused by chemicals that are thought to act as haptens.

[f] Common Environmental Precipitants of Asthma

There are many environmental precipitants of asthma. Although all asthmatic individuals do not react to all known precipitants, they are certainly at risk of reacting to any agent on the list.

Some common household precipitants include cat and dog dander (hair), cockroaches and house dust mites. Grasses, weeds (especially ragweed) and some trees are common plant allergens. Certain molds (fungi) can precipitate asthma.

Viral respiratory infections, exercise and cold air are very common causes of asthmatic attacks. These are nonspecific irritants. Drugs are another common precipitant, particularly aspirin. Tartrazine (a food color) and beta-blockers (beta-adrenergic receptor antagonists)[5] can also precipitate an asthmatic attack. Examples of the latter include propranolol (Inderal ®), a drug used in the treatment of arrhythmias (irregular heartbeat patterns), hypertension (high blood pressure) and angina pectoris (chest pain from sudden contraction of the blood vessels that supply the heart muscle); atenolol (Tenormin ®), used for hypertension; and metoprolol (Lopressor ®), also used for hypertension. Chemical triggers include those found in air pollution, cigarette smoke and a variety of occupational settings.

Certain foods have been thought to produce asthmatic attacks in some individuals, usually children, although this remains a matter of controversy.

[6]   The Spectrum of Asthmatic Conditions

People with asthma have often been classified into two groups: the extrinsic (also called allergic) and the intrinsic (also called idiosyncratic). The *extrinsic* group consists of individuals with allergies in whom IgE and IgE-related immunologic mechanisms are clearly demonstrable.[6]

In the *intrinsic* group, no clear immunologic mechanism can be found. Commonly the patient gets a viral infection (such as the common cold) and several days later begins to wheeze, cough and complain of shortness of breath. This syndrome can persist for months (McFadden, 1991). Some authors would call this hyper-reactive airway disease rather than asthma.

A syndrome of asthma, nasal polyps and chronic sinusitis has also been classified as intrinsic asthma. Patients with this condition generally react to aspirin, and the disease tends to progress with age.

This classification system is considerably less than perfect, with many patients actually found somewhere in between the two groups. In fact, increasingly, authors are abandoning the intrinsic-extrinsic

---

[5] See 17.01[5][a] *supra.*

[6] See 17.01[5][c] *supra.*

classification system, but it has been replaced by a confusing array of pathologic entities and terms, like *hyper-reactive* and *reactive* airways.

[7]   Hyper-reactive Airways, Reactive Airways and Bronchospasm

Although there is no question that all asthmatics have hyper-reactive airways, most authors describe syndromes of hyper-reactive airways that they do not consider to be asthma. In some cases, this is simply a question of the evolution of terminology. Many patients who might have been labeled as intrinsic asthmatics in the past are now given a diagnosis of hyper-reactive airways disease. This is particularly true of those who characteristically wheeze following a cold.

In other cases, the term *hyper-reactive airways* describes a segment of the general population that demonstrates a bronchospastic response to certain nonspecific irritants when tested, but who do not normally have symptoms.

The term *reactive airways dysfunction syndrome* also appears in the scientific literature. This was coined to refer to a variant of occupational asthma that occurs following single toxic exposure to certain chemicals (Brooks, et al., 1985). There is some controversy over whether this is a form of occupational asthma (Chan-Yeung, 1990). The underlying pathology appears to be the same as that seen in asthma (Bernstein, 1992).

Bronchospasm (the constriction of bronchi) occurs in asthma, in hyper-reactive airways disease and in other conditions. Bronchospasm may follow a variety of insults to the airway. It may complicate chronic bronchitis and other bronchial diseases, as well as a kind of heart failure (cardiac asthma) and pulmonary embolism (a blood clot in the blood vessels of the lung).

17.02   OCCUPATIONAL ASTHMA

Occupational asthma is a subspecies of asthma. It is defined as reversible or variable airway obstruction and airway hyper-responsiveness due to a specific occupational situation (Bernstein, 1992). It is, in fact, the most common compensable occupational lung disease in the United States, with a prevalence (number of cases in a given population) ranging from 2 to 15 percent (Bernstein and Bernstein, 1988).

Over 200 causative agents have been associated with occupational asthma, and the list continues to grow. In some cases, the link is strong, with large numbers of workers being affected by exposure to one agent. On the other hand, many reports consist of only a single case.

The association between an agent and asthma may also be influenced by other factors that are not always well understood. In some industries, some factories may report a high prevalence of asthma, while in others, the incidence remains low.

Occupational asthma is not a single pathologic entity. Several mechanisms produce the disorder. Clinically it may be an immediate reaction, a delayed reaction or both. It may occur early in one worker's career or after years of exposure in another's. When exposure ceases, the asthma may cease, or it may persist for as long as five years, as in workers exposed to western red cedar (wood dust) (Butcher and Salvaggio, 1986).[7]

In other cases, a single heavy exposure is all it takes. Symptoms may even persist for years in some workers who have had a single exposure (Chan-Yeung, 1990). This particular syndrome has been called *reactive airways dysfunction syndrome.*

In some cases, atopy[8] is clearly a risk for the development of occupational asthma among workers with a personal history of allergies. It is possible to screen workers for atopy by asking them to recall episodes of eczema, hay fever and other allergic reactions; however, many of these occur early in childhood and may not be remembered.

Atopy is not a factor in a number of cases. The majority of asthma cases induced by western red cedar, for example, occur in nonatopic individuals.

Asthma is a very common disease. Although it often begins in childhood, less well known is the fact that many cases also begin in adulthood. Therefore, it can be assumed that some cases of occupational asthma will occur in workers who would have developed asthma in any environment. It can also be assumed that these workers will not recover completely when they are removed from a particular work environment, since asthma typically runs a chronic course, with exacerbations over many years.

---

[7] *See* 17.03[3][c] *infra.*

[8] *See* 17.01[5] [d] *supra.*

Unfortunately these cases cannot easily be distinguished from those in which the occupational environment is the sole cause of asthma. Some clinicians would argue the point in the following scenario: The individual develops asthma at work, is removed from exposure and recovers, but several months after recovery, develops another attack. Is the work environment the cause of this new attack, or is this person one of those patients who would have developed asthma in any setting?

[1]   Pathophysiology

Despite all that has been learned about the origins of this disease, the pathophysiology of occupational asthma in many cases is not clear. Agents in the workplace can serve as nonspecific irritants or can behave as allergens by inducing an IgE-mediated reaction.[9] In other cases, such agents activate other, less well understood immunologic pathways.

Thus a number of possibilities exist. First, the worker may have a pre-existing allergic condition called atopy. This is a personal history of allergic respiratory symptoms, with or without a positive skin test. The condition involves an underlying bronchial hyper-reactivity, which can be exacerbated by irritant agents in the workplace. Atopy is so prevalent in the general population[10] that this scenario is very common. The offending agent may be a specific chemical or a nonspecific irritant, such as cold air. Does someone who works in a freezer and begins to wheeze on the job have occupational asthma? This is a matter of debate.

Second, the individual may never have been atopic but develops classic IgE-mediated asthma, without other manifestations of atopy, in response to work-related exposure.

Third, the individual may be nonatopic and develop a type of asthma that is idiosyncratic (has no demonstrable immunologic mechanism). The nonatopic worker wheezing in the freezer is an example of this, also. Airway hyper-reactivity can exist alone, without atopy or asthma.

Last, it appears that exposure to high concentrations of certain chemical agents can produce atopy in a previously nonatopic individual (Butcher and Salvaggio, 1986).

---

9 *See* 17.01[5] [c] *supra.*

10 *See* 17.01[5] [d] *supra.*

Symptoms do not always abate when exposure ceases. This may be due to:

- chronic persistent inflammation caused by the occupational agent;
- persistence of the agent in the body; or
- the fact that the worker actually has nonoccupational asthma.

[2] Risk Factors for Occupational Asthma

There are a number of compounding variables in the production of occupational asthma; many of them are not well understood. Two factors that have repeatedly been noted to increase the risk of an individual having occupational asthma are smoking and atopy.

[a] Smoking

Tobacco smoking has been shown to increase the risk of many types of occupational asthma (Burge, 1992). Workers who smoke at the time of exposure are at risk; those who give up smoking prior to exposure, however, are not at increased risk.

Cigarette smoke probably exerts its effects through several different mechanisms, including its ability to induce cellular responses in the airways that promote airway inflammation.

Reports of occupational asthma related to different agents do not all show an increased risk with smoking, as response varies with the agent. Asthmatic reactions to platinum salts, colophony (rosin) and possibly anhidrides appear to occur with increased frequency in smokers. This has not been found to be the case with western red cedar (wood dust) and azodicarbonamide (Burge, 1990).[11]

[b] Atopy

Atopy[12] is a condition in which a person, e.g., a worker, is predisposed to develop allergic reactions to a variety of stimuli. This predisposition can be identified by questioning the worker about past allergic reactions and by skin testing. Unfortunately, many allergic reactions that occur early in childhood may not be recalled.

Atopy is a risk factor for the development of asthmatic reactions to many agents that are found in the workplace, particularly those that

---

[11] See 17.03[3] [c] infra.

[12] See 17.01[5] [d] supra.

are derived from plants or animals (generally speaking, high molecular weight compounds). Reactions to some low molecular weight compounds are also associated with atopy.

Atopic reactions to agents in the workplace may begin soon after exposure begins, as, for example, when a worker starts a new job. More commonly, however, the worker is exposed for some time— months or even years—before he or she manifests an asthmatic reaction. This time between the onset of exposure and the appearance of an allergic response is referred to as the *sensitization period.* Once the allergic response is documented, either by symptoms or skin testing, the worker is said to be sensitized to the agent.

Studies of occupational asthma must contend with many variables that affect the data. One is the phenomenon of self-selection, that is, that workers with certain characteristics simply leave an industry when they become symptomatic. This applies to the study of the relationship between atopy and occupational asthma. It is quite possible that atopic workers find that they cannot tolerate certain work environments and leave to take up other work.

Thus, when a study finds that most asthmatic workers are not atopic at one particular plant, it might be because atopy does not affect the risk. But it might also be because atopy affects the risk to such a high degree that the atopic workers have all left and are therefore not available to participate in the study.

[3]   Clinical Syndromes of Occupational Asthma

Patients with occupational asthma are first seen with either:

- an immediate reaction;
- a late reaction; or
- a mixture of the two.

The immediate reaction begins within minutes of exposure and then resolves within about an hour. The late reaction begins hours after exposure, frequently after the worker has already left the workplace, and requires hours, days or even weeks to resolve. One type of late reaction consists of recurring symptoms at night. Asthmatics of all types are prone to attacks that occur in the early morning (often around 4 a.m.); these attacks are thought to be due to inflammation.

The classic symptoms of asthma are difficulty in breathing (dyspnea) and wheezing. A wheeze is a high-pitched musical sound that is made when air passes through narrowed bronchial tubes, usually on expiration (breathing out). As an asthmatic attack becomes severe, the characteristic wheeze often disappears. This is not a sign of improvement, however. Rather, it indicates that the air flow has become insufficient to produce sound and is thus regarded as ominous.

Chest pain, usually described as a tightness, also occurs frequently. Some patients cough, and in a few cases, such coughing may be the only symptom. The cough is usually nonproductive (dry, with nothing coughed up), although it may produce mucus or phlegm as the attack worsens. In other cases, shortness of breath on exertion may be the only symptom.

17.03 CAUSATIVE AGENTS

The agents that cause occupational asthma are manifold. They are generally classified into two groups, according to their molecular size. The two groups are:

- high molecular weight (HMW) substances, for the most part, derived from animal and vegetable products; and

- low molecular weight (LMW) substances, mostly consisting of minerals.

Each will be considered in turn.

[1] High Molecular Weight Agents

The high molecular weight group consists mostly of large, complex molecules, generally proteins, that are derived from animal or plant sources. Most elicit an IgE-mediated reaction and are considered to be true allergens.[13]

Most exposure to HMW allergens occurs through the inhalation of dusts or aerosols from grains, animals or animal products. Although the number of HMW agents is large, some substances are more likely to cause allergic reactions than others. (*See Table 17–1 and Table 17–2.*) Some of the most problematic agents are discussed in detail in a later section.[14]

---

[13] *See* 17.01[5][c] *supra.*

[14] *See* 17.03[3] *infra.*

Table 17–1
Animal Products Associated with Occupational Asthma

Agent/Organism	Occupations Affected
rodents	breeders, laboratory workers, veterinarians
cows	dairy workers
shellfish	shellfish processors
seashells	shell grinders
eggs	egg processing workers
bees	beekeepers
flies	sewerage workers
fishfeed	breeders
mealworms	bait producers, grain workers
silkworms, larvae, eggs	sericulture
cockroaches	laboratory workers
locusts	laboratory workers
grain mites	granary workers, farmers, dock workers
fowl mites	poultry workers
animal enzymes	medical personnel handling drugs

[2] Low Molecular Weight Agents

The low molecular weight (LMW) compounds associated with occupational asthma are mostly chemicals used in industrial settings. There is an impressive number of such chemicals. (*See Table 17–3.*) Some of these chemicals may induce an IgE-mediated type of asthma in some workers, but for others, the mechanism is not clear.

Table 17–2
Plant Products Associated with Occupational Asthma

Agent	Occupations Affected
grain	granary workers, millers, dockworkers
flour	bakers, millers, food processors
wood dusts	sawmill workers, carpenters
cotton dust	mill workers, textile workers
tobacco leaf	farmers and processors
tea	tea, food industry workers
garlic	food workers
coffee beans	food processors, coffee industry workers, longshoremen, seamen
soybeans	farmers, dockworkers
castor beans	longshoremen, fertilizer workers
cottonseeds	cottonseed oil producers, bakers, fertilizer workers
linseed	linseed oil producers
flaxseed	flax workers
sunflower pollen	agricultural workers
vegetable gums	food processors, hairdressers, printers, carpet manufacture workers
psyllium	pharmaceutical industry workers
latex	latex glove manufacturers and users
plant enzymes (papain)	food production workers

Table 17–3
Chemicals Associated with Occupational Asthma

Agent	*Occupations Affected*
di-isocyanates	isocyanate and urethane manufacture, foundries, polyurethane foam, plastics
anhydrides	plastics, epoxy resins, drugs, fire retardants, food wrapping
platinum salts	platinum refining
dyes	cloth dyeing, fur dyeing
colophony	electronics
epoxy resin curing agents	epoxy and other resins, plasticizers, fire retardants, dye, perfume and weed killer manufacture
antibiotics	pharmaceutical industry, poultry breeding
pharmaceuticals	pharmaceutical production, nursing
sterilizing agents	hospital, kitchen and abbatoir work
insecticides	manufacturing, farming, fumigation
metal fumes and salts	chemical industry, metal refining, plating, grinding, welding, smelters
vanadium pentoxide	aluminum smelters, vanadium refinery work
fluxes	aluminum smoldering, electronics, welding
amines	electronics, plastics, rubber industry, photography
formaldehyde	plywood particle board making
inks	printing, EKG technology
azodicarbonamide	manufacture of polyvinyl chloride and plastics cosmetology
ammonium thioglycolate	cosmetology
henna	cosmetology

| persulfate salts | cosmetology, use of hair bleach |
| ethylenediamine | cosmetology, plastics and rubber industries |

---

[3]   Specific Agents

With the exception of wood dust, animal and plant derivatives are HMW substances. The specific agent in wood dust associated with occupational asthma is LMW and thought to act as a hapten.[15] Enzymes, which may be derived from bacteria or plants, are also HMW.

[a]   Flour

Grain dusts and flour are a major source of allergens. Workers who are exposed to flour may contract a condition known as baker's asthma. This was first described as far back as the 1700s and today is said to affect 9 to 16 percent of all bakers (Bernstein, 1992; Burge, 1990). The precise agents responsible are gluten proteins in the flour itself, although molds and mites that are found in flour are also capable of inducing asthma. Wheat, rye and buckwheat flour have all been implicated.

Baker's asthma usually begins with rhinitis (inflammation of the nasal passages, the common "runny nose"). Symptoms may not appear until after years of exposure. Workers at highest risk are those who are directly handling or sprinkling flour, rather than those involved in baking, where concentrations of flour in the air are naturally lower.

[b]   Grain

Farmers, grain elevator workers, dockworkers and millers are exposed to a number of different agents in grain that are capable of inducing occupational asthma.

At harvest, molds on the grain are thought to be the primary agent. During storage, the grain can be contaminated not just with molds but with bacteria, mites and other organisms that can cause problems for grain elevator workers, dockworkers and others who are involved in the transport of grain. Grain workers are also at risk for other

---

[15] See 17.01[5][e] supra.

occupational lung diseases besides asthma, such as chronic obstructive pulmonary disease.

[c]   Wood Dusts

Wood dusts are capable of causing a severe, long-lasting form of occupational asthma. Sawmill workers are known to suffer from occupational asthma and as a result have been well studied, but carpenters and cabinet workers are also at risk. (It is important to note that the latter groups may also be exposed to varnishes and adhesives containing low molecular weight agents that are capable of producing asthma.)

A number of wood dusts and other tree products (such as gums and extracts) have been reported to cause occupational asthma. These include western red cedar, eastern white cedar, California redwood, African maple, Quillaja bark, mahogany, oak, acacia, cedar of Lebanon and others.

Although many types of wood dust are associated with occupational asthma, the most studied of these dust-induced illnesses is that connected with the western red cedar, a tree that grows in western Canada but is exported widely. It has been shown that about 4 percent of western red cedar sawmill workers develop asthma (Vedal, et al., 1986). The vast majority of affected workers are nonatopic (i.e., they have no personal history of atopic, or allergic, disease). However, it is possible that atopic workers tend to leave industries that involve exposure to western red cedar, which would skew the study data (Butcher and Salvaggio, 1986).[16]

Most affected workers initially develop rhinitis (inflammation of the nose) and conjunctivitis (inflammation of the conjunctiva, the delicate membrane of the eyelid), followed by asthma. A major problem with asthma related to exposure to western red cedar is that symptoms persist after exposure has ceased. In some cases, persistent symptoms have been noted for up to five years after exposure stops (Butcher and Salvaggio, 1986). Tests of lung function also do not show improvement, suggesting that some permanent injury has occurred (Burge, 1992).

---

[16] *See* 17.02[2][b] *supra.*

[d] Enzymes

Asthma has been reported to occur with high frequency among workers who manufacture detergents. The active agents appear to be enzymes derived from the bacterium *Bacillus subtilis,* which are inhaled. Atopy[17] is clearly a risk factor in such cases, as there is a direct correlation between atopy and the development of this form of occupational asthma (Butcher and Salvaggio, 1986).

Other enzymes used in the food industry (such as the meat tenderizing agent papain) and in medicine (for example, pancreatic enzymes) have also been reported to produce occupational asthma (Burge, 1990).

[e] Animals

Exposure to laboratory animals is associated with a high rate of occurrence of occupational asthma, particularly in workers who examine or feed the animals or clean the cages (Bernstein, 1992). Approximately a third of workers who handle rats, mice, guinea pigs and hamsters eventually develop some form of allergic reaction to them (Burge, 1990). The responsible agents may be in the animals' fur, urine or blood.

Locusts and other insects that are widely used in research have also been reported to cause asthma. The precise agent is found in the feces. Atopy is a risk for the development of locust allergy as well as for allergies to rodents.

Pigs, rabbits, bats, pigeons, parakeets, monkeys, deer and cows have also been reported to cause occupational asthma (Butcher and Salvaggio, 1986; Chan-Yeung, 1990; Burge, 1990). Veterinarians, breeders and other who work with these animals are at risk.

[f] Contaminated Ventilation Systems

Humidification and ventilation systems can become contaminated with microbes such as fungi or bacteria. Most are normally found in the air and at usual concentrations do not cause disease, but they can accumulate in humidification and air-conditioning systems.

Asthma related to this type of contamination has been reported in office buildings, but it is most common in the printing industries, where humidification is necessary and paper dust acts as an efficient transport medium. The contaminated dust is inhaled and causes

---

[17] *See* 17.01[5][d] *supra.*

bronchoconstriction (a narrowing of the lumen, or hollow interior, of the bronchial tubes). As a cause of occupational asthma, contaminated ventilation is somewhat controversial.

The clinical picture of asthma due to contaminated ventilation is different from that for other forms of occupational asthma. The symptoms are generally worse on the first day of exposure and then improve despite continued exposure. However, some workers do experience progression of symptoms.

Contaminated humidifiers have also been associated with other occupational diseases, notably humidifier fever, rhinitis (runny nose) and pulmonary alveolitis (inflammation of the air sacs of the lungs).

[g]   Drugs

Workers in the pharmaceutical industry may be exposed to agents that are capable of inducing occupational asthma. The specific agent may be a drug or some inert substance used in the manufacture of drug tablets (such as gum acacia). Nurses and other medical personnel may also be vulnerable to this cause of asthma.

Occupational asthma has been reported with the manufacture and handling of, among other agents, the following (Burge, 1990):

- antibiotics;
- cimetidine;
- alphamethyldopa;
- psyllium;
- piperaine;
- enfluorane;
- ispaghula;
- ipecacuanha;
- amprolium hydrochloride;
- aminophylline; and
- hepatitis B vaccine.

Other occupational allergic reactions besides asthma have been reported with exposure to pharmaceuticals, particularly anaphylaxis, a life-threatening reaction.

[h] Di-isocyanates

Di-isocyanates are a group of related compounds that are used to manufacture polyurethane, paints, foam insulation, coatings and adhesives. They are also frequently used in the manufacture of copper wire insulation and may be released during soldering (Burge, 1990). Car and airplane spray paints also contain isocyanates. These compounds include toluene di-isocyanate, methylene diphenyldiisocyanate and hexamethylene di-isocyanate. (There are others, but these are the most frequently used.)

Di-isocyanates are often a cause of occupational asthma. In one surveillance report, di-isocyanate–caused asthma actually represented 22 percent of all cases of occupational asthma (Meredith, et al., 1991). The exact mechanism by which these compounds induce asthma is not clear. Only a few affected workers develop specific IgE, and atopy is not a risk factor.

The symptoms can be severe, and they can persist after exposure ceases. In general, the longer the symptoms go undiagnosed, the more likely it is that they will persist after the individual is no longer in the workplace (Bernstein, 1992).

[i] Anhydrides

Anhydrides are used to make epoxy resins, which are important in the manufacture of adhesives, molding resins, surface coatings and plastics. Trimellitic anhydride, phthalic, hexahydrophthalic and tetra-chlorophthalic anhydrides are the most common of these agents to be associated with occupational asthma. Himic anhydride, which is used in fire retardants, has also been implicated.

At high concentrations, anhydrides are irritants that produce eye and nose symptoms. At lower concentrations, they are thought to combine with proteins in the body, and the combined molecule triggers the reaction (i.e., they act as haptens).[18] In terms of their ability to interact with the immune system, anhydrides are very reactive; some 25 percent of exposed workers have been reported to become sensitized (i.e., the body can be shown to be sensitive to the specific agent by objective testing) (Burge, 1990).

Workers who are exposed to anhydrides present varying syndromes with different pathogenetic mechanisms. Some develop an immediate

---

[18] *See* 17.01[5] [e] *supra.*

reaction consisting of rhinitis (runny nose) and asthma; testing shows that this is clearly IgE-mediated.[19] In others, a delayed reaction occurs composed of asthma and fever, and this appears to be IgG-mediated, involving a different immunologic mechanism.[20]

[j]   Colophony

Colophony is a derivative of pine tree resin that is used in electronic soldering flux. Asthma may occur in electronics workers when they are exposed to soldering fumes, and in rare cases, it may also occur when colophony is handled cold.

Workers who are atopic or who have had asthma prior to exposure are at higher risk for developing this type of occupational asthma (Bernstein, 1992). The risk also increases with the extent of exposure and with smoking (Burge, 1990).

At high concentrations, colophony can be an irritant. It has also been associated with occupational rhinitis (runny nose), allergic skin conditions and other lung disorders apart from asthma.

[k]   Platinum and Metallic Salts

Platinum, nickel, chromium, tungsten, cobalt and vanadium have been reported to cause occupational asthma. In alloy manufacturing, this has been referred to as *hard metal asthma*.

Platinum salts, principally hexachloroplatinate and tetrachloroplatinate, present the highest risk of occupational asthma from all causes. It has been reported that in platinum refineries, 20 to 50 percent of exposed workers will develop occupational asthma (Bernstein, 1992). The mechanism is an IgE-mediated immune reaction. Workers who smoke cigarettes are at an even higher risk for developing asthmatic reactions. Workers with pre-existing atopy[21] are also at risk, but to a lesser extent (Burge, 1990).

Some workers in the platinum industry become extremely sensitive to platinum salts and can react outside the workplace to small amounts on clothing or in hair. Their spouses may also have this reaction (Burge, 1990).

---

[19] *See* 17.01[5] [c] *supra.*

[20] *See* 17.01[5] [c] *supra.*

[21] *See* 17.01[5][d] *supra.*

The prognosis for asthma induced by platinum salts is better than that for other forms of occupational asthma. If exposure ceases, recovery is faster and more complete than is usually the case with other forms, particularly if exposure can be terminated early (Burge, 1990).

[l] Azodicarbonamide

Azodicarbonamide is used to manufacture polyvinyl chloride and plastics for coverings, insulation and packaging. Azodicarbonamide in dust has been reported to cause occupational asthma. Atopy and smoking did not appear to increase the risk of developing symptoms in this case (Burge, 1990).

[4] Byssinosis

A classic form of occupational lung disease is *byssinosis*. Also known as brown lung disease (a misnomer), it occurs among some textile workers who inhale dust arising from the processing of cotton and other fibers, such as flax, hemp, jute and sisal. Symptoms of byssinosis include chest tightness, coughing and dyspnea (shortness of breath). These symptoms are more pronounced upon returning to work after a brief absence, such as a weekend, hence the name "Monday morning asthma."

The main etiologic agents of byssinosis seem to be not the cotton itself but substances present in the brachts (leaves surrounding the cotton boll). What makes this disease somewhat unusual is that these substances are low molecular weight (LMW) agents, unlike most allergens of plant origin, which are high molecular weight (HMW) substances.

17.04 CLINICAL APPROACH TO OCCUPATIONAL ASTHMA

Two tasks are involved in evaluating a worker with symptoms of occupational asthma:

1. The diagnosis of asthma must be established.

2. It must be clear that the asthma is due to exposure in the workplace.

Of the two, the latter is usually the more complicated task.

In the assessment of a symptomatic worker, the astute clinician will manage these two tasks simultaneously, beginning with the patient's history.

[1]   History

Obtaining an accurate and a detailed patient history is absolutely essential to the evaluation of occupational asthma. This must include the patient's entire personal medical history, with attention to allergic reactions, as well as a detailed occupational history, including all military as well as civilian jobs. Information about any hobbies is also critical, as there may be exposure to suspect substances here also. With regard to the patient's current job, it is vital to know all the materials with which the patient and his or her co-workers are working. Eye,[22] nose and pulmonary symptoms are important to document as well.

It is very helpful if the worker can relate the onset of symptoms to a new job, but this is not always the case. There is commonly a so-called latent period between the initial exposure to an agent and the onset of symptoms. This period can be as short as a few weeks or as long as 20 years (Chan-Yeung, 1990).

When workers experience immediate reactions that occur within minutes of exposure, the link between occupation and symptoms is usually clear. However, many agents produce late reactions, i.e., ones that do not occur for several hours. Workers experiencing these late reactions will generally report symptoms after they leave work. This is particularly true when the asthma is caused by low molecular weight (LMW) agents (Chan-Yeung, 1990).[23]

Late reactions naturally obscure the relationship between work and disease. In some cases, the worker may note improvement on weekends or on vacation, which is a helpful sign.

[2]   Physical Examination

A complete physical examination is important in the diagnosis of asthma, primarily because it helps exclude other diseases. The eyes, ears, nose and throat may reveal evidence of ongoing allergic reactions. The chest exam usually normal, unless the patient is having an attack at the time of the exam or the asthma has progressed to become chronic.

---

[22] See 17.03[3][i] *supra.*

[23] See 17.03[2] *supra.*

Wheezes may be heard on expiration, especially if the patient is symptomatic at the time of the exam. Sometimes wheezing can be brought on simply by having the patient breathe out forcefully.

If the patient is very symptomatic at the time of the exam, there may be signs of respiratory distress, such as the use of additional muscles in the work of breathing, with reduced chest wall motion. In life-threatening attacks, there may be cyanosis (blue coloration of the skin due to lack of oxygen).

17.05   DIAGNOSTIC TESTING

Testing has become essential in the diagnosis of all types of asthma as well as in the specific diagnosis of occupational asthma. Testing provides objective evidence of airflow obstruction.

The most important tests are those of pulmonary function. Skin tests and other immunologic tests are also often used. Beyond these, the more conventional diagnostic tests are of limited usefulness. Chest x-rays are important to rule out other diseases or complicating processes, such as infection, but they often correlate poorly with physiologic findings (American Medical Association, 1993). Likewise, the use of blood tests, such as blood counts and blood chemistry analysis, is restricted to the evaluation of severe or complicated asthma and the assessment of patients in whom the diagnosis of asthma is in doubt.

One exception to this is the finding of eosinophilia on the blood count.[24] Eosinophils are a type of white blood cell that stains red in the conventional preparation of microscopic examinations of blood samples. Normally they make up only a very small proportion of the total white blood cell count. Eosinophilia is an abnormal increase in the number of eosinophils in the blood and is considered by some to be a hallmark of true allergic asthma (Lopez and Salvaggio, 1987).

[1]   Pulmonary Function Tests

Pulmonary function tests (PFTs) are procedures that examine the way a patient breathes. These include the following criteria:

- the speed with which the patient can breathe in and out;
- the volumes of air the patient can breathe; and

---

[24] *See* 17.01[3] *supra.*

- the extent to which air is trapped behind bronchial tubes that are in spasm.

Pulmonary function tests are used for diagnosis, to follow response to therapy and in the evaluation of impairment. In diagnosis, they may initially be performed without medication, but they may also be performed after an exposure (inhalational challenge) or after a therapeutic maneuver, such as inhalation of a beta-agonist drug.[25]

Another useful feature of PFTs is that they can be performed using portable equipment. Patients can be given small, hand-held instruments that measure one specific parameter. They can then test themselves at home as well as at work. This is very useful in determining the cause of the asthmatic episodes.

Pulmonary function is measured in terms of two parameters:

- the volume of air that is breathed; and
- the speed at which the patient can breathe, which is referred to as the flow rate.

Clinicians and investigators use these measurements extensively.

Patients perform these tests by breathing through a tube connected to a spirometer; PFTs may thus also be called spirometry. The spirometer measures volume and volume over time (flow rate).

[a] The FEV_1

One of the most useful measurements in the study of all obstructive lung diseases is the measurement of a single forced expiration, specifically, the volume of air a patient can exhale while exhaling as fast as she or he can. The patient exhales forcibly, and the volume of air that is exhaled in the first second is called the *forced expiratory volume* or FEV_1.

When airways become obstructed, the FEV_1 decreases. During an asthmatic attack, the FEV_1 is generally reduced; it increases back to baseline after the attack ends (unless the asthma has become chronic or permanent damage has supervened).

[b] Expiratory Flow Rates

When the airways are narrowed, more time is required to inhale and exhale, i.e., the rate of airflow slows. Several flow rate

---

[25] *See* 17.06 *infra.*

measurements are frequently used. The most common is the *peak expiratory flow rate* (PEFR). This is the flow rate at the height of expiration.

The PEFT is a popular measurement, because it can be assessed by a cheap, simple, hand-held device that the worker can take with him or her, to do serial measurements at different times of the day. However, accurate measurements depend on the user making a maximal effort to exhale.

Other flow rates that are often measured include the *maximal midexpiratory flow rate* (MMFR) and the *maximum expiratory flow rate* (MEFR).

[c]   Methacholine Challenge

The diagnosis of bronchial hyper-responsiveness rests on demonstrating a change in pulmonary function after inhalation of a nonspecific constrictor agent. Methacholine and histamine are frequently used for this purpose. In the methacholine challenge test, pulmonary function (i.e., FEV_1) is tested initially and then after the inhalation of methacholine. The dose of methacholine can then be increased, followed by further pulmonary function testing, and so on.

Patients with asthma and other forms of airway hyper-reactivity are anywhere from a hundred to a thousand times more sensitive to methacholine than those without these difficulties. This means that an asthmatic individual will demonstrate airway constriction at a dose of methacholine that is much lower than one that would cause a reaction in normal individuals.

It should be noted that as with all physiologic measurements, there is a range of reactions to methacholine in asymptomatic (normal) individuals. However, results are not reported in terms of a range but as either positive or negative. Thus, some people with positive methacholine challenge tests do not have symptoms and probably will never have them.

[d]   Bronchial Provocation Testing

The methacholine challenge test demonstrates nonspecific airway hyper-reactivity, i.e., that the airways are hyper-reactive, but it does not indicate which specific agents in the environment induce this response.

To find out the cause of hyper-reactivity, one must use bronchial provocation testing or blood tests for the presence of specific IgE.[26] Bronchial provocation testing aims to reproduce the work environment in the hospital laboratory. Initially a complete analysis of the work environment must be done to ascertain which agents are present and their particle sizes and concentrations. The worker then sits in a specially designed room where he or she can be exposed to agents one at a time, in the concentrations that occur in the work environment. Pulmonary function is measured serially.

Bronchial provocation tests using suspected offending agents must be performed with great caution, especially if underlying lung function is impaired. They should be done only under controlled conditions in laboratories experienced in such testing. In addition, standardization of these tests is very difficult, and not every agent is available for testing.

The methacholine challenge test is better standardized and more widely available. It, too, must be performed only in laboratories where there has been experience with the test.

Bronchial provocation testing is expensive and time consuming. In addition, it requires expertise and equipment that are generally found in only a few medical research centers. Obviously, therefore, it is not practical in all cases. Situations in which provocation testing probably would be useful include (Chan-Yeung, 1990):

- study of an agent that has not previously been recognized as a cause of occupational asthma;

- attempts to determine the precise cause in a complex working environment; and

- for medicolegal purposes.

A negative bronchial provocation test does not exclude the diagnosis of occupational asthma. First, a worker who has not been exposed in some time may have lost sensitivity to that agent. Second, the bronchial challenge may not have included all agents in the work environment. Other agents may be responsible for the patient's problem.

---

[26] *See* 17.01[5][c] *supra.*

[2] Immunologic Tests

Several immunologic tests have been designed to pinpoint the precise agent causing a patient's symptoms. Two types of tests are commonly used—skin tests and IgE tests—but each has its limitations.

[a] Skin Tests

In a skin test, a small amount of a known allergen is applied to the skin with a needle prick. If the patient already has specific IgE for this allergen, the skin will swell and redden (wheal and flare) within 15 minutes of the test. This indicates only that the patient is sensitized to the substance being tested. It does not mean that the substance is the cause of the respiratory symptoms, since sensitization often occurs in patients without symptoms.

When occupational asthma has been documented and the reaction is thought to be IgE-mediated (that is, triggered by a high molecular weight agent), skin tests can be helpful in identifying the responsible agent. Skin tests are most useful in determining whether a worker is atopic (has a history of childhood allergic reactions and is predisposed to developing a variety of IgE-mediated allergic reactions).

[b] IgE Tests

Tests exist for specific IgE antibodies in the blood. One such test is called a radioallergosorbent test (RAST), which describes the technique used. In common usage, it is referred to as a RAST test. RAST tests are available for some agents that are known to cause occupational asthma, but they are more expensive and less sensitive than skin testing. However, the RAST, when positive, is more specific than the skin test. Generally during the process of sensitization, the skin test becomes positive some time before the RAST test becomes positive. Symptoms may also appear before the RAST test is positive.

[3] Diagnosis of Occupational Asthma

The diagnosis of occupational asthma requires a demonstration that a patient's pulmonary function has undergone changes in a pattern that is related to work. This can be done by pre-and post-shift spirometry, using the FEV_1,[27] preferably over an entire work week. A decrease of 10 percent or more in the FEV_1 is considered significant

---

[27] *See* 17.05[1] [a] *supra.*

(Bernstein, 1992). However, this test is not considered to be very reliable (Chan-Yeung, 1990).

Most investigators prefer more frequent measurements, and this is done using serial PEFR measurements.[28] The worker performs the PEFR test every two to three waking hours for one to three weeks and, if it is possible, repeats this procedure for one to three weeks while away from work.

Variations of 20 percent or more on days the individual is at work, with resolution of variation when away from work, are considered diagnostic (Bernstein, 1992). The major problem with this method is that the measurements must be performed and recorded by the worker, who may not be trained or motivated to perform the test properly, or who may even be inclined to falsify the results (Chan-Yeung, 1990).

It should be noted that negative test results obtained outside the workplace do not exclude the diagnosis of occupational asthma. If the patient is not tested until some time after exposure ceases, he or she may have lost the sensitivity (Chan-Yeung, 1990).

[a] Differential Diagnosis

Occupational asthma must be differentiated from other types of asthma. Since asthma is common in the general population, it is common to find workers with pre-existing asthma (or airway hyper-reactivity) whose symptoms are exacerbated in the work environment because of irritating gases, dusts or vapors.

A variety of lung diseases can produce shortness of breath and other pulmonary symptoms. Emphysema, pneumoconioses (lung diseases caused by exposure to dust, such as "black lung"), hypersensitivity pneumonitis (inflammation of a small portion of the lung) and even heart failure may produce syndromes that resemble asthma. Usually the episodic nature of symptoms and the presence of wheezing are sufficient to point to the diagnosis of asthma, but this is not always the case. When the diagnosis is not clear, pulmonary function testing and a chest x-ray will distinguish asthma from other pulmonary conditions. However, asthma may coexist with these other lung diseases.

---

[28] *See* 17.05[1] [b] *supra.*

[b] Screening for Occupational Asthma

The methacholine challenge test is considered to be a good method of screening for occupational asthma. It should be performed at the end of the workday, after one to two weeks at work (Bernstein, 1992). However, results can be affected by variations in exposure that may occur in the workplace (McNutt, et al., 1991). Preferably the test should be conducted under controlled conditions.

17.06 TREATMENT

Occupational asthma is most effectively treated by removing the worker from the workplace where the exposure occurs. The earlier this is done the better, since symptoms can become severe and also frequently persist after exposure stops.

The acute symptoms of occupational asthma are treated the same way as those of other types of asthma. Considerable controversy is apparent in the medical literature as to which medications should be used and how they should be given with certain kinds of patients. Patient compliance is a major issue. Medications that are used in the treatment of asthma are briefly described here, along with their mode of delivery and possible side effects.

[1] Corticosteroids

Recent theories of the pathophysiology of asthma have placed much more emphasis on the role inflammation plays in the generation of symptoms. This has led to a trend toward increasing use of corticosteroids (cortisone, methylprednisolone and related drugs).

Corticosteroids act to prevent inflammation by inhibiting the action of various cells in the lung, especially polymorphonuclear leukocytes, macrophages and eosinophils. All these cells are capable of releasing mediators that cause bronchial inflammation. Corticosteroids may also act to prevent the release of mediators from epithelial cells lining the bronchial tree.

Steroid therapy may be given orally or parenterally (other than through the digestive system, e.g., by inhalation or intravenously), especially if the asthma is acute. Maintenance therapy can be given with small oral doses. However, steroid administration by inhalation is preferred for maintenance therapy and may be the treatment of choice for chronic asthma. Side effects due to steroid therapy are minimized by the use of nebulized steroids.

[2]   Methylxanthines

Methylxanthines are a class of chemicals found in common beverages. Theophylline, which originally was derived from tea, relaxes bronchial smooth muscles, increases the clearance of mucus and enhances the contractility of the diaphragm. Theophylline inhibits allergin-induced asthma reactions and inhibits the airway responsiveness to such stimuli in some patients.

There is a relatively narrow therapeutic range, however, within which theophylline must be given. Signs of toxicity include nausea, vomiting, dyspepsia, rapid heartbeat and other untoward effects, up to and occasionally including death (Newhouse and Lam, 1990). Methylxanthine therapy has become less common in treating chronic asthma, due to the beneficial effects of low-dose steroid therapy.

[3]   Sympathomimetic Amines

Rescue bronchodilator therapy (the emergency use of substances, such as beta agonists, that quickly bring about a dilation of the bronchial tubes in order to promptly relieve the dangerous symptoms of asthma) provides symptomatic relief by relaxing bronchoconstriction. Generally the duration of action of these agents is short, although longer-acting preparations are under development. Primary actions include, in addition to the basic bronchodilation, increased mucociliary clearance (necessary for the removal of mucus and phlegm from the air passages during an asthma attack), reduction in the cough reflex and reduction of mediator release, thereby decreasing airway inflammation. Frequency of use greater than 200 puffs per week definitely indicates that regular prophylactic therapy is required (Cochrane, 1990).

[4]   Cromolyn Sodium

Cromolyn sodium is used to prevent symptoms prior to exposure, but with continuous exposure to the agent that is activating the condition, this drug becomes much less effective.

17.07   PROGNOSIS

Most workers with occupational asthma do not recover completely after leaving the workplace (Chan-Yeung, 1990). Although improvement may occur, it is gradual and may take years. Recovery varies with the duration of the patient's exposure and the nature of the causative agent. Workers with asthma due to exposure to western red cedar, for example, show a permanent decrease in FEV_1 and are symptomatic for years following cessation of exposure (Burge, 1992).

Platinum refinery and laboratory animal workers tend to fare much better after exposure stops. Platinum refiners in Britain are reported to do very well when removed from exposure. In the United States, platinum refiners do less well, although they do better than workers exposed to other agents. The difference in prognosis between the two countries has been attributed to a delay in recognizing the problem in the United States (Burge, 1992).

Most workers with asthma due to isocyanates, colophony or some shellfish have persistent symptoms after exposure stops (Chan-Yeung, 1990).

Workers sometimes choose to continue exposure for social or economic reasons. Some of these individuals remain stable, and others deteriorate despite medical therapy. Some workers turn to protective measures, such as respirators, masks and airstream helmets, but these have not been consistently shown to prevent deterioration (Chan-Yeung, 1990).

Nevertheless, some physicians recommend that workers who opt to continue exposure should be provided with protective gear, although its effectiveness must be determined in each individual case (Chan-Yeung, 1990). Careful and regular monitoring of respiratory function is essential, and if further deterioration occurs, cessation of exposure is mandatory.

17.08 PREVENTION

Despite the fact that treatment for asthma is available, medical therapy is not an appropriate alternative to removing the worker from the offending worksite. Fatalities have been reported, including one worker who continued to be exposed after diagnosis (Chan-Yeung and Lam, 1986).

For that reason, prevention is a top priority. Several methods of prevention of workplace-induced asthma have been tried, with different degrees of success. One method is substitution, in which the offending agent is removed and a different agent is used in its place.

This does not always work, since the substitute may not be as effective in the industrial process or may turn out to be allergenic itself.

In other cases, changes in factory design can be used to minimize exposure and minimize the number of workers who are exposed. This is obviously expensive. Improvements in ventilation also may help. Detergent manufacturers have been successful in reducing the rate of asthma by using these mechanisms, as well as by switching from a very dusty form of the product to a pellet form. Larger particles are less likely to be inhaled (Burge, 1992).

As was mentioned earlier, personal protective equipment is not very helpful once sensitization has occurred.[29]

17.09   EVALUATION OF IMPAIRMENT

In general, an evaluation of impairment for occupational asthma should be carried out by a physician with expertise in lung disease, and the final rating of impairment must be left to the physician's own judgment.

An asthmatic person is generally considered impaired if he or she has a marked reduction in forced vital capacity (FVC) or forced expiratory volume (FEV) when tested in a qualified laboratory in three successive tests performed at least one week apart. The frequency of attacks is also taken into consideration when determining the level of impairment.

People whose asthma is caused by job-related exposure may occasionally be evaluated to determine their employability or to gauge their employment-related disability. The final determination relies only in part on medical evidence, however, and many researchers regard it as basically a nonmedical decision. The physician must thoroughly document the entire course of the asthmatic condition, as well as all nonmedical evidence, such as data on exposure and reports from supervisors and fellow employees.

Most authors recommend that the evaluation of permanent impairment be performed two years after exposure ceases. Most workers will have reached a plateau of improvement in symptoms and response to methacholine challenge[30] by this time. Pulmonary function tests

---

[29] *See* 17.07 *supra.*

[30] *See* 17.05[1][c] *supra.*

can be used to evaluate lung function for this purpose, but it must be emphasized that no universally accepted guidelines are currently available for the assessment of impairment due to asthma. The guidelines used for other pulmonary diseases do not apply (Chan-Yeung, 1990).

17.100   BIBLIOGRAPHY

Reference Bibliography

American Medical Association: Guides to the Evaluation of Permanent Impairment, 4th ed. Chicago: American Medical Association, 1993.

Bernstein, D. I.: Occupational Asthma. Med. Clin. N. Am. 76(4):917–934, July 1992.

Bernstein, D. I. and Bernstein, I. L.: Occupational Asthma. In: Middleton, E., et al. (Eds.): Allergies: Principle and Practice. St. Louis: Mosby, 1988.

Brooks, S. M., et al.: Reactive Airways Dysfunction Syndrome (RADS). Chest 88:376–383, 1985.

Burge, P. S.: New Developments in Occupational Asthma. Br. Med. Bull. 48(1):221–230, Jan. 1992.

Burge, P. S.: Occupational Asthma. In: Brewis, R. A. L., et al. (Eds.): Respiratory Medicine. Philadelphia: Bailliere Tindall, 1990.

Butcher, B. T. and Salvaggio, J. E.: Occupational Asthma. J. Allergy Clin. Immunol. 76(4):547–556, Oct. 1986.

Chan-Yeung, M.: A Clinician's Approach to Determine the Diagnosis, Prognosis, and Therapy of Occupational Asthma. Med. Clin. N. Am. 74(3):811–823, May 1990.

Chan-Yeung, M. and Lam, S.: State of the Art—Occupational Asthma. Am. Rev. Resp. Dis. 133(4):686–703, April 1986.

Clark, T. J. H.: Asthma. An Overview. In: Brewis, R. A. L., et al. (Eds.): Respiratory Medicine. Philadelphia: Bailliere Tindall, 1990.

Cochrane, G. M.: Bronchial Asthma and the Role of Beta$_2$-Agonists. Lung Suppl.:66–70, 1990.

Lopez, M. and Salvaggio, J. E.: Bronchial Asthma. Postgrad. Med. 82(5):177, Oct. 1987.

McFadden, E. R.: Asthma. In: Wilson, J. D., et al. (Eds.): Harrison's Principles of Internal Medicine. New York: McGraw-Hill, 1991.

McNutt, G. M., et al.: Screening for Occupational Asthma: A Word of Caution. J. Occup. Med. 33(1):19–22, Jan. 1991.

Meredith, S. K., et al.: Occupational Respiratory Disease in the United Kingdom 1989: A Report to the British Thoracic Society and the Society of Occupational Medicine by the SWORD Project Group. Br. J. Ind. Med. 48(5):292–298, May 1991.

Newhouse, M. T. and Lam, A.: Management of Asthma and Chronic Airflow Limitations: Are Methylxanthines Obsolete? Lung Suppl.:634–641, 1990.

Vedal, S., et al.: Symptoms and Pulmonary Function in Western Red Cedar Workers Related to Duration of Employment and Dust Exposures. Arch. Environ. Health 41(3):179–183, May-June 1986.

Additional References

Brisman, J. and Belin, L.: Clinical and Immunological Responses to Occupational Exposure to Alpha-Amylase in the Baking Industry. Br. J. Ind. Med. 48(9):604–608, Sept. 1991.

Brooks, S. M., et al.: Cold Air Challenge and Platinum Skin Reactivity in Platinum Refinery Workers: Bronchial Reactivity Precedes Skin Response. Chest 97(6):1401–1407, June 1990.

Guidelines for the Diagnosis of Occupational Asthma. Subcommittee on Occupational Allergy of the European Academy of Allergy and Clinical Immunology. Clin. Exp. Allergy 22(1):103–108, Jan. 1992.

Harber, P.: Assessing Disability from Occupational Asthma. A Perspective on the AMA Guides. Chest 98(5 Suppl.):232s–235s, Nov. 1990.

Kilburn, K. H. and Warshaw, R. H.: Irregular Opacities in the Lung, Occupational Asthma and Airways Dysfunction in Aluminum Workers. Am. J. Ind. Med. 21(6):845–853, 1992.

Malo, J. L., et al.: Is the Clinical History a Satisfactory Means of Diagnosing Occupational Asthma? Am. Rev. Resp. Dis. 143(3):528–532, March 1991.

Marcos, C., et al.: Occupational Asthma Due to Latex Surgical Gloves. Ann. Allergy 67(3):319–323, Sept. 1991.

Marks, G. B., et al.: Asthma and Allergy Associated with Occupational Exposure to Ispaghula and Senna Products in a Pharmaceutical

Work Force. Am. Rev. Respir. Dis. 144(5):1065–1069, Nov. 1991.

Reed, C. E.: Occupational Asthma in the Egg Processing Industry. Chest 98(2):261–262, Aug. 1990.

Rempel, D., et al.: Respiratory Effects of Exposure of Shipyard Workers to Epoxy Paints. Br. J. Ind. Med. 48(11):783–787, Nov. 1991.

Rosenman, K. D., et al.: Occupational Asthma in a Beet Sugar Processing Plant. Chest 101(6):1720–1722, June 1992.

Salvaggio, J. E.: Clinical and Immunologic Approach to Patients with Alleged Environmental Injury. Ann. Allergy 66(6):493–503, June 1991.

Uragoda, C. G. and Wijekoon, P. N.: Asthma in Silk Workers. J. Soc. Occup. Med. 41(3):140–142, Autumn 1991.

Vandenplas, O., et al.: Occupational Asthma Caused by a Prepolymer but Not the Monomer of Toluene Diisocyanate (TDI). J. Allergy Clin. Immunol. 89(6):1183–1188, June 1992.

CHAPTER 18

Contact Hypersensitivity and Other Skin Disorders

SCOPE

Skin diseases are among the most common occupational disorders. They may be caused by chemicals in the workplace; by physical factors such as trauma, friction or constant immersion in water; or by infectious agents. Among the conditions caused by occupational exposure are irritant contact dermatitis, allergic contact dermatitis, contact urticaria, dermatoses related to visual display terminals, pigmentation disorders, acne, skin infections and nail disorders. Treatment is generally aimed at promoting healing, controlling pain and preventing infection and permanent disfigurement; therapeutic measures may include bandages and soaks, topical or oral medication, and surgical debridement. Prevention of occupational skin disorders may involve improving safety practices, wearing protective clothing or removing the worker from exposure.

SYNOPSIS

18.01   INTRODUCTION

Skin diseases are among the most common occupational disorders and a leading cause of illness-related absence from work. According to the U.S. Department of Labor, work-related dermatoses (skin disorders) accounted for 20 percent of all reported occupational diseases in 1988 (Nethercott, 1990). This proportion is probably an underestimate of the true frequency of occupational skin disease; investigations of many different groups of workers have shown that such conditions often are not reported (Nethercott and Gallant, 1986).

Occupational dermatoses may be caused by chemicals in the workplace; by physical factors such as trauma, friction or constant immersion in water; or by infectious agents. These disorders may be aggravated by mechanical trauma, sunlight or the wearing of rubber gloves or other protective clothing.

For the most part, occupational dermatoses are clinically identical to corresponding skin diseases produced by nonoccupational exposures. Therefore, it is important to identify a history of occupational exposure in a worker with a skin disease that might be job related.

[1]   Skin Structure and Function

The skin functions as a barrier to protect the body from the external environment. Intact skin prevents (or sometimes allows) the penetration of chemicals into the body, prevents the entry of infectious agents, regulates the water content of the body and helps maintain a stable body temperature by means of sweating and blood circulation. Healthy skin and nails are also important in maintaining an individual's presentable appearance and self-image.

The epidermis (outermost of the skin's three layers) is very important in terms of occupational disease. It is made primarily of keratinocytes (cells that contain varying amounts of keratin, a protein that gives the outer layer of skin its stiffness and structural integrity). Keratin is also the primary constituent of the nails and hair.

Keratinocytes are formed in the innermost layer of the epidermis and migrate outward to the surface, progressively acquiring increased amounts of keratin in a process called keratinization. The outermost layer of the epidermis, the stratum corneum (horny layer), consists of highly keratinized cells embedded in a matrix. This layer forms a barrier against penetration by chemicals and other external agents.

The epidermis also contain melanocytes (cells containing the pigment melanin, which gives skin its color and protects against ultraviolet radiation) and Langerhans cells, which scavenge harmful substances and organisms that enter the skin. Occupational exposures to chemicals may result in depigmentation or hyperpigmentation (change in skin color resulting from either a reduction or an increase, respectively, in melanin).

Some cells of the epidermis form appendages (structures that extend into the dermis, the middle layer of skin). These include the sweat glands and the pilosebaceous unit, comprised of a paired hair follicle and a sebaceous gland (which secretes sebum, a fatty substance, onto the skin). Occupational acne[1] may result from chemicals that cause excessive keratinization of epidermal cells, which then create a plug in the pilosebaceous unit. The epidermal appendages may sometimes act as a route by which harmful chemicals can circumvent the epidermis.

The dermis, a thick layer of skin, is made of connective tissue and contains the epidermal appendages, fat, muscle and blood vessels. Blood vessels in the dermis contribute to the inflammatory reaction that is part of the syndromes of irritant and immunologic contact dermatitis.[2]

---

[1] See 18.06 infra.

[2] See 18.02 infra.

The innermost layer of the skin, the subcutaneous tissue, is not important as a site of occupational disease. (*See Figure 18–1.*)

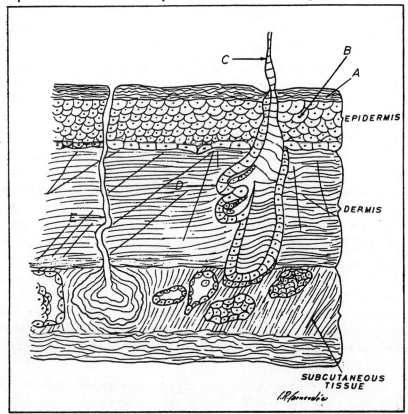

Fig. 18-1. Cross section of the skin, showing the three layers: epidermis, dermis and subcutaneous tissue. Other structures include (A) a keratinized (horny) layer of durable tissue; (B) epithelial cells, which form the covering of the skin; (C) hair shafts, which penetrate through the dermis and epidermis to the superficial skin; (D) sebaceous (oil-secreting) glands; and (E) sweat glands.

[2]   Skin Lesions and Eruptions

The skin has a limited range of responses to disease processes. In the physical examination of patients with skin diseases, characteristics of skin lesions and skin eruptions may provide important diagnostic clues. Dermatologists use a vocabulary of special terms to describe lesions and eruptions of the skin. Skin lesions or eruptions that may be features of occupational skin disorders include the following:

- papule—a small (less than 10 mm in diameter), elevated, solid lesion; may occur in occupational contact dermatitis;

- vesicle—a small (less than 5 mm) blister (elevated lesion containing serous fluid); may occur in occupational contact dermatitis;

- bulla—a large (greater than 5 mm) blister; may occur in occupational contact dermatitis;

- wheal—a raised, itchy, red or pale skin eruption that may be caused by irritation or an immune system response;

- urticaria—a transient skin eruption consisting of wheals; also called hives or a rash;

- lichenification—an area of thickened skin with accentuated markings; a feature of severe allergic contact dermatitis;

- pustule—a raised lesion containing pus; may be a feature of an occupational skin infection;

- comedone—the primary acne lesion, caused by blockage of a pilosebaceous unit and accumulation of sebum; closed comedones are also called whiteheads; open comedones usually become blackened from dirt and are also called blackheads;

- cyst—a lump that contains fluid; may occur in occupational acne; and

- nodule—a solid lump; also sometimes associated with acne.

Microtrauma may produce skin syndromes, some of which are characteristic of certain occupations. Microtrauma is damage to the superficial layers of the skin resulting from small cuts, abrasions, friction, etc. These mechanical injuries can produce blisters or calluses. Workers often take these lesions for granted as part of the job and do not report them as occupational injuries. However, they can disrupt the barrier function of the skin and may allow the penetration of irritants, allergens and infectious agents.

Pressure on the skin may aggravate an underlying skin condition such as psoriasis (chronic skin disease marked by the development of red patches on various parts of the body). Foreign bodies such as fiberglass may become embedded in the skin during work.

[3]   Workers at Risk

Workers in certain occupations are at risk for the development of occupational dermatoses because they come into direct contact with industrial chemicals, naturally occurring substances in the outdoor environment or infectious agents. Industries that have received special study with regard to cutaneous (relating to the skin) toxicity include agriculture, horticulture, petroleum, rubber and health care. In addition, people who work with wood, industrial machinery, hair, produce, meat, poultry and fish have also been studied (Adams, 1990; Maibach, 1987).

Nonspecific aspects of work also may contribute to the risk of cutaneous toxicity. These factors may interfere with the normal protective mechanisms of the skin by disrupting the integrity of the epidermis or by removing the skin's protective coating of oil. The risk is increased among workers who repeatedly wet and dry their hands, who use detergent soaps and whose hands are subjected to mechanical trauma such as small cuts, friction or abrasion.

Workers also vary among themselves in terms of their risk of developing dermatoses, given the same amount of exposure. Some variation in susceptibility probably results from genetic inheritance. Fair skin predisposes workers to develop irritant contact dermatitis and phototoxicity.[3] Increased age, hairiness, perspiration and poor personal hygiene all may increase the likelihood of occupational dermatosis.

Certain pathologic conditions of the skin are associated with risk for occupational dermatoses. Prominent among these is atopic dermatitis (a common, poorly understood chronic inflammatory skin disease that is associated with a family history of asthma and other allergies). Atopic dermatitis increases the individual's sensitivity to skin irritants.

Patients with psoriasis (chronic skin disease marked by the development of red patches on various parts of the body) also may have increased sensitivity to irritants and may suffer exacerbations of psoriasis as a result of exposure tro irritants or pressure on the skin. Acne-prone persons have increased sensitivity to the effects of occupational chemicals that cause acne. Some skin diseases— including lichen planus (marked by the presence of flat-topped papules, or elevations), keloids (thick scars resulting from excessive growth of fibrous tissue) and chronic fungal infections such as athlete's

---

[3] *See* 18.02 *infra.*

foot (infection of the skin of the foot)—may worsen under occupational conditions that expose the skin to heat, friction or trauma (Lammintausta and Maibach, 1987; Shmunes, 1988).

18.02 CONTACT DERMATITIS

Contact dermatitis is by far the most common occupational skin disease, representing about 90 percent of all cases. It is associated with eczema, an inflammation of the skin accompanied by itching, redness and sometimes the formation of papules (elevated solid lesions) or vesicles (small blisters). (The term "eczema" is sometimes used descriptively, but it has fallen into disfavor as a diagnostic term.)

Contact dermatitis is an inflammatory response that occurs at the site of contact with the offending substance—usually, but not always, the hands. About 80 percent of occupational contact dermatitis results from exposure to irritating substances; the remaining 20 percent results from exposure to allergens (substances that induce sensitivity or allergy) (Arndt and Bigby, 1988).

[1] Acute Irritant Contact Dermatitis

Acute irritant contact dermatitis develops after a single contact with an irritant chemical. Solvents, acids and alkalis may all cause acute irritant contact dermatitis, particularly when they are in contact with the skin under an occlusive cover such as rubber gloves or a hat band. Other irritants in the workplace include detergents, enzymes, strong salt solutions, epoxy resins, carbonless copy paper, insulating foams, cement powders, metallic oxide powders and airborne particles from plants, wood, dry plastics and stone (Fischer, 1986; Lammintausta and Maibach, 1990).

In people with acute irritant contact dermatitis, lesions appear on the site of skin contact with the irritant, usually the fingers and the backs and sides of the hands. The thick stratum corneum (outermost layer of the epidermis) that covers the palms generally protects them from irritation. If the chemical is airborne, lesions may appear first on the face. Irritant dermatitis also may develop at sites of skin disease, chapping or breaks in the skin; sensitive areas such as the eyelids; and areas of friction.

Acute irritant reactions are characterized by a burning pain at the site of exposure, followed by redness and, sometimes, the development of vesicles (small blisters) or bullae (large blisters). In severe reactions, the affected area of skin may turn white and then black, developing a border that separates it from normal skin. The tissue in the damaged area sloughs off, sometimes only superficially and sometimes to a considerable depth; the skin then heals, in some cases with residual scarring or pigmentary changes.

When a worker is exposed to an irritant, the irritant should be washed off the skin immediately; oil should be used if the chemical is not water-soluble. Subsequent treatment is aimed at promoting healing, controlling pain, and preventing infection and permanent disfigurement; therapeutic measures may include wet bandages and cool soaks, topical or oral antibiotics, and surgical debridement (removal of dead tissue).

These injuries can be prevented by educating workers about safe practices for handling irritant chemicals, providing gloves and other personal protective equipment, and implementing engineering controls designed to lower the level of airborne irritants in the workplace (Nethercott, 1990).

Typically, stronger irritants produce acute contact dermatitis after a single exposure, while weaker irritants produce chronic dermatitis as a result of cumulative exposures. However, a great deal of overlap exists between the categories of acute and chronic irritants, both because individual workers vary in their sensitivity to these substances and because many factors can increase the irritancy of a chemical, including its concentration and the nature of the exposure.

[2] Chronic Irritant Contact Dermatitis

Chronic irritant contact dermatitis, the most common type of occupational contact dermatitis, results from continued exposure to a low-grade irritant. The condition develops slowly, over a period of weeks to years. Chronic irritant contact dermatitis may develop as a result of contact with cutting oils, mild solvents and mildly acidic or alkaline substances.

The worker typically does not notice much irritation upon initial exposure to the chemical; however, the skin is damaged imperceptibly, and it cannot repair these injuries fully in the interval between exposures. Nonchemical factors in the workplace may exacerbate chronic irritant dermatitis or even produce a primary irritation. These factors include dry air, frequent hand washing (especially if harsh soap and an air dryer are used), high wind, heat, sweating, work that involves friction or abrasion to the skin, and occlusive clothing.

The initial injury in chronic contact dermatitis is chapping of the skin, with drying and fissures (cracks or splits in tissue) that may be shallow or deep. Workers do not usually seek medical treatment for chronic irritant dermatitis until the condition becomes relatively severe, with itching, pain, deep fissures and scaling of the skin. At this point, it is unlikely that treatment will result in a cure, but the symptoms of the condition can be ameliorated, and workers can usually continue at their jobs.

Treatment consists of frequent application of topical corticosteroids (drugs that control the symptoms of inflammation without, however, curing the underlying condition). Protective gloves, lubricating skin creams and the avoidance of harsh soaps can also improve the condition. By the time irritant contact dermatitis becomes chronic, stopping the exposure to the offending agent often does not result in an improvement (Nethercott, 1990).

[3] Photodermatitis

In phototoxic reactions, previous exposure to a chemical causes a skin reaction to ultraviolet radiation or to visible light. This reaction is nonimmunologic, in contrast to photoallergy.[4] Phototoxic chemicals consist of molecules that absorb radiation within a spectrum that differs from one chemical to another, so that different chemicals are phototoxic when acted upon by different portions of the ultraviolet spectrum or by visible light.

When a worker has a phototoxic chemical on the skin or has ingested a phototoxic chemical, exposure to sunlight causes an immediate reaction consisting of a burning sensation, redness and swelling, similar to the early stages of a severe sunburn. These symptoms appear only on sun-exposed skin and usually resolve within a day or so when the skin is shaded. Sometimes redness and swelling may appear from a few hours to a day or two after the sun exposure, rather than immediately. Blistering and hyperpigmentation occasionally occur as part of these reactions. Window glass does not protect the worker from phototoxicity, and phototoxic reactions have been reported' in indoor workers (Emmett, 1991).

---

[4] See 18.02[4][b] infra.

Coal tar, pitch and related substances can cause photodermatitis, particularly in light-skinned persons. Workers who may be exposed to these substances include roofers and road workers.[5] Persons who manufacture the dye Disperse blue 35 may also develop photodermatitis.

Another agent that frequently causes occupational photodermatitis is psoralen, a chemical naturally found in plants. Phytophotodermatitis is the rather cumbersome name for plant-induced photodermatitis. Psoralens occur in many wild and cultivated plants, in some herbs, and in some fruits and vegetables, including limes, celery and carrots. Workers who may develop phytophotodermatitis from psoralen exposure include agricultural workers, florists, cannery workers, pharmaceutical industry workers, forestry workers, workers in the cosmetics industry, bartenders, and supermarket produce clerks, cashiers and grocery baggers (Emmett, 1991; Nethercott, 1990).

The primary means to prevent phototoxicity is to reduce or prevent contact with phototoxic substances, by substituting an alternative chemical in an industrial process, plant engineering modifications and personal protective garments. Preventing exposure to solar radiation is less practical and less effective, though it may be necessary as an adjunctive measure.

[4]   Allergic Contact Dermatitis

Allergic contact dermatitis accounts for about 20 percent of cases of occupational contact dermatitis (Nethercott, 1990). Clinically it may resemble irritant contact dermatitis.[6] However, the mechanism by which this reaction occurs is entirely different, as are the timing of the reaction and most of the substances involved. The substances that cause allergic contact dermatitis are low molecular weight chemicals that can readily penetrate the skin. There they bind with a normally occurring protein to form a hapten, a kind of hybrid molecule that is capable of provoking an immune system response.

When the individual is first exposed to the allergenic substance, nothing happens that is clinically apparent. However, the body's immune system recognizes the hapten as an immunologically provocative foreign substance (an allergen or antigen) and begins to manufacture cells that are capable of reacting to the antigen the next time it

---

[5] See 18.06 and 18.07[2] infra.

[6] See 18.02[1] and 18.02[2] supra.

is encountered. This process, called sensitization, sets the stage for events that occur during all subsequent exposures.

After a latent period of about two weeks, during which time sensitization takes place, the immune system is capable of mounting an inflammatory response to the offending chemical, resulting in swelling of the skin, redness, itching and the formation of vesicles (small blisters) or bullae (large blisters). Although sensitization is sometimes lost, it is usual for the individual to mount an allergic response every time he or she is exposed to the allergenic chemical. Some allergens, such as poison ivy, are potent sensitizers, but most contact allergens produce sensitization in a small proportion of exposed people. Once the individual has been sensitized, the time between exposure and the skin reaction may range from 6 to 24 hours.

[a]   Workplace Allergens

Rhus, a chemical found in poison ivy, oak and sumac, is a very common cause of occupational allergic contact dermatitis. Other plant allergens are found in flowers and exotic woods. Outdoor workers (particularly forestry workers and forest fire fighters), gardeners and florists may be exposed to these substances.

Nickel is another cause of allergic contact dermatitis. Nickel sensitization usually does not result from handling nickel on the job—it may be caused by traumatic or prolonged contact, such as by ear piercing or wearing jewelry that contains nickel—but once sensitization occurs, it is possible to develop contact dermatitis as a result of occupational use of the substance.

Nickel sensitization may also be associated with sensitization to cobalt or chromate, other metals found in the industrial environment. Chromate is a potent occupational sensitizer; exposures may occur in construction workers and others exposed to wet cement and in cleaners, printers and engineers. Platinum is also a sensitizing metal (Menne, et al., 1987).

Penicillin and some other pharmaceutical agents may produce cutaneous allergy; at risk are pharmaceutical manufacturers, pharmacists, health care workers and veterinarians. Formaldehyde may produce sensitization in embalmers, pathologists, resin manufacturers, insulation workers and woodworkers. Dyes and cosmetics may affect hairdressers and beauticians. Rubber workers, tire manufacturers and persons who wear protective rubber clothing may be exposed to allergenic substances that are used to manufacture rubber. Epoxy resins and acrylic monomers are other allergens used in a variety of industrial processes (Nethercott, 1990).

[b] Photoallergy

Photoallergy involves the same immunologic mechanisms as ordinary allergic contact dermatitis.[7] However, exposure to ultraviolet radiation or visible light is required to convert the hapten (a kind of hybrid molecule that is capable of provoking an immune response) into an allergen. Ultraviolet A (rays having a wavelength of 320 to 400 nanometers) is the main radiation wavelength capable of provoking a photoallergic response. In very sensitive persons, sufficient exposure to ultraviolet A radiation can result from sunlight filtering through loosely woven clothing or from indoor fluorescent lighting (Emmett, 1991).

Photoallergic skin reactions usually develop a day or two after the sun exposure. The reactions usually resemble ordinary allergic dermatitis[8] and may extend to areas of the skin that were not exposed to the sun. As the skin reactions subside, there may be residual, slowly resolving skin thickening or pigmentary changes. After repeated exposures, patients may develop a persistent light reaction, with extreme photosensitivity even in the absence of the chemical allergen and with sensitivity to a broader spectrum of radiation.

The antibacterial agents hexachlorophene, tetrachlorosalicylanilide (TCSA) and related compounds may cause photoallergy. Occupational outbreaks have been reported following the use of antibacterial soaps and germicides containing these substances. Most have been removed from the market, but exposures may still occur occasionally. In rare instances, the sunscreen para-aminobenzoic acid (PABA), which can be used to treat people with photoallergy, may actually induce photoallergy. Photoallergy may also result from contact with certain plants (members of the *Compositae* family), pharmaceutical compounds (sulfanilamide and phenothiazines) and some fragrances used in perfumes and cosmetics (Emmett, 1991).

---

[7] *See* 18.02[4] *supra.*

[8] *See* 18.02[4] *supra.*

[c]   Patch Testing

A worker may be tested for sensitization to a chemical by applying a small amount to the skin and observing whether an allergic reaction takes place. Patch testing, as this technique is called, may be useful to identify a specific allergen and to distinguish allergic from irritant contact dermatitis;[9] however, it is of no use in confirming whether a particular substance has caused irritant contact dermatitis.

Patch tests are carried out using a device such as a specially made strip of occlusive material with a small absorbent pad in the center. The purified chemical is placed on the absorbent pad, and the pad is placed in contact with undamaged skin (usually on the back), under occlusion, for 48 hours. Concentrations of the chemical that are too low to produce an irritant reaction but high enough to provoke an allergic reaction should be used (unfortunately, the optimal concentration for patch testing is unknown for many industrial chemicals).

After the patch is removed and the area cleansed, the skin is observed immediately and at periodic intervals. Irritant reactions are sharply delineated and tend to appear immediately and fade rapidly, while allergic reactions develop gradually over 48 hours, become more intense with time and spread out from the original testing site (Nethercott, 1990; Tucker and Key, 1983).

Photopatch testing may be carried out if photoallergy is suspected. In this procedure, two patches of the test substance are applied to the skin, and light is subsequently applied to only one of the treated areas. In addition to possible occupational photosensitizers, patients should be tested with the sunscreen they usually use (Emmett, 1991).

Patch tests should be carried out with strict adherence to recommended protocols, and the results should be interpreted cautiously. It is easy to obtain a false-positive result if the procedure is not done correctly.

[d]   Treatment and Prevention

Treatment of the symptoms of allergic contact dermatitis is similar to that of irritant contact dermatitis.[10] Because sensitivity to a particular substance usually persists, workers who switch to a job in which they are no longer exposed may recover completely or at least

---

[9] *See* 18.02[1] and 18.02[2] *supra.*

[10] *See* 18.02[1] and 18.02[2] *supra.*

improve significantly. If the condition has gone untreated long enough to become chronic, complete recovery is less likely, even if the worker avoids contact with the allergen (Nethercott, 1990). Workers with photodermatitis can avoid future reactions not only by avoiding the offending chemical but by wearing clothing to protect themselves from sunlight, avoiding outdoor work during the brightest times of day and wearing a sunscreen that protects against ultraviolet A radiation (rays having a wavelength of 320 to 400 nanometers) (Emmett, 1991).

The allergenic potentials of some substances are well known. Others can be tested in laboratory animals before being introduced into the workplace. When allergenic chemicals are used, employers should minimize exposure by using alternative chemicals, instituting engineering controls, and providing gloves and other protective equipment. Patch tests using known or potential allergens should not be carried out as part of pre-employment medical screening; if a worker has not been previously exposed to one of these substances, such testing may actually induce sensitization (Nethercott, 1990).

18.03   CONTACT URTICARIA

Contact urticaria is an episode of hives that occurs within seconds or minutes after direct contact with a substance. It may be either immunologic or nonimmunologic in nature. Immunologic contact urticaria requires an initial sensitizing exposure, while nonimmunologic urticaria can occur upon the first exposure.

The symptoms of urticaria result from the release of histamine by mast cells (certain connective tissue cells) in the skin; other substances may be involved as well. Histamine is a chemical that causes fluid to leak from the blood vessels into the skin and immune system cells to migrate to the affected site, resulting in tissue edema (swelling) and inflammation.

Substances that induce nonimmunologic urticaria include many that are used as preservatives or flavorings in foods, cosmetics, toiletries and pharmaceuticals. These include benzoic acid, sorbic acid, cinnamic acid and balsam of Peru. Allergic contact urticaria also may result from contact with the dander, saliva or urine of small animals, and is a frequent problem in people who work with laboratory animals.

Persons who handle foods may come in contact with many foods that can induce contact urticaria, including meat, poultry, fish, shellfish, potatoes, apples, beans, carrots, eggs and beer. Antibiotics, the topical anesthetic benzocaine and the dermatologic drug nitrogen mustard can induce allergic contact urticaria in health care workers. Latex rubber gloves or the cornstarch they sometimes contain are also a frequent cause of contact urticaria in health care workers. Many of the substances that can cause allergic contact dermatitis[11] may also provoke allergic contact urticaria, including nickel, platinum, epoxy resins, wood and formaldehyde.

The symptoms of contact urticaria usually resolve within minutes to hours, unless the exposure continues. There is no specific treatment for contact urticaria; however, oral antihistamines may be given if further exposure cannot be avoided.

Some highly sensitive patients may develop an anaphylactic reaction (an excessive, sometimes life threatening response to exposure that may include respiratory collapse). Anaphylaxis may also occur during patch testing to identify the cause of contact urticaria. Anaphylaxis may be rapidly aborted by giving the patient epinephrine; for this reason, epinephrine and resuscitation equipment should be on hand when administering a patch test (Nethercott, 1990).

In a worker with known sensitivity to a particular substance, contact urticaria can easily be prevented by avoiding the substance. Protective clothing may help avoid contact. If the offending substance can be scrupulously avoided, the likelihood of a recurrence is low.

The physical urticarias are a group of syndromes in which a rash is produced by exposure to physical factors such as heat, cold, sunlight, pressure or exertion. They often appear in association with other symptoms, including headache, faintness and breathing difficulty (Kanerva, 1990).

18.04 DERMATOSES RELATED TO VISUAL DISPLAY TERMINALS

Skin problems have also been reported, although rarely, in persons who work with video display terminals (VDTs). The syndrome consists of a rash on the face or the hands, sometimes associated with itching or burning sensations. On occasion, symptoms have resolved when the worker was removed from the terminal, only to recur when exposure was resumed.

---

[11] *See* 18.02[4] *supra.*

Many patients who complain of skin disease after working at a VDT have an underlying skin disorder, such as acne or atopic dermatitis (a common, poorly understood, chronic inflammatory skin disease that is associated with a family history of asthma and other allergies), which is exacerbated by the exposure. Complaints of VDT-related skin disease occur most often when the weather is dry and cold, and they are reported most frequently in Scandinavian countries. No evidence exists that VDTs emit harmful radiation, and many other explanations for injury have been proposed, though none has been proved. VDT-related dermatoses usually respond to therapy directed at the symptoms, and affected workers do not have to stop working at the terminals (Marks, 1988; Wahlberg and Liden, 1988).

18.05   DISORDERS OF PIGMENTATION

Workplace exposure to chemicals, and other exposures, may produce local changes in the color of the skin by inducing either hyperpigmentation or hypopigmentation.

[1]   Hyperpigmentation

Hyperpigmentation, also called melanosis, is a darkening of the skin caused by increased production of the pigment melanin in the epidermis (outermost of the skin's three layers). It may occur following occupational exposure to coal tar pitch and related chemicals, and it may accompany coal tar acne[12] and phototoxicity.[13] Psoralens (chemicals that naturally occur in certain fruits and vegetables) can induce photosensitivity, resulting in hyperpigmentation. Workers who handle celery, figs and other plant foods that contain psoralen and who receive exposure to sunlight may develop the condition (Gellin, 1990).

Other workplace substances that can cause excessive production of melanin are the heavy metals silver, bismuth, arsenic and mercury (Emmett, 1991). Postinflammatory hyperpigmentation can occur in workers with irritant or allergic contact dermatitis.[14] Hyperpigmentation may also develop as a result of exposure to ionizing radiation (a type of electromagnetic energy that alters the atomic structure of materials it penetrates), nonionizing radiation or physical irritation of the skin by burns or superficial trauma (Cooke and Foulds, 1987).

---

12 *See* 18.06[2] *infra.*

13 *See* 18.02[3] *supra.*

14 *See* 18.02 *supra.*

[2] Hypopigmentation

Hypopigmentation is a deficiency of pigmentation in the skin. It may occur as a nonspecific consequence of irritant or allergic contact dermatitis, or as a result of chemical or thermal burns or radiodermatitis (skin inflammation caused by exposure to x-rays or other forms of radiation).

Leucoderma (whitening of the skin caused by loss of melanin) may also result from specific chemical exposures. In the workplace, depigmenting chemicals may be found in insecticides, paints, plastics and resins, synthetic rubbers, lubricating and motor oils, photographic chemicals, disinfectants, detergents and printing inks (Gellin, 1990).

Leucoderma is also called *occupational vitiligo,* to distinguish it from naturally occurring vitiligo, a spontaneous, patchy loss of pigment that affects about 1 percent of the population (Cooke and Foulds, 1987). Vitiligo can be disfiguring, particularly when it occurs on the face of dark-skinned people. Occupational vitiligo is rare in comparison to spontaneous vitiligo. It may develop in workers who are exposed to phenols and catechols (chemicals that are toxic to the melanin cells).

Occupational vitiligo usually affects the hands, wrists and forearms on both sides of the body. It may also affect distant sites on the body that the worker touches and, sometimes, even distant sites the worker does not touch. Leucoderma usually develops after at least two to four weeks of exposure and may become perceptible even more slowly.

Occupational vitiligo cannot be distinguished from spontaneous vitiligo on the basis of physical appearance or microscopic examination of tissue samples. Vitiligo is usually diagnosed as being occupational on the basis of exposure history. Outbreaks of occupational vitiligo may occur in groups of workers who were exposed to the same substances. However, not all exposed individuals may be affected, probably because individual susceptibility differs.

[3] Treatment and Prognosis

There is no treatment that can rapidly reverse either hyperpigmentation or hypopigmentation. Skin pigmentation usually returns to normal gradually after exposure to the toxic agent is discontinued, though in some cases following extreme inflammatory dermatitis, the skin color may never return completely to normal.

Patients with leucoderma on the face may wear cosmetics to camouflage the patches of whitened skin. Because the whitened skin lacks its normal protection from ultraviolet light, the patient should wear a sunscreen to prevent sunburn; on the other hand, deliberate exposure to ultraviolet radiation has been suggested as a treatment to increase the rate of repigmentation (Gellin, 1990; Nethercott, 1990).

18.06 OCCUPATIONAL ACNE

Occupational acne may be induced by exposure to oils and other petroleum products, coal tar products and certain chemicals. Some aspects of the pathogenesis and treatment of occupational acne are similar to those for ordinary acne, though the clinical appearance may differ somewhat.

Acne vulgaris, or ordinary acne, most often affects adolescents and young adults, but it also occurs in about 10 to 20 percent of mature adults (Lawley and Swerlick, 1991). The cause of acne vulgaris is not known; or rather, since acne is so common in adolescents, it is not known why some people develop acne and others do not.

Acne develops when the sebaceous glands begin to produce increased amounts of sebum (a fatty substance) during puberty. Acne lesions, called comedones, are caused by the blocking of a pilosebaceous unit (comprised of a paired hair follicle and a sebaceous gland) and retention of sebum. Comedones may be either open (blackheads) or closed (whiteheads).

Acne lesions sometimes become inflamed as a result of leakage of sebum into the surrounding skin; in more severe disease, patients may develop large cysts or nodular lesions that can result in permanent scarring. Comedones may be colonized by yeast or bacteria, which further increase inflammation. Acne may be aggravated by such external agents as mechanical trauma, cosmetics or medications.

Occupational acne develops when a comedogenic (acne-inducing) agent comes into contact with the skin, causing excessive keratinization (a process in which tissue becomes infiltrated with keratin, a protein that gives the outer layer of skin its stiffness and structural integrity) of the epidermis.

Acne may be induced by occupational exposures to chemicals, cosmetics (as may occur among actors, models and cosmeticians) and fluorescent light (in office workers and people who work in other indoor settings). Physical factors in the workplace that can increase the severity of acne include heat, friction and exposure of the skin to harsh detergents (Taylor, 1987). Unlike ordinary acne, bacterial infection is not a usual feature of occupational acne.

Treatment of occupational acne is the same as that of acne vulgaris. Gentle cleansing of the skin with mild detergents is recommended; too aggressive cleansing will only aggravate the condition. Topical drugs that can help eliminate comedones include benzoyl peroxide, salicylic acid and retinoic acid (a vitamin A derivative), but these must be taken with caution. Topical or oral antibiotics are useful not only for their antibacterial effects but also because of their apparent anti-inflammatory properties. Systemic treatment with isotretinoin, a vitamin A derivative, is very effective but is usually reserved for severe acne because it produces birth defects if taken by pregnant women (Lawley and Swerlick, 1991).

[1] Oil Acne

Oil acne, also called oil folliculitis, is the most common type of occupational acne (Ancona, 1986). It occurs most often in machinists and other workers who are exposed to light cutting oils, especially those with a high content of mineral oil. Mechanics who are exposed to grease and lubricating oils may also develop oil acne. The condition occurs infrequently in oilfield and refinery workers, who do not usually have direct skin contact with petroleum. A special type of oil acne may develop in young people who work in fast-food restaurants, as a result of exposure to frying oil and grease (Taylor, 1987; Zugerman, 1990).

Comedones develop in areas that come into direct contact with oil, such as the forearms and the backs of the hands. Oil acne may also affect parts of the body that are in contact with oil-soaked clothing, such as the thighs and buttocks. The comedones may become inflamed as a result of skin irritation from the oil and from leakage of sebum (a fatty substance) into the surrounding tissues. The lesions are often (but imprecisely) called oil boils (boils are infected skin lesions).

Workers with chronic oil acne may develop melanosis (darkening of the skin) and photosensitivity (excessive sensitivity to light). Prolonged cutaneous exposure to cutting oils is also a risk factor for skin cancer of the hands, arms and particularly the scrotum (Ancona, 1986).[15]

---

[15] *See also* ch. 15.

Treatment of oil acne consists of removing the worker from exposure and, if the acne does not clear up, administration of topical drugs that are used to treat ordinary acne. Oral antibiotics may also be required. If it remains untreated, the condition may persist for months after the worker is no longer exposed to oil.

To prevent oil acne and other adverse effects of exposure, cutting oils with a reduced content of mineral oil have been substituted for more comedogenic (acne-causing) oils in many industrial operations. Exposure may also be reduced by redesigning machinery to reduce oil splashing, using protective curtains and goggles, and ventilating the workplace to remove oil mists. Workers who are exposed to light oils should be instructed to bathe frequently and to wear fresh clothing every day. Workers cannot usually wear protective gloves on the job because of the danger of catching them in machinery.

[2] Coal Tar Acne

Coal tar acne results from the comedogenic properties of coal tar and related compounds such as coal tar oils, pitch and creosote oils. Workers who may be exposed to these substances include those employed in coal tar plants as well as roofers, road workers and construction workers.

Coal tar acne typically occurs on exposed parts of the body, particularly the cheeks. This anatomic distribution suggests that workers are exposed to these compounds as fumes in the air. Unlike other forms of chemical acne, comedones are usually the only type of lesion present; inflamed lesions and cysts do not develop.

In addition to their comedogenic properties, coal tar and related substances are also phototoxic. They can produce burning sensations, reddening of the skin and watering of the eyes with exposure to sunlight. They may also produce hyperpigmentation of the skin.[16] Certain components of these substances are carcinogenic (cancer-causing).[17] Coal tar acne is treated by discontinuation of exposure and, if necessary, therapy with ordinary acne treatments. Workers in at-risk jobs should have regular screening for skin cancer and premalignant skin lesions. Other preventive measures include enclosure and ventilation of the workplace and provision of shower facilities, clean work

---

[16] *See* 18.05[1] *infra.*

[17] *See also* ch. 15.

clothes every day and double lockers to prevent contamination of workers' street clothes (Ancona, 1986).

[3] Chloracne

Although chloracne is a rare syndrome, it has become well known to the public because of its association with Agent Orange and with accidental exposures of residential areas (such as Times Beach, Missouri) to dioxin as a result of sprayings or industrial accidents (Zugerman, 1990). Chloracne occurs as part of a syndrome of poisoning with various halogenated aromatic hydrocarbon compounds (compounds of chlorine, iodine, bromine or fluorine combined with carbon and hydrogen, in which the carbon atoms are linked in the form of a ring) that are used as herbicides, pesticides, insulators and industrial fluids. Substances that can cause chloracne include:

- polychlorinated biphenyls (PCBs), a large group of substances with many industrial applications, now used only in closed industrial processes;

- chloronaphthalenes, which have been mostly phased out of American industry but are still used to insulate electrical wire coils;

- chlorobenzenes, used to manufacture pesticides and herbicides; and

- dioxins, substances with no industrial use that are given off as waste products of pesticide manufacture and use.

[a] Clinical Presentation and Diagnosis

Chloracne is diagnosed on the basis of its typical clinical appearance and the patient's history of exposure. It usually appears as numerous small, straw-colored cysts, ranging in size from 1 mm to 1 cm, associated with even more numerous small open comedones (blackheads). The cheeks, the "crow's feet" around the eyes and the areas behind the ears are the parts of the face and head that are most often affected; lesions may also occur on the penis and scrotum. The nose is rarely involved.

In severe cases, large cysts or abscesses may appear, particularly on the back and buttocks. Lesions that occur on covered body sites indicate that the chemical has been absorbed into the body. In addition to acne lesions, other skin abnormalities that may develop include hyperpigmentation,[18] dry skin and conjunctivitis (inflammation of the mucous membranes of the eyes).

Substances that produce chloracne usually do so as a result of direct contact, but they are sometimes inhaled or ingested (Ancona, 1986). Chloracne may occur in the family members of workers as a result of contact with contaminated clothing. Once exposure to a chloracnegenic substance has occurred, acne lesions usually first appear after a delay of two to four or more weeks. They grow worse for a while, then subside over a four-to six-month period. After severe exposures, chloracne skin lesions may persist for decades, even if no additional exposure occurs (Zugerman, 1990).

Some experts believe chloracne to be an infallible sign of internal poisoning with a halogenated aromatic hydrocarbon compound. At the very least, the appearance of chloracne is strong evidence that poisoning has occurred (Zugerman, 1990). The dose of a substance that is needed to produce chloracne is lower than the dose required for systemic poisoning (Ancona, 1986).

Systemic effects of poisoning with chloracnegenic chemicals include liver toxicity and central or peripheral neurologic toxicity (relating to the brain and spinal cord, or the nerves emanating from the brain and spinal cord to the rest of the body, respectively). Neurologic symptoms of poisoning include peripheral nerve involvement with pain and numbness, headache, paresthesias (sensory disturbances), dizziness and disturbed coordination. Other systemic effects include kidney and pancreas toxicity, psychiatric disturbances and elevated blood levels of cholesterol or triglycerides (Taylor, 1987).

[b]   Treatment and Prevention

The symptoms of chloracne are treated in the same manner as those of acne vulgaris.[19] Because scarring may result from severe cases of chloracne, patients who are left with scars after recovery may be candidates for dermabrasion. In this surgical procedure, the outer layer of the dermis (layer of skin beneath the epidermis) is removed to eliminate or improve the appearance of scars.

Accidental exposures to chloracnegens may be prevented by improving safety practices. In industrial operations, the use of these

---

[18] *See* 18.05[1] *supra.*

[19] *See* 18.02 *supra.*

substances should be restricted to closed processes, and workers should wear protective clothing.

18.07 SKIN INFECTIONS

Almost any kind of infectious organism can spread to the skin as a result of occupational exposure. An existing skin injury or dermatosis (skin disease) may serve as the portal of entry for a microorganism into the skin. Contagion is sometimes facilitated in warm or wet environments.

[1] Bacterial Infections

Bacterial infection is the most common occupational infectious dermatosis (Arndt and Bigby, 1988). Infections with *Streptococci* or *Staphylococci* are common in construction workers, farm workers and butchers, all of whom may experience frequent small injuries and lacerations of the skin, and some of whom are in jobs that expose them to bacterial contamination. Also at risk are barbers and beauticians, who may work with customers with contagious skin diseases such as impetigo (an inflammatory skin disease). Less common bacterial skin infections include brucellosis and, very rarely, anthrax, which may occur in persons who work with animals or animal products. Erysipeloid, which is nearly always occupational, affects workers who handle fish, shellfish and poultry.

In workers with bacterial skin infections, the nature of the infectious organism should be identified by culture (growth of bacteria on an artificial medium). These infections usually respond to treatment with systemic antibiotics. Preventive measures include plant sanitation, wearing protective gloves and avoiding cuts or other injuries on the hands.

[2] Viral Infections

Most of the viral infections of the skin that are occupational are acquired via exposure to animals. The exception is herpes simplex, which can affect dentists and other health care workers who are exposed to the human mouth.

Viral skin diseases that can be acquired from animals include orf (a disease of the hands in people who work with sheep and goats), cat-scratch disease (in small-animal veterinarians), milker's nodules (in dairy workers and large-animal veterinarians) and viral warts (in meat and poultry handlers). All these infections are mild and/or self-limited; some, such as herpes simplex or warts, have specific topical drug treatments of uncertain efficacy, but most people are treated only for relief of symptoms while the condition subsides (Ancona, 1990).

[3]   Fungal Infections

Occupational hand infections with *Candida,* a yeast, are fairly common. *Candida* infection may occur in people who habitually work with wet hands, such as dishwashers and food handlers. Because cutting oils irritate the skin and remove protective skin oils, machinists are also at risk for *Candida* infections.

Occupational infection with dermatophytes (the fungus that causes ringworm and athlete's foot) may occur as a result of exposure to infected animals or people, or from organisms that live in the soil. Dermatophyte contagion among humans occurs in jobs that involve microtrauma to the skin and that take place in a humid environment. Farmers, ranchers and people who work with laboratory animals are also at risk for dermatophyte infection. These infections are treated with topical or oral antifungal drugs.

[4]   Parasitic Infections

Parasitic skin infestations may occasionally occur as a result of occupational exposure—for example, in lifeguards, farm workers and sewer workers. Outdoor workers may be exposed to ticks, mites, spiders and stinging or biting insects. People who work around lakes may become infected with hookworm, the cutaneous phase of which is called cutaneous larva migrans. Scabies, caused by a mite, is a hazard for employees in hospitals and nursing homes.

Exposure to these parasites sometimes causes severe skin or systemic allergic reactions. Preventive measures include wearing protective clothing and avoiding these organisms' known habitats.

18.08   NAIL DISORDERS

Because the nails protect the ends of the fingers, they are subject to occupational injuries and exposures to irritants, allergens and infectious agents. Nail disorders make up about 5 to 10 percent of dermatologic practice and a significant proportion of occupational dermatologic complaints (Scher, 1988).

The nail plates grow out from the nail matrix, which is located beneath the skin of the nail fold (edge of skin overlapping the nail at its sides and at the root). The nail bed, located under the nail plate itself, is made up of skin and connective tissue.

Repeated traumatic injury of the nail plate, leading eventually to its destruction, is common in shoemakers, butchers, rope makers and silk weavers. Destruction of the nails may also predispose these workers to develop infections or detachment of the nail plate from the nail bed. Cold, burns, ionizing radiation and microwaves can damage the nail plate or the nail matrix (Baran, 1990). Workers in certain occupations may develop brittle nails as a result of exposure to chemicals; these workers include engravers, etchers, glaziers, photo developers and woodworkers.

Traumatic pterygia is a characteristic scarring fingernail deformity particular to carpenters and construction workers, caused by hitting the nail with a hammer (Scher, 1988). Hand-held vibrating tools, especially pneumatic drills, may cause nail thickening, brittleness and splitting along the edges (Baran, 1990).

Immersion in water containing high concentrations of alkali, chlorine or detergents can soften and destroy the nails, as can exposure to solvents and motor oils. Formaldehyde, oxalic acid and hydrofluoric acid are common industrial chemical irritants that affect the nails.

Allergic contact dermatitis[20] involving the tissues surrounding the nails may be associated with occupational exposure to turpentine (in artists), anesthetics (in dentists) and acrylic-based glues used in nail wrapping and to make artificial nails (in manicurists). Rhus (poison ivy) and contact allergy to tulip bulbs may affect the nails in persons who work outdoors or with plants.

Infectious paronychia (infection of the skin surrounding the nails) can occur with many occupational dermatologic pathogens (disease-causing organisms). Certain infections of the nail area are associated with specific occupations. Infection with the bacterium *Pseudomonas*, which causes a green discoloration of the nails, can affect persons whose work involves frequent immersion of the hands in water, such as bartenders, dishwashers and laundry workers. Infections caused by mixed organisms are seen in kitchen workers and farm workers.

---

[20] *See* 18.02[4] *supra.*

Workers who handle meat, poultry or fish may develop a variety of nail infections, including warts, *Candida* (yeast) and bacterial infections. *Candida* infections may also occur in workers whose hands are wet for long periods. Herpes simplex may infect the nail region in dentists, nurses, surgeons and anesthetists.

18.09   EVALUATION OF IMPAIRMENT

When symptoms are treated and further exposure is avoided, occupational dermatoses may not result in permanent disability. However, it is not uncommon for the cause of occupational dermatosis to remain unidentified, for dermatitis to continue after exposure has been discontinued or for the worker to wish to put up with mild discomfort to continue working. In fact, occupational contact dermatitis remains chronic in half or more of cases. Reduced earning power or job loss also affects a surprising proportion of patients with occupational skin disease (Nethercott and Gallant, 1986). Furthermore, cosmetic disfigurement, such as scarring or depigmentation, may be a permanent consequence of occupational skin disease.

Permanent impairment of the skin is considered if functional abnormality or loss persists after medical treament and rehabilitation, following a sufficient amount of time to permit regeneration (American Medical Association, 1993). Some sequelae of scars and disfigurement are considered for other reasons. Behavioral changes resulting from disfigurement, such as withdrawal from society, are evaluated as part of the criteria for mental illness. Loss of function resulting from pain or limited movement in a scar is also evaluated using nondermatologic criteria. Interference in daily living resulting from such alterations as hair or nail loss or depigmentation (and consequent inability to tolerate sunlight) are part of the criteria for dermatologic disability evaluation.

The American Medical Association criteria (1993), expressed as proportional impairment of the whole person, are as follows:

- Class 1—0 percent to 9 percent: Physical signs or symptoms of skin disorder may be intermittently to constantly present, but there is no limitation of usual daily activity most of the time;

- Class 2—10 percent to 24 percent: Signs and symptoms of skin disorder may be intermittently to constantly present, treatment may be required and performance of some activities of daily living is limited;

- Class 3—25 percent to 54 percent: Signs and symptoms are present, intermittent to continuous treatment is required and performance of many activities of daily living is limited;

- Class 4—55 percent to 84 percent: Signs and symptoms are always present, treatment is required intermittently to constantly, and performance of many activities of daily living is limited (which may involve periodic confinement at home or in a treatment setting);

- Class 5—85 percent to 95 percent: Signs and symptoms are always present, intermittent to continuous treatment is required, and performance of daily activities is severely limited (which necessitates occasional or permanent confinement).

18.100   BIBLIOGRAPHY

Reference Bibliography

Adams, R. M. (Ed.): Occupational Skin Disease, 2nd ed. Philadelphia: Saunders, 1990.

American Medical Association: Guides to the Evaluation of Permanent Impairment. Chicago: American Medical Association, 1993.

Ancona, A. A.: Biologic Causes. In: Adams, R. M. (Ed.): Occupational Skin Disease, 2nd ed. Philadelphia: Saunders, 1990.

Ancona, A. A.: Occupational Acne. Occup. Med. 1(2):229–243, Apr.-June 1986.

Arndt, K. A. and Bigby, M.: Skin Disorders. In: Levy, B. S. and Wegman, D. H. (Eds.): Occupational Health. Recognizing and Preventing Work-Related Disease, 2nd ed. Boston: Little, Brown, 1988.

Baran, R. L.: Occupational Nail Disorders. In: Adams, R. M. (Ed.): Occupational Skin Disease, 2nd ed. Philadelphia: Saunders, 1990.

Cooke, M. A. and Foulds, I. S.: Occupational Skin Disease. In: Howard, J. K. and Tyrer, F. H.: Textbook of Occupational Medicine. Edinburgh: Churchill Livingstone, 1987.

Emmett, E. A.: Toxic Responses of the Skin. In: Amdur, M. O., et al. (Eds.): Casarett and Doull's Toxicology: The Basic Science of Poisons, 4th ed. New York: Pergamon, 1991.

Fischer, T.: Prevention of Irritant Dermatitis. Occup. Med. 1(2):335–342, Apr.-June 1986.

Gellin, G. A.: Pigmentary Changes. In: Adams, R. M. (Ed.): Occupational Skin Disease, 2nd ed. Philadelphia: Saunders, 1990.

Gellin, G. A.: Physical and Mechanical Causes of Occupational Dermatoses. In: Maibach, H. (Ed.): Occupational and Industrial Dermatology, 2nd ed. Chicago: Year Book, 1987.

Kanerva, L.: Physical Causes of Occupational Skin Disease. In: Adams, R. M. (Ed.): Occupational Skin Disease, 2nd ed. Philadelphia: Saunders, 1990.

Lammintausta, K. and Maibach, H.: Contact Dermatitis Due to Irritation. In: Adams, R. M. (Ed.): Occupational Skin Disease, 2nd ed. Philadelphia: Saunders, 1990.

Lawley, T. J. and Swerlick, R. A.: Eczema, Psoriasis, Cutaneous Infections, Acne, and Other Common Skin Disorders. In: Wilson, J. D., et al. (Eds.): Harrison's Principles of Internal Medicine. New York: McGraw-Hill, 1991.

Maibach, H. (Ed.): Occupational and Industrial Dermatology, 2nd ed. Chicago: Year Book, 1987.

Marks, J. G., Jr.: Dermatologic Problems of Office Workers. Dermatol. Clin. 6(1):75–79, Jan. 1988.

Menne, T., et al.: Epidemiology of Allergic Contact Sensitization. Monogr. Allerg. 21:132–161, 1987.

Nethercott, J. R.: Occupational Skin Disorders. In: LaDou, J. (Ed.): Occupational Medicine. Norwalk, Conn.: Appleton & Lange, 1990.

Nethercott, J. R. and Gallant, C.: Disability Due to Occupational Contact Dermatitis. Occup. Med. 1(2):199–203, Apr.-June 1986.

Scher, R. K.: Occupational Nail Disorders. Dermtol. Clin. 6(1):27–33, Jan. 1988.

Shmunes, E.: Predisposing Factors in Occupational Skin Diseases. Dermatol. Clin. 6(1):7–13, Jan. 1988.

Taylor, J. S.: The Pilosebaceous Unit. In: Maibach, H. (Ed.): Occupational and Industrial Dermatology, 2nd ed. Chicago: Year Book, 1987.

Tucker, S. B. and Key, M. M.: Occupational Skin Disease. In: Rom, W. N. (Ed.): Environmental and Occupational Medicine. Boston: Little, Brown, 1983.

Wahlberg, J. E. and Liden, C.: Is the Skin Affected by Work at Visual Display Terminals? Dermatol. Clin. 6(1):81–85, Jan. 1988.

Zugerman, C.: Chloracne, Chloracnegens, and Other Forms of Environmental Acne. In: Adams, R. M. (Ed.): Occupational Skin Disease, 2nd ed. Philadelphia: Saunders, 1990.

Additional Bibliography

Buring, J. E. and Hennekens, C. H.: Carbonless Copy Paper: A Review of Published Epidemiologic Studies. J. Occup. Med. 33(4):486–495, Apr. 1991.

Engasser, P. G.: Cosmetics and Contact Dermatitis. Dermatol. Clin. 9(1):69–80, Jan. 1991.

Fisher, A. A.: Management of Allergic Contact Dermatitis Due to Rubber Gloves in Health and Hospital Personnel. Cutis 47(5):301–302, May 1991.

Jensen, J. S., et al.: Delayed Contact Hypersensitivity and Surgical Glove Penetration with Acrylic Bone Cements. Acta Orthop. Scand. 62(1):24–28, Feb. 1991.

Lewinsohn, H. C. and Ott, M. G.: A Review of Medical Surveillance Records of Employees Exposed to Ethyleneamines. J. Occup. Med. 33(2):148-154, Feb. 1991.

Salkie, M. L.: The Prevalence of Atopy and Hypersensitivity to Formaldehyde in Pathologists. Arch. Pathol. Lab. Med. 115(6):614–616, June 1991.

CHAPTER 19

Acquired Immunodeficiency Syndrome (AIDS)

SCOPE

Acquired immunodeficiency syndrome (AIDS) is both a blood-borne and a sexually transmitted disease caused by the human immunodeficiency virus (HIV). The organism invades cellular material, seriously damaging the host's ability to defend against potentially life threatening infections and malignancies. The illness is diagnosed by a positive (reactive) HIV antibody test and the presence of one or more of the diseases characteristic of the syndrome. *Pneumocystis carinii* pneumonia and Kaposi's sarcoma are the most commonly observed opportunistic infection and cancer, respectively, that afflict individuals suffering with AIDS. Homosexual men and intravenous drug users are at great risk for developing AIDS, as are their sexual partners. The prevalence of HIV infection increased from 1984 to 1992, with a greater relative increase among women than men. In addition, health care providers, emergency medical technicians, police officers and firefighting personnel are regularly exposed to the virus in the course of their work. Consequently necessary precautions must be taken to avoid the low but significant risk of acquiring the virus as a result of occupational transmission.

SYNOPSIS

19.01   INTRODUCTION

Acquired immunodeficiency syndrome (AIDS) is a blood-borne and sexually transmitted condition in which HIV (human immunodeficiency virus) invades the body, seriously impairing the ability of the immune system to fight off disease.

In AIDS, the damaged immune system loses its ability to launch an effective defense against attack by other infectious agents. AIDS is often first diagnosed when the patient develops an opportunistic infection—a disease that is only likely to occur when the body's immune system is in a weakened state.

Although AIDS was first reported in the United States in 1981, subsequent investigation indicates that the current epidemic in this country actually began earlier, in the late 1970s. In May of 1983, researchers at the renowned Pasteur Institute in Paris succeeded in isolating the human immunodeficiency virus (HIV), the agent we now know to be the cause of AIDS.

AIDS is not one isolated disease but, rather, a severe late manifestation of the many infections that are associated with the virus. HIV invades critical cells of the human immune response system, leaving the host vulnerable to a variety of opportunistic infections and malignancies. It accomplishes this attack by invading and destroying T helper lymphocytes, white blood cells formed in lymph tissue that are crucial to proper functioning of the immune system.

HIV has the ability to target cells, gain access and then use the living cellular material to manufacture copies of the virus. This process is termed *replication.*

All viruses have a similar basic structure: a strand of raw genetic material—deoxyribonucleic acid (DNA) or ribonucleic acid (RNA)—surrounded by a protective protein coat. The viral DNA or RNA contains complete instructions for making identical copies of itself.

The AIDS virus belongs to a group of RNA viruses called retroviruses. Retroviruses are characterized by their unique replication process: They possess a special enzyme, called reverse transcriptase, that reverses the normal direction of transcription (transfer of genetic code information) and produces DNA copies of the viral RNA that are then inserted into the DNA of the host cell. (*See Figure 19-1.*)

Protein structures on the surface of the virus, called antigens, enable the virus to attach itself to specific sites on the surface of its target

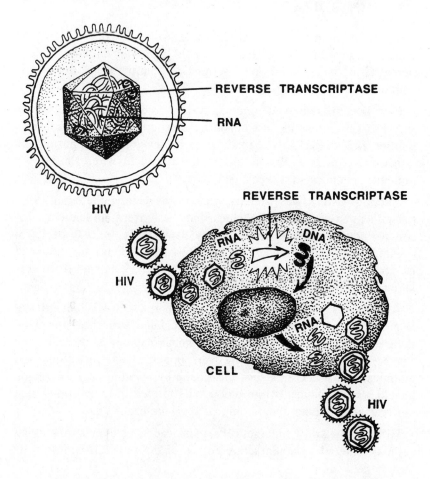

Fig. 19-1. The human immunodeficiency virus (HIV) is a retrovirus that uses a special enzyme, reverse transcriptase, to make DNA copies of viral RNA.

cell. However, viral antigens are a two-edged sword: On one hand, they enable the virus to latch onto its target cell. On the other hand, these same antigens contain proteins that are foreign to the host; these foreign proteins may betray the presence of the virus to the host and trigger the body's immune response to fight against the virus, basically by producing antibodies to it.

19.02   THE HUMAN IMMUNE SYSTEM

The immune system is the body's natural response to disease-bearing organisms. The cells of the immune system are located in lymph nodes (glands) scattered throughout the body. They are connected by channels called the lymphatics.

The complex network of interdependent elements protects the body against infection and, to some degree, the development of certain forms of cancer. The immune system is also responsible for hypersensitivity reactions to allergens and to organ transplants that have been rejected by the body.

The immune system is composed of a variety of elements, including several types of white blood cells and specialized circulating molecules. The blood cells include neutrophils (mature leukocytes, white blood cells with the ability to engulf bacteria and other foreign bodies), lymphocytes, macrophages (scavenger cells) and natural killer cells (white blood cells that are toxic to other cells). The molecular structures that participate in the immune response include immunoglobulins (antibodies), components of complement (a group of proteins found in the plasma of blood that destroy foreign organisms) and lymphokines (substances released by lymphocytes).

Two types of lymphocytes react to antigens (foreign molecules not usually present in the body, which cause certain responses when induced into the body): T cells (thymus-derived[1]) and B cells (bone-marrow-derived); these are responsible for production of antibodies (chemical weapons, or immunoglobulins, directed to a specific invader of the body).

---

[1] *See* 19.04 *infra.*

19.03   CELL ENTRY

Helper cells—T helper lymphocytes—are derived from the thymus, a glandlike organ in the front part of the chest. They are crucial to the proper functioning of the immune system and are responsible for cell-mediated immunity, in which immune cells directly attack the invaders. These and other targeted cells are vulnerable to infection by HIV because they carry a specific antigen (a protein) on their surface membranes. This antigen—called CD4 or T4—represents a receptor molecule for the virus. Scientists have been exploring the effects of neutralizing CD4 molecules, but the results have largely been disappointing. CD4 is necessary but not sufficient to permit HIV entry into the host cells; another factor present in human cells is also required. A number of experimental drugs are being investigated in the effort to block this stage of the cell entry process.

Helper T cells that are infected by HIV lose their ability to detect antigens. The affected cells become unable to mobilize the immune system into a defensive mode, leaving the host susceptible to a variety of diseases. Over the course of the patient's illness, the decreasing number of T cells results in severe impairment of the body's immune system.

The virus destroys the T cell population using several methods. One involves the direct killing of infected helper T cells by active viral replication. Production of these viral cells eventually causes the rupture of the targeted cell and release of the virus into the bloodstream.

A second mechanism involves syncytium formation, a process by which HIV-infected cells fuse with uninfected cells to form large clusters, and healthy T cells are gradually removed from circulation.

A third mechanism is an autoimmune response (a reaction of the host's own immune system) that suppresses the proliferation of helper T cells. In the laboratory, researchers have been able to reproduce this process and even kill T cell populations using the patient's autoantibodies.

A helper T cell count of less than 400 cells/mm is considered abnormal, and the risk of opportunistic infection rises sharply when the count falls below 200 cells/mm.

[1] Co-receptors

Since 1986, it has been known that a "co-factor" of CD4 is needed for HIV cell entry. In May-June 1996, two different membrane proteins were identified as co-receptors for the HIV virus.

Fusin is a protein that is probably part of the family of G-protein-coupled receptors. It enables CD4-expressing cells to be infected by HIV, preferentially for the viral strains that infect T cell lines (Feng, 1996).

CC CKR5 is a receptor for the three chemokines RANTES, MIP-1a and MIP-1b. These chemokines are substances produced by CD8 T cells that have been found to cause suppression of the HIV infection, particularly for the viral strains that infect macrophages (Cocchi, 1995). CC CKR5 is also a co-receptor for HIV (Alkhatib, 1996).

[2] Natural History of HIV Infection

In the case of sexual transmission or occupational mucocutaneous (pertaining to the mucous membranes and skin) exposure, the virus gets across the mucocutaneous barrier and reaches the regional lymph tissue, presumably by dendritic cells (part of the nervous system) within days after exposure. Then massive viremia (presence of virus in the blood) is achieved (this is the first step in cases of percutaneous transmission), and the virus arrives at the lymph tissue within days or weeks. This phase corresponds to the acute retroviral infection. The immune response appears in weeks or months with partial control. HIV replication is persistent, with low-level viremia and CD4 cell depletion over several—usually eight to ten—years. Massive destruction of the immune system is evident, with susceptibility to opportunistic pathogens and opportunistic tumors (Pantaleo,1993).

[3] Classification of AIDS

The AIDS surveillance case definition for adolescents and adults done by the Centers for Disease Control and Prevention (CDC) was changed in 1993. It uses three CD4 cell categories:

- 1—CD4 count greater than $500/mm^3$);
- 2—CD4 count between 200 and $499/mm^3$); and
- 3—CD4 count less than $200/mm^3$).

This classification also has three clinical categories: A, B and C, each of which is subdivided into the three CD4 categories. The clinical categories are:

- A: asymptomatic, persistent generalized lymphadenopathy (PGL) or acute HIV infection;

- B: symptomatic (not A or C); and

- C: AIDS indicator condition. (In 1987, a list was published of the clinical conditions that permit the diagnosis of AIDS. Thereafter, three new conditions were added. In general, these conditions are severe infections, cancer or other manifestations of advanced HIV infection.)

In the current classification, categories A3, B3, C1, C2 and C3 are reported as AIDS (CDC,1992).

[4] Acute Infection Syndrome

Some patients show no initial signs of infection by HIV, while others develop flulike symptoms within several weeks of the exposure. Symptoms of this acute infection phase include fever, sore throat, night sweats, fatigue, nausea, loss of appetite (anorexia), swollen lymph glands, muscle aches, headaches, light sensitivity (photophobia) and severe diarrhea. A maculopapular skin rash (characterized by flat or raised pigmented spots) may break out over the face, trunk or extremities. Aseptic meningitis (viral infection of the membranes that cover the brain and spinal cord) or neurologic symptoms may also develop during this acute phase of the illness. Most of these symptoms subside within two weeks, but lymph gland involvement may persist or even become a chronic mononucleosis-type of condition called persistent generalized lymphadenopathy (PGL).

Laboratory studies during this phase have shown a high concentration of HIV in the blood, accompanied by a negative serologic test for HIV antibody. There is also a transient decrease in the CD4 cell counts. The spontaneous recovery is possibly due to the cytotoxic T lymphocytic response. This stage is also marked by low-level plasma viremia and increased CD4 cell counts.

[5] Seroconversion

The incubation period between infection and seroconversion (when a patient begins to manufacture antibodies, which can be detected in the blood) may be as short as four weeks and as long as five years. Consequently, particularly in the early years of the epidemic, health care and laboratory personnel were routinely and unknowingly in contact with HIV-infected patients who were not yet demonstrating the overt symptoms of AIDS.

Once seroconversion occurs, patients usually remain seropositive for life, although some rare individuals have been observed to revert to a seronegative state and have demonstrated no detectable HIV antibodies.

[6] Asymptomatic Infection

During this phase, the patient is asymptomatic or may have persistent generalized lymphadenopathy (PGL). There is usually a gradual decline in the CD4 cell count averaging 30 to 60/mm^3/year, but this is extremely variable. The CD4 depletion seems to be a direct consequence of the persistent viral replication. Some individuals will have a rapid decline within a few months to a few years, and they are called *rapid progressors*. Other patients remain with a CD4 cell count above 500 for more than eight years; these are called *long-term nonprogressors*.

19.04 HIV ANTIBODY TESTING

When AIDS was first described in the early 1980s, the primary purpose of HIV antibody testing revolved around ensuring that the virus would no longer be spread by contaminated blood and plasma transfusions. Since 1985, there has been a tremendous decrease in the number of HIV transmissions caused in this manner. This is due to the improved screening of donated blood and the heat treatment of clotting factor concentrates required by hemophiliacs. However, there is still a 3 percent false-negative rate (incorrect readings of no involvement) associated with the test.

Today, in addition to its use in blood screening for transfusion, laboratory detection of HIV antibodies in an individual's serum is also used to provide evidence of past or present exposure to the virus. Although the tests do not demonstrate the status of a patient's infection, they can play a significant role in providing prompt diagnosis and appropriate medical intervention. In fact, there appears to be some correlation between early intervention and longevity. Unfortunately, HIV antibody testing by initial screening test is fraught with a high rate of false-positive results (instances in which no HIV antibodies actually exist and yet the test yields positive results).

Because of this difficulty, the initial screening test should be confirmed with a second test with a lower rate of false positives: the Western blot test.

[1]   ELISA (Enzyme-Linked Immunosorbent Assay)

Enzyme-linked immunosorbent assay (ELISA) tests are the initial screening tests used to detect the presence of antibodies to HIV infection. These tests are administered by adding a sample of the patient's serum (blood) to protein components of HIV (antigens). Then prepared immunoglobulin (Ig; antibody) chemically bound to an enzyme molecule and able to bind the human antibodies is added.

If the patient's blood contains antibody to HIV, that antibody will bind to both the HIV antigen and to the immunoglobulin-enzyme combination. The binding process alters the chemical structure of the enzyme molecule. The final step consists of adding a color indicator solution. When the preparation comes into contact with the enzyme molecule in the presence of HIV antibody, the color will change to yellow-green.

Sensitive instruments can detect even subtle alterations in color. A spectrophotometer is used to measure whether color was produced and, if so, with what degree of intensity. The degree of color change can be calibrated precisely. Generally the greater the color change, the greater the likelihood that positive test results are true positives.

Occasionally false-negative findings have been associated with ELISA tests. There are several explanations for this phenomenon. For one, there may not have been enough antibody in the serum for the test to react positively. Also, the chemical characteristics of the antibody produced may not coincide with those for which the test was designed. Another possibility is that the test was not properly performed or that the blood sample was improperly labeled.

Generally the rate of false-negatives associated with ELISA is quite low. However, further confirmatory testing would seem prudent if exposure is recent. Positive results must be confirmed by further testing, using one of the following methods.

[2]   Western Blot Test

This is a confirmatory test used in identifying antibodies to specific components of the HIV virus in a blood sample. Despite its extreme sensitivity and reliability, the Western blot test does have certain drawbacks. For one, it is a complicated procedure that is awkward to perform. More important, however, is that the test sometimes yields ambiguous results. Lack of standardized methods among the myriad laboratories that perform the test further complicates the results.

Administering the test involves lysing (dissolving) quantities of HIV and then fractionating (separating) the various individual components of the virus by electrophoresis (use of an electric current). In this manner, the purified specimen is transferred to a nitrocellulose sheet that is cut into strips. Samples of the patient's blood are then absorbed into the sheet to observe the presence of antibodies to specific components of the sample virus. Any antibodies present are located with the aid of radioactively labeled immunoglobulin that is known to bind with human antibody.

[3]   Radio Immune Assay (RIA)

This test is administered by extracting a purified protein component (antigen) of the virus. Then a laboratory animal is inoculated with the protein to produce antibodies. The patient's serum is then added to radioactively labeled HIV antigen. If antibody to the virus is present in the sample, it will inhibit the subsequent reaction of the animal antibody with the HIV protein.

[4]   Indirect Immunofluorescent Assay (IFA)

This test is performed by incubating human serum on human cells infected by HIV. Any material that does not bind together is rinsed away, and labeled immunoglobulin is added. It is expected that this immunoglobulin will bind with any HIV antibody present in the serum. Immunofluorescence (coating of test cells with antibodies) will occur if anti-HIV antibody is present (Lenette, 1987).

[5]   Latex Agglutination (LA)

Latex agglutination is administered by attaching viral antigen to polystyrene beads. Then the sample to be tested is added, and any that causes the beads to agglutinate (clump) is thought to contain HIV antibody.

19.04   HIV VIRAL TESTING

These tests directly measure one component of the virus—the genetic material. They do not test the antibodies that are part of the immune response to the infection.

[1]   Polymerase Chain Reaction

This extremely sensitive test is capable of detecting even trace amounts of viral genetic material (Eisenstein, 1990). Unfortunately the test is not yet readily available in any but the largest health care institutions. Another disadvantage is the high cost and inconvenience of propagating viral cultures. However, with patients whose previous tests have proved inconclusive, polymerase chain reaction may be the only reliable method of detecting the presence of infection.

[2]   Viral Load

There are two kinds of viral load tests: the PCR test and the branched DNA test. Both tests measure what is called HIV ribonucleic acid (RNA). RNA is the part of the human immunodeficiency virus that knows how to make more virus. Scientists can find HIV RNA in the blood of the patient by creating a mirror image of some known parts of the HIV RNA and matching them with the original if it is present in the patient's blood.

The PCR test encourages the HIV RNA to make more of itself in a laboratory test tube. Then, the amount of RNA that was originally in the sample of the patient's blood is measured to obtain a *quantitative PCR*.

The *branched DNA* (bDNA) test sets off a chemical reaction with the HIV RNA so that it gives out light. Then the amount of light is measured in order to show how much HIV RNA was found.

These two tests are standardized, reliable, quantitative assays (tests) of HIV RNA in the patient's plasma. Their results are useful in assessing the patient's prognosis, guiding the initiation of therapy and assessing the patient's response to therapy (Mellors, et al., 1996).

19.06   DISEASES ASSOCIATED WITH AIDS

Certain illnesses have become characteristically associated with AIDS. These include *Pneumocystis carinii* pneumonia, tuberculosis, and various viral and fungal infections. Also, particular types of cancer, such as Kaposi's sarcoma and lymphomas, and neurologic disorders are common to AIDS patients.

[1]   Pneumocystis Carinii Pneumonia (PCP)

Pneumocystis carinii pneumonia (PCP) is one of the most devastating of the opportunistic infections striking immunosuppressed patients with T4 counts of less than 200 cells/mm. This virulent form of pneumonia is considered to be a classic symptom of full-blown AIDS.

In the past, PCP was observed only in cancer patients and transplant recipients receiving corticosteroids or other immunosuppressive therapy. Today PCP ultimately strikes at least once in more than 80 percent of patients with AIDS (Kovacs, 1989).

The initial clinical signs of PCP are fever, shortness of breath and a persistent, dry cough. Most PCP patients have an abnormal chest x-ray, with diffuse infiltrate in one or both lungs. Some patients, however, may have only minimal respiratory symptoms and a normal-appearing chest film. (*See Figure 19-2.*)

A physical examination may reveal a rapid pulse, abnormal breathing sounds (rales), a high-pitched sound caused by passage of air through swollen bronchial tubes (rhonchi) or wheezing. PCP should be suspected in a patient who is in a high-risk group for AIDS and who has diffuse pneumonia, a worsening cough, unexplained shortness of breath or insufficient oxygenation of blood.

Although open lung biopsy has long been the standard procedure for definitive diagnosis of PCP, a number of other procedures are available to confirm the presence of the parasite microorganism that causes this type of pneumonia. Transbronchial lung biopsy involves passing a fiberoptic bronchoscope through the patient's mouth, down the bronchial tube and through the bronchial wall to extract samples of lung tissue. This test is extremely sensitive and is usually able to establish diagnosis in more than 90 percent of patients with symptoms of PCP (Kovacs, 1989).

One disadvantage of bronchoscopy is its invasive nature. A number of complications can result from this procedure, including collapsed lung (pneumothorax). Also, bronchoscopy is a relatively expensive procedure. Some physicians opt not to subject their patients with suspected PCP to this uncomfortable ordeal. (*See Figure 19-3.*)

Tissue and sputum specimens may also be used in diagnosis. If the organism is found in the lung tissue, respiratory secretions or lavage (washing) specimens, the definitive diagnosis of PCP is confirmed.

Monoclonal immunofluorescence, another diagnostic method for *Pneumocystis carinii* pneumonia, involves analyzing the sputum sample by using a staining method to demonstrate the presence of the organism that causes PCP.

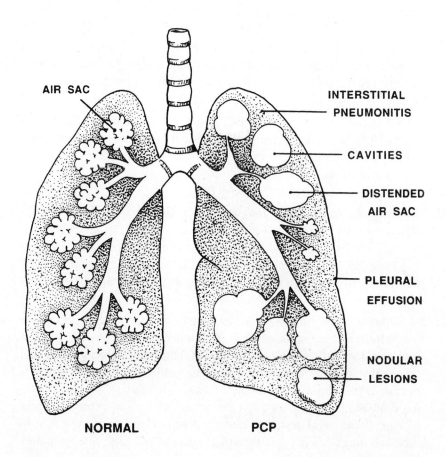

Fig. 19-2. A healthy lung (left) and a lung infected with *Pneumocystis carinii* pneumonia (right). PCP is often the first opportunistic infection to appear in AIDS patients.

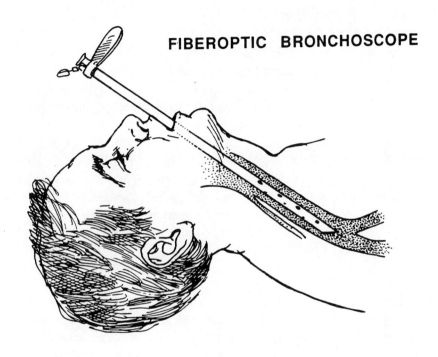

FIBEROPTIC BRONCHOSCOPE

Fig. 19-3. Transbronchial lung biopsy may be performed to diagnose *Pneumocystis carinii* pneumonia and other pulmonary problems in AIDS patients. This method, in which a fiberoptic bronchoscope is used to obtain lung tissue specimens, is usually preferable to open lung biopsy.

[2]   Fungal Infections

Oral candidiasis (thrush) has been estimated to affect almost 90 percent of AIDS patients. Thrush is diagnosed by the appearance of curdlike lesions on the sides of the mouth, the back portion of the roof of the mouth and the tongue. There may be mild or severe pain.

Other areas prone to candidiasis are the esophagus (the portion of the digestive canal between the pharynx, or throat, and the stomach), the skin and the vagina. If the disease settles in the esophagus, patients may have pain upon swallowing. Confirmation of the disease can only be made by taking a biopsy of the esophageal mucosa to demonstrate the specific characteristics of these esophageal ulcerations.

Candida vaginitis is diagnosed by the presence of a cheesy vaginal discharge. Patients often have pain and itching in the vaginal area. Microscopic examination of the oral plaques or the vaginal exudate confirms the diagnosis by demonstrating the presence of yeast and pseudohyphae (a type of fungus).

[3]   Tuberculosis

Tuberculosis is one of the AIDS-related opportunistic infections necessitating special precautions. To date, at least six multiple transmissions of tuberculosis have been reported in association with the care of HIV-infected patients in hospitals, clinics and hospices (Rhame, 1992).

Patients with a persistent (chronic) cough, abnormal chest x-ray and suspicious sputum smears should be treated with caution. Repeat sputum smears and bacilli cultures confirm the diagnosis. The detection of mycobacteria is usually considered indicative of the disease.

Precautionary measures that have been instituted in some health care facilities include instructing personnel to wear special masks, increasing the air change frequency, altering ventilation systems to change or reduce outflow air where HIV-positive patients are being treated by pentamidine, and isolating patients with particularly virulent cases. Patients with AIDS who require aerosol therapy should be carefully monitored to prevent transmission of tuberculosis and other infections via droplets.

[4] Viral Infections

Certain viral infections are common among AIDS patients, including cytomegalovirus, Epstein-Barr virus, herpes simplex and herpes zoster.

[a] Cytomegalovirus (CMV)

One of the most common opportunistic infections afflicting HIV-infected individuals is cytomegalovirus (CMV), a member of the herpes group. Eventually almost all AIDS patients develop CMV, and the results can prove life threatening. A gradual loss of vision progressing to blindness is the most common symptom associated with CMV.

Cytomegalovirus can affect almost any organ in the body, including the retina of the eye, the lungs, the esophagus, the gastrointestinal tract, the liver, the adrenal glands and the brain. Standard antiviral drugs have not proved effective in treating CMV. However, gancyclovir is the antiviral drug that seems to control CMV infection, even though some patients develop toxic reactions to the medication.

[b] Epstein-Barr Virus

Epstein-Barr is a common virus affecting the population as a whole. The illness causes acute mononucleosis and has recently been implicated as a factor in the proliferation of HIV.

[c] Herpes Simplex

Herpes simplex type I is a common virus affecting the general population. It often causes gingivostomatitis, an inflammation of the mucosal membranes of the mouth.

Herpes simplex type II usually affects the genitalia and the rectum. It is particularly prevalent among homosexual men and can prove to be intensely uncomfortable. Herpes I and II were among the first opportunistic infections to be observed in AIDS patients, for whom the oral and perirectal ulcerations can be quite painful.

Culturing the lesions usually confirms the diagnosis, but sometimes biopsy and histologic (cell) examination are required. Although the herpetic lesions are initially responsive to antiviral therapy, the relapse rate remains high.

[d] Herpes Zoster (Shingles)

Herpes zoster occurs in two separate stages—a primary infection and a reactivation of the infection. Initial infection by herpes zoster is called varicella (chickenpox) and usually affects children. After the patient recovers, the virus goes into a latent stage; it may be reactivated much later in the patient's life, at which time the illness is called shingles.

If it is reactivated in an HIV-infected patient, the virus can have severe consequences. Subsequent disease (shingles) can be limited to skin surfaces or can become systemic, involving the brain, the liver, the pancreas and the central nervous system. If the disease disseminates to the lungs, liver or central nervous system, the results can be fatal. Acyclovir is the standard antiviral agent used in the treatment of herpes zoster.

[5] Cancers Associated with AIDS

In addition to the opportunistic infections associated with AIDS, several forms of cancer are being seen with increasing frequency among patients with HIV. The most common malignancies in this group are Kaposi's sarcoma and non-Hodgkin's lymphoma.

[a] Kaposi's Sarcoma

This used to be a rare form of cancer that almost exclusively affected elderly men of Mediterranean or eastern European Jewish ancestry. The disease usually progressed slowly, and the patient ultimately died as a result of a different ailment. However, the outbreak of the AIDS pandemic (worldwide epidemic) has resulted in a new, more aggressive strain of Kaposi's sarcoma.

Epidemic Kaposi's primarily affects homosexual and bisexual males under the age of 40. Some evidence suggests a genetic predisposition toward development of this form of cancer, which has four stages: patch, plaque, nodular and ulcerative.

The lesions characteristic of Kaposi's are diagnosed in the patch stage or in the plaque stage. Lesions may appear anywhere on the body, including the mouth, palms, soles, ears, scalp and anus. (*See Figure 19-4.*) The patch stage consists of lesions early in their development, varying in size from as small as a pinpoint to several centimeters in diameter. They are flat lesions ranging in color from a light pink to purple in light-skinned individuals to blue in dark-skinned individuals. As the illness progresses, the lesions may become hyperpigmented and turn brown.

If the patches harden and thicken, they are said to have entered the plaque stage. As the disease progresses, discrete tumor nodules develop (nodular stage). At this point, the plaques may become hyperpigmented, turning dark purple, blue or brown. In the ulceration stage, the nodules break through the skin surface and may contain pus.

KAPOSI'S SARCOMA

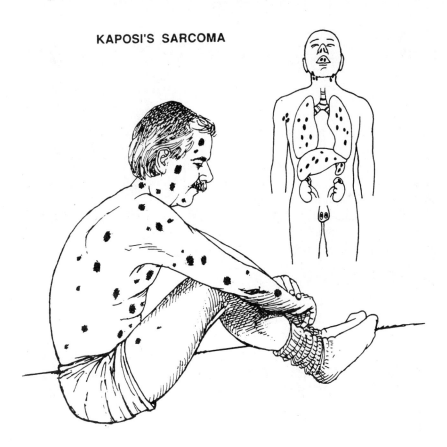

Fig. 19-4. Clinical presentation of Kaposi's sarcoma as it appears in AIDS patients. The characteristic lesions can differ in size, color, texture and area of involvement, depending on the state of development.

The ulcerative lesions may involve subcutaneous tissue, deep fascial tissue (connective tissue) or underlying bone. The tumor may spread to lymph nodes, lung tissue and the gastrointestinal tract. Edema (fluid-filled swelling) may develop. A clinical diagnosis requires biopsy and histologic evaluation, as the lesions may resemble other dermatologic disorders.

The disease is slow in progressing, sometimes spanning a decade or more. Patients have survived between 8 to 15 years, and death usually results from another disease common to the AIDS population.

Analysis of the Kaposi's sarcoma tissues obtained from patients with AIDS showed that in more than 90 percent of the cases, there was DNA of a herpesvirus called Kaposi's-sarcoma-associated herpesvirus (Chang, 1994), also known as human herpesvirus 8 (Moore, 1996).

Treatment of Kaposi's presents a medical dilemma. The most effective regimen is a combination of chemotherapy and radiation, both of which result in bone marrow suppression. This additional immunosuppression leaves the AIDS patient more susceptible to opportunistic infections. Interferon-alpha, administered in large doses, seems to result in at least partial tumor regression in a large proportion of patients. Radiation therapy usually produces a rapid and effective response (tumor shrinkage) and improves the quality of life in the short term. Unfortunately, the prognosis remains poor for the long term.

[b] Lymphomas

Lymphomas are aggressive cancers in which certain white blood cells proliferate in an uncontrolled fashion. Diagnosis of lymphoma is based on microscopic and histologic (cellular) evaluation.

In patients with HIV, the type of lymphoma that occurs with alarming regularity is called non-Hodgkin's lymphoma. This disease is indicative of HIV infection, and the Centers for Disease Control and Prevention (CDC) has included the disease in its surveillance case definition for AIDS.

These tumors often appear in the brain but may also appear in bone marrow, skin tissue, small intestine, stomach, liver, spleen and inside the mouth. Some unusual sites have been reported in AIDS patients, including the heart, lung, rectum and common bile duct.

Chemotherapy is the only treatment currently in use, but the prognosis is generally very poor, with patients with primary brain lymphoma generally surviving only two or three months after diagnosis.

[6] Neurologic and Psychiatric Symptoms

Neurologic complications are a significant component of HIV infection. The central nervous system (brain and spinal cord) is an early area of infection and may serve as a reservoir for the virus. However, many individuals with evidence of HIV in the central nervous system do not exhibit clinical signs or symptoms of neurologic disease.

Two different types of neurologic complications arise from HIV infection, both of which can coexist in the same patient. The first consists of primary complications caused by direct HIV infection of the nervous system. HIV encephalopathy (AIDS dementia complex) is the most common of these. The second consists of secondary neurologic complications of the opportunistic infections or cancers that result from the immunodeficiency produced by HIV.

[a] HIV Encephalopathy (AIDS Dementia Complex)

Research has demonstrated that the central nervous system is an early site of HIV infection. HIV has been found to replicate in the central nervous system, including the brain and cerebrospinal fluid, and in peripheral nerves. HIV encephalopathy (AIDS dementia complex) is the most common neurologic complication and is marked by clinical findings of disabling cognitive and/or motor dysfunction interfering with occupation or activities of daily living. Symptoms include forgetfulness and loss of concentration. Severe psychiatric disturbances, such as psychosis or psychotic behavior and hallucinations, may also be present.

The onset of dementia is often insidious, with gradual deterioration over a period of months, especially without medical intervention. As the disease progresses, patients characteristically develop a wide-eyed stare. They may appear either apathetic or indifferent to their environment. Eventually the disease causes severe global (overall) cognitive dysfunction. Many patients demonstrate symptoms of motor dysfunction, including leg weakness, progressive loss of balance and deterioration in handwriting.

Motor dysfunctions may also include partial paralysis of the lower (distal) extremities (paraparesis), bladder and bowel incontinence, intermittent muscle spasms (myoclonus) and tremors. Computed tomography (CT) scan and magnetic resonance imaging (MRI) are used for making the clinical diagnosis. Zidovudine (AZT) has proved effective in reducing the neurologic symptoms of HIV encephalopathy.

[b]   Peripheral Neuropathy

The peripheral nerves are those outside the brain and spinal cord. HIV is responsible for causing two types of peripheral nerve damage—sensory and demyelinating.

HIV-caused sensory neuropathy affects 10 to 20 percent of AIDS patients. Generally the condition manifests itself at an advanced stage of the illness. Symptoms include nerve palsy, numbness or tingling in the lower (distal) extremities. Some patients experience intense pain. Symptoms either remain stable or worsen gradually. Treatment includes a regimen of narcotics, antidepressants and anticonvulsants.

Demyelinating neuropathy generally has motor symptoms and occurs at an earlier stage of HIV infection. The symptoms may manifest themselves in an acute form over a period of several hours or in a chronic form spanning a period from days to weeks. Unfortunately there is no established treatment, although a process called plasmapheresis has recently begun to be used. This involves separating plasma from other blood cells, washing them, suspending them in a saline solution and then injecting the purified plasma back into the patient.

[7]   Dermatologic Disorders

Hairy leukoplakia is a disease characterized by thickened patches on the mucosal membranes of the gums, mouth and tongue. The cellular structures become distorted and result in hairlike projections. Evidence has suggested a link between this disease and the Epstein-Barr virus. Retin-A solution is used as a topical remedy, but the lesions usually recur.

19.07   ANTIVIRAL AGENTS

Successful treatment of human immunodeficiency virus infection will most likely require activity on three fronts:

- control or destruction of the virus;
- repair of damage to the immune system; and

- successful treatment of the secondary manifestations of HIV infection—the opportunistic infections and cancers associated with the virus.

Conventional treatments are available for these latter conditions, but their effectiveness varies, depending on the disease and on the state of the patient's immune system.

[1] Analogues

A group of drugs called reverse transcriptase inhibitors act to block the replication of the virus.[4] One type of treatment uses nucleoside analogues—counterfeit agents that look like the substances that form the building blocks for DNA and RNA—to trick the virus into using it to make new copies of itself, which are then unable to make further copies. These drugs include compounds like zidovudine (AZT), dideoxycytidine (DDC) and dideoxyinosine (DDI). Other analogues have recently been developed, among them didehydrodeoxythymidine (D4T) and lamivudine (3TC).

The nucleoside analogues work by deceiving the virus with a decoy of the genetic material it requires for replication. Although the analogues seem to impede the progress of viral reproduction, eventually the deception is recognized. In addition, HIV mutates rapidly, resulting in a new and different strain of the virus. The combination therapy may delay or prevent the emergence of drug resistance. Studies of combination therapy using two nucleoside analogues, with or without a member of the new drug group called protease inhibitors, indicate that this treatment appears to have more potent antiretroviral activity.

The most common side effect of AZT is bone marrow suppression with progressive anemia (deficiency of red blood cells or hemoglobin, the iron-carrying portion of blood), leukopenia (insufficient number of leukocytes, a type of white blood cell) or thrombocytopenia (abnormally small number of platelets, irregularly shaped discs found in the blood). Frequent blood count monitoring is recommended, therefore, for patients who are taking AZT. Other adverse side effects that have been described in the early course of AZT treatment include fever, rash, severe headaches, nausea, muscle pain, insomnia and nail pigmentation changes. If neurotoxicity (destruction of nerve cells) occurs, the patient may develop seizures or dementia.

---

[4] See 19.01 supra.

The toxicity of AZT in healthy, nonpregnant females is reported to be relatively low; however, it has been found to affect spermatozoa adversely (Goldsmith, 1990). Although there are gastrointestinal and hematologic manifestations of AZT toxicity, these appear to be completely reversible (Rhame, 1992).

Some concerns have been raised about the possible carcinogenicity of zidovudine, but to date, results of studies attempting to ascertain this have been unconvincing.

AZT monotherapy was used in a trial to prevent maternal-to-fetal transmission in women with CD4 counts above 200 and almost no prior experience with AZT therapy. The results showed a reduction in transmission from 24.9 percent to 7.8 percent. Recent observational studies have shown reduced transmission associated also with prior AZT therapy (Fiscus, 1996).

DDC and DDI are dioxynucleosides—compounds that, like AZT, inhibit reverse transcriptase, effectively interfering with the virus's replication process. Unfortunately the high dose required often results in peripheral neuropathy. The most common symptom of this toxicity in a significant percentage of patients is painful feet. DDI also has serious side effects, including peripheral neuropathy and pancreatitis (inflammation of the pancreas). Nevertheless, the drug was approved by the Food and Drug Administration (FDA) in 1991.

DDC, a nucleoside with properties similar to those of AZT and DDI, was approved by the FDA in 1992. The most significant side effect of this drug is peripheral neuropathy. However, because of the low incidence of hematologic (pertaining to blood) toxicity, DDC is being administered in combination therapy with AZT. This treatment is resulting in increasing counts of CD4 cells and decreasing levels of HIV.

Lamivudine (3TC) is a new nucleoside analogue that acts as a reverse transcriptase inhibitor. Strains resistant to AZT are sensitive to 3TC. Its few side effects include nausea, vomiting and headaches and, on rare occasions, hair loss and pancreatitis. It is been used in combination therapy with very encouraging preliminary results.

[2] Protease Inhibitors

These drugs block a part of the virus called protease. Protease inhibitors force the human immunodeficiency virus to make copies of itself that cannot infect new cells. The drugs appear to have fewer side effects than the AZT-type drugs, but each one is different.

Several drugs of this group have been approved by the FDA in record time due to the preliminary results of testing. Saquinavir was one of the first in this group. It is not well absorbed by the body.

Ritonavir is better absorbed. The side effects described with this drug are nausea (affecting a fourth of the people who take it), vomiting, weakness, numbness around the mouth and elevated levels of liver enzymes. This drug also can affect the way other drugs are absorbed by the body. It is very important, therefore, to check the list of drugs the patient takes before administering ritonavir.

Indinavir is another drug in this classification that is also more potent than saquinavir. A study done with indinavir in combination with AZT and 3TC showed that 90 percent of the patients taking it had no detectable HIV in their blood after 24 weeks of treatment. Their CD4 cell counts also rose significantly. This is very exciting news, because it is the first therapy to have this effect on HIV, but it is still too early to know the magnitude and durability of the clinical benefits associated with plasma viral RNA suppression. The most common side effects are kidney stones and temporary elevation of the levels of a liver enzyme called bilirubin. Bilirubin usually returns to normal levels on its own. Kidney stones, which are present in 4 percent of the patients, can be avoided by drinking plenty of water (at least 48 ounces of fluid per day while taking indinavir).

[3]   Antibiotics

Recently a class of antibiotics known as aminoglycosides has demonstrated the ability to block a step that is vital to the HIV replication process. The most effective of these aminoglycosides is neomycin B, which attaches itself to the RNA molecules of the virus, intervening at an initial stage in the sequence of events required for HIV to successfully invade a targeted cell. Because it is then unable to move into the cytoplasm of the cell, the RNA molecules pile up in the cell nucleus, rendering them impotent and unable to reproduce.

Unfortunately, neomycin B has serious side effects: Large doses of the drug are known to cause renal (kidney) damage. Consequently neomycin is currently being used only for bowel cleaning prior to certain surgical procedures. Another treatment approach involves a method of designing drugs to combat HIV by targeting the molecule that carries the genetic message within cells. Investigators hope to chemically modify the antibiotics to effectively thwart viral replication without harming the patient (Hirsch, 1993).

[4]   Vaccines

Strains of HIV have been found to vary throughout the world. Therefore, it is an extremely challenging task to develop a vaccine that would be effective against all strains of the virus. Researchers are not confident that a vaccine derived from one strain of the virus will necessarily protect patients from all the others.

19.08   UNIVERSAL PRECAUTIONS FOR PREVENTING OCCUPATIONAL HIV TRANSMISSION

The Centers for Disease Control (CDC) first issued "universal precautions" in 1987. More recently (1988), the CDC issued "Universal Precautions for Prevention of Transmission of HIV, Hepatitis B Virus and Other Bloodborne Pathogens in Health-Care Settings." In addition, there are now recommendations for preventing transmission of HIV during exposure-prone invasive procedures (CDC, 1991). The underlying principle of these precautions is the assumption that until a negative test has been confirmed, all blood and certain other body fluids are to be considered potentially infectious.

In October of 1991, the CDC recommendations achieved the force of law when Congress required state public health officials to certify that the recommendations or equivalent guidelines would be instituted within one year.

[1]   Potentially Infectious Body Fluids

The body fluids the CDC deems hazardous include any fluid containing white blood cells. These include semen, blood and plasma; synovial, pleural, peritoneal, pericardial and amniotic fluids; vaginal secretions and bone marrow. Urine, feces, sweat, saliva, vomitus and tears are not considered hazardous unless they contain visible blood (Rhame, 1992). However, merely locating the virus in a particular body fluid does not indicate how readily it can be transmitted through that fluid. The virus is very rare in tears and saliva, and when it does appear, the levels are probably too low to cause infection.

Any unfixed tissue or organ (other than intact skin) from a live or deceased human being infected with the virus is potentially infectious. This has necessarily complicated the field of organ transplantation.

HIV-containing cells, tissue cultures, organ cultures, culture media or specimens from experiment animals infected by HIV can be hazardous, especially to laboratory personnel.

[2] Use of Barrier Precautions

Some of the basic elements of the CDC guidelines include:

- Wearing gloves prior to contact with all body fluids and blood-soaked articles of clothing or linens. Used gloves are to be discarded before treating the next patient.

- Barrier equipment is to be worn during surgery, including masks, eye wear, gowns and aprons. This is especially important during procedures that are likely to produce splashing of blood and body fluids (pelvic surgery, for example).

- Used needles are to be disposed of in puncture-resistant containers. They are not to be recapped or bent by hand.

- Disposable mouthpieces and resuscitation bags (ambubags) are to be employed whenever feasible to prevent direct contact with a patient requiring ventilation assistance whose HIV status is not known.

- Employees with open scratches or exudative wounds should not engage in direct patient care.

- Hands and skin must be washed immediately if they become contaminated by blood or body fluids.

19.09 CDC GUIDELINES FOR INVASIVE MEDICAL PROCEDURES

The Centers for Disease Control and Prevention (CDC) has issued guidelines that encourage, but do not require, all health care workers who perform exposure-prone (invasive) procedures to be voluntarily tested for HIV antibodies.

[1] Definitions

Examples of invasive procedures that carry a high risk of HIV transmission include abdominal, gynecologic and heart surgeries, tooth extractions and root canals. These surgical procedures involve organs with small and so-called blind areas. Surgery in these confined body cavities poses a risk of blood and body fluid exchange between patient and surgeon.

Invasive procedures have been described by the Centers for Disease Control and Prevention (CDC) as entry into tissues, cavities or organs and repair of major traumatic injuries. These exposure-prone procedures are regularly performed in various health care settings, including operating rooms, delivery rooms and emergency rooms. These procedures are also regularly being performed in outpatient settings, including physicians' and dentists' offices. The manipulation, cutting or removal of any oral tissue or tooth structure has the potential for extensive bleeding.

[2]   Precautions for Invasive Procedures

Health care employees who participate in the performance of invasive procedures must routinely use appropriate barrier protections to prevent skin and mucous-membrane contact with the blood and bodily fluids of their patients. Gloves and surgical masks must be worn during all invasive procedures. Protective eye wear (goggles, glasses) or chin-length eye shields should be employed during procedures that result in droplets and splashing of blood and other body fluids or the generation of sharp shards of bone. Gowns or surgical aprons must be worn as well to provide adequate protection.

A single infected health care provider who performs invasive procedures can infect many more patients than a seropositive patient can infect providers (Brennan, 1991). The CDC recommends that HIV-positive health care workers who perform exposure-prone procedures modify their practices as advised by an expert review panel to be designated locally.

A significant CDC recommendation states that HIV testing of health care workers be voluntary and not mandatory (CDC, 1991). One court has allowed mandatory testing of health care workers, however, reasoning that the welfare of patients outweighs the rights of workers to privacy (Brennan, 1991).

Several public and private employers have opted for mandatory HIV screening for their current personnel and job applicants. The Pentagon, for example, tests all potential employees for the armed services and routinely rejects any applicant who is seropositive. A plan is also in effect for testing the more than 2 million men and women already employed by the army, navy, air force and marines.

The American Medical Association (AMA) has recommended that a physician who knows he or she has an infectious disease should not engage in any activity that creates a risk of transmission of the disease to others (Gerbert, et al., 1991). Many authorities believe that seropositive health care providers have an ethical responsibility to inform patients of their HIV status or cease practicing (Brennan, 1991).

19.10 OCCUPATIONAL TRANSMISSION OF HIV

Approximately 7 million people are employed in hospitals, health clinics and hospices across the country. Occupational exposure to HIV poses a low, although ever-present, risk to these workers (Rhame, 1992). Transmission of the virus in these settings has most commonly occurred from percutaneous (through the skin) exposure to "sharps" (needles, scalpels and other sharp instruments) that have been contaminated with HIV-infected blood or body fluids.

Although surgeons, dentists, nurses and other health care workers would appear to be the individuals who are most clearly at risk of transmitting or receiving the virus in the course of their daily activities, other employees are also at risk for acquiring HIV from occupational means. These workers include laboratory and blood bank technicians, dialysis personnel, medical examiners (coroners), morticians, personal service workers (housekeepers, laundry workers) and virtually any employee whose job involves contact with blood, secretions, other hazardous body fluids or corpses. The list of at-risk occupations also includes paramedics, emergency medical technicians, law enforcement personnel, firefighters, lifeguards and others whose job entails first-response medical care.

[1] Surgical Procedures

The opportunity for occupational transmission of HIV from patient to health care provider is especially significant in the field of surgery. The CDC has reported that surgeons, for example, come into direct contact with the blood of patients during one out of every five surgeries (Lowenfels, 1989). The specific vehicles of transmission can be scalpels, needles and other devices that come into direct contact with the patient's blood; blood splashing in the eyes, mouth, nose or skin;

and hospital gowns and shoes being soaked with the patient's blood or body fluids. Even the most experienced of orthopedic surgeons are regularly cut by the sharp shards of bone generated by the surgical procedures.

The possibility of patient-to-surgeon HIV transmission has made for some changes in the operating room. Some surgeons use electro-cautery devices rather than scalpels for incisions. Instruments are being passed in basins instead of from hand to hand, and staples are increasingly being used in lieu of stitches.

The probability of surgeon-to-patient HIV transmission is estimated to be between 1 per 100,000 and 1 per 1 million operations (Rosner, et al., 1992). The exposure rate is strongly linked with the type of surgery being performed. Ophthalmic (eye) surgery has the lowest risk, whereas pelvic surgery has the highest risk (Rosner, et al., 1992). There is the potential for substantial bleeding during vaginal or cesarean deliveries and other invasive procedures, including hysterectomy. The same principle holds true for cardiac surgery, including bypass, cardiac catheterization and angiographic procedures (Pate, 1990).

The CDC estimates that surgeons cut themselves at least 2 times out of every 100 procedures, with patients coming into direct contact with the surgeon's blood about 30 percent of the time. By the mid-1990s, perhaps 100 patients may have been infected by HIV-positive surgeons and dentists countrywide (Banta, 1993).

[2]   Obstetric Procedures

All health care workers who perform or assist obstetricians or nurse-midwives in vaginal or cesarean deliveries must wear gloves and gowns during the handling of the placenta and the umbilical cord. Amniotic fluid and blood must be removed from the infant's skin before barrier precautions can be abandoned.

[3]   Dental Procedures

Blood, saliva and gingival fluid from all dental patients must be considered potentially infective. Therefore, all dentists, dental assistants and dental students should wear surgical masks, protective eye wear or chin-length plastic face shields during dental procedures that are likely to result in splashing of fluids. Rubber dams and the high-speed evacuation of fluids are just two of the many methods available to minimize the generation of fluids and droplets.

Other intra-oral devices, such as impressions, that may be contaminated by HIV should be cleaned and disinfected before being handled by a dental technician. Dental equipment and environmental surfaces should be sterilized and disinfected before being used on a subsequent patient. Most important, the dentist, dental hygienist and dental technician must discard used surgical gloves and replace them before seeing the next patient.

In one well-known instance, genetic testing has positively linked a dentist who died of AIDS with the strain of virus shared by five patients who had been treated by him. According to the CDC, DNA assay revealed that the dentist's and his patients' viral sequences displayed the extent of similarity expected for epidemiologically linked individuals (CDC, 1990). Unique patterns of nucleotide not found in any other virus isolate were shared between the dentist and the patient (Gerbert, et al., 1991).

The American Dental Association (ADA) has therefore called on HIV-infected dentists to stop performing invasive procedures or to disclose their HIV status to patients who are scheduled for surgery (Rosner, et al., 1991).

[4] Nurses

Nurses are exposed during their regular daily rounds administering medications both orally and by injection. Clearly, nurses who work full-time with AIDS patients are at high risk for occupational exposure to the virus.

[5] Dialysis Workers

HIV-positive patients who are undergoing maintenance dialysis for kidney disease require the insertion of a device called a dialyzer. Although some health care centers instruct workers to discard the dialyzer after only one use, some facilities reuse it by issuing one to a specific patient, using it on that patient exclusively, then disinfecting the device for future use by that patient. This practice increases the exposure of workers who must perform the disinfection.

[6] Coroners and Morticians

Postmortem procedures necessitate the use of barrier protection, including gloves, masks, protective eye wear, gowns, splatter-proof aprons and shoe covers (Sale, 1991).

Instruments and environmental surfaces used during autopsies need to be decontaminated with an appropriate chemical germicide that has been deemed a "sterilant" by the U.S. Environmental Protection Agency (EPA). Studies have demonstrated that HIV is inactivated shortly after being exposed to commonly used chemical germicides at relatively low concentrations. Embalming fluid is one germicide that has been found to completely inactivate the virus.

In addition to the chemical germicide preparations that are commercially available, a solution of common household bleach (sodium hypochlorite) and water has been found to be an effective and inexpensive germicide. The proportions are 1 part bleach to 10 parts water.

[7]   Medical Students

Many medical students in residents' training programs express the fear that they may become victims of the virus through occupational transmission. Mangone and colleagues have suggested that the fatality rate from HIV infection may become four times higher among hospital interns than among California police officers (Brennan, 1991). There is evidence that medical students have become selective about choosing clinical specialties based on the degree of contact with AIDS. However, one recent study (Loring, 1993) shows that newer students are more willing to care for HIV patients and that their career choices are not particularly influenced by the AIDS epidemic.

[8]   Emergency Room (ER) Personnel

Emergency room personnel—especially those working in urban health care facilities—are regularly exposed to HIV-infected individuals in the course of their everyday duties. The high volume of trauma cases treated by physicians and nurses puts them at risk for coming into contact with possibly contaminated blood and other body fluids. Those health care employees who handle needles, bandages and other equipment used to treat seropositive patients are at particular risk.

The wearing of protective barrier equipment (gowns, gloves, goggles, etc.) only partially mitigates the risk of exposure. Despite the very best of precautions, the frenzied pace of the emergency department may contribute to accidental transmission of the virus. Furthermore, given the pressures that are present in most trauma centers, it is unlikely that full compliance with regard to wearing protective gear will ever be fully achieved.

[9] Personal Service Workers

These are individuals whose jobs bring them into close personal contact with the public (manicurists, cosmetologists, etc.). Also, certain occupations require the performance of procedures involving penetration of clients' skin with needles or other sharp instruments (acupuncture, tattooing and ear piercing, for example). HIV transmission may occur from personal service worker to client, or vice versa. In addition, unsterilized instruments that are recently contaminated can transmit the virus from one client to another.

19.11 NEEDLE-STICK AND OTHER "SHARPS" INJURIES

Statistics indicate that almost a third of all sharps injuries arise from two-handed recapping of needles (Rhame, 1992). The recapping of needles is to be discouraged, but when the procedure is absolutely necessary, needles should be recapped with one hand. In recent years, many self-sheathing devices and other built-in protectors have been developed for use by the medical community. Puncture-resistant disposable containers clearly displaying the biohazard logo are necessary in today's health care setting. These receptacles must be within easy reach of the health care provider and must be large enough to accommodate the full range of instruments and devices being discarded. Containers must be emptied or replaced on a regular basis.

Hollow and large-bore needles freshly removed from a seropositive patient pose a more significant hazard than do faint scratches or needles that have been used for piggyback connections to other intravenous tubing, for example.

Research indicates that more than half of reported needle-stick injuries occurred to the index finger of the nondominant hand (Weiss, 1992). The addition of reinforcement of this area of surgical gloves or the use of a thimblelike barrier might therefore dramatically reduce the incidence of occupational exposures. Double gloving would also decrease contamination rates. Many surgeons are now including a thin cloth between glove and fingers in an effort to decrease the incidence of needle-stick injuries. Latex gloves appear to be preferred over vinyl gloves, with less tearing and perforation reported. However, the quality of disposable and sterile gloves is not yet standardized.

19.12   OCCUPATIONAL EXPOSURE EVALUATION

Contact of a fresh (i.e., sustained within the previous 24 hours) wound or abrasion with blood or hazardous body fluid constitutes an exposure. The CDC also considers extensive skin contact with blood to be a significant exposure (Rhame, 1992).

A health care worker can sustain parenteral (through injection) exposure to blood or other body fluids, for example, from a needle-stick or cut, or mucous membrane exposure, for example, from a splash to the eye or mouth. Exposure may also be cutaneous when skin is chapped, abraded or afflicted with dermatitis. Mucocutaneous exposures accounted for 12 percent of the HIV infections documented to be due to occupational exposure (CDC, 1992). The risk associated with occupational exposure to HIV through mucocutaneous route is 0.1 percent (Ippoloto, 1993).

In the case of a sharps injury, the wound requires examination. If the basement membrane (a thin layer beneath the skin surface) has been penetrated by a sharp contaminated with blood or another hazardous body fluid, the health care worker is thought to have sustained significant injury (Rhame, 1992). The volume of blood involved in percutaneous exposures may also prove to be an important determinant of risk. The type and gauge of needle used, the depth of penetration and use of gloves all affect the amount of blood transferred during simulated needle sticks (Mast, 1993).The risk associated through percutaneous injuries involving needles and other HIV contaminated devices was 0.3 percent (Tokars, 1993).

If the source patient is diagnosed as being HIV positive, the health care worker should be evaluated clinically and serologically for the presence of the human immunodeficiency virus. Periodic testing for at least six months after exposure is recommended. If the source patient has no evidence of HIV infection, no further follow-up of the health care worker is necessary. If the source patient cannot be identified, decisions regarding appropriate follow-up procedures should be individualized based on the type of exposure and the likelihood that the source patient was infected.

Postexposure prophylaxis with AZT has been associated with a decrease of approximately 79 percent in the risk of HIV seroconversion after percutaneous exposure to HIV-infected blood in a case-control study among health-care workers (CDC, 1995). Because of the new information, provisional recommendations for chemoprophylaxis after occupational exposure to HIV have been published (CDC, 1996). These new recommendations should be implemented in consultation with persons having expertise in antiretroviral therapy and HIV transmission.

Chemoprophylaxis should be recommended to exposed workers after occupational exposure associated with the highest risk for HIV transmission. These highest risk conditions are: (1) a deep injury, (2) visible blood on the device causing the injury, (3) injury with a device previously placed in the source patient's vein or artery and (4) a source patient who died as a result of AIDS within 60 days postexposure.

For exposures with lower risk, prophylaxis should be offered. For exposures with negligible risk (e.g., urine exposure), prophylaxis is not justified.

Chemoprophylaxis should include AZT, because it is the only agent for which data support the efficacy of postexposure prophylaxis in the clinical setting. The drug 3TC should usually be added, due to studies showing the efficacy of this drug. A protease inhibitor (preferably indinavir) should be added for exposures with the highest risk of HIV transmission.

Chemoprophylaxis should be initiated promptly, preferably within one to two hours postexposure. Initiating therapy after a longer interval (e.g., one to two weeks) may be considered for the highest risk exposure, since even if infection is not prevented, early treatment of acute HIV infection may be beneficial. The optimal duration of prophylactic therapy is unknown, but the recommended duration is four weeks, if the individual tolerates it.

If the source patient or the patient's HIV status is unknown, initiation of therapy should be decided on a case-by-case basis. Exposed personnel must be counseled to avoid unprotected sex and needle sharing for at least three months and to postpone donating blood for at least one year (Rhame, 1992). Female employees who are or who may become pregnant must be specifically warned that transmission to the fetus may occur if HIV infection becomes established (Rhame, 1992), and the beneficial effect that AZT has in preventing transmission of the HIV infection to the infant should be explained. Follow-up counseling should be offered, as the psychological trauma of such an exposure may be significant. As always, confidentiality and privacy must be maintained to prevent discrimination and any other negative fallout that may result.

The need to maintain confidentiality may require the development of protocols for processing blood for serologic testing, for communicating any positive test results and for preparing and distributing exposure incident reports (Rhame, 1992).

The HIV-infected physician is also a patient and therefore has the same rights to privacy and confidentiality as any other patient. Both the physician and the patient have a responsibility to disclose their HIV status when appropriate, so that both can make informed decisions regarding treatment (Rosner, 1992).

19.13   EDUCATION OF EMPLOYEES

Transmission of AIDS is a concern that extends across many occupations. In educating the staff of both medical and nonmedical workplaces, management has a responsibility to ensure employees that people with AIDS or HIV do not pose a risk of transmitting the virus to co-workers through ordinary contact.

Health care workers need to be educated as to the methods that are available for preventing accidental occupational transmission of HIV. In addition, strategies must be designed for monitoring and increasing compliance with such guidelines. Management can disseminate educational materials and accurate scientific data about AIDS. Also, it is the responsibility of management to ensure that any necessary special equipment is in place. Formal programs need to be set in motion for the surveillance of occupational transmission of HIV.

Some hospitals have developed special teams of personnel who are available to answer medical questions about AIDS and to provide emotional support for both hospital employees and patients. The personnel that might comprise such a team include psychiatrists, infection control nurses, psychiatric social workers, a nursing administrator and a patient advocate.

19.14   AIDS RESEARCH

Three federal agencies are involved in AIDS research: the National Institutes of Health (NIH), the Food and Drug Administration (FDA) and the Defense Department. The National Library of Medicine, a branch of NIH, has compiled an extensive data base pertaining to AIDS, HIV and various licensed and experimental drugs being tested. The four AIDS-related data bases include:

- Aidsline, which lists more than 90,000 references to journals, articles, books, audiovisuals and conference abstracts;

- Aidstrials, which contains current information about more than 500 clinical trials of drugs and vaccines;

- Aidsdrugs, which lists the licensed anti-HIV drugs currently being evaluated; and

- Dirline, which lists more than 2,300 organizations and services that provide information to the general public about AIDS and HIV.

19.15   EVALUATION OF IMPAIRMENT

The American Medical Association's *Guides to the Evaluation of Permanent Impairment* determines the overall stage of HIV disease according to the patient's CD4 cell count. Less than 500 cells/mm^3 indicates the need to begin antiretroviral therapy; a count of 5 cells/mm^3 indicates that the patient is near death. However, the patient's symptoms must also be taken into consideration, since these can vary dramatically even within established categories or stages. If several organ systems are involved, the whole-person impairment percentages related to all the systems are combined (American Medical Association, 1993).

19.100   BIBLIOGRAPHY

Reference Bibliography

Alkhatib, G., et al.: CC CKR5: A RANTES, MIP-1α and MIP-1β Receptor as a Fusion Cofactor for Macrophage-tropic HIV-1. Science 272:1955-1958, 1996.

Altman, L.: U.S. Data on AIDS to Be Free. N.Y. Times, Jan. 25, 1994, p. C6.

Altman, L.: New Strategy Backed for Fighting AIDS. N.Y. Times, Nov. 2, 1993, p. C1.

American Academy of Orthopedic Surgeons Task Force on AIDS and Orthopedic Surgery: Recommendations for the Prevention of Human Immunodeficiency Virus in the Practice of Orthopedic Surgery. Park Ridge, Ill.: American Academy of Orthopedic Surgeons, 1989.

American Medical Association: Guides to the Evaluation of Permanent Impairment, 4th ed. Chicago: American Medical Association, 1993.

Banta, W.: AIDS in the Workplace. New York: Macmillan, 1993.

Brennan, T. A.: Transmission of the Human Immunodeficiency Virus in the Health Care Setting—Time for Action. N. Engl. J. Med. 324:1504-1509, 1991.

Centers for Disease Control and Prevention: Update: Provisional Public Health Service Recommendations for Chemoprophylaxis After Occupational Exposure to HIV. From the Centers for Disease Control and Prevention. M.M.W.R. Morbid. Mortal. Wkly. Rep. 45:468-472, 1996.

Centers for Disease Control and Prevention: CDC Case-Control Study of HIV Seroconversion in Health-Care Workers after Percutaneous Exposure to HIV-Infected Blood—France, United Kingdom and United States, January 1988–August 1994. M.M.W.R. Morbid. Mortal. Wkly. Rep. 44:929-33, 1995.

Centers for Disease Control and Prevention: Surveillance for Occupationally Acquired HIV Infection—United States, 1981–1992. M.M.W.R. Morbid. Mortal. Wkly. Rep. 41:823-825, 1992.

Centers for Disease Control and Prevention: Recommendations for Preventing Transmission of Human Immunodeficiency Virus and

Hepatitis B Virus to Patients During Exposure-Prone Invasive Procedures. M.M.W.R. Morbid. Mortal. Wkly. Rep. 40(RR-8):1, 1991.

Centers for Disease Control and Prevention: Possible Transmission of Human Immunodeficiency Virus to a Patient During an Invasive Dental Procedure. M.M.W.R. Morbid. Mortal. Wkly. Rep. 39:489-492, 1990.

Centers for Disease Control: Update: Universal Precautions for Prevention of Transmission of Human Immunodeficiency Virus, Hepatitis B Virus and Other Bloodborne Pathogens in Health Care Settings. M.M.W.R. Morbid. Mortal. Wkly. Rep. 37:377-382, 1988.

Chang, Y., et al.: Identification of Herpesvirus-like DNA Sequences in AIDS-Associated Kaposi's Sarcoma. Science 266:1865-1869, 1996.

Cocchi, F., et al.: Identification of RANTES, MIP-1α and MIP-1β as the Major HIV-suppressive Factors Produced by CD8 T Cells. Science 270:1811-1815, 1995.

Cuisini, M., et al.: AIDS in the Workplace. Clin. Dermatol. 2:201-224, Apr.-June 1992.

DeVita, V. T., et al.: AIDS Etiology, Diagnosis, Treatment and Prevention. Philadelphia: Lippincott, 1988.

Eisenstein, B.: The Polymerase Chain Reaction: A New Method of Using Molecular Genetics for Medical Diagnosis. N. Engl. J. Med. 322:178, 1990.

Feng, Y., et al.: HIV-1 Entry Co-factor: Functional c DNA Cloning of a Seven-Transmembrane, G Protein-Coupled Receptor. Science 272:872-877,1996.

Fiscus, S.A., et al.: Perinatal HIV Infection and the Effect of Zidovudine Therapy on Transmission in Rural and Urban Counties. JAMA 275:1483-1488, 1996.

Gerberding, J. L., et al.: Risk of Exposure of Surgical Personnel to Patients' Blood During Surgery at San Francisco General Hospital. N. Engl. J. Med. 322:1788-1793, 1990.

Gerbert, B., et al.: Possible Health Care Professional-to-Patient HIV Transmission: Dentists' Reactions to a Centers for Disease Control Report. J.A.M.A. 265:1845-1848, 1991.

Goldsmith, M. F.: Even "In Perspective," HIV Specter Haunts Health Care Workers Most. J.A.M.A. 263:2413-2420, 1990.

Hayward, R. A. and Shapiro, M. F.: A National Study of AIDS and Residency Training: Experiences, Concerns, and Consequences. Ann. Intern. Med. 114:23-32, 1991.

Henderson, D. K.: Postexposure Chemoprophylaxis for Occupational Exposure to Human Immunodeficiency Virus Type I: Current Status and Prospects for the Future. Am. J. Med. 91(3B):312s-319s, Sept. 16., 1991.

Hirsch, M. S.: Chemotherapy of Human Immunodeficiency Virus Infections: Current Practice and Future Prospects. J. Infect. Dis. 161 (845):1990, 1993.

Ippolito, G., et al.: The Risk of Occupational Human Immunodeficiency Virus Infection in Health Care Workers: Italian Multicenter Study. Arch. Intern. Med. 153:1451-1458, 1993.

Karon, J. M., et al.: Prevalence of HIV Infection in the United States, 1984 to 1992. JAMA 276:126-131, 1996.

Kolata, G.: Antibiotics Block HIV in Laboratory Studies. N.Y. Times, Sept. 28, 1993.

Kovacs, J. A.: Diagnosis, Treatment and Prevention of Pneumocystis Carinii Pneumonia in HIV-Infected Patients. AIDS Updates 2(1), 1989.

Lenette, E. T., et al.: Indirect Immunofluorescence Assay of Antibodies to Human Immunodeficiency Virus. J. Clin. Microbiol. 25:199, 1987.

Loring, K. E., et al.: The Influence of Perceived Risk of Exposure to Human Immunodeficiency Virus on Medical Students' Planned Specialty Choices. Am. J. Emerg. Med. 11:143-148, 1993.

Lowenfels, A.: Frequency of Puncture Injuries in Surgeons and Estimated Risk of HIV Infection. Arch. Surg. 124(11):1284-1286, Nov. 1989.

Mast, S. T., et al.: Efficacy of Gloves in Reducing Blood Volumes Transferred During Simulated Needlestick Injury. J. infect. Dis. 168:1589-1592, 1993.

Mellors, J. W., et al.: Prognosis in HIV-1 Infection Predicted by the Quantity of Virus in Plasma. Science 272:1167-1170, 1996.

Moore, P. S., et al.: Primary Characterization of a Herpesvirus-Like Agent Associated with Kaposi's Sarcoma. J. Virol. 70:549-558, 1996.

Pantaleo, G., et al.: The Immunopathogenesis of Human Immunodeficiency Virus Infection. N. Engl. J. Med. 328:327-335, 1993.

Pate, J. W.: Risks of Blood Exposure to the Cardiac Surgical Team. Ann. Thorac. Surg. 50(2):248-250, Aug. 1990.

Rhame, F. S.: Preventing HIV Transmission. Strategies to Protect Clinicians and Patients. Postgrad. Med. 91(8):141-144, June 1992.

Rosner, F., et al.: Ethical Considerations Concerning the HIV-Positive Physician. N.Y. State J. Med. 92(4):151-155, Apr. 1992.

Sale, G. E.: Acquired Immunodeficiency Syndrome and the Pathologist [Letter]. Arch. Pathol. Lab. Med. 115(8):741, Aug. 1991.

Schmalz, J.: N.Y. Times Magazine, Nov. 28, 1993, p. 57.

Tokars, J. I., et al.: Surveillance of HIV Infection and Zidovudine Use Among Health Care Workers After Occupational Exposure to HIV-Infected Blood. Ann. Intern. Med. 118:913-919, 1993.

Weiss, S.: Occupational Issues Related to the HIV Epidemic in AIDS and other Manifestations of HIV Infection. In: Wormser, G. (Ed.): New York: Raven Press, 1992.

Additional Bibliography

Armstrong, F. P., et al.: Investigation of a Health-Care Worker with Symptomatic Human Immunodeficiency Virus Infection: An Epidemiologic Approach. Milit. Med. 152:414, 1987.

Baker, J. L.: What is the Occupational Risk to Emergency Care Providers from the Human Immunodeficiency Virus? Ann. Emerg. Med. 17(7):700-703, July 1988.

Barondess, J. A., et al.: The Risk of Contracting HIV Infection in the Course of Health Care. J.A.M.A. 265:1872-1873, 1991.

Bland, A.: CDC to Change Guidelines for Infected Surgeons, Dentists. AIDS Alert 5:1610-1665, 1990.

Breo, D. L.: The "Slippery Slope": Handling HIV-Infected Health Workers. J.A.M.A. 264:1464-1466, 1990.

Camilleri, A. E., et al.: Needlestick Injury in Surgeons: What is the Incidence? J. R. Coll. Surg. Edinb. 36(5):317-318, Oct. 1991.

Centers for Disease Control: Update: Transmission of HIV Infection During Invasive Dental Procedures. M.M.W.R. 40:377, 1991.

Chamberland, M. E., et al.: Health Care Workers With AIDS: National Surveillance Update. J.A.M.A. 266:3459, 1991.

Comer, R. W., et al.: Management Considerations for an HIV Positive Dental Student. J. Dent. Educ. 55:187, 1991.

Elford, J.: Health Care Workers and HIV/AIDS. AIDS Care 2(4):367-370, 1990.

Gallacher, W.: Needle Stick Injuries [Letter]. Can. J. Anaesth. 39(5 Pt. 1):518-519, May 1992.

Gerberding, J. L.: Does Knowledge of Human Immunodeficiency Virus Infection Decrease the Frequency of Occupational Exposure to Blood? Am. J. Med. 91(3B):308S-311S, Sept. 16, 1991.

Gerberding, J. L.: Reducing Occupational Risk of HIV Infection. Hosp. Pract. 26(6):103, 1991.

Gerberding, J. L.: Current Epidemiologic Evidence and Case Reports of Occupationally Acquired HIV and Other Bloodborne Diseases. Infect. Contrl. Hosp. Epidemiol. 11(10 Suppl.):558-560, Oct. 1990.

Gerberding, J. L., et al.: Surgery and AIDS. Reducing the Risk [Editorial; Comment]. J.A.M.A. 265(12):1572-1573, March 27, 1991.

Goldsmith, M. F.: Physicians and Dentists Tell the CDC: "Avoid Quick Fix for a Tough Problem." J.A.M.A. 265:1221-1222, 1991.

Ippolito, G., et al.: Risk of HIV Transmission Among Health Care Workers: A Multicentre Study. Scand. J. Infect. Dis. 22:245-246, 1990.

Jagger, J., et al.: Universal Precautions: Still Missing the Point on Needlesticks [Editorial]. Infect. Control Hosp. Epidemiol. 12(4):211-213, April 1991.

Klein, R. S.: Universal Precautions for Preventing Occupational Exposures to Human Immunodeficiency Virus Type 1. Am. J. Med. 90:141-144, 1991.

McCormick, R. D., et al.: Epidemiology of Hospital Sharps Injuries: A 14-Year Prospective Study in the pre-AIDS and AIDS Eras. Am. J. Med. 91(3B):301S-307S, Sept. 16, 1991.

Panlilio, A. L., et al.: Blood Contacts During Surgical Procedures. J.A.M.A. 265:1533-1537, 1991.

Price, D. M. L.: What Should We Do About HIV-Positive Health Professionals? Arch. Intern. Med. 151:658-659, 1991.

Quebbeman, E. J., et al.: Risk of Blood Contamination and Injury to Operating Room Personnel. Ann. Surg. 214(5):614-620, Nov. 1991.

Raub, W.: Risk of Occupational Transmission of Human Immunodeficiency Virus Evaluated. J.A.M.A. 265:706, 1991.

Smith, R. V., et al.: Human Immunodeficiency Virus: Transmission Concerns in Clinical Practice. Ear Nose Throat J. 70(5):271-289, May 1991.

Stevens, C. K., et al.: The Human Immunodeficiency Virus: Knowledge and Precautions Among Anesthesiology Personnel [See Comments]. J. Clin. Anesth. 3(4):266-275, July-Aug. 1991.

Street, A.: Compensation for Medically Acquired AIDS [Letter]. Lancet 339(8809):1615, June 27, 1992.

Wall, S. D., et al.: AIDS Risk and Risk Reduction in the Radiology Department. A.J.R. Am. J. Roentgenol. 157(5):911-917, Nov. 1991.

INDEX

I–1

[References are to Sections.]

[References are to Sections.]

[References are to Sections.]

[References are to Sections.]

[References are to Sections.]

[References are to Sections.]

**ATHEROSCLEROTIC HEART DIS-
EASE**
Generally . . . 12.03[1]
Complicated lesions associated with . . .
12.03[1][b]
Etiology . . . 12.03[1]
Fibrous plaques associated with . . . . .
12.03[1][a]

ATOPIC DERMATITIS
Generally . . . 18.01[3]

ATTENTION DEFICITS
Head injuries, associated with . . . . . .
11.08[1][b]

ATTENTION-SEEKING DISORDERS
Head injuries, associated with . . . . . .
11.08[4][c]

AUDIOMETRIC TESTING
Generally . . . 10.12[5]; 10.15
Goals of . . . 10.15[2]
Precautionary measures . . . 10.15[1]
Pure-tone audiometry tests . . 10.15[4],
[a]-[c]
Speech audiometry tests . . 10.15[5], [a],
[b]
Types of tests . . . 10.15[3]

AURAMINE EXPOSURE
Bladder cancer caused by . . 15.08[1][a]

**AUTOMOBILES (See MOTOR VEHI-
CLES)**

AUTONOMIC HYPERREFLEXIA
Spinal cord injury, complication of . . .
5.08[7], [9]

AVASCULAR NECROSIS
Proximal humeral fractures, complication
of . . . 2.11[2][a]

AVULSION INJURIES
Hand, of . . . 1.05[1], [3]

AZODICARBONAMIDE
Occupational asthma from . . . .
17.02[2][a]; 17.03[3][l]: Table 17-3

**BACTERIA AND BACTERIAL PROD-
UCTS**
Asthma from . . . 17.03[3][b], [d], [f]
Skin infections . . . 18.07[1]

BENZENE
Heart diseases associated with exposure to
. . . 12.04[4]

BERYLLIUM
Carcinogenicity of . . . 15.04[1][d]

BICEPS TENDONITIS
Generally . . . 8.06[2]
Impingement syndrome associated with
. . . 2.17[2]

BILIARY TRACT CANCERS
Generally . . . 15.07[5]
Anatomical considerations . . 15.07, [5]:
Fig. 15-3
Asbestos exposure causing . . . .
15.07[5][a]
Diagnostic procedures . . . 15.07[5][b]
Epidemiology . . . 15.07[5], [a]
Prognosis . . . 15.07[5][b]
Treatment . . . 15.07[5][b]

BIRTH DEFECTS
Generally . . . 14.03[1][b]
Environmental chemicals associated with
. . . 14.03[1][b]
Hernias predisposed by (See HERNIAS,
subhead: Congenital anomalies predis-
posing to)
Teratogenicity, definition of . . . 14.01

BISMUTH
Hyperpigmentation caused by exposure to
. . . 18.05[1]

BLADDER CANCER
Generally . . . 15.08[1]
4-Aminobiphenyl exposure causing . . .
15.08[1][a]
Anatomical considerations . . . .
15.08[1][b]: Fig. 15-4
Auramine exposure causing . . . .
15.08[1][a]
Benzidine exposure causing . . . .
15.08[1][a]
Diagnostic procedures . . 15.08[1][b],
[c]: Fig. 15-4
Epidemiology . . . 15.08[1], [a]
MDA exposure causing . . . 15.08[1][a]
MOCA exposure causing . . 15.08[1][a]
2-Naphthylamine exposure causing . . .
15.08[1][a]
Pesticide exposure causing . . . .
15.08[1][a]
Polycyclic aromatic hydrocarbon exposure
causing . . . 15.08[1][a]
Prognosis . . . 15.08[1][b]
Screening of employees . . . 15.08[1][c]
Treatment . . . 15.08[1][b]

[References are to Sections.]

[References are to Sections.]

[References are to Sections.]

CARPAL TUNNEL SYNDROME—
Cont.
Differential diagnosis . . . 8.09[4]
Electrodiagnostic testing . . . 8.09[4]
Mechanism of injury . . . 8.09[2]
Muscle weakness as symptom . . . . . .
8.09[3]
Occupations associated with . . . 8.09[6]
Predisposing factors . . . 8.09[2]
Prevalence . . . 8.09[6]
Risk factors . . . 8.09[2], [6]; 8.10, [2]
Sensory loss as symptom . . . 8.09[3]
Signs and symptoms . . . 8.09[3]
Surgical decompression treatment . . . .
8.09[5]
Tenosynovitis as predisposing factor . .
8.09[2]
Thoracic outlet syndrome and . . 2.19[3]
Treatment . . . 8.09[5]
Vascular disorders associated with . . . .
8.09[2]
Vibration as cause . . . 8.10, [2]
Work associated with . . . 8.09[6]

**CAUDA EQUINA-CONUS MEDUL-
LARIS SYNDROME**
Generally . . . 5.04[8]

CAUDA EQUINA SYNDROME
Generally . . . 6.08[2]

CENTERS FOR DISEASE CONTROL
AIDS, guidelines for invasive medical procedures in . . . 19.09, [1], [2]

CENTRAL CORD SYNDROME
Generally . . . 5.04[7][a]

CERVICAL SPINE (See NECK INJU-
RIES)

CERVICOBRACHIAL DISORDERS
Generally . . . 2.18
Hyperabduction syndrome . . 8.08[1][b]
Myofascial pain syndrome . . . 8.05[2]
Nerve compression syndromes . . . . . .
8.08[1]-[e]: Fig. 8-6
Occupational cervicobrachial disorder (See
OCCUPATIONAL CERVICO-
BRACHIAL DISORDER (OCD))
Scapulocostal syndrome . . . 8.08[1][c]
Suprascapular nerve syndrome . . . . . .
8.08[1][d]

CHEMICAL BURNS
Foot injuries . . . 3.05[4][b]

CHEMICAL BURNS—Cont.
Hand injuries . . . 1.08[3][c]
Upper extremity injuries . . . 1.08[3][c];
2.06[4]

CHILDREN
Cancer, childhood . . . 14.04[2][c]
Maternal exposure to toxic substances,
effects of
Generally . . . 14.04; 14.04[2]
Behavioral toxicity . . 14.04[2][b]
Breast milk . . . 14.04[2][a]
Childhood cancers . . . 14.04[2][c]
Low birth weight . . . 14.04[1]
Prematurity . . . 14.04[1]

CHLORACNE
Generally . . . 18.06[3]
Agent Orange as cause of . . . 18.06[3]
Diagnosis . . . 18.06[3][a]
Dioxin as cause of . . . 18.06[3]
PCBs as cause of . . . 18.06[3]
Pesticides as cause of . . . 18.06[3]
Prevention programs . . . 18.06[3][b]
Signs and symptoms . . . 18.06[3][a]
Treatment . . . 18.06[3][b]

CHLOROFLUOROCARBONS (CFCs)
Heart diseases associated with exposure to
. . . 12.04[4]

CHLOROMETHYL ETHERS
Exposure levels, control of . . . .
15.12[4][b]
Lung cancer, risk of . . . 15.04[1][d]

CHONDROMALACIA PATELLAE
Generally . . . 4.06[5]

CHROMIUM
Asthma from exposure to chromium salts
. . . 17.03[3][k]

**CHRONIC IRRITANT CONTACT
DERMATITIS**
Generally . . . 18.02[2]

**CHRONIC OBSTRUCTIVE PULMO-
NARY DISEASE (COPD)**
Etiology . . . 15.04[2]
Grain workers, in . . . 17.03[3][b]
Host factors . . . 15.04[2]
Smoking as factor . . . 15.04[2]

CIRRHOSIS
Hernia rupture from . . . 9.04[3]

[References are to Sections.]

[References are to Sections.]

[References are to Sections.]

[References are to Sections.]

[References are to Sections.]

[References are to Sections.]

[References are to Sections.]

[References are to Sections.]

[References are to Sections.]

[References are to Sections.]

HIP INJURIES—Cont.
History of patient . . . 4.04[1]
Ischiogluteal bursitis . . . 4.05[1][a]; 8.12
Magnetic resonance imaging (MRI) as diagnostic tool . . . 4.04[3]
Mechanisms of injury . . . 4.03, [1], [4]
Physical examination . . . 4.04[2]
Repetitive motion disorders
    Generally . . . 8.12: Fig. 8-11
    Bursitis . . 4.03[4]; 4.05[1]-[b]; 8.12: Fig. 8-11
Sitting injuries . . . 4.03[4]
Trochanteric bursitis . . 4.05[1][b]; 8.12: Fig. 8-11
X-ray as diagnostic tool . . . 4.04[3]

HIV (See AIDS)

HIV ANTIBODY TESTING
Generally . . . 19.04
ELISA (Enzyme-linked immunosorbent assay) . . . 19.04[1]
False-negative results . . . 19.04[1]
False-positive results . . . 19.04
Indirect immunofluorescent assay (IFA) . . . 19.04[4]
Latex agglutination (LA) . . . 19.04[5]
Radio immune assay (RIA) . . 19.04[3]
Western blot test . . . 19.04; 19.04[2]

HIV ENCEPHALOPATHY
Generally . . . 19.06[6][a]

HIV VIRAL TESTING
Branched DNA test . . . 19.05[2]
DNA tests . . . 19.05[2]
PCR test . . . 19.05[2]
Polymerase chain reaction . . . 19.05[1]
Viral load . . . 19.05[2]

HODGKIN'S DISEASE
Generally . . . 15.11

HORMONES
Reproductive system, affecting . . . . . . 14.02[1][b], [c], [2][a]

HUMERAL FRACTURES
Distal . . . 2.13 et seq.
Humeral shaft . . . 2.12, [1], [2]
Nerve injuries associated with . . . . . . 2.19[1]
Proximal . . . 2.11 et seq.

HYDROCARBONS
Halogenated hydrocarbons as cause of heart disease . . . 12.04[4]

HYDROCARBONS—Cont.
Polycyclic aromatic hydrocarbons (See POLYCYCLIC AROMATIC HYDROCARBONS (PAHs))
Reproductive disorders associated with (See REPRODUCTIVE DISORDERS)

HYPERABDUCTION SYNDROME
Generally . . . 8.08[1][b]

HYPERPIGMENTATION
Generally . . . 18.05[1]

HYPERREACTIVE AIRWAY
Generally . . . 17.01[6]; 17.02[1]
Asthma and . . . 17.01[3], [6], [7]
Atopy and . . . 17.01[5][d]; 17.02[1]
Bronchial provocation testing . . . . . . 17.05[1][d]
Methacholine challenge test . . . . 17.05[1][c]

HYPERSENSITIVITY PNEUMONITIS
Asthma differentiated from . . . . 17.05[3][a]

HYPERTENSION
Generally . . . 12.06[1]
Evaluation of . . . 12.06[1]
Treatment of . . . 12.06[1]; 13.07[1]

HYPOPIGMENTATION
Generally . . . 18.05[2]

HYPOTHERMIA
Spinal cord injuries, treatment for . . . . 5.07[5][d]

HYSTERECTOMY
Hernia, as risk factor for . . . 9.03[4]

IFA TEST
HIV antibody testing . . . 19.04[4]

INCARCERATED HERNIA
Generally . . . 9.02[3]; 9.03[3][e]
Clinical classification . . . 9.02[3]
Management . . . 9.07[2]
Prognosis . . . 9.09
Reduction of . . . 9.07[2], [a]
Signs and symptoms . . . 9.06[2], [3]
Traumatic hernia . . . 9.04[3]; 9.08[4][a]

INCISIONAL HERNIA
Generally . . . 9.03[3]
Anatomical considerations . . 9.03[3][c]
Complications . . . 9.03[3][c]

[References are to Sections.]

[References are to Sections.]

[References are to Sections.]

[References are to Sections.]

[References are to Sections.]

[References are to Sections.]

[References are to Sections.]

[References are to Sections.]

[References are to Sections.]

[References are to Sections.]

[References are to Sections.]

[References are to Sections.]

[References are to Sections.]

[References are to Sections.]

[References are to Sections.]

[References are to Sections.]

[References are to Sections.]

[References are to Sections.]

SPINAL CORD INJURIES

Generally . . . 5.01; 5.02

Alignment as treatment . . . 5.07[3]

Anatomical considerations . . . 5.01[2]:
Figs. 5-1, 5-2; 6.02[2]

Anorectal function impairment, evaluation
of . . . 5.11[1][e]

Anterior cord syndrome . . . 5.05[7][b]

Autonomic hyperreflexia as complication
. . . 5.08[7], [9]

Bladder function impairment . . . .
5.08[7][a]; 5.11[1][d]

Blunt trauma . . . 5.02, [1]; 5.04[5]

Brown-Séquard syndrome . . 5.04[7][c]

Bruises . . . 5.04[5]

Cardiorespiratory complications . . . . .
5.08[4]

Cauda equina-conus medullaris syndrome
. . . 5.04[8]

Causes (See subhead: Etiology)

Central cord syndrome . . . 5.04[7][a]

Cervical cord injuries . . . . 5.03[1][a];
5.07[3]

Circulatory complications . . . 5.08[4]

Classification (See subhead: Types of lesions)

Closed injuries
Complete injuries . . . 5.04[2]
Etiology . . . 5.02, [1]
Incomplete injuries . . . 5.04[2]
Mechanisms of injury . . . 5.03[1],
[a]-[d]: Figs. 5-5, 5-6

Complete injuries . . . 5.04[2]

Complications
Medical complications . . . .
5.08[1]-[9]; 5.11[2][a]
Psychosocial complications . . 5.09

Compression injuries
Generally . . . 5.01[2]; 5.04[6]
Closed injuries . . . 5.03[1]: Fig.
5-6
Etiology . . . 5.04[6]
Mechanism of injury . . . 5.03[1]:
Fig. 5-6
Nerve root compression . . . . . .
5.03[1][d]
Pathology . . . 5.04[6]
Surgical decompression as treatment
. . . 5.07[3]: Fig. 5-11

Computed tomography as diagnostic tool
. . . 5.06[2], [3]

Concussion . . . 5.04[4]

Construction industry injuries . . . . . .
5.05[1][a], [c]

SPINAL CORD INJURIES—Cont.

Contusion . . . 5.04[5]

CT myelography as diagnostic tool . . .
5.06[3]

Decompression as treatment . . 5.07[3]:
Fig. 5-11

Depression as complication . . . 5.09

Dermatologic complications . . 5.08[6];
5.11[2][a]

Design planning in prevention of workplace injuries . . . 5.05[2]

Diagnostic procedures
Generally . . . 5.06[1]-[7]
Early diagnosis . . 5.07[2]-[b]: Fig.
5-10

Dimethyl sulfoxide (DMSO) therapy . .
5.07[5][c]

Disability evaluations
Generally . . . 5.11, [1][a]-[f]
Function recovery from rehabilitation
. . . 5.10[2][a]

Drug therapy . . . 5.07[5]-[c]

Early diagnosis . . . 5.07[2]-[b]: Fig.
5-10

Electromyography as diagnostic tool . .
5.06[5]

Emergency care
Generally . . . 5.07, [1]
Early diagnosis . . 5.07[2]-[b]: Fig.
5-10
Transfer of patient from accident site
. . . 5.07[1]
Ventilation requirements . . 5.07[1]

Epidemiology
Generally . . . 5.01[1]
Work-related injuries (See subhead:
Work-related injuries)

Etiology
Generally . . . 5.01[1]; 5.02
Blunt trauma . . . 5.02, [1]
Closed injuries . . . 5.02[1]
Compression injuries . . . 5.04[6]
Falls . . . 5.05[1], [2]
Penetrating trauma . . . 5.02[2]
Work-related injuries . . . 5.05[1],
[a]-[b]

Factory injuries . . . 5.05[1][c]

Falls as cause . . . 5.05[1], [2]

Flexion injuries . . . 5.03[1]: Fig. 5-5

Frankel classification system . . 5.04[2];
5.10[2][a]

Function recovery from rehabilitation
. . . 5.10[2][a]

[References are to Sections.]

[References are to Sections.]

[References are to Sections.]

[References are to Sections.]

[References are to Sections.]

[References are to Sections.]

[References are to Sections.]

ZIDOVUDINE (AZT)
Generally . . . 19.07[1]
HIV encephalopathy . . . 19.06[6][a]

ZIDOVUDINE (AZT)—Cont.
Prophylactic use . . . 19.07[1]; 19.12